Windows Programming Made Easy: Using Object Technology, COM, and the Windows Eiffel Library

ISBN 0-13-028977-9

90000

9 780130 289773

OBJECT AND COMPONENT TECHNOLOGY SERIES

Bertrand Meyer, *Series Editor*

FORTHCOMING

MEYER, *Design by Contract*
2001—0-13-088921-0

CURRENT

BROWN, *Large-Scale, Component-Based Development*
2000—0-13-088720-X

COLEMAN et al., *Object-Oriented Development: The Fusion Method*
1994—0-13-338823-9

COOK and DANIELS, *Designing Object Systems: Object-Oriented Modelling with Syntropy*
1994—0-13-203860-9

HENDERSON-SELLERS, *Object-Oriented Metrics: Measures of Complexity*
1996—0-13-239872-9

HOPKINS, *Smalltalk: An Introduction to Application Development Using VisualWorks*
1996—0-13-318387-4

JOYNER, *Objects Unencapsulated: Java, Eiffel and C++*
1999—0-13-014269-7

KRIEF, *Using Object-Oriented Languages for Rapid Prototyping*
1996—0-13-014713-3

LORENZ, *Object-Oriented Software Development: A Practical Guide*
1993—0-13-726928-5

LORENZ and KIDD, *Object-Oriented Software Metrics*
1994—0-13-179292-X

MAUGHAN and SIMON, *Windows Programming Made Easy: Using Object Technology, COM and The Eiffel Library*
2001—0-13-028977-9

MEYER, *Object-Oriented Software Construction, 2/e*
1997—0-13-629155-4

MEYER, *Eiffel: The Language*
1990—0-13-247925-7

MEYER, *Object Success: A Manager's Guide to Object-Oriented Technology and Its Impact on the Corporation*
1995—0-13-192833-3

MEYER and BÉZIVIN, *Tools 4: Technology of Object-Oriented Languages and Systems*
1992—0-13-923160-9

NIERSTRASZ and TSICHRITZIS, *Object-Oriented Software Composition*
1995—0-13-220674-9

POMBERGER and BLASCHEK, *Object Orientation and Prototyping in Software Engineering*
1996—0-13-192626-8

WIENER, *An Object-Oriented Introduction to Computer Science Using Eiffel*
1996—0-13-183872-5

WIENER, *An Object-Oriented Introduction to Data Structures Using Eiffel*
1997—0-13-185588-3

Windows Programming Made Easy: Using Object Technology, COM, and the Windows Eiffel Library

Glenn Maughan, PhD

Raphael Simon

PH PTR

Prentice Hall PTR
Upper Saddle River, NJ 07458
www.phptr.com

Library of Congress Cataloging-in-Publication Data available.

Editorial/Production Supervision: *Jan H. Schwartz*
Acquisitions Editor: *Paul Petralia*
Editorial Assistant: *Justin Somma*
Marketing Manager: *Bryan Gambrel*
Manufacturing Manager: *Alexis Heydt*
Cover Design Director: *Jerry Votta*
Cover Design: *Nina Scuderi*
Art Director: *Gail Cocker-Bogusz*
Series Interior Design: *Meg VanArsdale*

© 2001 Prentice Hall PTR
Prentice-Hall, Inc.
Upper Saddle River, NJ 07458

Prentice Hall books are widely used by corporations and government agencies for training,
marketing, and resale.

The publisher offers discounts on this book when ordered in bulk quantities.
For more information, contact Corporate Sales Department, phone: 800-382-3419;
fax: 201-236-7141; e-mail: corpsales@prenhall.com
or write: Prentice Hall PTR, Corporate Sales Department, One Lake Street, Upper Saddle River, NJ 07458

All product names mentioned herein are the trademarks or registered trademarks
of their respective owners.

Printed in the United States of America
10 9 8 7 6 5 4 3 2 1

ISBN 0-13-028977-9

Prentice-Hall International (UK) Limited, **London**
Prentice-Hall of Australia Pty. Limited, **Sydney**
Prentice-Hall Canada Inc., **Toronto**
Prentice-Hall Hispanoamericana, S.A., **Mexico**
Prentice-Hall of India Private Limited, **New Delhi**
Prentice-Hall of Japan, Inc., **Tokyo**
Pearson Education Asia Pte. Ltd.
Editora Prentice-Hall do Brasil, Ltda., **Rio de Janeiro**

CONTENTS

NINETEEN   EIFFELCOM   687

FOREWORD

The dominant platform of the day, Microsoft Windows, started out not so long ago as a mere GUI (Graphical User Interface) on top of DOS, but quickly evolved into a full operating system in its own right, the basis for all current Microsoft offerings. It has branched out into a number of variants, from Windows 3.11 to Windows 95, Windows 98, Windows CE, and Windows ME on the consumer side and from Windows for Workgroups to Windows NT and Windows 2000 on the professional side. Even though some of these offerings are internally very different, they provide a common look and feel both to end users, through a shared GUI, and to application writers, through a shared API (Application Programming Interface). These offerings cover not only graphics but also the mechanisms for exchanging information between applications, known previously as OLE and more recently as COM (Component Object Model), which this book explores along with the graphics part of Windows.

The GUI has won the hearts of the end-user masses, but programming to the API remains the privilege of a small developer elite. The developer must understand hundreds of C and C++ routine specifications, with numerous parameters, and figure out what will happen in all possible cases. The sheer size of popular books, such as Charles Petzold's *Programming Windows,* shows the amount of detail that must be mastered. Tools such as Visual Basic and Delphi provide some relief, but to produce an ambitious system with a sophisticated

GUI, using all the advanced interface techniques and glitzy controls that today's users expect as a matter of course, developers can't avoid the plunge. They end up fighting with a myriad of low-level details, and trying to write successful programs through a painful process of trial and error.

These comments apply even more to COM. Although interapplication communication is a sine qua non of most modern software developments, mastering the intricacies of COM requires extensive effort on the developers' part, especially those who are using a language other than C++, since the C++ computational model is plastered all over the COM design.

Along with complexity, reliability is a constant concern. Because developers end up playing with C and C++ pointers, and pointers are well known for the propensity to go wild, developers never quite know if a wrong manipulation somewhere—whether due to software or to users—will freeze a system or bring the dreaded "blue screen of death." Since the underlying languages are not garbage-collected, developers are never immune from memory leaks; an application may seem to work well for a while but inexorably consume more and more resources until a long session ends up in rigor mortis.

There is a better way. Combined with the breadth and effectiveness of the Windows mechanisms, the power of object technology and Design by Contract enables developers to build attractive GUI applications with less effort, shorter development times, and far shorter debugging times, producing results that are far more reliable and easier to maintain. This book describes an approach, based on WEL (Windows Eiffel Library) and the EiffelCOM library and wizard, that achieves these goals.

Neither WEL nor EiffelCOM is the topic of the book. The topic is the Windows API itself, including COM, and how to use it effectively to build excellent interactive, multicomponent applications. As the title—*Windows Programming Made Easy*—indicates, developers can use this book to learn about programming Windows through a smooth, pleasurable process.

The language, library, and wizard serve as tools to implement the goals of rapid development and high-quality results. Eiffel provides the simple object-oriented framework—classes with single and multiple inheritance, genericity, polymorphism, automatic memory management through garbage collection, dynamic binding, strong typing, simplicity, and clarity of the language and its syntax—that enables developers to forget the language and concentrate on their applications and GUIs. WEL is a beautiful packaging of the Windows API, shielding developers from all the messy details, yet providing the power and flexibility expected of modern applications.

Particularly important is the application of Design by Contract principles, which for the first time equip the Windows interface with precise specifications of its functionalities, enabling the Windows developer, through WEL, to build robust applications that will not crash at the first sign of trouble. Design by Contract—embodied in the WEL classes' preconditions, postconditions, and invariants—pervades this book and constantly facilitates the programming life (and possibly the social life too, as peace of mind is always to be appreciated) of the Windows developer.

Glenn Maughan and Raphael Simon are particularly qualified to write this book. Both have had years of experience with large-scale object-oriented development and the practical application of Design by Contract. In his thesis on object-oriented restructuring at Monash University, and then in his work as a consultant for leading Australian companies, Glenn accumulated much of the experience that shows throughout this book. Raphael played a key role in the development of WEL at ISE (Interactive Software Engineering) and was the project leader for the EiffelCOM library and wizard, both coming to fruition as this book is released. Both Glenn and Raphael have taught the concepts of this book in TOOLS conference tutorials and to other industrial audiences. Throughout this book they maintain a practical, hands-on approach to transfer their own accumulated experience to you.

The Windows API doesn't have to be scary; learning to program to it doesn't have to be painful. This book combines the best of object technology and the best of Windows to make the process easy and enjoyable

—Bertrand Meyer

PREFACE

BUILDING WINDOWS SOFTWARE

The construction of Windows software is an immensely satisfying activity. It is satisfying to write software that is easy to use and that meets the needs of its users. Microsoft Windows software gives you the benefit of a standard graphical interface composed of prebuilt user interface components which can be combined to construct a myriad of software applications.

Building Windows software is also challenging. Very challenging! The number and variety of components that you can use is daunting. The latest application programming interface (API) for Windows 32-bit applications consists of hundreds of interface components and thousands of functions used to create and manipulate each of them. Assembling an application from these components requires careful design, and usually a great deal of experience, before it will meet its requirements and attain one of the ultimate software goals: being user-friendly.

Windows software has traditionally been constructed using the C programming language in conjunction with the standard Windows API library. More recently, applications have been built using C++ and a class library, such as the Microsoft Foundation Classes (MFC) or the Borland Object Windows Library (OWL), built on top of the Windows API. C has long been praised for its low-level power and expressiveness. It is said to be suitable for Windows programming because the Windows API itself is implemented in C and therefore provides the closest possible programming link between the application and the Windows libraries. However, C has also been criticized for its low-level power and expressiveness—C is sometimes *too* close to the bone. The language can beguile a programmer into concentrating on internal structure, physical layout, and mechanical capabilities, rather than on business requirements. For instance, more time is typically spent managing program execution flow, organizing how the data structures are laid out in memory, how the data structures are accessed, and occasionally even how the executable is constructed. Little time is left to concentrate on what the program is supposed to do and what it is supposed to provide for its users. When you combine the complexities of the Windows API with the complexity of using C or C++ as an implementation language, it adds up to one *very* complex and error-prone software development process.

AN ALTERNATIVE APPROACH

A number of alternative approaches exist. One of the most popular is to generate the Windows source code semiautomatically using fourth generation languages (4GLs), or so-called *visual programming languages.* Examples include Microsoft's Visual Basic, IBM's VisualAge, and Borland's Delphi. Each is a development environment that provides a fast way to interactively create Windows applications. In practice, this approach is very productive. However, these environments (and others like them) tend to restrict the range of Windows programming facilities to which the programmer has access. When a really tricky problem arises, these types of tools can thwart the implementation of a good solution.

The tools and environments also tend to be based on older style programming languages, such as BASIC and Pascal. Even though such languages have their merits, they tend to be based on outdated software development principles and often have not incorporated newer techniques, such as object-orientation, as thoroughly or effectively as would be hoped. Both VisualBasic and Delphi have attempted to incorporate object-oriented principles into newer versions of the language. However, concepts such as inheritance, parameterized types, and polymorphism have been only partially integrated, or not integrated at all; in some cases, the language has become more complex, rather than simpler, as a result.

For software to be successful in today's market, it must be *engineered,* as opposed to just constructed. Well-engineered software has a better chance of exhibiting *quality.* The attributes of software quality include correctness, robustness, and extensibility. That is, the system meets the user requirements, does not crash or fail unexpectedly (possibly causing disastrous results, like the loss of expensive spacecraft), and can be easily adapted to meet new and changing user requirements. Producing quality software using traditional software development techniques can be very difficult and sometimes, especially when it comes to the maintenance of that software, even impossible.

Object-orientation is a leap (not a step) in the right direction. The techniques and structures available in an object-oriented language allow a programmer to concentrate more on *what* needs to be programmed. That is, *what* abstractions are needed, *what* functionality the abstractions need to provide, and *what* data structures are needed to support the abstractions. In a pure object-oriented environment, *how* these abstractions and data structures are implemented can be effectively hidden from the programmer.

An object-oriented approach requires at least three components: an object-oriented language that provides proper support for object-oriented concepts, an object-oriented encapsulation of the Windows API library, and a set of base, or kernel, classes that provide a solid collection of data structures and abstractions needed to build software.

The language used in this book is Eiffel. Eiffel is a pure object-oriented language designed from the ground up to support the production of quality software. The API encapsulation library is the Windows Eiffel Library (WEL), produced by Interactive Software Engineering (ISE), that provides a well-designed encapsulation of the Win32 API. The base library is the EiffelBase library, also produced by ISE and available in the public domain, that provides all the data structure and support classes needed for most applications.

These three tools provide a surprisingly powerful way of engineering quality Windows software. This is exactly the alternative that we are looking for! We get all the benefits of a pure object-oriented language, the benefits of a well-designed encapsulation of the Windows API library, and collectively, an environment for building quality, well-engineered Windows software.

Finally, the language, compiler, libraries, and other development tools should be accessible to the developer from within a productive and integrated development environment. The examples in this book were developed using ISE's EiffelBench.

We mentioned earlier not to rule out the tools that provide an automated approach to Windows code generation. An object-oriented approach, using the tools listed above, is not the golden "this-is-so-easy-now" solution. With an object-oriented approach, Windows programming is easier and less error-prone, but it is still challenging. Using visual tools in *conjunction* with an object-oriented method can improve the overall quality of applications and speed the development of components.

INTENDED AUDIENCE

This book is aimed at intermediate programmers. You should have a reasonable level of competence in general programming, programming algorithms, and a little mathematics (for graphics programming). You should also be competent in object-oriented programming. However, the Eiffel language is sufficiently easy to read and understand that this requirement is not a strict prerequisite.

The book concentrates on the WEL. In fact, it provides a complete programmer's reference for this library. Examples in the book also rely heavily on the EiffelBase library for its data structures and other abstractions.

You will need to have access to an Eiffel compiler, the ISE WEL library, and either the EiffelBase library or an equivalent substitute. A number of free (and trial) implementations of Eiffel are available, and a trial version of the ISE Eiffel compiler and its associated libraries is included on the CD that comes with this book, so you can get started immediately.

The book presents an easy way to write Windows software that addresses quality attributes including correctness, robustness, and extendibility. If you write Windows software using another programming language, then this book will still give you valuable insight and advice to help construct quality Windows software. The book may even help to convince you to use Eiffel on your next development project.

ORGANIZATION OF THE BOOK

There are two goals in the organization of this book. The first is to present an easy way to construct Windows software using Eiffel and the Windows Eiffel Library. The second goal is to provide a complete reference for WEL. To meet both of these goals, we have organized the book using the following structure.

Each chapter introduces one particular area of interest—for instance windows, composite windows, or controls. The introduction is followed by a discussion on the theory underlying the topic, including answers to the relevant *what, why,* and *how* questions: What does this type of Windows component provide for me? Why would I use it in one of my applications? And finally, how do I use it? The reference material for the library component is then presented with numerous programming examples illustrating particular features and behavior of the component.

In order to provide a complete view of the WEL, a medium-sized application is constructed incrementally throughout the book. This application is introduced in detail in the section "Directory Tree Analyzer" in Chapter 2, "Applications." Many chapters include a section titled "Implementing the Example ————," in which the chapter's components and concepts are demonstrated using the sample application. For example, the use of composite windows in the sample application is discussed in the section "Implementing Composite Windows" in Chapter 5, "Composite Window."

ACKNOWLEDGMENTS

This book has taken longer than expected to write. Almost three years, in fact. It would never have been completed without you—the proud owner of your own copy! Your frequent questions via e-mail and via the newsgroup *comp.lang.eiffel* have reignited our motivation to finish every time. Thank you.

We would also like to thank a number of individuals who have helped throughout the project. In particular, Bertrand Meyer and Christine Mingins for encouraging us to write the book in the first place; Daryl Foy, Per Grape, Jim McKim, Robin van Ommeren, Arnaud Pichery, Margot Postema, and Kim Walden for helping to review and class test early material; and our editor, Paul Petralia, of Prentice-Hall, for getting everything done so quickly.

Finally, we would like to thank our families and friends for their patience, encouragement, fun, and laughter.

LIST OF EXAMPLES

The Windows Eiffel Library

Introducing the Windows Eiffel Library

The Windows Eiffel Library (WEL) is an Eiffel source library enabling the development of Windows applications in an object-oriented environment. The library was developed by Interactive Software Engineering in 1994, and is constantly updated in line with Microsoft's operating system versions. WEL relies on the open source EiffelBase library for its data structures and currently includes about 350 classes distributed in nine clusters.

WEL is more than just another object-oriented windows library. It offers many advantages compared to other more conventional approaches. The use of true multiple inheritance and Design by Contract, combined with the simplicity of the Eiffel language, considerably increases the ease of use of the library. Building a WEL system is nothing more than choosing graphical components and combining them. However, WEL also gives access to the low-level capabilities of Windows should you need to access them. You get the best of both worlds—the ease of use of high-level languages with the power of low-level approaches.

The Purpose

Every Windows application has to provide a common set of features to communicate with the operating system. This so-called "plumbing code" is ideal for reuse. WEL provides a powerful framework that has been thoroughly tested by many users. Windows applications can be built quickly and can benefit from a wide range of existing classes. Although a thin wrapper, WEL offers a higher level of abstraction than do the raw Windows APIs, and WEL frees the developer from having to know all the low-level details.

Design by Contract

Design by Contract (DBC) is used extensively in the Eiffel classes that constitute WEL. DBC is a method of formally specifying the relationships between a client and a supplier—a client uses a service or component, and a supplier supplies services and components. The rights and obligations of each party are specified precisely in the form of contracts. Contracts are specified using assertions in the form of class invariants, routine preconditions, and routine postconditions. The precondition defines the rights and obligations of the client, while the postcondition and class invariant define those of the supplier. The main advantages include improved reusability and self-documented code—the interface of a class defines the available functionality, while DBC describes how the functionality can be used and what it will do for you.

Contracts are extremely useful when applied to features that use system calls. Windows functionality is available to the developer through APIs. These can be cumbersome to use because the context in which they should be called is not always obvious. DBC allows us to specify that context. It can define the range of possible values for API function arguments as well as how arguments interact with each other.

DBC also reduces the time needed to debug a system. If the system is well-contracted, each possible problem will result in a contract violation that will give extensive information on the source of the failure. Bugs are caught earlier and thus are easier to fix. The nature of the broken contract also helps to locate the source of the error—a precondition violation indicates a problem in the calling feature, while a postcondition violation indicates a problem in the feature itself. Finally, class invariants define the context in which the class is intended to be instantiated.

WEL inherits other benefits from the Eiffel language. The ability to efficiently use multiple inheritance is one of them. The class hierarchy can be defined without worries about the actual implementation. This allows the WEL inheritance tree to follow a natural mapping of human concepts. Add this to the

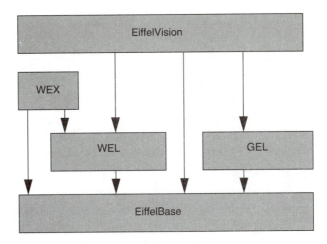

FIGURE 1.1. Position of WEL in relation to other ISE Eiffel libraries.

simplicity of the Eiffel language and you get the rationale behind the title of the book—programming Windows applications becomes easy and straightforward.

Positioning WEL

WEL relies on the EiffelBase library for its data structures and support abstractions. It also provides a basis on which other libraries can be constructed. The ISE Eiffel product uses WEL as the Windows implementation for its EiffelVision library and also provides a WEL extension library, called WEX, for multimedia capabilities. Figure 1.1 illustrates the positioning of WEL in relation to other ISE Eiffel libraries.

EiffelBase provides a comprehensive set of data structure and support classes. WEL provides the Windows API encapsulation. GEL (GTK Eiffel Library) provides an encapsulation of the GTK Windows toolkit found on many UNIX platforms. WEX (WEL Extension Library) provides multimedia extensions to the WEL library. And finally, EiffelVision provides a platform-independent GUI library that utilizes either WEL or GEL.

WEL STRUCTURE

The WEL delivery includes eleven directories. Nine of them are clusters containing the WEL classes. The directory *spec* contains C header files containing C macros used to call Windows API functions. The directory *extra* includes the source files of the *H2E* utility (see "The H2E Utility" in Chapter 7, "Resources"). Table 1.1 enumerates the WEL clusters.

Each cluster is a group of semantically related classes. They define the context in which the classes should be reused. For example, classes in the *WEL_CONSTANTS* cluster contain definitions for Windows constants and should be inherited by classes that need to use those constants.

Windows

The most fundamental cluster is *WEL_WINDOWS*. This cluster defines the principal kinds of windows that can be created using WEL. The Business Object Notation[1] diagram in Figure 1.2 describes the hierarchy of the cluster main classes.

The ancestor of all windows classes is *WEL_WINDOW*. This class defines the attributes common to any window, such as its geometry, its current display status (shown or hidden), its text, and common commands including positioning commands (maximize, minimize), display commands (show, hide), and message handling commands.

Every WEL application needs to register a main window that will handle messages coming from the operating system or other running applications (see Chapter 3, "Messages"). Such a window can be of two types: a frame window or a dialog. Frame windows include a title bar and a client area in which text can be displayed. They can also contain a menu, a tool bar, scroll bars, and a status bar (see Chapter 4, "Windows"). Dialogs contain a set of controls instead of a client area (see Chapter 9, "Dialogs").

Only dialogs that are instances of *WEL_MAIN_DIALOG* can be the main window of an application; different types of frame windows can serve this

TABLE 1.1   *WEL Library Clusters*

CLUSTER NAME (DIRECTORY NAME)	CONTENT
WEL_CONSTANTS (consts)	Flags and constants
WEL_CONTROLS (controls)	Standard controls
WEL_GDI (gdi)	Graphics Device Interface management classes
WEL_GDI_STOCK (gdistock)	Stock fonts, brushes, and pens
WEL_MESSAGES (messages)	Common Windows messages
WEL_STANDARD_DIALOGS (stddlgs)	Standard dialogs
WEL_STRUCTURES (structs)	Windows data structures
WEL_SUPPORT (support)	Miscellaneous
WEL_WINDOWS (windows)	Windows types

1. See *Seamless Object-Oriented Software Architecture*, K. Walden and J. M. Nerson, Prentice-Hall, 1995.

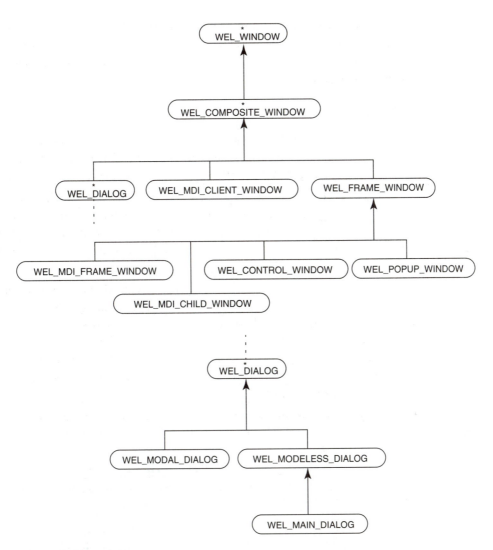

FIGURE 1.2. Window cluster hierarchy.

purpose. For applications that require a simple main window, the class *WEL_FRAME_WINDOW* provides a full implementation of a standard window. It can be inherited from to perform customization such as changing default position, size, style, or default display status.

You may also use an instance of *WEL_MDI_FRAME_WINDOW* if you are building an editor-like application where each editing session requires its own window (e.g., Microsoft Word 6). All child windows are contained within a window and can be rearranged in different ways. For example, they can be tiled, cascaded, or maximized. Regardless of your choice, the principle remains the same—inherit and customize. This principle applies to any kind of window, be it a standard window, a dialog, or a control.

The Support Cluster

Although the hardest to qualify, the support cluster is another central cluster of WEL. The first goal of this cluster is to provide classes that are used by the internal mechanisms of the library. The cluster also provides helper classes that are used to accomplish specific tasks such as manipulating bit flags, displaying a dialog box or setting the delay for mouse double-clicks.

Essential to any WEL system is *WEL_APPLICATION*. The root class of all WEL systems has to inherit from this class. All the mechanisms needed to create a Windows application are provided as part of its implementation. This class also provides the placeholder used to specify the main window. See Chapter 2, "Applications," for additional information on how WEL applications are built.

Another support class worth mentioning is *WEL_ANY*. It is the common ancestor for all classes wrapping a Windows construct, including windows, window structures, and resources. This class defines two major attributes, *item* and *shared*. The former holds a pointer to the actual underlying Windows construct, while the latter specifies whether multiple instances of Eiffel classes share that resource. All Windows constructs need to be freed explicitly, which goes against the automatic garbage-collection nature of Eiffel. The solution adopted in WEL consists of releasing the Windows construct automatically when the Eiffel object is garbage-collected. This can work only if the Windows construct is not wrapped by multiple Eiffel objects, in which case the system would crash when the second Eiffel object tries to free the construct that was already released. This is why we have the *BOOLEAN* attribute *shared*. When *shared* is *True* the Eiffel runtime will not free the underlying construct when garbage-collected; instead, the application has to free it explicitly by calling the corresponding API function.

All the WEL classes dealing with resources are also part of the support cluster. They include wrappers for icons, cursors, menus, and keyboard shortcuts. See Chapter 7 for a description of each resource class.

WEL_SUPPORT includes numerous classes that are needed for the internals of WEL. These classes implement mechanisms such as the Context → Event → Command (CEC) protocol or the messages dispatch engine (see Chapter 3).

Standard Controls

Controls are types of windows that provide visual feedback on user interactions. They include push buttons, radio buttons, tool bars, combo boxes, tree views, and a growing list of others.

The *WEL_CONTROLS* cluster contains classes that wrap the Windows standard controls. All the control classes inherit from *WEL_CONTROL,* which in turn inherits from *WEL_WINDOW.* All types of controls have a font and an identifier associated with them. The font is used to draw any text displayed on the control (e.g., button title or list box content), and the identifier allows you to create the control from a resource definition and allows the parent to process the messages it generates. The hierarchy is illustrated in Figure 1.3.

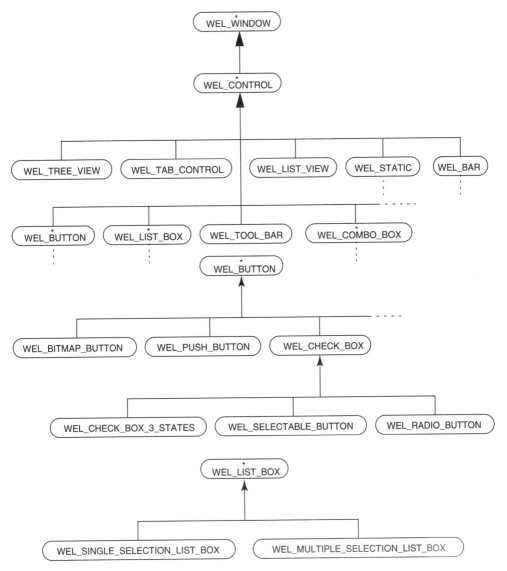

FIGURE 1.3. Control cluster hierarchy. *(continued)*

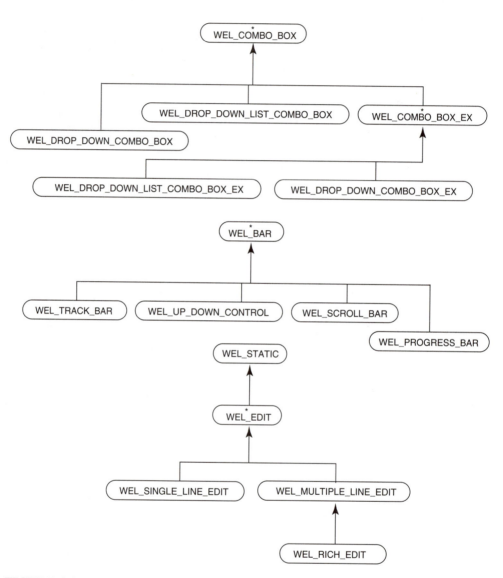

FIGURE 1.3. *(continued)*

The *WEL_CONTROLS* classes supply abstractions that implement application windows. Refer to Chapter 11, "Controls," for additional information on how to use standard controls with WEL.

GDI Management

The Graphics Device Interface (GDI) allows you to draw text and figures on different devices in a uniform way. The drawing code is independent from the actual device, be it a plotter, a printer, or a display, that you are drawing on. The *WEL_GDI* cluster, shown in Figure 1.4, includes the classes used to access the Graphics Device Interface APIs.

The GDI classes all inherit from *WEL_GDI_ANY*, which defines operations to load and free GDI resources. The *WEL_GDI_STOCK* cluster contains Eiffel classes that wrap the standard Windows GDI objects, including pens, brushes, palettes, and fonts. The steps involved in using the GDI with WEL are described in detail in Chapter 10, "Graphics Device Interface."

Messages

Messages are the heart of any Windows application. They allow different windows of the same application, or even from different applications, to exchange information in a simple and powerful way. The main Windows' messages are wrapped by Eiffel classes in the *WEL_MESSAGES* cluster. These classes

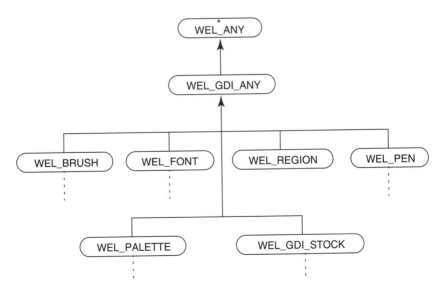

FIGURE 1.4. GDI cluster hierarchy.

expose helper features to access information related to a given message. One class may wrap multiple messages if the information that they carry is similar. Wrapped messages include mouse, keyboard, menu selection, window resizing, window movement, and timer messages.

All the message classes inherit from *WEL_MESSAGE_INFORMATION*, which includes attributes that hold the data carried by the message. They are used in the message processing mechanisms of WEL, as described in Chapter3.

Standard Dialogs

The standard dialog cluster, shown in Figure 1.5, includes classes that wrap the standard Windows dialogs. These dialogs are used to choose a color from a palette, to choose a font from a list of available fonts, to open or save a file, and to perform other standard operations.

All the dialog classes inherit from *WEL_STANDARD_DIALOG*. They can be used as suppliers of classes that need to display the corresponding dialogs. See Chapter 9 for additional information on dialogs.

Structures

Windows defines numerous data structures used throughout the API. WEL provides Eiffel classes that wrap all the structures used by the library. These structure classes are all grouped in the *WEL_STRUCTURE* cluster and they all inherit from the class *WEL_ANY* with its attribute, *item*, pointing to the actual underlying data.

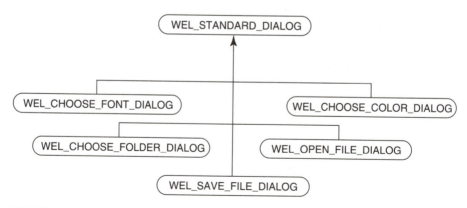

FIGURE 1.5. Standard dialog cluster hierarchy.

Flags and Constants

The classes contained in the *WEL_CONSTANTS* cluster provide a collection of Windows constant declarations. Example 1.1 shows the declaration for the Windows *Swp_nosize* constant.

Example 1.1 WEL Constant Declaration

```
Swp_nosize: INTEGER is
      external
          "C [macro %"wel.h%"]"
      alias
          "SWP_NOSIZE"
      end
```

Each of the declarations are *external* routines referring to the definition of a constant in a Windows header file. Because they are constants and not standard C functions, they are defined using a *macro* external. The *wel.h* header file can be found in the *spec\windows\include* directory of your Eiffel installation. This file contains a reference to the main Windows header file *windows.h*, which in turn points to the header files containing the definition of the constant. The actual names of the Windows constants appear after the *alias* keyword.

The *WEL_CONSTANTS* classes should be inherited to access specific Windows constants.

SUMMARY

The Windows Eiffel Library provides a true object-oriented encapsulation of the Win32 API library. Each Windows abstraction, such as a window, control, constant, and structure, is encapsulated by its own class. Semantically related classes are grouped into different clusters (physical directories) to assist you in locating the right classes for your applications.

Now that you know where to find the classes, we will explore how they interact with each other and the steps you need to follow to build your Windows application. In the next chapter, we construct our first WEL application and learn the basics of WEL programming.

T   W   O

APPLICATIONS

INTRODUCING APPLICATIONS

A Windows application requires at least one window. The main window of an application presents you with the initial application interface. You use the controls and menus attached to the main window to perform different tasks. The main window may allow you to load and edit documents, draw diagrams, or load application subsystems.

THE ROOT CLASS OF A WEL APPLICATION

Every WEL application contains a single instance of *WEL_APPLICATION*, usually as its root object. The *WEL_APPLICATION* class provides a deferred interface for creating and initializing an application and its main window. Every Windows application requires the processing of an *event loop*. The event loop processes Windows messages, such as notification of mouse movement or selection of push buttons. Each message received is passed to the Windows component in which it occurred. The *WEL_APPLICATION* class provides routines for automatically processing the Windows event loop and for distributing messages to the relevant components. In a typical application, you do not need to implement a message processing loop. Compare this with a Windows application written in the C programming language. A C programmer must implement a loop that collects and processes each message for that application. The following C code fragment illustrates a typical message processing loop:

```
while( GetMessage( &msg, NULL, 0 0))
{
        if (TranslateAccelerator (hwnd, hAccel, &msg))
        {
                TranslateMessage( &msg );
                DispatchMessage( &msg );
        }
}
```

This code fragment is usually followed by an implementation of a large case statement that performs the required action for each message received. Both the message processing loop and message dispatching intelligence are built into the WEL libraries, relieving the programmer of this coding burden. Messages are automatically received by the components in which they occurred. You can customize message processing by redefining message hook routines in each component type. See Chapter 3, "Messages," for more detail.

When creating a WEL application you must inherit from the *WEL_APPLICATION* class and implement the *main_window* function to create and return the required main window object. A main window can take the form of any composite window provided by the WEL library. For instance, the main window may be a frame window, a popup window, or an MDI window, depending on the needs of the application interface.

The type of main window is determined by declaring the return type of the *main_window* function. For example, if an application requires a frame window as its main window, then the following implementation of *main_window* would suffice:

```
main_window: WEL_FRAME_WINDOW is
                -- A frame main window
        once
                create Result.make_top ("Main Window")
        end
```

The main window must be declared as a once function to ensure that there is only one main window in the application. The function type specifies the kind of main window that will be used in the application—in this case a *WEL_FRAME_WINDOW*. A main window can be either a frame, a popup, a dialog, or an MDI frame.

CREATING A MINIMAL APPLICATION

A minimal WEL application can be implemented by simply creating the main window. For example, an application with a frame window that can be displayed and closed could be implemented with the Eiffel code listed in Example 2.1.

Example 2.1 Minimal Application (app\minimal)

```
class APPLICATION
inherit
    WEL_APPLICATION
creation
    make
feature -- Access

    main_window: WEL_FRAME_WINDOW is
            -- Frame main window
        once
            create Result.make_top ("Main Window")
        end

end -- class APPLICATION
```

Class *MINIMAL_APPLICATION* inherits from the deferred class *WEL_APPLICATION* and implements its only deferred feature, *main_window.* The default creation procedure, *make,* is used to create and initialize the application. Compiling and running this class produces the output shown in Figure 2.1. The main window is created using default settings and can be moved, resized, maximized, minimized, and closed. *MINIMAL_APPLICATION* is not very useful as an application. However, it demonstrates the ease of creating a simple application using the WEL library.

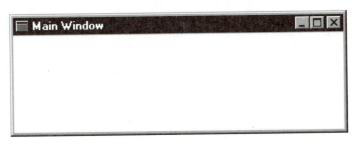

FIGURE 2.1. A minimal WEL application.

The *WEL_APPLICATION* Interface

In addition to declaring the main window, the *WEL_APPLICATION* class provides a number of features for extending and customizing your applications. You can implement code to display the main window in a particular style, such as minimized or maximized; you can implement a routine which will run when the system is idle; and you can set keyboard accelerators.

This section explores each of the features available in *WEL_APPLICATION*.

Constructing an Application

You must write a descendant class of *WEL_APPLICATION* to create an application. The descendant class must effect (i.e., provide an implementation of) the *main_window* feature and specify a creation procedure to be called—typically the default *make* found in *WEL_APPLICATION*.

```
make
       -- Create the application's dispatcher,
       -- set the application's main window and run
       -- the application.
       -- (export status {NONE})

main_window: WEL_COMPOSITE_WINDOW
       -- Must be defined as a once function to create the
       -- application's main_window.
   require
     once_declaration: application_main_window = void
   ensure
     result_not_void: Result /= void;
     parent_main_window_is_void: Result.parent = void
```

The default *make* routine creates the dispatcher, initializes and stores the main window, and then runs the application. This routine is normally sufficient for most applications. If further customization is necessary, then the *make* routine of *WEL_APPLICATION* can be redefined and the parent's version called via the Precursor command (as shown in Example 2.2).

You must ensure that the functionality implemented in *WEL_APPLICATION's make* is actually performed in your application. Ensure that the dispatcher and main window are initialized; in most cases, as in this example, it is sufficient to call the parent's *make* procedure.

Showing the Main Window

Class *WEL_APPLICATION* also provides a function to determine the layout of a main window when it is first displayed on the screen. Normally, a window is displayed using default settings. The minimal application, shown in Figure 2.1,

---

Example 2.2 Minimal Application Version 2, *APPLICATION* Class (app\minimal2)

```
class APPLICATION
inherit
      WEL_APPLICATION
           redefine
                make
           end
creation
      make
feature {NONE} -- Initialization

      make is
              -- Customized make routine
          do
              -- perform customized processing here
              Precursor
          end
  feature -- Access

      main_window: WEL_FRAME_WINDOW is
              -- Frame main window
          once
              create Result.make_top ("Main Window")
          end

  end -- class APPLICATION
```

---

uses the default layout for the frame window. A window can be shown in many different forms, including maximized and minimized.

Function *default_show_command* returns an integer value representing the type of window layout to use when displaying the main window for the first time. You can redefine this function to return a value representing a different layout style. The default definition of *default_show_command* returns the show command passed to the application from the operating system. This is usually the best result because it allows the user to select different show commands using the Windows environment. If your application must override this setting (for instance, if your application must start as an icon) then it can redefine the *default_show_command* to return a fixed result.

```
      default_show_command: INTEGER
              -- Default command used to show 'main_window'.
              -- May be redefined to have a maximized window for
              -- instance.
              -- See class WEL_SW_CONSTANTS for values.
```

The values that can be returned by the *default_show_command* are located in the show window constant class, namely *WEL_SW_CONSTANTS*. Table 2.1 lists the available constants and their general use.

The usual way to use a constant class is to inherit from the class and use the features directly, within the descendant class. A constant class can also be used in a client supplier relationship, using either local variables or attributes within the routine or class. In most cases, this book uses the inheritance method of using constant classes.

An application that shows its main window maximized when first executed can be implemented as shown in Example 2.3.

The inheritance clause lists an additional parent of type *WEL_SW_CONSTANTS*. The export status of the features inherited from *WEL_SW_CONSTANTS* is changed to *NONE,* effectively making them private. The redefinition of *default_show_command* now returns a constant value *Sw_show-*

TABLE 2.1 *Show Window Constants (WEL_SW_CONSTANTS)*

CONSTANT	DESCRIPTION
Sw_hide	Hide the window.
Sw_minimize	Minimize the window.
Sw_otherunzoom	Window is being uncovered because a maximized window was restored or minimized.
Sw_otherzoom	Window is being covered by another window that has been maximized.
Sw_parentclosing	Window's owner window is being minimized.
Sw_parentopening	Window's owner window is being restored.
Sw_restore	Restore the window from its maximized or minimized size to its normal size.
Sw_show	Show the window (that may be hidden) in its normal size and activate it.
Sw_showmaximized	Show the window maximized and activate it.
Sw_showminimized	Show the window minimized and activate it.
Sw_showminnoactivate	Show the window minimized without activating it.
Sw_showna	Show the window in its normal size without activating it.
Sw_shownoactivate	Show the window in its normal size without activating it (same effect as *Sw_showna*).
Sw_shownormal	Show the window in its normal size and activate it.

Example 2.3 Application Main Window Initialization, *APPLICATION* Class (app\initmain)

```
class APPLICATION
inherit
    WEL_APPLICATION
        redefine
            default_show_command
        end
    WEL_SW_CONSTANTS
        export
            {NONE} all
        end
creation
    make
feature {NONE}

    make is
            -- Customized make routine
        do
            -- perform customized processing here
            Precursor
        end
feature {ANY}

    main_window: WEL_FRAME_WINDOW is
            -- Frame main window
        once
            create Result.make_top ("Main Window")
        end
    default_show_command: INTEGER is
            -- Initially show the main window
            -- maximized
        once
            Result := Sw_showmaximized
        end

end -- class APPLICATION
```

maximized, which ensures that the window will be maximized when first shown on the screen.

You can use code similar to Example 2.4 to implement the same functionality using a client supplier relationship with *WEL_SW_CONSTANTS*.

In this case, you do not need to inherit *WEL_SW_CONSTANTS*. An expanded local variable of type *WEL_SW_CONSTANTS* is added to the *default_show_command* routine. The local variable is declared as expanded to reduce the overhead of accessing an object via a reference. This technique can

Example 2.4 Main Window Initialization Using a Client, *APPLICATION* Class (app\initclnt)

```
class APPLICATION
inherit
    WEL_APPLICATION
        redefine
            default_show_command
        end
creation
    make
feature {ANY}

    main_window: WEL_FRAME_WINDOW is
            -- Frame main window
        once
            create Result.make_top ("Main Window")
        end
    default_show_command: INTEGER is
            -- Initially show the main window
            -- maximized
        local
            sw_constants: expanded WEL_SW_CONSTANTS
        once
            Result := sw_constants.Sw_showmaximized
        end

end -- class APPLICATION
```

be useful for constant classes because an expanded object does not need to be accessed via a dereference—it becomes part of the containing object.

Accessing the Main Window of an Application

All windows hold a shared instance of the class *WEL_APPLICA-TION_MAIN_ WINDOW*. As shown in Figure 2.2, this class is also inherited by *WEL_APPLICATION* and is used to initialize and store the main window.

The *WEL_APPLICATION_MAIN_WINDOW* class provides access to the application's main window and to the application itself (i.e., the instance of *WEL_APPLICATION*).

You can use the function *is_application_main_window* to determine if a window is the main window of an application. The window in question is passed as the sole argument. For example, an application may provide the functionality to minimize all child windows when the main window is minimized. To implement this, the following code would need to be implemented in the minimize message routine of the main window:

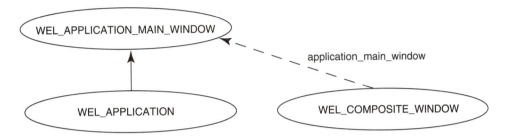

FIGURE 2.2. WEL application class structure.

```
if application_main_window.is_application_main_window (Current) then
    -- code to minimize all child windows
end
```

This allows you to have a number of instances of the main window type, but only one of those instances is actually the main window. A call to *is_application_main_window* returns *True* if the current object is the main window (initialized in *WEL_APPLICATION*); otherwise, the call returns *False*.

Running the Application

In order to begin the execution of a Windows application, the main window must be initialized and shown on the screen, and the message processing loop must be started. In most applications, these tasks are performed by the default implementation of *make* in *WEL_APPLICATION*. The last line of code in *make*

```
application: WEL_APPLICATION
        -- Current application
        -- (from WEL_APPLICATION_MAIN_WINDOW)

application_main_window: WEL_COMPOSITE_WINDOW
        -- Application's main window
        -- (from WEL_APPLICATION_MAIN_WINDOW)

is_application_main_window (window: WEL_COMPOSITE_WINDOW): BOOLEAN
        -- Is 'window' the application's main window?
        -- (from WEL_APPLICATION_MAIN_WINDOW)
    require -- from WEL_APPLICATION_MAIN_WINDOW
        window_not_void: window /= void
    ensure -- from WEL_APPLICATION_MAIN_WINDOW
        Result = (window = application_main_window)

is_dialog: BOOLEAN
        -- Is the main window a dialog box?
```

```
runable: BOOLEAN
         -- Can the application be run?
         -- (True by default)
         -- The user may want to return False if the application
         -- cannot be executed for any reason.
```

invokes *WEL_APPLICATION's run* procedure, which initializes the main window, shows it on the screen (in the style defined by *default_show_command*), and begins the message loop. The loop reads and dispatches all messages received by the application.

You can stop an application from running by redefining the feature *runnable* to return *False*. For example, you might want to stop an application from running if the user does not have sufficient access rights to start it.

The following code fragment implements this requirement:

```
inherit
        WEL_APPLICATION
                redefine
                        runnable
                end
feature
        runnable: BOOLEAN is
                        -- Allow the application to run only if the
                        -- user has sufficient access rights.
                do
                        Result:= sufficient_user_rights
                end
feature {NONE}
        sufficient_user_rights: BOOLEAN is
                        -- Does the user have sufficient user rights
                        -- to use this application?
                do
                        -- check rights and return boolean result,
                        -- true if rights exist, false otherwise
                end
```

Setting an Idle Routine

A Windows application is idle while waiting for input from the user. During this idle time, it is sometimes useful to perform some background processing, such as running an animation, updating a real-time clock, or caching database query information.

Class *WEL_APPLICATION* provides four related features for setting and enabling an idle routine. An application can have only one idle routine at a

```
idle_action_enabled: BOOLEAN
          -- Is the idle action enabled?
          -- (False by default)
disable_idle_action
          -- Disable the call to 'idle_action' when the message
          -- queue is empty.
    ensure
          idle_action_disabled: not idle_action_enabled
          enable_idle_action
          -- Enable the call to 'idle_action' when the message
          -- queue is empty.
    ensure
          idle_action_enabled: idle_action_enabled
idle_action
          -- Called when the message queue is empty.
          -- Useful to perform background operations.
    require
          idle_action_enabled: idle_action_enabled
```

time, although you can, through the use of flags, code this routine in any reasonable manner to simulate multiple idle routines. The idle routine features allow you to enable and disable the idle routine, check whether the idle routine is enabled, and implement the idle routine.

If the application is idle and has no messages to process, then the routine *idle_action* is called. The application tests whether to call the idle action routine via the function *idle_action_enabled*. This flag can be set using the procedures *disable_idle_action* and *enable_idle_action*.

The default implementation of *idle_action* (as found in class *WEL_APPLICATION*) does nothing. Therefore, to implement your own idle routine you must redefine *idle_action* in the *WEL_APPLICATION* descendant. The following example uses an idle routine to repeatedly display a message in a window. Figure 2.3 shows the output of the application at one particular point in time.

When you run the application, you can pause the idle routine by moving or resizing the window or by opening the window control menu. At all other times, the idle routine will be running and continually displaying the message *Waiting* with a series of dots trailing.

First, the *make* routine enables the idle action, then it calls the precursor *make* routine. The idle routine initializes a static text control to display a message and attaches it to the main window (we examine the creation of controls in more detail in later chapters). Once the text control has been initialized, the routine appends a full stop to the end of the message until it has appended more than 40 full stops, then it starts from the beginning again.

Example 2.5 Application Idle Routine, *APPLICATION* Class (app\idle)

```
class APPLICATION
inherit
    WEL_APPLICATION
        redefine
            make,
            idle_action
        end
creation
    make

feature
    make is
            -- Initialize application with an idle routine enabled
        do
            enable_idle_action
            Precursor
        end
    main_window: WEL_FRAME_WINDOW is
            -- Frame main window
        once
            create Result.make_top ("Main Window")
        end
    idle_action is
            -- Display "waiting" message on screen
        do
            if text = Void then
                create text.make (main_window, "Waiting",
                    0, 0, main_window.width, main_window.height, -1)
                create message.make (60)
                message.append ("Waiting")
            else
                if count > 40 then
                    count := 1
                    message.wipe_out
                    message.append ("Waiting")
                end
                message.append_character ('.')
                text.set_text (message)
                count := count + 1
            end
        end
    text: WEL_STATIC
            -- Static text control for message
    count: INTEGER
            -- Counter for message dots
    message: STRING
            -- Current message to display
end -- class APPLICATION
```

FIGURE 2.3. Application with idle action.

The solution above provides a simple mechanism for performing actions when an application is idle. However, the idle routine takes 100 percent of the CPU and should be used with care. In particular, the idle handler should be reset once the work has been completed.

Using Keyboard Accelerators

Keyboard accelerators provide user shortcuts for performing various operations. A keyboard accelerator is a particular key sequence that the user can press to invoke an action. The action might be a menu item or an arbitrary command.

To implement keyboard accelerators, you have to build a keyboard accelerator table and add it to your application resources. This can be done using a resource editor or by manually typing the resource text into a resource file. See Chapter 7, "Resources," for more detail. Once you have created an accelerator table resource, you need to load it into your application. The easiest way to do this is to redefine the feature *accelerators* of class *WEL_APPLICATION*.

The feature *accelerators* should be redefined as a once function that returns an instance of the class *WEL_ACCELERATORS*, representing the accelerator keys for your application. Once the accelerator table has been loaded, you can detect accelerator key events and perform appropriate application operations.

The following example uses three accelerators for the function keys F1, F2, and F3. Each accelerator is given a unique identification number and the

```
accelerators: WEL_ACCELERATORS
        -- Application's accelerators
        -- May be redefined (in once) to associate accelerators.
```

accelerator table itself is also given a number. These identifiers are defined in the class *APPLICATION_IDS*. The *APPLICATION_IDS* class is typically generated automatically from the resource files, as discussed in Chapter 7. Example 2.6 shows the text of class *APPLICATION_IDS*. The accelerator table is loaded using the *WEL_APPLICATION* accelerators feature.

Example 2.6 Keyboard Accelerator Keys, APPLICATION_IDS Class (applic\keys)

```
class
      APPLICATION_IDS
feature - Access
      Idr_f3_constant: INTEGER is 40003
      Idr_f1_constant: INTEGER is 40005
      Idr_f2_constant: INTEGER is 40004
      Idr_accelerator1_constant: INTEGER is 101
end -- class APPLICATION_IDS
```

When the user presses one of the defined function keys, a message box is shown, indicating which accelerator key was pressed. The *APPLICATION* class (see Example 2.7) gains access to the accelerator table constants by inheriting from *APPLICATION_IDS*. The *Idr_accelerator1_constant* represents the accelerator table as a whole and is used to construct the *WEL_ACCELERATOR* instance. We leave the description of accelerator key event handling until a later chapter (see "On a Composite Window Keyboard Accelerator Message" in Chapter 5, "Composite Windows").

Modifying Application Initialization

Two features are provided to customize the way an application is initialized, namely, *init_instance* and *init_application*. The routines are used to perform processing before the first instance of the application is created or before the current instance is created, respectively. The default implementation of both routines (as found in *WEL_APPLICATION*) performs no processing. You can redefine the routines to perform any initialization you require. A common initialization requirement is to load dynamic-link libraries (DDLs) used by the application.

The *init_instance* routine is currently not implemented. Future versions of the WEL libraries will allow initialization of the first application instance.

If an application requires a DLL to be loaded before beginning execution, it can add the DLL loading code to a redefined version of *init_application*. For example, a Windows application may require the common controls DLL to be

---

**Example 2.7 Keyboard Accelerator Keys, APPLICATION Class
(applic\keys)**

```
class APPLICATION
inherit
      WEL_APPLICATION
            redefine
                  accelerators
            end
      APPLICATION_IDS
            export
                  {NONE} all
            end
creation
      make
feature
      main_window: MAIN_WINDOW is
                  -- Frame main window
            once
                  create Result.make
            end
      accelerators: WEL_ACCELERATORS is
                  -- Application's accelerators
            once
                  create Result.make_by_id (Idr_accelerator1_constant)
            end
end -- class APPLICATION
```

---

loaded so that it can use extended components. The application class in Example 2.8 would do the job.

The redefined implementation of *init_application* creates an instance of *WEL_COMMON_CONTROLS_DLL*, which loads the dynamic-link library. Additional DLL classes can be created in this routine to load any required libraries.

```
init_application
          -- Called for each instance of the application.
          -- May be defined to load DLLs.
init_instance
          -- Called for the first instance
          -- of the application.
          -- Not yet implemented, for future release.
```

Example 2.8 Application Initialization (app\init)

```
class APPLICATION
inherit
    WEL_APPLICATION
        redefine
            init_application
        end
creation
    make
feature {ANY}
    main_window: WEL_FRAME_WINDOW is
            -- Frame main window
        once
            create Result.make_top ("Main Window")
        end
    init_application is
            -- Load requred Win32 DLL library
        do
            create win32_dll.make
        end

    win32_dll: WEL_COMMON_CONTROLS_DLL

end -- class APPLICATION
```

SUMMARY

Every WEL application is composed of a main window and at least one class that inherits from *WEL_APPLICATION*. The main window of an application can be any type of *WEL_COMPOSITE_WINDOW* and typically takes the form of a frame, popup, or MDI window.

Class *WEL_APPLICATION* provides features for storing and accessing the main window of the application, initializing the main window, setting an idle action, and defining keyboard accelerators.

An application built using the WEL libraries does not have to implement its own message-processing loop. This is performed by the *WEL_APPLICA-TION* class itself. All messages are automatically forwarded to the relevant window or control in which they occurred.

SAMPLE APPLICATION

DIRECTORY TREE ANALYZER

We would like to demonstrate the use of WEL in the construction of a complete application. The application stems from our experience with the UNIX operating system. One of the many useful tools available on UNIX is the *du* command, which provides a textual listing of disk usage for a selected directory and its subdirectories. A graphical Windows version of this tool is useful and requires a wide coverage of WEL features for its implementation. The tool is called Directory Tree Analyzer (DTA).

WHICH DIRECTORIES ARE USING ALL THE DISK SPACE?

Have you ever needed to find extra space on your hard drive to fit the latest Eiffel compiler (or firstperson shoot-em-up game!) only to find that you don't know which directories are using up all the space? A solution would be a small utility that can explore a directory and all of its subdirectories to examine the number and size of files in each directory and display the resulting information in a sorted list. Beginning with this chapter, we explore the construction of Directory Tree Analyzer, a possible solution to the problem. At the end of many chapters throughout the book, we expand the example. This chapter begins with a description of the requirements and a description of problem domain classes used to collect and analyze directory information.

THE SOLUTION

The general requirements we wanted to meet include the ability to

- mirror UNIX's *du* command
- select a specific directory where the analysis will begin
- change the depth that the analysis will traverse when collecting information
- display directory usage in bytes, kilobytes, or megabytes
- display directory usage in a graphical percentage bar form to easily identify directories using more space than others

Directory Information

First, we need a way of traversing a directory tree to collect information about the number and size of files in each directory. To do this we wrote two classes, *DIRECTORY_PARSER* and *DIRECTORY_INFO*. *DIRECTORY_PARSER* provides a feature that collects information for each directory parsed and stores the information, including the number of files, the total size of the files, the path name, and the number of subdirectories, in an instance of *DIRECTORY_INFO*. Example 2.9 shows the code for *DIRECTORY_INFO*.

Example 2.9 DIRECTORY_INFO Class for the Directory Tree Analyzer

```
1     class DIRECTORY_INFO
2     inherit
3           COMPARABLE;
4           DIRECTORY_INFO_CONSTANTS
5                 undefine
6                       is_equal
7                 end
8     create
9           make
10    feature -- Initialization
11          make (a_name: like name) is
12                      -- Set 'name' with 'a_name'.
13                      -- Set default ordering.
14                require
15                    non_void_name: a_name /= void;
16                    valid_name: not a_name.empty
17                do
18                    name := a_name
19                    order_by (ordered_by_name)
20                ensure
21                    name_set: name.is_equal (a_name);
22                    name_order: ordered_by = ordered_by_name
23                end;
24
25    feature -- Access
26
27          file_count: INTEGER;
28                      -- Number of files
29
30          directory_count: INTEGER;
31                      -- Number of sub-directories
32
33          name: STRING;
34                      -- Full path name
35
36          total_usage: INTEGER;
37                      -- Total space usage in bytes
38                      -- i.e., sum of file sizes
```

```
39
40          total_byte_usage: STRING is
41                  -- Formatted 'total_usage' in bytes
42              do
43                  Result := byte_formatter.formatted
                        (total_usage)
44                  Result.append (byte_symbol)
45              end;
46
47          total_kb_usage: STRING is
48                  -- Formatted total space usage in kilobytes
49              do
50                  Result := formatter.formatted (total_usage /
                        kilobyte)
51                  Result.append (kilobyte_symbol)
52              end;
53
54          total_mb_usage: STRING is
55                  -- Formatted total space usage in megabytes
56              do
57                  Result := formatter.formatted (total_usage /
                        megabyte)
58                  Result.append (megabyte_symbol)
59              end;
60
61          total_optimised_usage: STRING is
62                  -- Total space usage in largest byte size.
63              do
64                  if total_usage > megabyte then
65                          Result := total_mb_usage
66                  elseif total_usage > kilobyte then
67                          Result := total_kb_usage
68                  else
69                          Result := total_byte_usage
70                  end
71              end;
72
73          ordered_by: INTEGER;
74                  -- Ordering field
75
76          Kilobyte: INTEGER is 1024;
77                  -- Number of bytes in a Kilobyte
78
79          Megabyte: INTEGER is 1048576;
80                  -- Number of bytes in a Megabyte
81
82      feature -- Status report
83
84          infix "<" (other: like Current): BOOLEAN is
85                  -- Is current object less than 'other'?
                    -- Depends on 'ordered_by'
86                  -- flag to indicate the fields to compare.
87              do
```

```
88                      if ordered_by = ordered_by_name then
89                             Result := name < (other.name)
90                      elseif ordered_by = ordered_by_file_count then
91                             Result := file_count <
                                  (other.file_count)
92                      elseif ordered_by = ordered_by_directory_count
                           then
93                             Result := directory_count < (other.
                                  directory_count)
94                      else
95                             Result := total_usage <
                                  (other.total_usage)
96                      end
97               end;
98
99      feature -- Status setting
100
101            order_by (order_field: INTEGER) is
102                      -- Set the order comparison field
103                  require
104                      valid_order_by: valid_order_by (order_field)
105                  do
106                      ordered_by := order_field
107                  end;
108
109            set_name (new_name: like name) is
110                      -- Set 'name' with 'new_name'.
111                  require
112                      non_void_name: new_name /= void;
113                      valid_name: not new_name.empty
114                  do
115                      name := new_name
116                  ensure
117                      name_set: name.is_equal (new_name)
118                  end;
119
120            set_file_count (count: like file_count) is
121                      -- Set 'file_count' with 'count'.
122                  require
123                      valid_count: count >= 0
124                  do
125                      file_count := count
126                  ensure
127                      file_count_set: file_count = count
128                  end;
129
130            set_directory_count (count: like directory_count) is
131                      -- Set 'directory_count' with 'count'.
132                  require
133                      valid_count: count >= 0
134                  do
135                      directory_count := count
136                  ensure
137                      directory_count_set: directory_count = count
```

```
138            end;
139
140        set_total_usage (usage: like total_usage) is
141                   -- Set 'total_usage' with 'usage'.
142            require
143                valid_total_usage: usage >= 0
144            do
145                total_usage := usage
146            ensure
147                total_usage_set: total_usage = usage
148            end;
149
150  feature {NONE} -- Implementation
151
152        formatter: FORMAT_DOUBLE is
153                   -- Total space usage formatter
154            once
155                create Result.make (10, 2)
156                Result.no_justify
157            end;
158
159        byte_formatter: FORMAT_INTEGER is
160                   -- Total byte space usage formatter
161            once
162                create Result.make (12)
163                Result.no_justify
164            end;
165
166  end -- class DIRECTORY_INFO
```

The *DIRECTORY_INFO* class is used to create objects that store information about a single directory. The class defines attributes for holding the name of the directory, number of files contained in the directory, number of subdirectories, and the total usage in bytes of all the files in the directory. The total usage can be converted to different size representations, including kilobytes, megabytes, and optimized (depends on the closest size match). Each of these routines use an EiffelBase library class to format the numbers as strings. The once function *formatter* (returning an instance of *FORMAT_DOUBLE*) is used to format usage in kilobytes and megabytes. Formatting in bytes is performed using the singleton object *byteformatter* (of type *FORMAT_INTEGER*).

DIRECTORY_INFO inherits from *COMPARABLE* so that each instance can be compared using a total order relation to another *DIRECTORY_INFO* instance. This allows us to easily sort information by storing it in a *SORTED_LIST* or one of its descendants. As a descendant of *COMPARABLE*, *DIRECTORY_INFO* inherits one deferred feature, *is_equal*. To become truly comparable, *DIRECTORY_INFO* must effect *is_equal* to return *True* if the current instance is equal to another instance (passed as parameter *other*). In most descendants of *COMPARABLE*, this is straightforward—compare one or more attributes of each instance and return the result of the comparison. For example, we could have just compared the *name* of each instance using *is_equal,* of class *STRING,* and returned the result of that comparison. However, we need to do more than that—we need the ability to sort *DIRECTORY_INFO* instances by name, usage, number of files in each, and number of directories in each. One solution is to define a flag that indicates the type of comparison that we want to apply for a particular *sort* operation. Feature *ordered_by* (line 73) performs this function. Our implementation of *is_equal* (lines 84–97) checks the current value of *ordered_by* and performs an appropriate comparison of attributes. The order types are defined in class *DIRECTORY_INFO_CONSTANTS* shown in Example 2.10. The feature group "Status Setting" (lines 99–149) provides routines for setting each of the *DIRECTORY_INFO* attributes, including the current order setting for *is_equal.*

Example 2.10 DIRECTORY_INFO_CONSTANTS Class for the Directory Tree Analyzer

```
1    class DIRECTORY_INFO_CONSTANTS
2    feature -- Access
3
4        Byte_symbol: STRING is "B";
5                    -- Byte unit symbol
6
7        Kilobyte_symbol: STRING is "Kb";
8                    -- Kilobyte unit symbol
9
10       Megabyte_symbol: STRING is "Mb";
11                   -- Megabyte unit symbol
12
13       Ordered_by_name: INTEGER is 1;
14
15       Ordered_by_file_count: INTEGER is 2;
16
17       Ordered_by_directory_count: INTEGER is 3;
18
19       Ordered_by_usage: INTEGER is 4;
20
21       valid_order_by (field: INTEGER): BOOLEAN is
22                   -- Is 'field' a valid ordering type
23           do
24               Result := field = ordered_by_name or field =
                     ordered_by_file_count
25                   or field = ordered_by_directory_count or
                         field = ordered_by_usage
26           end;
27
28   end -- class DIRECTORY_INFO_CONSTANTS
```

Directory Parsing

The class that does most of the real work in our application is *DIRECT-ORY_PARSER* (see Example 2.11). This class implements the logic for recursively traversing a directory structure and accumulating information on each directory as it descends. The routine that does all the work is *collect*. Information collected during a traversal is stored in a sorted list in the attribute *directory_infos*. The *collect* routine (beginning at line 30) takes three parameters—*start*, of type *FILE*, representing the directory from which the collection should begin; *sort_order*, of type *INTEGER*, representing the initial ordering criteria for *DIRECTORY_INFO* instances; and *callback*, of type *ROUTINE*, representing a routine that is called for each directory traversed. The agent can be a feature of any type (thus the first generic parameter is type *ANY*) and must take one parameter of type *STRING* (thus *TUPLE [STRING]*). The agent is useful for providing information on the progress of a *collect* call. Our example uses the agent to display the current progress of the traversal in the main window. If the callback parameter is *Void*, then it is ignored during the *collect* operation.

**Example 2.11 DIRECTORY_PARSER Class for the Directory
Tree Analyzer**

```
1     class DIRECTORY_PARSER
2     inherit
3            SHARED_DATA
4                   export
5                          {NONE} all
6                   end;
7            DIRECTORY_INFO_CONSTANTS
8                   export
9                          {NONE} all;
10                         {ANY} valid_order_by
11                  end
12    create
13           make
14
15    feature -- Initialization
16
17        make is
18                   -- Initialize
19             do
20                    create directory_infos.make
21             end;
22
23    feature -- Access
24
25           directory_infos: SORTED_TWO_WAY_LIST [DIRECTORY_INFO];
26                   -- Sorted list of directory information
```

```
27
28      feature -- Basic operations
29
30          collect (start: FILE; sort_order: INTEGER; callback: ROUTINE [ANY,
                  TUPLE [STRING]]) is
31                  -- Reset the current 'directory_infos' and collect
32                  -- directory information beginning at 'start'.
33                  -- Sort the directories by 'sort_order' type.
34                  -- If 'callback' is not Void then call 'callback' at
35                  -- each folder.
36              require
37                  start_valid: start /= void;
38                  start_exists: start.exists;
39                  start_is_directory: start.is_directory;
40                  valid_sort_type: valid_order_by (sort_order)
41              do
42                  start_directory := start.name
43                  total_size := 0
44                  total_file_count := 0
45                  total_directory_count := 0
46                  directory_infos.wipe_out
47                  sort := sort_order
48                  notify_callback := callback
49                  collect_directory_info (start, 0)
50              end;
51
52      feature -- Access
53
54          start_directory: STRING;
55                  -- Start directory of last parse. Void if no parse
56                  -- performed.
57
58          largest_directory_size: INTEGER is
59                  -- Return the size of the largest directory
60              require
61                  valid_directory_info: directory_infos /= void
62              local
63                  largest: INTEGER
64              do
65                  from
66                          directory_infos.start
67                  until
68                          directory_infos.exhausted
69                  loop
70                          Result := Result.max (directory_infos.item.total_usage);
71                          directory_infos.forth
72                  end
73              ensure
74                  size_greater_or_equal_to_zero: Result >= 0
75              end;
76
77          total_size: INTEGER;
78                  -- Total usage of all directories
```

```
79
80          total_mb_size: STRING is
81                  -- Total usage of all directories in Megabytes
82              require
83                  valid_directory_info: directory_infos /= void
84              local
85                  formatter: FORMAT_DOUBLE
86              do
87                  create formatter.make (10, 2);
88                  formatter.no_justify;
89                  Result := formatter.formatted (total_size / 1048576);
90                  Result.append (megabyte_symbol)
91              end;
92
93          total_file_count: INTEGER;
94                  -- Total number of files in all directories
95
96          total_directory_count: INTEGER;
97                  -- Total number of subdirectories in all directories
98
99      feature {NONE} -- Implementation
100
101         notify_callback: ROUTINE [ANY, TUPLE [STRING]];
102                  -- Callback to call for each directory name parsed.
103                  -- Can be Void.
104
105         sort: INTEGER;
106                  -- Sort order for new directory information
107
108         collect_directory_info (start: FILE;
                current_depth: INTEGER) is
109                  -- Collection information on all directories under
110                  -- and including 'start'
111             require
112                 start_valid: start /= void;
113                 start_exists: start.exists;
114                 start_is_directory: start.is_directory;
115                 positive_current_depth: current_depth >= 0;
116                 within_fixed_depth: not shared_preferences.is_traversal_
                        infinite
117                     implies current_depth <= shared_
                        preferences.traversal_depth
118             local
119                 directory: DIRECTORY;
120                 contents: ARRAYED_LIST [STRING];
121                 info: DIRECTORY_INFO;
122                 file_count, directory_count, usage: INTEGER;
123                 next: STRING;
124                 next_file: RAW_FILE;
125                 next_path: STRING
126             do
127                 create info.make (start.name);
128                 if notify_callback /= void then
```

```
129                         notify_callback.call ([<<start.name>>])
130                     end;
131                     from
132                         create directory.make (start.name);
133                         contents := directory.linear_representation;
134                         contents.start
135                     until
136                         contents.exhausted
137                     loop
138                         if not (contents.item.is_equal (".") or
                                 contents.item.is_equal ("..")) then
139                             next_path := clone (start.name);
140                             if next_path.item (next_path.count) /= '\' then
141                                 next_path.append_string ("\")
142                             end;
143                             next_path.append_string (contents.item);
144                             create next_file.make (next_path);
145                             if next_file.is_directory then
146                                 directory_count := directory_count + 1;
147                                 if shared_preferences.is_traversal_infinite then
148                                     collect_directory_info (next_file,
                                             current_depth + 1)
149                                 elseif current_depth < shared_preferences.
                                     traversal_depth then
150                                     collect_directory_info (next_file,
                                             current_depth + 1)
151                                 elseif shared_preferences.sum_last_folder then
152                                     sum_directory_info (next_file)
153                                 end
154                             else
155                                 file_count := file_count + 1;
156                                 usage := usage + next_file.count
157                             end
158                         end;
159                         contents.forth
160                     end;
161             info.set_file_count (file_count);
162             info.set_directory_count (directory_count);
163             info.set_total_usage (usage);
164             info.order_by (sort);
165             directory_infos.extend (info);
166             total_size := total_size + usage;
167             total_file_count := total_file_count + file_count;
168             total_directory_count := total_directory_count +
                     directory_count
169         end;
170
171     sum_directory_info (start: FILE) is
172             -- Sum the total directory usage within 'file' and store
173             -- in one directory info
174         require
175             start_valid: start /= void;
176             start_exists: start.exists;
```

```
177                     start_is_directory: start.is_directory
178             local
179                     info: DIRECTORY_INFO;
180                     str: STRING
181             do
182                     str := (start.name;
183                     str.append ("+");
184                     create info.make (str);
185                     sum_directory_info_recurse (start, info);
186                     info.order_by (sort);
187                     directory_infos.extend (info);
188                     total_size := total_size + info.total_usage;
189                     total_file_count := total_file_count + info.file_count;
190                     total_directory_count := total_directory_count +
191                         info.directory_count
192             end;

193         sum_directory_info_recurse (start: FILE; info: DIRECTORY_INFO) is
194             require
195                     start_valid: start /= void;
196                     start_exists: start.exists;
197                     start_is_directory: start.is_directory;
198                     info_not_void: info /= void
199             local
200                     directory: DIRECTORY;
201                     contents: ARRAYED_LIST [STRING];
202                     file_count, directory_count, usage: INTEGER;
203                     next: STRING;
204                     next_file: RAW_FILE;
205                     next_path: STRING
206             do
207                     if notify_callback /= void then
208                             notify_callback.call (<<start.name>>)
209                     end;
210                     from
211                             create directory.make (start.name);
212                             contents := directory.linear_representation;
213                             contents.start
214                     until
215                             contents.exhausted
216                     loop
217                      if not (contents.item.is_equal (".") or
                            contents.item.is_equal ("..")) then
218                             next_path := clone (start.name);
219                             if next_path.item (next_path.count) /= '\' then
220                                 next_path.append_string ("\")
221                             end;
222                             next_path.append_string (contents.item);
223                             create next_file.make (next_path);
224                             if next_file.is_directory then
225                                 directory_count := directory_count + 1;
226                                 sum_directory_info_recurse (next_file, info)
227                             else
```

```
228                                     file_count := file_count + 1;
229                                     usage := usage + next_file.count
230                            end
231                    end;
232                    contents.forth
233             end;
234             info.set_file_count (info.file_count + file_count);
235             info.set_directory_count (info.directory_count + directory_count);
236             info.set_total_usage (info.total_usage + usage)
237          end;
238
239   end -- class DIRECTORY_PARSER
```

The *collect* routine calls *collect_directory_info,* which performs the re-cursive traversal of a directory according to the current user preferences. Recall that the application must allow the user to select whether the depth of traversal will be infinite or fixed at a certain level. If a fixed level is chosen, then the user must also be able to choose whether any further subdirectory information is included in the information for the fixed level. If a fixed traversal depth is chosen and further information should be accumulated, then *collect_direc-tory_info* calls *sum_directory_info,* which in turn calls *sum_directory_info_ recurse* to collect and accumulate subdirectory information.

Shared Application Data

The current user preferences are accessible via a once function inherited from class *SHARED_DATA.* Example 2.12 shows the two shared variables in class *SHARED_DATA,* namely *shared_preferences* and *print_dialog* (we discuss the *print_dialog* function later in the book). The once function definitions make sure that any descendants of *SHARED_DATA* always access the same instance of the function values.

Application Preferences

The routine *collect_directory_info* in *DIRECTORY_PARSER* checks the pref-erences *is_traversal_infinite, traversal_depth,* and *sum_last_folder* during the traversal process to determine the path of execution to be taken. For example, if *is_traversal_infinite* is *True,* then the traversal continues with a standard re-cursive call on *collect_directory_info* (line 147 of *DIRECTORY_PARSER*). If *is_traversal_infinite* is *False,* then *current_depth* is compared with the user se-lected *traversal_depth,* and if the traversal depth has not been reached, then a standard recursive call is executed (line 149); otherwise, the *sum_last_folder*

Example 2.12 SHARED_DATA Class for the Directory Tree Analyzer

```
1      class SHARED_DATA
2      feature -- Access
3              shared_preferences: PREFERENCES is
4                          -- Settings used to display list view
5              once
6                      create Result.make
7              end;
8          print_dialog: WEL_PRINT_DIALOG is
9                          -- Print setting dialog
10             once
11                     create Result.make
12             end;
13     end -- class SHARED_DATA
```

---

preference is checked to see if traversal should continue to collect subdirectory sizes via a call to *sum_directory_info* (line 151). Recursion stops when all directories have been traversed, when the fixed traversal depth has been reached, or when the fixed traversal depth has been reached and all remaining subdirectories have been traversed and their information accumulated.

The user can also choose how directory size information is displayed, a heading for printed output, and the font that printed output will use. All of the preferences are stored in an instance of class *PREFERENCES* (see Example 2.13). The *PREFERENCES* class provides an attribute for each preference and a *set_ routine* used to change each preference.

Example 2.13 PREFERENCES Class for the Directory Tree Analyzer

```
1    class PREFERENCES
2    inherit
3          WEL_WINDOWS_ROUTINES
4              export
5                  {NONE} all
6              end;
7          APPLICATION_IDS
8              export
9                  {NONE} all
10             end
11   create
12         make
13   feature {NONE} -- Initialization
14
15       make is
16               -- Initialize preferences with defaults
17           do
```

```
18                          traversal := traversal_infinite
19                          traversal_depth := 1
20                          size := size_optimal
21                          page_title := resource_string_id
                               (ids_default_page_title_constant)
22                          create row_font.make (12, "System")
23                  ensure
24                          infinite_traversal: traversal = traversal_infinite;
25                          size_in_kilobytes: size = size_optimal
26                  end;
27      feature - Access
28
29          traversal: INTEGER;
30                      -- Type of traversal
31
32          traversal_depth: INTEGER;
33                      -- Depth of traversal (-1 if infinite)
34
35          sum_last_folder: BOOLEAN;
36                      -- Should subfolders at the last level of traversal be
37                      -- collected and added to the size of the parent folder?
38
39          size: INTEGER;
40                      -- Type of display for directory sizes
41
42          selected_path: STRING;
43                      -- Path to analyze
44
45          is_traversal--infinite: BOOLEAN is
46                      -- Should depth of directory traversal be infinite or
47                      -- fixed?
48              do
49                  Result := traversal = traversal_infinite
50              end;
51
52          Size_bytes: INTEGER is unique;
53                      -- Possible directory sizes types
54
55          Size_kilobytes: INTEGER is unique;
56                      -- Possible directory sizes types
57
58          Size_megabytes: INTEGER is unique;
59                      -- Possible directory sizes types
60
61          Size_optimal: INTEGER is unique;
62                      -- Possible directory sizes types
63
64          Traversal_fixed: INTEGER is unique;
65                      -- Possible traversal types
66
67          Traversal_infinite: INTEGER is unique;
68                      -- Possible traversal types
69
```

```
70        is_valid_size (an_integer: INTEGER): BOOLEAN is
71                    -- Is 'an_integer' a valid size type?
72            do
73                    Result := an_integer = size_bytes or an_integer =
                          size_kilobytes
74                        or an_integer = size_megabytes or an_integer =
                              size_optimal
75            end;
76
77        page_title: STRING;
78                    -- Page title for printing
79
80        row_font: WEL_LOG_FONT;
81                    -- Font for printing detail rows
82
83    feature -- Settings
84
85        set_traversal_infinite is
86                    -- Set infinite traversal.
87            do
88                    traversal := traversal_infinite
89            ensure
90                    traversal_infinite: is_traversal_infinite
91            end;
92
93        set_traversal_fixed (depth: like traversal_depth) is
94                    -- Set fixed traversal with depth 'depth'.
95            require
96                    positive_depth: depth >= 0
97            do
98                    traversal := traversal_fixed
99                    traversal_depth := depth
100           ensure
101                   traversal_fixed: not is_traversal_infinite;
102                   traversal_depth_set: traversal_depth = depth
103           end;
104
105       set_sum_last_folder (flag: BOOLEAN) is
106           do
107                   sum_last_folder := flag
108           end;
109
110       set_size (a_size: like size) is
111                   -- Set 'size' with 'a_size'.
112           require
113                   valid_size: is_valid_size (a_size)
114           do
115                   size := a_size
116           ensure
117                   size_set: size = a_size
118           end;
119
120       set_selected_path (a_path: like selected_path) is
```

```
121                    -- Set 'selected_path' with 'a_path'.
122              require
123                  non_void_path: a_path /= void;
124                  valid_path: not a_path.empty
125              do
126                  selected_path := a_path
127              ensure
128                  selected_path_set: selected_path.is_equal (a_path)
129              end;
130
131          set_page_title (new_title: like page_title) is
132                  -- Set 'page_title' to 'new_title'
133              require
134                  new_title_exists: new_title /= void
135              do
136                  page_title := new_title
137              end;
138
139          set_row_font (new_font: like row_font) is
140                  -- Set 'row_font' to 'new_font'
141              require
142                  new_font_exists: new_font /= void
143              do
144                  row_font := new_font
145              end;
146
147      invariant
148
149          valid_traversal: traversal = traversal_fixed or traversal =
                  traversal_infinite;
150          valid_traversal_depth: not is_traversal_infinite implies
                  traversal_depth >= 0;
151          valid_size: is_valid_size (size);
152          valid_page_title: page_title /= void;
153          valid_row_font: row_font /= void;
154
155      end -- class PREFERENCES
```

The example classes we have explored so far provide the inner workings of the Directory Tree Analyzer application. The abstractions used to explore a directory tree, store information about each directory, and maintain user preferences have been shown. We currently have nothing, apart from the occasional mention of fonts and a single mention of a string resource, that indicates that these classes will be used in a Windows application. In fact, there is no reason that the classes could not be used, without modification, in a command-line or console application.

THE APPLICATION

Given that this chapter explores the creation of a Windows application, we look at one last class: *APPLICATION*. As you can see in Example 2.14, the code for the *APPLICATION* class is very brief. Only a minimal implementation of *WEL_APPLICATION* is needed to identify and instantiate the main window of the Directory Tree Analyzer application.

Example 2.14 APPLICATION Class for the Directory Tree Analyzer

```
1    class APPLICATION
2    inherit
3           WEL_APPLICATION
4    create
5           make
6    feature
7
8           main_window: MAIN_WINDOW is
9                         -- Frame main window
10             once
11                     create Result.make
12             end;
13
14   end -- class APPLICATION
```

T   H   R   E   E

MESSAGES

INTRODUCING MESSAGES

A Windows application reacts to user interaction and to its working environment—a button, when pressed, should provide visual feedback and cause an action. A window should stretch when the user drags the resize handles and it should close cleanly when its close button is clicked. Windows notifies an application of user events and changes to the working environment by passing messages. Each message notifies the application of a particular event, such as mouse movement, a mouse button click, or keyboard key press events.

The message-passing protocol provides programmers with a great deal of flexibility. Your applications can register interest in particular messages and quietly ignore others. Windows provides default processing for most messages, so any messages that your application ignores will be passed to Windows to process. If your application needs to perform an action when a button is pressed, then it can register interest in the button click message and perform the necessary processing whenever the message notification is received.

The WEL library provides three methods of handling messages—*message operations,* the *context → event → command* protocol, and *default message processing.* Each of these methods provides a different degree of control and flexibility and can be used simultaneously in one application.

This chapter explores the use of each message-handling method in detail. We begin with a general description of messages and then describe the message-handling approaches.

WINDOWS MESSAGES

It is interesting to explore the button click example further. Let's say your application needs to display a message to the user whenever a button is clicked. Figure 3.1 shows just such an application.

This seems like a simple application to write—create a window, capture the button click message, and display a message box with the relevant message as its text. We will see how to create a window and display a message box in subsequent chapters. For now, we are interested in how to capture the button click message and how to perform an operation when it arrives.

Capturing Messages

When the user clicks on a button, three different messages are sent to the application. First, a button press message is sent, followed by a button release message, and then a button click message. The three messages may also differ depending on whether the right or left mouse button was pressed.

The messages sent to a window are defined in the class *WEL_WM_CON-STANTS*. Each constant name is prefixed with *Wm_* (which stands for Window Message), and they range from *Wm_activate* (sent when a window is activated or deactivated) to *Wm_wininichange* (sent to notify an application that the

FIGURE 3.1. Button click message application.

WIN.INI file has been modified). There are approximately 130 different window messages. A number of the messages are also used in different circumstances.

The message *Wm_command* is used to notify an application of specific child window control actions. In our example, the window is notified of a button click by receiving a *Wm_command* message. The *Wm_notify* message is also used in a similar fashion to notify a dialog window of dialog control actions. The *Wm_command* message can be processed in a number of ways. The simplest way is to capture and process the message using a *message hook.*

Message Hooks

A WEL library component, such as a window, implements a set of routines for processing the most common messages that the component receives. Each message routine is named with a prefix *on_* and the message name as the remainder. For example, the *Wm_command* message has a corresponding message hook defined in the class *WEL_COMPOSITE_WINDOW,* called *on_control_command.* The routine *on_control_command* is called whenever a window receives a *Wm_command* message from a child control. Similar message hooks exist for the messages *Wm_size, Wm_close, Wm_notify,* and many others. Each message hook is passed parameters relevant to the message call. For instance, the *on_control_command* routine is passed a reference to the control in which the *Wm_command* message originated, and the *on_size* routine is passed the new dimensions of the window that has been resized.

The default implementation of all message hooks is empty and does not perform any action. The implementation of *on_control_command* in class *WEL_COMPOSITE_WINDOW* is

```
on_control_command (control: WEL_CONTROL) is
        -- A command has been received from 'control'
    require
        exists: exists
        control_not_void: control /= Void
        control_exists: control.exists
    do
    end
```

Redefining Message Hooks

You need to redefine a message hook to have it perform an action when called. In our button example, we implement a descendant of *WEL_FRAME_WINDOW* (itself a descendant of *WEL_COMPOSITE_WINDOW*) called *MAIN_WINDOW,* as shown in Example 3.1.

Example 3.1 Message Hooks, MAIN_WINDOW Class (messages/button)

```
class MAIN_WINDOW
inherit
    WEL_FRAME_WINDOW
            redefine
                on_control_command
            end
creation
    make
feature

    make is
            -- Initialize the main window
        do
            make_top ("Main Window")
            resize (300, 255)
            create message_button.make (Current, "Button", 10, 30,
                90, 35, -1)
        end

    message_button: WEL_PUSH_BUTTON
            -- Push button

    on_control_command (control: WEL_CONTROL) is
            -- A command has been received from 'control'.
        local
            message_result: INTEGER
        do
            if control = message_button then
                message_result := message_box ("You pressed my
                    button!",
                    "Button Parent", Mb_ok)
            end
        end

end -- class MAIN_WINDOW
```

The creation procedure *make* of *MAIN_WINDOW* builds the main window. The procedure then adds a push button to the top left corner of the newly created window. The *MAIN_WINDOW* inheritance clause specifies that the inherited feature *on_control_command* will be redefined. The new implementation appears near the end of the class. The routine is fairly simple. First, the *control* parameter is checked to see if it is the message button and if so, a message box is displayed with the message "You pressed my button!" If the control parameter is not the message button, then the message is ignored.

To complete this example, you need an implementation of *WEL_APPLI-CATION* that creates an instance of *MAIN_WINDOW*. Example 3.2 shows a typical implementation of the application class.

Other messages can be captured and processed in a similar manner. We can extend our example to capture the *Wm_size* message and resize the push button to automatically fit the entire window whenever the window changes size. Example 3.3 shows the modified *MAIN_WINDOW* class.

The first modification appears in the inheritance clause. The inherited feature *on_size* is also declared as redefined. Secondly, the class *WEL_SIZE_CONSTANTS* is inherited to provide access to the different size event constants for the *on_size* routine. The export status of the inherited features are changed to *NONE,* hiding them from the public interface of the class. In this example, we need to size the push button to the current size of the window. The code is modified to defer the creation of the button until a *Wm_size* message has been received and the associated *on_size* routine is called. When *on_size* is called, the *message_button* attribute is examined to see if the push button has been created. If not, it is created and then sized to fit the new window. If the button already exists, and the *on_size* routine has not been called as a result of a minimize, then it is resized to the new width and height of the window.

The *on_size* routine is passed three parameters. The first parameter indicates what type of sizing operation has occurred. In a typical Windows application, the user can resize a window in a number of ways, including maximizing to the full screen size and minimizing to an icon. In the button example, it is

Example 3.2 Message Hooks, APPLICATION Class (messages/button)

```
class APPLICATION

inherit
     WEL_APPLICATION
creation
     make
feature

     main_window: MAIN_WINDOW is
             -- Frame main window
         once
             create Result.make
         end

     end -- class APPLICATION
```

Example 3.3 Message Hooks, MAIN_WINDOW Class (messages/button)

```
class MAIN_WINDOW
inherit
    WEL_FRAME_WINDOW
        redefine
            on_control_command,
            on_size
        end
    WEL_SIZE_CONSTANTS
        export
            {NONE} all
        end
creation
    make

feature

    make is
            -- Initialize the main window
        do
            make_top ("Main Window")
            resize (300, 255)
        end
    message_button: WEL_PUSH_BUTTON
            -- Push button
    on_control_command (control: WEL_CONTROL) is
            -- A command has been received from 'control'.
        local
            message_result: INTEGER
        do
            if control = message_button then
                message_result := message_box ("You pressed my
                    button!",
                    "Button Parent", Mb_ok)
            end
        end
    on_size (size_type: INTEGER; a_width, a_height: INTEGER) is
            -- Wm_size message
            -- See class WEL_SIZE_CONSTANTS for 'size_type' values
        do
            if message_button = Void then
                create message_button.make (Current, "Button", 0, 0,
                    a_width, a_height, -1)
            elseif size_type /= Size_minimized then
                message_button resize (a_width, a_height)
            end
        end

end -- class MAIN_WINDOW
```

not necessary to resize the push button when the window is being minimized. In this case, the window is removed from the screen and the effect of resizing the button would go unnoticed. Restoring the window to its normal size causes a new *Wm_size* message to be sent, effectively resizing the button correctly when the window reappears on the screen.

The second and third parameters of *on_size* specify the new width and height of the window, respectively.

Checking the Message Result

Many Windows messages return a result that provides information indicating the outcome of the message. Some messages return a status result to indicate whether their execution was successful or not, while others return a result that provides further information as requested by the message.

Class *WEL_WINDOW* has two features available that allow you to determine the result returned by a message and to set the message return value. The features are *message_return_value* and *set_message_return_value*, respectively.

Routine *set_message_result_value* is normally used internally by WEL, and you should rarely have to call it in your own applications. You may need to use these features if you are creating your own custom controls and will be wrapping your own Windows API messages. The feature *set_message_return_value* is mainly used in conjunction with the redefinition of *on_wm_erasebkgnd*, since this message requires a non-zero return value to tell Windows that it was handled.

Who Sent the Message?

We have briefly examined the process of redefining message hooks to perform actions for common Windows messages. The full collection of message hooks is explored in later chapters. In particular, see Chapter 4, "Windows" and Chapter 11, "Controls" for detailed descriptions of supported message hooks.

```
message_return_value: INTEGER
        -- Value to be returned to Windows after message
           processing.

set_message_return_value (v: INTEGER)
        -- Set 'v' to 'message_return_value'.
    ensure
        message_return_value_set: message_return_value = v
```

Message hooks provide the simplest way to capture and perform actions for common messages. The technique requires you to redefine any message hooks for the messages that you are interested in and implement appropriate processing. However, message hooks do not exist for all of the messages that Windows uses. If this were the case, then the class definitions for a number of WEL components would be huge! Only the most common messages for each component have a corresponding message operation. Less common messages can be processed in two different ways, either by using the *context → event → command* protocol or by redefining the *default_message_processing* routine.

Before describing the two remaining methods of message processing, we need to delve deeper into the origins of messages to gain an understanding of when they are sent and where they end up.

A message can originate from a number of sources. The predominant source is user interaction. An application is notified of user actions by receiving messages that indicate what type of interaction the user performed. For example, a message is sent whenever the user moves a mouse over an application's window or when a mouse or keyboard button is pressed and released. Windows generates a specific message for each of these user actions and sends the message to the window that currently has the *input focus*. Only one window at a time can have the input focus, and all user-event messages are sent to this window for processing. The window with the input focus may be a frame, a child, or a window control. If a frame window has the input focus, then this is indicated by its highlighted title bar. When a push button has the input focus, it is highlighted by a dotted box surrounding the text of the button.

The second source of messages is built in to the Windows operating system. We have already seen an example of Windows sending a message to an application. Example 3.3 relies on the fact that calling *resize* on a window will cause a *Wm_size* message to be sent to that window. The example initializes the size of the main window with the following call:

```
resize (300, 255)
```

This call causes the size of the window to change (in this case from its default size) to a width of 300 pixels and a height of 255 pixels. As a side effect of this call, Windows sends a *Wm_size* message to the window, informing it that its size has changed. WEL automatically calls *on_size*. The *Wm_size* message is sent as a side effect of another procedure. Another common example is the *Wm_paint* message. This message is sent whenever the contents of a window must be repainted as a result of being erased, resized, or obscured. You can also cause a *Wm_paint* message to be sent by calling the routine *invalidate* or *update*. Painting and invalidating are explored in more detail in Chapter 10, "Graphics Device Interface." Thus, the message may be sent as a result of different operations. All you need to do is handle the message in an appropriate manner.

Finally, a message can originate from your program code. You can send messages to components to request information or cause some action. The WEL library handles much of this message sending for you and provides a simpler interface for collecting and setting information on components. When programming in a language such as C, you typically need to send messages to components to get their current state. For example, to determine whether a check box is checked, you need to send a message to the check box and examine the result returned to you. In WEL, you can ask a check box instance directly for its current state (provided you have a reference to it). WEL performs the message passing under the covers and returns the relevant information via a standard Eiffel function.

The Context → Event → Command Protocol

Message hooks provide a simple way of processing the most common messages received by Windows components. This type of message processing is more than sufficient for most applications. However, as an application becomes more sophisticated and demands more of the Windows environment, message hooks may not provide enough flexibility for your needs. This is because only a small number of messages have associated message hooks. The WEL library implements message hooks only for the most common messages. A different approach is needed if your application has to use less common messages. The Context → Event → Command (CEC) protocol provides a more flexible approach in terms of both an unlimited range of messages supported and the additional reusability and generality of abstractions that can be built.

The CEC protocol is taken from the ISE EiffelVision Library. Eiffel-Vision provides a portable graphics layer on top of both WEL and the GTK Eiffel Library (GEL) and uses the CEC protocol very effectively for processing messages. This protocol has been recently incorporated into the WEL libraries, in addition to the existing message hook support.

CEC is based on the notion of a *command* associated with an *event* originating from a *context*. The command is an instance of a *WEL_COMMAND* descendant and implements the processing that needs to occur when it is invoked. The event relates directly to a particular message and the context is the receiver of the message. Put simply, when a particular message (event) is sent to a component (context), the associated processing (command) is performed. For example, we can associate a command that implements the resizing of our push button (Example 3.3) with the *Wm_size* message of the main window. In this case, we don't need to redefine the *on_size* message operation.

Enabling Context → Event → Command Processing

To reduce message-handling overhead, CEC processing is not enabled unless explicitly turned on. When CEC processing is enabled, WEL must check every arriving message to determine whether a command has been registered for that message in the current component. However, the overhead of CEC processing is relatively minimal (one look-up for each message received) and can be turned on or off for particular component types and individual component instances.

To turn CEC processing on, you can call the feature *enable_commands* of class *WEL_WINDOW*. Similarly, to turn CEC processing off, you can call *disable_commands*. The current status of CEC processing is available via the function *commands_enabled*.

If CEC processing is enabled, then each arriving message is first checked to see if it has an associated command. If the message does have a registered command, then it is executed. The relevant message hook is then called, if it exists. When CEC processing is disabled, message processing begins with execution of message hooks followed by *default_message_processing* (see below).

Modifying our example to use CEC processing requires the redefinition of *on_size* to be removed from the inheritance clause and CEC processing to be enabled in the creation procedure. We can also remove the inheritance of *WEL_SIZE_CONSTANTS*. Example 3.4 shows the modified *MAIN_WINDOW* class. Note, this class is not yet complete. The *Wm_size* message handling is added later.

```
commands_enabled: BOOLEAN
      -- Is the command execution enabled?

enable_commands
      -- Enable commands execution
    ensure
      commands_enabled: commands_enabled

disable_commands
      -- Disable commands execution
    ensure
      commands_disabled: not commands_enabled
```

**Example 3.4 Enabling CEC Processing, MAIN_WINDOW
Class (messages\command)**

```
class MAIN_WINDOW
inherit
    WEL_FRAME_WINDOW
           redefine
               on_control_command
           end
creation
    make
feature
    make is
               -- Initialize the main window
           do
               make_top ("Main Window")
               enable_commands
               create message_button.make (Current, "Button", 0, 0,
                   width, height, -1)
               resize (300, 255)
           end

    message_button: WEL_PUSH_BUTTON
               -- Push button
    on_control_command (control: WEL_CONTROL) is
               -- A command has been received from 'control'.
           local
               message_result: INTEGER
           do
               if control = message_button then
                   message_result := message_box ("You pressed my
                       button!",
                           "Button Parent", Mb_ok)
               end
           end

    end -- class MAIN_WINDOW
```

Notice that the call to *enable_commands* appears before the call to resize. This ensures that the *Wm_size* message will be handled by our CEC command. We also simplify *Wm_size* message processing by moving the creation of the message button back into the procedure *make*. The button, in this case, is created to fit the initial default size of the window.

Creating a Command Instance

We have talked about associating a command with a context and event, and subsequently executing that command. So what is a command object and how do we execute one? A command, or more specifically, a *WEL_COMMAND*, is an abstraction that represents an operation that can be applied to an arbitrary argument. The deferred class *WEL_COMMAND* provides an abstract interface for an executable command. It specifies one deferred feature, namely *execute,* that must be implemented in a descendant to perform the command processing. The full interface of class *WEL_COMMAND* includes two additional features, *message_information* and *set_message_information.*

The additional features provide information relevant to the message being processed. Descendants of the class *WEL_MESSAGE_INFORMATION* exist for a number of message types, including the class *WEL_SIZE_MESSAGE* for the *Wm_size* message. Table 3.1 lists the message information classes available in WEL, the message that each class pertains to, and a description of its use.

For our example, we need a command that will resize a button to the new size of the main window. More generally, we need a command that will resize a window's children to conform to the new window's size. The *execute* feature of *WEL_COMMAND* allows us to pass an arbitrary object of any type as its argument. We use this argument to pass the parent window that has been resized. Example 3.5 shows an implementation of the *MAIN_WINDOW_SIZE_COMMAND* class.

The class is a direct descendant of *WEL_COMMAND.* Class *WEL_SIZE_CONSTANTS* is also inherited to allow access to the size type constant values. The *execute* routine then redefines the parameter *argument* to the more specific type *MAIN_WINDOW,* allowing us to pass an instance of *MAIN_WINDOW* to the

```
deferred class interface WEL_COMMAND
feature -- Access

    message_information: WEL_MESSAGE_INFORMATION
            -- Information associated to the message
feature -- Execution

    execute (argument: ANY)
            -- Execute the command with 'argument'
        deferred
feature -- Element change

    set_message_information (mi: WEL_MESSAGE_INFORMATION)
            -- Set 'message_information to 'mi'
        ensure
            message_information_set: message_information = mi

end -- class WEL_COMMAND
```

TABLE 3.1   *Message Information Structures*

STRUCTURE	MESSAGE	INFORMATION
WEL_COMMAND_MESSAGE	*Wm_command*	Information about message *Wm_command* sent when the user selects a command from a menu, when a control sends a notification message to its parent window, or when an accelerator keystroke is translated.
WEL_KEY_MESSAGE	*Wm_char, Wm_sys-char, Wm_keydown, Wm_keyup, Wm_sys-keydown, Wm_syskeyup*	Stores information about a keyboard message, including the keycode and key modifier data.
WEL_MENU_SELECT_MESSAGE	*Wm_menuselect*	Information about a menu select message sent to a menu's owner window when the user highlights a menu item.
WEL_MESSAGE_INFORMATION	N/A	Generic message information. Ancestor of all message information structure classes.
WEL_MOUSE_MESSAGE	*Wm_mousemove, Wm_lbuttondown, Wm_rbuttondown, Wm_mbuttondown, Wm_lbuttonup, Wm_rbuttonup, Wm_mbuttondown, Wm_lbuttondblclk, Wm_rbuttondblclk, Wm_mbuttondblclk*	Information about a mouse message, sent when the user clicks a mouse button or moves the mouse.
WEL_MOVE_MESSAGE	*Wm_move*	Information about a *Wm_move* message, sent when a window has been moved.
WEL_NOTIFY_MESSAGE	Wm_notify	Information about the *Wm_notify* event sent to the parent of a control when an event occurs in the control or when the control requires some information.
WEL_SHOW_WINDOW_MESSAGE	*Wm_showwindow*	Information about a *Wm_showwindow* message, sent when a window is about to be hidden or shown.
WEL_SIZE_MESSAGE	*Wm_size*	Information about a *Wm_size* message, sent after a window has changed its size.
WEL_SYSTEM_COM-MAND_MESSAGE	*Wm_syscom*	Information about message *Wm_syscommand*, sent when the user chooses a command from the System menu (also known as the Control menu) or when the user chooses the Maximize or Minimize buttons.

(continued)

TABLE 3.1   *Message Information Structures (continued)*

STRUCTURE	MESSAGE	INFORMATION
WEL_TIMER_MESSAGE	Wm_timer	Information about the *Wm_timer* message, sent after each interval specified in the *set_time* procedure used to install a timer. See Chapter 4.
WEL_WINDOW_POSI-TION_MESSAGE	Wm_window-poschanged, Wm_windowposchanging	Information about the messages *Wm_windowposchanged* and *Wm_windowposchanging*. These messages are sent to a window whose size, position, and Z-order have changed or are about to be changed, respectively.

execute routine. Be careful with this approach, however, as many Eiffel compilers do not fully check systemwide validity constraints. If an object other than an instance of *MAIN_WINDOW* is passed as the argument (i.e., a nonconforming type), then you may experience a semantic error that is not caught by the compiler. We can protect against this problem by adding a check statement that will raise an exception if a nonconforming object is passed.

For example, the first check statement provides some protection in our routine and specifies that the argument must not be *Void*. The next two statements,

```
        size_information ?= message_information
check
            size_message: size_information /= Void
end
```

assign the stored message information structure to the variable *size_information* declared of type *WEL_SIZE_MESSAGE*. The assignment attempt is necessary because the *message_information* type does not conform to the *size_information* type. Following the assignment attempt, if the variable *size_information* is not *Void,* then we can assert that the call has been made as a consequence of a *WM_SIZE_Message* and that *message_information* contained an object whose type conformed to *WEL_SIZE_MESSAGE*. The *MAIN_WINDOW_SIZE_COMMAND* should be executed only as a consequence of a *Wm_size* message; therefore, the check statement labeled *size_message* specifies that the assignment attempt should never fail. As well as specifying this property, the check statement provides an invaluable aid in debugging. If this command was executed as a result of a different message, such as *Wm_paint,* then the check statement would fail and an exception would

Example 3.5 CEC Size Command, MAIN_WINDOW_SIZE_COM-MAND Class (messages\command)

```
class MAIN_WINDOW_SIZE_COMMAND

inherit
    WEL_COMMAND

    WEL_SIZE_CONSTANTS
            export
                {NONE} all
            end
feature -- Execution

    execute (argument: MAIN_WINDOW) is
            -- Resize message button of 'argument' to
            -- accommodate the new window size.
        local
            size_information: WEL_SIZE_MESSAGE
        do
            check
                    valid_argument: argument /= Void
            end
            size_information ?= message_information
            check
                    size_message: size_information /= Void
            end
            if size_information.size_type /= Size_minimize then
                    argument.message_button.resize (size_informa-
                        tion.width,
                        size_information.height)
            end
        end

end -- class MAIN_WINDOW_SIZE_COMMAND
```

be raised in the program. The failure could then be traced back to where the command was called.

The last four lines of code test the resize type (accessible through the *size_information* structure) and resizes the button to the new width and height (also accessible through *size_information*). The message button is accessed via the *argument* parameter of the *execute* routine. In this case, the parameter is a reference to the main window and the attribute *message_button* (of *MAIN_WINDOW*) is publicly accessible.

The *execute* method has effectively only five lines of code—equivalent to the original implementation of *on_size* in Example 3.3. Recall that assertions (including check statements) are normally discarded when generating a final executable. They are used for specification, documentation, testing, and debugging purposes.

A second version of *MAIN_WINDOW_SIZE_COMMAND,* called *MAIN_WINDOW_SIZE_2,* uses a creation procedure to store the argument locally. In this example, the parameter to execute is unused and the main window is retrieved from a local variable *main_window.*

Example 3.6 shows how to avoid the system validity weakness of the preceding version. In this example, the command parameter is set during creation and does not need to be passed to the *execute* routine. Notice that the first check statement, in *execute,* has been discarded and the main window is now accessed through an attribute of the class. Deciding on which style of command class to use depends on the requirements of your application. If you need to pass more than one parameter to the *execute* routine, then using *argument* does not suffice. Instead, you can use a creation procedure to store the data in attributes.

Registering a Command with a Context and Event

A command instance is registered by associating it with a particular context and event. The context is the component in which the event will take place and the event is the type of message that will cause the command's execution. The feature *put_command* defined in *WEL_WINDOW* is used to register a command.

Routine *put_command* takes three arguments: a command instance, a message number, and a reference to an object that will be passed as the argument to the *execute* routine of the command. The precondition specifies that the command must not be *Void* and that the message number must be positive. This ensures that you cannot associate a nonexistent command object or an invalid message number. The available message numbers are defined in the class *WEL_WM_CONSTANTS.* Many of the messages will not be familiar to you at this stage; later chapters will describe their use in more detail.

```
put_command (a_command: WEL_COMMAND; message: INTEGER; arg: ANY)
        - Put 'a_command' associated to 'message'.
    require
        a_command_not_void: a_command /= Void
        possitive_message: message >= 0
    ensure
        command_added: command (message) = a_command and
            command_argument (message) = arg
```

Example 3.6 CEC Size Command Version 2, MAIN_WINDOW_SIZE_2 Class (messages\command2)

```
class MAIN_WINDOW_SIZE_2

inherit
    WEL_COMMAND

    WEL_SIZE_CONSTANTS
        export
            {NONE} all
        end
creation
    make
feature -- Initialization

    make (window: MAIN_WINDOW) is
            -- Store the main window argument locally
        require
            valid_window: window /= Void
        do
            main_window := window
        ensure
            window_set: main_window = window
        end
feature -- Execution
    main_window: MAIN_WINDOW
            -- Reference to the main window
    execute (argument: ANY) is
            -- Resize message button of 'main_window' to
            -- accomodate the new window size.
        local
            size_information: WEL_SIZE_MESSAGE
        do
            size_information ?= message_information
            check
                size_message: size_information /= Void
            end

            if size_information.size_type /= Size_minimize then
                main_window.message_button.resize (
                    size_information.width,
                    size_information.height)
            end
        end

end -- class MAIN_WINDOW_SIZE_2
```

The routine guarantees (through its postcondition) that the command associated with *message* is equal to *a_command* and that the command argument is equal to *arg*. The two routines *command* and *command_argument* are used to check the status of a registered command.

We need to modify *MAIN_WINDOW's* creation procedure *make* to register our new command. The new procedure can be coded as

```
make is
            -- Initialize the main window
    local
        size_command: MAIN_WINDOW_SIZE_COMMAND
    do
        make_top ("Main Window")
        enable_commands
        create size_command
        put_command (size_command, Wm_size, Current)
        create message_button.make (Current, "Button",
        0, 0, width, height, -1)
            resize (300, 255)
    end
```

The two lines

```
create size_command
put_command (size_command, Wm_size, Current)
```

create an instance of *MAIN_WINDOW_SIZE_COMMAND* and associate it with the *Wm_size* message. The argument for the execute routine is set to the current object—the main window itself. The variable *size_command* is declared as a local variable and could have been declared as an attribute of the *MAIN_WINDOW* class. Only a temporary reference is needed because the *MAIN_WINDOW_SIZE_COMMAND* instance is stored through the routine *put_command* and can be obtained at a later time using the function *command*.

If our application required the use of the *MAIN_WINDOW_SIZE_2* class instead of *MAIN_WINDOW_SIZE_COMMAND*, then the two lines above would need to be modified to read

```
create size_command.make (Current)
put_command (size_command, Wm_size, Void)
```

First, the size command is created by passing the current object to its creation procedure, and second the *put_command* is passed *Void* as the argument to the execute routine.

Unregistering a Command

Use the routine remove_command to remove a registered command.

```
remove_command (message: INTEGER)
        -- Remove the command associated to 'message'.
    require
        positive_message: message >= 0
        command_exists: command_exists (message)
    ensure
        command_removed: not command_exists (message)
```

Function *command_exists* is used by the precondition to ensure that the command already exists. If the command does exist and the message number is valid, then the command association is removed.

The code to remove the *Wm_size* command association would be

```
remove_command (Wm_size)
```

As this routine suggests, only one command can be associated with a message at any given time. However, the commands you construct can be as simple or as complex as you require. This means that the restriction does not hinder your designs.

You can change the command associated with a message by removing the existing command and associating a new command, or by calling *put_command* with a new command association to overwrite the existing command.

Checking the Status of Registered Commands

The routines *command* and *command_argument* provide the means to check the status of a CEC association. For a particular message number, you can ascertain what command is registered and what argument will be passed to the command's *execute* routine. In addition, the function *command_exists* lets you determine if a command has been registered for a particular message.

Before calling *command* or *command_argument,* you must ensure that the message association you are interested in does have a command registered by calling *command_exists*. This is enforced by the preconditions labeled *command_exists* of both *command* and *command_argument*.

```
command_exists (message: INTEGER): BOOLEAN
      -- Does a command associated to 'message' exist?
  require
      positive_message: message >= 0
command (message: INTEGER): WEL_COMMAND
      -- Command associated to 'message'
  require
      positive_message: message >= 0
      command_exists: command_exists (message)
  ensure
      result_not_void: Result /= Void
command_argument (message: INTEGER): ANY
      -- Command argument associated to 'message'
  require
      positive_message: message >= 0
      command_exists: command_exists (message)
```

If you need more control over your command associations or direct access to the collection of commands, you can access the command manager structure through the feature *commands*.

```
commands: WEL_COMMAND_MANAGER
      -- Command manager associated to the current window
```

This feature returns the instance of *WEL_COMMAND_MANAGER* for the current window. Class *WEL_COMMAND_MANAGER* is a direct descendant of *HASH_TABLE* and provides a specialized collection for storing *message* → *command* associations. Be careful when directly accessing this object. Do not break any existing command associations or add any incorrect associations. It is safer to access this structure through the features command, *command_argument* and *command_exists*.

Combining Message Operations and the CEC Protocol

It is easy to combine the two message-handling approaches in one application. For instance you may implement the processing of the *Wm_paint* routine for an owner draw button (see "Owner Draw Buttons" in Chapter 12) using the message operation *on_paint,* while the button actions can be implemented using a CEC association with the *Wm_command* message. The combination of approaches provides a simple way to build highly reusable components—the specialized behavior of the owner draw button is implemented using redefinition through inheritance, while the general notion of the action the button takes when pressed is implemented by CEC commands. Example 3.7 shows a framework for building such a button.

Example 3.7 Combination of Message Operations and CEC Protocol (messages\combination)

```
class MY_DRAW_BUTTON

inherit
      WEL_OWNER_DRAW_BUTTON
         redefine
             on_paint
         end

creation
      make
      make_by_id
feature

      on_paint (paint_cd: WEL_PAINT_CD; invalid_rect: WEL_RECT) is
             -- Paint the button surface
         do
             -- paint implementation omitted
         end

   end -- class MY_DRAW_BUTTON
```

To create and use an instance of *MY_DRAW_BUTTON*, we need to associate a command with the *Wm_command* message.

```
button: MY_DRAW_BUTTON
command: MY_BUTTON_COMMAND
command2: MY_OTHER_BUTTON_COMMAND

...
-- create one button
create button.make (Current, x_pos, y_pos, width, height)
create command
button.put_command (command, Wm_command, Void)

-- create another button with a different command association
create button.make (Current, x_pos + 10, y_pos + 10, width, height)
create command2
button.put_command (command2, Wm_command, Void)

...
```

The button creation procedure is passed the current object as its parent and the position and dimensions of the button window (see "Creating a Button" in Chapter 12). The command object is then created and associated with the button's *Wm_command* message. In this instance, *Void* is passed as the command argument. However, a more specific argument can be passed if needed. More than one instance of *MY_DRAW_BUTTON* can be created with different actions associated with the *Wm_command* message. You can also define a CEC message handler and a message hook for the same message. The CEC command will be called before the message hook.

Windows Default Message Processing

After a message has been handled by a CEC association or message hook, it is typically passed on to the default Windows procedure to be processed. In most applications, it is essential to pass all unhandled messages to the default processing procedure to ensure a correctly running application interface.

Enabling and Disabling Default Message Processing

You do, however, have the ability to turn default window message processing on or off. The routines *enable_default_processing* and *disable_default_processing* provide this functionality.

```
enable_default_processing
        - Enable default window processing.
        - The standard window procedure will be called for
        - each message received by the window and then the
        - normal behavior will occur.
    ensure
        default_processing_enabled: default_processing_enabled
disable_default_processing
        - Disable default window processing.
        - The standard window procedure will not be called for
        - each message received by the window and then the
        - normal behavior will not occur.
    ensure
        default_processing_disabled: not default_processing_
        enabled
```

The current status of default window processing can be determined using the feature *default_processing_enabled.*

```
default_processing_enabled: BOOLEAN
        -- Is the default window processing enabled?
        -- If True (by default) the standard window
        -- procedure will be called. Otherwise, the standard
        -- window procedure will not be called and the
        -- normal behavior will not occur.
```

ADVANCED MESSAGE HANDLING

You should be well satisfied with the message-handling functionality provided by both message operations and the CEC protocol. Most message-handling requirements can be implemented using one of the two approaches, or a combination of both. Another form of message handling is provided for the rare requirement that cannot be directly supported by these approaches. The *default_process_message* routine is called for any message that is not handled by a message hook or a CEC association. Although different from the default Windows message procedure, the *default_process_message* routine is called under the same circumstances—when a message is not handled by either a CEC association or a message hook.

The following sections describe the WEL message-processing architecture in more detail and show you how you can modify the way WEL processes Windows messages to suit any requirement you may encounter.

WEL Message-Processing Architecture

WEL insulates you from the complexity of Windows message processing by providing message hooks and the CEC framework. If you need to implement nonstandard (or unsupported) message processing, then you will need a greater understanding of the internals of WEL message-processing logic. To do this, we need to explore how WEL processes different types of messages and dispatches them to appropriate objects.

Three classes in a WEL application collaborate to process and dispatch messages: *WEL_APPLICATION*, *WEL_MSG*, and *WEL_DISPATCHER*. *WEL_APPLICATION* manages the main message processing loop and uses *WEL_MSG* to translate and forward the messages to the WEL dispatcher. The WEL dispatcher (class *WEL_DISPATCHER*) controls the dispatch of messages to relevant message-processing procedures. The dispatcher first determines if the message's target is a dialog window or a normal window. If the target of the message is a dialog window, then the procedure may perform additional initialization on the dialog, such as setting the window handle. Otherwise, the message is handled normally by calling the relevant window message hook and, if enabled, the default window procedure. Figure 3.2 shows the processing logic of the WEL dispatcher.

This logic is implemented in *WEL_DISPATCHER's* procedure *process_message*. Once the message type has been determined, the *process_message* procedure of the target window object is called. The correct version of

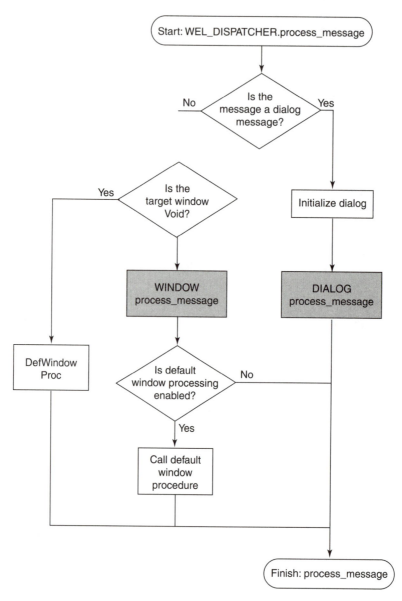

FIGURE 3.2. Dispatcher message-processing logic.

process_message is called depending on the dynamic type of the target window object. For example, if the message target is an instance of *WEL_FRAME_WINDOW*, then the version of *process_message* implemented in *WEL_FRAME_WINDOW* is called. Currently, four versions of *process_message* exist in the WEL library. There are implementations in *WEL_WINDOW, WEL_COMPOSITE_WINDOW, WEL_FRAME_WINDOW,*

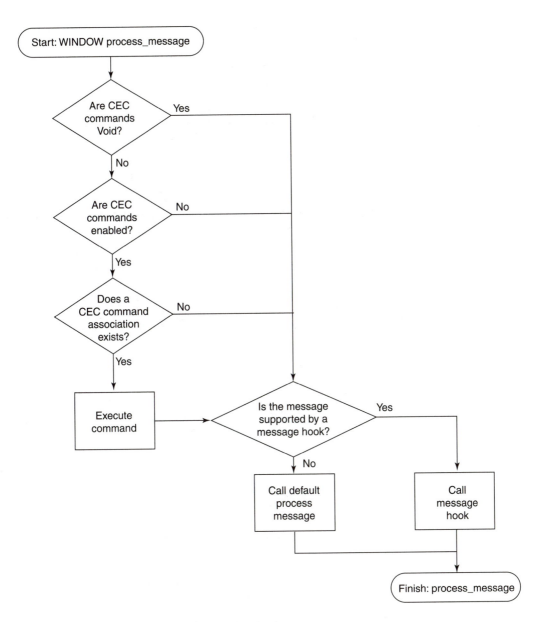

FIGURE 3.3. Window message-processing logic.

and WEL_DIALOG. Additional redefinitions may be added in future versions of WEL or may be implemented in your own applications. Figure 3.3 shows the processing that occurs in the *process_message* procedure of class *WEL_WINDOW*.

Initially, the procedure tests whether CEC commands are enabled and whether a command association for the message is registered. If so, the command is executed. The procedure then checks if the message is a known window message and executes the appropriate hook. If the message is not recognized, then the default process message routine is called.

Descendants of *WEL_WINDOW,* including *WEL_COMPOSITE_WIN-DOW, WEL_FRAME_WINDOW,* and *WEL_DIALOG,* all redefine *process_message* to perform their own message processing. As shown in Figure 3.4, *WEL_COMPOSITE_WINDOW* first calls the *process_message* procedure of *WEL_WINDOW* before processing its own messages. In a similar fashion, *WEL_FRAME_WINDOW* and *WEL_DIALOG* call the *WEL_COMPOSITE_WINDOW, process_message* procedures (See Figure 3.5).

The process logic described previously is a simplified version of the actual process performed to handle messages. In Chapter 11, we expand on the processing flow to include the handling of control notification messages. For the time being, and for the intervening chapters, the description above will suffice.

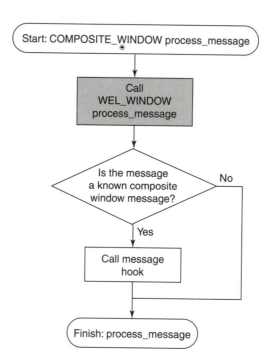

FIGURE 3.4. Composite window message-processing logic.

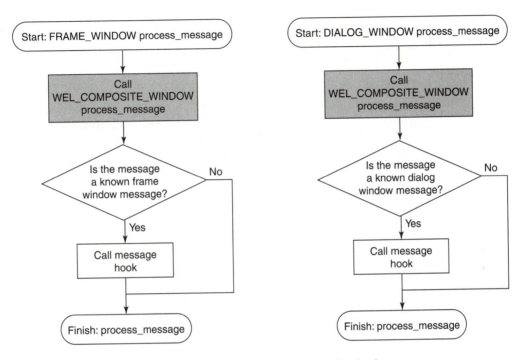

FIGURE 3.5. Frame window and dialog message-processing logic.

The Default Process Message Routine

In a traditional programming language, you are required to process the parameters of a Windows message depending on the type of message being sent. The parameters arrive in the form of two integers named *lparam* and *wparam.* The names of the parameters have historical significance and are used to represent the type of integer being sent—*lparam* was a long-size integer and *wparam* was a word-size integer.[1] As a C programmer, you would be required to extract high or low words of the *lparam* parameter to ascertain message information. For example, the *wparam* of the *Wm_size* message represents the size type, while the low word of *lparam* represents the new width, and the high word represents the new height. The WEL library hides these operations by providing message hooks and CEC message information classes. However, the *default_process_message* routine reverts back to this form of parameter passing. You are required to perform parameter decoding yourself. The routine receives three parameters; *msg, wparam,* and *lparam,* representing the message type and the *wparam* and *lparam* of the message, respectively.

---

1. In Windows 95, and later versions, *lparam* and *wparam* are the same size.

```
default_process_message (msg, wparam, lparam: INTEGER)
     - Process 'msg' which has not been processed by
     - 'process_message'.
```

The default implementation of *default_process_message* is empty. You can redefine the routine in a descendant of *WEL_WINDOW* to perform your own processing. Note, the routine is not public and therefore, will not appear in the flat-short forms of *WEL_WINDOW*. The private routines *cwin_low_word* and *cwin_high_word* of class *WEL_WORD_OPERATIONS* can assist in the decoding of message parameters.

SUMMARY

A Windows application communicates via messages—it interacts with them, sends them to notify other components of events, and receives them to find out about its surroundings. All of your Windows applications will need to perform at least rudimentary message processing, if only to catch a *Wm_close* message to close down. Typical applications exhibit more complicated message processing to meet their user interface requirements.

Three forms of message handling are available in the WEL library. The first and simplest approach is provided in the form of message hooks. Many classes in the WEL library implement message hooks that can be redefined to perform actions when certain messages are received. The second approach is the Context → Event → Command protocol in which a particular component and message can be associated with the execution of a command. This form of message handling provides a very flexible and powerful way of building reusable user interface components. The third and final approach is to handle and decode messages by overriding the *default_process_message* procedure.

Message handling is introduced in class *WEL_WINDOW* and is specialized in its descendants for more specific message handling. For example, the message *Wm_paint* is not introduced until class *WEL_COMPOSITE_WINDOW*, a direct descendant of *WEL_WINDOW*, while *Wm_size* is introduced in *WEL_WINDOW*. Individual message operations are discussed in more detail in later chapters.

WINDOWS

INTRODUCING WINDOWS

Windows are the most fundamental elements of a Microsoft Windows application. They are the basis of every visible application component, from the main window to the individual controls, such as buttons, lists, and check boxes, that make up the interface. A window is displayed as a rectangular area of the screen and may overlap other windows. It can also have an optional frame that allows it to be moved to a different position and to have its dimensions changed.

Windows can be overlaid upon other windows to build an interface. For instance, a main window will usually have other windows attached to its client area, providing user interaction controls. A top-level window can be displayed in an arbitrary position on the screen, while its child windows can be displayed only within its client area. Every window has a parent except for the the top-level window, whose parent is implicitly the desktop. The parent of a child window is the window to which the child window is attached, or the window that controls the child window (in the case of a popup window).

This chapter describes the general notion of all window types found in WEL.

TYPES OF WINDOWS

The most abstract form of a window is implemented in the class *WEL_WINDOW*. Specialized forms of windows inherit from this class. Figure 4.1 shows the top two levels of the WEL window class hierarchy. The abstract class *WEL_WINDOW* implements behavior common to all window types and the descendants, *WEL_COMPOSITE_WINDOW* and *WEL_CONTROL,* introduce specialized behavior. The class hierarchy extends further than these three classes. In particular, descendants of *WEL_COMPOSITE_WINDOW* implement framed windows, popup windows, dialogs, and MDI windows. Descendants of *WEL_CONTROL* implement many different types of controls, including buttons, lists, and check boxes.

A composite window is a window that can contain other windows, known as its children. See Chapter 5, "Composite Windows," for a detailed description. A control, on the other hand, is a window that provides or retrieves information, such as static text messages or push buttons, to and from the user. Although many controls are implemented as a collection of child windows on a common parent, you cannot add additional child windows to a control in your applications.

Abstract Window Class

Class *WEL_WINDOW* is the parent of all window classes. It provides all of the common features that can be applied to any window. When you are using a window, irrespective of its actual type, you should consult the features in *WEL_WINDOW* for the full interface or generate a flat-short interface of the class to show you all of the inherited features.

The following sections describe the features available in *WEL_WINDOW.*

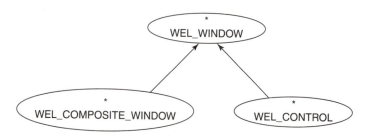

FIGURE 4.1. WEL window class hierarchy.

Creating a Window

You cannot create a direct instance of *WEL_WINDOW* because it is a deferred class. However, *WEL_WINDOW* provides a procedure that can be used as a default creation procedure in descendant classes. In addition, a number of descendants of *WEL_WINDOW* implement their own creation procedures. For instance, frame windows have two creation procedures—one for creating the window as a top-level window and another for creating it as a child.

For most windows, you must specify the new window's parent (a window itself). Frame and MDI frame windows allow you to create windows without a parent. See Chapter 5, and Chapter 6, "Multi-Document Windows," for windows without parents.

Testing a Window for Existence

A window exists if the window object and the underlying Windows data structures have been successfully created and initialized. The creation procedures of each window class guarantee that the window exists at the completion of the routine. One exception is if the window object is explicitly destroyed. See the next section, "Destroying a Window."

To test the existence of a window object, you can query the window's *exists* feature.

```
exists: BOOLEAN
         -- Does the window exist?
```

For example, given a reference to a window instance *my_window,* you can test its existence with the following code:

```
my_window.exists
```

The feature *exists* returns *True* if the window has been successfully created (i.e., its creation procedure was successfully executed) or *False* if the creation procedure did not execute successfully.

Destroying a Window

You can call feature *destroy* of *WEL_WINDOW* to remove a window from the screen and, if appropriate, delete the underlying Windows data structures. However, the Eiffel window object will still remain.

You can destroy a window only if it exists. That is, the window must have been created and initialized successfully. The window does not necessarily have to be visible on screen to be destroyed.

```
destroy is
        -- Destroy the window.
    require
        exists: exists
    ensure
        not_exists: not exists
```

Destroying a window causes the feature *exists* to return *False*, indicating a nonexistent window. Once a window is destroyed, most of the following features cannot be called.

Showing and Hiding a Window

A window can be either shown, where it becomes visible on the screen, or hidden. Four features are provided in *WEL_WINDOW* to show and hide a window. They can be used to temporarily hide a window and then show it again later.

The routines are *shown, hide, show,* and *show_with_option.*

```
shown: BOOLEAN
        -- Is the window shown?
    require
        exists: exists

hide
        -- Hide the window
    require
        exists: exists
    ensure
        hidden: not shown

show
        -- Show the window
    require
        exists: exists

show_with_option (cmd_show: INTEGER)
        -- Set the window's visibility with cmd_show.
        -- See class WEL_SW_CONSTANTS for cmd_show value.
    require
        exists: exists;
        parent_shown: parent /= void implies parent.exists and
            parent.shown
```

The query *shown* determines whether a window is currently visible on screen. Call *show* to make a window visible and *hide* to make a window invisible. Command *show_with_option* allows you to show a window in a particular form. For example, maximized, minimized, or restored. This is similar to the *default_show_command* of *WEL_APPLICATION*. Refer to Chapter 2, Table 2.1, for a list of *cmd_show* parameters.

The example below shows how to use each of these features. We first create a main window and a child window. The child window is shown when the user clicks on the show button of the main window; it is hidden when the hide button is clicked. If the user clicks on the minimize push button, then the window is shown minimized by calling *show_with_option* with the parameter *Sw_showmin* from class *WEL_SW_CONSTANTS*. Note, class *WEL_SW_CONSTANTS* does not need to be inherited by *MAIN_WINDOW* because it is already inherited indirectly by *WEL_FRAME_WINDOW*. Example 4.1 shows the source code required to perform the show and hide actions, depending on which button is clicked. Don't be to concerned about the inner workings of this example; all will be revealed in later chapters. Concentrate only on the shaded lines of code.

Figure 4.2 shows the output of this example with the popup window shown.

Finding the Parent of a Window

A window's parent can be reached through the feature *parent*. If a window does not have a parent, possibly because it was created using *make_top*, then the parent will be *Void*.

Example 4.1 Showing and Hiding a Window (windows\showhide)

```
class MAIN_WINDOW

inherit
    WEL_FRAME_WINDOW
        redefine
            on_control_command
        end
creation
    make
feature -- Initialization

    make is
            -- Initialize the main window, its buttons and
            -- the popup window.
        do
            make_top ("Main Window")
            resize (300, 255)
            create show_button.make (Current, "Show", 10, 30, 90, 35, -1)
            create hide_button.make (Current, "Hide", 10, 70, 90, 35, -1)
            create minimize_button.make (Current, "Minimize", 10, 110,
                90, 35,-1)
```

```
            create popup.make_child (Current, "Child Window")
            popup.resize (200, 100)
        end
feature {NONE} -- Implementation

        show_button, hide_button, minimize_button: WEL_PUSH_BUTTON
            -- Push buttons

        popup: WEL_POPUP_WINDOW
            -- Popup window to show and hide
        on_control_command (control: WEL_CONTROL) is
            -- A command has been received from `control'.
        do
            if control = show_button then
                if not popup.shown then
                        popup.show
                end
            elseif control = hide_button then
                if popup.shown then
                        popup.hide
                end
            elseif control = minimize_button then
                popup.show_with_option (Sw_showminimized)
            end
        end
end -- class MAIN_WINDOW
```

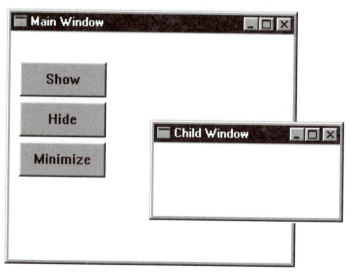

FIGURE 4.2. Hide and show window example.

```
parent: WEL_COMPOSITE_WINDOW
          -- Parent window
```

The query *parent* returns a composite window. This is because only composite windows can have children, and therefore a child can only have a composite window as its parent.

Enabling and Disabling Input in a Window

When a window is shown and activated, it is normally ready to accept input from the user through either the keyboard or a pointing device. This default behavior can be changed by enabling or disabling input for a particular window. Class *WEL_WINDOW* provides three features for enabling and disabling input, namely, *enabled, enable,* and *disable.* Feature *enabled* lets you query the current input state—if input is allowed, then *enabled* returns *True;* otherwise, it returns *False.* You call *enable* to allow user input, and *disable* to disallow input.

```
enabled: BOOLEAN
          -- Is the window enabled for mouse and keyboard input?
   require
       exists: exists

disable
          -- Disable mouse and keyboard input
   require
       exists: exists
   ensure
       disabled: not enabled

enable
          -- Enable mouse and keyboard input.
   require
       exists: exists
   ensure
       enabled: enabled
```

Capturing the Keyboard Focus in a Window

Only one window at a time can have the input focus (also known as the *keyboard focus*). When a window has the input focus, its title bar is highlighted and it receives keyboard input messages from the operating system. A user can use keyboard interaction with a window only when it has the input focus. Class *WEL_WINDOW* provides a number of features for changing the input focus and determining which window currently has focus.

```
focused_window: WEL_WINDOW
          -- Current window which has the focus.
     require
          exists: exists

has_focus: BOOLEAN
          -- Does this window have the focus?
     require
          exists: exists

set_focus
          -- Set the focus to Current
     require
          exists: exists
```

Example 4.2 shows how to change the input focus between two popup windows. The example initially shows both popup windows and changes the input focus between the windows, depending on which button is clicked on the main window.

Example 4.2 Setting the Input Focus of a Window (windows\focus)

```
class MAIN_WINDOW

inherit
     FRAME_WINDOW
          redefine
              on_control_command
          end
creation
     make
feature -- Initialization

     make is
              -- Initialize the main window, its buttons and the pop windows
          do
              make_top ("Main Window")
              resize (300, 255)
              create focus_1_button.make (Current, "Focus 1", 10, 30,
                  90, 35, -1)
              create focus_2_button.make (Current, "Focus 2", 10, 70,
                  90, 35, -1)
              create popup_1.make_child (Current, "Child Window 1")
              popup_1.resize (200, 100)
              popup_1.move (100, 100)
              create popup_2.make_child (Current, "Child Window 2")
              popup_2.resize (200, 100)
              popup_2.move (300, 100)
          end
feature -- Implementation

     focus_1_button, focus_2_button: WEL_PUSH_BUTTON
              -- Push buttons
```

```
popup_1, popup_2: WEL_POPUP_WINDOW
        -- Popup windows to focus
on_control_command (control: WEL_CONTROL) is
        -- A command has been received from 'control'.
    do
        if control = focus_1_button then
            if focused_window /= popup_1 then
                if not popup_1.shown then
                    popup_1.show
                end
                popup_1.set_focus
            end
        elseif control = focus_2_button then
            if not popup_2.has_focus then
                if not popup_2.shown then
                    popup_2.show
                end
                popup_2.set_focus
            end
        end
    end
end -- class MAIN_WINDOW
```

If *focus_1_button* is pressed, then *popup_1* is given the input focus. Likewise, if *focus_2_button* is pressed, then *popup_2* is given the input focus. The code fragment also demonstrates two different ways of determining which window currently has the input focus. The first method uses the feature *focused_window*. In this case, we test *focused_window* to see if it references *popup_1*. Feature *focused_window* can be called from any window in an application. It returns the currently focused window. The second method uses the *has_focus* function to ask the popup itself if it currently has the input focus.

Figure 4.3 shows the output generated by this example after *focus_1_button* has been pressed and the input focus has been set to *popup_1* (Child Window 1), as indicated by its highlighted title bar.

Capturing the Mouse in a Window

In a multiwindow application, a single window can capture all mouse events. When a window has captured input, it receives notification of all mouse events performed in any of the application's windows. This is similar to the behavior of a modal dialog (see Chapter 9, "Dialogs"). Only one window at a time can capture mouse input, and a window should release a capture as soon as it is not needed.

Class *WEL_WINDOW* provides five features for setting and querying the current state of window capture. You can determine whether a window has captured input, determine which window has the capture, and set and release the capture on a window.

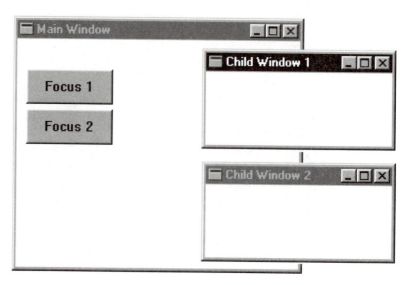

FIGURE 4.3. Set focus example window.

```
captured_window: WEL_WINDOW
        -- Current window which has been captured.
    require
        exists: exists;
        window_captured: window_captured

has_capture: BOOLEAN
        -- Does this window have the capture?
    require
        exists: exists

window_captured: BOOLEAN
        -- Has a window been captured?

release_capture
        -- Release the mouse capture after a call
        -- to set_capture.
    require
        exists: exists
    ensure
        not_has_capture: not has_capture

set_capture
        -- Set the mouse capture to the Current window.
        -- Once the window has captured the mouse, all
        -- mouse input is directed to this window, regardless
        -- of wheter the cursor is over that window. Only
        -- one window can have the mouse capture at a time.
    require
        exists: exists
    ensure
        has_capture: has_capture
```

In order to demonstrate input capture, we need an example application with more than one window. The example uses a main window and one popup window. The main window reacts to two messages—a *left button up* message sets the capture on the main window and a *right button up* message releases the capture. When capture is set, pressing the right mouse button in either the main window or the popup window causes the mouse event to be sent to the main window, thus demonstrating the capture of mouse events. You will also notice that a left click in the popup window (while input is captured) does not have an effect. Example 4.3 shows the processing required in each mouse message routine (See the section "On a Window Mouse Message" later in this chapter for a description of the *on_left_button_up* and *on_right_button_up* routines.)

Example 4.3 Capturing the Mouse Input (windows\capture)

```
class MAIN_WINDOW

inherit
      WEL_FRAME_WINDOW
         redefine
             on_left_button_up,
             on_right_button_up,
             on_set_focus
         end
creation
      make
feature -- Initialization

      make is
             -- Initialize the main window and the popup window.
         do
             make_top ("Main Window")
             resize (300, 255)
             create message.make (Current, "Not captured", 0, 0,
             width, height, -1)
             create popup.make_child (Current, "Child Window")
             popup.resize (200, 100)
             popup.move (100, 100)
         end
feature -- Implementation

      popup: WEL_POPUP_WINDOW
             -- The popup window

      message: WEL_STATIC
             -- The message text box
      on_set_focus is
             -- Show the popup when the main window receives the input focus
         do
             if not popup.shown then
```

```
            popup.show
        end
    end
on_left_button_up (keys, x_pos, y_pos: INTEGER) is
        -- Capture the window
    do
        if not has_capture then
            set_capture
            message.set_text ("Captured, click right button anywhere%
                % in application to release")
        end
    end
on_right_button_up (keys, x_pos, y_pos: INTEGER) is
        -- Release the window
    do
        if has_capture then
            release_capture
            message.set_text ("Not captured, click left button to
                capture")
        end
    end
```

Changing the Dimensions of a Window

The dimensions of a window are determined by its width and height attributes.
Both attributes can be set to an integer value. You can use the following features from *WEL_WINDOW* to query the size of a window.

```
height: INTEGER
        -- Window height
    require
        exists: exists
    ensure
        result_small_enough: Result <= maximal_height;
        result_large_enough: Result >= minimal_height

width: INTEGER
        -- Window width
    require
        exists: exists
    ensure
        result_small_enough: Result <= maximal_width;
        result_large_enough: Result >= minimal_width
```

To set the width and height of a window, use the features *set_height* or
set_width. You can also set both attributes in one call with the *resize* routine.

```
set_height (a_height: INTEGER)
        -- Set height with a_height
    require
        exists: exists;
        a_height_small_enough: a_height <= maximal_height;
        a_height_large_enough: a_height >= minimal_height;
        not_minimized: not minimized
    ensure
        height_set: height = a_height

set_width (a_width: INTEGER)
        -- Set width with a_width
    require
        exists: exists;
        a_width_small_enough: a_width <= maximal_width;
        a_width_large_enough: a_width >= minimal_width;
        not_minimized: not minimized
    ensure
        width_set: width = a_width

resize (a_width, a_height: INTEGER)
        -- Resize the window with a_width, a_height.
    require
        exists: exists;
        a_width_small_enough: a_width <= maximal_width;
        a_width_large_enough: a_width >= minimal_width;
        a_height_small_enough: a_height <= maximal_height;
        a_height_large_enough: a_height >= minimal_height;
        not_minimized: not minimized
    ensure
        width_set: width = a_width;
        height_set: height = a_height
```

Example 4.4 demonstrates the different ways you can resize a window. The example creates a main window and a popup window that is always shown when the main window is open. If the user clicks on the *small_button,* then the window is resized to a smaller size. If the user clicks on the *big_button,* then the window is resized to a larger size.

Example 4.4 Resizing a Window (windows\size)

```
class MAIN_WINDOW

inherit
    WEL_FRAME_WINDOW
        redefine
            on_control_command,
            on_set_focus
        end
```

```
creation
    make
feature -- Initialization

    make is
            -- Initialize the main window, the buttons and the popup
            -- window.
        do
            make_top ("Main Window")
            resize (300, 255)
            create big_button.make (Current, "Big", 10, 30, 90, 35, -1)
            create small_button.make (Current, "Small", 10, 70, 90, 35, -1)
            create popup.make_child (Current, "Child Window")
            popup.resize (200, 100)
        end
    on_set_focus is
            -- Show the popup when the main window receives the
input focus
        do
            if not popup.shown then
                popup.show
            end
        end
    on_control_command (control: WEL_CONTROL) is
            - A command has been received from 'control'.
        do
            if control = big_button then
                popup.set_width (400)
                popup.set_height (200)
            elseif control = small_button then
                popup.resize (200, 100)
            end
        end

end - class MAIN_WINDOW
```

The example uses two methods of resizing. When resizing to a large window, two separate calls are used—one to size the width *(set_width)* and the other to size the height *(set_height)*. When resizing to a small window, one call to *resize* is used to set both the width and height.

Specifying Window Size Constraints

The window sizing features enforce a number of constraints on the arguments of the routines. For example, *set_height* requires that the window exists, the height is between *maximal_height,* and *minimal_height,* and that the window is not minimized. The user can resize a window by grabbing hold of a resize bar on the frame of the window, allowing a resize to arbitrary dimensions. In some cases, it is necessary to restrict the minimum or maximum size of a window.

WEL_WINDOW provides features which will set the maximum and mini-mum size of a window. The default implementations of these functions return four values: zero, the screen height, zero, and the screen width, respectively. Therefore, if you do not redefine these functions to return other values, windows can be resized in increments from an empty window to the full size of the screen.

```
maximal_height: INTEGER
        -- Maximal height allowed for the window
    ensure
        result_large_enough: Result >= minimal_height

maximal_width: INTEGER
        -- Maximal width allowed for the window
    ensure
        result_large_enough: Result >= minimal_width

minimal_height: INTEGER
        -- Minimal height allowed for the window
        -- Zero by default.
    ensure
        positive_result: Result >= 0;
        result_small_enough: Result <= maximal_height

minimal_width: INTEGER
        -- Minimal width allowed for the window
        -- Zero by default.
    ensure
        positive_result: Result >= 0;
        result_small_enough: Result <= maximal_width
```

For example, we can redefine these features to specify the ranges within which the new width and height should fall after a resize. The following inheritance clause redefines all of the size restriction functions.

```
WEL_FRAME_WINDOW
        redefine
            on_control_command,
            on_set_focus,
            minimal_width, minimal_height,
            maximal_width, maximal_height
        end
```

The new definitions allow the window to be shrunk to three hundred by two hundred fifty-five pixels, and to increase to 600 by 400 pixels. The features are implemented as follows:

```
minimal_width: INTEGER is
            -- The minimum width of the window
      do
            Result := 300
      end

minimal_height: INTEGER is
            -- The minimum height of the window
      do
            Result := 255
      end

maximal_width: INTEGER is
            -- The maximum width of the window
      do
            Result := 600
      end

maximal_height: INTEGER is
            -- The maximal height of the window
      do
            Result := 400
      end
```

In this case, we implement each feature as a function. We could have re-defined each feature to be a constant. For instance,

```
maximal_height: INTEGER is 300
            -- The maximal height of the window
```

is equivalent (and more efficient) than the function redefinition of *maximal_height*.

To constrain a window to a particular fixed size, you can set both the maximal and minimal values of either width or height to the same values. For example, setting *maximal_width* and *minimal_width* to three hundred pixels can be used to restrict the width of the window to that size. Recall, these values only provide the recommended maximum and minimum sizes of a window. You must redefine either *on_get_min_max_info* or *on_window_pos_changing* message operations of *WEL_COMPOSITE_WINDOW* to actually restrict the values (see the sections "On a Composite Window Minimum Maximum Message" and "On a Composite Window Position Message" in Chapter 5).

Changing the Position of a Window

A window is positioned on screen using x and y coordinates relative to its parent window. Therefore, a top-level window is positioned relative to the top left corner of the screen, while a child window is positioned relative to the top left corner of the parent's client area (see "Window Dimensions as a Rectangle" in this chapter for a description of client areas). This allows you to easily position child windows on other windows. If all coordinates were relative to the top left corner of the screen, then positioning child windows, such as controls, would be very difficult.

Four *WEL_WINDOW* features allow you to query and set the position of a window. The features are *x, y, set_x,* and *set_y.*

```
x: INTEGER
        -- Window x position
    require
        exists: exists
    ensure
        parent = void implies Result = absolute_x

y: INTEGER
        -- Window y position
    require
        exists: exists
    ensure
        parent = void implies Result = absolute_y

set_x (a_x: INTEGER)
        -- Set x with a_x
    require
        exists: exists;
        not_minimized: not minimized
    ensure
        x_set: x = a_x

set_y (a_y: INTEGER)
        -- Set y with a_y
    require
        exists: exists;
        not_minimized: not minimized
    ensure
        y_set: y = a_y
```

Example 4.5 demonstrates querying a window's current position. The example creates a main window and a popup child window. When you click on *pos_button,* the current positions of both windows are displayed. If you move the popup window on the screen and then click the *pos_button,* the new coordinates of the popup window are displayed.

Example 4.5 Positioning a Window (windows\pos)

```
class MAIN_WINDOW

inherit
    WEL_FRAME_WINDOW
        redefine
            on_control_command,
            on_set_focus
        end
creation
    make
feature -- Initialization

    make is
            -- Initialize the main window, the button, popup window
            -- and message areas.
        do
            make_top ("Main Window")
            resize (300, 255)
            create message.make (Current, "", 0, 0, width, 30, -1)
            create pos_button.make (Current, "Position", 10, 30, 90,
                35, -1)
            create popup.make_child (Current, "Child Window")
            popup.resize (200, 200)
            create popup_message.make (popup, "", 0, 0,
            popup.width, popup.height, -1)
        end
feature -- Implementation

    pos_button: WEL_PUSH_BUTTON
            -- Push button

    message, popup_message: WEL_STATIC
            -- Message areas

    on_set_focus is
            -- Show the popup
        do
            if not popup.shown then
                popup.show
            end
        end
    on_control_command (control: WEL_CONTROL) is
            -- A command has been received from 'control'.
        local
            s: STRING
        do
            if control = pos_button then
                -- show current window position
                create s.make (30)
                s.append ("x=")
```

```
                s.append_integer (x)
                s.append (", y=")
                s.append_integer (y)
                message.set_text (s)
                -- show the popup window position
                create s.make (30)
                s.append ("x=")
                s.append_integer (popup.x)
                s.append (", y=")
                s.append_integer (popup.y)
                popup_message.set_text (s)
            end
        end

    end -- class MAIN_WINDOW
```

Figure 4.4 shows the output of the application with the main window positioned near the top corner of the screen and the child positioned on the main window.

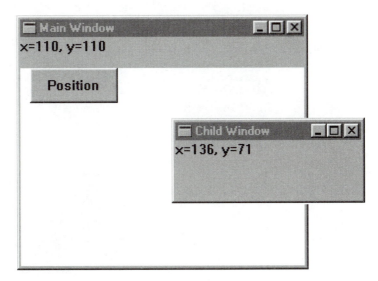

FIGURE 4.4. Positioning windows example.

An application can also query a window for its *absolute* x and y positions relative to the top left corner of the screen. The features *absolute_x* and *absolute_y* provide this information.

```
absolute_x: INTEGER
        -- Absolute x position
    require
        exists: exists
    ensure
        Result = window_rect.x

absolute_y: INTEGER
        -- Absolute y position
    require
        exists: exists
    ensure
        Result = window_rect.y
```

Figure 4.5 shows the output of a modified version of Example 4.5. The application prints both the absolute and relative positions of each window.

Example 4.6 shows the code used in *MAIN_WINDOW* to display absolute coordinates. This is a modified version of Example 4.5.

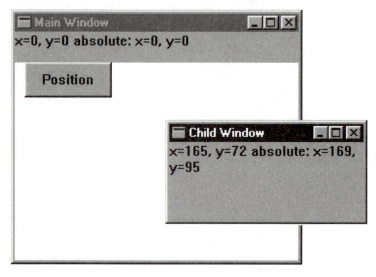

FIGURE 4.5. Absolute and relative window positions example.

Example 4.6 Positioning a Window Using Absolute Coordinates (windows\abspos)

```
class MAIN_WINDOW
inherit
    WEL_FRAME_WINDOW
        redefine
            on_control_command,
            on_set_focus
        end
creation

    make
feature

    make is
            -- Initialize the main window
        do
            make_top ("Main Window")
            resize (300, 255)
            create message.make (Current, "", 0, 0, width,
                30, -1)
            create pos_button.make (Current, "Position", 10, 30, 90,
                35, -1)
            create popup.make_child (Current, "Child Window")
            popup.resize (200, 200)
            create popup_message.make (popup, "", 0, 0,
            popup.width, popup.height, -1)
        end
    on_set_focus is
            -- Show the popup
        do
            if not popup.shown then
                popup.show
            end
        end
    pos_button: WEL_PUSH_BUTTON
            -- Push button

    message, popup_message: WEL_STATIC
            -- Message areas

    popup: WEL_POPUP_WINDOW
            -- The popup
    on_control_command (control: WEL_CONTROL) is
            -- A command has been received from 'control'.
        local
            s: STRING
```

```
        do
            if control = pos_button then
                -- show current window position
                create s.make (30)
                s.append ("x=")
                s.append_integer (x)
                s.append (", y=")
                s.append_integer (y)
                message.set_text (s)
                -- show the absolute window position
                s.append(" absolute: x=")
                s.append_integer(absolute_x)
                s.append(" y=")
                s.append_integer(absolute_y)
                -- show the popup window position
                create s.make (30)
                s.append ("x=")
                s.append_integer (popup.x)
                s.append (", y=")
                s.append_integer (popup.y)
                popup_message.set_text (s)
            end
        end

end -- class MAIN_WINDOW
```

Routine *move* allows you to move a window to a different position. It requires two parameters, representing the new x and y coordinates.

```
move (a_x, a_y: INTEGER)
        — Move the window to 'a_x', 'a_y'.
    require
        exists: exists
        not_minimized: not minimized
    ensure
        x_set: x = a_x
        y_set: y = a_y
```

move_and_resize allows you to move and resize a window in a single call. This routine requires five parameters representing the new x and y positions, the new width and height, and a Boolean flag indicating whether a repaint of the window should occur.

```
move_and_resize (a_x, a_y, a_width, a_height: INTEGER; repaint: BOOLEAN)
        — Move the window to 'a_x', 'a_y' position and
        — resize it with 'a_width', 'a_height'.
    require
        exists: exists
        a_width_small_enough: a_width <= maximal_width
        a_width_large_enough: a_width >= minimal_width
        a_height_small_enough: a_height <= maximal_height
        a_height_large_enough: a_height >= minimal_height
        not_minimized: not minimized
    ensure
        x_set: x = a_x
        y_set: y = a_y
        width_set: width = a_width
        height_set: height = a_height
```

Maximizing and Minimizing a Window

You can maximize and minimize a window using the title bar controls or the window control menu. You can also maximize and minimize a window programmatically. *WEL_WINDOW* provides two query functions for determining the current visible state of a window and three procedures for maximizing, minimizing, or restoring a window.

To determine the current state of a window, use the functions *minimized* or *maximized*.

```
minimized: BOOLEAN
        -- Is the window minimized?
    require
        exists: exists
maximized: BOOLEAN
        -- Is the window maximized?
    require
        exists: exists
```

Call *maximize* to *maximize*, and *minimize* to minimize a window. Routine *restore* restores a window to its original size (from either a maximized or minimized form).

```
minimize
            -- Minimize the window and display its icon
    require
            exists: exists
    ensure
            minimized: minimized

maximize
            -- Maximize the window
    require
            exists: exists
    ensure
            maximized: maximized

restore
            -- Restore the window to its
            -- original size and position after
            -- 'minimize' or 'maximize'
    require
            exists: exists
```

Using Scroll Bars with a Window

If the client area of a window is larger than a window's dimensions, then additional portions of the client window can be accessed using scroll bars. When a window contains scroll bars, it effectively acts as a *viewport* onto a larger area. In order to view different portions of a window, the viewport can be moved within the client area.

A window can have both vertical and horizontal scroll bars, and they can be turned on and off at arbitrary times during the execution of an application. Class *WEL_WINDOW* provides a number of features for working with scroll bars.

```
has_vertical_scroll_bar: BOOLEAN
            -- Does this window have a vertical scroll bar?
    require
            exists: exists

has_horizontal_scroll_bar: BOOLEAN
            -- Does this window have a horizontal scroll bar?
    require
            exists: exists

show_scroll_bars
            -- Show the horizontal and vertical scroll bars.
```

```
    require
        exists: exists

show_vertical_scroll_bar
            -- Show the vertical scroll bar.
    require
        exists: exists

show_horizontal_scroll_bar
            -- Show the horizontal scroll bar.
    require
        exists: exists

hide_scroll_bars
            -- Hide the horizontal and vertical scroll bars.
    require
        exists: exists

hide_vertical_scroll_bar
            -- Hide the vertical scroll bar.
    require
        exists: exists

hide_horizontal_scroll_bar
            -- Hide the horizontal scroll bar.
    require
        exists: exists
```

Figure 4.6 shows a window with both horizontal and vertical scroll bars enabled. The window receives messages indicating scroll actions by the user. Your application needs to implement the functionality for adjusting the client area appropriately.

FIGURE 4.6. Scroll bar window example.

Scrolling a Window

You can scroll the client area of a window using the feature *scroll* from class *WEL_WINDOW*.

```
scroll (a_x, a_y: INTEGER)
        -- Scroll the contents of the window's
        -- client area.
        -- 'a_x' and 'a_y' specify the amount of
        -- horizontal
        -- and vertical scrolling.
  require
        exists: exists
```

The two parameters of *scroll* specify the amount of scrolling to perform in the horizontal and vertical directions. We show an example of using *scroll* when we examine the message operations for scrolling in composite windows.

Changing the Text of a Window

One of the most important properties of a window is its *text*. The text of a window is a string of characters that is displayed either as its label, title, or contents. For example, a frame window displays its text in the title bar, while a push button displays its text as a label.

The creation of a window usually requires the window text to be specified. This technique has been used in many of the examples presented so far. For instance, when creating the main window of the example applications, we set the text (in this case, the window title) to "Main Window" using the following line of code:

```
make_top ("Main Window")
```

In many circumstances, it is necessary to change the text of a window while the application is running—for example, dynamically changing the text of labels on buttons or changing the title bar of a window to include the current document name. *WEL_WINDOW* provides three features for window text manipulation—one to query the current window text, another to query the length of the text, and finally, a routine to set the text to a new value.

```
text: STRING
        -- Window text
    require
        exists: exists
    ensure
        result_not_void: Result /= void

text_length: INTEGER
        -- Text length
    require
        exists: exists
    ensure
        positive_result: Result >= 0

set_text (a_text: STRING)
        -- Set the window text
    require
        exists: exists;
        a_text_not_void: a_text /= void
    ensure
        text_set: text.is_equal (a_text)
```

Query *text* returns the current window text as a string, query *text_length* returns the length of the current window text, and *set_text* allows you to set the text to a different value. Example 4.7 includes a push button that changes the text of the main window when pressed.

Example 4.7 Window Text Manipulation (windows\text)

```
class MAIN_WINDOW

inherit
    WEL_FRAME_WINDOW
        redefine
            on_control_command
        end
creation
    make
feature -- Initialization

    make is
            -- Initialize the main window and the push button.
        do
            make_top ("Main Window")
            resize (300, 255)
            create text_button.make (Current, "Set Text", 10, 30, 90,
                35, -1)
```

```
            end
feature -- Implementation

        text_button: WEL_PUSH_BUTTON
                -- Push button
        on_control_command (control: WEL_CONTROL) is
                -- A command has been received from 'control'.
            local
                s: STRING
            do
                if control = text_button then
                    s := "Length of last title was: "
                    s.append_integer (text_length)
                    set_text (s)
                end
            end

    end -- class MAIN_WINDOW
```

Routine *on_control_command* checks to see if the *text_button* has been clicked, and if so, changes the window's text to a string that indicates the length of the previous window text. The query *text_length* is used to determine the length of the previous text, and the routine *set_text* is used to change the text to the string stored in the local variable *s*. Figure 4.7 shows the output of the application after clicking the text button once.

Using Timers with a Window

Timers can be used to schedule periodic events in your applications, such as updating an animated picture, notifying the user of appointments, and scheduling automatic document saves. Timers schedule registered events that fire after a specified period in milliseconds. In WEL, you can set a restricted number of

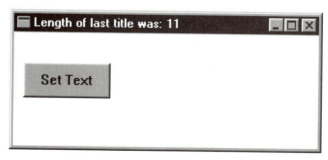

FIGURE 4.7. Window text example.

timers on a window. The restriction arises from the operating system you are programming in; Win32s allows a total of 12 timers, Windows 95 allows over 2,500 timers, and Windows NT allows approximately 10,000 timers. Each timer is given a unique identification number to distinguish it from others associated with the same window.[1]

When a timer fires, a message is sent to the window on which the timer was set. An application can redefine the *on_timer* message hook to perform any required action (see "On a Window Timer Message" later in this chapter). Call *set_timer* to set a timer specifying the identification number and the time-out period in milliseconds. You can reset a timer's interval by calling *set_timer* with the same timer identification number. A timer will continue to be processed even after it has fired. If the timer interval has not been changed, it will fire again after the original time period has elapsed. You must call *kill_timer* to stop a timer.

```
set_timer (timer_id, time_out: INTEGER)
        -- Set a timer idenfied by 'timer_id' with a
        -- 'time_out' value (in milliseconds).
    require
        exists: exists
        positive_timer_id: timer_id > 0
        positive_time_out: time_out > 0

kill_timer (timer_id: INTEGER)
        -- Kill the timer identified by 'timer_id'.
    require
        exists: exists
        positive_timer_id: timer_id > 0
```

Feature *set_timer* requires a unique timer identification number and a time out value in milliseconds. Both parameters must be positive. Feature *kill_timer* requires a timer identifier as its sole parameter.

Example 4.8 demonstrates how to create a timer on a window. A constant integer is used as the timer identifier. In this case, the Eiffel keyword **unique** has been used to generate the constant value automatically. You could also use a fixed constant.

---

[1]Timers are not asynchronous. They are just messages and therefore may not be very precise.

Example 4.8 Window Timers (windows\timer)

```
class MAIN_WINDOW

inherit
    WEL_FRAME_WINDOW
        redefine
            on_control_command,
            on_timer
        end
creation
    make
feature -- Initialization

    make is
            -- Initialize the main window, the buttons and message area
        do
            make_top ("Main Window")
            resize (300, 255)
            create start_button.make (Current, "Start", 10, 30, 90,
                35, -1)
            create stop_button.make (Current, "Stop", 10, 70, 90, 35, -1)
            create message.make (Current, "", 0, 0, width, 30, -1)
        end
feature — Implementation

    Main_timer: INTEGER is unique
            -- Constant for main timer id
    count: INTEGER
            -- Count of how many timers the timer has fired.
    start_button, stop_button: WEL_PUSH_BUTTON
            -- Push buttons
    mesage: WEL_STATIC
            -- Message area
    on_control_command (control: WEL_CONTROL) is
            -- A command has been received from 'control'.
        do
            if control = start_button then
                set_timer (Main_timer, 2000)
                message.set_text ("Timer started...")
            elseif control = stop_button then
                kill_timer (Main_timer)
                count := 0
                message.set_text ("Timer stopped.")
            end
        end
    on_timer (timer_id: INTEGER) is
            -- Set timer fired message
        local
            s: STRING
        do
            if timer_id = Main_timer then
count := count + 1
```

```
            s := "Timer fired "
            s.append_integer (count)
            s.append (" times...")
            message.set_text (s)
        end
    end

end -- class MAIN_WINDOW
```

When you click on the start button, a timer is started with the id *Main_timer*. The timer is set to fire every 2,000 milliseconds (every two seconds). Every time the timer fires, the *on_timer* routine is called and a message is displayed indicating how many times the timer has fired. If you click on the stop button, the timer is killed and the counter is reset. Application output after the timer has fired three times is shown in Figure 4.8.

Manipulating Child Windows

All windows on the screen are stored in a stacking order from the bottom window to the top. The ordering is known as the *z-order*.[2] A window at the bottom of the z-order appears to be under all other windows, and windows higher in the z-order obscure windows lower in the order. The z-order of a window can be changed by calling *set_z_order*.

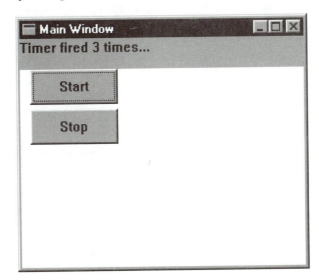

FIGURE 4.8. Timer window example.

---

[2]The name *z-order* comes from the third dimension in a three-dimensional coordinate system with dimensions x, y, and z.

```
set_z_order (z_order: INTEGER)
        -- Set the z-order of the window.
        -- See class WEL_HWND_CONSTANTS for 'z_order' values.
    require
        exists: exists
        valid_hwnd_constant: valid_hwnd_constant (z_order)
```

Values that can be passed as the *z_order* parameter can be found in the class *WEL_HWND_CONSTANTS*.[3] Table 4.1 lists the constants in WEL_HWND_CONSTANTS that are used for z-ordering. Using these parameter values, a window can be moved either to the top of the z-order, the bottom, above the topmost window, or below the topmost window.

You typically do not need to inherit from the *WEL_HWND_CONSTANTS* class because *WEL_FRAME_WINDOW* already indirectly inherits it through *WEL_WINDOW*. The example below provides four buttons. Each button changes the z-order of a second window according to the table below.

TABLE 4.1 *Window Handle Z-Order Constants (WEL_HWND_CONSTANTS)*

CONSTANT	DESCRIPTION
Hwnd_bottom	Place window at the bottom of the z-order.
Hwnd_notopmost	Specify that the window will not remain topmost.
Hwnd_top	Place window at the top of the z-order.
Hwnd_topmost	Make a window remain on top of all other windows not specified topmost. This setting will make a window stay on top of all other windows.

Example 4.9 Window Z-Ordering (windows\z_order)

```
class MAIN_WINDOW

inherit
    WEL_FRAME_WINDOW
        redefine
            on_control_command,
            on_set_focus
        end
```

---

[3]The HWND acronym comes from the Windows API libraries. It stands for a *handle to a window*.

```
creation
    make
feature -- Initialization

    make is
            -- Initialize the main window, the buttons and the second
frame
            -- window.
        do
            make_top ("Main Window")
            resize (300, 255)
            create top_button.make (Current, "Top", 10, 30, 90, 35, -1)
            create bottom_button.make (Current, "Bottom", 10, 70, 90,
                35, -1)
            create top_most_button.make (Current, "TopMost", 10, 110,
                90, 35,-1)
            create notop_most_button.make (Current, "Not TopMost",
                10, 150, 90, 35, -1)
            create child.make_top ("Second Window")
            child.resize (200, 100)
        end
feature -- Implementation

    top_button, bottom_button, top_most_button, notop_most_button;
        WEL_PUSH_BUTTON
            -- Push buttons
    child: WEL_FRAME_WINDOW
            -- Second frame window

    on_set_focus is
            -- Show the second window
        do
            if not child.shown then
                child.show
            end
        end
    on_control_command (control: WEL_CONTROL) is
            -- A command has been received from 'control'.
        do
            if control = top_button then
                child.set_z_order (Hwnd_top)
            elseif control = bottom_button then
                child.set_z_order (Hwnd_bottom)
            elseif control = top_most_button the
                child.set_z_order (Hwnd_topmost)
            elseif control = notop_most_button then
                child.set_z_order (Hwnd_notopmost)
            end
        end

end -- class MAIN_WINDOW
```

Each button calls *set_z_order* with a different constant value from *WEL_HWND_CONSTANTS.* You can also set the z-order of windows relative to other windows. The feature *insert_after* inserts the current window after another in the z-order.

```
insert_after (a_window: WEL_WINDOW)
        -- Insert the current window after 'a_window'.
    require
        exists: exists
        a_window_not_void: a_window /= Void
        a_window_exists: a_window.exists
        a_window_not_current: a_window /= Current
```

The parameter to *insert_after* must be another window existing in your application. The current window is inserted after *a_window* in the z-order. For example, given two windows, *window_1* and *window_2,* the following code inserts *window_1* after *window_2:*

```
window_1.insert_after (window_2)
```

This routine is useful if you need to layer, or stack, a set of windows in a particular order. You can traverse such a set, inserting each window in the correct position.

Window Dimensions as a Rectangle

Each window contains two parts—the border area and the client area. The border area of a window contains border decorations, such as resize handles, title bar, and icons. The client area is the area within the border of a window on which child windows are attached. Figure 4.9 shows a typical frame window and indicates the border and client areas.

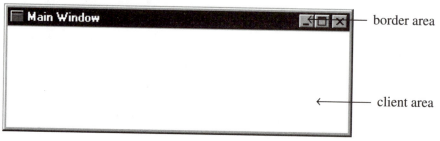

FIGURE 4.9. Border and client areas of a window.

Class *WEL_WINDOW* provides two features for determining the current dimensions of both the client area and the entire window (including the border area). Feature *client_rect* returns the client area dimensions as a rectangle, while feature *window_rect* returns the dimensions of the entire window.

```
client_rect: WEL_RECT
          -- Client rectangle
    require
       exists: exists
    ensure
       result_not_void: Result /= Void

window_rect: WEL_RECT
          -- Window rectangle (absolute position)
    require
       exists: exists
    ensure
       result_not_void: Result /= Void
```

Both features return a *WEL_RECT* that holds the top left corner coordinates and the width and height of the bounding rectangle.

Changing the Placement of a Window

Window placement information specifies where a window will be positioned when maximized, minimized, and restored, and in what form the window will be shown. Setting the placement information of a window allows you to set a number of properties using one call. Two *WEL_WINDOW* features allow you to query and set a window's placement information.

```
placement: WEL_WINDOW_PLACEMENT
          -- Window placement information
    require
       exists: exists
    ensure
       result_not_void: Result /= void

set_placement (a_placement: WEL_WINDOW_PLACEMENT)
          -- Set placement with a_placement
    require
       exists: exists;
       a_placement_not_void: a_placement /= void
```

Feature *placement* returns an instance of *WEL_WINDOW_PLACE-MENT*, holding the window placement information for the window. You can also create an instance of *WEL_WINDOW_PLACEMENT* directly by passing the target window to its creation procedure *make*. For example, given the two attributes *my_window* and *placement_info*

```
my_window: WEL_WINDOW
placement_info: WEL_WINDOW_PLACEMENT
```

Creating an instance of *WEL_WINDOW_PLACEMENT* directly using

```
create placement_info.make (my_window)
```

is equivalent to asking the window for the information using

```
placement_info := my_window.placement
```

However, in most cases it is best to ask a window for its placement information instead of creating an instance for yourself. Once you have hold of the window's placement information, you can modify the settings and reset the window to the new placement information using *set_placement*. The short public interface of class *WEL_WINDOW_PLACEMENT* is shown next. Features of *WEL_WINDOW_PLACEMENT* that are inherited from *WEL_RESOURCE* are not shown here for brevity. (See Chapter 7, "Resources," for more information on the missing features.)

Class *WEL_WINDOW_PLACEMENT* provides features that let you query the current window placement information and features you can use to set the placement information.

```
class interface
      WEL_WINDOW_PLACEMENT
creation
      make

feature - Access

      flags: INTEGER
               -- Flags that control the position of the
               -- minimized window and the method by which
               -- the window is restored.
               -- See class WEL_WPF_CONSTANTS for possible values.

      maximum_position: WEL_POINT
```

```
                        -- Coordinates of the window's upper left
                        -- corner when the window is maximized.
            ensure
                  result_not_void: Result /= void


      minimum_position: WEL_POINT
                        -- Coordinates of the window's upper left
                        -- corner when the window is minimized.
            ensure
                  result_not_void: Result /= void


      normal_position: WEL_RECT
                        -- Window's coordinates when the
                        -- window is in the restored position
            ensure
                  result_not_void: Result /= void


      show_command: INTEGER
                        -- Show state of the window.
                        -- See class WEL_SW_CONSTANTS for possible values

feature -- Element change
      set_flags (a_flags: INTEGER)
                        -- Set 'flags' with 'a_flags'
            ensure
                  flags_set: flags = a_flags


      set_maximum_position (a_point: WEL_POINT)
                        -- Set 'maximum_position' with 'a_point'
                        -- maximum_position_set: maximum_position = a_point
            require
                  a_point_not_void: a_point /= void


      set_minimum_position (a_point: WEL_POINT)
                        -- Set 'minimum_position' with 'a_point'
                        -- minimum_position_set: minimum_position = a_point
            require
                  a_point_not_void: a_point /= void


      set_normal_position (a_rect: WEL_RECT)
                        -- Set 'normal_position' with 'a_rect'
                        -- normal_position_set: normal_position = a_rect
            require
                  a_rect_not_void: a_rect /= void


      set_show_command (a_show_command: INTEGER)
                        -- Set 'show_command' with 'a_show_command'
            ensure
                  show_command_set: show_command = a_show_command
end -- class WEL_WINDOW_PLACEMENT
```

TABLE 4.2 *Window Placement Flag Constants (WEL_WPF_CONSTANTS)*

CONSTANT	DESCRIPTION
Wpf_setminposition	When this flag is set, the x and y positions of the minimized window can be set. If you set the minimized position by calling *set_minimum_position*, then you must also ensure that this flag is set.
Wpf_restoretomaximized	When this flag is set, the window will be maximized when it is restored, regardless of whether it was maximized before being minimized. The flag only affects the next time the window is restored and does not change the default restoration behavior. The flag takes effect only when the *Sw_show-minimized* flag is specified for the show command.

The window placement flags can be set to either *Wpf_setminposition* or *Wpf_restoretomaximized*, or to a combination of both values. Table 4.2 describes the use of these flag values. Set the flags by calling *set_flags*, passing an integer that represents the flags to be set. The following instruction would set both flags:

```
set_flags (Wpf_setminposition + Wpf_restoretomaximized)
```

The value of the placement flags can be determined by calling the feature *flags* and comparing the value using the helper class *WEL_BIT_OPERATIONS*.

WEL_WINDOW_PLACEMENT holds three positions. Two are coordinates that represent the minimized and maximized window positions, and the third is a rectangle that represents the restored size of the window. The values of these positions are determined by calling the features *minimum_position, maximum_position,* and *restored_position,* respectively. Each has a corresponding set operation that can be used to change its value. The maximum and minimum positions are set using a *WEL_POINT* that holds the x and y position coordinates, and the restored position takes a *WEL_RECT* that holds a coordinate for the top left-hand corner and a width and height of the bounding rectangle.

The final piece of information available in *WEL_WINDOW_PLACE-MENT* is the *show_command*. This attribute can be set to any of the constants in *WEL_SW_CONSTANTS* (see Chapter 2, Table 2.1).

Changing the Style of a Window

The style of a window is normally set by the window class used to create the window. You can modify all of the style parameters of a window either before or after it is displayed on the screen. Typical style settings include settings for the type of window, the buttons and controls on the title bar, and clipping settings. Class *WEL_WINDOW* provides two features for manipulating the style—one for querying and the other for setting.

```
style: INTEGER
          — Window style
      require
          exists: exists

set_style (a_style: INTEGER)
          — Set style with a_style.
      require
          exists: exists
      ensure
          style_set: style = a_style
```

Available styles are located in the class *WEL_WS_CONSTANTS*. Table 4.3 lists the constants found in this class.[4] Each of the values can be combined using addition. However, many of the values are mutually exclusive, and the combined values may cause unusual and unexpected behavior. For example, it does not make sense to combine *Ws_border* with *Ws_thickframe* because *Ws_border* specifies a thin border and *Ws_thickframe* specifies a thick border. Trying to use both border styles in the same window will only confuse Windows.

TABLE 4.3   *Window Style Constants (WEL_WS_CONSTANTS)*

CONSTANT	DESCRIPTION
Cw_usedefault	Uses default value as determined by Windows.
Ws_border	Adds a thin border to the window.
Ws_caption	Adds a title bar to the window. This implies the *Ws_border* style and cannot be used with *Ws_dlgframe*.
Ws_child	Creates a child window or control. *Ws_popup* cannot be used with this style.
Ws_childwindow	Same as *Ws_child*.
Ws_clipchildren	Used when creating parent windows. Clips around children when painting occurs, i.e., the areas occupied by child windows are excluded when painting the parent.
Ws_clipsiblings	Clips child windows relative to each other when painting occurs.

(continued)

---

[4]The *ex_* in some of the style constants represents extended window styles introduced in recent versions of Windows.

TABLE 4.3 *Window Style Constants (WEL_WS_CONSTANTS) (continued)*

CONSTANT	DESCRIPTION
Ws_disabled	Creates a window that has input initially disabled.
Ws_dlgframe	Adds a frame suitable for dialogs. Windows with dialog frames cannot have title bars.
Ws_ex_acceptfiles	Creates a window that will accept drag-drop files.
Ws_ex_clientedge	Creates a window with a 3D look, i.e., the window has a border with a sunken edge.
Ws_ex_dlgmodalframe	Creates a window that has a double-size border. To add a title, specify *Ws_caption* also.
Ws_ex_noparentnotify	Turns off *Wm_parentnotify* messages.
Ws_ex_topmost	Creates a window that will remain on top of all other windows not specified topmost.
Ws_ex_transparent	Creates a window that is transparent. Siblings of this window will receive the paint message first, thus creating the appearance of transparency.
Ws_group	Marks the first control in a group. The next control found with *Ws_group* is marked as the end of the group.
Ws_hscroll	Adds a horizontal scroll bar to the window.
Ws_iconic	Creates a window that is initially iconic.
Ws_maximize	Creates a window that is initially maximized.
Ws_maximizebox	Adds a maximize icon to the title bar.
Ws_minimize	Creates a window that is initially minimized.
Ws_minimizebox	Adds a minimize icon to the title bar.
Ws_overlapped	Creates a window with a title bar and a border.
Ws_overlappedwindow	Combination of *Ws_overlapped, Ws_caption, Ws_sysmenu, Ws_minimize_box,* and *Ws_maximize_box.* In addition, the window is given a sizing frame.
Ws_popup	Creates a popup window. *Ws_child* cannot be used with this style.
Ws_popupwindow	Combination of *Ws_border, Ws_popup,* and *Ws_sysmenu.* To make the system menu visible, *Ws_caption* must also be specified.
Ws_sizebox	Adds a sizebox to the window.
Ws_sysmenu	Adds a system menu icon to the title bar.
Ws_tabstop	Specifies a control that the tab key will stop on.
Ws_thickframe	Adds a sizing border to the window.
Ws_tiled	Synonym of *Ws_overlapped.*
Ws_tiledwindow	Synonym of *Ws_overlappedwindow.*
Ws_visible	Creates a window that is initially visible.

(continued)

TABLE 4.3   *Window Style Constants (WEL_WS_CONSTANTS) (continued)*

CONSTANT	DESCRIPTION
Ws_vscroll	Adds a vertical scroll bar to the window.
Ws_ex_contexthelp	Includes a question mark icon in the title bar of the window. When clicked, the cursor changes to a question mark with a pointer. If the user clicks a child window with the question mark pointer, the child receives a *Wm_help* message.
Ws_ex_controlparent	Allows the user to navigate among the child windows of the window by using the tab key.
Ws_ex_left	Gives the window generic left-aligned properties. This is the default.
Ws_ex_leftscrollbar	Places a vertical scroll bar to the left of the client area.
Ws_ex_mdichild	Creates an MDI child window.
Ws_ex_overlappedwindow	Combination of *Ws_ex_clientedge* and *Ws_ex_windowedge* styles.
Ws_ex_palettewindow	Combination of *Ws_ex_windowedge* and *Ws_ex_topmost* styles.
Ws_ex_right	Gives a window generic right-aligned properties. This depends on the window class.
Ws_ex_rightscrollbar	Places a vertical scroll bar (if present) to the right of the client area. This is the default.
Ws_ex_rtlreading	Displays the window text using right-to-left reading order properties.
Ws_ex_staticedge	Creates a window with a three-dimensional border style intended to be used for items that do not accept user input.
Ws_ex_toolwindow	Creates a window intended for use as a floating tool bar. The window has a short title bar and the title text is drawn using a smaller font. A tool window does not appear in the task bar or in the window that appears when the user presses ALT+TAB.
Ws_ex_windowedge	Specifies that a window has a border with a raised edge.

Example 4.10 illustrates what can be done using different styles. Each WEL window class creates a window with a given style (see Chapter 5 and Chapter 6, for more information). Example 4.10 modifies the *MAIN_WINDOW* creation procedure to change the main window's style.

Example 4.10 Window Styles (window\style)

```
class MAIN_WINDOW

inherit
    WEL_FRAME_WINDOW
creation
    make
feature -- Initialization
```

```
make is
            -- Initialize the main window with a different style
    do
        make_top ("Main Window")
            set_style (Ws_overlapped + Ws_thickframe + Ws_caption)
    end
end -- class MAIN_WINDOW
```

The default style set in the call to *make_top* is overridden with a call to *set_style*. New style settings include *Ws_overlapped, Ws_thickframe,* and *Ws_caption.* The window created by this example includes a title bar and border, a thick frame, and a caption. It does not contain a system menu, minimize icon, or maximize icon (as it would if the style wasn't overridden). Figure 4.10 shows the window displayed with these style settings.

Validating the Client Area of a Window

When a window first appears on the screen, is resized, or is restored from a minimized state, its client area must be validated. Validation is the process of ensuring that all visible areas of a window are up-to-date and painted correctly. Normally, validation occurs automatically—a window receives a paint message and forwards the paint message to any child windows for them to paint themselves. Therefore, a window with controls will normally be painted correctly when it first appears. However, in some cases it is necessary to manually perform client area validation. For example, when a client area contains drawings or bitmaps, you must ensure these are redrawn if the client area becomes invalid. A client area may become invalid if it changes size or if another window obscuring the client area is moved out of the way.

You can also force a client area (or a portion of it) to become invalid. When a client area becomes invalid, it is usually updated by the operating system sending a paint message to the affected window.

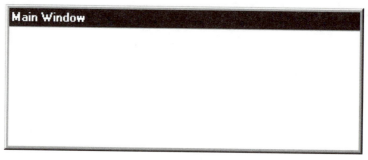

FIGURE 4.10. Window style example.

WEL_WINDOW provides a number of features for invalidating client areas and updating invalid areas. You can call *update* to force an update of a client area, thus sending a paint message to the parent window. Validation can be performed on a portion of the client area using the features *validate_rect* and *validate_region*.

```
update
        -- Update the client area by sending a Wm_paint message.
    require
        exists: exists
validate_rect (rect: WEL_RECT)
        -- Validate the area 'rect'.
    require
        exists: exists;
        rect_not_void: rect /= void
validate_region (region: WEL_REGION)
        -- Validate the area 'region'.
    require
        exists: exists;
        region_not_void: region /= void;
        region_exists: region.exists
```

A *WEL_RECT* holds the coordinates of the top left corner, the width, and the height of a rectangle; a *WEL_REGION* is a rectangular, polygonal, or elliptical area that can be manipulated.

Call *invalidate* to invalidate a window. Three variants of invalidate allow you to invalidate an area without clearing the background, invalidate a portion of the client area within a rectangle, or invalidate a portion within a region. The *BOOLEAN* flag *erase_background* causes the background to be cleared if *True*. You can also invalidate the entire client area without first erasing the background with the routine *invalidate_without_background*.

```
invalidate
            -- Invalide the entire client area of the window. The
            -- background will be erased before.
    require
        exists: exists

invalidate_rect (rect: WEL_RECT; erase_background: BOOLEAN)
            -- Invalidate the area 'rect' and erase
            -- the background if erase_background is True.
    require
        exists: exists;
        rect_not_void: rect /= void
```

```
invalidate_region (region: WEL_REGION; erase_background: BOOLEAN)
        -- Invalidate the area region and erase
        -- the background if erase_background is True.
    require
        exists: exists;
        region_not_void: region /= void;
        region_exists: region.exists

invalidate_without_background
        -- Invalide the entire client area of the window. The
        -- background will not be erased.
    require
        exists: exists
```

Examples of the use of these features can be found in the discussion on graphics programming in Chapter 10, "Graphics Device Interface."

Adding User Help to a Window

A user can invoke help by clicking on help buttons by choosing help from a menu bar, or by selecting context help topics. Your applications should provide facilities for the user to get help in each to these ways. Once the facilities are implemented, you can use the *WEL_WINDOW* feature *win_help* to load a help window for a particular topic.

The *win_help* feature requires a string representing the help file name, an integer representing the type of help command requested by the user, and an integer representing arbitrary data used by the command. The value of the command parameter can be selected from the constants implemented in class *WEL_HELP_CONSTANTS*. Table 4.4 lists each constant, the purpose of the constant, and what the data parameter represents for each.

Message Hooks in a Window

Message hooks are defined for the most common messages that a window receives.You can either redefine the relevant message hook or use a Context → Event → Command (CEC) association to capture and perform actions on window events. Class *WEL_WINDOW* implements the message operations listed in Table 4.5.

On a Window Resize Message

The *on_size* routine is called whenever a window changes size and receives a *Wm_size* message from the operating system.

TABLE 4.4   *Help Constants (WEL_HELP_CONSTANTS)*

CONSTANT	DESCRIPTION
Help_command	Executes a help macro or macro string. The data represents the address of a string that specifies the name of the help macro(s) to execute. You can pass the address of a string by using the *to_c* routine of class *STRING* in Eiffel.
Help_contents	Displays the topic specified by the Contents option in the [OPTIONS] section of the help file. This is obsolete in Win32 and you should use the *Help_finder* command instead.
Help_context	Displays the topic identified by the specified context identifier defined in the [MAP] section of the help file. The data represents an integer containing the context identifier for the topic.
Help_contextpopup	Displays the topic identified by the specified context identifier defined in the [MAP] section of the help file in a popup window. The data represents an integer containing the context identifier for the topic.
Help_forcefile	Ensures that WinHelp is displaying a particular file. If WinHelp is not displaying the specified file, then it will be loaded in place of the file currently being displayed. The data is ignored for this command.
Help_helponhelp	Displays help on how to use Windows Help. The data is ignored.
Help_index	Displays the index in the help topics box. This command is obsolete in Win32 and *Help_finder* command should be used in its place.
Help_key	Displays the topic in the keyword table that matches the specified keyword, if there is an exact match. If there is more than one match, displays the index with the Topics Found list box. Pass an address of a *STRING* as the data to specify the topic.
Help_multikey	Displays the topic specified by a keyword in an alternative keyword table. The data represents the address of a MULTIKEYHELP structure. Pass an address of a *STRING* as the data that represents the alternative keyword.
Help_partialkey	Displays the topic in the keyword table that matches the specified keyword, if there is an exact match. If there is more than one match, displays the Index tab. To display the Index without passing a keyword (the third result), you should use a pointer to an empty string. To specify a partial key, pass a pointer to a *STRING* that holds the key value.
Help_quit	Informs the Help application that is it no longer needed. If no other applications have asked for Help, Windows will close the Help application. The data is ignored.
Help_setcontents	Specifies the Contents topic. The Help application displays the topic when the user clicks the Contents button. The data is an integer containing the context identifier for the Contents topic.
Help_setindex	Specifies a keyword table to be displayed in the Index of the Help Topics dialog box. Data is an integer containing the context identifier for the topic.
Help_setwinpos	Displays the Help window if it is minimized or in memory, and sets its size and position. Data is an address of a HELPWININFO structure that specifies the size and position of the window.

TABLE 4.5 *Window Message Hooks*

MESSAGE HOOK	DESCRIPTION
on_char	A key down message has been translated.
on_destroy	The window has been removed from the screen.
on_hide	The window is about to be hidden.
on_key_down	A nonsystem key has been pressed.
on_key_up	A nonsystem key has been released.
on_kill_focus	The window is about to lose the keyboard focus.
on_left_button_double_click	Left mouse button has been double-clicked, possibly with keyboard modifiers.
on_left_button_down	Left mouse button has been pressed, possibly with keyboard modifiers.
on_left_button_up	Left mouse button has been released, possibly with keyboard modifiers.
on_mouse_move	The cursor has moved, possibly with keyboard modifiers.
on_move	The window has been moved.
on_notify	Notification of an event in a child control window.
on_right_button_double_click	Right mouse button has been double-clicked, possibly with keyboard modifiers.
on_right_button_down	Right mouse button has been pressed, possibly with keyboard modifiers.
on_right_button_up	Right mouse button has been released, possibly with keyboard modifiers.
on_set_cursor	Cursor has moved within a window and mouse input is not captured.
on_set_focus	The window has gained the keyboard focus.
on_show	The window is about to be shown.
on_size	Window has been maximized, minimized, restored, or shown.
on_sys_char	A system key down message has been translated.
on_sys_key_down	A key has been pressed with the Alt key or when no other window has keyboard focus.
on_sys_key_up	A key has been released with the Alt key or when no other window has keyboard focus.
on_timer	A timer has fired.

TABLE 4.6   *Window Size Constants (WEL_SIZE_CONSTANTS)*

CONSTANT	DESCRIPTION
Size_maxhide	Sent to all popup windows when another window has been hidden.
Size_maximized	Window has been maximized.
Size_maxshow	Sent to all popup windows when another window has been restored to its original size.
Size_minimized	Window has been minimized.
Size_restored	Size has been resized, but neither *Size_maximized* or *Size_minimized* apply.

Three parameters are passed to *on_size*. The first parameter gives the reason for the resize event; the second and third parameters specify the new width and height of the *client area* within the newly sized window. The reason for the resize is represented by one of the constants found in class *WEL_SIZE_CONSTANTS*, which are itemized in Table 4.6.

Recall, Example 3.3 in Chapter 3, "Messages," illustrates the use of this message operation by resizing a button to fill its parent window's client area whenever the parent window is resized.

On a Window Move Message

The *on_move* routine is invoked when a window is moved. This routine is passed the new x and y positions for the client area of the window that has moved.

```
on_move (x_pos, y_pos: INTEGER)
        -- Wm_move message.
        -- This message is sent after a window has been moved.
        -- 'x_pos' specifies the x-coordinate of the upper-left
        -- corner of the client area of the window.
        -- 'y_pos' specifies the y-coordinate of the upper-left
        -- corner of the client area of the window.
    require
        exists: exists
```

Example 4.11 uses the *on_move* routine to display the current position of the main window in a static text control. Using the same method as the previous example, *on_move* is redefined from the parent *WEL_FRAME_WINDOW* (see also Example 4.5).

Example 4.11 On Move Message Operation (windows\on_move)

```
class MAIN_WINDOW

inherit
    WEL_FRAME_WINDOW
        redefine
            on_move
        end
creation
    make
feature -- Initialization

    make is
            -- Initialize the main window and the static text
        do
            make_top ("Main Window")
            message.make (Current, 0, 0, width, height, -1)
        end
feature -- Implementation

    on_move (new_x, new_y: INTEGER) is
            -- Wm_move message received. Display the current position
            -- in the message control.
        local
            s: STRING
        do
            create s.make (20)
            s.append ("[")
            s.append_integer (new_x)
            s.append (", ")
            s.append_integer (new_y)
            s.append ("]")
            message.set_text (s)
        end

end -- class MAIN_WINDOW
```

On a Window Mouse Message

Mouse events can be detected and processed using a group of six routines in
WEL_WINDOW. A window is notified of mouse button clicks and movement
through separate messages. You can redefine the routines *on_left_button_down*
or *on_right_button_down* to perform particular processing when a mouse button is pressed. You can also detect when a button has been released with the
routines *on_left_button_up* or *on_right_button_up*. A mouse button release
message is usually used to capture mouse click events.

A combination of these routines is useful for implementing drag-and-drop operations where a drag is initialized upon a mouse button down event and completed when the mouse button up event is received.

```
on_left_button_down (keys, x_pos, y_pos: INTEGER)
        -- Wm_lbuttondown message
        -- See class WEL_MK_CONSTANTS for 'keys' value
    require
        exists: exists

on_left_button_up (keys, x_pos, y_pos: INTEGER)
        -- Wm_lbuttonup message
        -- See class WEL_MK_CONSTANTS for 'keys' value
    require
        exists: exists

on_right_button_down (keys, x_pos, y_pos: INTEGER)
        -- Wm_rbuttondown message
        -- See class WEL_MK_CONSTANTS for 'keys' value
    require
        exists: exists

on_right_button_up (keys, x_pos, y_pos: INTEGER) is
        -- Wm_rbuttonup message
        -- See class WEL_MK_CONSTANTS for 'keys' value
    require
        exists: exists
```

The *keys* parameter holds more information about what mouse key was pressed and if any modifier keys (shift or control) were held at the time. For example, the *keys* parameter can hold information about whether the left, right, or middle button was pressed and also if the shift or control keys were held down at the time of the mouse key press. This parameter can be compared with the values in *WEL_MK_CONSTANTS* shown in Table 4.7.

TABLE 4.7 *Mouse and Key Constants (WEL_MK_CONSTANTS)*

CONSTANT	DESCRIPTION
Mk_control	The control key was held down at the time of the mouse button press.
Mk_lbutton	The left mouse button was pressed.
Mk_mbutton	The middle mouse button was pressed. (This can be simulated on a two-button mouse by pressing both buttons at the same time).
Mk_rbutton	The right mouse button was pressed.
Mk_shift	The shift key was held down at the time of the mouse button press.

The routines *on_left_button_double_click* and *on_right_button_double_click* can be redefined to detect mouse button double-clicks. Finally, *on_mouse_move* can be used to detect mouse movement.

```
on_left_button_double_click (keys, x_pos, y_pos: INTEGER)
        -- Wm_lbuttondblclk message
        -- See class WEL_MK_CONSTANTS for 'keys' value
    require
        exists: exists

on_right_button_double_click (keys, x_pos, y_pos: INTEGER)
        -- Wm_rbuttondblclk message
        -- See class WEL_MK_CONSTANTS for 'keys' value
    require
        exists: exists

on_mouse_move (keys, x_pos, y_pos: INTEGER)
        -- Wm_mousemove message
        -- See class WEL_MK_CONSTANTS for 'keys' value
    require
        exists: exists
```

Example 4.12 illustrates all of the mouse event routines in one application. The application displays a message in the main window whenever a mouse event occurs. The current mouse position (when in the main window) is displayed and updated. Also, whenever a button is clicked or double-clicked, a message indicates that the event occurred.

Example 4.12 Mouse Message Operations

```
class MAIN_WINDOW

inherit
    WEL_FRAME_WINDOW
        redefine
            on_left_button_down, on_right_button_down,
            on_left_button_up, on_right_button_up,
            on_left_button_double_click, on_right_button_double_click,
            on_mouse_move
        end
creation
    make
feature -- Initialization

    make is
            -- Initialize the main window and the message controls.
```

```eiffel
        do
            -- Implementation omitted
        end
feature -- Implementation

    left_message, right_message, click_message, move_message: WEL_STATIC
            -- Message controls
    on_left_button_down (keys, x_pos, y_pos: INTEGER) is
            -- Show left button down message
        do
            left_message.set_text ("Left button down")
        end
    on_right_button_down (keys, x_pos, y_pos: INTEGER) is
            -- Show right button down message
        do
            right_message.set_text ("Right button down")
        end
    on_left_button_up (keys, x_pos, y_pos: INTEGER) is
            -- Show left button up message
        do
            left_message.set_text ("Left button up")
        end
    on_right_button_up (keys, x_pos, y_pos: INTEGER) is
            -- Show right button up message
        do
            right_message.set_text ("Right button up")
        end
    on_left_button_double_click (keys, x_pos, y_pos: INTEGER) is
            -- Show left double click message
        do
            click_message.set_text ("Left button double click")
        end
    on_right_button_double_click (keys, x_pos, y_pos: INTEGER) is
            -- Show right double click message
        do
            click_message.set_text ("Right button double click")
        end
    on_mouse_move (keys, x_pos, y_pos: INTEGER) is
            -- Show mouse movement message
        local
            s: STRING
        do
            create s.make (30)
            s.append ("Mouse moved to: [")
            s.append_integer (x_pos)
            s.append (", ")
            s.append_integer (y_pos)
            s.append ("]")
            move_message.set_text (s)
        end
end -- class MAIN_WINDOW
```

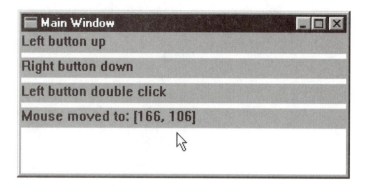

FIGURE 4.11. Mouse message operation example.

Figure 4.11 shows the output of this example after the user has double-clicked and held the left button. The current position of the mouse is at screen coordinates (166, 106).

On a Window Keyboard Message

Keyboard messages are handled in a manner similar to mouse events. A message is sent to the window whenever a key is pressed and released. In addition, distinct messages are sent to the window depending on whether the key pressed is a system key (i.e., pressed with Alt key held down) or a normal key.

Use either *on_key_down* or *on_sys_key_down* to detect when a keyboard key is pressed.

```
on_key_down (virtual_key, key_data: INTEGER)
        -- Wm_keydown message
    require
        exists: exists
on_sys_key_down (virtual_key, key_data: INTEGER)
        -- Wm_syskeydown message
    require
        exists: exists
```

Features *on_key_up* and *on_sys_key_up* detect a key release.

```
on_key_up (virtual_key, key_data: INTEGER)
        — Wm_keyup message
    require
        exists: exists
on_sys_key_up (virtual_key, key_data: INTEGER)
        — Wm_syskeyup message
    require
        exists: exists
```

TABLE 4.8   *Key Data Bit Values*

BITS	USAGES
0-15	Specifies the repeat count. This value is the number of times the key has been repeated as a result of the user holding down the key. This count is always one for an *on_key_up* message.
16-23	Specifies the original equipment manufacturer (OEM) scan code.
24	Specifies whether the key is an extended key, such as a key on an enhanced 102-key keyboard. The value is one if this is an extended key, zero otherwise.
25-28	Reserved.
29	Specifies the context code. This value is always zero for an *on_key_down* and *on_key_up* message. For an *on_char* message, this value is one if the Alt key is pressed.
30	Previous key state. The value is one if the key is down before the message is sent; otherwise the value is zero.
31	Specifies the transition state. The value is one if the key is being released, zero if the key is being pressed.

All of the keyboard routines defined above are passed two parameters, *virtual_key* and *key_data,* representing the virtual key code and any additional key data. The key data parameter provides a set of values in different *bits* of the variable. Table 4.8 lists the use of each bit.

A keyboard key press also causes an *on_char* message or *on_sys_char* message to be sent. The interfaces of these messages are

```
on_char (character_code, key_data: INTEGER)
        -- Wm_char message
    require
        exists: exists
on_sys_char (character_code, key_data: INTEGER)
        -- Wm_syschar message
    require
        exists: exists
```

Both of these messages are passed the ASCII character code of the key that was pressed. The key data values are also passed. The *on_sys_char* message represents a key press that occurred when the Alt key was held down.

Example 4.13 illustrates the use of the key press message routines. The example captures each type of key event and displays in the main window the value of the key pressed. Each key message routine is redefined in class *MAIN_WINDOW.*

Example 4.13 Keyboard Message Operations (windows\keys)

```
class MAIN_WINDOW

inherit
    WEL_FRAME_WINDOW
        redefine
            on_key_down, on_sys_key_down,
            on_key_up, on_sys_key_up,
            on_char, on_sys_char
        end
creation
    make
feature -- Initialization

    make is
            -- Initialize the main window and the message controls.
        do
            -- Implementation omitted
        end
feature -- Implementation

    key_message, sys_key_message, char_message, sys_char_message:
        WEL_STATIC
        -- Message controls
    on_key_down (virtual_key, key_data: INTEGER) is
            -- Key down message
        local
            s: STRING
        do
            s := "Key down: "
            s.append_integer (virtual_key)
            key_message.set_text (s)
        end
    on_sys_key_down (virtual_key, key_data: INTEGER) is
            -- Sys key down message
        local
            s: STRING
        do
            s := "System key down: "
            s.append_integer (virtual_key)
            sys_key_message.set_text (s)
        end
    on_key_up (virtual_key, key_data: INTEGER) is
            — Key up message
        local
            s: STRING
        do
            s := "Key up: "
            s.append_integer (virtual_key)
            key_message.set_text (s)
        end
    on_sys_key_up (virtual_key, key_data: INTEGER) is
```

```
                -- Sys key up message
        local
            s: STRING
        do
            s := "System key up: "
            s.append_integer (virtual_key)
            sys_key_message.set_text (s)
        end
    on_char (virtual_key, key_data: INTEGER) is
            -- Char message
        local
            s: STRING
        do
            s := "Key pressed: "
            s.append_integer (virtual_key)
            char_message.set_text (s)
        end
    on_sys_char (virtual_key, key_data: INTEGER) is
            -- Sys char message
        local
            s: STRING
        do
            s := "System key pressed: "
            s.append_integer (virtual_key)
            sys_char_message.set_text (s)
        end
end -- class MAIN_WINDOW
```

Figure 4.12 shows the output of the example after key *a* has been pressed with and without the Alt key. The scan code for key *a* is 65, while the character code, as given by the *on_char* message, is 97.

The virtual key value passed to any of the key input routines can also be interpreted using virtual key code constants defined in class *WEL_VK_CON-STANTS*. Each key code is given a symbolic name representing the key. For example, special keys such as function keys are given symbolic names like

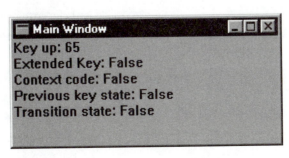

FIGURE 4.12. Keyboard message example.

Vk_f1, Vk_f2, and *Vk_f3,* representing function keys 1, 2, and 3, respectively. Table 4.9 lists the virtual key codes available in Windows and defined in *WEL_VK_CONSTANTS.* The keys are listed in numeric order according to their virtual key code.

TABLE 4.9 *Virtual Key Constants (WEL_VK_CONSTANTS)*

CONSTANT	DESCRIPTION
Vk_0 to *Vk_9*	Numeric keys
Vk_A to *Vk_Z*	Alphabetic keys
Vk_add	Add key
Vk_back	Backspace key
Vk_cancel	Control-break
Vk_capital	Caps Lock key
Vk_clear	Clear key
Vk_control	Control key
Vk_decimal	Decimal key
Vk_delete	Del key
Vk_divide	Divide key
Vk_down	Down Arrow key
Vk_end	End key
Vk_escape	Esc key
Vk_execute	Execute key
Vk_f1 to *Vk_f24*	Function keys
Vk_help	Help key
Vk_home	Home key
Vk_insert	Ins key
Vk_lbutton	Left mouse button
Vk_left	Left Arrow key
Vk_mbutton	Middle mouse button on a three-button mouse
Vk_menu	Alt key
Vk_multiply	Multiply key
Vk_next	Page Down key
Vk_numlock	Num Lock key
Vk_numpad0 to *Vk_numpad9*	Numeric keypad keys
Vk_pause	Pause key

(continued)

TABLE 4.9 *Virtual Key Constants (WEL_VK_CONSTANTS) (continued)*

Constant	Description
Vk_prior	Page Up key
Vk_rbutton	Right mouse button
Vk_return	Enter key
Vk_right	Right Arrow key
Vk_scroll	Scroll Lock key
Vk_select	Select key
Vk_separator	Separator key
Vk_shift	Shift key
Vk_snapshot	Print Screen key for Windows 3.0 and later
Vk_space	Spacebar
Vk_subtract	Subtract key
Vk_tab	Tab key
Vk_up	Up Arrow key

On a Window Input Focus Message

When a window receives the input focus, its title bar is changed to signify to the user that the window has now gained focus. It is also possible to capture a message whenever the window gains or loses focus in order to perform other actions. For example, your application may need to display a message in a status bar when input focus is gained.

Two message hooks, *on_set_focus* and *on_kill_focus,* perform actions whenever a window gains focus or loses focus.

```
on_set_focus
        -- Wm_setfocus message
   require
        exists: exists

on_kill_focus
        -- Wm_killfocus message
   require
        exists: exists
```

Routine *on_set_focus* is called after a window gains the input focus; *on_kill_focus* is called immediately before a window loses the input focus. Example 4.14 uses *on_set_focus* and *on_kill_focus* to display a message in the main window client area that indicates the current input focus status.

Example 4.14 Window Keyboard Focus (windows\on_focus)

```
class MAIN_WINDOW
inherit
    WEL_FRAME_WINDOW
        redefine
            on_set_focus, on_kill_focus
        end
creation
    make
feature

    make is
            -- Initialize the main window
        do
            make_top ("Main Window")
            resize (300, 255)
            create text_message.make (Current, "", 0, 0, width,
                height, -1)
        end
    text_message: WEL_STATIC
            -- Message
    on_set_focus is
            -- Input focus has been gained.
        do
            text_message.set_text ("Gained input focus.")
        end
    on_kill_focus is
            -- Input focus is about to be lost.
        do
            text_message.set_text ("Lost input focus.")
        end
end -- class MAIN_WINDOW
```

Figure 4.13 shows the window produced by this example with the window currently having input focus. If you click a window of another application, then the main window of this example loses the input focus and the message in the main window indicates the change.

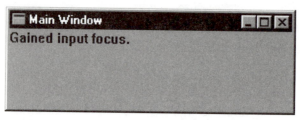

FIGURE 4.13. On input focus example.

On a Window Cursor Message

The *on_set_cursor* message hook is invoked whenever the mouse causes the cursor to move into a window that has not captured the mouse. The *on_set_cursor* interface is as follows:

```
on_set_cursor (hit_code: INTEGER): BOOLEAN
            -- Wm_setcursor message.
            -- See class WEL_HT_CONSTANTS for valid 'hit_code' values.
            -- If True further processing is halted.
            -- (False by default)
        require
            exists: exists
```

The *hit_code* parameter specifies the current status of the mouse as it *hit* the window. Table 4.10 shows the possible values of *hit_code* as defined in class *WEL_HT_CONSTANTS*.

TABLE 4.10   *Mouse Hit Test Constants (WEL_HT_CONSTANTS)*

CONSTANT	DESCRIPTION
Hterror	On the screen background or on a dividing line between windows. Same as *Htnowhere,* except that a system beep is produced.
Httransparent	In a window currently covered by another window.
Htnowhere	On the screen background or on a dividing line between windows.
Htclient	In a client area.
Htcaption	In a title bar.
Htsysmenu	In a System menu or in a Close button in a child window.
Htmenu	In a menu.
Hthscroll	In the horizontal scroll bar.
Htvscroll	In the vertical scroll bar.
Htminbutton	In Minimize button.
Htmaxbutton	In Maximize button.
Htleft	In the left border of a window.
Htright	In the right border of a window.
Httop	In the upper horizontal border of a window.
Httopleft	In the upper left corner of a window border.
Httopright	In the upper right corner of a window border.

(continued)

TABLE 4.10 *Mouse Hit Test Constants (WEL_HT_CONSTANTS)*
(continued)

CONSTANT	DESCRIPTION
Htbottom	In the lower horizontal border of a window.
Htbottomleft	In the lower left corner of a window border.
Htbottomright	In the lower right corner of a window border.
Htborder	In the border of a window that does not have a sizing border.
Htgrowbox	In a size box (same as *Htsize*).
Htreduce	In a minimize button.
Htzoom	In a maximize button.

On a Window Timer Message

The *on_timer* message hook is invoked when a timer fires. The routine is passed the identification number of the timer that fired. The identification number is set when the timer is created using the *set_timer* routine. Refer to "Using Timers with a Window" for an example of timers in an application.

```
on_timer (timer_id: INTEGER)
        -- Wm_timer message.
        -- A Wm_timer has been received from 'timer_id'
    require
        exists: exists
        positive_timer_id: timer_id > 0
```

On a Windows Show or Hide Message

When a window is about to be shown on screen or hidden from the screen, perhaps as a result of a call to *show* or *hide,* the window is notified of the new state via the two message hooks *on_show* and *on_hide.*

```
on_show
                -- Wm_showwindow message
                -- The window is being shown
        require
            exists: exists

on_hide
                -- Wm_showwindow message
                -- The window is being hidden
        require
            exists: exists
```

The messages that invoke these hooks are sent immediately prior to the window becoming visible (in the case of *on_show*) or prior to the window becoming invisible *(on_hide)*.

On a Control Notification Message

A window receives notification of any notification event that occurs in a child control through the *on_notify* message hook. The *on_notify* hook takes two parameters—the control in which the event occurred and an integer identifying the type of event.

```
on_notify (control_id: INTEGER; info: WEL_NMHDR)
    require
        exists: exists;
        info_not_void: info /= void
```

Using Default Window Processing

After a window message has been handled by either a message operation or a CEC association, it is typically passed on to a default processing routine. In a WEL application, Windows default message processing is normally enabled. You can disable default processing if your application does not need the default actions. However, this is not recommended because Windows performs a great deal of housekeeping during default message processing. Without this behind-the-scenes processing, your applications may behave strangely.

Class *WEL_WINDOW* provides features for enabling and disabling default processing for an individual window. You can also check whether default processing is enabled.

```
default_processing_enabled: BOOLEAN
            -- Is the default window processing enabled?
            -- If True (by default) the standard window
            -- procedure will be called. Otherwise, the standard
            -- window procedure will not be called and the
            -- normal behavior will not occur.

enable_default_processing
            -- Enable default window processing.
            -- The standard window procedure will be called for
            -- each messages received by the window and then the
            -- normal behavior will occur.
    ensure
        default_processing_enabled: default_processing_enabled
```

```
disable_default_processing
            -- Disable default window processing.
            -- The standard window procedure will not be called for
            -- each messages received by the window and then the
            -- normal behavior will not occur.
        ensure
            default_processing_disabled: not default_processing_
            enabled
```

These class interfaces have been duplicated from "Enabling and Disabling Default Message Processing" in Chapter 3, which provides additional information on the types of default message processing.

SUMMARY

Windows form the basic building blocks of a Microsoft Windows application. Each application must have at least one main window, which in turn may create other child windows. Each child window can take the form of a control, a frame window, or a popup window.

The abstract window class *WEL_WINDOW* introduces the functionality that is available to *all* kinds of windows. It provides features for showing and hiding windows, and for setting size and positional information, and provides message hooks for many windows messages.

The following three chapters introduce specific types of windows—composite windows, MDI windows, and controls. Each window type is a descendant of *WEL_WINDOW*.

COMPOSITE WINDOWS

INTRODUCING COMPOSITE WINDOWS

Most of the examples we have seen so far have used a composite window, or more specifically, a *WEL_FRAME_WINDOW*. A composite window is so called because it can be composed of other windows. That is, a composite window can hold other windows as its children. The child windows may be controls or other composite windows, such as popup windows. As you have seen, composite windows are often used for the main window of an application. They are also used for dialog boxes, message boxes, and other compound interface components.

Three different composite windows exist in the WEL library—frames, popups, and multiple-document interfaces. All of these window types are descendants of class *WEL_COMPOSITE_WINDOW*. Figure 5.1 shows the inheritance relationships between these classes, including the superclass of all windows, *WEL_WINDOW*.

The classes *WEL_FRAME_WINDOW* and *WEL_POPUP_WINDOW* are described in this Chapter. Class *WEL_MDI_FRAME_WINDOW* and its related classes are described in Chapter 6, "Multi-Document Windows." Class *WEL_WINDOW* was described in the previous chapter.

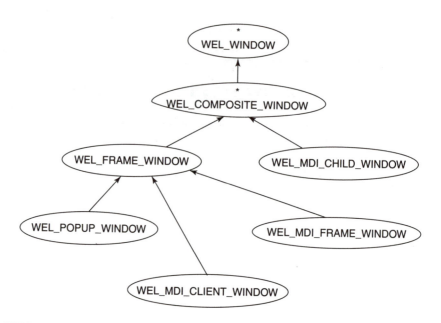

FIGURE 5.1. Composite window class hierarchy.

Abstract Composite Window Class

The abstract class, *WEL_COMPOSITE_WINDOW,* implements general behavior of all the composite window types. Specifically, a composite window has access to its children, it can have a menu bar and control over the system menu, and it provides extended control for scrolling its client area. The following sections describe each of the features introduced in *WEL_COMPOSITE_WINDOW.* Recall that *WEL_COMPOSITE_WINDOW* is a direct descendant of *WEL_WINDOW,* and therefore, all features available in *WEL_WINDOW* are also available in *WEL_COMPOSITE_WINDOW.*

Creating a Composite Window

The class *WEL_COMPOSITE_WINDOW* is similar to *WEL_WINDOW* in that it is deferred and therefore cannot be instantiated. The default creation procedures defined in *WEL_WINDOW* are typically used to create an instance of a *WEL_COMPOSITE_WINDOW* descendant. No additional creation procedures are introduced in *WEL_COMPOSITE_WINDOW.*

Finding the Children of a Composite Window

When a window is created, it is passed the window that will be its parent. For example, creating a push button as a child of another window can be coded as

```
create push_button.make (parent, x_pos, y_pos, width, height, id)
```

where *parent* is the parent window of the push button. In the examples presented so far, this has typically been *Current* (to specify the current object).

A window can find its parent through the feature *parent* from *WEL_WINDOW* (see "Finding the Parent of a Window" in Chapter 4, "Windows"). A composite window can also determine the reverse of this relationship through the feature *children*. The *children* feature constructs a linear representation of the window's current children. This linear structure can be traversed to perform operations on all of the children or to find a particular child window.

```
children: LINKED_LIST [WEL_WINDOW]
        -- Construct a linear representation of the children.
    require
        exists: exists
    ensure
        result_not_void: Result /= Void
```

Example 5.1 demonstrates the use of *children*. The example creates a single window with three buttons and a static text area. The *on_control_command* feature displays the text of each child in the static text field by iterating over the list returned by the call to *children*. In more detail, if the *find_children* button is pressed, the list of current children is stored in a local variable. The routine then iterates over all of the elements in the list, concatenating the text of each child to the local variable *s*. Finally, the text of the *text_area* control is set to the string *s*. If you need to iterate over the elements in the children list, or perform a number of tasks on the list itself, then ensure that you store the value of *children* in a local variable or attribute because each call to *children* generates a new list.

Example 5.1 Composite Window Children (comp\children)

```
class MAIN_WINDOW

inherit
    WEL_FRAME_WINDOW
        redefine
            on_control_command
        end
creation
    make
feature -- Initialization

    make is
            --Initialize the main window, buttons and text area.
```

```
            do
                make_top ("Main Window")
                resize (350, 140)
                create button_1.make (Current, "Button 1", 10, 10, 90, 35, -1)
                create button_2.make (Current, "Button 2", 10, 50, 90, 35, -1)
                create find_children.make (Current "Find Children", 10,
                    90, 90, 35, -1)
                create text_area.make (Current, "", 110, 10, width - 130,
                    height - 20,c -1)
            end
        feature -- Implementation

            button_1, button_2, find_children: WEL_PUSH_BUTTON
                    -- Push buttons

            text_area: WEL_STATIC
                    -- Text field
        on_control_command (control: WEL_CONTROL) is
                -- Show the popup
            local
                children_list: LINEAR [WEL_WINDOW]
                s: STRING
            do
                if control = find_children then
                    from
                        children_list := children
                        create s.make (30)
                        children_list.start
                    until
                        children_list.exhausted
                    loop
                        if children_list.item /= text_area then
                            s.append (children_list.item.text)
                            s.append_character ('%N')
                        end
                        children_list.forth
                    end
                    text_area.set_text (s)
                end
            end
        end -- class MAIN_WINDOW
```

When the Find Children button is pressed, the text of each child window (the buttons and text area) is displayed in the text area. Figure 5.2 shows the resulting window after clicking the Find Children button.

Using a System Menu on a Composite Window

A composite window may have a system menu from which operations such as maximize, minimize, move, size, and close can be selected. The system menu is typically activated by the user clicking on the application icon in the title bar

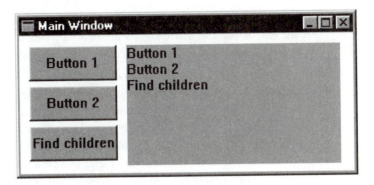

FIGURE 5.2. Composite window children example.

or right-clicking in the title bar itself (under Windows 9x, NT 4.0, or Windows 2000). A system menu is added to a window if *Ws_sysmenu* is included in the window style (see "Changing the Style of a Window" in Chapter 4). You can determine if a window has a system menu through the function *has_system_menu*, and the menu itself can be accessed through the feature *system_menu*.

```
has_system_menu: BOOLEAN
        -- Does the window have a system menu?
    require
        exists: exist

system_menu: WEL_MENU
        -- Associated system menu
    require
        exists: exists
        has_system_menu: has_system_menu
    ensure
        result_not_void: Result /= Void
```

Feature *system_menu* returns a *WEL_MENU* object that represents the current system menu. You can modify this menu by adding and removing items or changing the text of existing items. See Chapter 8, "Menus," for a detailed description.

Using a Menu on a Composite Window

A composite window can also have a menu bar attached to the top of the client area. A menu bar can provide access to all of an application's operations and facilities. In particular, it is recommended that every application have at least

File and *Help* menus and, optionally, an *Edit* menu. Figure 5.3 illustrates the menu bar of the ISE EiffelBench application, which provides access to file, edit, compile, debug, format, special, window, and help operations.

Adding a menu bar to a composite window requires a *WEL_MENU* to be constructed and attached. To attach a menu to a composite window, you can pass a *WEL_MENU* object to the *set_menu* operation. The *set_menu* call redraws the window to show the new menu bar, effectively shortening the available height of the client area. To detach a menu from the window, you can call *unset_menu*. The currently attached menu can be accessed through the feature *menu* (after determining if a menu currently exists by calling *has_menu*).

```
menu: WEL_MENU
        -- Associated menu
    require
        exists: exists
        has_menu: has_menu
    ensure
        result_not_void: Result /= Void
has_menu: BOOLEAN
        -- Does the window have a menu?
    require
        exists: exists
set_menu (a_menu: WEL_MENU)
        -- Set 'menu' with 'a_menu'.
    require
        exists: exists
        a_menu_not_void: a_menu /= Void
        a_menu_exists: a_menu.exists
    ensure
        has_menu: has_menu
        menu_set: menu.item = a_menu.item
unset_menu
        -- Unset the current menu associated with the window.
    require
        exists: exists
    ensure
        menu_unset: not has_menu
```

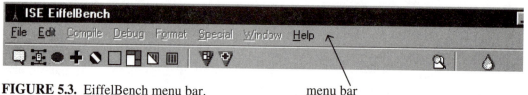

FIGURE 5.3. EiffelBench menu bar.   menu bar

Finally, if you change the menu after it has been set, then you need to call *draw_menu* for the changes to appear. This ensures that the menu bar appears and is configured according to the current set menu instance.

```
draw_menu
        -- Draw the menu bar associated with the window.
    require
        exists: exists
        has_menu: has_menu
```

Example 5.2 shows how to create and set a simple menu bar on a composite window. The menu bar is defined as a once function. This is useful to ensure that only one instance of the menu bar is created and that only that instance is accessed through the feature *main_menu*. The main window is notified of its new menu bar through the call to *set_menu*. Creating menus is described in more detail in Chapter 8.

Example 5.2 Menu Bar (comp\menu)

```
class MAIN_WINDOW

inherit
    WEL_FRAME_WINDOW
creation
    make
feature -- Initialization

    make is
            -- Initialize the main window and its menu bar
        do
            make_top ("Main Window")
            resize (350, 140)
            set_menu (main_menu)
        end
feature -- Implementation

    Id_file_menu, Id_edit_menu, Id_help_menu: INTEGER is unique

    main_menu: WEL_MENU is
            -- The menu bar
        once
            create Result.make
            Result.append_string ("&File", Id_file_menu)
            Result.append_string ("&Edit", Id_edit_menu)
            Result.append_string ("&Help", Id_help_menu)
        end

end -- class MAIN_WINDOW
```

Figure 5.4 shows the resulting main window with its menu bar. The menu bar has three items: File, Edit, and Help. None of the menu items in this example actually perform any function. We will see how to create a version of *on_control_command* that handles menu item selection in Chapter 8.

Setting Scroll Properties of a Composite Window

A composite window can have a vertical scroll bar, a horizontal scroll bar, or both, active at any time. When these scroll bars are active, the window receives notification of user events such as scroll bar button clicks or page up and page down commands. These events are processed by the message hooks *on_vertical_scroll* and *on_horizontal_scroll* (see "On a Composite Window Control Scroll Message" later in this chapter). When activating a scroll bar, you need to set its properties so that it will operate appropriately for your application. You need to set the range of values that the scroll bars can use and set their initial positions.

To determine the current position of a scroll bar, you can call *horizontal_position* or *vertical_position*. Both of these features return an *INTEGER* representing the current scroll position of either the horizontal or vertical scroll bars, respectively.

```
horizontal_position: INTEGER
        -- Current position of the horizontal scroll box
    require
        exists: exists
    ensure
        result_small_enough: Result <= maximal_horizontal_position;
        result_large_enough: Result >= minimal_horizontal_position
vertical_position: INTEGER
        -- Current position of the vertical scroll box
    require
        exists: exists
    ensure
        result_small_enough: Result <= maximal_vertical_position;
        result_large_enough: Result >= minimal_vertical_position
```

FIGURE 5.4. Simple composite window menu bar.

Similarly, you can query the maximum and minimum ranges of scroll bars by calling the features *maximum_horizontal_position, minimum_horizontal_position, maximum_vertical_position,* and *minimum_vertical_position.*

```
maximal_horizontal_position: INTEGER
        -- Maximum position of the horizontal scroll box
    require
        exists: exists
    ensure
        result_large_enough: Result >= minimal_horizontal_position

maximal_vertical_position: INTEGER
        -- Maxium position of the vertical scroll box
    require
        exists: exists
    ensure
        result_large_enough: Result >= minimal_vertical_position

minimal_horizontal_position: INTEGER
        -- Minimum position of the horizontal scroll box
    require
        exists: exists
    ensure
        result_small_enough: Result <= maximal_horizontal_position

minimal_vertical_position: INTEGER
        -- Minimum position of the vertical scroll box
    require
        exists: exists
    ensure
        result_small_enough: Result <= maximal_vertical_position
```

The state of a horizontal scroll bar can be changed programmatically using the features *set_horizontal_position* and *set_horizontal_range* to set the current position and to set the maximum and minimum allowable values.

```
set_horizontal_position (position: INTEGER)
        -- Set 'horizontal_position' with 'position'.
    require
        exists: exists;
        position_small_enough: position <=
            maximal_horizontal_position;
        position_large_enough: position >=
            minimal_horizontal_position
    ensure
        horizontal_position_set: horizontal_position = position
```

```
set_horizontal_range (minimum, maximum: INTEGER)
          -- Set 'minimal_horizontal_position' and
          -- 'maximal_horizontal_position' with 'minimum' and
          -- 'maximum'.
   require
          exists: exists;
          consistent_range: minimum <= maximum
   ensure
          minimal_horizontal_position_set: minimal_horizontal_
               position = minimum;
          maximal_horizontal_position_set: maximal_horizontal_
               position = maximum
```

The vertical scroll bar has corresponding features for updating its position and range.

```
set_vertical_position (position: INTEGER)
          -- Set 'vertical_position' with 'position'.
   require
          exists: exists;
          position_small_enough: position <=
             maximal_vertical_    position;
          position_large_enough: position >=
             minimal_vertical_    position
   ensure
          vertical_position_set: vertical_position = position

set_vertical_range (minimum, maximum: INTEGER)
          -- Set 'minimal_vertical_position' and
          -- 'maximal_vertical_position' with 'minimum' and
          -- 'maximum'.
   require
          exists: exists;
          consistent_range: minimum <= maximum
   ensure
          minimal_vertical_position_set: minimal_vertical_position =
               minimum;
          maximal_vertical_position_set: maximal_vertical_position =
               maximum
```

Updating the Scroll Bars of a Composite Window

The features *horizontal_update* and *vertical_update* provide a way of updating the current position of composite window scroll bars using both an increment value and a new position. When called, the window is scrolled by *inc* amount and the scroll bar is positioned at *position*.

```
horizontal_update (inc, position: INTEGER)
        -- Update the window and the horizontal scroll box with
        -- 'inc' and 'position'.
    require
        exists: exists;
        position_small_enough: position <=
            maximal_horizontal_position;
        position_large_enough: position >=
            minimal_horizontal_position
    ensure
        horizontal_position_set: horizontal_position = position

vertical_update (inc, position: INTEGER)
        -- Update the window and the vertical scroll box with
        -- 'inc' and 'position'.
    require
        exists: exists;
        position_small_enough: position <=
            maximal_vertical_position;
        position_large_enough: position >=
            minimal_vertical_position
    ensure
        vertical_position_set: vertical_position = position
```

Conditionally Closing a Composite Window

If the user selects *Close* from the system menu or clicks on the Close icon, the application first checks to see whether the window can be closed by calling the function *closeable*. The function *closeable* returns *True* by default, indicating that the window can be closed at any time. It is often necessary to check the current state of an application before allowing its main window to be closed. For instance, an application may need to prompt the user to save any unsaved documents. To implement this type of conditional closing, you can redefine the feature *closeable* from *WEL_COMPOSITE_WINDOW*.

```
closeable: BOOLEAN
        -- Can the user close the window?
        -- Yes by default
```

As the header comment of *closeable* states, the function returns *True* by default. You can implement any necessary checking in *closeable* to determine if a window can be closed or not. If *False* is returned, then the close operation is aborted and normal processing continues. If the routine returns *True,* then the window is closed.

Example 5.3 uses the closeable function to pop up a dialog that requests confirmation to close the application. If the user selects *Yes* then the *closeable* routine returns *True,* indicating that the window (in this case, the entire application) can be closed. Otherwise the application continues to run as normal.

Example 5.3 Conditional Closing (comp\closeable)

```
class MAIN_WINDOW
inherit
    WEL_FRAME_WINDOW
        redefine
            closeable,
            on_control_command
        end
    WEL_ID_CONSTANTS
        export
            {NONE} all
        end
creation
    make

feature -- Initialization

    make is
            -- Initialize the main window
        do
            make_top ("Main Window")
            resize (350, 140)
            create close_button.make (Current, "Close", 10, 30, 90, 35, -1)
        end
feature -- Implementation
    close_button: WEL_PUSH_BUTTON
            -- Push button
    msg_box: WEL_MSG_BOX
            -- Message box
    closeable: BOOLEAN is
            -- Confirm that the application should be closed.
        do
            create msg_box.make
            msg_box.question_message_box (Current, "Do you want to exit?"",
                "Exit")
            Result = msg_box.message_box_result = Idyes
        end
    on_control_command (control: WEL_CONTROL) is
            -- Check for a close command
        do
            if control = close_button then
                if closeable then
                        destroy
                end
```

```
            end
        end

    end -- class MAIN_WINDOW
```

The *closeable* function is called automatically when the user attempts to close the window via the system menu close option or the close icon on the title bar. If the user clicks the Close button on the main window, then the *on_control_command* message hook is called and the *closeable* function is tested explicitly.

Figure 5.5 shows the main window and popup confirmation message box after the user has clicked on the Close button. If the user clicks *Yes* in the message box, then the application will be closed; otherwise, the application will continue running.

Moving a Composite Window

In addition to the positioning operations in *WEL_WINDOW* (see "Changing the Position of a Window" in Chapter 4), class *WEL_COMPOSITE_WINDOW* introduces an additional feature for changing the position of a window on the screen: *move_absolute*. Feature *move_absolute* allows a composite window to be positioned using absolute coordinates. Absolute coordinates extend from the top left corner of the screen.

```
move_absolute (a_x, a_y: INTEGER)
        -- Move the window to 'a_x', 'a_y' absolute position.
    require
        exists: exists
```

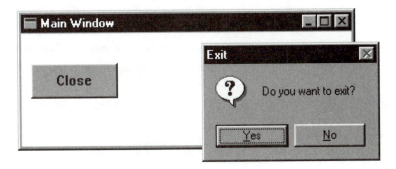

FIGURE 5.5. Close confirmation example.

Message Hooks in a Composite Window

A composite window responds to a number of messages in addition to the messages of *WEL_WINDOW*. A composite window can also respond to the messages listed in Table 5.1.

TABLE 5.1   *Composite Window Message Hooks*

MESSAGE HOOK	DESCRIPTION
notify	Either a button, edit control, or combo-box notification message is received.
on_accelerator_command	An accelerator key with a specific id has been pressed.
on_color_control	A child control is requesting the foreground and background colors that it should use to paint itself.
on_control_command	A command has been received from a specific control.
on_control_id_command	A command has been received from a control with a specific id.
on_draw_item	An owner-draw control has changed and must be redrawn.
on_get_min_max_info	The size of the window is about to change.
on_horizontal_scroll	A horizontal scroll message has been received. Usually passed on to the scroller object if it exists.
on_horizontal_scroll_command	A horizontal scroll message has been received from a user-defined scroll bar.
on_menu_command	A menu item with a specific id has been chosen from a menu.
on_menu_select	A menu item of a menu has been highlighted.
on_paint	A paint message has been received. The window must paint the specified rectangle area.
on_palette_changed	The window has realized its logical color palette.
on_palette_is_changing	Window is about to realize its logical color palette.
on_query_new_palette	The window is about to receive input focus and can realize its logical color palette.
on_sys_command	A system menu item has been selected from the system menu.
on_vertical_scroll	A vertical scroll message has been received. Usually passed on to the scroller object if it exists.
on_vertical_scroll_command	A vertical scroll message has been received from a user-defined scroll bar.
on_window_pos_changed	The size, position, or place in the z-order of this window has changed as a result of a call to move or resize.
on_window_pos_changing	The size, position, or place in the z-order of this window is about to change.

On a Composite Window Notify Message

A window receives a notify message from a control attached to itself whenever an event occurs in the control or whenever the control requires some information. Typical notification events include button clicks, edit control content updates, and list box selection changes. Notification messages often overlap with control messages. For example, a push button click event is received as both an *on_control_command* message and a *notify* message. You need to decide which of the two message notifications will be used.

The *notify* message operation is passed the control in which the event occurred and an integer representing the type of event. Different controls have different notify events that can occur. A push button, for example, can send only a button click notify event, while a list box can send a notification event indicating focus gained, focus lost, selection changed, and double-click selection.[1]

```
notify (control: WEL_CONTROL; notify_code: INTEGER)
        -- A 'notify_code' is received for 'control'.
    require
        exists: exists
        control_not_void: control /= Void
        control_exists: control.exists
```

The notification codes for different controls are defined in separate classes. For instance, the notification codes for push buttons appear in the class *WEL_BN_CONSTANTS*. Similar constant classes exist for all of the control types. We describe each group of event notification codes when we look at controls in Chapter 11, "Controls."

Example 5.4 shows how to capture a button click event using the *notify* message hook instead of *on_control_command*. The only changes are to redefine the *notify* feature, check the control when a notify event occurs, and check the notify code to see if it is a *Bn_clicked* event. This example is a modification of Example 5.3 and performs the same function.

---

[1]Note that a push button actually defines a number of additional notification codes. However, these codes are for an obsolete button style and will not be sent in current Windows implementations.

Example 5.4 Notification Message Operations (comp\notify)

```
class MAIN_WINDOW
inherit
    WEL_FRAME_WINDOW
        redefine
            closeable,
            notify
        end
    WEL_BN_CONSTANTS
        export
            {NONE} all
        end
    WEL_ID_CONSTANTS
        export
            {NONE} all
        end
creation
    make
feature -- Initialization
    make is
            -- Initialize the main window
        do
            make_top ("Main Window")
            resize (350, 140)
            create close_button.make (Current, "Close", 10, 30, 90,
                35, -1)
        end
feature -- Implementation
    close_button: WEL_PUSH_BUTTON
            -- Push button
    msg_box: WEL_MSG_BOX
            -- Message box
    closeable: BOOLEAN is
            -- Confirm that the application should be closed.
        do
            create msg_box.make
            msg_box.question_message_box (Current, "Do you want to exit"",
                "Exit")
            Result = msg_box.message_box_result = Idyes
        end
    notify (control: WEL_CONTROL; notify_code: INTEGER) is
            -- Check for a close command
        do
            if control = close_button then
                if notify_code = Bn_clicked then
                    if closeable then
                        destroy
                    end
                end
            end
        end
    end
end -- class MAIN_WINDOW
```

On a Composite Window Control Message

One of the most often used message hooks is *on_control_command*. Feature *on_control_command* is used to capture and act on events from child window controls. Whenever a child control is activated it causes a *Wm_command* message to be sent to its parent window. WEL translates this message into an invocation of *on_control_command* and can take different forms depending on the type of control. For example, a push button is activated when it is clicked (the *Wm_command* message is actually sent when the mouse button is released while the cursor is within the button window), while a check box is activated when the mouse is clicked anywhere in its window.

The *on_control_command* message hook is passed the control from which the *Wm_command* message originated.

```
on_control_command (control: WEL_CONTROL)
        -- A command has been received from 'control'.
    require
        exists: exists
        control_not_void: control /= Void
        control_exists: control.exists
```

Thus, when processing *on_control_command*, you can determine the origin of the event and act accordingly. You can also examine the current state of the control directly through the *control* reference.

There are multiple ways in which a window is notified of control actions. You need to decide which method your application will use. In actual fact, a *Wm_command* message is handled multiple times according to the following criteria: When a *Wm_command* message is received, first call *on_control_id_command*. If the associated window and control exist, then also call *on_control_command* and *notify*. Finally, if the control exists, allow the control to process the notification for itself (by calling the private routine *process_notification* in *WEL_CONTROL*).

Therefore, one *Wm_command* message may be handled by up to four separate message operations. To keep your application design simple, you should choose one or two methods and use them consistently. Mixing multiple methods can create confusing and inconsistent designs.

The *on_control_id_command* is used primarily for controls that have been created with a unique identification number. This typically occurs when creating a control from a Windows resource file in which an identification number is used to access the resource (see Chapter 7, "Resources"). If a control has been created from a resource file, then its *Wm_command* message can only be processed using the *on_control_id_command*.

```
on_control_id_command (control_id: INTEGER)
        -- A command has been received from 'control_id'.
    require
        exists: exists
```

The difference between *on_control_command* and *on_control_id_command* is the parameter that is passed; *on_control_command* is passed a reference to the actual control object, while *on_control_id_command* is passed the identification number of the control. You will recall when creating a control, such as a push button, that the last parameter to the creation procedure *make* is an id.

```
create push_button.make (parent, x_pos, y_pos, width, height, id)
```

In the examples so far, we have used *-1* as the identification number. This effectively gives the control a dummy identification number, which will not be used later in the application. We could have given our controls a specific identification number by specifying it in the last parameter position (again, refer to Chapter 7 for more information on control ids).

On a Composite Window Menu Message

We saw earlier how a simple menu bar can be attached to a composite window. We also saw that each menu item in the menu bar has a unique menu identification number. Recall

```
Id_file_menu, Id_edit_menu, Id_help_menu: INTEGER is unique

main_menu: WEL_MENU is
                -- The menu bar
    once
            create Result.make
            Result.append_string ("&File", Id_file_menu)
            Result.append_string ("&Edit", Id_edit_menu)
            Result.append_string ("&Help", Id_help_menu)
    end
```

Notice that each menu item string (appended with *append_string*) is given a unique integer identification number. It is this number that is passed to the *on_menu_command* message hook when a menu item is chosen from a menu.

```
on_menu_command (menu_id: INTEGER)
        -- The 'menu_id' has been choosen from the menu.
    require
        exists: exists
```

With this newly acquired knowledge, we can now extend Example 5.2 to perform a task when each menu item is chosen. The menu bar example is extended to show a message window notifying the user of which menu item was chosen. Example 5.5 shows the changes required. Figure 5.6 shows the output of this example after the *Help* menu item has been selected.

Example 5.5 Menu Activation (comp\menu2)

```
class MAIN_WINDOW
inherit
    WEL_FRAME_WINDOW
        redefine
            on_menu_command
        end
creation
    make

feature -- Initialization
    make is
            -- Initialize the main window and its menu bar
        do
            make_top ("Main Window")
            create msg_box.make
            resize (350, 140)
            set_menu (main_menu)
        end
feature -- Implementation
    Id_file_menu, Id_edit_menu, Id_help_menu: INTEGER is unique
    main_menu: WEL_MENU is
            -- The menu bar
        once
            create
            Result.make
            Result.append_string ("&File", Id_file_menu)
            Result.append_string ("&Edit", Id_edit_menu)
            Result.append_string ("&Help", Id_help_menu)
        end

    msg_box: WEL_MSG_BOX
            -- Message box
    on_menu_command (menu_id: INTEGER) is
            -- Process the selected menu item
        local
            s: STRING
        do
            if menu_id = Id_file_menu then
                s := "File menu item selected"
            elseif menu_id = Id_edit_menu then
                s := "Edit menu item selected"
            elseif menu_id = Id_help_menu then
                s := "Help menu item selected"
```

```
        else
            s := "Unknown menu item selected"
        end
        msg_box.information_message_box (Current, s,
            "Selected Menu Item")
    end
end -- class MAIN_WINDOW
```

On a Composite Window System Menu Command

Menu item selection can also occur on the system menu. When the user chooses a system menu item, such as *Close,* then the *on_sys_command* message hook is invoked. Feature *on_sys_command* is passed three parameters—the system menu command identifier, and the current x and y coordinates of the mouse.

```
on_sys_command (command, x_pos, y_pos: INTEGER)
        -- Wm_syscommand message.
        -- This message is sent when the user selects a command
        -- from the system menu or when the user selects the
        -- Maximize or Minimize button.
        -- See class WEL_SC_CONSTANTS for 'command' values.
        -- 'x_pos' and 'y_pos' specify the x and y coordinates
        -- of the cursor.
    require
        exists: exists
```

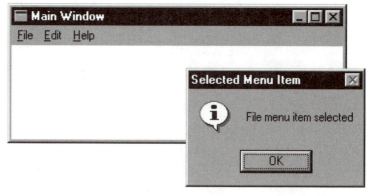

FIGURE 5.6. Menu bar item selection.

Each system menu item is given a unique identification number. These identifiers are defined in the class *WEL_SC_CONSTANTS*. Table 5.2 lists each constant name and the menu item it represents. For example, if the *Close* menu item is chosen from the system menu, then the *on_sys_command* operation is called with the value *Sc_close* as the first parameter.

Under most circumstances, your applications will not need to perform any additional processing other than the default processing that Windows performs for you—for instance, when the user chooses *Close* from the system menu and Windows automatically calls *closeable* to determine if the window can be closed, and then closes the window, if allowed. Similarly, most other system menu options have an appropriate default implementation.

On a Composite Window Menu Selection

In a typical application, it doesn't make sense for all menu items to be enabled at one time. Consider an application that allows cutting and pasting to the Windows clipboard. It does not make sense to allow a paste operation when the clipboard contains no data. It also does not make sense to cut or copy text to

TABLE 5.2   *System Menu Command Constants (WEL_SC_CONSTANTS)*

CONSTANT	DESCRIPTION
Sc_size	Size menu item selected.
Sc_move	Move menu item selected.
Sc_minimize	Minimize menu item selected.
Sc_maximize	Maximize menu item selected.
Sc_nextwindow	Next window menu item selected.
Sc_prevwindow	Previous window menu item selected.
Sc_close	Close menu item selected.
Sc_vscroll	Vertical scroll menu item selected.
Sc_hscroll	Horizontal scroll menu item selected.
Sc_mousemenu	Mouse menu item selected.
Sc_keymenu	Key menu item selected.
Sc_arrange	Arrange menu item selected.
Sc_restore	Restore menu item selected.
Sc_tasklist	Task list menu item selected.
Sc_screensave	Screensave menu item selected.
Sc_hotkey	Hot key menu item selected.

the clipboard if no text has been selected. In both of these cases, we would like to enable and disable relevant menu items depending on the current state of the application. The easiest way to do this is by using the *on_menu_select* message hook. Feature *on_menu_select* is called whenever a menu item is highlighted or selected. It can be used to modify the state of the selected menu or menu item just before it is highlighted (or opened, in the case of a submenu). Feature *on_menu_select* is passed the identification number of the menu item, a set of flags representing the state of the menu, and a new menu object representing the menu from which the selection occurred (this parameter may be *Void* if no menu exists).

```
on_menu_select (menu_item, flags: INTEGER; a_menu: WEL_MENU)
      -- The 'menu_item' from 'a_menu' is currently
      -- highlighted by the selection bar. `flags'
      -- indicates the state of 'a_menu'.
      -- The selection does not mean that the user has
      -- choosen the option, the option is just highlighted.
   require
      exists: exists
```

Let's modify Example 5.2 again. This time we add a multiline text edit control, and implement cut, copy, and paste to allow interaction with the Window's clipboard. Given no easy way to determine the menu (or submenu, in this case) that has been selected, we enable and disable the edit menu items when any menu item is selected. Example 5.6 implements both *on_menu_ select,* to enable and disable the edit menu items, and *on_menu_command,* to perform the actual edit operations. The user is also presented with a multiple line edit control in which to type text (see Chapter 13, "Edit Controls").

Example 5.6 Menu Selection (comp\menu_sel)

```
class MAIN_WINDOW
inherit
    WEL_FRAME_WINDOW
        redefine
            on_menu_select,
            on_menu_command
        end
creation
    make
feature -- Initialization
    make is
            -- Initialize the main window and its menu bar
```

```
        do
                make_top ("Main Window")
                resize (350, 140)
                set_menu (main_menu)
                create text_area.make (Current, "", 0, 0,
                    client_area.width, client_area.height, -1)
                create clipboard
        end
feature -- Implementation
    text_area: WEL_MULTIPLE_LINE_EDIT
                -- Text area
    Id_file_menu, Id_help_menu: INTEGER is unique
    clipboard: WEL_CLIPBOARD
                -- Clipboard
    main_menu: WEL_MENU is
                -- The menu bar
        once
                create Result.make
                Result.append_string ("&File", Id_file_menu)
                Result.append_popup (edit_menu, "&Edit")
                Result.append_string ("&Help", Id_help_menu)
        end
    Id_edit_cut, Id_edit_copy, Id_edit_paste: INTEGER is unique
    edit_menu: WEL_MENU is
                -- The edit menu
        once
                create Result.make
                Result.append_string ("&Cut", Id_edit_cut)
                Result.append_string ("&Copy", Id_edit_copy)
                Result.append_string ("&Paste", Id_edit_paste)
        end
    on_menu_select (menu_item, flags: INTEGER; a_menu: WEL_MENU) is
                -- Set the edit popup menu according to the current text
                -- area state.
        do
                if text_area.has_selection then
                    edit_menu.enable_item (Id_edit_cut)
                    edit_menu.enable_item (Id_edit_copy)
                else
                    edit_menu.disable_item (Id_edit_cut)
                    edit_menu.disable_item (Id_edit_copy)
                end
                clipboard.open_clipboard (Current)
                    if clipboard.is_clipboard_format_available
                (clipboard.Cf_text) then
                    edit_menu.enable_item (Id_edit_paste)
                else
                    edit_menu.disable_item (Id_edit_paste)
                end
                clipboard.close_clipboard
        end
    on_menu_command (menu_id: INTEGER) is
                -- Process the selected menu item
```

```
      do
          inspect menu_id
          when Id_edit_cut then
              text_area.clip_cut
          when Id_edit_copy then
              text_area.clip_copy
          when Id_edit_paste then
              text_area.clip_paste
          else
              -- ignore all other menu selections
          end
      end
end -- class MAIN_WINDOW
```

The *on_menu_select* message hook enables or disables the cut and copy edit menu items depending on whether the *text_area* currently has a selection. This test is performed every time a menu item is selected. This may seem inefficient (and in a way, it is). However, because of the difficulty of testing the selected menu item, the code is difficult to improve. The *on_menu_command* operation processes each menu selection as it occurs. The implementation of cut, copy, and paste is simply to delegate the operation to the text control itself. All other menu items are ignored, including File and Help.

On a Composite Window Keyboard Accelerator Message

Keyboard accelerators provide keystroke shortcuts for menu items and other application functions. It is common practice to provide shortcut accelerators for common menu items. For instance, the menu items in an Edit menu, such as Cut, Copy, and Paste, typically have shortcuts that allow them to be performed using a single keystroke—for example, Control-C or Control-Ins for a copy operation.

A keyboard accelerator table is loaded by the *WEL_APPLICATION* class (see Chapter 2, "Using Keyboard Accelerators") and resides in memory for the lifetime of the application. Each keyboard accelerator is given a unique identification number that can be tested in the *on_accelerator_command* message hook to determine the correct action to take. The message hook *on_accelerator_command* is called whenever a keyboard accelerator is pressed by the user. The operation is passed the identification number of the accelerator.

```
on_accelerator_command (accelerator_id: INTEGER)
        -- The 'acelerator_id' has been activated.
    require
        exists: exists
```

You can use the *on_accelerator_command* hook to parallel the *on_menu_command* feature. For example, if you define keyboard accelerators for common edit operations, such as Ctrl-X for cut, Ctrl-C for copy and Ctrl-Y for paste, you can perform the same operations as the *on_menu_command* feature for the relevant accelerators. If you functionally decompose your applications sufficiently, then you will most likely have separate features for each edit operation, and the relevant menu selection and accelerator key press can simply call the appropriate feature. Furthermore, you can assign the same identifier to an accelerator key and a menu item that perform the same operation. You can then delegate the processing of the operation to one message hook (see Example 5.15, "MAIN_WINDOW Event Hooks").

On a Composite Window Paint Message

When a window is exposed, such as when the window is initially shown on screen or when another window obscuring part of the window is moved or minimized, the window has to paint its client area. Windows sends a *Wm_paint* message to any window exposed in this manner, allowing each to then paint its client area as needed. The *on_paint* message hook can be used to handle the *Wm_paint* message.

```
on_paint (paint_dc: WEL_PAINT_DC; invalid_rect: WEL_RECT)
         -- Wm_paint message.
         -- May be redefined to paint something on
         -- the 'paint_dc'. 'invalid_rect' defines
         -- the invalid rectangle of the client area that
         -- needs to be repainted.
   require
         paint_dc_not_void: paint_dc /= Void
         paint_dc_exists: paint_dc.exists
         invalid_rect_not_void: invalid_rect /= Void
```

The message hook *on_paint* takes receives two parameters, a *WEL_PAINT_DC* and a *WEL_RECT,* named *paint_dc* and *invalid_rect,* respectively. The *paint_dc* parameter is the device context on which you need to paint, and the *invalid_rect* parameter identifies the area of the device context that needs to be repainted.

To illustrate how you can paint the client area of a window, we redefine the message hook *on_paint* in a composite window. The *on_paint* routine draws consecutive ellipses in rectangles of increasing size. Example 5.7 shows the class text for the *MAIN_WINDOW.*

Example 5.7 Composite Window Paint Example, MAIN_WINDOW Class (comp\paint)

```
class MAIN_WINDOW
inherit
    WEL_FRAME_WINDOW
        redefine
            on_paint
        end
creation
    make
feature -- Initialization
    make is
            -- Initialize the main window
        do
            make_top ("Main Window")
            resize (300, 255)
        end

    Ellipse_size_increment: INTEGER is 15

    on_paint (paint_dc: WEL_PAINT_DC; invalid_rect: WEL_RECT) is
            -- Paint on the window
        local
            current_size: INTEGER
        do
            paint_dc.set_background_transparent
            from
                current_size := Ellipse_size_increment
            variant
                height - current_size
            until
                current_size > height
            loop
                paint_dc.ellipse (0, 0, current_size, current_size)
                current_size := current_size + Ellipse_size_increment
            end
        end
end -- class MAIN_WINDOW
```

Figure 5.7 shows the resulting window after the *on_paint* message hook has executed. If you subsequently resize the window, the *on_paint* message will be called again and will draw fewer or more ellipses, depending on the new height of the window.

Recall from "Validating the Client Area of a Window" in Chapter 4 that you can force the *Wm_paint* message to be sent by calling *update* and *invalidate*.

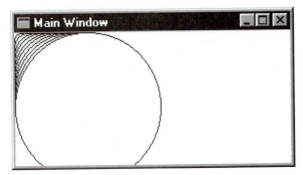

FIGURE 5.7. Composite window paint example.

On a Composite Window Control Scroll Message

If a composite window has scroll bar or track bar controls, then it receives notification of events through the *on_vertical_scroll_control* and *on_horizontal_ scroll_control* message hooks. Both hooks are passed a scroll code indicating the type of event that the user has invoked and a position indicating the new scroll bar position. The scroll codes represent events, including single-line up, single-line down, page up, page down, and so on. Table 5.3 lists the scroll codes that these operations can receive. The scroll or track bar that was the source of the event is indicated by the bar parameter. We explore this feature in more detail when we discuss bar controls in Chapter 16, "Bar Controls."

```
on_vertical_scroll_control (scroll_code, position: INTEGER;
      bar: WEL_BAR)
      -- Vertical scroll is received with a
      -- 'scroll_code' type. See class WEL_SB_CONSTANTS
      -- for 'scroll_code' values. 'position' is the new
      -- scroll box position. `bar' indicates the scroll bar
      -- or track bar control activated.
  require
      exists: exists
      bar_not_void: bar /= Void
      bar_exists: bar.exists

on_horizontal_scroll_control (scroll_code, position: INTEGER;
      bar: WEL_BAR)
      -- Horizontal scroll is received with a
      -- 'scroll_code' type. See class WEL_SB_CONSTANTS
      -- for 'scroll_code' values. 'position' is the new
      -- scrollbox position. 'bar' indicates the scroll bar
      -- or track bar control activated.
  require
      exists: exists
      bar_not_void: bar /= Void
      bar_exists: bar.exists
```

TABLE 5.3   *Scroll Bar Command Constants (WEL_SB_CONSTANTS)*

CONSTANT	DESCRIPTION
Sb_lineup	Scroll one line up.
Sb_lineleft	Scroll one line left.
Sb_linedown	Scroll one line down.
Sb_lineright	Scroll one line right.
Sb_pageup	Scroll one page up.
Sb_pageleft	Scroll one page left.
Sb_pagedown	Scroll one page down.
Sb_pageright	Scroll one page right.
Sb_thumbposition	Scroll to an absolute position.
Sb_thumptrack	Drag scroll box to specified position.
Sb_top	Scroll to upper left.
Sb_left	Scroll to far left.
Sb_bottom	Scroll to lower right.
Sb_right	Scroll to far right.
Sb_endscroll	End scroll.
Sb_horz	Enable or disable the arrows on the horizontal scroll bar associated with the window.
Sb_vert	Enable or disable the arrows on the vertical scroll bar.
Sb_ctl	Identify the scroll bar as a scroll bar control.
Sb_both	Enable or disable the arrows on both the horizontal and vertical scroll bars.

If the composite window has its own scroll bars activated, then it will receive similar message notifications via the message hooks *on_vertical_scroll* and *on_horizontal_scroll*. Both operations are passed a scroll code and scroll bar position representing the same information as the scroll control operations above.

WEL processes these scroll messages automatically. *on_vertical_scroll* processes a vertical scroll message using the *scroller* feature (shown below) while *on_horizontal_scroll* processes a horizontal scroll message using the *scroller*.

```
on_vertical_scroll (scroll_code, position: INTEGER)
                -- Vertical scroll is received with a
                -- 'scroll_code' type. See class WEL_SB_CONSTANTS for
                -- 'scroll_code' values. 'position' is the new
                -- scrollbox position.
        require
                exists: exists
on_horizontal_scroll (scroll_code, position: INTEGER)
                -- Horizontal scroll is received with a
                -- 'scroll_code' type. See class WEL_SB_CONSTANTS for
                -- 'scroll_code' values. 'position' is the new
                -- scrollbox position.
        require
                exists: exists
```

It is sometimes useful to determine the current state of the window's scroll bars when implementing scroll events. Feature *scroller* provides access to this scroll information, including the current scroll positions, scroll ranges, and page sizes. The scroll message hooks use this object to process scroll messages automatically.

```
scroller: WEL_SCROLLER
            -- Scroller object for processing scroll messages.
```

On a Composite Window Color Control Message

Each control sends a message to its parent window just before it paints its background. You can intercept this message to adjust the background, foreground, and brush settings that the control uses to draw. WEL notifies a composite window of such messages by calling *on_color_control*. Procedure *on_color_control* receives a reference to the control being painted (of type *WEL_COLOR_CONTROL*) and to the paint device context that will be used to paint the control. The controls that send this message include list boxes, static controls, edit controls, and scroll bars, each of which is a descendant of *WEL_COLOR_CONTROL*.

```
on_color_control (control: WEL_COLOR_CONTROL; paint_dc:
   WEL_PAINT_DC)
              -- Wm_ctlcolorstatic, Wm_ctlcoloredit, Wm_ctlcolorlistbox
              -- and Wm_ctlcolorscrollbar messages.
              -- To change its default colors, the color-control 'control'
              -- needs :
              -- 1. a background color and a foreground color to be selected
              --    in the 'paint_dc',
              -- 2. a backgound brush to be returned to the system.
   require
          exists: exists;
          control_not_void: control /= void;
          control_exists: control.exists;
          paint_dc_not_void: paint_dc /= void;
          paint_dc_exists: paint_dc.exists
```

A typical implementation of *on_color_control* needs to set the background and foreground colors and select a brush in to the device context. For example,

```
paint_dc.set_text_color (control.foreground_color)
paint_dc.set_background_color (control.background_color)
create brush.make_solid (control.background_color)
set_message_return_value (brush.to_integer)
disable_default_processing
```

sets the background and foreground colors and the brush to the current settings of the control.

On a Composite Window Draw Item Message

A special type of control is the owner-draw control. This type of control is a normal window that implements its own paint procedure used to paint its surface. Owner-draw controls can be used for any type of custom control that you may need. Graphics drawing applications often use owner-draw buttons to provide push buttons for drawing lines, ellipses, boxes, and so on. The surface of each button is drawn by the application—for example, a crooked line for the line button and a circle for an ellipse button. This type of control is explored further in the section "Owner-Draw Buttons" in Chapter 12, "Buttons."

Owner-draw buttons are important in the context of composite windows because whenever an owner-draw button needs painting, its parent is notified through the message hook *on_draw_item*. When implementing a composite window, you need to be aware of all owner-draw buttons that may be attached as children. Each button must be drawn by the parent. However, we can design our owner-draw buttons so that they draw themselves whenever the parent asks. An example of *on_draw_item* is left to "Owner-Draw Buttons" in Chapter 12. The second parameter of type *WEL_DRAW_ITEM_STRUCT* is also described in the forthcoming chapter.

```
on_draw_item (control_id: INTEGER; draw_item: WEL_DRAW_ITEM_STRUCT)
        -- Wm_drawitem message.
        -- A owner-draw control identified by 'control_id' has
        -- been changed and must be drawn. 'draw_item' contains
        -- information about the item to be drawn and the type
        -- of drawing required.
    require
        exists: exists
        draw_item_not_void: draw_item /= Void
```

On a Composite Window Minimum Maximum Message

Before a window is resized, the *on_get_min_max_info* message hook is invoked. When *on_get_min_max_info* is executed, you can modify the settings in the *min_max_info* parameter to override the new position and size. If you need to restrict a window to a certain size, *on_get_min_max_info* is where to do it.

```
on_get_min_max_info (min_max_info: WEL_MIN_MAX_INFO)
        -- Wm_getminmaxinfo message.
        -- The size or position of the window is about to
        -- change. An application can change 'min_max_info' to
        -- override the window's default maximized size and
        -- position, or its default minimum or maximum tracking
        -- size.
    require
        exists: exists
        min_max_info_not_void: min_max_info /= Void
```

The *min_max_info* parameter passed to *on_get_min_max_info* is an instance of *WEL_MIN_MAX_INFO*. This object holds the position coordinates, width, and height that the window is changed to. You can modify all of the settings to override any of the changes. The window is repositioned and resized to the settings in *min_max_info* after the call to *on_get_min_max_info* has returned.

Used in conjunction with the window size constraints (see "Specifying Window Size Constraints" in Chapter 4), the feature *on_get_min_max_info* provides a simple way of constraining the size of windows. Example 5.8 demonstrates how to restrict a window size to a width of 300 pixels and a height of 300 pixels.

Example 5.8 Window Minimum Maximum Restriction (comp\minmax)

```
class MAIN_WINDOW
inherit
    WEL_FRAME_WINDOW
        redefine
            on_get_min_max_info,
            maximal_width, maximal_height
        end
creation
    make
feature -- Initialization
    make is
            -- Initialize the main window
        do
            make_top ("Main Window")
            resize (100, 100)
        end
feature -- Implementation
    maximal_width: INTEGER is 300
            -- Maximum width of this window
    maximal_height: INTEGER is 300
            -- Maximum height of this window
    on_get_min_max_info (min_max_info: WEL_MIN_MAX_INFO) is
            -- The size or position of the window is about to change.
            -- Restrict the size.
        local
            p: WEL_POINT
        do
            create p.make (maximal_width.min
                (min_max_info.max_track_size.x),
                maximal_height.min (min_max_info.max_track_size.y))
            min_max_info.set_max_track_size (p)
        end
end -- class MAIN_WINDOW
```

The *on_get_min_max_info* redefinition sets the maximum tracking size to the minimum value of either the maximal settings or the current maximum tracking size in the *min_max_info* structure. The tracking size is the size of the window when the user drags the borders of a window. This fragment of code ensures that the maximum tracking size will not increase beyond *maximal_width* and *maximal_height*.

On a Composite Window Position Message

Two additional message hooks provide similar capabilities—feature *on_window_pos_changed* is sent whenever a window has changed its position, size, and/or z-order, while feature *on_window_pos_changing* is sent just before a window position, size, and/or z-order is changed.

Both of the features are passed an instance of a *WEL_WINDOW_POS* structure that represents the new position information, either after the change (for an *on_window_pos_changed*) or before the change (for *on_window_pos_changing*). The *WEL_WINDOW_POS* structure holds the size, position, z-ordering, and a set of flags for additional information.

```
on_window_pos_changed (window_pos: WEL_WINDOW_POS)
        -- Wm_windowpschanged message.
        -- This message is sent to a window whose size,
        -- position, or place in the z order has changed as a
        -- result of a call to 'move' or 'resize'.
    require
        exists: exists
        window_pos_not_void: window_pos /= Void

on_window_pos_changing (window_pos: WEL_WINDOW_POS)
        -- Wm_windowposchanging
        -- This message is sent to a window whose size,
        -- position or place in the z order is about to change
        -- as a result of a call to 'move', 'resize'.
        -- 'window_pos' can be changed to override the default
        -- values.
    require
        exists: exists
        window_pos_not_void: window_pos /= Void
```

The *on_window_pos_changing* message hook allows you to change the settings in its *window_pos* parameter to override any positional information. The *on_window_pos_changed* message hook gives you the resulting positional information after the change has occurred.

On a Composite Window Palette Message

Changes to the colors in the system palette can affect the appearance of the windows on the desktop. Windows sends a set of messages to notify applications of changes to the system palette. Your application can use these messages to help manage its logical palette and to ensure that the applied colors match the intended colors as closely as possible.

The operations include *on_query_new_palette,* received just before an application is about to gain the input focus; *on_palette_is_changing,* received when a window is about to realize its logical palette; and *on_palette_changed,* received after the window with the input focus has realized its logical palette.

```
on_palette_is_changing (window: WEL_WINDOW)
          -- Wm_paletteischanging.
          -- Inform that an application is going to realize its
          -- logical palette. 'window' identifies the window
          -- that is going to realize its logical palette.
    require
          exists: exists

on_palette_changed (window: WEL_WINDOW)
          -- Wm_palettechanged message.
          -- This message is sent after the window with the
          -- keyboard focus has realized its logical palette.
          -- 'window' identifies the window that caused the
          -- system palette to change
    require
          exists: exists

on_query_new_palette
          -- Wm_querynewpalette message.
          -- Inform an application that is about to receive the
          -- keyboard focus, giving the application an opportunity
          -- to realize its logical palette when it receives the
          -- focus. If the window realizes its logical palette,
          -- it must return True; otherwise it must return False.
          -- (False by default)
    require
          exists: exists
```

Frame Windows

A frame window is one of the most common types of windows. Class
WEL_FRAME_WINDOW is the first concrete (nonabstract) window class we
have encountered. Both *WEL_WINDOW* and *WEL_COMPOSITE_WINDOW*
are abstract classes and therefore cannot be instantiated. Class
WEL_FRAME_WINDOW, on the other hand, is fully implemented and can be
instantiated.

A frame window presents to the user a composite window with a client
area, a title bar, and a border. The title bar may include different icons representing system menu functions and may also include a textual description
of the window, such as the application name. The style of a frame window
can be modified to include additional title bar icons, different borders (or
none at all), and different creation, message handling, and painting policies. (See "Changing the Default Style of a Frame Window" later in this
chapter.)

Creating a Frame Window

A frame window can be created as either a child of another composite window or as a top-level window (a child of the desktop). The two features *make_child* and *make_top* instantiate a frame window as either a child window or top-level window, respectively.

```
make_child (a_parent: WEL_COMPOSITE_WINDOW; a_name: STRING)
        -- Make the window as a child of 'a_parent' and
        -- 'a_name' as a title.
    require
        a_parent_not_void: a_parent /= Void
        a_parent_exists: a_parent.exists
    ensure
        parent_set: parent = a_parent
        exists: exists
        name_set: text.is_equal (a_name)
make_top (a_name: STRING)
        -- Make a top window (without parent) with 'a_name'
        -- as a title.
    require
        a_name_not_void: a_name /= Void
    ensure
        parent_set: parent = Void
        exists: exists
        name_set: text.is_equal (a_name)
```

The creation procedure *make_child* is passed a reference to the composite window that will be its parent. Both *make_child* and *make_top* are passed the window title in the form of a *STRING*.

Almost all of the examples presented so far have used a frame window as the application's main window, and it has typically been created with a call to *make_top*:

```
make_top ("Main Window")
```

To create a frame window as a child, the code would have read

```
make_child (parent_window, "Main Window")
```

where *parent_window* was a reference to another composite window.

Changing the Default Settings of a Frame Window

A number of default settings on a frame window can be changed by redefining the functions *class_cursor*, *class_icon*, *class_background*, *class_style*, *class_menu_name*, *class_name*, and *class_window_procedure*. Each of these functions returns an object that represents the default value. For example, *class_icon* returns the default icon for a frame window, *class_cursor* returns the default cursor, and so on. All of the functions are defined as "once functions" to ensure that the object is shared among all instances of that particular type of frame window. In most cases, your redefinitions should also be implemented as once functions. The following sections describe each of the class setting routines and how you can redefine them.

Changing the Default Cursor of a Frame Window

Most of the time, the cursor takes the shape of an arrow pointing towards the left. It is possible to change the cursor shape, depending on which window the pointer is currently within. For instance, you have probably noticed the cursor change to a vertical bar when the pointer is inside a text edit control or change to resize handles when over a window's borders. You can set the shape of the cursor for each type of window in your application by redefining the feature *class_cursor. class_cursor* should return a cursor instance of a particular shape.

```
class_cursor: WEL_CURSOR
        -- Standard arrow cursor used to create the window
        -- class.
        -- Can be redefined to return a user-defined cursor.
    ensure
        result_not_void: Result /= Void
        result_exists: Result.exists
```

The *WEL_FRAME_WINDOW* implementation of *class_cursor* returns an instance of *WEL_CURSOR* representing the default cursor shape (the left facing arrow). *WEL_CURSOR* is a class that represents a Windows cursor. You can create a cursor and set its shape to a bitmap or a Windows resource. More detail (and an example) can be found in the section "Cursors" in Chapter 7.

Changing the Default Icon of a Frame Window

When a window is minimized, Windows displays an icon in its place. The icon is displayed either in the task bar (for Windows 9x and Windows 2000) or on the desktop (for older versions of Windows NT and Windows 3.x). By default, a WEL frame window uses an icon that depicts an empty window frame. You can change the icon of each frame window in your applications by redefining the feature *class_icon*.

```
class_icon: WEL_ICON
            -- Standard application icon used to create the
            -- window class.
            -- Can be redefined to return a user-defined icon.
       ensure
            result_not_void: Result /= Void
            result_exists: Result.exists
```

Feature *class_icon* returns an instance of a *WEL_ICON* that represents the icon that will be used when the frame window is minimized. An icon can be created from a Windows resource. Refer to "Icons" in Chapter 7 for more details on creating and manipulating icons.

Changing the Default Background of a Frame Window

Each frame window can also have a particular background pattern or color that will be drawn whenever the client area of the window is erased. The background pattern can be set by redefining the feature *class_background*.

```
class_background: WEL_BRUSH
            -- Standard window background color used to create the
            -- window class.
            -- Can be redefined to return a user-defined brush.
       ensure
            result_not_void: Result /= Void
            result_exists: Result.exists
```

A *WEL_BRUSH* can be created from a system color, a bitmap, or a hatch pattern (see "Brushes" in Chapter 10, "Graphics Device Interface"). The brush returned by this feature will be used when the client area of the window is erased.

Changing the Default Style of a Frame Window

The class style of a frame window specifies a number of additional behavioral settings, such as performance enhancements, device context creation, message handling, and clipping policies. The feature *class_style* returns an integer value representing the conjunction of a selection of style constants taken from class *WEL_CS_CONSTANTS*.

```
class_style: INTEGER
            -- Standard style used to create the window class.
            -- Can be redefined to return a user-defined style.
```

Table 5.4 lists all of the class style constants and describes what each is used for. You can group a number of style constants by adding them together in the *class_style* function. For example, the default implementation of *class_style* is defined as

```
Result := Cs_hredraw + Cs_vredraw + Cs_dblclks
```

specifying that the entire frame window should be redrawn when either the width or height of the window is modified and that double-click messages should be sent for this frame window.

TABLE 5.4   *Class Style Constants (WEL_CS_CONSTANTS)*

CONSTANT	DESCRIPTION
Cs_bytealignclient	Aligns the window's client area on a byte boundary (in the x direction) to enhance performance during drawing operations. This style affects the width of the window and its horizontal placement on the display.
Cs_bytealignwindow	Aligns the window on a byte boundary (in the x direction) to enhance performance during operations that involve moving or sizing the window. This style affects the width of the window and its horizontal placement on the display.
Cs_classdc	Allocates one device context to be shared by all windows in the class.
Cs_dblclks	Instructs Windows to send a double-click message to the window procedure when the user double-clicks the mouse while the cursor is within a window belonging to the class.
Cs_globalclass	Specifies that the window class is an application global class.
Cs_hredraw	Specifies that the entire window is to be redrawn if a movement or size adjustment changes the width of the client area.
Cs_noclose	Disables the *Close* command on the System menu.
Cs_owndc	Allocates a unique device context for each window in the class.
Cs_parentdc	Sets the clipping rectangle of the child window to that of the parent window so that the child can draw on the parent. A window with the *Cs_parentdc* style receives a regular device context from the system's cache of device contexts. It does not give the child the parent's device context or device context settings. Specifying *Cs_parentdc* enhances an application's performance.
Cs_savebits	Saves as a bitmap the portion of the screen image obscured by a window. Windows uses the saved bitmap to recreate the screen image when the window is removed. Windows displays the bitmap at its original location and does not invoke *on_paint* for windows obscured by the window if other screen actions have not invalidated the stored image. Use this style for small windows that are displayed briefly and

(continued)

TABLE 5.4   *Class Style Constants (WEL_CS_CONSTANTS) (continued)*

CONSTANT	DESCRIPTION
	then removed before other screen activity takes place (for example, menus or dialog boxes). This style increases the time required to display the window because the operating system must first allocate memory to store the bitmap.
Cs_vredraw	Specifies that the entire window is to be redrawn if a movement or size adjustment changes the height of the client area.

Changing the Default Menu Name of a Frame Window

When a frame window is created, you can have a default menu bar added to the window. Normally a frame window will not have a class menu. However, if you redefine the routine *class_menu_name* to return the name of a menu resource, then that resource will be used as the menu bar of all frame windows of that type.

```
class_menu_name: STRING
          -- Window's menu used to create the window class.
          -- Can be redefined to return a user-defined menu.
          -- (None by default).
     ensure
          result_not_void: Result /= Void
```

You can override the menu bar by using the routine *set_menu* (see "Using a Menu on a Composite Window" earlier in this chapter). By default, this routine returns an empty string, thus specifying no default menu bar for frame windows of this type.

Changing the Default Creation Values of a Frame Window

A frame window's default style, position, dimensions, and identifier are determined by the following functions:

```
default_style: INTEGER
          -- Overlapped window style.
          -- By default, a frame window is not visible
          -- at the creation time. 'show' needs to be called.
          -- This solution avoids a bad visual effect when
          -- the children are created one by one inside
          -- the window.

default_x, default_y, default_width, default_height: INTEGER
          -- Default position and dimension when the window is
          -- created.

default_id: INTEGER
          -- Default window id.
          -- (Zero by default).
```

Feature *default_style* returns in integer value that represents the style of the window. Normally this returns *Ws_overlappedwindow*. The default style function can be redefined to return a different style (or combination of styles) as defined in the class *WEL_WS_CONSTANTS* (see Table 4.3 in Chapter 4).

The features *default_x*, *default_y*, *default_width*, and *default_height* specify the initial position and size of the window when it is first created. Each of these functions returns *Cw_usedefault* (also defined in Table 4.3) to use the default value as determined by Windows. Each of these functions can be redefined to return integer values to specify the initial position or size of a frame window.

Finally, the *default_id* function returns an integer value that represents the default identification number of the window. This value is zero by default and can be changed by redefining *default_id* to return another integer value.

Popup Windows

A popup window is a window that can move outside of its parent's client area. A popup window is very similar to a frame window created with *make_child*. The difference is in the window style—a popup window uses the style setting

```
Ws_overlapped + Ws_popup
```

while a frame window's style is just *Ws_overlapped*. The *Ws_popup* style creates a popup window.

Creating a Popup Window

A popup window can be used by creating an instance of class *WEL_POP-UP_WINDOW*. The window can be created in an identical fashion to a frame window. Both features *make_top* and *make_child* are available and create a popup window without a parent and with a parent, respectively. The class *WEL_POPUP_WINDOW* is a direct descendant of *WEL_FRAME_WINDOW* and redefines the feature *class_style*.

SUMMARY

Composite windows allow other windows to be attached as children. Typical Windows application interfaces are constructed by using a composite window as the main window and child windows (in the form of controls or other composite windows) attached to the main window.

Two types of composite windows can be directly instantiated—frame windows and popup windows. A frame window is the most commonly used and provides a client area surrounded by a title bar and a border. A popup window is a type of window that can move outside of its parent (as opposed to control windows that are clipped if moved outside the client area of their parents) and can be used to show temporary information or can even be used as the main window of an application.

DIRECTORY TREE ANALYZER

IMPLEMENTING COMPOSITE WINDOWS

The main window of the Directory Tree Analyzer application provides the central user interface from which all user actions are invoked and in which all generated information is displayed. Almost all applications have a main window, whether it be a frame window, a dialog window, or even a hidden window. The window serves the purpose of providing a central area of user interface.

The example's main window provides a menu bar where all application functionality can be performed, an icon bar from which commonly used functionality can be performed, a tab control showing information in both list and graphical form, and finally, a status bar used to indicate application status and operation progress as shown in Figure 5.8.

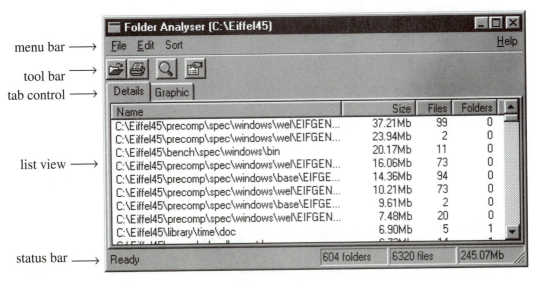

FIGURE 5.8. Directory Tree Analyzer in textual list mode.

The Main Window

The Directory Tree Analyzer uses a frame window as its main window, thus providing a window with borders, title bar, and a customizable client area. Accordingly, the *MAIN_WINDOW* class inherits from *WEL_FRAME_WINDOW* (line 3 of Example 5.9).

Other parents of *MAIN_WINDOW* include WEL constant classes for the controls used in the application, a utility class *WEL_WINDOW_ROUTINES* that provides useful window operations, and the application-specific *SHARED_DATA*, *APPLICATION_IDS,* and *DIRECTORY_INFO_CONSTANTS* classes.

Example 5.9 MAIN_WINDOW Class for the Directory Tree Analyzer

```
1    class MAIN_WINDOW
2    inherit
3        WEL_FRAME_WINDOW
4            redefine
5                on_size, on_menu_command, on_accelerator_command,
                 on_control_id_command
6            end;
7        SHARED_DATA
8            export
9                {NONE} all
10           end;
11       WEL_SIZE_CONSTANTS
12           export
13               {NONE} all
14           end;
15       APPLICATION_IDS
16           export
17               {NONE} all
18           end;
19       WEL_IDC_CONSTANTS
20           export
21               {NONE} all
22           end;
23       DIRECTORY_INFO_CONSTANTS
24           export
25               {NONE} all;
26               {ANY} valid_order_by
27           end;
28       WEL_WINDOWS_ROUTINES
29           export
30               {NONE} all
31           end
```

Example 5.10 shows the *MAIN_WINDOW* creation procedure and the Access feature group. The creation procedure of *MAIN_WINDOW* first initializes the frame window by calling the inherited feature *make_top*. Each of the child controls on the window are then initialized by calling their relevant creation procedures and passing the main window as their parent. Finally, a number of application defaults, such as the initial sorting criteria and window size, are set.

The control objects are declared in the feature group labeled *Access*, along with a *DIRECTORY_PARSER* and *SORTED_TWO_WAY_LIST [DIRECTORY_INFO]*, used to collect and store directory information, respectively.

Example 5.10 MAIN_WINDOW Creation Procedure

```
32  create
33        make
34  feature -- Initialization
35        make is
36               -- Initialize the main window
37           do
38               make_top (resource_string_id (ids_app_name_constant))
39               create tool_bar.make (Current)
40               create status_bar.make (Current)
41               create msg_box.make
42                  status_bar.set_status_part (resource_string_id
                       (ids_app_ready_constant))
43               create tab_window.make (Current, 0, tool_bar.height, width,
44                       height - tool_bar.height - status_bar.height, - 1)
45               initialize_tab_window
46               tool_bar.update_icons (directory_infos)
47               create main_menu.make
48               main_menu.update (directory_infos)
49               set_menu (main_menu)
50               resize (450, 270)
51               sort_reverse := False
52               sort_by_name
53               create printer
54           end;
55  feature -- Access
56        tab_window: WEL_TAB_CONTROL;
57                   -- Tab control for list and graphical view
58        list_view: LIST_VIEW;
59                   -- Analysis results display
60        graph_view: GRAPH_VIEW;
61                   -- Graphic results display
62        main_menu: MENU_BAR;
63                   -- Main menu bar
64        tool_bar: TOOL_BAR;
65                   -- Tool bar
66        status_bar: STATUS_BAR;
67                   -- Status bar
68        msg_box: WEL_MSG_BOX;
69                   -- Error message box
```

```
70          directory_infos: SORTED_TWO_WAY_LIST [DIRECTORY_INFO];
71                    -- Analyzed directory information
72          analyzer: DIRECTORY_PARSER;
73                    -- Directory tree analyzer
74          printer: DIR_INFO_PRINTER;
75                      -- Print engine for printing directory
                        -- information
```

The Basic Operations feature group includes the feature *analyze_directory* (Example 5.11, lines 77–107), which is used to initiate a directory analysis, beginning at the specified directory name (see Example 5.11). This routine makes use of the *analyzer* object to perform the analysis, and if the analysis is successful, updates relevant controls with collected information or displays an error message to the user, using a message dialog box.

The *parse_directory* routine (lines 108–118) prompts the user for a directory to parse using a *WEL_CHOOSE_FOLDER_DIALOG*, and if a valid directory is selected, calls *analyze_directory*. The remaining routines in this group show dialog boxes to the user, including dialogs for "about" information, printer setup, find, and configuration.

Example 5.11 MAIN_WINDOW Basic Features

```
76  feature -- Basic Operations
77      analyze_directory (directory: STRING) is
78              -- Perform directory analysis
79          require
80              directory_valid: directory /= void
81          local
82              file: RAW_FILE;
83              largest: INTEGER
84          do
85              create file.make (directory);
86              if file.exists then
87                  if file.is_directory then
88                      create analyzer.make;
89                      analyzer.collect (file, sort_type,
                            ~update_status_callback (?));
90                      largest := analyzer.largest_directory_size;
91                      directory_infos := analyzer.directory_infos;
92                      update_list_content;
93                      update_status_bar_content;
94                      tool_bar.update_icons (directory_infos);
95                      main_menu.update (directory_infos);
96                      update_title_bar (directory)
97                  else
```

```
 98                              msg_box.error_message_box (Current,
 99                                  resource_string_id (ids_file_er-
                                         ror_constant),
100                                  resource_string_id (ids_file_not_di-
                                         rectory_constant))
101                          end
102                  else
103                      msg_box.error_message_box (Current,
104                          resource_string_id (ids_file_er-
                                 ror_constant),
105                          resource_string_id (ids_file_non_exist-
                                 ent_constant))
106                  end
107              end;
108      parse_directory is
109              -- Show open file dialog and parse the selected directory.
110          do
111              open_dialog.activate (Current)
112              if open_dialog.selected then
113                  wait_cursor.set
114                  shared_preferences.set_selected_path (clone
                         open_dialog.folder_name))
115                  analyze_directory (shared_preferences.selected_path)
116                  wait_cursor.restore_previous
117              end
118          end;
119      configure_preferences is
120              -- Show preferences dialog and configure
121              -- directory analyzer with chosen settings.
122          do
123              pref_dialog.activate
124          end;
125      find_text is
126              -- Show find dialog.
127          do
128              find_dialog.activate
129          end;
130      page_setup is
131              -- Show page setup dialog
132          do
133              page_setup_dialog.activate
134          end;
135      print_info is
136              -- Show print dialog.
137          do
138              print_dialog.activate (Current)
139              if print_dialog.selected then
140                  printer.set_analyzer (analyzer)
141                  printer.set_directory_infos (directory_infos)
142                  printer.set_sort_reverse (sort_reverse)
143                  printer.print_info (print_dialog)
144              end
```

```
145            end;
146     about is
147                     --Show about dialog.
148            do
149                     about_dialog.activate
150            end;
```

Directory information collected by the application can be sorted in different ways (see Example 5.12). The user may choose to sort the information alphabetically, using directory names, or numerically, using the size of directories. The routines *sort_by_name* through *sort_by_usage* change the current configuration of the application to sort by a chosen criterion (see Example 5.12). Each sort type can also be reversed using routine *reverse_sort*. For example, the user can choose to sort by reverse directory size—from largest to smallest rather than from smallest to largest.

Example 5.12 MAIN_WINDOW Sort Features

```
151     sort_by_name is
152                     -- Sort directory information by name
153            do
154                    if sort_type = ordered_by_name then
155                            toggle_reverse_sort
156                    else
157                            sort_type := ordered_by_name
158                    end
159                    main_menu.clear_sort_menus
160                    main_menu.check_item (idm_sort_name_constant)
161                    if directory_infos /= void then
162                            update_for_sort
163                    end
164            end;
165     sort_by_files is
166                     -- Sort directory information by number of
                        files
167            do
168                    if sort_type = ordered_by_file_count then
169                            toggle_reverse_sort
170                    else
171                            sort_type := ordered_by_file_count
172                    end
173                    main_menu.clear_sort_menus
174                    main_menu.check_item (idm_sort_files_constant)
175                    if directory_infos /= void then
```

```
176                             update_for_sort
177                 end
178            end;
179        sort_by_directories is
180                    -- Sort directory information by number of
                          directories
181            do
182                    if sort_type = ordered_by_directory_count then
183                            toggle_reverse_sort
184                    else
185                            sort_type := ordered_by_directory_count
186                    end
187            main_menu.clear_sort_menus
188            main_menu.check_item (idm_sort_direc-
                          tories_constant)
189                    if directory_infos /= void then
190                            update_for_sort
191                    end
192            end;
193        sort_by_usage is
194                    -- Sort directory information by usage
195            do
196                    if sort_type = ordered_by_usage then
197                            toggle_reverse_sort
198                    else
199                            sort_type := ordered_by_usage
200                    end
201            main_menu.clear_sort_menus
202            main_menu.check_item (idm_sort_usage_constant)
203                    if directory_infos /= void then
204                            update_for_sort
205                    end
206            end;
207        toggle_reverse_sort is
208                    -- Toggle the current reverse sort setting
209            do
210                    sort_reverse := not sort_reverse
211                    if sort_reverse then
212                            main_menu.check_item (idm_sort_re-
                                      verse_constant)
213                    else
214                            main_menu.uncheck_item (idm_sort_re-
                                      verse_constant)
215                    end
216            end;
```

The routines listed in Example 5.13 provide helper functionality for updating the user interface when different events occur. For instance, when the sorting criterion is changed by the user, the *update_for_sort* routine (lines 217–227) is called to reorder any collected directory information and update relevant display controls. Routine *update_for_display* (lines 228–236) is used when the user changes display preferences, such as how to display directory sizes. Neither of these routines require a reanalysis of the directory structure. However, if the user selects a different traversal depth, then a reanalysis of directories is required. Thus, the *update_for_traversal_depth* routine (lines 237–245) calls *analyze_directory* to perform a reanalysis.

Example 5.13 MAIN_WINDOW Update Features

```
217     update_for_sort is
218                     -- Update the list content order for a new sort type
219         require
220                 non_void_directories: directory_infos /= void
221         do
222                 wait_cursor.set
223                 set_order_by (sort_type)
224                 directory_infos.sort
225                 update_list_content
226                 wait_cursor.restore_previous
227         end;
228     update_for_display is
229                     -- Update the list content for a new display
                        -- preference
230         require
231                 non_void_directories: directory_infos /= void
232         do
233                 wait_cursor.set
234                 update_list_content
235                 wait_cursor.restore_previous
236         end;
237     update_for_traversal_depth is
238                     -- Update the list content order for a new
                        -- traversal depth
239         require
240                 non_void_directories: directory_infos /= void
241         do
242                 wait_cursor.set
243                 analyze_directory (shared_preferences.
                        selected_path)
244                 wait_cursor.restore_previous
245         end;
```

Line 89 of routine *analyze_directory* (see Example 5.11) passes a routine agent to the collect procedure of *DIRECTORY_PARSER*. The *DIRECTORY_PARSER* uses this agent (similar to a function pointer or high-order procedure in other programming languages) to register a callback routine to call during the analysis process. The callback routine used is *update_status_callback,* as shown in Example 5.14. This routine updates the status bar of the main window to notify the user of progress during a directory parse. Recall line 89:

```
analyzer.collect (file, sort_type, ~update_status_callback (?))
```

The routine *update_status_callback* is passed as a delayed call to the collect routine. Its only parameter is left unbound. During the analysis process, the routine is invoked for every directory entered. Line 129 of routine *collect_directory_info* in class *DIRECTORY_PARSER* (see the section "Directory Parsing" in Chapter 2, "Applications") invokes the routine.

```
notify_callback.call ([<<start.name>>])
```

where *notify_callback* is an attribute of type *ROUTINE* and the expression *start.name* returns the name of the current directory as a *STRING*. The name is passed to the routine invocation as the sole element of a *TUPLE* object.

Example 5.14 MAIN_WINDOW Agent Callback

```
246  feature
247          update_status_callback (message: STRING) is
248                     -- Update the status bar with 'message'
249             require
250                 message_not_void: message /= void
251             do
252                 status_bar.set_status_part (message)
253             end;
```

The Directory Tree Analyzer uses message hooks to capture and process user events. The feature group labeled *Events* (in Example 5.15) defines the message hooks used by the main window. The first message processed by the main window is *Wm_size* and is handled by the *on_size* message hook (lines 255–269). *on_size* appropriately repositions and resizes all child controls for the new window size.

The only other messages directly handled by the main window are messages resulting from a user action, including menu item selection, tool bar icon selection, and accelerator key presses. Through careful designation of event codes, it is possible to handle all of these message types with one procedure. The message hook *on_menu_command* (lines 270–303) is used to handle all user application events by inspecting the *menu_id* passed as a parameter (see Example 5.15). The remaining message hooks, *on_control_id_command* and *on_accelerator_command,* use *on_menu_command* to do the processing for them. This works because each user event is given a single event code (defined in class *APPLICATION_IDS*). For example, both the open menu item and the open tool bar icon pass the value of `Idm_file_open_constant` as the event code.

Example 5.15 MAIN_WINDOW Event Hooks

```
254  feature -- Events
255      on_size (size_type, new_width, new_height: INTEGER) is
256              -- Resize controls
257          local
258              column, next_position: INTEGER;
259              edges: ARRAY [INTEGER]
260          do
261              if size_type = size_maximized or size_type = size_restored
262                      or size_type = size_maxshow then
263                  tool_bar.set_width (new_width);
264                  status_bar.initialize (new_width);
265                  status_bar.reposition;
266                  tab_window.move_and_resize (0, tool_bar.height,
                          new_width,
267                          new_height - tool_bar.height - status_bar.height,
                          True)
268              end
269          end;
270      on_menu_command (menu_id: INTEGER) is
271              -- Perform menu command actions
272          do
273              inspect menu_id
274              when idm_sort_reverse_constant then
275                  toggle_reverse_sort;
276                  if directory_infos /= void then
277                      update_for_sort
278                  end
279              when idm_sort_usage_constant then
280                  sort_by_usage
281              when idm_sort_directories_constant then
282                  sort_by_directories
283              when idm_sort_files_constant then
284                  sort_by_files
285              when idm_sort_name_constant then
286                  sort_by_name
287              when idm_about_constant then
288                  about
289              when idm_page_setup_constant then
290                  page_setup
291              when idm_file_print_constant then
292                  print_info
293              when idm_edit_find_constant then
294                  find_text
295              when idm_edit_preferences_constant then
296                  configure_preferences
297              when idm_file_exit_constant then
298                  destroy
299              when idm_file_open_constant then
300                  parse_directory
301              else
```

```
302                         end
303                 end;
304         on_control_id_command (control_id: INTEGER) is
305                         -- Perform control id command actions
306                 do
307                         on_menu_command (control_id)
308                 end;
309         on_accelerator_command (accelerator_id: INTEGER) is
310                         -- Perform accelerator command actions
311                 do
312                         on_menu_command (accelerator_id)
313                 end;
```

Example 5.16 lists helper routines and variables used by the routines described previously. The variables specify the current sort criteria. The routines help to simplify updates to controls and changes to the sorting order of directory information.

Example 5.16 MAIN_WINDOW Implementation Features

```
314   feature -- Implementation
315       sort_type: INTEGER;
316                         -- Sort order to use for new directory search
317       sort_reverse: BOOLEAN;
318                         -- Should the sort type be performed in reverse?
319       update_list_content is
320                         -- Reset the current view to the new directory information
321           require
322                   valid_list: list_view.exists
323           do
324                   list_view.reset_content
325                   if sort_reverse then
326                       from
327                             directory_infos.finish
328                       until
329                             directory_infos.exhausted
330                       loop
331                             list_view.add_info (directory_infos.item);
332                             directory_infos.back
333                       end
334                   else
335                       from
336                             directory_infos.start
337                       until
338                             directory_infos.exhausted
339                       loop
```

```
340                              list_view.add_info (directory_infos.item);
341                              directory_infos.forth
342                        end
343                  end
344              graph_view.invalidate
345              graph_view.update
346        end;
347  update_status_bar_content is
348              -- Reset the status bar information
349        require
350              valid_status_bar: status_bar.exists;
351              analyzer_valid: analyzer /= void
352        local
353              str: STRING
354        do
355              status_bar.set_status_part (resource_string_id
                    (ids_app_ready_constant));
356              create str.make (20);
357              if analyzer.directory_infos /= void then
358                    str.append (analyzer.directory_infos.count.out);
359                    str.append (" folders");
360                    status_bar.set_folders_part (str);
361                    status_bar.set_size_part (analyzer.total_mb_size);
362                    str.wipe_out;
363                    str.append (analyzer.total_file_count.out);
364                    str.append (" files");
365                    status_bar.set_files_part (str)
366              end
367        end;
368  update_title_bar (str: STRING) is
369              -- Update the title bar with the application name
370              -- with 'str' appended. If 'str' is Void just use the
371              -- application name.
372        local
373              new_title: STRING
374        do
375              new_title := clone (resource_string_id (ids_app_name_
                    constant));
376              if str /= void then
377                    new_title.append (" (");
378                    new_title.append (str);
379                    new_title.append_character (')')
380              end;
381              set_text (new_title)
382        end;
383  set_order_by (sort: INTEGER) is
384              -- Update all directory information to sort by 'sort'
385        require
386              valid_sort: valid_order_by (sort);
387              info_exists: directory_infos /= void
388        do
389              from
```

```
390                         directory_infos.start
391             until
392                         directory_infos.exhausted
393             loop
394                         directory_infos.item.order_by (sort);
395                         directory_infos.forth
396             end
397       end;
```

The dialog windows used by the application are defined as once functions (see Example 5.17) to ensure that only a single instance of each dialog is used. Using a single instance makes retaining dialog state easy—when a dialog is shown to the user for a second or subsequent time, it contains the same state as last set by the user. For instance, the page setup dialog is displayed with the last settings selected by the user without the need for explicit reinitialization of the dialog.

Example 5.17 MAIN_WINDOW Variables

```
398       wait_cursor: WEL_CURSOR is
399                     -- Window cursor
400           once
401                     create Result.make_by_predefined_id (idc_wait)
402           end;
403       open_dialog: WEL_CHOOSE_FOLDER_DIALOG is
404                     -- Directory open dialog
405           once
406                     create Result.make
407           end;
408       pref_dialog: IDD_PREFERENCES_DIALOG is
409                     -- Preferences dialog
410           once
411                     create Result.make (Current)
412           end;
413       find_dialog: IDD_FIND_DIALOG is
414                     -- Find dialog
415           once
416                     create Result.make (Current)
417           end;
418       about_dialog: IDD_ABOUT_DIALOG is
419                     -- About dialog
420           once
421                     create Result.make (Current)
```

```
422             end;
423         page_setup_dialog: IDD_PAGE_SETUP_DIALOG is
424                     -- Page setup dialog
425             once
426                     create Result.make (Current)
427             end;
```

The final routine defined by the *MAIN_WINDOW* class is a helper routine for initializing the tab view control (see Example 5.18). Basically, two tab windows are created—the first with a list view attached and the second with an empty window used to graphically display information. The labels for each tab are initialized, and the tab windows are registered with the tab control.

Example 5.18 MAIN_WINDOW Initialization

```
428         initialize_tab_window is
429                 -- Create tab control window and tab items
430             local
431                 tab: WEL_TAB_CONTROL_ITEM;
432                 system_font: WEL_ANSI_VARIABLE_FONT
433             do
434                 create system_font.make;
435                 tab_window.set_vertical_font (system_font);
436                 create tab.make_with_window (tab_window);
437                 create list_view.make (tab_window, Current, 0,
                        10, width, 10, list_view_id_constant);
438                 tab.set_window (list_view);
439                 tab.set_text ("Details");
440                 tab_window.insert_item (0, tab);
441                 create tab.make_with_window (tab_window);
442                 create graph_view.make (tab_window, Current);
443                 tab.set_window (graph_view);
444                 tab.set_text ("Graphic");
445                 tab_window.insert_item (1, tab)
446             end;
447 end -- class MAIN_WINDOW
```

S   I   X

MULTIPLE-DOCUMENT WINDOWS

INTRODUCING MDI WINDOWS

The multiple-document interface (MDI) specification defines a set of window types that can be used to build applications that support multiple documents. MDI windows are implemented by three classes: *WEL_MDI_FRAME_WINDOW*, *WEL_MDI_CLIENT_WINDOW*, and *WEL_MDI_CHILD_WINDOW*. Using these windows, you can build applications such as word processing applications that handle multiple documents and spreadsheet applications that handle multiple worksheets. Each document in an MDI application is displayed in a separate child window contained within the client area of the application's main window. Figure 6.1 shows an example of an MDI application.

The frame window in this application contains three child windows. The child windows are contained within the client window of the frame window. Every MDI frame window automatically has a client window attached that is sized to take up all of the remaining client area excluding space for an optional menu bar and tool bar. The child windows are actually attached to the client window of the MDI frame window, and the client window controls the display of each child window—each child window can be moved within the client window but cannot be moved outside.

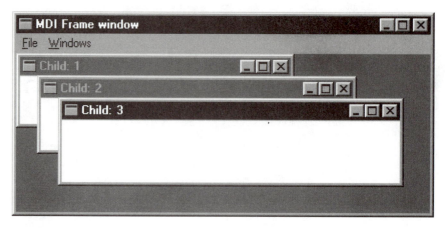

FIGURE 6.1. MDI example.

MDI Frame Windows

The MDI frame window is typically the main window of an MDI application and contains an MDI client window and a number of MDI child windows. The classes used in each case are *WEL_MDI_FRAME_WINDOW, WEL_MDI_CLIENT_WINDOW,* and *WEL_MDI_CHILD_WINDOW.* You need only create a *WEL_MDI_FRAME_WINDOW* and a number of *WEL_MDI_CHILD_WINDOWs.* The class *WEL_MDI_CLIENT_WINDOW* is created and used internally by *WEL_MDI_FRAME_WINDOW.* Figure 6.2 shows the relationships between the three MDI classes.

The MDI frame window holds a single instance of an MDI client window through the feature *client_window.* This client window is also accessible through the feature *children* of *WEL_COMPOSITE_WINDOW.* Both the MDI

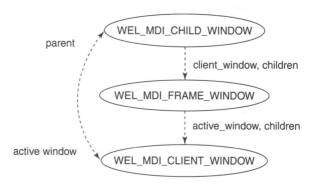

FIGURE 6.2. MDI class relationships.

client window and MDI frame window can access the currently active child window through the feature *active_window*. One interesting relationship is that the parent of the MDI child window is not the MDI client window, as would be first thought. The parent of all MDI child windows is *always* the MDI frame window and is accessible through the feature *parent*.

Both *WEL_MDI_FRAME_WINDOW* and *WEL_MDI_CHILD_WINDOW* inherit from *WEL_FRAME_WINDOW*. Therefore, both of these classes have the same facilities as a frame window, including a border and system menu. On the other hand, class *WEL_MDI_CLIENT_WINDOW* inherits from *WEL_COMPOSITE_WINDOW* and has the same facilities as *WEL_COMPOSITE_WINDOW*.

Creating an MDI Frame Window

Every MDI application has one MDI frame window. The window must also be the main window of the application and should be defined and instantiated in your application class. To create and initialize an MDI frame window, you need to call the creation procedure *make_top*.

```
make_top (a_name: STRING; a_menu: WEL_MENU; first_child: INTEGER)
        -- Make an MDI frame window named 'a_name' using
        -- 'a_menu' as the application's Window menu.
        -- 'first_child' specifies the child window identifier
        -- of the first MDI child window created. Windows
        -- increments the identifier for each additional
        -- MDI child window the application creates. These
        -- identifiers are used in 'on_command_control_id' when
        -- a child window is chosen from the Window menu; they
        -- should not conflict with any other command
        -- identifiers.
        -- (export status {NONE})
    require
        a_name_not_void: a_name /= void;
        a_menu_not_void: a_menu /= void;
        a_menu_exists: a_menu.exists
    ensure
        parent_set: parent = void;
        exists: exists;
        name_set: text.is_equal (a_name);
        client_window_not_void: client_window /= void;
        client_window_exists: client_window.exists
```

The creation procedure *make_top* takes three parameters—the window name, a reference to the Window menu, and an integer representing the numeric identifier that the first child window will receive. The *a_name* parameter is the same as all other window creation procedures. It is used to set the text of the window (the title, in the case of a frame window).

The parameter *a_menu* is used to refer to the pull-down menu of the MDI frame window's menu bar that will be modified to contain a list of the MDI child windows. When a child window is created, a menu item is automatically added to the pull-down menu referenced by *a_menu*. The user is then able to activate a particular MDI child window via the menu bar. When the first MDI child window is created, it is assigned the integer specified in the *first_child* parameter. This integer is used as the menu command id for the menu item that is added to the menu bar. Subsequent child windows receive an identification number one greater than the previous number. You must ensure that the *first_child* integer and all potential child window values following this number do not conflict with any other menu item command identifiers.

Example 6.1 lists the code needed to create a very simple MDI application. We extend this example to add child windows in the next section.

Example 6.1 Simple MDI Frame Window Example (mdi\frame)

```
class MAIN_WINDOW
inherit
    WEL_MDI_FRAME_WINDOW
creation
    make
feature {NONE} -- Initialization
    make (new_name: STRING) is
            -- Build an MDI frame window with a simple menu bar.
        require
            valid_name: new_name /= Void
        do
            make_top (new_name, window_menu, 100)
            set_menu (menu_bar)
        end
feature - Menu
    File_exit: INTEGER is 10
    Window_arrange_icons: INTEGER is 11
    Window_cascade_windows: INTEGER is 12
    Window_tile_horizontally: INTEGER is 13
    Window_tile_vertically: INTEGER is 14
    menu_bar: WEL_MENU is
            -- Construct the menu bar main menu.
        once
            create Result.make
            Result.append_popup (file_menu, "&File")
            Result.append_popup (window_menu, "&Windows")
        end
    file_menu: WEL_MENU is
```

```
                    -- Construct the file popup menu
            once
                create Result.make
                Result.append_string ("E&xit", File_exit)
            end
        window_menu: WEL_MENU is
                -- Construct the window menu
            once
                create Result.make
                Result.append_string ("&Arrange Icons",
                    Window_arrange_icons)
                Result.append_string ("&Cascade", Window_cascade_windows)
                Result.append_string ("Tile &Horizontally",
                    Window_tile_horizontally)
                Result.append_string ("Tile &Vertically", Window_tile_
                    vertically)
            end
    end -- class MAIN_WINDOW
```

The creation procedure *make* initializes the MDI frame window by calling *make_top* from *WEL_MDI_FRAME_WINDOW* and passing the title for the window, a reference to the Window menu, and a starting child id of 100. The remaining routines create a very simple menu bar with two pull-down menus: File and Window. Don't worry too much about how the menu is constructed and what it does; we explore menus fully in Chapter 8, "Menus."

Example 6.1 does not attach any actions to the menu items. All it does is create an instance of a *WEL_MDI_FRAME_WINDOW*. The output of the program is shown in Figure 6.3. As you can see, an MDI frame window looks identical to a normal frame window (only our example includes a menu bar).

What isn't immediately apparent is that an instance of *WEL_MDI_CLI-ENT_WINDOW* has also been created as a child of the MDI frame window.

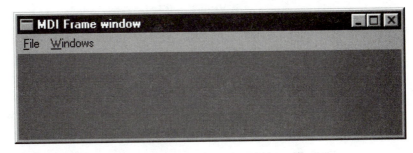

FIGURE 6.3. MDI frame window.

The MDI client window covers all of the area below the menu bar. It is this window that MDI child windows are attached to, and more importantly, contained within. One obvious difference to a normal frame window client area is that the MDI client window background color defaults to gray instead of white.

Finding the Client Window of an MDI Frame Window

The MDI client window of an MDI frame window is accessible through the feature *client_window*.

```
client_window: WEL_MDI_CLIENT_WINDOW
        -- MDI client window which contains child windows
```

Most interaction with an MDI interface occurs either through the MDI frame window or directly with the MDI child windows. You will rarely have to access the MDI client window. WEL uses this function internally.

Finding the Active Child Window of an MDI Frame Window

Only one of an MDI frame window's children can be active at one time. When an MDI child window is active, it is displayed on top of all other child windows and its title bar is highlighted. Each MDI client window maintains its own z-order of child windows, and the child window at the top of the z-order is the active window.[1] Two features of *WEL_MDI_FRAME_WINDOW* allow you to access the current active child window (if any): *active_window* and *has_active_window*.

```
active_window: WEL_MDI_CHILD_WINDOW
        -- Window currently active
    require
        exists: exists;
        client_window_not_void: client_window /= void;
        client_window_exists: client_window.exists;
        has_active_window: has_active_window

has_active_window: BOOLEAN
        -- Is a window currently active?
    require
        exists: exists;
        client_window_not_void: client_window /= void;
        client_window_exists: client_window.exists
```

Feature *active_window* returns the currently active child window. For this function to succeed, it is necessary for a child window to be active, thus the following precondition must be *True:*

---

[1]You can use the same z-order window settings, as defined in "Manipulating Child Windows" in Chapter 4, "Windows," to modify the ordering of MDI child windows.

```
has_active_window: has_active_window
```

The function *has_active_window* returns *True* if a child window is currently active, or *False* if not. You typically need to check the value of this function before calling *active_window*. For example, the following code may be used to access the active child window of an MDI frame window *f* and store a reference to it in a variable *c:*

```
if f.has_active_window then
        c := f. active_window
end
```

Arranging the Child Windows of an MDI Frame Window

You can arrange the child windows of an MDI frame window as a group. Different arrangements are available, including cascaded, tiled, or iconized. When child windows are cascaded, each window is sized equally and positioned so that the title bar of each window is visible, while the titled arrangement sizes and positions all windows in a tile pattern so that all of the child windows take up an equal amount of space. The features of *WEL_MDI_FRAME_WINDOW* that provide this arrangement functionality are *cascade_children, tile_children_horizontal*, and *tile_children_vertical*.

When child windows are iconized, their icons are positioned at the bottom of the MDI client window. The icons can be arranged automatically to line up evenly along the bottom of the MDI client window by using one of the arrangement features of MDI frame window, namely *arrange_icons*.

```
arrange_icons
        -- Arrange iconized child windows.
    require
        exists: exists

cascade_children
        -- Cascade the child windows.
    require
        exists: exists

tile_children_horizontal
        -- Horizontally tile the child windows.
    require
        exists: exists

tile_children_vertical
        -- Vertically tile the child windows.
    require
        exists: exists
```

The two versions of tile children provide different ways of arranging the children. Feature *tile_children_vertical* tiles all child windows horizontally down the MDI client window. Each child window is sized to the full width of the MDI client window. The height of the MDI client window is evenly distributed among all child windows so that each child window is visible. The *tile_children_horizontal* works in a similar manner, only the child windows are given enough width to be visible across the MDI client window.

You will typically provide child window arrangement functionality via a menu bar. Example 6.2 extends the previous example by adding menu item actions for arranging the child windows. The example also adds the ability to create a child window.

Example 6.2 Arranging MDI Child Windows (mdi\arrange)

```
class MAIN_WINDOW
inherit
     WEL_MDI_FRAME_WINDOW
          redefine
               on_menu_command
          end
creation
     make
feature {NONE} -- Initialization
     make (new_name: STRING) is
               -- Build an MDI frame window with a simple menu bar.
          require
               valid_name: new_name /= Void
          do
               make_top (new_name, window_menu, 100)
               set_menu (menu_bar)
          end
feature — Messages
     on_menu_command (menu_id: INTEGER) is
               -- Perform the menu actions for the selected menu
               -- item represented by 'menu_id'.
          do
               inspect menu_id
               when File_new then
                    create_new_child_window
               when File_exit then
                    destroy
               when Window_arrange_icons then
                    arrange_icons
               when Window_cascade_windows then
                    cascade_children
               when Window_tile_horizontally then
                    tile_children_horizontal
               when Window_tile_vertically then
                    tile_children_vertical
```

```
            else
                -- unknown menu id, do nothing
            end
        end
feature {NONE} -- Implemenatation
    child_number: INTEGER
            -- Unique number for each new child beginning at one.
            -- Should be incremented before use.
    create_new_child_window is
            -- Build a new child window and attach it to this
            -- MDI frame window
        local
            new_child: WEL_MDI_CHILD_WINDOW
            name: STRING=
        do
            child_number := child_number + 1
            name := "Child: "
            name.append_integer (child_number)
            create new_child.make (Current, name)
        end
feature — Menu
    File_new: INTEGER is 9
    File_exit: INTEGER is 10
    Window_arrange_icons: INTEGER is 11
    Window_cascade_windows: INTEGER is 12
    Window_tile_horizontally: INTEGER is 13
    Window_tile_vertically: INTEGER is 14
    menu_bar: WEL_MENU is
            -- Construct the menu bar main menu.
        once
            create Result.make
            Result.append_popup (file_menu, "&File")
            Result.append_popup (window_menu, "&Windows")
        end
    file_menu: WEL_MENU is
            -- Construct the file popup menu
        once
            create Result.make
            Result.append_string ("&New", File_new)
            Result.append_separator
            Result.append_string ("E&xit", File_exit)
        end
    window_menu: WEL_MENU is
            -- Construct the window menu
        once
            create Result.make
            Result.append_string ("&Arrange Icons", Window_arrange_icons)
            Result.append_string ("&Cascade", Window_cascade_windows)
            Result.append_string ("Tile &Horizontally", Window_tile_horizontally)
            Result.append_string ("Tile &Vertically", Window_tile_vertically)
        end
end -- class MAIN_WINDOW
```

Figure 6.4 shows the output from this example after selecting the Cascade, Tile Horizontal and Tile Vertical menu items with three child windows.

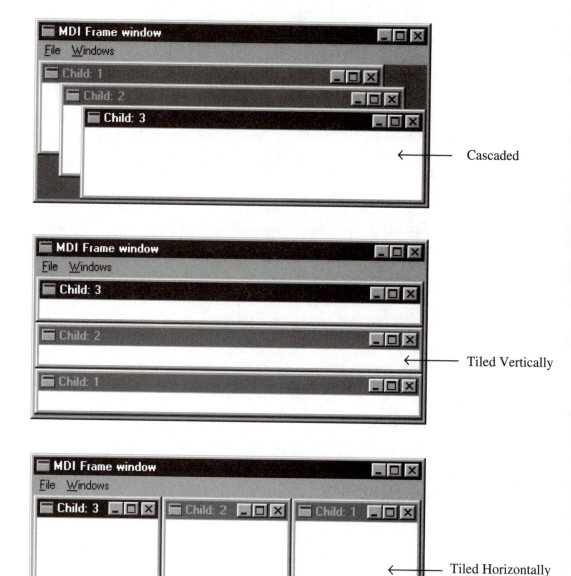

FIGURE 6.4. Cascaded and tiled MDI child windows.

MDI Client Windows

A single MDI client window is created automatically by each MDI frame window. You do not need to create an MDI client window directly in your applications. You can, however, access the client window using the feature *client_window* of *WEL_MDI_FRAME_WINDOW*. Once you have hold of the client window, you can access it just like any other composite window. For instance, you can get the dimensions of the window, set its background color, and arrange its child windows. In fact, when an MDI frame window arranges child windows through the routines *cascade_children, tile_children_vertical,* and *tile_children_horizontal,* the window actually forwards the request to the client window. For example, when you call *cascade_children* on an MDI frame window, the frame window actually calls

```
client_window.cascade_children
```

asking the client window to perform the desired operation.

Destroying an MDI Child Window of an MDI Client Window

One interesting feature of an MDI client window is how it deletes its child windows. An MDI child window must be deleted via its parent client window. You cannot delete an MDI child window directly. The routine *destroy_window* of *WEL_MDI_CLIENT_WINDOW* destroys the child window passed as a parameter.

```
destroy_window (child: WEL_MDI_CHILD_WINDOW)
        -- Destroy the child window 'child'.
    require
        exists: exists;
        child_not_void: child /= void;
        child_exists: child.exists
```

This routine ensures that the child window is destroyed and removed from the client window (and subsequently from the frame window) cleanly and correctly. In the WEL library, you can treat the destruction of a *WEL_MDI_CHILD_WINDOW* as you would a normal frame window. Calling *destroy* of *WEL_MDI_CHILD_WINDOW* will actually call *destroy_window* of the child's parent client window.

MDI Child Windows

An MDI child window is identical to a frame window, only it has a *WEL_MDI_FRAME_WINDOW* as its parent. Therefore, all features available to a *WEL_FRAME_WINDOW* are available to a *WEL_MDI_CHILD_WINDOW*.

Creating an MDI Child Window

To create an MDI child window, you need to call the creation procedure *make*.

```
make (a_parent: WEL_COMPOSITE_WINDOW; a_name: STRING)
       -- (from WEL_FRAME_WINDOW)
   require -- from WEL_FRAME_WINDOW
       a_parent_not_void: a_parent /= void;
       a_parent_exists: a_parent.exists;
       a_name_not_void: a_name /= void
   ensure -- from WEL_FRAME_WINDOW
       parent_set: parent = a_parent;
       exists: exists;
       name_set: text.is_equal (a_name)
```

The creation procedure *make* takes two parameters and performs the same functionality as *make_child* of class *WEL_FRAME_WINDOW* (see "Creating a Composite Window" in Chapter 5, "Composite Windows"). In Example 6.2, the routine *create_new_child_window* creates a new child window with its parent set to the enclosing class. The line of code that actually performed the creation was

```
create new_child.make (Current, name)
```

where the parameter *a_parent* was bound to the current object and the *a_name* parameter was bound to a local string variable. After executing the *make* creation procedure, the new child window immediately appears within the frame window's client area.

Finding the MDI Frame Window of an MDI Child Window

As mentioned earlier, the parent of an MDI child window is the enclosing MDI frame window. Therefore, when you access the feature *parent* of *WEL_MDI_CHILD_WINDOW,* you receive a reference to the parent window of type *WEL_MDI_FRAME_WINDOW*. Contrast this with the *parent* feature of class *WEL_WINDOW,* which returns a reference to a *WEL_COMPOSITE_WINDOW* and not a *WEL_MDI_FRAME_WINDOW* (see "Finding the

Parent of a Window" in Chapter 4). The interface for feature *parent* in *WEL_MDI_CHILD_WINDOW* is defined as

```
parent: WEL_MDI_FRAME_WINDOW
        -- Parent window
```

SUMMARY

The MDI application framework provides a simple way to build applications that need to support multiple documents. Using the classes *WEL_MDI_FRAME_WINDOW* and *WEL_MDI_CHILD_WINDOW,* you can build very powerful applications, such as word processors, spreadsheet applications, and databases. Many of the applications you find on the Windows platform use an MDI interface to control multiple documents and provide a consistent way of accessing them.

However, the MDI interface concept has come under criticism in recent times as being difficult to learn and understand. Initially, it was also difficult to program an application to use an MDI interface. Recent libraries, such as WEL, have simplified that process considerably. Newer applications are moving towards more document-oriented models, such as workspaces and workbooks.

RESOURCES

INTRODUCING RESOURCES

Resources consist of data kept separately from the application. They are defined in a resource script that is compiled and linked with the application during compilation. The data does not include any logic and only describes the appearance of a variety of application elements.

These elements can be of different natures, including bitmaps, icons, menus, accelerators, cursors, strings, and dialog templates. The resource script describes all the resources that will be used in the system. The description consists of a set of attributes, with associated values for each resource. Attributes can include size, position, font (if applicable), filename (for bitmaps, icons, and cursors) and other resource specific characteristics. Each resource is given an identifier that can then be used to bind to the resource from within an application.

This chapter describes how resources are used in WEL. It does not cover menus and dialogs; they are discussed in Chapter 8, "Menus," and Chapter 9, "Dialogs."

Types of Resources

The WEL classes corresponding to a Windows resource all inherit from *WEL_RESOURCE*. There is one Eiffel class per resource kind (except for string tables, which are explained later in this chapter in the section "Creating a String from a Resource"). Table 7.1 lists the types of resources and their encapsulating WEL classes.

When an application is started, resources are not loaded directly into memory. Instead, Windows loads a resource *just in time* and discards it when it is no longer needed. This, and the ability to change resources without having to recompile the whole application, are the main advantages of using resources over standard application data.

Abstract Resource Class

Initialization is the only aspect in which resources have a common behavior. Hence, *WEL_RESOURCE* includes features that are to be used as creation routines in its descendants.

Creating a Resource by an Identifier

Resources are declared in a resource script. Each resource is associated with a 16-bit integer identifier or a unique name. The feature *make_by_id* provides a way of initializing a resource according to its integer identifier. It requires that the identifier is positive because the use of negative identifiers is discouraged by Microsoft. The ensure clause guarantees that the resource is not shared by another instance and may be freed when the Eiffel object is garbage-collected.

TABLE 7.1   *Resource Types*

RESOURCE	EIFFEL CLASS	DESCRIPTION
Accelerators	*WEL_ACCELERATOR*	Application specific keyboard shortcuts
Icons	*WEL_ICON*	Symbolic bitmaps associated with an application
Cursors	*WEL_CURSOR*	Mouse pointers
String Tables	*WEL_WINDOWS_ROUTINES*	Predefined strings (e.g., for help messages)
Bitmaps	*WEL_BITMAP*	Arrays of bits that correspond to pixels on a device
Dialog Templates	*WEL_DIALOG*	See "Dialogs" (Chapter 9)
Menus	*WEL_MENU*	See "Menus" (Chapter 8)

```
make_by_id (id: INTEGER)
        -- Load the resource by an 'id'
        -- (export status {NONE})
    require
        valid_id: id > 0
    ensure
        not_shared: not shared
```

After *make_by_id* has been called, the underlying Windows structure is initialized and the resource is ready to be loaded in memory.

Creating a Resource by a Windows Predefined Identifier

Windows includes a number of predefined identifiers for commonly used resources. They can be used in Eiffel by using the creation routine *make_by_predefined_id*. Such resources are shared between all Windows applications and should not be freed by WEL. This is why *make_by_predefined_id* ensures that the structure is *shared* and as such should not be released when the Eiffel object is garbage-collected.

The predefined identifiers can be found in the classes listed in Table 7.2.

```
make_by_predefined_id (id: INTEGER)
        -- Load the resource by an 'id', predefined by
        -- Windows
        -- (export status {NONE})
    ensure
        shared: shared
```

TABLE 7.2   *Predefined Resource Identifier Classes*

CLASS	DESCRIPTION
WEL_IDC_CONSTANTS	Predefined cursors. These constants can be used as argument to *make_by_predefined_id* of *WEL_CURSOR*.
WEL_IDI_CONSTANTS	Predefined message box icons. These constants can be used as argument to *make_by_predefined_id* of *WEL_ICON*.
WEL_STANDARD_TOOL_BAR_BITMAP_CONSTANTS	Predefined standard tool bar bitmap icons. These constants can be used as argument for *make_by_predefined_id* of *WEL_TOOL_BAR_BITMAP*.

Creating a Resource by a Resource Name

Resources may also be identified with unique names instead of integer values. The creation procedure *make_by_name* takes the name of a resource as an argument and creates the structure according to its definition in the resource script. The name may not be equal to *Void* or empty (it should contain at least one character). *make_by_name* ensures that the resource is not *shared* and thus may be freed when the Eiffel object is garbage-collected.

```
make_by_name (name: STRING)
        -- Load the resource by a 'name'
        -- (export status {NONE})
    require
        name_not_void: name /= void;
        name_not_empty: not name.empty
    ensure
        not_shared: not shared
```

Creating a Resource from a Pointer

The last common creation routine for all WEL resources is inherited from *WEL_ANY—make_from_pointer*. This routine creates a resource from a pointer to an already existing Windows structure. It is not generally advised to use this creation routine, as it ensures that *item* will be *shared* and therefore will not be freed when the Eiffel objects referencing the underlying Windows structure are garbage-collected. (See Chapter 1, "The Windows Eiffel Library," for more details.) WEL makes extensive use of this routine internally.

```
make_by_pointer (a_pointer: POINTER) is
        -- Set 'item' with 'a_pointer'.
        -- Since 'item' is shared, it does not need
        -- to be freed.
        -- Caution: 'a_pointer' must be a pointer
        -- coming from Windows.
        -- (from WEL_ANY)
        -- (export status {NONE})
    ensure -- from WEL_ANY
        item_set: item = a_pointer;
        shared: shared
```

Manipulating Resource Scripts

The Eiffel compiler automatically takes care of compiling a resource script for your applications. The standard extension for a file that includes such a script is *.rc*. If no resource script file is specified, EiffelBench creates one in the project folder. You may provide your own resource script as long as the name of the file matches the system name as specified in the Ace file (excluding the *.rc* extension). For example, if your system name is *test,* then the resource file must be named *test.rc* for it to be compiled and linked with the executable. The given resource script is compiled and linked with the executable during C compilation of the system. Consequently, using custom resource scripts implies freezing the system at least once before running the application.

Also, remember to refreeze (C compile) your application if you modify the resource script. Otherwise, your changes will not be linked in and may result in unexpected runtime errors.

Accelerators

Accelerators are user-defined keyboard shortcuts usually associated with a command. For example, pressing Ctrl-Shift-F under EiffelBench triggers a freeze of the current system.

Defining Accelerator Resources

Accelerators are defined in accelerator tables. The syntax used in a resource script to declare an accelerator table is

```
table_name ACCELERATORS
BEGIN
    event, idvalue, [type] [options]
    . . .
END
```

where *table_name* is a unique name or 16-bit unsigned integer identifying the table, and *ACCELERATORS* is the resource definition keyword used to declare an accelerator table. In the remaining lines, the *BEGIN* and *END* keywords delimit the accelerator list and each accelerator is defined using *event, type,* and *options.*

The *event* clause specifies the keystroke used for the accelerator. It may be specified using either a character, a control character, an ASCII code, or a virtual-key code. The virtual-key code values are defined in class *WEL_VK_CONSTANTS.* The *type* clause specifies the type of accelerator event; *ASCII* for ASCII or *VIRTKEY* for a virtual key. The default type for a character is *ASCII.* When a *code* is used, *ASCII* or *VIRTKEY* must be specified. In addition, if *type* is *ASCII,* then *event* is case-sensitive.

The *options* clause is used to describe the modifiers that must be used together with the accelerator key. The possible values are combinations of *ALT,*

SHIFT, and *CONTROL. SHIFT* and *CONTROL* may only be used when *type* is *VIRTKEY.* The *options* clause may also be used to differentiate the accelerator from the corresponding top-level menu shortcuts by adding the parameter *NOINVERT.* If *NOINVERT* is specified, then the corresponding top-level menu will not be highlighted when the accelerator is activated.

Example 7.1 illustrates the declaration of an accelerator table. The table represents a sample of the accelerator keys used in the ISE EiffelBench application.

Example 7.1 Declaring Accelerators in a Resource Script

```
ID_EBENCH_ACCEL_TABLE   ACCELERATORS
BEGIN
   "n",    ID_NEW_PROJECT,     VIRTKEY, CONTROL Ctrl-N.
   15,     ID_OPEN_PROJECT, ASCII    ;Ctrl-O. Ctrl-Shift-O also
           works.
   "^F",   ID_FIND     ;Ctrl-F. Ctrl-Shift-F overwritten by
           ID_FREEZE.
   "m",    ID_MELT, VIRTKEY, SHIFT, CONTROL ;Ctrl-Shift-M.
   "q",    ID_QUICK_MELT, VIRTKEY, SHIFT, CONTROL
   "F",    ID_FREEZE, VIRTKEY, SHIFT, CONTROL;;Ctrl-Shift-F. Over-
           writes ID_FIND.
   "P",    ID_PRECOMPILE, VIRTKEY, SHIFT, CONTROL;;Ctrl-Shift-P.
   "^R",   ID_RUN      ;Ctrl-R. Ctrl-Shift-R also works.
   "^E",   ID_END_RUN ;Ctrl-E. Ctrl-Shift-E also works.
   "^L",   ID_CURRENT_OBJECT  ;Ctrl-L. Ctrl-Shift-L also works.
   "^T",   ID_TEXT_FORMAT      ;Ctrl-T. Ctrl-Shift-T also works.
   "p",    ID_PROJECT_WINDOW,ALT ;Alt-P. Case sensitive.
   "n",    ID_NOT_USED_1,VIRTKEY, ALT;;Alt-N. Case insensitive.
   VK_F1, ID_NOT_USED_2,VIRTKEY ;F1
END
```

This example requires that all the identifiers are defined before the declaration of the accelerator table, such as within an include file. An identifier is defined as follows:

```
#define ID_EBENCH_ACCEL_TABLE 1000
```

This resource script should also include the file *windows.h,* as it uses the Windows defined constant *VK_F1.* A file may be included in a resource script using the a *#include* clause, such as

```
#include <windows.h>
```

Using Accelerators in Eiffel

Accelerators can be used in Eiffel using the class *WEL_ACCELERATORS*. The available creation routines are *make_by_name* and *make_by_id*. The following Eiffel code can be written to access the accelerator table defined earlier:

```
accelerators: WEL_ACCELERATORS
...
create accelerators.make_by_id (Id_ebench_accel_table)
```

It requires that the integer constant *Id_ebench_accel_table* has been defined with the same value as in the resource script, for example, by using the *H2E* utility. (See "The H2E Utility" later in this chapter for more information.)

The next step consists of plugging the newly created accelerators into the WEL message processing mechanism by redefining the feature *accelerators* of *WEL_APPLICATION*.

```
accelerators: WEL_ACCELERATORS
        -- Application's accelerators
        -- May be redefined (in once) to associate accelerators
```

This feature is a once function since accelerators are shared between all windows of the application. The redefined feature should return the Eiffel accelerator table created with *make_by_name* or *make_by_id*.

Whenever an accelerator is activated, a message is sent by the feature *message_loop* of *WEL_APPLICATION* to the main window procedure (not the current window). This prevents the duplication of the code-handling accelerators in every window of an application—an accelerator always triggers a message sent to the main window of a WEL application. This message is then processed by the feature *process_message* of *WEL_COMPOSITE_WINDOW*. *process_message* calls *on_wm_command* as accelerator-related information is coded in *WM_COMMAND* messages. Finally, *on_wm_command* calls the feature *on_accelerator_command* of *WEL_COMPOSITE_WINDOW*, which may be redefined to implement the correct behavior.

```
on_accelerator_command (accelerator_id: INTEGER)
        -- The 'accelerator_id' has been activated.
    require
            exists: exists
```

The parameter *accelerator_id* corresponds to the identifier associated with the accelerator. The implementation of *on_accelerator_command* generally requires an *inspect* statement to distinguish between the different accelerator identifiers. The precondition *exists* prevents the processing of any translator message before the creation of the main window.

Creating Accelerators in Eiffel

Accelerators may be directly declared in Eiffel with the class *WEL_ACCELERATOR* (singular). However, accelerators may not be registered "on the fly" when the application is running. The class *WEL_ACCELERATOR* inherits from *WEL_STRUCTURE* and only provides a convenient wrapper of the corresponding Windows structure.

Accelerators are very useful and quite easy to implement, as their support is built in to Windows. Although style rules may apply to their use (mainly to avoid clashes with Windows predefined accelerators, such as *Ctrl-C*), accelerators should be extensively used in any nontrivial Windows application.

Icons

Icons are small pictures used in an application to represent something graphically. Icons can be used to represent an application itself, different functions of an application, or different types of objects manipulated by an application. Windows displays the icon of an application in its *Explorer* program, in the Start menu, in the upper left corner of the windows associated with the application, and in any other places where there is a reference to it.

Defining Icon Resources

Icons are defined in resource scripts using an ICON clause

```
nameID ICON filename
```

which defines an icon in a resource script with *nameID* as the identifier of the icon, *ICON* the resource definition keyword, and *filename* naming the file containing the icon's bitmap. As with accelerators, *nameID* can be either a string or a 16-bit integer.

Using Icons in Eiffel

Icons can be used in a WEL application through the class *WEL_ICON*. Any of the creation routines described earlier in "Abstract Resource Class" can be called to initialize an instance of *WEL_ICON*. Furthermore, *WEL_ICON* adds a new creation routine to the list: *make_by_file*. Routine *make_by_file* initializes an icon, given an icon file from which to read the bitmap data.

```
make_by_file (file_name: FILE_NAME)
        -- Load an icon file named 'file_name'.
        -- Only Windows 95.
        -- (export status {NONE})
    require
        file_name_not_void: file_name /= void
```

As expected, it requires that the filename given is not equal to *Void*. This functionality is not supported by Windows NT 4.0 and should be used only on Windows 95, Windows 98, or Windows 2000.

Instances of *WEL_ICON* may be used to specify the icon associated to a window class by redefining the *class_icon* feature of the class *WEL_FRAME_WINDOW* (see Chapter 4, "Windows"). The icon should be defined using a once function to ensure that the same icon instance is used for the window class.

Example 7.2 demonstrates the use of a *WEL_ICON* in the redefinition of *class_icon*. This example causes every instance of *WEL_FRAME_WINDOW* and *MAIN_WINDOW* to have a new custom cursor. If you need to have different icons for frame windows, then redefine *class_name* to return a unique name for the underlying window class.

Example 7.2 Icon Example, MAIN_WINDOW Class (resources\icons)

```
class MAIN_WINDOW
inherit
    WEL_FRAME_WINDOW
        redefine
            class_icon,
            on_paint
        end
    APPLICATION_IDS
        export
            {NONE} all
        end
creation
    make
feature
    make is
            -- Initialize the main window
        do
```

```
            make_top ("Main Window")
      end

feature -- Events

    on_paint (paint_dc: WEL_PAINT_DC; invalid_rect: WEL_RECT) is
            -- Paint the icon on the client area
        do
            paint_dc.draw_icon (draw_icon, 0, 0)
        end

feature {NONE}

    draw_icon: WEL_ICON is
            -- Load the icon to draw in the client area
        once
            create Result.make_by_id (Idi_draw_icon_constant)
        end

    class_icon: WEL_ICON is
            -- Define the window class icon
        once
            create Result.make_by_id (Idi_application_icon_constant)
        end

end -- class MAIN_WINDOW
```

The example sets the class icon to a yellow letter A with the identifier *Idi_application_icon_constant*. A second icon, this time the letter B, is drawn in the client area of the window using *draw_icon* (see "Drawing Bitmaps, Cursors, and Icons" in Chapter 10, "Graphics Device Interface"). Figure 7.1 shows the first icon in the title bar of the window and the second icon drawn at the top left corner of the client area.

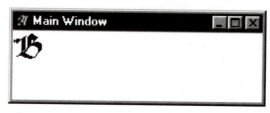

FIGURE 7.1. Icon example.

Null Icons

Null icons are created via the class *WEL_NULL_ICON*. This class inherits from *WEL_ICON* and does not have any creation routine. *item* is consequently set to *default_pointer*. As the default implementation of *exists* compares *item* with *default_pointer*, it is redefined in *WEL_NULL_ICON* to always return *True*. Null icons may be used in a window class, in which case the icon of the corresponding application must be drawn manually using *draw_icon*.

Cursors

Cursors are used to display the mouse pointer on the screen. Each window may use its own cursor and the shape of the cursor is updated whenever the underlying window changes.

Defining Cursor Resources

Cursors are declared in the same way as icons in resource scripts. For example,

```
nameID CURSOR filename
```

defines a cursor with *nameID* as the identifier of the cursor (either a unique name or 16-bit integer), *CURSOR* the resource definition keyword, and *filename* naming the file containing the bitmap of the cursor.

Creating a Cursor

Cursors may be initialized using any of the creation routines seen in "Abstract Resource Class" earlier in this chapter. As with Icons, it is also possible to use *make_by_file*. The standard extension for a cursor file is *.cur*.

```
make_by_file (file_name: FILE_NAME)
        -- Load a cursor file named 'file_name'.
        -- Only Windows 95.
        -- (export status {NONE})
    require
        file_name_not_void: file_name /= void
```

Cursors can also be created via the creation routine *make_by_bitmask*, with the two first arguments, *x_hot_spot* and *y_hot_spot*, specifying the position of the active pixel in the cursor bitmap. The position should be positive and lesser than or equal to the maximum cursor size allowed by Windows. This active pixel represents the coordinates of the cursor on the screen. Whenever an event relative to the cursor occurs (e.g., a mouse click), this pixel is used to find out the target of the event (e.g., the underlying button). The last two arguments, *and_plane* and *xor_plane,* specify the *and* and *exclusive or* planes of the cursor bitmap. They should be coded into arrays of characters.

```
make_by_bitmask (x_hot_spot, y_hot_spot: INTEGER; and_plane,
        xor_plane: ARRAY [CHARACTER])
        -- Make a cursor using bitmask arrays.
        -- 'and_plane' and 'xor_plane' points to an array of
        -- byte that contains the bit values for the AND and XOR
        -- bitmasks of the cursor, as in a device-dependent
        -- monochrome bitmap. 'x_hot_spot', and 'y_hot_spot'
        -- specify the horizontal and vertical position of
        -- the cursor's hot spot.
        -- (export status {NONE})
    require
        x_hot_spot_large_enough: x_hot_spot >= 0;
        x_hot_spot_small_enough: x_hot_spot < cursor_width;
        y_hot_spot_large_enough: y_hot_spot >= 0;
        y_hot_spot_small_enough: y_hot_spot < cursor_height;
        and_plane_not_void: and_plane /= void;
        xor_plane_not_void: xor_plane /= void;
        and_plane_not_empty: not and_plane.empty;
        xor_plane_not_empty: not xor_plane.empty
```

Setting the Cursor of a Window

Class *WEL_FRAME_WINDOW* defines the *class_cursor* to be the default pointer cursor. You can change this cursor to one of your own for all frame windows by redefining *class_cursor,* or for a particular set of windows by redefining both *class_cursor* and *class_name.*

The following example sets the cursor of all frame windows to a custom-built cursor in the shape of a cross hair with a large, centered circle. The cursor is also drawn in the client area of the *MAIN_WINDOW* using *draw_cursor* from *WEL_DC* (see "Drawing Bitmaps, Cursors, and Icons" in Chapter 10).

**Example 7.3 Cursor Example, MAIN_WINDOW Class (resources\
cursors)**

```
class MAIN_WINDOW
inherit
    WEL_FRAME_WINDOW
        redefine
            class_cursor,
            on_paint
```

```
                end
          APPLICATION_IDS
             export
                  {NONE} all
             end
      creation
          make
      feature

          make is
                  -- Initialize the main window
             do
                  make_top ("Main Window")
             end

      feature -- Events

          on_paint (paint_dc: WEL_PAINT_DC; invalid_rect: WEL_RECT) is
                  -- Paint the cursor on the client area
             do
                  paint_dc.draw_cursor (class_cursor, 0, 0)
             end

      feature {NONE}

          class_cursor: WEL_CURSOR is
                  -- Define the window class cursor
             once
                  create Result.make_by_id (Idc_main_cursor_constant)
             end

      end -- class MAIN_WINDOW
```

Figure 7.2 shows the window with the cursor drawn in the top left corner of the client area. This screen capture also includes the custom mouse cursor positioned near the center of the window.

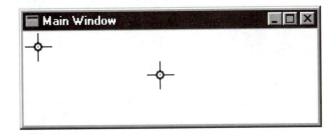

FIGURE 7.2. Cursor example.

Saving and Restoring a Cursor

The shape of a cursor may depend on the current state of the application rather than on the underlying window (e.g., the hourglass cursor is typically used whenever an application is busy). The class *WEL_CURSOR* provides the functionality to temporarily save the current shape of the cursor and then restore it at a later time.

```
previous_cursor: WEL_CURSOR
        -- Previously assigned cursor
set
        -- Set the current cursor for the entire application and
        -- save the old one in 'previous_cursor' if there was
        -- one.
    require
        exists: exists
restore_previous
        -- Restore the 'previous_cursor'.
    require
        previous_cursor_not_void: previous_cursor /= void
    ensure
        previous_cursor_void: previous_cursor = void
```

Routine *set* changes the shape of the current application cursor with the instance of *WEL_CURSOR* on which it is called. *restore_previous* changes the current shape of the application cursor back to the previous one and sets *previous_cursor* to *Void*. It requires that *set* was called first.

Null Cursors

Null cursors are the equivalent of null icons for mouse pointers. They refer to an empty Windows structure (*item* is always equal to *default_pointer*). The class *WEL_NULL_CURSOR* inherits from *WEL_CURSOR* and should be used when the cursor is to be drawn manually using *draw_cursor* from *WEL_DC*. As with null icons, null cursors are rarely used.

Strings

One can also define string tables in resource scripts. The main advantage of using the resource script to define strings instead of coding them directly in the sources is the ability to modify them without having to recompile the whole system (only a relink is needed). Using predefined strings is also more efficient than using text files loaded at runtime.

Defining String Resources

The syntax used to declare a string table follows:

```
STRINGTABLE
BEGIN
    stringID string
    . . .
END
```

where **STRINGTABLE** is the resource definition keyword used to declare string tables. **BEGIN** and **END** delimit the string list and each string is identified with a 16-bit integer: *stringID*. string may be a 4,097 character string and it should be written on one line with the character sequence \012 used to insert new lines.

Creating a String from a Resource

There is no specific class in WEL related to string tables. Instead, the feature *resource_string_id* from *WEL_WINDOWS_ROUTINES* should be used to load a string according to its *stringID* identifier.

```
resource_string_id (an_id: INTEGER): STRING
        -- String identified by 'an_id' in the resource file.
    ensure
        result_not_void: Result /= Void
```

The class *WEL_WINDOW_ROUTINES* is typically inherited so that its facilities are available in the descendant. Example 7.4 uses the inherited feature *resource_string_id* to retrieve three strings from a resource table and display them in the client area of the window. Figure 7.3 shows the resulting window.

Example 7.4 String Resource Example, MAIN_WINDOW Class (resources\strings)

```
class MAIN_WINDOW
inherit
    WEL_FRAME_WINDOW
        redefine
            on_paint
        end
    APPLICATION_IDS
        export
            {NONE} all
```

```
            end
        WEL_WINDOWS_ROUTINES
            export
                {NONE} all
            end
creation
    make
feature

    make is
            -- Initialize the main window
        do
            make_top ("Main Window")
        end

feature -- Events

    on_paint (paint_dc: WEL_PAINT_DC; invalid_rect: WEL_RECT) is
            -- Paint the cursor on the client area
        do
            paint_dc.text_out (0, 0, resource_string_id
                (Ids_string1_constant))
            paint_dc.text_out (0, 20, resource_string_id
                (Ids_string2_constant))
            paint_dc.text_out (0, 40, resource_string_id
                (Ids_string3_constant))
        end

end -- class MAIN_WINDOW
```

Bitmaps

Bitmaps are arrays of bits describing a picture that can be drawn on devices such as a screen or a printer. Bitmaps can have different color depths, ranging from monochrome (one bit per pixel) to True Color (24 or 32 bits per pixel).

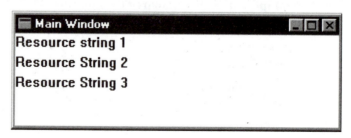

FIGURE 7.3. String resource example.

The appearance of a bitmap depends on the device on which it is drawn. In particular, the number of available colors can differ between devices. Windows introduces the notion of device-independent bitmap (DIB) to allow the developer to handle bitmaps independently of any device. When the bitmap is rendered, Windows automatically maps the bitmap to the device. The class *WEL_BITMAP* corresponds to a device-dependent bitmap (DDB), while the class *WEL_DIB* wraps the DIB structure.

Defining Bitmap Resources

Bitmaps are defined in resource scripts as follows:

```
nameID BITMAP "eiffel.bmp"
```

where *nameID* is the identifier of the bitmap, *BITMAP* the resource script keyword used to declare a bitmap, and *"eiffel.bmp"* the name of the bitmap file.

Creating Bitmaps in Eiffel

The standard way of initializing a bitmap from a resource is to use the creation routine *make_by_id* from the class *WEL_BITMAP*. The routine is passed the bitmap integer identifier as its argument. If the identifier is a unique name, then the creation routine *make_by_name* should be used instead. In both cases, the DDB loaded in memory is compatible with the display, which implies that it can be rendered only on the current screen.

There are two other ways of creating a bitmap—from a DIB to target a specific device, or from a bitmap description. The first possibility is used to convert a DIB into a DDB. The device the bitmap is to be compatible with is specified as the *a_dc* argument of the creation routine.

```
make_by_dib (a_dc: WEL_DC; dib: WEL_DIB; mode: INTEGER)
        -- Create a WEL_BITMAP from a `dib' in the 'a_dc'
        -- using 'mode'. See class 'WEL_DIB_COLORS_CONSTANTS'
        -- for 'mode' values.
require
    a_dc_not_void: a_dc /= void;
    a_dc_exists: a_dc.exists;
    dib_not_void: dib /= void;
    valid_mode: valid_dib_colors_constant (mode)
ensure
    bitmap_created: item /= item.default;
```

The last argument *mode* specifies the color coding used in the DIB. The precondition *valid_mode* enforces its possible values, as listed in Table 7.3.

TABLE 7.3   *Device-Independent Bitmap Color Mode Constants (WEL_DIB_COLORS_CONSTANTS)*

CONSTANT	DESCRIPTION
Dib_rgb_colors	Match the colors in the color table to the logical palette associated with the device context.
Dib_pal_colors	Entries in the color table are treated as word indexes into the logical palette associated with the device context.

The creation routine *make_compatible* initializes a blank DDB compatible with the device and with the size specified as arguments. The width and the height of the bitmap cannot be negative, and the device should be correctly initialized.

```
make_compatible (a_dc: WEL_DC; a_width, a_height: INTEGER)
            -- Initialize current bitmap to be compatible
            -- with 'a_dc' and with 'a_width' as 'width',
            -- 'a_height' as 'height'.
    require
        a_dc_not_void: a_dc /= void;
        a_dc_exists: a_dc.exists;
        positive_width: a_width >= 0;
        positive_height: a_height >= 0
    ensure
        bitmap_created: item /= default_pointer
```

The last creation routine uses an instance of *WEL_LOG_BITMAP* as its argument. This data structure includes all the information required to create a DDB without having to specify the device. The developer specifies the characteristics of the bitmap instead of Windows extracting them from a device.

```
make_indirect (a_log_bitmap: WEL_LOG_BITMAP)
            -- Make a bitmap using 'a_log_bitmap'.
    require
        a_log_bitmap_not_void: a_log_bitmap /= void
        a_log_bitmap_exists: a_log_bitmap.exists
    ensure
        bitmap_created: item /= default_pointer
```

THE H2E UTILITY

H2E is part of the standard delivery of ISE Eiffel on Windows. This utility converts integer constants defined in header or resource files into Eiffel. Any line of the form

```
#define my_constant 1
```

will be converted into the corresponding Eiffel declaration

```
My_constant: INTEGER is 1
```

As many resources are associated with constants, this utility helps prevent constant mismatches between Eiffel and the C declaration.

H2E can be launched from the start menu of Windows (Programs $\rightarrow$ Eiffel x.x $\rightarrow$ h2e) and will present the user with the dialog shown in Figure 7.4. The first line in the H2E dialog specifies the path of the file to be converted (either a header or a resource file), and the second line contains the path to the generated file. Finally, the last field contains the generated class name.

When all these fields are filled, the *Translate* button can be clicked to generate the Eiffel class. It is possible to convert multiple files in one session by following the same steps. When the session is over, a click on *Close* terminates the application.

The sources of H2E are available as an example of a WEL application in the *extra* directory of the WEL delivery.

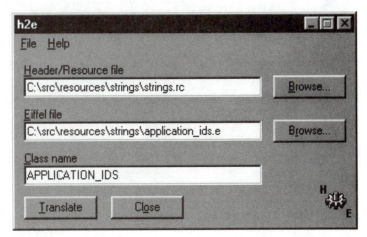

FIGURE 7.4. Using H2E.

RESOURCE BENCH

Resource Bench is a more powerful version of H2E. Not only does it convert constants into Eiffel, it also translates resources defined in a resource script into appropriate Eiffel code.

Resource Bench can be launched in the same way as H2E (Programs → Eiffel x.x → Resource Bench). The first step is to choose the resource script to be converted. Resource Bench then analyzes the script and displays the different resources under a tree view, as shown in Figure 7.5. Icons, cursors, and bitmaps can be displayed by simply clicking on their names.

The only resources that require the generation of Eiffel code are dialog templates. The generation may be customized using the right panel of Resource Bench, as shown in Figure 7.6.

The generated dialog inherits from the type corresponding to the selected radio button. If the dialog is to be modal, then it should inherit from *WEL_MODAL_DIALOG*. If it has to be modeless, then it should inherit from *WEL_MODELESS_DIALOG*. If it is the main window of the application, then it should inherit from *WEL_MAIN_DIALOG*. (See Chapter 9 for more detail about dialog types.)

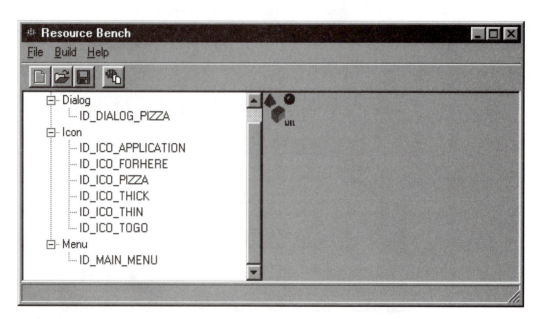

FIGURE 7.5. Using Resource Bench.

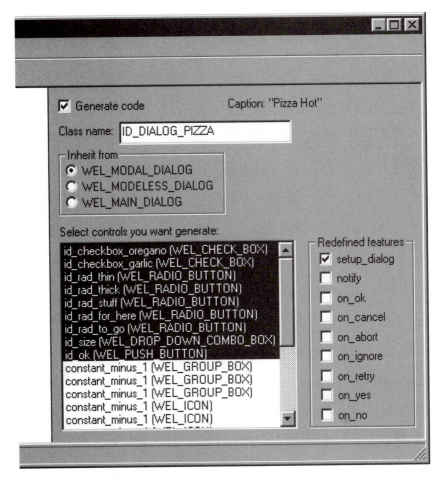

FIGURE 7.6. Generating Dialogs with Resource Bench.

The generated class includes the declaration and the initialization of the highlighted controls. The controls that are not highlighted still appear when the dialog box is activated, the difference being that they cannot be accessible from the Eiffel code. They usually include static texts and group boxes for which there is no associated logic.

Finally, the features that are checked in the *Redefined features* box will be generated with a skeleton implementation that does nothing. They should be edited to perform desired tasks. For example, if you want to initialize a text field to a certain value when the dialog is activated, you should check the *setup_dialog* box and then edit the generated code to perform the correct initialization.

Resource Bench generates one class per dialog template (given that the check boxes named *Generate code* are all checked) plus an additional class for the constants: *APPLICATION_IDS*. The content of this class is similar to what H2E would have generated on the same resource script.

SUMMARY

Using resources is not compulsory when developing a WEL application. For example, null icons and null cursors can be used to draw icons and cursors manually. Menus as well as dialogs can be created on the fly, and accelerator logic can be hand-coded. However, such burden can add unnecessary complexity to a system. Also, tools such as Microsoft Visual Studio or Borland Visual Resource Builder can be used to quickly build the resources for an application. Tools such as Resource Bench can then translate the generated resource script into Eiffel.

Resources can also be used to quickly modify the appearance of an application without having to recompile it entirely. Resources are typically a part of any serious WEL application development.

MENUS

INTRODUCING MENUS

An application generally needs to provide a simple and convenient way for users to select its functions. This is particularly important when your application provides more than a handful of operations. A menu is one of the most common ways of providing access to application features.

A menu, either in bar format at the top of the window or in track format, provides a hierarchical set of categorized menu items. A menu item activates a command or displays a popup submenu of additional menu items when chosen.

Menu

Class *WEL_MENU* provides an encapsulation of the Windows menu resources. *WEL_MENU* can be used to create and manipulate menu bars, popup menus, and track menus, and can represent new menu objects created in your applications or menus stored as resources.

Creating a Menu

When creating a new menu, you first need to create an empty menu structure by calling *make* on class *WEL_MENU*. *make* initializes the menu structure and provides you with a menu object that you can use. Once the menu object has been initialized, you can add popup menus and/or menu items as needed. See "Adding Menu Items to a Menu" later in this chapter. Creating a menu in this way provides the most flexible approach and is typically used when you need menus that change dynamically or menus that are created on the fly, depending on application state.

```
make

make_by_id (id: INTEGER)
        -- (from WEL_RESOURCE)
    require -- from WEL_RESOURCE
        valid_id: id > 0
    ensure -- from WEL_RESOURCE
        not_shared: not shared

make_by_name (name: STRING)
        -- (from WEL_RESOURCE)
    require -- from WEL_RESOURCE
        name_not_void: name /= void;
        name_not_empty: not name.empty
    ensure -- from WEL_RESOURCE
        not_shared: not shared

make_track
```

Finally, you can create a menu that tracks the position of the mouse, known as a *track menu,* by calling *make_track.* This type of menu is typically used for context-sensitive menus activated by a right mouse click.

Creating a Menu from a Resource

The most common way to create a complicated menu is to use a resource and create the *WEL_MENU* instance by calling *make_by_id.* Many development environments come with tools for building menu resources. The menu bar we constructed has two pull-down menus, File and Edit. Each of the menus has a number of menu items. For instance, the Edit menu has nine menu items that the user will be able to select from.

Once you have constructed a menu bar and associated appropriate identifiers to the menu and to all of its menu items, you can create the necessary identifier constant class using the Resource Bench or H2E utilities (see "Resource Bench" and "The H2E Utility" in Chapter 7, "Resources").

Example 8.1 shows an *APPLICATION_IDS* class generated by Resource Bench for the menu bar described above. Each menu item and the menu bar itself has a unique identifier. The identifiers are used to create and access the

Example 8.1 Menu Bar Example, APPLICATION_IDS Class (menus\bar)

```
class
        APPLICATION_IDS
feature -- Access
        Id_editgotoend_constant: INTEGER is 40008
        Id_editcut_constant: INTEGER is 40002
        Id_editselectall_constant: INTEGER is 40006
        Id_editpaste_constant: INTEGER is 40004
        Id_editunselect_constant: INTEGER is 40010
        Id_editgotostart_constant: INTEGER is 40007
        Id_fileexit_constant: INTEGER is 40001
        Id_editcopy_constant: INTEGER is 40003
        Id_editundo_constant: INTEGER is 40009
        Id_editdelete_constant: INTEGER is 40005
        Id_mainmenu_constant: INTEGER is 101
end -- class APPLICATION_IDS
```

menu items and to identify a menu item selected by the user in a menu command event.

To use a menu bar, we need to attach it to a composite window using the *set_menu* routine of *WEL_COMPOSITE_WINDOW*. Example 8.2 uses a once function to initialize the menu bar via a resource and to pass this result to the *set_menu* command. That's all there is to it. The frame window now has a menu bar attached to the top of window. Windows automatically reduces the height of the client area so that any other controls attached to the client area are not obscured by the menu bar and sends notification events for menu item activation and selection.

To receive notification of menu bar command events (for instance, the selection of a menu item by the user) you need to redefine the *on_menu_command* message hook defined in *WEL_COMPOSITE_WINDOW*. This message hook receives the menu item identifier (as defined in *APPLICATION_IDS*) to uniquely identify the menu item that was selected. You can inspect this value to determine what course of action needs to take place. In Example 8.2, *on_menu_command* shows a message box with the text of the selected menu item. The routine also checks to see if the Exit menu item *(Idm_fileexit_constant)* has been selected and exits the application if so.

Example 8.2 Menu Bar Example, MAIN_WINDOW Class (menus\bar)

```
class MAIN_WINDOW
inherit
      WEL_FRAME_WINDOW
            redefine
```

```
                    on_menu_command
            end
        APPLICATION_IDS
            export
                {NONE} all
            end
creation
    make
feature
    make is
            -- Initialize the main window
        do
            make_top ("Main Window")
            -- add the menu and controls to the window
            set_menu (main_menu)
            resize (360, 100)
        end
    on_menu_command (menu_id: INTEGER) is
            -- Check for a menu command
        do
            show_message (main_menu.id_string (menu_id))
            inspect menu_id
            when Id_fileexit_constant then
                destroy
            else
                -- ignore
            end
        end
feature {NONE} -- Implementation
    main_menu: WEL_MENU is
            -- Main menu created from a menu resource
        once
            create Result.make_by_id (Id_mainmenu_constant)
        end
    show_message (message: STRING) is
            -- Show an information message box with 'message'.
        require
            valid_message: message /= Void
        do
            popup_message_box.information_message_box (Current,
                message, "Menu Item Selected")
        end
    popup_message_box: WEL_MSG_BOX is
            -- Message box
        once
            create Result.make
        end
end -- class MAIN_WINDOW
```

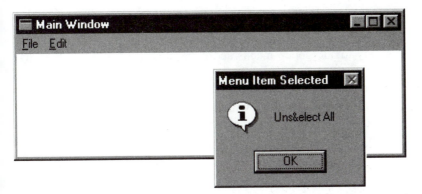

FIGURE 8.1. Menu bar example.

Figure 8.1 shows the output of this example with the dialog showing that the user selected the Unselect All menu item of the Edit pull-down menu.

Accessing a Popup Menu from a Menu

Both a popup menu and a menu bar are represented by the *WEL_MENU* class. A menu's submenus are accessible via the feature *popup_menu,* which takes an *INTEGER* parameter specifying the zero-based position of the popup menu required. That is, passing zero retrieves the first popup menu, passing one retrieves the second, and so on.

```
popup_menu (position: INTEGER): WEL_MENU
        -- Popup menu at the zero-based relative 'position'
    require
        exists: exists;
        position_large_enough: position >= 0;
        position_small_enough: position < count;
        popup_exists: popup_exists (position)
    ensure
        result_not_void: Result /= void
```

Before you call *popup_menu,* you can test to see if the popup menu you require actually exists. The *popup_exists* routine takes the same zero-based parameter and returns *True* if a popup menu exists at that location, or *False* if not.

```
popup_exists (position: INTEGER): BOOLEAN
        -- Does a popup menu exists at the zero-based position?
    require
        exists: exists;
        positive_position: position >= 0
```

Adding Menu Items to a Menu

When constructing a menu by hand (i.e., without the use of a resource), you need the ability to add popup menus and menu items to the menu. You may also need to dynamically add menu items to an existing menu. For instance, if your application requires a window menu that lists all the currently open windows in your application, then you will need to dynamically add (and remove) menu items, depending on how many windows are open at any one time.

The easiest way to add menu items is to use the append routines *append_bitmap, append_popup, append_separator,* and *append_string.* Each appends a particular type of menu element to the end of the menu. *append_string* and *append_separator* are the most commonly used and provide the ability to add a standard menu item (represented by a *STRING*) and a menu item separator to an existing menu. Routine *append_bitmap* allows you to add a bitmap image as a menu item rather than as a string, and routine *append_popup* provides the ability to add another menu as a submenu to an existing menu.

```
append_bitmap (bitmap: WEL_BITMAP; an_id: INTEGER)
        -- Append 'bitmap' with the identifier 'an_id' to the
        -- menu.
    require
        exists: exists;
        bitmap_not_void: bitmap /= void;
        bitmap_exists: bitmap.exists;
        positive_id: an_id > 0;
        item_not_exists: not item_exists (an_id)
    ensure
        new_count: count = old count + 1;
        item_exists: item_exists (an_id)

append_popup (a_menu: WEL_MENU; a_title: STRING)
        -- Append a popup menu 'a_menu' with 'a_title' to the
        -- current menu.
        -- 'a_menu' must be shared since Windows will
        -- destroy it automatically with 'Current'.
    require
        exists: exists;
        a_menu_not_void: a_menu /= void;
        a_menu_exists: a_menu.exists;
        a_title_not_void: a_title /= void
    ensure
        new_count: count = old count + 1

append_separator
        -- Append a separator to the current menu.
    require
        exists: exists
```

```
    ensure
        new_count: count = old count + 1

append_string (a_string: STRING; an_id: INTEGER)
        -- Append 'a_string' with the identifier 'an_id' to the
        -- menu.
    require
        exists: exists;
        a_string_not_void: a_string /= void;
        positive_id: an_id > 0;
        item_not_exists: not item_exists (an_id)
    ensure
        new_count: count = old count + 1;
        item_exists: item_exists (an_id);
        string_set: id_string (an_id).is_equal (a_string)
```

Example 8.3 uses code, rather than a resource, to build the same menu as shown in Example 8.2. The once function appends two popups, *file_menu* and *edit_menu*, to a new menu. Similarly, *file_menu* and *edit_menu* are defined as once functions and use *append_string* (and in some cases, *append_separator*) to build the required menus. The remaining code has not changed from the previous example.

Example 8.3 Menu Bar Code Example, MAIN_WINDOW Class (menus\codebar)

```
class MAIN_WINDOW
inherit
    WEL_FRAME_WINDOW
        redefine
            on_menu_command
        end
    APPLICATION_IDS
        export
            {NONE} all
        end
creation
    make
feature
    make is
            -- Initialize the main window
        do
            make_top ("Main Window")
            -- add the menu and controls to the window
            set_menu (main_menu)
            resize (360, 100)
        end
    on_menu_command (menu_id: INTEGER) is
```

```
                    -- Check for a menu command
            do
                show_message (main_menu.id_string (menu_id))
                inspect menu_id
                when Id_fileexit_constant then
                    destroy
                else
                    -- ignore
                end
            end
feature {NONE} -- Implementation
        main_menu: WEL_MENU is
                -- Main menu created from a menu resource
            once
                create Result.make
                Result.append_popup (file_menu, "&File")
                Result.append_popup (edit_menu, "&Edit")
            end
        file_menu: WEL_MENU is
                -- File menu
            once
                create Result.make
                Result.append_string ("E&xit", Id_fileexit_constant)
            end
        edit_menu: WEL_MENU is
                -- Edit menu
            once
                create Result.make
                Result.append_string ("&Undo", Id_editundo_constant)
                Result.append_separator
                Result.append_string ("Cu&t", Id_editcut_constant)
                Result.append_string ("&Copy", Id_editcopy_constant)
                Result.append_string ("&Paste", Id_editpaste_constant)
                Result.append_string ("&Delete", Id_editdelete_constant)
                Result.append_separator
                Result.append_string ("Select A&ll",
                    Id_editselectall_constant)
                Result.append_string ("Uns&elect All",
                    Id_editunselect_constant)
                Result.append_separator
                Result.append_string ("Go to &Start",
                    Id_editgotostart_constant)
                Result.append_string ("Go to E&nd", Id_editgoto-
                    end_constant)
            end
        show_message (message: STRING) is
                -- Show an information message box with 'message'.
            require
                valid_message: message /= Void
            do
                popup_message_box.information_message_box (Current,
```

```
                    message, "Menu Item Selected")
          end
      popup_message_box: WEL_MSG_BOX is
              -- Message box
          once
              create Result.make
          end
  end -- class MAIN_WINDOW
```

Inserting Menu Items in a Menu

Features *insert_bitmap, insert_popup, insert_separator,* and *insert_string* insert a menu item at a specified position (indicated by the *a_position* parameter). Each routine requires that the position already exist and that the item being added (as identified by *an_id*) is not already present in the menu. This ensures that you cannot have more than one menu item with the same identifier.

```
insert_bitmap (bitmap: WEL_BITMAP; a_position, an_id: INTEGER)
          -- Insert 'bitmap' at zero-based 'a_position' with
          -- `an_id'.
      require
          exists: exists;
          a_position_large_enough: a_position >= 0;
          a_position_small_enough: a_position <= count;
          bitmap_not_void: bitmap /= void;
          bitmap_exists: bitmap.exists;
          positive_id: an_id > 0;
          item_not_exists: not item_exists (an_id)
      ensure
          new_count: count = old count + 1

insert_popup (a_menu: WEL_MENU; a_position: INTEGER; a_title:
STRING)
          -- Insert a popup menu 'a_menu' at zero-based 'a_position'
          -- with 'a_title'.
      require
          exists: exists;
          a_menu_not_void: a_menu /= void;
          a_menu_exists: a_menu.exists;
          a_title_not_void: a_title /= void;
          a_position_large_enough: a_position >= 0;
          a_position_small_enough: a_position <= count
```

```
        ensure
                new_count: count = old count + 1;
                popup_menu_set: popup_menu (a_position).item = a_menu.item

insert_separator (a_position: INTEGER)
                -- Insert a separator at zero-based 'a_position'.
        require
                exists: exists;
                a_position_large_enough: a_position >= 0;
                a_position_small_enough: a_position <= count
        ensure
                new_count: count = old count + 1

insert_string (a_string: STRING; a_position, an_id: INTEGER)
                -- Insert 'a_string' at zero-based 'a_position' with
                -- 'an_id'.
        require
                exists: exists;
                a_position_large_enough: a_position >= 0;
                a_position_small_enough: a_position <= count;
                a_string_not_void: a_string /= void;
                positive_id: an_id > 0;
                item_not_exists: not item_exists (an_id)
        ensure
                new_count: count = old count + 1;
                string_set: id_string (an_id).is_equal (a_string)
```

Modifying Existing Menu Items in a Menu

Modifying the text of an existing menu item can be performed by using *modify_string*. This routine is useful if you need to change the text of a menu item from *Close* to *Close & Save*, depending on the state of your application. The menu item to change is identified by its command identifier.

```
modify_string (a_string: STRING; an_id: INTEGER)
                -- Modify the menu title identified by 'an_id' to
                -- 'a_string'.
        require
                exists: exists;
                a_string_not_void: a_string /= void;
                positive_id: an_id > 0;
                item_exists: item_exists (an_id)
        ensure
                string_set: id_string (an_id).is_equal (a_string)
```

Removing Menu Items from a Menu

A menu item can be removed from a menu by calling *delete_item*, passing the menu item's identifier. This routine removes the menu item from the menu in which it is held. All menu items below the removed item are repositioned.

If you know the position of a menu item to be removed, but don't necessarily know its identifier, then you can use *delete_position* and specify the zero-based menu item position.

```
delete_item (an_id: INTEGER)
        -- Delete 'an_id' from the menu.
    require
        exists: exists;
        positive_id: an_id > 0;
        item_exists: item_exists (an_id)
    ensure
        new_count: count = old count - 1;
        item_not_exists: not item_exists (an_id)

delete_position (position: INTEGER)
        -- Delete the item at zero-based 'position'.
    require
        exists: exists;
        position_large_enough: position >= 0;
        position_small_enough: position < count
    ensure
        new_count: count = old count - 1
```

Accessing Menu Items in a Menu

The number of menu items (and separators) in a menu can be determined by calling *count*. Feature *count* returns the total number of elements in the menu.

```
count: INTEGER
        -- Number of items
    require
        exists: exists
    ensure
        positive_result: Result >= 0
```

The text displayed for a menu item can be retrieved using *id_string*, passing the command identifier of a menu item. If you need to check whether a particular menu item exists, call *item_exists*, passing the command identifier.

Also, if you have inadvertently lost the menu identifier for a menu, you can retrieve it by calling *position_to_item_id* with the zero-based position of a menu item. The menu identifier will be returned for the menu item at that position.

```
id_string (an_id: INTEGER): STRING
              -- String associated with 'an_id'
      require
              exists: exists;
              positive_id: an_id > 0;
              item_exists: item_exists (an_id)
      ensure
              result_not_void: Result /= void

item_exists (an_id: INTEGER): BOOLEAN
              -- Does 'an_id' exist in the menu?
      require
              exists: exists;
              positive_id: an_id > 0

position_to_item_id (position: INTEGER): INTEGER
              -- Retrieve the menu item identifier of a menu item at
              -- the zero-based 'position'.
              -- Return 0 if the item at the zero-based
              -- 'position' is a separator or a pop-up menu.
      require
              exists: exists;
              position_large_enough: position >= 0;
              position_small_enough: position < count
```

Enabling Menu Items in a Menu

Many applications require different menu items to be enabled and disabled at different times. For example, you may want to enable a Copy menu item only when text has been selected in a document, and similarly, only enable a Paste menu item when the clipboard has some content.

Enabling and disabling menu items can be performed by specifying a menu identifier or position, using the *enable_item, enable_position, disable_item*, and *disable_position* routines.

```
enable_item (an_id: INTEGER)
        -- Enable the item idenfied by 'an_id'.
    require
        exists: exists;
        positive_id: an_id > 0;
        item_exists: item_exists (an_id)
    ensure
        item_enabled: item_enabled (an_id)

enable_position (position: INTEGER)
```

```
        -- Enable the item at zero-based 'position'.
    require
        exists: exists;
        position_large_enough: position >= 0;
        position_small_enough: position < count
    ensure
        position_enabled: position_enabled (position)

disable_item (an_id: INTEGER)
        -- Disable the item identified by 'an_id'.
    require
        exists: exists;
        positive_id: an_id > 0;
        item_exists: item_exists (an_id)
    ensure
        item_disabled: not item_enabled (an_id)

disable_position (position: INTEGER)
        -- Disable the item at zero-based 'position'.
    require
        exists: exists;
        position_large_enough: position >= 0;
        position_small_enough: position < count
    ensure
        position_disabled: not position_enabled (position)
```

You can check the current enabled status of a menu item by calling *item_enabled* or *position_enabled*.

```
item_enabled (an_id: INTEGER): BOOLEAN
        -- Is the item idenfied by 'an_id' enabled?
    require
        exists: exists;
        positive_id: an_id > 0;
        item_exists: item_exists (an_id)

position_enabled (position: INTEGER): BOOLEAN
        -- Is the item at zero-based 'position' enabled?
    require
        exists: exists;
        position_large_enough: position >= 0;
        position_small_enough: position < count
```

Checking Menu Items in a Menu

A menu item can behave like a check box or a radio box, whereby a single toggle selection or group toggle selection can be made using the menu item. When a menu is checked, a check mark appears to the left of the menu text. Typically, this is a small tick symbol. When unchecked, the check mark disappears. However, unlike a radio box control, a menu item used in this fashion does not manage the selection of one mutually exclusive item at a time. You must implement code that will uncheck corresponding menu items in the group.

To check or uncheck a menu item, you need to pass the identifier of the item to either *check_item* or *uncheck_item*. An example of using check marks with menus can be found in the Directory Tree Analyzer example at the end of this chapter.

```
check_item (an_id: INTEGER)
        -- Put a check mark for the item identified by 'an_id'.
    require
        exists: exists;
        positive_id: an_id > 0;
        item_exists: item_exists (an_id)
    ensure
        item_checked: item_checked (an_id)

uncheck_item (an_id: INTEGER)
        -- Remove the check mark for the item identified
        -- by 'an_id'.
    require
        exists: exists;
        positive_id: an_id > 0;
        item_exists: item_exists (an_id)
    ensure
        item_unchecked: not item_checked (an_id)
```

To determine the current checked status of a menu item, call *item_checked*, passing the identifier of the item. *item_checked* returns *True* if the item is checked, *False* otherwise.

```
item_checked (an_id: INTEGER): BOOLEAN
        -- Is the item idenfied by 'an_id' checked?
    require
        exists: exists;
        positive_id: an_id > 0;
        item_exists: item_exists (an_id)
```

Highlighting Menu Items in a Menu

A menu item can be highlighted and unhighlighted programmatically, using *hilite_menu_item* and *unhilite_menu_item*. Both of these routines require an additional parameter representing the parent window of the menu to change.

```
hilite_menu_item (window: WEL_COMPOSITE_WINDOW; an_id: INTEGER)
              -- Hilite the item identified by 'an_id' in the
              -- 'window''s menu.
      require
            exists: exists;
            window_not_void: window /= void;
            window_exists: window.exists;
            positive_id: an_id > 0;
            item_exists: item_exists (an_id)
unhilite_menu_item (window: WEL_COMPOSITE_WINDOW; an_id: INTEGER)
              -- unhilite the item identified by 'an_id' in the
              -- 'window's menu.
      require
            exists: exists;
            window_not_void: window /= void;
            window_exists: window.exists;
            positive_id: an_id > 0;
            item_exists: item_exists (an_id)
```

Showing a Track Menu

The *show_track* operation can be used to show a shortcut menu at a particular location and have Windows track the selection of menu items on the menu. The menu appears at the location specified by parameters *x* and *y*, and all menu command events are sent to *window*.

```
show_track (x, y: INTEGER; window: WEL_COMPOSITE_WINDOW)
              — Show a track popup menu at the 'x' and 'y' absolute
              — position. 'window' will receive the selection in
              — 'on_menu_command'.
      require
            exists: exists;
            not_empty: count > 0;
            window_not_void: window /= void;
            window_exists: window.exists

show_track_with_option (x, y: INTEGER; window: WEL_COMPOSITE_WIN-
      DOW; option: INTEGER; rect: WEL_RECT)
              -- Show a track popup menu with 'option' at
              -- the 'x' and 'y' absolute position.
              -- 'window' will receive the selection in
              -- 'on_menu_command'.
              -- 'rect' specifies the portion of the screen
              -- in which the user can select without
              -- dismissing the popup menu. If this parameter
              -- is Void the popup menu is dismissed if the
              -- user clicks outside the popup menu
```

```
require
    exists: exists;
    not_empty: count > 0;
    window_not_void: window /= void;
    window_exists: window.exists
```

Operation *show_track* displays a shortcut menu with the default options of *Tpm_leftbutton*. You can display a shortcut menu with different options by calling *show_track_with_option*. The possible values for *option* are listed in Table 8.1. Operation *show_track_with_option* also takes a rectangle that specifies the portion of the screen in which the user can select a menu item without dismissing the menu. If you pass *Void* for the *rect* parameter, then the menu will be dismissed whenever the user clicks outside the popup menu's border.

Example 8.3 can be modified to use a shortcut menu rather than a menu bar. Three changes need to be made. First, we no longer need to call *set_menu* in the creation procedure of the *MAIN_WINDOW*. Second, we need to capture an event that will activate the menu. In this case, we use a right-button-up notification event. A redefinition of *on_right_button_up* calls *show_track* to display the shortcut menu at the current cursor position. When the user clicks the right mouse button, the menu is displayed and notification of the user selecting a menu item is sent to the *MAIN_WINDOW*. Finally, we need to initialize the menu by calling *make_track* rather than *make* in the *main_menu* once function. Example 8.4 highlights the modified code.

TABLE 8.1   *Track Popup Menu Option Constants (WEL_TPM_CONSTANTS)*

CONSTANT	DESCRIPTION
Tpm_centeralign	The shortcut menu is centered horizontally relative to the coordinate specified by the *x* parameter.
Tpm_leftalign	The shortcut menu is positioned so that its left side is aligned with the coordinate specified by the *x* parameter.
Tpm_leftbutton	The shortcut menu tracks the left mouse button.
Tpm_rightalign	The shortcut menu is positioned so that its right side is aligned with the coordinate specified by the *x* parameter.
Tpm_rightbutton	The shortcut menu tracks the right mouse button.

Example 8.4 Track Menu Example (menus\track)

```
class MAIN_WINDOW
inherit
    WEL_FRAME_WINDOW
        redefine
            on_menu_command,
            on_right_button_up
        end
    APPLICATION_IDS
        export
            {NONE} all
        end
creation
    make
feature
    make is
            -- Initialize the main window
        do
            make_top ("Main Window")
            resize (360, 100)
        end
    on_menu_command (menu_id: INTEGER) is
            -- Check for a menu command
        do
            show_message (main_menu.id_string (menu_id))
            inspect menu_id
            when Id_fileexit_constant then
                destroy
            else
                -- ignore
            end
        end
    on_right_button_up (keys, x_pos, y_pos: INTEGER) is
            -- Show track menu
        local
            point: WEL_POINT
        do
            create point.make (x_pos, y_pos)
            point.client_to_screen (Current)
            main_menu.show_track (point.x, point.y, Current)
        end
feature {NONE} -- Implementation
    main_menu: WEL_MENU is
            -- Main menu created from a menu resource
        once
            create Result.make_track
            Result.append_popup (file_menu, "&File")
            Result.append_popup (edit_menu, "&Edit")
        end
    file_menu: WEL_MENU is
            -- File menu
```

```
        once
            -- code as before
        end
    edit_menu: WEL_MENU is
            -- Edit menu
        once
            -- code as before
        end
    show_message (message: STRING) is
            -- Show an information message box with 'message'.
        require
            valid_message: message /= Void
        do
            popup_message_box.information_message_box (Current,
                message, "Menu Item Selected")
        end
    popup_message_box: WEL_MSG_BOX is
            -- Message box
        once
            create Result.make
        end
end -- class MAIN_WINDOW
```

SUMMARY

The WEL library provides support for menus in a single class, *WEL_MENU*. This class can be used to manipulate menus created via a resource or created by hand. A *WEL_MENU* can be attached to a composite window as a menu bar by calling *set_menu* of *WEL_COMPOSITE_WINDOW*. Or a menu can be used as a shortcut menu by calling *make_track* and *show_track* to initialize the menu and show it at a particular location.

Menus provide a simple way to present a large number of commands to the user. You can group similar commands in popup menus and provide a hierarchy of menus to provide access to an application's complete functionality. The Windows style guidelines recommend that every application has (at a minimum) a File, Edit, and Help menu. Therefore, the *WEL_MENU* class is commonly used in Windows applications.menus

DIRECTORY TREE ANALYZER

IMPLEMENTING THE MENUS

A single menu is used in the Directory Tree Analyzer application. The menu is attached to the main window as a menu bar. It is defined using a resource and initialized in the *MAIN_WINDOW's* creation procedure.

The Menu Bar

Class *MENU_BAR* is a direct descendant of *WEL_MENU,* and therefore provides standard menu features and behavior. The creation procedure of *MENU_BAR* initializes the menu from a resource, using the identifier *Idr_main_menu_constant* (as defined in class *APPLICATION_IDS*).

Two additional routines are provided that assist in the initialization of the menu items, depending on the application state. The first routine, in Example 8.5, *update* (lines 24–36), takes a *CONTAINER* (an abstract ancestor of *TWO_WAY_SORTED_LIST*) as a parameter. The *MAIN_WINDOW* uses this routine to enable and disable particular menu items, depending on whether a directory has been parsed or not. That is, if the *CONTAINER* reference is *Void,* then it implies that no directory information has been gathered and therefore no directory has been parsed.

The second routine, *clear_sort_menus* (lines 38–47), is used by *MAIN_WINDOW* whenever the sort criterion is changed so that the correct sort menu item can be checked—all other sort menu items are unchecked first.

Example 8.5 MENU_BAR Class for the Directory Tree Analyzer

```
1    class MENU_BAR
2
3    inherit
4            WEL_MENU
5                    rename
6                            make as menu_make
7                    end;
8            APPLICATION_IDS
9                    export
10                           {NONE} all
11                   end
12   create
13           make
```

```
14   feature
15
16        make is
17                         -- Initialization
18                    do
19                         make_by_id (idr_main_menu_constant)
20                    end;
21
22   feature -- make
23
24        update (directory_infos: CONTAINER [ANY]) is
25                         -- Element change
26                    require
27                         menu_exists: exists
28                    do
29                         if directory_infos = void then
30                              disable_item (idm_file_print_constant)
31                              disable_item (idm_edit_find_constant)
32                         else
33                              enable_item (idm_file_print_constant)
34                              enable_item (idm_edit_find_constant)
35                         end
36                    end;
37
38        clear_sort_menus is
39                         -- update
40                    require
41                         valid_menu: exists
42                    do
43                         uncheck_item (idm_sort_name_constant)
44                         uncheck_item (idm_sort_files_constant)
45                         uncheck_item (idm_sort_directories_constant)
46                         uncheck_item (idm_sort_usage_constant)
47                    end;
48
49   end -- class MENU_BAR
```

The *MAIN_WINDOW* class responds to menu commands via the *on_menu_command* message hook. The code for *on_menu_command* is as follows:

```
on_menu_command (menu_id: INTEGER) is
             -- Perform menu command actions
        do
             inspect menu_id
             when Idm_file_open_constant then
                  parse_directory
             when Idm_file_exit_constant then
```

```
                    destroy
            when Idm_edit_preferences_constant then
                    configure_preferences
            when Idm_edit_find_constant then
                    find_text
            when Idm_file_print_constant then
                    print_info
            when Idm_page_setup_constant then
                    page_setup
            when Idm_about_constant then
                    about
            when Idm_sort_name_constant then
                    sort_by_name
            when Idm_sort_files_constant then
                    sort_by_files
            when Idm_sort_directories_constant then
                    sort_by_directories
            when Idm_sort_usage_constant then
                    sort_by_usage
            when Idm_sort_reverse_constant then
                    toggle_reverse_sort
                    if directory_infos /= Void then
                            update_for_sort
                    end
            else
                    -- ignore
            end
        end
```

The *menu_id* is examined and the appropriate application function is called. If the menu identifier is unknown, then it is ignored. When we discuss the application's tool bar, you will notice that this routine is reused exactly as is because each tool bar button is defined with the same command identifier (see "Implementing Bar Controls" at the end of Chapter 16, "Bar Controls," if you can't resist jumping ahead).

DIALOGS

INTRODUCING DIALOGS

A dialog box is most often used to collect detailed information from a user. A dialog box is often invoked by a menu item (whose label normally ends with an ellipsis) and is composed of a popup window with a number of child window controls. The dialog box is shown to the user, and the information that the user enters in the control is collected, validated, and acted upon.

The WEL library supports dialog boxes defined as resources. That is, you must first construct the dialog box using a resource builder tool and link it with your application. The dialog boxes behave in the manner described in this chapter.

TYPES OF DIALOG

A dialog box is either modal or modeless. A modal dialog must be explicitly dismissed before the user can interact with another part of the application. A modal dialog box is typically dismissed by clicking its OK or Cancel button. All user input is captured and sent to the dialog.

On the other hand, a modeless dialog box does not need to be dismissed before further application interaction can take place. A modeless dialog box can be shown to the user, and the user can interact with it and the rest of the application. Common examples of modeless dialog boxes include property sheets and text search dialogs.

WEL supports a third type of dialog that is suitable for use as an application's main window. A main window dialog is a type of modeless dialog box that is used as the main (or first visible) window of an application. This form of dialog is useful when you need to construct the main window using a resource editor tool.

The hierarchy of classes used to define dialog boxes is shown in Figure 9.1. Each type of dialog inherits general functionality and behavior from the deferred class *WEL_DIALOG*. The relationship between a modeless dialog and a main window dialog is represented by the inheritance of *WEL_MODELESS_DIALOG* by *WEL_MAIN_DIALOG*.

Abstract Dialog Class

The abstract class *WEL_DIALOG* introduces features used to create dialog boxes and features that implement the general behavior of dialog boxes, including initialization, activation, deactivation, and return of user responses.

Creating a Dialog

When instantiating a dialog box, you must indicate the name or identification number of the dialog template resource. You must also supply a reference to a parent window. The parent window essentially becomes the controlling

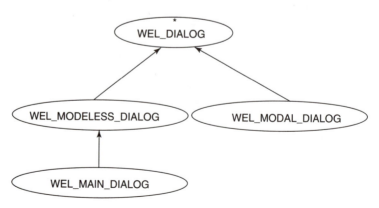

FIGURE 9.1. WEL dialog class hierarchy.

window of the dialog and affects its position on the screen and its z-order—initially, a dialog box is displayed at the center and on top of its parent window.

```
make_by_id (a_parent: WEL_WINDOW; an_id: INTEGER)
        -- Initialize a loadable dialog box identified by
        -- 'an_id' using 'a_parent' as parent.
   require -- from WEL_DIALOG
      parent_exists: a_parent /= void implies a_parent.exists
   ensure -- from WEL_DIALOG
      parent_set: parent = a_parent;

make_by_name (a_parent: WEL_COMPOSITE_WINDOW; a_name: STRING)
        -- Initialize a loadable dialog box identified by
        -- 'a_name' using 'a_parent' as parent.
   require — from WEL_DIALOG
      parent_exists: a_parent /= void implies a_parent.exists;
      name_not_void: a_name /= void;
      name_not_empty: not a_name.empty
   ensure -- from WEL_DIALOG
      parent_set: parent = a_parent;
```

The creation procedures *make_by_id* and *make_by_name instantiate* a dialog box by referencing its dialog resource template using an identifier or name, respectively. In both procedures, the parent must exist for the call to succeed.

Activating a Dialog

The creation procedures of *WEL_DIALOG* do not actually create any underlying Windows dialog structures. This occurs when you call *activate*. The *activate* routine initializes the necessary Windows structures and shows the dialog box. Windows, in turn, sends a *Wm_initdialog* message to the dialog when the dialog is ready. *WEL_DIALOG* captures this message, initializes child controls, and calls *setup_dialog*.

You can call *activate* as many times as you need. Only the underlying Windows dialog structures are reinitialized on each call. Any information you store in the dialog object itself is retained.

```
activate
        -- Activate the dialog box.
        -- Can be called several times.
   require
      parent_exists: parent /= void implies parent.exists;
      not_exists: not exists
```

Initializing a Dialog

The *setup_dialog* routine is called whenever a dialog is activated. You can redefine the default *setup_dialog* routine to perform any dialog initialization you
require. For example, you may want to set default values in the dialog's child
controls, or enable or disable different controls. The examples below show you
how you can store information locally in your dialog classes for use in the
setup_dialog routine.

```
setup_dialog
        -- May be redefined to setup the dialog and its
        -- children.
    require
        exists: exists
```

Accessing the Result of a Dialog

An identifier representing the control used to dismiss a dialog box is stored in
the *result_id* attribute. The value of *result_id* can be one of the constants defined in *WEL_ID_CONSTANTS*, listed in Table 9.1.

```
result_id: INTEGER
        -- Last control id used to close the dialog.
        -- See class WEL_ID_CONSTANTS for the different values.
```

TABLE 9.1 *Dialog Result Identification Constants*
(WEL_ID_CONSTANTS)

CONSTANT	DESCRIPTION
Idabort	"Abort" button was selected.
Idcancel	"Cancel" button was selected.
Idignore	"Ignore" button was selected.
Idok	"OK" button was selected.
Idretry	"Retry" button was selected.
Idyes	"Yes" button was selected.
Idno	"No" button was selected.

Once a dialog box has been dismissed, you can check this attribute to determine which control the user selected. For example, a typical dialog box will contain an OK and a Cancel button. The application may only need to apply the changes made in the dialog box if the user selected OK to close it; otherwise, the changes could be ignored.

A shortcut function also exists that lets you determine if the dialog was closed by the user pressing the OK button—*ok_pushed* returns *True* if the dialog box was dismissed by its OK button.

```
ok_pushed: BOOLEAN
        -- Has the OK button been pushed?
```

Terminating a Dialog

A dialog box is normally terminated when the user selects one of the standard dialog buttons, such as OK or Cancel. You can preempt the termination by calling *terminate* and specifying a result to indicate the type of termination.

```
terminate (a_result: INTEGER)
        -- Terminate the dialog with 'a_result'.
        -- 'result_id' will contain 'a_result'.
```

For example, to simulate a dialog termination by an OK button, you can call

```
terminate(Id_ok)
```

You can also simulate the termination of a dialog box by the Cancel button by calling *destroy,* which calls *terminate* with *Idcancel* as the *result* parameter.

```
destroy
        -- Terminate the dialog.
```

Message Hooks in a Dialog Box

Table 9.2 lists the message hooks that are defined in *WEL_DIALOG.* One of these hooks is called whenever the corresponding dialog button is pressed. You can redefine the message hooks to perform customized processing for button press events.

TABLE 9.2   *Dialog Box Message Hooks*

MESSAGE HOOK	DESCRIPTION
on_abort	"Abort" button was pressed.
on_cancel	"Cancel" button was pressed.
on_ignore	"Ignore" button was pressed.
on_no	"No" button was pressed.
on_ok	"OK" button was pressed.
on_retry	"Retry" button was pressed.
on_yes	"Yes" button was pressed.

On a Button Press Message in a Dialog Box

Each *WEL_DIALOG* message hook has the same signature—they take no parameters and require that the dialog box exists. For instance, the interface for *on_abort* is shown next.

```
on_abort
      -- Button Abort has been pressed.
   require
      exists: exists
```

If you redefine any of the dialog message hooks, make sure you include a call to the precursor implementation to ensure that the standard processing occurs (i.e., that the dialog terminates with the correct result). For example, a redefinition of *on_abort* should look similar to the following code fragment:

```
on_abort
         -- Perform abort operation
      do
         -- perform custom processing
         Precursor
      end
```

MODAL DIALOGS

To demonstrate modal dialogs, we use a small class that represents personal details of a person and a dialog to view and update the attributes of the person. Example 9.1 shows the code for the class *PERSON*. Each *PERSON* instance holds name, gender, address, and country details, and can be initialized via the creation procedure *make*.

Example 9.1 Modal Dialog, PERSON Class (dialogs\modal)

```
class
    PERSON
creation
    make
feature -- Initialization
    make (new_name, new_address, new_country: STRING;
        male: BOOLEAN) is
            -- Initialize a new person with the specified details
        require
            valid_name: new_name /= Void
            valid_address: new_address /= Void
            valid_country: new_country /= Void
        do
            name := new_name
            address := new_address
            country := new_country
            is_male := male
        end
feature -- Access
    name: STRING
    address: STRING
    country: STRING
    is_male: BOOLEAN
feature -- Update
    set_name (new_name: STRING) is
        require
            valid_name: new_name /= Void
        do
            name := new_name
        ensure
            name_set: name = new_name
        end
    set_address (new_address: STRING) is
        require
            valid_address: new_address /= Void
        do
            address := new_address
        ensure
            address_set: address = new_address
        end
    set_country (new_country: STRING) is
        require
            valid_country: new_country /= Void
        do
            country := new_country
        ensure
            country_set: country = new_country
        end
    set_gender (male: BOOLEAN) is
        do
            is_male := male
        ensure
```

```
        gender_set: is_male = male
    end
end -- class PERSON
```

The dialog resource used in this example was created using a resource editor. The dialog contains three text fields for the name, address, and country attributes, two radio buttons for the gender, and OK and Cancel buttons. Each of the controls has been given a unique resource identifier. For instance, the text controls have identifiers *Idc_name, Idc_address,* and *Idc_country.* The next step was to create a descendant class of *WEL_DIALOG* that encapsulated the dialog and managed its behavior. The Resource Bench tool was used to create this class.

Resource Bench examined the definition of the dialog box resource and displayed a list of controls and message hooks that can be generated. Figure 9.2 shows the information Resource Bench displayed for our dialog box. We generated redefinition code for the *setup_dialog* routine and *on_ok* message hook. We also generated attributes for each of the text controls and radio buttons. It was not necessary to generate code for the static controls because we did not need to manipulate them in any way.

Lastly, we selected the type of dialog that we would use. That is, one of *WEL_MODAL_DIALOG, WEL_MODELESS_DIALOG,* or *WEL_MAIN_DIALOG.* In this case we chose WEL_MODAL_DIALOG.

When we clicked the Generate code button, Resource Bench created two classes: *APPLICATION_IDS* and *IDD_DIALOG.* Class *APPLICATION_IDS,* as shown in Example 9.2, includes constant definitions for all of the resource identifiers for our dialog box.

Example 9.2 Modal Dialog, APPLICATION_IDS Class (dialogs\modal)

```
class
    APPLICATION_IDS
feature -- Access
    Idc_static_constant: INTEGER is -1
    Idc_country_constant: INTEGER is 1002
    Idc_name_constant: INTEGER is 1000
    Idc_address_constant: INTEGER is 1001
    Idd_dialog_constant: INTEGER is 101
    Idc_male_constant: INTEGER is 1004
    Idc_female_constant: INTEGER is 1005
end -- class APPLICATION_IDS
```

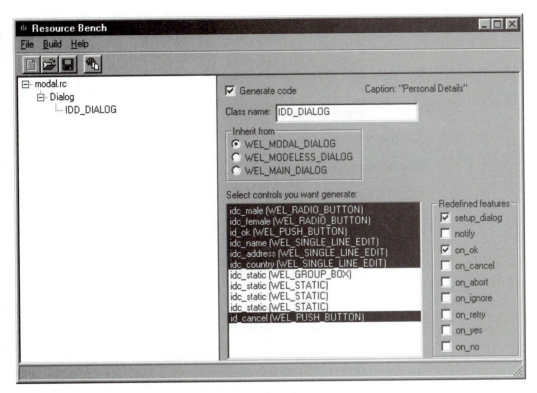

FIGURE 9.2. Modal dialog in ISE Resource Bench.

The generated *IDD_DIALOG* class provides a skeleton implementation of our dialog box wrapper. The class compiles cleanly; however, it did not perform any useful tasks without modification. The generated code includes the inheritance of *WEL_MODAL_DIALOG* and *APPLICATION_IDS,* a complete creation procedure *make,* attributes for each control, and empty redefinitions of *setup_dialog* and *on_ok*. Example 9.3 shows the generated code after we modified it to work with our application. The shaded areas of code highlight the changes and additions.

Example 9.3 Modal Dialog, IDD_DIALOG Class (dialogs\modal)

```
indexing
    description: "IDD_DIALOG class created by Resource Bench."
class
    IDD_DIALOG
```

```
inherit
    WEL_MODAL_DIALOG
        redefine
            setup_dialog, on_ok
        end
    APPLICATION_IDS
        export
            {NONE} all
        end
creation
    make
feature {NONE} -- Initialization
    make (a_parent: WEL_COMPOSITE_WINDOW) is
            -- Create the dialog.
        require
            a_parent_not_void: a_parent /= Void
            a_parent_exists: a_parent.exists
        do
            make_by_id (a_parent, Idd_dialog_constant)
            create idc_male.make_by_id (Current, Idc_male_constant)
            create idc_female.make_by_id (Current, Idc_female_
                constant)
            create id_ok.make_by_id (Current, Idok)
            create idc_name.make_by_id (Current, Idc_name_constant)
            create idc_address.make_by_id (Current, Idc_address_
                constant)
            create idc_country.make_by_id (Current, Idc_country_
                constant)
            create id_cancel.make_by_id (Current, Idcancel)
        end
feature -- Initialization
    setup_dialog is
            -- Initialize the dialog from the current person object
        do
            if person.is_male then
                idc_male.set_checked
            else
                idc_female.set_checked
            end
            idc_name.set_text (person.name)
            idc_address.set_text (person.address)
            idc_country.set_text (person.country)
        end
    set_person (new_person: PERSON) is
            -- Set the person object that this dialog will
            -- be initialized from
        require
            valid_person: new_person /= Void
        do
            person := new_person
        ensure
```

```
              person_set: person = new_person
        end
feature -- Basic Operations
    on_ok is
              -- Capture the new person values and terminate
              -- the dialog.
        do
              person.set_name (idc_name.text)
              person.set_address (idc_address.text)
              person.set_country (idc_country.text)
              person.set_gender (idc_male.checked)
              Precursor
        end
feature -- Access
    person: PERSON
    idc_male: WEL_RADIO_BUTTON
    idc_female: WEL_RADIO_BUTTON
    id_ok: WEL_PUSH_BUTTON
    idc_name: WEL_SINGLE_LINE_EDIT
    idc_address: WEL_SINGLE_LINE_EDIT
    idc_country: WEL_SINGLE_LINE_EDIT
    id_cancel: WEL_PUSH_BUTTON
end -- class IDD_DIALOG
```

First, we added an attribute *person* of type *PERSON,* and a corresponding *set_person* routine to set the *person* object. Second, code was added to the *setup_dialog* routine to use the current values of *person* as the default values for the dialog box controls. Finally, we added code to *on_ok* to update the person object with the new values from the dialog box controls and then to terminate normally by calling *Precursor.*

The following *MAIN_WINDOW* class in Example 9.4 shows how we can use our newly created dialog box. The *MAIN_WINDOW* creates and initializes a new *PERSON* object and an *IDD_DIALOG* object. The dialog is notified of the new person via a call to *set_person.*

When the user clicks on the Personal Details button, the dialog is activated. If the user dismisses the dialog by clicking the OK button, then the person details are updated; otherwise, they are left unchanged.

Example 9.4 Modal Dialog, MAIN_WINDOW Class (dialogs\modal)

```
class MAIN_WINDOW
inherit
    WEL_FRAME_WINDOW
        redefine
            on_control_command
        end
creation
    make
feature -- Initialization
    make is
            -- Initialize the main window
        do
            make_top ("Main Window")
            resize (300, 255)
            create get_button.make (Current, "Personal Details", 10,
                30, 120, 35, -1)
            create dialog.make (Current)
            create person.make ("Glenn Maughan", "Melbourne",
                "AUSTRALIA", True)
            dialog.set_person (person)
        end
    get_button: WEL_PUSH_BUTTON
            -- Push button
    dialog: IDD_DIALOG
            -- Personal Details dialog
    person: PERSON
            -- Person object for dialog
    on_control_command (control: WEL_CONTROL) is
            -- A command has been received from 'control'.
        do
            if control = get_button then
                dialog.activate
            end
        end
end -- class MAIN_WINDOW
```

Figure 9.3 shows the main window and the personal details dialog with the initial values of the person in each of the dialog box controls.

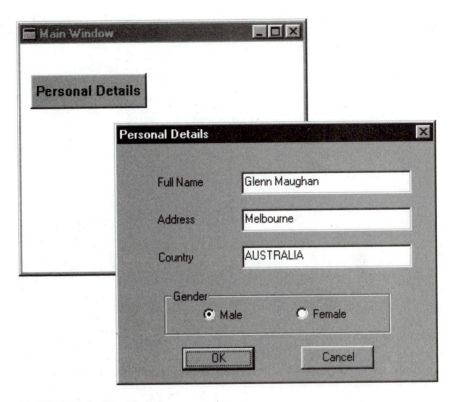

FIGURE 9.3. Modal dialog example.

MODELESS DIALOGS

It is a simple exercise to modify the previous example to use a modeless dialog rather than a modal dialog. To do this, we would have initially chosen *WEL_MODELESS_DIALOG* in Resource Bench before we generated the dialog skeleton code (see Figure 9.4), or we could have modified the generated code to inherit from *WEL_MODELESS_DIALOG*.

In either case, Example 9.5 shows the result. The only change occurs in the inheritance clause—the class now inherits from *WEL_MODELESS_DIALOG* rather than from *WEL_MODAL_DIALOG*. All other code remains identical.

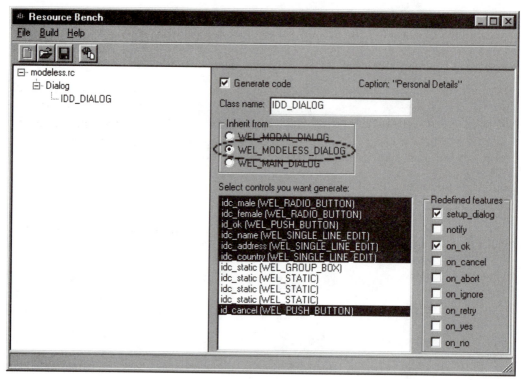

FIGURE 9.4. Modeless dialog in ISE Resource Bench.

Example 9.5 Modeless Dialog, IDD_DIALOG Class (dialogs\modeless)

```
indexing
    description: "IDD_DIALOG class created by Resource Bench."
class
    IDD_DIALOG
inherit
    WEL_MODELESS_DIALOG
        redefine
            setup_dialog, on_ok
        end
    APPLICATION_IDS
        export
            {NONE} all
        end
creation
    make
feature -- Initialization

    -- remainder of class as before
end -- class IDD_DIALOG
```

With the above changes, the dialog box now operates in a modeless form. That is, the user can now interact with the rest of the system while the dialog is active. Contrast this with the modal dialog, where the user could not interact with the rest of the application.

We now need to modify the *MAIN_WINDOW* class to take the new behavior into account. The user can now click the Personal Details button while the Personal Details dialog is active. The modifications shown in Example 9.6 check whether the dialog is already active, and if so, it shows a warning message box.

Example 9.6 Modeless Dialog, MAIN_WINDOW Class (dialogs\modal)

```
class MAIN_WINDOW
inherit
    WEL_FRAME_WINDOW
        redefine
            on_control_command
        end
creation
    make
feature -- Initialization
    make is
            -- Initialize the main window
        do
            make_top ("Main Window")
            resize (300, 255)
            create get_button.make (Current, "Personal Details", 10,
                30, 120, 35, -1)
            create dialog.make (Current)
            create message.make
            create person.make ("Glenn Maughan", "Melbourne",
                "AUSTRALIA", True)
            dialog.set_person (person)
        end
    get_button: WEL_PUSH_BUTTON
            -- Push button
    dialog: IDD_DIALOG
            -- Personal Details dialog
    person: PERSON
            -- Person object for dialog
    message: WEL_MSG_BOX
            -- Message box
    on_control_command (control: WEL_CONTROL) is
            -- A command has been received from 'control'.
        do
            if control = get_button then
```

```
                    if not dialog.exists then
                            dialog.activate
                    else
                            message.error_message_box (Current,
                                    "You are already editing personal in-
                                    formation.", "Error")
                    end
            end
        end
end -- class MAIN_WINDOW
```

If the user clicks on the Personal Details button while the Personal Details dialog is active, then the warning dialog is shown as illustrated in Figure 9.5.

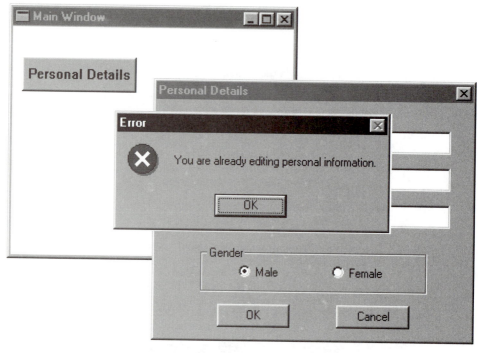

FIGURE 9.5. Modeless dialog example.

MAIN WINDOW DIALOGS

Class *WEL_MAIN_DIALOG* simplifies the task of using a dialog box as the main window of an application. Modifying our example, this time to use a *WEL_MAIN_DIALOG,* is simple. Either use Resource Bench to generate skeleton code with *WEL_MAIN_DIALOG* as the parent, or modify the existing dialog code. The result should look similar to Example 9.7.

Example 9.7 Main Dialog, IDD_DIALOG Class (dialogs\main)

```
indexing
    description: "IDD_DIALOG class created by Resource Bench."
class
    IDD_DIALOG
inherit
    WEL_MAIN_DIALOG
        redefine
            setup_dialog, on_ok
        end
    APPLICATION_IDS
        export
            {NONE} all
        end
creation
    make
feature {NONE} -- Initialization

    -- remaining features as before
end -- class IDD_DIALOG
```

The *MAIN_WINDOW* class of previous examples is now redundant. We define the *IDD_DIALOG* class to be the main window of the application in our *APPLICATION* class. The *APPLICATION* class in Example 9.8 serves the purpose of creating a new *PERSON* object, activating the Personal Details dialog on that person, and exiting when the dialog is dismissed.

Example 9.8 Main Dialog, APPLICATION Class (dialogs\main)

```
class APPLICATION
inherit
    WEL_APPLICATION
    APPLICATION_IDS
creation
    make
feature
```

```
    person: PERSON
    main_window: IDD_DIALOG is
            -- Dialog main window
        once
            create Result.make
            create person.make ("Glenn Maughan", "Melbourne",
                "AUSTRALIA", True)
            Result.set_person (person)
        end
end -- class APPLICATION
```

STANDARD DIALOGS

The Windows API provides a number of prebuilt dialogs for use in applications. Standard dialogs exist for opening and saving files, printing, choosing fonts, choosing colors, and choosing folders. Each of the standard dialogs has a corresponding class in WEL. For example, the standard Windows print dialog is encapsulated by the *WEL_PRINTER_DIALOG,* and the open file dialog by the *WEL_OPEN_FILE_DIALOG.*

Each of the standard dialogs inherit from *WEL_STANDARD_DIALOG,* either directly or indirectly, as in the case of *WEL_OPEN_FILE_DIALOG* and *WEL_SAVE_FILE_DIALOG* (see Figure 9.6).

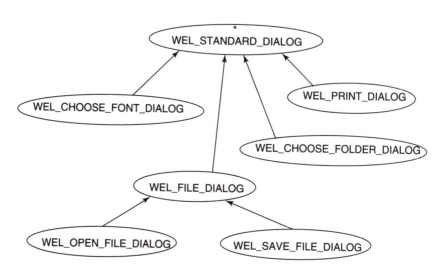

FIGURE 9.6. Standard dialog classes.

One example is sufficient to demonstrate the use of each standard dialog. Example 9.9 shows the code for a *MAIN_WINDOW* that provides a menu bar from which each of the standard dialogs can be activated.

Example 9.9 Standard Dialog, MAIN_WINDOW Class (dialogs\standard)

```
class MAIN_WINDOW
inherit
    WEL_FRAME_WINDOW
        redefine
            on_menu_command
        end
    APPLICATION_IDS
        export
            {NONE} all
        end
create
    make
feature
    make is
            -- Initialize the main window
        do
            make_top ("Main Window")
            set_menu (main_menu)
            resize (300, 255)
        end
    on_menu_command (id: INTEGER) is
        do
            inspect id
            when idm_fileexit_constant then
                destroy
            when idm_dialog_openfile_constant then
                file_open_dialog.activate (Current)
            when idm_dialog_savefile_constant then
                file_save_dialog.activate (Current)
            when idm_dialog_print_constant then
                print_dialog.activate (Current)
            when idm_dialog_choosefont_constant then
                choose_font_dialog.activate (Current)
            when idm_dialog_choosecolor_constant then
                choose_color_dialog.activate (Current)
            else
            end
        end
feature {NONE} -- Implementation
    main_menu: WEL_MENU is
        once
            create Result.make_by_id (idr_main_menu_constant)
        end
    file_open_dialog: WEL_OPEN_FILE_DIALOG is
```

```
      once
           create Result.make
      end
    file_save_dialog: WEL_SAVE_FILE_DIALOG is
      once
           create Result.make
      end
    print_dialog: WEL_PRINT_DIALOG is
      once
           create Result.make
      end
    choose_font_dialog: WEL_CHOOSE_FONT_DIALOG is
      once
           create Result.make
      end
    choose_color_dialog: WEL_CHOOSE_COLOR_DIALOG is
      once
           create Result.make
      end
  end -- class MAIN_WINDOW
```

Activating a Standard Dialog

The creation routines of a standard dialog differ from resource-based dialog
boxes because they do not require a parameter for the parent window. Instead,
each type of standard dialog defines its own creation procedure to perform any
required initialization. The parent window is passed to a standard dialog when
it is activated. This allows you to reuse a single instance of a standard dialog
with different parent windows. Thus the signature for *activate* in *WEL_STAN-
DARD_DIALOG* differs from *WEL_DIALOG*.

```
activate (a_parent: WEL_COMPOSITE_WINDOW)
        -- Activate the dialog box (modal mode) with
        -- 'a_parent' as owner.
    require
        a_parent_not_void: a_parent /= void;
        a_parent_exists: a_parent.exists
```

Retrieving the Chosen Value from a Standard Dialog

A standard dialog also indicates the results of user interaction differently from
resource dialogs. Once the dialog has been dismissed, the *WEL_STAN-
DARD_DIALOG* attribute *selected* indicates whether the user selected an element within the dialog and clicked OK, or clicked Cancel.

```
selected: BOOLEAN
            -- Has the user selected something (file,
            -- color, etc.)?
            -- If True, the OK button has been chosen.
If False,
            -- the Cancel button has been chosen.
```

Choose Color Dialog

Figure 9.7 shows a fully expanded Choose Color dialog. The dialog allows the user to select from a set of basic colors or to define and choose custom colors. You can customize the dialog by disabling custom color controls before the dialog is activated.

Retrieving the Chosen Color from a Choose Color Dialog

The color selected by the user can be accessed by calling the *rgb_result* function to return a *WEL_COLOR_REF* object representing the color. This function can be called only if the user actually selected a color and the dialog was not dismissed by pressing Cancel.

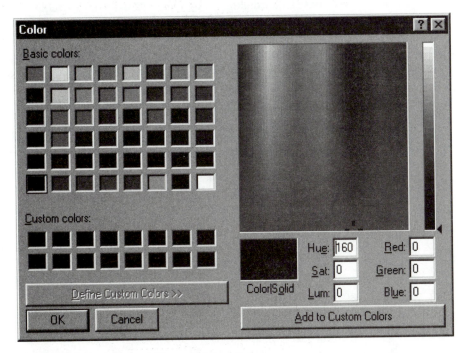

FIGURE 9.7. Standard Choose Color dialog.

```
rgb_result: WEL_COLOR_REF
        -- Color selected by the user and default color
        -- selected when the dialog box is created.
    require
        selected: selected
    ensure
        result_not_void: Result /= void
```

The custom colors defined by the user (if any) are accessible by calling *custom_colors*. This routine returns a *WEL_CUSTOM_COLORS* structure that provides access to each of the 16 user defined custom colors.

```
custom_colors: WEL_CUSTOM_COLORS
        -- Custom colors chosen by the user
```

Customizing a Choose Color Dialog

The Choose Color dialog has two main parts—the basic color selection controls and the custom color selection controls. You can modify a Choose Color dialog by allowing or disallowing custom color selection. Features *allow_full_open* and *prevent_full_open* allow and prevent the user from opening the custom color selection controls. The *prevent_full_open* operation effectively disables the Define Custom Colors button. The current status of this setting can be determined by calling *full_open_allowed*.

```
full_open_allowed: BOOLEAN
        -- Is the define custom colors button enabled?
        -- This button allows the user to create custom colors.

allow_full_open
        -- Enable the define custom colors button,
        -- allowing the user from creating custom colors.
    ensure
        full_open_allowed: full_open_allowed

prevent_full_open
        --.Disable the define custom colors button,
        -- preventing the user from creating custom colors.
    ensure
        full_open_prevented: not full_open_allowed
```

When a Choose Color dialog is activated, the color black is initially selected. You can modify this behavior by calling *set_rgb_result* to set the color
that will be initially selected on activation. The set of defined custom colors
can also be modified by supplying a *WEL_CUSTOM_COLORS* structure to the
set_custom_colors operation.

```
set_rgb_result (color: WEL_COLOR_REF)
        -- Set 'rgb_result' with 'color'
    require
        color_not_void: color /= void
    ensure
        color_set: rgb_result.is_equal (color)
set_custom_colors (a_custom_colors: WEL_CUSTOM_COLORS)
        -- Set 'custom_colors' with 'a_custom_colors'.
    require
        a_custom_colors_not_void: a_custom_colors /= void
    ensure
        custom_colors_set: custom_colors = a_custom_colors
```

Fine-grained customization of the Choose Color dialog can be performed
by setting and unsetting customization flags. The attribute *flags* holds the
current set of flags for the dialog. Features *add_flag* and *remove_flag* add and
remove a single flag to the existing set, respectively. *set_flags* can be used to
replace the current set of flags with a new set. And *has_flag* can be used to
determine if a particular flag is already set.

```
flags: INTEGER
        -- Dialog box creation flags.
        -- Can be a combination of the values defined in
        -- class WEL_CHOOSE_COLOR_CONSTANTS.

has_flag (a_flags: INTEGER): BOOLEAN
        -- Is 'a_flags' set in 'flags'?
        -- See class WEL_CHOOSE_COLOR_CONSTANTS for 'a_flags'
        -- values.

add_flag (a_flags: INTEGER)
        -- Add 'a_flags' to 'flags'.
        -- See class WEL_CHOOSE_COLOR_CONSTANTS for 'a_flags'
        -- values.
    ensure
        has_flag: has_flag (a_flags)

remove_flag (a_flags: INTEGER)
```

```
        -- Remove 'a_flags' from 'flags'.
        -- See class WEL_CHOOSE_COLOR_CONSTANTS for 'a_flags'
        -- values.
    ensure
        has_not_flag: not has_flag (a_flags)

set_flags (a_flags: INTEGER)
        -- Set 'flags' with 'a_flags'.
        -- See class WEL_CHOOSE_COLOR_CONSTANTS for 'a_flags'
        -- values.
    ensure
            flags_set: flags = a_flags
```

The customization flags for a Choose Color dialog are listed in Table 9.3. Individual flags can be combined using addition. For example, to set both *Cc_fullopen* and *Cc_showhelp* using the *set_flags* operation you can use

```
    set_flags (Cc_fullopen + Cc_showhelp)
```

Choose Font Dialog

The standard Choose Font dialog is shown in Figure 9.8. The dialog provides controls for selecting a font face, style, and size. The list of available fonts is configurable and can be targeted to a particular device context.

Retrieving the Chosen Font from a Choose Font Dialog

The information for a selected font is available via a set of functions, or collectively via a logical font structure. The font color, type, and point size can be accessed using the functions *color, font_type,* and *point_size*, respectively.

TABLE 9.3   *Choose Color Customization Constants*
(WEL_CHOOSE_COLOR_CONSTANTS)

CONSTANT	DESCRIPTION
Cc_fullopen	Shows the dialog with the custom color section open. If this flag is not specified, then the user will have to click on the Define Custom Colors button before the custom color controls are displayed.
Cc_preventfullopen	Disables the Define Custom Colors button.
Cc_rdbinit	Forces the dialog to use the color specified in *rgb_result* as the initial color selection.
Cc_showhelp	Causes the dialog to display the Help button.

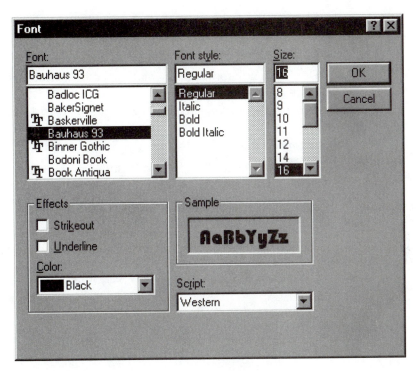

FIGURE 9.8. Standard Choose Font dialog.

```
color: WEL_COLOR_REF
        -- Font color
    require
        exits: exists
    ensure
        result_not_void: Result /= void

font_type: INTEGER
        -- Type of the selected font.
        -- See class WEL_FONT_TYPE_CONSTANTS for values.
    require
        selected: selected
    ensure
        valid_font_type: valid_font_type_constant (Result)

log_font: WEL_LOG_FONT
        -- Information about the selected font

point_size: INTEGER
        -- Size of the selected font (in units of 1/10 of
        -- a point)
    require
        selected: selected
```

The *font_type* value indicates the type of font selected by the user. It will be one of the values listed in Table 9.4 and identifies the weight of the font and the type. The type of font can be one of screen, printer, or simulated.

Detailed font information is available in the logical font structure stored in the attribute *log_font*. You can easily create a *WEL_FONT* from this structure by calling the creation procedure *make_log of WEL_FONT*.

Customizing a Choose Font Dialog

The Choose Font dialog can be customized in a number of ways. First, the type of font that the user can select can be restricted. Second, the maximum and minimum sizes of the selectable font can be adjusted. And finally, the font initially selected in the dialog can be set.

The maximum and minimum selectable font size is determined by the *maximum_size* and *minimum_size* attributes. The sizes can be changed by calling *set_maximum_size* and *set_minimum_size,* respectively.

```
maximum_size: INTEGER
        -- Maximum point size a user can select
minimum_size: INTEGER
        -- Minimum point size a user can select
```

The initial color of the font can be set by calling *set_color* and passing a *WEL_COLOR_REF* that represents the desired color. Further font details can be preselected by calling *set_log_font,* passing an instance of *WEL_LOG_FONT* with the desired font metrics initialized.

Finally, you can set the target device context from which fonts will be selected and subsequently used by calling *set_dc*. This routine takes any type of device context and affects the list of available fonts and font metrics.

TABLE 9.4   *Font Type Constants (WEL_FONT_TYPE_CONSTANTS)*

CONSTANT	DESCRIPTION
Bold_fonttype	The font weight is bold.
Italic_fonttype	The italic font attribute is set.
Printer_fonttype	The font is a printer font.
Regular_fonttype	The font weight is regular.
Screen_fonttype	The font is a screen font.
Simulated_fonttype	The font is simulated by the graphics device interface.

```
set_color (a_color: WEL_COLOR_REF)
        -- Set 'color' with 'a_color'.
    ensure
        color_set: color.is_equal (a_color)
set_dc (a_dc: WEL_DC)
        -- Set a device context 'a_dc' of the printer whose
        -- fonts will be listed in the dialog box.
    require
        a_dc_not_void: a_dc /= void;
        a_dc_exists: a_dc.exists
set_log_font (a_log_font: WEL_LOG_FONT)
        -- Set 'log_font' with 'a_log_font'.
    require
        a_log_font_not_void: a_log_font /= void
    ensure
        log_font_set: log_font.item = a_log_font.item
set_maximum_size (size: INTEGER)
        -- Set 'maximum_size' with 'size'.
    ensure
        maximum_size_set: maximum_size = size
set_minimum_size (size: INTEGER)
        -- Set 'minimum_size' with 'size'.
    ensure
        minimum_size_set: minimum_size = size
```

A Choose Font dialog can be further customized by setting and unsetting dialog box creation flags. The Choose Font dialog supports each of the flag operations described for the Choose Color dialog. The flags available for customizing a Choose Font dialog are listed in Table 9.5.

File Dialogs

Two standard File dialogs are supported by WEL. Actually, both dialogs are a derivative of the same Windows File Open dialog, only they each have different settings. The *WEL_FILE_OPEN_DIALOG* provides a standard Windows interface for selecting a file either on any local disk or across a network. *WEL_FILE_SAVE_DIALOG* provides the same interface for saving a file in any location.

Both dialogs are highly customizable and can be used in a variety of filename selection and path selection operations. They each have a common set of features defined in their common parent *WEL_FILE_DIALOG*.

Retrieving File Information from a Standard File Dialog

The information about a selected file can be accessed through a group of functions defined in *WEL_FILE_OPEN_DIALOG*. The functions include *file_extension_offset,* used to find the position of the file extension in the full

TABLE 9.5   *Choose Font Customization Constants*
(WEL_CF_CONSTANTS)

CONSTANT	DESCRIPTION
Cf_apply	Causes the dialog box to display the Apply button. A hook procedure should be provided to handle the *WM_COMMAND* messages for the Apply button.
Cf_both	Causes the dialog to list both printer and screen fonts.
Cf_effects	Allows the user to select strikeout, underline, and text color effects.
Cf_fixedpitchonly	Only fixed pitch fonts will be listed.
Cf_forcefontexist	The dialog will indicate an error condition if the user attempts to select a font or style that does not exist.
Cf_initlogfontstruct	Specifies that the dialog should initialize the selected font from the *log_font* structure.
Cf_limitsize	Limits the selectable font sizes to the range within *maximum_size* and *minimum_size*.
Cf_nofacesel	When initializing the selected font from the *log_font* structure, this flag causes the dialog to ignore the font face.
Cf_noemfonts	Same as *Cf_novectorfonts*.
Cf_nosimulations	The dialog will not allow graphics device interface font simulations.
Cf_nosizesel	Ignore the font size when initializing the selected font from the *log_font* structure.
Cf_nostylesel	Ignore the font style when initializing the font from the *log_font* structure.
Cf_novectorfonts	The dialog will not list vector fonts.
Cf_printerfonts	Lists only those fonts supported by the printer represented by the specified device context.
Cf_scalableonly	The dialog will only allow selection of scalable fonts.
Cf_screenfonts	The dialog will list only screen fonts supported by the system.
Cf_showhelp	Causes the dialog to display the Help button.
Cf_ttonly	The dialog will list only TrueType fonts.
Cf_usestyle	Specifies that the dialog should initialize the Font Style combo box.
Cf_wysiwyg	The dialog will list only fonts available on both the printer and display.

filename; *file_name*, which returns the full filename including the path; *file_name_offset*, which returns the position of the filename in the complete filename; and *file_title*, which returns the filename (not including the path) from the complete filename.

```
file_extension_offset: INTEGER
            -- Specifies the offset from the beginning of the path
            -- to the filename extension in the string 'file_name'.
    require
        selected: selected
    ensure
        result_greater_than_or_equal_to_one: Result >= 1

file_name: STRING
            -- Filename selected (including path).
    require
        selected: selected
    ensure
        result_not_void: Result /= void

file_name_offset: INTEGER
            -- Specifies the offset from the beginning of the path
            -- to the filename in the string `file_name'.
    require
        selected: selected
    ensure
        result_greater_than_or_equal_to_one: Result >= 1

file_title: STRING
            -- Title of the selected file (without path).
    require
        selected: selected
    ensure
        result_not_void: Result /= void
```

Setting a Filename Filter in a File Open Dialog

The standard File dialog provides facilities for filtering the list of files in the selection control. A typical application requires that the user select a file of a particular type (i.e., with a particular file extension). For instance, the user might be requested to select a text file (with extension *.txt*) for a text editor, or a document file (*.doc*) for a word processor.

In your applications, you can set a filename filter using the *set_filter* routine. *set_filter* takes two parameters of type *ARRAY [STRING]* that specify the names of each filter and the filename pattern of each filter. For example, if your application needs to support both text and document files, you would use the following code to set two file filters. The code also adds an additional filter, *All files,* that will match all filenames.

```
set_filter (<<"Text files", "Document files", "All files">>,
    <       <"*.txt", "*.doc", "*.*">>)
```

```
filter_index: INTEGER
        -- Index of the selected filter
    require
        selected: selected
    ensure
        positive_result: Result >= 0

set_filter (filter_names, filter_patterns: ARRAY [STRING])
        -- Set the file type combo box.
        -- 'filter_names' is an array of string containing
        -- the filter names and 'filter_patterns' is an
        -- array of string containing the filter patterns.
        -- Example:
        --   filter_names = <<"Text file", "All file">>
        --   filter_patterns = <<"*.txt", "*.*">>
    require
        filter_names_not_void: filter_names /= void;
        filter_patterns_not_void: filter_patterns /= void;
        same_count: filter_names.count = filter_patterns.count;
        no_void_name: not filter_names.has (void);
        no_void_pattern: not filter_patterns.has (void)

set_filter_index (a_filter_index: INTEGER)
        -- Set 'filter_index' with 'a_filter_index'.
    require
        positive_filter_index: a_filter_index >= 0
    ensure
        filter_index_set: filter_index = a_filter_index
```

To set the default filter before the File dialog is activated, you can call *set_filter_index* and pass the zero-based index of the filter you want selected. If you do not call *set_filter_index,* then the first filter in the *set_filter* call will be used.

If the user changes the filter during the file selection process, then the selected filter will be indicated by the *filter_index* function. *filter_index* returns the zero-based index of the currently selected file filter.

Customizing a Standard File Dialog

The text of the File dialog's title bar can be changed using *set_title.* The current title bar text is available in function *title.* WEL uses both of these routines (and *set_default_title*) internally to initialize the title bar of *WEL_OPEN_FILE_DIALOG* and *WEL_SAVE_FILE_DIALOG* instances.

```
title: STRING
            -- Title of the current dialog
        ensure
            result_not_void: Result /= void

set_default_title
            -- Set the title bar with the default value ("Save As"
            -- or "Open")
        ensure
            default_title_set: title.is_equal ("")

set_title (a_title: STRING)
            -- Set 'title' with 'a_title' and use this string to
            -- display the title.
        require
            a_title_not_void: a_title /= void
        ensure
            title_set: title.is_equal (a_title)
```

When a File dialog is first activated, it displays the current default directory. The default directory is typically the My Documents folder of the current user or the last folder opened by the user. You can modify the initial directory by calling *set_initial_directory* or *set_initial_directory_as_current*. Routine *set_initial_directory* is used to set the directory to a particular path, as specified by the *directory* parameter, and *set_initial_directory_as_current* sets the directory to the current directory as selected by the operating system.

```
set_initial_directory (directory: STRING)
            -- Set the initial directory with 'directory'.
        require
            directory_not_void: directory /= void
set_initial_directory_as_current
            -- Set the initial directory as the current one.
```

If the user enters a filename without a file extension, you can have the File dialog automatically add one. For example, your application may handle text files and you want the user to be able to enter a filename without the *.txt* extension. Calling *set_default_extension* with *.txt* as the *extension* parameter provides the required behavior.

The initial filename can be set using *set_file_name*. This initializes the filename edit control with the specified filename. The routine does not affect the path that the dialog is viewing; only the filename is initialized. *set_file_name* is useful for a Save File dialog where your application provides a default filename for new documents. For example, the application may initialize a new document with the name *Document1.doc*. You can initialize a File Save dialog with this name so that the user can use the default name if he or she desires.

```
set_default_extension (extension: STRING)
        -- Set the default extension with 'extension'.
        -- This extension will be automatically added to the
        -- filename if the user fails to type an extension.
    require
        extension_not_void: extension /= void

set_file_name (a_file_name: STRING)
        -- Set 'file_name' with 'a_file' and initialize
        -- the file name edit control.
    require
        a_file_name_not_void: a_file_name /= void;
        a_file_name_count_ok: a_file_name.count <=
            max_file_name_length
    ensure
        file_name_set: file_name.is_equal (a_file_name)
```

The customization flags of a File dialog are listed in Table 9.6. Included are flags that allow multiple file selection, restricted file selection based on read-only, network, or shared files, and validation of files according to existence or nonexistence. The standard dialog flag routines are used to set and unset each of these flags.

Open File and Save File Dialogs

Figure 9.9 shows a standard Open File dialog viewing a project folder of the author's workstation. The dialog provides a folder selection pull-down control; icons for navigating through folders, showing the desktop, creating new folders, and changing the view; a file list view; a selected file text control; and a file filter drop-down control.

The Open File dialog is encapsulated by the class *WEL_OPEN_FILE_DIALOG*. The Save File dialog, *WEL_SAVE_FILE_DIALOG*, is identical except for a different title (Save As) and a different label on the default button (Save).

Print Dialog

The standard Print dialog, *WEL_PRINT_DIALOG*, provides an interface for selecting printing options, including the target printer, page ranges to print, and number of copies as shown in Figure 9.10. The target printer can also be configured via the Properties button next to the printer name.

TABLE 9.6   *File Dialog Constants (WEL_OFN_CONSTANTS)*

CONSTANT	DESCRIPTION
Ofn_allowmultiselect	Allows multiple selection of files.
Ofn_createprompt	If the user selects a file that does not exist, the dialog will prompt the user for permission to create the file. If the user chooses to create the file, the dialog closes and returns the specified name; otherwise, the dialog remains open.
Ofn_extensiondifferent	Specifies that the user typed a filename extension that differs from the default extension.
Ofn_filemustexist	Specifies that the user can only type names of existing files. A warning message box is displayed if the file does not exist.
Ofn_hidereadonly	Hides the Read Only check box.
Ofn_nochangedir	Restores the current directory to its original value if the user changes the directory while searching for files.
Ofn_nolongnames	Causes the dialog to use short file names.
Ofn_nonetworkbutton	Hides the Network button.
Ofn_notestfilecreate	Specifies that the file is not created before the dialog box is closed.
Ofn_novalidate	Allows invalid characters in the returned filename.
Ofn_overwriteprompt	Causes a Save As dialog box to generate a message box if the selected file already exists. The user must confirm whether to overwrite the file.
Ofn_pathmustexist	The user can type only valid paths and filenames.
Ofn_readonly	Causes the Read Only check box to be checked initially when the dialog box is created.
Ofn_shareaware	Specifies that if the open file fails because of a network sharing violation, the error is ignored and the dialog box returns the selected filename.
Ofn_sharefallthrough	Accepts the filename when a sharing violation occurs.
Ofn_sharenowarn	Reject the filename but do not warn the user.
Ofn_showhelp	Causes the dialog box to show the Help button.

Retrieving Print Information from a Print Dialog

Once the user has dismissed a Print dialog, you can determine the selections made through a number of functions and attributes. The following set of functions provides access to the number of copies selected and the range of pages that should be printed.

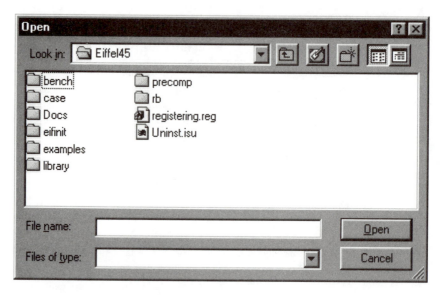

FIGURE 9.9. Standard Open File dialog.

```
copies: INTEGER
        -- Number of copies for the Copies edit control

from_page: INTEGER
        -- Value for the starting page edit control
    ensure
        positive_result: Result >= 0

maximum_page: INTEGER
        -- Maximum value for the range of pages specified
        -- in the From and To page edit controls

minimum_page: INTEGER
        -- Minimum value for the range of pages specified
        -- in the From and To page edit controls

to_page: INTEGER
        -- Value for the ending page edit control
    ensure
        positive_result: Result >= 0
```

Fine-grain settings can be determined by examining the following functions. The information includes the type of page range selected, whether the output should be saved in a file, and whether multiple copies should be collated.

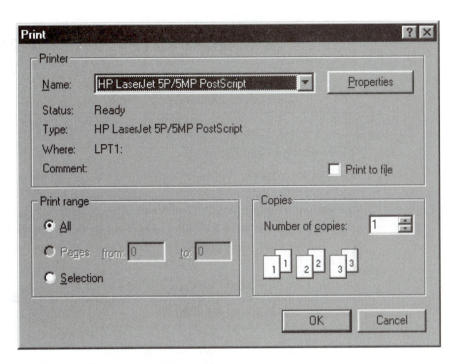

FIGURE 9.10. Standard Print dialog.

```
all_pages_selected: BOOLEAN
        -- Is the "All pages" radio button selected?
collate_checked: BOOLEAN
        -- Is the "Collate" check box checked?
page_numbers_selected: BOOLEAN
        -- Is the "Page" radio button selected?
print_to_file_checked: BOOLEAN
        -- Is the "Print to file" check box checked?
selection_selected: BOOLEAN
        -- Is the "Selection" radio box selected?
```

Retrieving the Printer Device Context from a Print Dialog

The most important piece of information selected by the user is the target printer. Each type and brand of printer has different capabilities, including the supported page sizes and resolutions. The *dc* function returns a printer device context (*WEL_PRINTER_DC*) that represents the paper size and resolution metrics for the selected printer. This device context should be used when painting output for the printer.

```
dc: WEL_PRINTER_DC
        -- Device context associated to the selected printer
    require
        selected: selected
    ensure
        result_not_void: Result /= void
```

Customizing a Print Dialog

Each of the controls on the Print dialog can be initialized, enabled, disabled, and sometimes hidden altogether. Your applications may need only a subset of the options available on the Print dialog. For instance, an application may not support the selection of a range of pages, or it may not support printing to a file. Both of these requirements can be supported by customizing the Print dialog using one or more of the following operations.

```
set_copies (number: INTEGER)
        -- Set 'copies' with 'number'.
    ensure
        copies_set: copies = number
set_from_page (page: INTEGER)
        -- Set 'from_page' with 'page'.
    ensure
        from_page_set: from_page = page
set_maximum_page (page: INTEGER)
        -- Set 'maximum_page' with 'page'.
    ensure
        maximum_page_set: maximum_page = page
set_minimum_page (page: INTEGER)
        -- Set 'minimum_page' with 'page'.
    ensure
        minimum_page_set: minimum_page = page
set_to_page (page: INTEGER)
        -- Set 'to_page' with 'page'.
    ensure
        to_page_set: to_page = page
page_numbers_enabled: BOOLEAN
        -- Is the "Page numbers" radio button enabled?
print_setup_enabled: BOOLEAN
        -- Is the Print setup dialog box enabled?
print_to_file_enabled: BOOLEAN
        -- Is the "Print to file" check box enabled?
print_to_file_shown: BOOLEAN
        -- Is the "Print to file" check box shown?
selection_enabled: BOOLEAN
        -- Is the "Selection" radio button enabled?
```

```
warning_enabled: BOOLEAN
        -- Is the warning message from being displayed when
        -- there is no default printer enabled?
check_collate
        -- Check the "Collate" check box.
    ensure
        collate_checked: collate_checked
check_print_to_file
        -- Check the "Print to file" check box.
    ensure
        print_to_file_checked: print_to_file_checked
disable_page_numbers
        -- Disable the "Page numbers" radio button.
    ensure
        page_numbers_disabled: not page_numbers_enabled
disable_print_setup
        -- Disable the system to display the Print setup dialog
        -- box rather than the Print dialog box.
    ensure
        print_setup_disabled: not print_setup_enabled
disable_print_to_file
        -- Disable the "Print to file" check box.
    ensure
        print_to_file_disabled: not print_to_file_enabled
disable_selection
        -- Disable the "Selection" radio button.
    ensure
        selection_disabled: not selection_enabled
disable_warning
        -- Disable the warning message from being displayed when
        -- there is no default printer.
    ensure
        warning_disabled: not warning_enabled
enable_page_numbers
        -- Enable the "Page numbers" radio button.
    ensure
        page_numbers_enabled: page_numbers_enabled
enable_print_setup
        -- Enable the system to display the Print setup dialog
        -- box rather than the Print dialog box.
    ensure
        print_setup_enabled: print_setup_enabled
enable_print_to_file
        -- Enable the "Print to file" check box.
    ensure
        print_to_file_enabled: print_to_file_enabled
enable_selection
        -- Enable the "Selection" radio button.
    ensure
        selection_enabled: selection_enabled
enable_warning
        -- Enable the warning message from being displayed when
```

```
            -- there is no default printer.
        ensure
            warning_enabled: warning_enabled
    hide_print_to_file
            -- Hide the "Print to file" check box.
        ensure
            print_to_file_hidden: not print_to_file_shown
    select_all_pages
            -- Select the "All pages" radio button.
        ensure
            all_pages_selected: all_pages_selected
    select_page_numbers
            -- Select the "Page numbers" radio button.
        ensure
            page_numbers_selected: page_numbers_selected
    select_selection
            -- Select the "Selection" radio button.
        ensure
            selection_selected: selection_selected
    show_print_to_file
            -- Show the "Print to file" check box.
        ensure
            print_to_file_shown: print_to_file_shown
    uncheck_collate
            -- Uncheck the "Collate" check box.
        ensure
            collate_unchecked: not collate_checked
    uncheck_print_to_file
            -- Uncheck the "Print to file" check box.
        ensure
            print_to_file_unchecked: not print_to_file_checked
```

Customization flags can also be used to modify the available controls and behavior of a standard Print dialog. The standard flag setting routines, namely *set_flag, unset_flag, has_flag,* and *set_flags,* are available. The possible flag values are listed in Table 9.7. Many of these capabilities can also be modified using the customization operations described earlier.

MESSAGE BOXES

A message box is a type of dialog that provides a simple way of presenting information to a user, or of receiving a simple Yes or No answer from a user. Typical uses of message boxes include notifying the user of an incorrect action, allowing the user to confirm some action, or warning the user of application failure.

TABLE 9.7   *Print Dialog Constants (WEL_PD_CONSTANTS)*

CONSTANT	DESCRIPTION
Pd_allpages	Indicates that the All radio button is initially selected.
Pd_collate	Places a check mark in the Collate check box. Also indicates that the user selected the Collate button and the printer driver does not support collation.
Pd_disableprinttofile	Disables the Print to File check box.
Pd_hideprinttofile	Hides the Print to File check box.
Pd_nopagenums	Disables the Pages radio button and the associated edit controls.
Pd_noselection	Disables the Selection radio button.
Pd_nowarning	Prevents the warning message from being displayed when there is no default printer.
Pd_pagenums	Causes the Pages radio button to be in the selected state when the dialog box is created.
Pd_printsetup	Causes the system to display the Print Setup dialog box rather than the Print dialog box.
Pd_printtofile	Causes the Print to File check box to be checked when the dialog box is created.
Pd_returndc	Causes a device context to be returned that matches the user's selections.
Pd_returndefault	Returns the default printer device context. Does not display the Print dialog.
Pd_returnic	Returns an information device context for the default printer. Does not display the Print dialog.
Pd_selection	Causes the Selection radio button to be in the selected state when the dialog is created.
Pd_showhelp	Causes the dialog to show the Help button.
Pd_usedevmodecopies	Disables the Copies edit control if the printer driver does not support multiple copies, and disables the Collate checkbox if the printer driver does not support collation.

WEL provides a class *WEL_MSG_BOX* with features for displaying messsage boxes in your application. Four prebuilt message box types are provided: *information_message_box* for displaying general information messages to the user, *warning_message_box* for messages such as confirmation of an action, *error_message_box* for critical and significant errors, and *question_message_box* for simple Yes or No questions.

Creating a Message Box

Creating a message box is a two-step process. First, create an instance of
WEL_MSG_BOX. Second, call the relevant message box routine for the type of
message box required. It is common for the *WEL_MSG_BOX* instance to be
reused many times, and in some cases, by many classes (if defined as a once
function). You can call the message box routines as many times as needed.

To create an instance of *WEL_MSG_BOX,* you need to call the creation
procedure *make,* which initializes the message box language.

```
make
        -- initialize language
```

Changing the Message Box Language

The message box language specifies the language that the message box uses.
This facility is typically used by multilingual applications. The language is
specified in two parts—the language itself and a sublanguage. Values for the
language and sublanguage are defined in the class *WEL_LANGUAGE_CON-
STANTS,* and the features *language* and *sublanguage* store the current settings.

```
language: INTEGER
        -- Actual language for "push buttons"
sublanguage: INTEGER
        -- Sublanguage of language for "push buttons"
```

The language settings can be changed by calling *set_language* and specifying new language and sublanguage identifiers.

```
set_language (a_language_id, a_sublanguage_id: INTEGER)
        -- set language to a_language_id
        -- and sublanguage to a_sublanguage_id
    require
        valid_langid: a_language_id > 0;
        valid_sublangid: a_sublanguage_id > 0
    ensure
        language_set: language = a_language_id;
        sublanguage_set: sublanguage = a_sublanguage_id
```

Displaying a Message Box

Each type of message box is supported by one routine; for an error box, use *error_message_box;* for an information box, use *information_message_box;* and so on. Each of the routines takes three parameters, including a parent window (*a_window*), the text of the message (*a_text*), and a message box title (*a_title*). The parent window becomes the controlling window for the message box and influences the position and z-order location of the dialog.

```
error_message_box (a_window: WEL_WINDOW; a_text, a_title: STRING)
        -- Show an error message box with message 'a_text'
        -- and caption 'a_title'
    require
        text_not_void: a_text /= void;
        title_not_void: a_title /= void

information_message_box (a_window: WEL_WINDOW; a_text, a_title:
    STRING)
        -- Show an information message box with message 'a_text'
        -- and caption 'a_title'
    require
        text_not_void: a_text /= void;
        title_not_void: a_title /= void

question_message_box (a_window: WEL_WINDOW; a_text, a_title:
STRING)
        -- Show a question message box with message 'a_text'
        -- and caption 'a_title'
    require
        text_not_void: a_text /= void;
        title_not_void: a_title /= void

warning_message_box (a_window: WEL_WINDOW; a_text, a_title: STRING)
        - Show a warning message box with message 'a_text'
        - and caption 'a_title'
    require
        text_not_void: a_text /= void;
        title_not_void: a_title /= void
```

To illustrate the use of message boxes, Example 9.10 uses four buttons to create a message box of each type supported by WEL.

Example 9.10 Window Message Boxes (windows\message)

```
class MAIN_WINDOW
inherit
    WEL_FRAME_WINDOW
```

```
            redefine
                on_control_command
            end
    creation
        make
    feature
        make is
                -- Initialize the main window
            do
                make_top ("Main Window")
                resize (300, 255)
                -- initialize the message box
                create popup_message_box.make
                create error_button.make (Current, "Error", 10, 30, 90, 35, -1)
                create info_button.make (Current, "Info", 10, 70, 90, 35, -1)
                create question_button.make (Current, "Question", 10,
                    110, 90, 35, -1)
                create warning_button.make (Current, "Warning", 10, 150,
                    90, 35, -1)
            end
        info_button, warning_button, error_button, question_button:
    WEL_PUSH_BUTTON
                -- Push buttons
        on_control_command (control: WEL_CONTROL) is
                -- A command has been received from 'control'.
            do
                if control = error_button then
                    popup_message_box.error_message_box (Current,
                        "This is a serious error.", "Error")
                elseif control = info_button then
                    popup_message_box.information_message_box (Current,
                        "This is a multi line message%Nfor your informa-
                            tion",
                        "For your Information")
                elseif control = question_button then
                    popup_message_box.question_message_box (Current,
                        "Are you sure?", "Confirm")
                elseif control = warning_button then
                    popup_message_box.warning_message_box (Current,
                        "This is a warning!", "Warning! Warning!")
                end
            end
        popup_message_box: WEL_MSG_BOX
                -- Message box
    end -- class MAIN_WINDOW
```

When a message box is displayed, it appears centered on the screen. A message box is also modal, meaning that you must acknowledge it by clicking on a button (usually OK or Cancel) before you can continue working in your application. Figure 9.11 shows the four types of message boxes as they appear on the screen.

Displaying a Custom Message Box

The four standard message boxes are actually constructed using different sets of customization flags. The flags indicate the icon to be displayed, the buttons that appear, and which button has the input focus when the message box is activated.

You can build your own custom message boxes using *basic_message_box* or *user_icon_message_box*. Routine *basic_message_box* is the same as the previous message box routines, only you also need to specify an integer that represents the style. The style parameter should be a combination of values from class *WEL_MB_CONSTANTS* (see Table 9.8) containing one value for the icon, one for the buttons, and one for the default button.

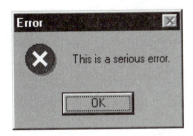

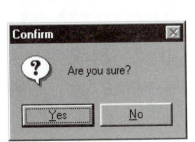

FIGURE 9.11. Message box example.

```
basic_message_box (a_window: WEL_WINDOW; a_text, a_title: STRING;
    a_style: INTEGER)
        -- Show a basic message box with 'a_text' inside and
        -- 'a_title' using 'a_style'. Basic means 'a_style' should
        -- not contain
        -- the flag 'MB_USERICON'.
        -- See class WEL_MB_CONSTANTS for 'a_style' value.
    require
        basic_message_box: basic_msg_box (a_style);
        text_not_void: a_text /= void;
        title_not_void: a_title /= void

user_icon_message_box (a_window: WEL_WINDOW; a_text, a_title:
    STRING; a_style, an_id: INTEGER)
        -- Show a message box with a user icon 'an_id',
        -- 'a_text' inside and 'a_title' using 'a_style'.
        -- the flag 'MB_USERICON' must be present in 'a_style'.
        -- See class WEL_MB_CONSTANTS for 'a_style' value.
    require
        user_message_box: not basic_msg_box (a_style);
        text_not_void: a_text /= void;
        title_not_void: a_title /= void
```

Routine *user_icon_message_box* allows you to use a custom icon rather than one of the predefined message box icons. The additional parameter *an_id* specifies a resource identifier for the icon.

TABLE 9.8   *Message Box Style Constants (WEL_MB_CONSTANTS)*

CONSTANT	DESCRIPTION
Mb_ok	Message dialog box contains an OK push button.
Mb_okcancel	Message dialog box contains OK and Cancel push buttons.
Mb_abortretrycancel	Message dialog box contains Abort, Retry, and Cancel push buttons.
Mb_yesnocancel	Message dialog box contains Yes, No, and Cancel push buttons.
Mb_yesno	Message dialog box contains Yes and No push buttons.
Mb_retrycancel	Message dialog box contains Retry and Cancel push buttons.
Mb_iconhand	The message dialog box contains a stop sign icon.
Mb_iconquestion	The message dialog box contains a question mark.
Mb_iconexclamation	The message dialog box contains an exclamation mark.

Mb_iconasterisk	The message dialog box contains an icon consisting of a lowercase letter i.
Mb_iconinformation	The message dialog box contains an icon consisting of a lowercase letter i. Same as *Mb_iconasterisk*.
Mb_iconstop	The message dialog box contains a stop sign icon.
Mb_defbutton1	Make the first button the default button.
Mb_defbutton2	Make the second button the default button.
Mb_defbutton3	Make the third button the default button.
Mb_applmodal	Make the message box window application modal. The user must answer the message box before continuing to work in the application. Other applications are not affected.
Mb_systemmodal	Make the message box window system modal. The user must answer the dialog box before continuing to work in any running application. Unless *Mb_iconhand* is also specified, the dialog box does not become modal until it is created.
Mb_taskmodal	Make the message box window task modal. All top-level windows of this application are disabled. The user must answer the dialog box before continuing in the current application.
Mb_nofocus	Do not give the message box window focus when it first appears.
Mb_default_desktop_only	The desktop currently receiving input must be a default desktop; otherwise the function fails. A default desktop is one an application runs on after the user has logged on.
Mb_help	Adds a Help button to the message box.
Mb_right	Right-justify the text.
Mb_rtlreading	Displays the text in right-to-left reading order for Arabic and Hebrew systems.
Mb_setforeground	The message box becomes the foreground window.
Mb_topmost	The message box becomes the topmost window.

Example 9.11 illustrates how you can create custom message boxes by creating both a standard message box and a message box with a user-defined icon.

Example 9.11 Custom Message Box Example (dialogs\custmsg)

```
class MAIN_WINDOW
inherit
    WEL_FRAME_WINDOW
```

Example 9.11 Custom Message Box Example (dialogs\custmsg)

```
        redefine
            on_control_command
        end
    APPLICATION_IDS
        export
            {NONE} all
        end
creation
    make
feature
    make is
            -- Initialize the main window
        do
            make_top ("Main Window")
            resize (300, 255)
            create message_button.make (Current, "Message", 10, 30,
                90, 35, -1)
            create usericon_button.make (Current, "User Icon", 10,
                70, 90, 35, -1)
            create popup_message_box.make
        end
    message_button, usericon_button: WEL_PUSH_BUTTON
            -- Push buttons
    on_control_command (control: WEL_CONTROL) is
            -- A command has been received from `control'.
        local
            message_result: INTEGER
        do
            if control = message_button then
                popup_message_box.basic_message_box (Current,
                    "Do you want to continue?", "Confirm",
                    Mb_yesno + Mb_iconquestion + Mb_defbutton2)
                if popup_message_box.message_box_result = Idyes then
                    popup_message_box.information_message_box
                        (Current, "You selected Yes",
                            "Confirm Answer")
                elseif message_result = Idno then
                    popup_message_box.information_message_box
                        (Current, "You selected No", "Confirm
                        Answer")
                end
            elseif control = usericon_button then
                popup_message_box.user_icon_message_box (Current,
                    "Do you like my custom icon?",
                        "User Icon", Mb_yesno + Mb_usericon + Mb_def-
                            button1,
                        Idi_customquestion_constant)
            end
        end
    popup_message_box: WEL_MSG_BOX
end -- class MAIN_WINDOW
```

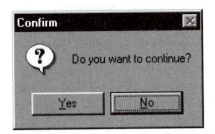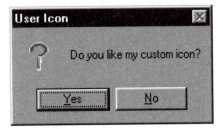

FIGURE 9.12. Custom message box examples.

Figure 9.12 shows the custom message boxes created by Example 9.11. The first message box was created by calling *basic_message_box,* specifying the question icon and Yes and No buttons, and the second message box was created by *user_icon_message_box,* specifying a user defined icon.[1]

Determining the Result of a Message Box

If a message box has more than one button, you may need to determine which button the user pressed. This value is stored in the *message_box_result* attribute of *WEL_MSG_BOX.* You can examine this value and compare it with the values in *WEL_ID_CONSTANTS* (see Table 9.9) to determine which button was used.

```
message_box_result: INTEGER
        -- Last result for all 'xxx_message_box' routines.
        -- See class WEL_ID_CONSTANTS for values.
```

TABLE 9.9   *Message Box Return Results (WEL_ID_CONSTANTS)*

CONSTANT	DESCRIPTION
Idok	OK button was selected.
Idcancel	Cancel button was selected.
Idabort	Abort button was selected.
Idretry	Retry button was selected.
Idignore	Ignore button was selected.
Idyes	Yes button was selected.
Idno	No button was selected.

---

[1]Given my icon drawing skills, it's no wonder graphic artists are in high demand!

SUMMARY

Three types of dialogs are supported in WEL—user defined resource dialogs, standard dialogs, and message boxes. An application will often contain many instances of each, including resource dialogs used to define application properties and settings, standard dialogs for opening and saving documents and/or files, and message boxes for confirmation questions and notifying the user of errors and information. The Directory Tree Analyzer application uses each type of dialog for exactly those reasons.

DIRECTORY TREE ANALYZER

IMPLEMENTING THE DIALOGS

The Directory Tree Analyzer uses dialog boxes to perform a wide variety of functionality, from a simple About dialog box used to show application information to a relatively complicated Preferences dialog used to set user preferences.

About Dialog

The About dialog box displays application version information and memory statistics, as shown in Figure 9.13. The only user action available in the dialog is an OK button used to dismiss the dialog.

Creating the dialog was a three-step process. First, the layout and design of the dialog window and its controls were created in a visual resource editor. Each control was given a unique identifier so that it could be referenced symbolically later on. Second, the resource file created by the resource editor was fed through the Resource Bench utility to generate Eiffel code representing the defined resources. Finally, the generated dialog code was edited to perform relevant application functionality—in this case, to display memory usage information collected from the *MEMORY* class.

Resource Bench generated all of the code required to initialize the dialog box and create its child controls. The only feature that needed additional code was the *setup_dialog* routine, which is called every time the dialog is displayed to the user. In this case, we collect memory usage information and insert it in the relevant static text controls (see lines 34–45 in Example 9.12).

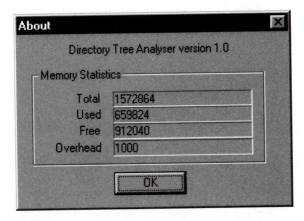

FIGURE 9.13. Directory Tree Analyzer About dialog.

Example 9.12 IDD_ABOUT_DIALOG for the Directory Tree Analyzer

```
1     class IDD_ABOUT_DIALOG
2
3     inherit
4            WEL_MODAL_DIALOG
5                redefine
6                        setup_dialog
7                end;
8            APPLICATION_IDS
9                export
10                       {NONE} all
11               end
12
13    create
14           make
15
16    feature {NONE} -- Initialization
17
18           make (a_parent: WEL_COMPOSITE_WINDOW) is
19                       -- Create the dialog.
20                require
21                       a_parent_not_void: a_parent /= void;
22                       a_parent_exists: a_parent.exists
23                do
24                       make_by_id (a_parent, idd_about_dialog_
                             constant)
25                       create id_ok.make_by_id (Current, idok)
26                       create id_total.make_by_id (Current, idc_
                             memory_total_constant)
27                       create id_used.make_by_id (Current, idc_
                             memory_used_constant)
28                       create id_free.make_by_id (Current, idc_
                             memory_free_constant)
```

```
29                              create id_overhead.make_by_id (Current,
                                  idc_memory_overhead_constant)
30              end;
31
32  feature -- Behavior
33
34          setup_dialog is
35              local
36                      mem_info: MEM_INFO
37              do
38                      create memory;
39                      memory.full_collect;
40                      mem_info := memory.memory_statistics
                             (memory.total_memory);
41                      id_total.set_text (mem_info.total.out);
42                      id_used.set_text (mem_info.used.out);
43                      id_free.set_text (mem_info.free.out);
44                      id_overhead.set_text (mem_info.overhead.out)
45              end;
46
47  feature -- Access
48
49          id_ok: WEL_PUSH_BUTTON;
50          id_total: WEL_STATIC;
51          id_used: WEL_STATIC;
52          id_free: WEL_STATIC;
53          id_overhead: WEL_STATIC;
54
55  feature {NONE} -- Implementation
56
57          memory: MEMORY;
58
59  end -- class IDD_ABOUT_DIALOG
```

Preferences Dialog

The Preferences dialog is a little more complicated. This dialog needs to display and modify the application preferences and settings, including the parsing depth and display options (see Figure 9.14). Four of the standard modal dialog routines, namely *setup_dialog, notify, on_ok,* and parent, are redefined to implement the dialog (see line 5 in Example 9.13).

Routine *setup_dialog* is implemented to initialize the dialog controls to the settings stored in *shared_preferences* so that relevant controls are enabled and disabled. For example, if an infinite parse depth is selected, then the traversal depth control is disabled.

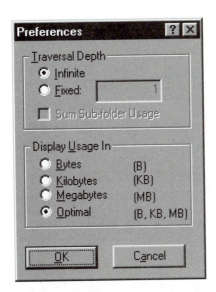

FIGURE 9.14. Directory Tree Analyzer Preferences dialog.

Routine *notify* is implemented to capture control events occurring within the dialog. If the event results in a change in parse traversal type (from infinite to fixed and vice versa), then appropriate controls are enabled and disabled to reflect the change.

Message hook *on_ok* is called whenever the user dismisses the dialog by clicking the OK button. This routine collects the values of the child controls set by the user and updates the *shared_preferences*. If necessary, *on_ok* notifies the parent window that it needs to update collected information.

Example 9.13 IDD_PREFERENCES_DIALOG for the Directory Tree Analyzer

```
1    class IDD_PREFERENCES_DIALOG
2    inherit
3            WEL_MODAL_DIALOG
4                redefine
5                    setup_dialog, notify, on_ok, parent
6                end;
7            SHARED_DATA
8                export
9                    {NONE} all
10               end;
11           APPLICATION_IDS
```

```
12              export
13                  {NONE} all
14              end;
15          WEL_BN_CONSTANTS
16              export
17                  {NONE} all
18              end
19  create
20          make
21
22  feature {NONE} -- Initialization
23
24      make (a_parent: MAIN_WINDOW) is
25              -- Create the dialog.
26          require
27              a_parent_not_void: a_parent /= void;
28              a_parent_exists: a_parent.exists
29          do
30              make_by_id (a_parent, idd_preferences_dia-
                    log_constant)
31              create idc_traversal_depth_infinite.make_by_id
32                  (Current, idc_traversal_depth_infinite_con-
                    stant)
33              create idc_traversal_depth_fixed.make_by_id
34                  (Current, idc_traversal_depth_fixed_constant)
35              create idc_size_bytes.make_by_id (Current,
                    idc_size_bytes_constant)
36              create idc_size_kilobytes.make_by_id (Current,
                    idc_size_kilobytes_constant)
37              create idc_size_megabytes.make_by_id (Current,
                    idc_size_megabytes_constant)
38              create idc_size_optimal.make_by_id (Current,
                    idc_size_optimal_constant)
39              create id_ok.make_by_id (Current, idok)
40              create idc_traversal_depth.make_by_id (Current,
                    idc_traversal_depth_constant)
41              create id_cancel.make_by_id (Current, idcancel)
42              create idc_sum_last_folder.make_by_id (Current,
                    idc_sum_last_folder_constant)
43          end;
44
45  feature -- Behavior
46
47      setup_dialog is
48          do
49              if shared_preferences.sum_last_folder then
50                  idc_sum_last_folder.set_checked
51              else
52                  idc_sum_last_folder.set_unchecked
53              end
54          if shared_preferences.traversal = shared_prefer-
                ences.traversal_infinite then
```

```
55              idc_traversal_depth_infinite.set_checked
56              idc_traversal_depth_fixed.set_unchecked
57              idc_traversal_depth.disable
58              idc_sum_last_folder.disable
59          else
60              idc_traversal_depth_infinite.set_unchecked
61              idc_traversal_depth_fixed.set_checked
62              idc_traversal_depth.enable
63              idc_sum_last_folder.enable
64          end
65          idc_traversal_depth.set_text (shared_pref-
                erences.traversal_depth.out)
66          idc_size_bytes.set_unchecked
67          idc_size_kilobytes.set_unchecked
68          idc_size_megabytes.set_unchecked
69          idc_size_optimal.set_unchecked
70          if shared_preferences.size = shared_pref-
                erences.size_bytes then
71              idc_size_bytes.set_checked
72          elseif shared_preferences.size = shared_prefer-
                ences.size_kilobytes then
73              idc_size_kilobytes.set_checked
74          elseif shared_preferences.size = shared_prefer-
                ences.size_megabytes then
75              idc_size_megabytes.set_checked
76          elseif shared_preferences.size = shared_prefer-
                ences.size_optimal then
77              idc_size_optimal.set_checked
78          end
79      end;
80
81      notify (control: WEL_CONTROL; notify_code: INTEGER) is
82          do
83              if notify_code = bn_clicked then
84                  if control = idc_traversal_depth_infinite then
85                      idc_traversal_depth.disable
86                      idc_sum_last_folder.disable
87                  elseif control = idc_traversal_depth_fixed
                    then
88                      idc_traversal_depth.enable;
89                      idc_sum_last_folder.enable
90                  end
91              end
92          end;
93
94      on_ok is
95          -- Set user selected preferences
96          local
97              original_traversal: INTEGER;
98              original_depth: INTEGER;
99              reparse: BOOLEAN
100         do
```

```
101              original_traversal := shared_preferences.traversal;
102              original_depth := shared_preferences.tra-
                     versal_depth;
103              shared_preferences.set_sum_last_folder
                     (idc_sum_last_folder.checked);
104              if idc_traversal_depth_infinite.checked then
105                  shared_preferences.set_traversal_infinite
106              elseif idc_traversal_depth_fixed.checked then
107                  shared_preferences.set_traversal_fixed
                         (idc_traversal_depth.text.to_integer)
108              else
109                  shared_preferences.set_traversal_fixed (1)
110              end;
111              if original_traversal /= shared_preferences.
                     traversal
112                  or original_depth /= shared_preferences.
                         traversal_depth then
113                  reparse := True
114              end;
115              if idc_size_bytes.checked then
116                  shared_preferences.set_size (shared_pref-
                         erences.size_bytes)
117              elseif idc_size_kilobytes.checked then
118                  shared_preferences.set_size (shared_pref-
                         erences.size_kilobytes)
119              elseif idc_size_megabytes.checked then
120                  shared_preferences.set_size (shared_pref-
                         erences.size_megabytes)
121              elseif idc_size_optimal.checked then
122                  shared_preferences.set_size (shared_pref-
                         erences.size_optimal)
123              end;
124              if parent.directory_infos /= void then
125                  if reparse then
126                          parent.update_for_traversal_depth
127                  else
128                          parent.update_for_display
129                  end
130              end;
131                Precursor
132          end;
133
134  feature -- Access
135
136      idc_traversal_depth_infinite: WEL_RADIO_BUTTON;
137      idc_traversal_depth_fixed: WEL_RADIO_BUTTON;
138      idc_size_bytes: WEL_RADIO_BUTTON;
139      idc_size_kilobytes: WEL_RADIO_BUTTON;
140      idc_size_megabytes: WEL_RADIO_BUTTON;
141      idc_size_optimal: WEL_RADIO_BUTTON;
142      idc_sum_last_folder: WEL_CHECK_BOX;
143      id_ok: WEL_PUSH_BUTTON;
```

```
144        idc_traversal_depth: WEL_SINGLE_LINE_EDIT;
145        id_cancel: WEL_PUSH_BUTTON;
146
147        parent: MAIN_WINDOW;
148                -- Parent window
149
150 end -- class IDD_PREFERENCES_DIALOG
```

GRAPHICS DEVICE INTERFACE

INTRODUCING THE GRAPHICS DEVICE INTERFACE

Windows provides device-independent graphics through the Graphics Device Interface (GDI). The GDI incorporates a standard set of API routines that can be used to draw on any graphical device, such as a screen, printer, or plotter. The GDI is actually used for every drawing operation in Windows, including drawing the desktop, windows, and their controls.

THE DEVICE CONTEXT

Before you can start to call GDI routines, you must let Windows know what type of device you will be drawing on. It is not necessary to tell Windows all the details about the device — just what type of device it is. For example, if you are drawing on a printer, you need to tell Windows only that it is a printer, not that it is a color laser printer with 600dpi resolution.

Windows uses a structure called a device context to represent different types of graphics devices. The device context helps Windows to draw on the device efficiently and to identify the capabilities of each device.

Types of Device Contexts

The abstract form of a device context is class *WEL_DC*. *WEL_DC* provides an abstract interface to the functionality of a device context, including the selection of drawing tools, determining device capabilities, and drawing. Descendants of *WEL_DC* implement different types of concrete device contexts. Device contexts are also used to draw on different areas of the screen and for drawing on a printer. The WEL library also supports a number of device contexts that may not be immediately familiar, such as memory device contexts. This type of device context can be used to create an area in memory that is compatible with another existing device context. Figure 10.1 shows the inheritance relationships between each of the device context types available in WEL.

As we will see next, types of device contexts allow you to paint on different areas of the Windows screen, ranging from the entire screen (*WEL_SCREEN_DC*) to a client area of a particular window (*WEL_CLIENT_DC*). Other device contexts allow painting in memory (*WEL_MEMORY_DC*) or painting on a printer (*WEL_PRINTER_DC*). The following sections describe how to construct and use each type of device context.

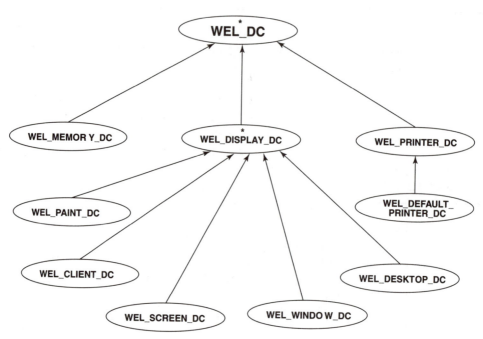

FIGURE 10.1. GDI Device context types.

Creating a Memory Device Context

A memory device context allows you to treat an area of memory as a bitmap. You can create a memory device context and then draw on it as you would draw on the screen. When a memory device context is first created, Windows initializes the context in memory so that it is compatible with the application's current screen. At this stage, the device context is just a placeholder for drawing and contains a bitmap with 1 pixel × 1 pixel dimensions. Before you can begin to draw on it, you must first select a bitmap of the required width and height into the device context. See "Selecting a Bitmap" later in this chapter.

A memory device context has two creation procedures, *make* and *make_by_dc*. The first creates a new memory device context that is compatible with the application's current screen, and the second creates a memory device context that is compatible with another existing device context.

```
make
        -- Make a memory dc compatible with the application's
        -- current screen.

make_by_dc (a_dc: WEL_DC)
        -- Make a memory dc compatible with 'a_dc'.
    require
        a_dc_not: a_dc /= Void;
        a_dc_exists: a_dc.exists
```

Creating a Paint Device Context

A paint device context is used when Windows sends the *Wm_paint* message. Windows creates the paint device context for you and passes it to the message processing loop, which in turn is passed to the *on_paint* routine of your window. You rarely have to create a paint device context in your own application code.

If you do need to create a paint device context, its creation procedure takes a reference to a window as its sole parameter. The paint device context is created for the specified window.

```
make (a_window: WEL_WINDOW)
        -- Makes a DC associated with 'a_window'
    require
        a_window_not_void: a_window /= Void;
        a_window_exists: a_window.exists
    ensure
        window_set: window = a_window
```

A *WEL_PAINT_DC* instance contains a reference to a *WEL_PAINT_STRUCT* object that specifies a number of parameters for the paint operation. Typically, if Windows created the paint device context, then this paint structure information will be set correctly to notify you whether the background needs to be erased and also to define the invalid rectangle of the window that needs re-painting. If you create a paint device context in your own code, ensure that the *WEL_PAINT_STRUCT* information is correct.

Creating a Client Device Context

A client device context is one of the most commonly used device context types. As its name suggests, the client device context is used to draw on the client area of a window. Specifically, a client device context allows you to draw on the area contained within the *client_rect* of a particular window. See "Window Dimensions as a Rectangle" in Chapter 4, "Windows," for more information on feature *client_rect*.

To create a client device context, you need to specify a reference to a window as the parameter to the creation procedure *make*. You can also specify a pointer to a preexisting Windows client device context if you are interfacing with external code by using the creation procedure *make_by_pointer* from class *WEL_ANY*.

```
make (a_window: WEL_WINDOW)
        -- Makes a DC associated with 'a_window'
    require
        a_window_not_void: a_window /= Void;
        a_window_exists: a_window.exists
    ensure
        window_set: window = a_window
```

Creating a Window Device Context

Creating a window device context allows you to draw on the entire rectangle of a window, including its title bar and borders. You may want to use such a de-vice context to draw your own borders and title bar. To create a window device context, you must pass a reference to a window to the creation procedure *make* of class *WEL_WINDOW_DC*.

```
make (a_window: WEL_WINDOW)
    require
        a_window_not_void: a_window /= Void;
        a_window_exists: a_window.exists
    ensure
        window_set: window = a_window
```

Creating a Screen Device Context

A screen device context can be used to draw on any part of the screen. For example, drawing graphics on the desktop or drawing cockroaches that hide under windows can be implemented using a screen device context.

The class *WEL_SCREEN_DC* does not declare any creation procedures; therefore, you can create a screen device context by using the creation instruction on its own.

Creating a Desktop Device Context

Desktop device contexts allow you to draw on the Windows desktop. A desktop device context is typically used to draw desktop icons. Like the screen device context, a desktop device context does not define any creation procedures; therefore, you can create an instance by using the creation instruction on its own.

Using Display Device Contexts

Each of the display device contexts, including *WEL_PAINT_DC*, *WEL_CLIENT_DC*, *WEL_SCREEN_DC*, *WEL_WINDOW_DC*, and *WEL_DESK-TOP_DC*, inherit from *WEL_DISPLAY_DC*. Deferred class *WEL_DIS-PLAY_DC* declares two deferred features, *get* and *release*.

```
get
          -- Get the device context.
      require
          not_exists: not exists
      ensure
          exists: exists

release
          -- Release the device context.
      require
          exists: exists
      ensure
          not_exists: not exists
```

The routine *get* is used to initialize the device context and ready it for drawing. You cannot draw on a device context before calling *get*. Feature *release* is used to release the resources used by the device context. It should be called when you have finished using it. For all descendants of *WEL_DIS-PLAY_DC*, except (in some circumstances) *WEL_PAINT_DC*, you must call *get* and *release* in your application code. If you receive a *WEL_PAINT_DC* as a parameter to *on_paint*, then you don't need to call *get* and *release*—the WEL library takes care of it for you.

GDI TOOLS

When drawing on a device context, the GDI relies on a number of tools to determine how the result will be painted. The tools include bitmaps, fonts, pens, brushes, palettes, and regions. Each tool can be separately selected (known as selecting a tool into a device context) and affects a different aspect of the drawing operation. A selected font changes the typeface, point size, and effects of any painted text; a pen changes the appearance of any drawn lines; a brush changes the appearance of any filled areas; a palette changes the choice of colors; a region changes the drawing area; and a bitmap changes a memory device context's background.

Unselecting All GDI Tools

One feature exists in *WEL_DC* that affects all tools—routine *unselect_all* unselects and restores all selected tools to the previously selected tool (if any) or to the default device context tool.

```
unselect_all
        -- Deselect all objects and restore the old ones
    require
        exists: exists
    ensure
        pen_not_selected: not pen_selected;
        brush_not_selected: not brush_selected;
        region_not_selected: not region_selected;
        palette_not_selected: not palette_selected;
        font_not_selected: not font_selected;
        bitmap_not_selected: not bitmap_selected
```

Bitmaps

When Windows creates a memory device context, it reserves a 1 × 1 area of memory. The size of this memory area is usually insufficient for most situations and needs to be resized. To resize a memory device context, you must select a bitmap into the context. The dimensions of the device context will match those of the selected bitmap.

The selected bitmap can be created from a resource (*make_by_id* or *make_by_name*), indirectly via a device independent bitmap (*make_by_dib*), indirectly via a logical bitmap (*make_indirect*), or compatibly with a particular device context (*make_compatible*).

The class interface for *WEL_BITMAP* is shown next.

```
class interface
      WEL_BITMAP
create

      make_by_id (id: INTEGER)
            -- (from WEL_RESOURCE)
          require - from WEL_RESOURCE
            valid_id: id > 0
          ensure - from WEL_RESOURCE
            not_shared: not shared
      make_by_name (name: STRING)
            -- (from WEL_RESOURCE)
          require - from WEL_RESOURCE
            name_not_void: name /= Void;
            name_not_empty: not name.empty
          ensure -- from WEL_RESOURCE
            not_shared: not shared
      make_by_dib (a_dc: WEL_DC; dib: WEL_DIB; mode: INTEGER)
          require
            a_dc_not_void: a_dc /= Void;
            a_dc_exists: a_dc.exists;
            dib_not_void: dib /= Void;
            valid_mode: valid_dib_colors_constant (mode)
          ensure
            bitmap_created: item /= item.default
      make_compatible (a_dc: WEL_DC; a_width, a_height: INTEGER)
          require
            a_dc_not_void: a_dc /= Void;
            a_dc_exists: a_dc.exists;
            positive_width: a_width >= 0;
            positive_height: a_height >= 0
      make_indirect (a_log_bitmap: WEL_LOG_BITMAP)
          require
            a_log_bitmap_not_void: a_log_bitmap /= Void
feature -- Access

      height: INTEGER
            -- Bitmap height
          require
            exists: exists
          ensure
            positive_result: Result >= 0
      log_bitmap: WEL_LOG_BITMAP
            -- Log bitmap structure associated to 'Current'
          require
            exists: exists
          ensure
            result_not_void: Result /= Void
      width: INTEGER
            -- Bitmap width
          require
            exists: exists
```

```
            ensure
                positive_result: Result >= 0
    feature {ANY} -- Status report

        valid_dib_colors_constant (c: INTEGER): BOOLEAN
                -- Is 'c' a valid dib colors constant?
                -- (from WEL_DIB_COLORS_CONSTANTS)
    feature - Basic operations

        set_di_bits (a_dc: WEL_DC; start_line, length: INTEGER; dib:
            WEL_DIB; mode: INTEGER)
                -- Set the bits of the current bitmap to the values
                -- given in 'dib', starting at line 'start_line'
                -- during 'length' lines, using 'mode'.
                -- See class WEL_DIB_COLORS_CONSTANTS for 'mode'
                -- values.
            require
                exists: exists;
                a_dc_not_void: a_dc /= Void;
                a_dc_exists: a_dc.exists;
                dib_not_void: dib /= Void;
                valid_mode: valid_dib_colors_constant (mode)

    end -- class WEL_BITMAP
```

Selecting a Bitmap

Once you have created an appropriately sized bitmap, you can select it into your memory device context by calling *select_bitmap*. The currently selected bitmap can be accessed by calling *bitmap*, and you can determine if a bitmap is currently selected by calling *bitmap_selected*.

Finally, the selected bitmap can be unselected with the feature *unselect_bitmap*.

```
bitmap: WEL_BITMAP
        -- Current bitmap selected

bitmap_selected: BOOLEAN
        -- Is a bitmap selected?

select_bitmap (a_bitmap: WEL_BITMAP)
        -- Select the 'a_bitmap' as the current bitmap.
    require
        exists: exists;
        a_bitmap_not_void: a_bitmap /= Void;
        a_bitmap_exists: a_bitmap.exists
```

```
    ensure
        bitmap_set: bitmap = a_bitmap;
        bitmap_selected: bitmap_selected

unselect_bitmap
        -- Deselect the bitmap and restore the old one
    require
        exists: exists;
        bitmap_selected: bitmap_selected
    ensure
        bitmap_not_selected: not bitmap_selected
```

Brushes

A brush can be used to fill any closed area, including rectangles, ellipses, polygons, and paths, with a color or hatch pattern. When a brush is selected, it is used to paint the interior of the area being drawn. For example, you may have a drawing application that provides the functionality to draw filled rectangles or ellipses. When drawing these shapes, you need to select a brush into the device context to fill the shape with a particular pattern or color. A brush has a style, a color, and a hatch pattern. The style determines if the brush is solid, hollow, or hatched, and the hatch pattern determines what type of pattern is used from a predefined set of patterns.

Two types of brushes exist in the WEL library, *WEL_BRUSH* and *WEL_LOG_BRUSH*. Class *WEL_BRUSH* defines a physical brush that can be selected in a device context, while a *WEL_LOG_BRUSH* is a logical definition of a physical brush. Once a *WEL_BRUSH* has been created, its settings, including the style, color, and hatch pattern, cannot be changed. In contrast, the settings of a *WEL_LOG_BRUSH* can be changed, and a physical *WEL_BRUSH* can be created from a logical brush at any time.

The interface of *WEL_BRUSH* includes a number of creation procedures for creating brushes, as well as features for setting brush properties and determining what the brush's properties are.[1]

```
class interface
    WEL_BRUSH
creation

    make_by_sys_color (sys_color: INTEGER)
        -- Make a brush using the system color 'sys_color'.
```

[1]Features inherited from *WEL_GDI_ANY* have been omitted.

```
               -- See class WEL_COLOR_CONSTANTS for 'sys_color' value.
               -- Use only this creation routine for a WNDCLASS brush.
          ensure
               shared: shared

     make_solid (a_color: WEL_COLOR_REF)
               -- Make a brush that has the solid 'a_color'
          require
               a_color_not_void: a_color /= Void
          ensure
               color_set: exists implies color.is_equal (a_color)

     make_hatch (a_hatch: INTEGER; a_color: WEL_COLOR_REF)
               -- Make a brush that has the
               -- 'hatch_style' pattern and 'a_color'
               -- See class WEL_HS_CONSTANTS for 'a_hatch'
          require
               a_color_not_void: a_color /= Void
          ensure
               hatch_set: exists implies hatch = a_hatch;
               color_set: exists implies color.is_equal (a_color)

     make_by_pattern (bitmap: WEL_BITMAP)
               -- Make a brush with the specified 'bitmap' pattern.
          require
               bitmap_not_void: bitmap /= Void;
               bitmap_exists: bitmap.exists

     make_indirect (a_log_brush: WEL_LOG_BRUSH)
               -- Make a brush using 'a_log_brush'
          require
               a_log_brush_not_void: a_log_brush /= Void

feature -- Access

     color: WEL_COLOR_REF
               -- Brush color
          require
               exists: exists
          ensure
               result_not_void: Result /= Void

     hatch: INTEGER
               -- Brush hatch
          require
               exists: exists

     log_brush: WEL_LOG_BRUSH
               -- Log brush structure associated to 'Current'
          require
               exists: exists
```

```
        ensure
            result_not_void: Result /= Void
    style: INTEGER
            -- Brush style
        require
            exists: exists

invariant
        -- from GENERAL
    reflexive_equality: standard_is_equal (Current);
    reflexive_conformance: conforms_to (Current);
end -- class WEL_BRUSH
```

Creating a Stock Brush

The most common brushes, including black, white, gray, and null brushes, can be created using GDI stock object classes. For example, if you need to create a solid black brush, you can create an instance of *WEL_BLACK_BRUSH,* which is a specialized type of WEL_BRUSH. Table 10.1 lists each of the stock brushes available in WEL.

Creating a stock brush is the easiest method of constructing brushes, and in most applications, stock brushes are all that is needed. To create a stock brush, say a solid black brush, you would need

```
black_brush: WEL_BLACK_BRUSH
...
create black_brush.make
```

You can then select the new brush into a device context using *select_ brush.* See the section "Selecting a Brush" later in this chapter.

TABLE 10.1   *Stock Brushes*

STOCK BRUSH CLASS	DESCRIPTION
WEL_BLACK_BRUSH	Solid black brush.
WEL_DARK_GRAY_BRUSH	Solid dark gray brush.
WEL_GRAY_BRUSH	Solid gray brush.
WEL_HOLLOW_BRUSH	Hollow brush. Nothing is drawn.
WEL_LIGHT_GRAY_BRUSH	Solid light gray brush.
WEL_NULL_BRUSH	Same as *WEL_HOLLOW_BRUSH.*
WEL_WHITE_BRUSH	Solid white brush.

Creating a System Color Brush

A brush can be created in many ways, including using a system color, a general color, from a hatch pattern, a bitmap, or indirectly from a logical brush.

To create a brush that represents a solid system color, you need to call *make_by_sys_color,* specifying a system color value. System colors are set by the user in Windows and are used to color general system components such as borders, title bars, buttons, and backgrounds. The symbolic names for system colors are all defined in class *WEL_COLOR_CONSTANTS,* shown in Table 10.2.

TABLE 10.2   *System Color Constants (WEL_COLOR_CONSTANTS)*

CONSTANT	DESCRIPTION
Color_activeborder	Active window border.
Color_activecaption	Active window caption.
Color_appworkspace	Background color of multiple document interface (MDI) applications.
Color_background	Background desktop.
Color_btnface	Face color for three-dimensional display elements.
Color_btnhighlight	Highlight color for three-dimensional display elements. Shown on the edges facing the light source.
Color_btnshadow	Shadow color for three-dimensional display elements. Shown on the edges facing away from the light source.
Color_btntext	Text on push buttons.
Color_captiontext	Text in scroll bar arrow boxes, size boxes, and captions.
Color_greytext	Disabled text.
Color_highlight	Item(s) selected in a control, such as a list box.
Color_highlighttext	Text of item(s) selected in a control.
Color_inactiveborder	Inactive window border.
Color_inactivecaptiontext	Text of an inactive window border.
Color_menu	Menu background.
Color_menutext	Text in menus.
Color_scrollbar	Scroll bar gray area.
Color_window	Window background.
Color_windowframe	Window frame.
Color_windowtext	Text in windows.

Creating a Solid Color Brush

You can also create a brush for any other color using *make_solid*. This procedure initializes a solid brush to the color you specify in the *a_color* parameter. The color is represented by an instance of *WEL_COLOR_REF* that holds the red, green, and blue intensity values for the color. The intensity values for a color range from 0 to 255, with 0 representing the lowest intensity and 255 representing the highest. Therefore, setting the three intensity values at 0, 0, 0, creates black, and at the other end of the scale, setting the values at 255, 255, 255 creates white.

Creating a color reference is simple—either initialize the color with separate values for red, green, and blue or initialize the color using a system color as specified in Table 10.2. You can also create a color reference without specifying the color intensities or a system color, in which case the color reference will be black (i.e., 0, 0, 0).

The interface of *WEL_COLOR_REF* contains the creation procedures *make, make_rgb,* and *make_system.* Access functions are also present to determine the current red, green, and blue intensities. Finally, routines are included to set the color intensities individually and as a group.

```
class interface
    WEL_COLOR_REF
creation
    make
            -- Make a black color
        ensure
          red_set: red = 0;
          green_set: green = 0;
          blue_set: blue = 0
    make_rgb (a_red, a_green, a_blue: INTEGER)
            -- Set 'red', 'green', 'blue' with
            -- 'a_red', 'a_green', 'a_blue'
        require
          valid_red_inf: a_red >= 0;
          valid_red_sup: a_red <= 255;
          valid_green_inf: a_green >= 0;
          valid_green_sup: a_green <= 255;
          valid_blue_inf: a_blue >= 0;
          valid_blue_sup: a_blue <= 255
        ensure
          red_set: red = a_red;
          green_set: green = a_green;
          blue_set: blue = a_blue
    make_system (index: INTEGER)
            -- Make a system color identified by 'index'.
```

```
                    -- See WEL_COLOR_CONSTANTS for 'index' values.
            require
               valid_color_constant: valid_color_constant (index)
feature -- Access

       blue: INTEGER
               -- Intensity value for the blue component
       green: INTEGER
               -- Intensity value for the green component
       red: INTEGER
               -- Intensity value for the red component
feature -- Element change

       set_blue (a_blue: INTEGER)
               -- Set 'blue' with 'a_blue'
            require
               valid_blue_inf: a_blue >= 0;
               valid_blue_sup: a_blue <= 255
            ensure
               blue_set: blue = a_blue
       set_green (a_green: INTEGER)
               -- Set 'green' with 'a_green'
            require
               valid_green_inf: a_green >= 0;
               valid_green_sup: a_green <= 255
            ensure
               green_set: green = a_green
       set_red (a_red: INTEGER)
               -- Set 'red' with 'a_red'
            require
               valid_red_inf: a_red >= 0;
               valid_red_sup: a_red <= 255
            ensure
               red_set: red = a_red
       set_rgb (a_red, a_green, a_blue: INTEGER)
               -- Set 'red', 'green', 'blue' with
               -- 'a_red', 'a_green', 'a_blue'
            require
               valid_red_inf: a_red >= 0;
               valid_red_sup: a_red <= 255;
               valid_green_inf: a_green >= 0;
               valid_green_sup: a_green <= 255;
               valid_blue_inf: a_blue >= 0;
               valid_blue_sup: a_blue <= 255
            ensure
               red_set: red = a_red;
               green_set: green = a_green;
               blue_set: blue = a_blue
invariant
       -- from GENERAL
       reflexive_equality: standard_is_equal (Current);
       reflexive_conformance: conforms_to (Current);
```

```
    exists: exists;
    valid_red_inf: red >= 0;
    valid_red_sup: red <= 255;
    valid_green_inf: green >= 0;
    valid_green_sup: green <= 255;
    valid_blue_inf: blue >= 0;
    valid_blue_sup: blue <= 255;

end -- class WEL_COLOR_REF
```

To create a solid green brush using a color, you need to code

```
brush: WEL_BRUSH
green: WEL_COLOR_REF
...
create green.make_rgb (0, 255, 0)
create brush.make_solid (green)
```

Two variables are needed—one a brush and the other a color reference. The color can then be created with maximum green intensity, and the color reference can be used to create the solid brush.

Using Standard Colors

A simpler way of creating a standard color is to use the class *WEL_STAN-DARD_COLORS*. This class defines all of the standard colors as once functions that return a *WEL_COLOR_REF*. You can therefore use this class when you require a color such as red, green, blue, black, white, and so on. The colors available in this class are

```
Black                Dark_red
Blue                 Dark_yellow
Cyan                 Green
Dark_blue            Grey
Dark_cyan            Magenta
Dark_green           Red
Dark_grey            White
Dark_magenta         Yellow
```

To use one of these features, you can inherit from *WEL_STANDARD_COLORS* and call the functions directly. For example, the inherit clause of a class *A*, may include

```
inherit
        WEL_STANDARD_COLORS
                export
                        {NONE} all
        end
```

and then a feature of class *A* can construct standard colors by calling the functions of *WEL_STANDARD_COLORS* directly

```
brush: WEL_BRUSH
...
-- can now refer to a standard color directly
create brush.make_solid (Blue)
```

In this case, the code creates a solid blue brush by calling the function Blue from class *WEL_STANDARD_COLORS*.

You can also declare *WEL_STANDARD_COLORS* as an attribute or local variable of a class or feature. Because the *WEL_STANDARD_COLORS* class consists entirely of constants (once functions, in this case) and does not have a creation procedure, it can be declared as an expanded type to provide more efficient access than if it were declared as a reference type. To use the local variable method, you would need the following code in a feature declaration:

```
local
      sc: expanded WEL_STANDARD_COLORS
do
      create brush.make (sc.Blue)
end
```

Creating a Hatch Pattern Brush

The third way to construct a brush is to use a hatch pattern. A hatch pattern is a small bitmap that is used to fill an area. It is drawn continuously, starting at its origin (usually the top left corner of the device context painting surface). If you are filling an area, then the hatch pattern is clipped so that it is painted within that area only.

A number of predefined hatch styles is available. Table 10.3 lists each hatch style as defined in class *WEL_HS_CONSTANTS*.

TABLE 10.3   *Brush Hatch Style Constants (WEL_HS_CONSTANTS)*

CONSTANT	DESCRIPTION
Hs_bdiagonal	Backward diagonal lines.
Hs_cross	Vertical and horizontal crossed lines.
Hs_diagcross	Diagonal crossed lines both forward and back.
Hs_fdiagonal	Forward diagonal lines.
Hs_horizontal	Horizontal lines.
Hs_vertical	Vertical lines.

To create a red hatch brush with a diagonal cross pattern, you need the following fragment of code:

```
red: WEL_COLOR_REF
brush: WEL_BRUSH
hs: expanded WEL_HS_CONSTANTS

...

create red.make_rgb (255, 0, 0)
create brush.make_hatch (hs.Hs_diagcross, red)
```

In this example, we create a red color reference (with maximum red intensity) and create the brush with the new color and a hatch style of *Hs_diagcross*. The *Hs_diagcross* constant is accessed via an expanded instance of *WEL_HS_CONSTANTS*. We could just as easily have inherited from *WEL_HS_CONSTANTS* rather than use an expanded attribute.

Creating a Bitmap Pattern Brush

To create a brush with a custom hatch pattern, you can use a bitmap. To do this, you first need to create a bitmap, either by reading a bitmap from a file or resource, or by creating the bitmap in memory (possibly using a memory device context). The *WEL_BRUSH* creation procedure *make_by_pattern* is used to initialize a brush with a bitmap. The following code shows how you might create a brush with a bitmap pattern if the bitmap was stored in a resource with the resource id *Bm_bitmap1*. (See Chapter 7, "Resources," for more information on resources.)

```
bitmap: WEL_BITMAP
brush: WEL_BRUSH

...

create bitmap.make_by_id (Bm_bitmap1)
create brush.make_by_pattern (bitmap)
```

The first creation instruction instantiates and initializes a bitmap from a resource. The second instantiates a brush using the newly created bitmap.

Creating a Brush Indirectly

Once a brush has been created, its settings cannot be changed. For example, if you need to change the hatch style of a brush, you must create a new brush. If you find your application uses a large number of different brush types, it is sometimes more efficient to use a logical brush to define the brush settings and create physical brush objects from the logical brush.

The interface of a logical brush, defined in class *WEL_LOG_BRUSH,* is similar to *WEL_BRUSH,* only there are two creation procedures and the interface includes features to set the relevant attributes, including the style, color and hatch pattern. The two creation procedures *make* and *make_by_brush* allow you to create a new logical brush with particular settings and to create a logical brush that mirrors an existing brush's settings.

```
make (a_style: INTEGER; a_color: WEL_COLOR_REF; a_hatch: INTEGER)
        -- Make a log brush using 'a_style', 'a_color' and
        -- 'a_hatch' type.
        -- See class WEL_BRUSH_STYLE_CONSTANTS for 'a_style'
        -- values.
        -- See class WEL_HS_CONSTANTS for 'a_hatch' values.
    require
        color_not_void: a_color /= Void
    ensure
        style_set: style = a_style;
        color_set: color.is_equal (a_color);
        hatch_set: hatch = a_hatch

make_by_brush (brush: WEL_BRUSH)
        -- Make a log brush using the information of 'brush'.
    require
        brush_not_void: brush /= Void;
        brush_exists: brush.exists
    ensure
        style_set: style = brush.style;
        color_set: color.is_equal (brush.color);
        hatch_set: hatch = brush.hatch
```

Using *WEL_LOG_BRUSH,* you can create many different brushes efficiently by changing settings in the logical brush and then creating the physical brushes indirectly using the *make_indirect* creation procedure. For example, to create two different brushes from one logical brush (with different hatch styles), you could use the following code:

```
logical_brush: WEL_LOG_BRUSH
green: WEL_COLOR_REF
bs: expanded WEL_BS_CONSTANTS
hs: expanded WEL_HS_CONSTANTS
brush1, brush2: WEL_BRUSH
...
create green.make_rgb (0, 255, 0)
create logical_brush.make (bs.Bs_hatched, green, hs.Hs_vertical)
create brush1.make_indirect (logical_brush)
logical_brush.set_hatch (hs.Hs_horizontal)
create brush2.make_indirect (logical_brush)
```

TABLE 10.4   *Brush Style Constants (WEL_BS_CONSTANTS)*

CONSTANT	DESCRIPTION
Bs_dibpattern	A pattern brush defined by a device independent bitmap. The *a_hatch* parameter must contain a pointer to an existing device-independent bitmap. You can use *to_integer* of *WEL_DIB* to convert the bitmap pointer to an integer for passing.
Bs_hatched	Hatched brush.
Bs_hollow	Hollow brush. Nothing is drawn.
Bs_null	Same as *Bs_hollow*.
Bs_pattern	Pattern brush defined by a memory bitmap.
Bs_solid	Solid brush.

One thing to note is the use of the *WEL_BS_CONSTANTS* class and one of its features, *Bs_hatched*. When creating a *WEL_BRUSH*, the brush style is set by its creation procedure. This is useful because it allows you to create the most common types of brushes with a minimum of coding effort. However, when you create a logical brush, you need to select the style of brush that you are creating. The brush styles you have seen so far include *Bs_solid* (used by *make_solid*), *Bs_hatched* (used by *make_hatch*), and *Bs_pattern* (used by *make_pattern*). Other brush styles include *Bs_hollow*, *Bs_dibpattern*, and *Bs_null*. Table 10.4 lists each of the brush styles available in Windows and a description of their purposes.

Selecting a Brush

Once you have created a brush, you need to select it into the device context you will be drawing on. As with all other tools, you can determine whether a brush is currently selected in the device context, you can access the brush, and you can select a new brush. The features available in *WEL_DC* for selecting brushes are *brush*, *brush_selected*, *select_brush*, and *unselect_brush*.

```
brush: WEL_BRUSH
        -- Current brush selected

brush_selected: BOOLEAN
        -- Is a brush selected?

select_brush (a_brush: WEL_BRUSH)
        -- Select the 'a_brush' as the current brush.
    require
        exists: exists;
        a_brush_not_void: a_brush /= Void;
```

```
        a_brush_exists: a_brush.exists
    ensure
        brush_set: brush = a_brush;
        brush_selected: brush_selected

unselect_brush
        -- Deselect the brush and restore the old one
    require
        exists: exists;
        brush_selected: brush_selected
    ensure
        brush_not_selected: not brush_selected
```

When you first create a device context, a solid white brush is selected by default. This causes all areas you draw to be filled with solid white. To change the default brush, you need to create a new brush and select it into the device context. For example,

```
dc: WEL_CLIENT_DC
null_brush: WEL_NULL_BRUSH
. . .
create dc.make (a_window)
dc.get
create null_brush.make
dc.select_brush (null_brush)
. . .
dc.release
```

The code above declares a client device context for an arbitrary window we have called *a_window* and declares a stock null brush. The device context is created and initialized and the brush is created and selected. Any drawing routines called following the selection of the brush use the selected brush to fill areas.

When you unselect a brush by calling *unselect_brush,* the previously selected brush is reselected. This includes the default solid white brush that is selected when a device context is first created.

To illustrate the use of brushes, Example 10.1 draws a filled rectangle for each of the stock brushes and a filled rectangle for each of the hatch pattern brushes.

Example 10.1 Stock and Hatch Brushes (gdi\brush)

```
class
    MAIN_WINDOW
inherit
```

```
        WEL_FRAME_WINDOW
            redefine
                on_paint
            end
creation
        make
feature

        make is
            -- Initialize the main window
            do
                make_top ("Main Window")
                resize (350, 140)
            end

    feature {NONE} -- Implementation

        black: WEL_COLOR_REF is
            once
                create Result.make
            end

        on_paint (paint_dc: WEL_PAINT_DC; invalid_rect: WEL_RECT) is
            -- Draw stock brushes and hatch pattern brushes.
            local
                pen: WEL_BLACK_PEN
            do
                create pen.make
                paint_dc.select_pen (pen)
                draw_stock_brushes (paint_dc)
                draw_hatch_pattern_brushes (paint_dc)
            end

        draw_stock_brushes (paint_dc: WEL_PAINT_DC) is
            -- Draw a line of rectangles representing each stock brush.
            require
                valid_paint_dc: paint_dc /= Void and then paint_dc.exists
            local
                count: INTEGER
                rect: WEL_RECT
                rec_width: INTEGER
            do
                from
                    create rect.make (0, 0, client_rect.width //
                        stock_brushes.count, 20)
                    count := stock_brushes.lower
                    rec_width := (client_rect.width -- (Rectangle_gap
                        stock_brushes.count)) // stock_brushes.count
                variant
                    (stock_brushes.count) -- count
```

```
        until
            count > stock_brushes.upper
        loop
            -- draw label
            paint_dc.draw_centered_text (stock_brush_labels.item
                (count), rect)
            -- select the next stock brush
            paint_dc.select_brush (stock_brushes.item (count))
            -- draw rectangle
            paint_dc.rectangle (Rectangle_gap + ((rec_width +
                Rectangle_gap) * (count - 1)),
                20, (Rectangle_gap + rec_width) * count, 60)
            -- reposition for the next rectangle and label
            rect.offset (client_rect.width // stock_brushes.count, 0)
            count := count + 1
        end
    end

Rectangle_gap: INTEGER is 5
        -- Spacing between brush rectangles

stock_brushes: ARRAY [WEL_BRUSH] is
        -- Available stock brushes
    local
        brush: WEL_BRUSH
    once
        create Result.make (1, 6)
        create {WEL_BLACK_BRUSH} brush.make
        Result.put (brush, 1)
        create {WEL_DARK_GRAY_BRUSH} brush.make
        Result.put (brush, 2)
        create {WEL_GRAY_BRUSH} brush.make
        Result.put (brush, 3)
        create {WEL_HOLLOW_BRUSH} brush.make
        Result.put (brush, 4)
        create {WEL_LIGHT_GRAY_BRUSH} brush.make
        Result.put (brush, 5)
        create {WEL_WHITE_BRUSH} brush.make
        Result.put (brush, 6)
    end


stock_brush_labels: ARRAY [STRING] is
        -- Labels for each of the stock brushes
    once
        Result := << "Black", "DarkGray", "Gray",
            "Hollow/Null", "LightGray", "White" >>
    ensure
        same_number: stock_brushes.count = Result.count
    end
```

```
draw_hatch_pattern_brushes (paint_dc: WEL_PAINT_DC) is
    -- Draw a line of rectangles representing each hatch pattern.
require
    valid_paint_dc: paint_dc /= Void and then paint_dc.exists
local
    count: INTEGER
    rect: WEL_RECT
    rec_width: INTEGER
    brush: WEL_BRUSH
do
    from
        create rect.make (0, 80, client_rect.width //
            hatch_patterns.count, 100)
        count := hatch_patterns.lower
        rec_width := (client_rect.width -- (Rectangle_gap *
            hatch_patterns.count)) // hatch_patterns.count
    variant
        (hatch_patterns.count) -- count
    until
        count > hatch_patterns.upper
    loop
        -- draw label
        paint_dc.draw_centered_text (hatch_pattern_labels.item
            (count), rect)
        -- create and select the next stock brush
        create brush.make_hatch (hatch_patterns.item (count),
            black)
        paint_dc.select_brush (brush)
        -- draw rectangle
        paint_dc.rectangle (Rectangle_gap + ((rec_width +
            Rectangle_gap) * (count - 1)),
            100, (Rectangle_gap + rec_width) * count, 140)
        -- reposition for the next rectangle and label
        rect.offset (client_rect.width // hatch_patterns.count, 0)
        count := count + 1
    end
end

hatch_patterns: ARRAY [INTEGER] is
    -- Available hatch patterns
local
    hs: expanded WEL_HS_CONSTANTS
once
    Result := << hs.Hs_bdiagonal, hs.Hs_cross, hs.Hs_diagcross,
        hs.Hs_fdiagonal, hs.Hs_horizontal, hs.Hs_vertical >>
end

hatch_pattern_labels: ARRAY [STRING] is
    -- Labels for each hatch pattern
once
```

```
      Result := << "Hs_bdiagonal", "Hs_cross", "Hs_diagcross",
          "Hs_fdiagonal", "Hs_horizontal", "Hs_vertical" >>
   ensure
      same_number: hatch_patterns.count = Result.count
   end

end -- class MAIN_WINDOW
```

The *on_paint* routine of this example first selects a black pen for drawing text and rectangle outlines. It then calls two routines, *draw_stock_brushes* and *draw_hatch_pattern_brushes,* to display all of the stock brushes and all of the hatch brush styles. The two draw routines draw a text label and a rectangle filled with each type of brush. Figure 10.2 shows the window painted by this example.

Fonts

Windows uses the currently selected font to determine a piece of text's font family, style, width, height, and other display attributes. If you do not explicitly select a font, then Windows uses the default font—usually the system font.

To select a font into a device context, you first need to create a font with the desired settings. Class *WEL_FONT* provides an encapsulation of an actual Windows font and can be instantiated to represent any font supported by your Windows environment. You can create a font either by passing the required font settings to the creation procedure *make,* passing an instance of *WEL_LOG_FONT* to the procedure *make_indirect,* or by referring to an existing font by calling *make_by_pointer.*

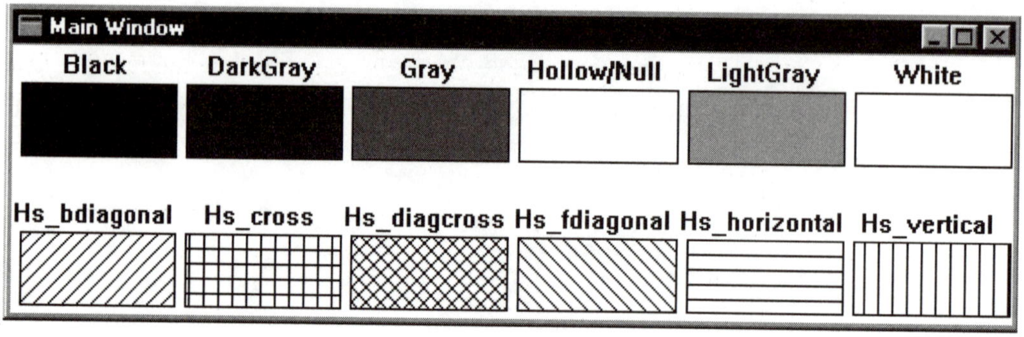

FIGURE 10.2. Stock and hatch brush examples.

Once an instance of *WEL_FONT* has been created, it cannot be modified. If you need to use a new font, you must create a new instance of *WEL_FONT*. The public interface of *WEL_FONT* therefore provides features for creating a font object and for determining the font's current attributes (indirectly via an instance of *WEL_LOG_FONT*). It does not include any features for changing the values, once set.

```
class interface
    WEL_FONT

creation
    make (height, width, escapement, orientation, weight, italic,
      underline,
        strike_out, charset, output_precision, clip_precision, quality,
        pitch_and_family: INTEGER; a_face_name: STRING)
        require
            a_face_name_not_void: a_face_name /= Void
    make_indirect (a_log_font: WEL_LOG_FONT)
        require
            a_log_font_not_void: a_log_font /= Void

feature -- Access
    log_font: WEL_LOG_FONT
            -- Log font structure associated to 'Current'
        require
            exists
        ensure
            result_not_void: Result /= Void
    class -- WEL_FONT
```

Selecting a Font

A font is selected into a device context by calling *select_font* and passing an instance of *WEL_FONT*. The font can be subsequently unselected by calling *unselect_font. unselect_font* restores the previously selected font.

The currently selected font can be accessed by calling the function *font*, and determining whether a font has been selected can be done via a call to *font_selected.*

```
font: WEL_FONT
        -- Current font selected

font_selected: BOOLEAN
        -- Is a font selected?
```

```
select_font (a_font: WEL_FONT)
        -- Select the 'a_font' as the current font.
    require
        exists: exists;
        a_font_not_void: a_font /= Void;
        a_font_exists: a_font.exists
    ensure
        font_set: font = a_font;
        font_selected: font_selected

unselect_font
        -- Deselect the font and restore the old one
    require
        exists: exists;
        font_selected: font_selected
    ensure
        font_not_selected: not font_selected
```

Determining Selected Font Typeface

The type face of a selected font can be found by querying the graphics context directly with a call to *text_face*. *text_face* returns a *STRING* with the name of the font's type face.

```
text_face: STRING
        -- Typeface name of the font that is currently selected
    require
        exists: exists
    ensure
        result_not_void: Result /= Void
```

Determining Selected Font Text Sizes

The dimensions of a string using the currently selected font can be calculated before painting by calling the features *string_height, string_width,* and *string_size.* The functions *string_height* and *string_width* return an *INTEGER* representing the height or width of a particular string. *string_size* returns the same dimensional information, only in the form of a *WEL_SIZE* object.

```
string_height (s: STRING): INTEGER
        -- Height of the string 's' using the selected font
    require
        exists: exists;
```

```
          s_exists: s /= Void
      ensure
          positive_result: Result >= 0

  string_size (s: STRING): WEL_SIZE
          -- Size of the string 's' using the selected font
      require
          exists: exists;
          s_exists: s /= Void
      ensure
          result_exists: Result /= Void;
          positive_width: Result.width >= 0;
          positive_height: Result.height >= 0

  string_width (s: STRING): INTEGER
          -- Width of the string 's' using the selected font
      require
          exists: exists;
          s_exists: s /= Void
      ensure
          positive_result: Result >= 0
```

Determining Selected Font Tabbed Text Sizes

The previous text-size queries ignore all tabulation in the *STRING* parameter.
To take tabulation into account, you need to call one or more of the following
functions.

```
  tabbed_text_height (text: STRING): INTEGER
          -- Height of a tabbed 'text'
      require
          exists: exists;
          text_not_void: text/=Void
      ensure
          positive_height: Result >= 0

  tabbed_text_size (text: STRING): WEL_SIZE
          -- Size of a tabbed 'text'
      require
          exists: exists;
          text_not_void: text /= Void
      ensure
          result_not_void: Result /= Void;
          positive_width: Result.width >= 0;
          positive_height: Result.height >= 0

  tabbed_text_size_with_tabulation (text: STRING;
      tabulations: ARRAY [INTEGER]): WEL_SIZE
```

```
                -- Size of a tabbed 'text', with 'tabulations' as
                -- tabulation positions.
        require
            exists: exists;
            text_not_void: text /= Void;
            tabulations_not_void: tabulations /= Void
        ensure
            result_not_void: Result /= Void;
            positive_width: Result.width >= 0;
            positive_height: Result.height >= 0

tabbed_text_width (text: STRING): INTEGER
                -- Width of a tabbed 'text'
        require
            exists: exists;
            text_not_void: text /= Void
        ensure
            positive_width: Result >= 0
```

The functions *tabbed_text_height, tabbed_text_width,* and *tabbed_text_size* all return the appropriate text-size information, with tab stops expanded to eight times the average character width. If you need to specify your own tabulation settings, you can call *tabbed_text_size_with_tabulation.* The *tabulations* parameter must be an *ARRAY* of *INTEGER* containing at least one value. If the array contains only one value, then regular tab stops are separated by this value; otherwise, each value in the array represents one tab stop position.

Palettes

Palettes define a set of colors that can be used to draw on the output device. Devices that can generate many colors, but can display only a subset of them at any given time, use palettes to define that subset. The number of color entries in a palette is device-dependent and can be requested using the feature *device_caps* from *WEL_DC* by passing the constant *Size_palette* as argument. Each palette entry can be retrieved independently by calling the feature *palette_index* from *WEL_PALETTE.* As with other GDI resource classes, a palette can be instantiated from its logical representation, defined in an instance of *WEL_LOG_PALETTE.*

```
class interface
    WEL_PALETTE
create

    make (a_log_palette: WEL_LOG_PALETTE)
```

```
        require
            a_log_palette_not_void: a_log_palette /= Void
feature -- Access

    palette_index (i: INTEGER): WEL_COLOR_REF
            - Color number 'i' of the palette
        require
            exists: exists
        ensure
            result_not_void: Result /= Void
end -- class WEL_PALETTE
```

WEL_LOG_PALETTE enumerates each palette entry as an instance of *WEL_PALETTE_ENTRY*. Each entry defines a color with its red, green, and blue components and is associated with a flag that defines how it should be realized (see "Realizing a Palette" in this chapter).

Note, there is no need for palettes with display devices that are in *True Color* mode (24 bits per pixel or higher) since all the colors can be displayed at once.

Selecting a Palette

Devices that support palettes always have one—and only one—palette selected. The default palette is automatically selected when the device context is created. Because colors in the default palette cannot be modified, applications that need to use different colors have to create a new logical palette. The palette can then be associated with the device, using the feature *select_palette* from *WEL_DC*. The query *palette_selected* indicates whether a palette, other than the default palette, was selected into the device. The current selected palette is accessible through the query *palette*. Finally, an application may restore the previously selected palette by calling the feature *unselect_palette*.

```
palette: WEL_PALETTE
        -- Current palette selected

palette_selected: BOOLEAN
        -- Is a palette selected?

select_palette (a_palette: WEL_PALETTE)
        -- Select the 'a_palette' as the current palette.
    require
        exists: exists;
        a_palette_not_void: a_palette /= Void;
        a_palette_exists: a_palette.exists
```

```
unselect_palette
          -- Deselect the palette and restore the old one
    require
          exists: exists;
          palette_selected: palette_selected
    ensure
          palette_not_selected: not palette_selected
```

Realizing a Palette

Once a palette has been selected into a device, the application has to call the feature *realize_palette* to map the system palette colors to the colors defined in the logical palette. The system searches for the best match for each color in the logical palette. If no exact match is found, it adds a new entry in the system palette with the new color. If the system palette is full, it mixes multiple colors to reproduce the new color. This process is known as dithering.

```
realize_palette
          -- Map palette entries from the current logical
          -- palette on the system palette
    require
          exists: exists;
          palette_selected: palette_selected
```

Pens

Whenever you draw a line using the GDI drawing routines, the currently se-lected pen is used to determine the style, width, and color of the line. Only one pen can be selected in the device context at one time. Therefore, you must se-lect a new pen into the device context in between drawing operations to change the style of the line to be drawn.

Once a pen has been created, its style, width, and color cannot be changed. To do this, you must create a new pen. You can, however, create a *logical pen* that does allow its settings to be changed and can be used to create a physical pen. The two classes that define a pen and a logical pen are *WEL_PEN* and *WEL_LOG_PEN,* respectively. As mentioned earlier, a pen can be created only with certain settings and selected into a device context giving the following interface:[2]

---

[2]The interface for *WEL_PEN* is not entirely complete. Features inherited from *WEL_GDI_ ANY* have been omitted.

```
class interface
     WEL_PEN
creation
     make (a_style, a_width: INTEGER; a_color: WEL_COLOR_REF)
         require
             valid_pen_style_constant: valid_pen_style_constant
                (a_style);
             positive_width: a_width >= 0;
             color_not_void: a_color /= Void
         ensure
             style_set: exists implies style = a_style;
             width_set: exists implies width = a_width;
             color_set: exists implies color.is_equal (a_color)

     make_solid (a_width: INTEGER; a_color: WEL_COLOR_REF)
         require
             positive_width: a_width >= 0;
             a_color_not_void: a_color /= Void
         ensure
             width_set: exists implies width = a_width;
             color_set: exists implies color.is_equal (a_color)

     make_indirect (a_log_pen: WEL_LOG_PEN)
         require
             a_log_pen_not_void: a_log_pen /= Void

feature -- Access

     color: WEL_COLOR_REF
             -- Pen color
         require
             exists: exists
         ensure
             result_not_void: Result /= Void

     log_pen: WEL_LOG_PEN
             -- Log pen structure associated to 'Current'
         require
             exists: exists
         ensure
             result_not_void: Result /= Void

     style: INTEGER
             -- Pen style
         require
             exists: exists
         ensure
             valid_result: valid_pen_style_constant (Result)

     width: INTEGER
             -- Pen width
```

```
        require
            exists: exists
        ensure
            positive_result: Result >= 0

feature {ANY} -- Status report

    valid_pen_style_constant (c: INTEGER): BOOLEAN
            -- Is 'c' a valid pen style constant?
            --- (from WEL_PS_CONSTANTS)

end -- class WEL_PEN
```

Creating a Pen

You can create a pen in four different ways: by passing all settings *(make)*, by passing just the width and color *(make_solid)*, by using the settings of a logical pen *(make_indirect)*, or by using a pointer *(make_by_pointer)*. The creation procedure *make_pointer* can be useful if you are interfacing with external code, such as C, and have a pointer to a pen that you need to create a *WEL_PEN* from.

After creating a pen, you can access its settings through the features *color, style,* and *width*. As mentioned earlier, you cannot change these settings once the pen has been created. You can also access a logical pen representation through the function *log_pen*.

The final feature in the interface, *valid_pen_style_constant,* is inherited from the *WEL_PS_CONSTANTS* class and can be used to determine if an arbitrary integer is a valid pen style. This routine is used in the precondition of the creation procedures that accept a style as a parameter. You can use it to validate an integer that will be used to represent a pen style. Table 10.5 lists the pen styles defined in class *WEL_PS_CONSTANTS*.

TABLE 10.5   *Pen Styles (WEL_PS_CONSTANTS)*

CONSTANT	DESCRIPTION
Ps_dash	A dashed line.
Ps_dashdot	A dashed line with dashes separated by a single dot.
Ps_dashdotdot	A dashed line with dashes separated by two dots.
Ps_dot	A dotted line.
Ps_insideframe	A solid line that will be drawn inside its bounding box. Can be used to ensure an object is drawn entirely within its dimensions.
Ps_null	A null line. Nothing will be drawn.
Ps_solid	A solid line.

A pen with a width greater than one will appear as a solid line, regardless of the style setting. This is a limitation of the Windows library and may be removed in the future.

Creating a Stock Pen

Three stock GDI pens can be created using the classes *WEL_BLACK_PEN, WEL_NULL_PEN,* and *WEL_WHITE_PEN.* When instantiated, these classes create a solid black pen, a null (hollow) pen, and a solid white pen, respectively. The creation procedure *make* of the stock pen classes takes no parameters; therefore, the code needed to create a stock pen is very simple. For instance, the following code

```
black_pen: WEL_BLACK_PEN
...
create black_pen.make
```

is all that is required to create a solid black pen.

Using Standard Color Pens

As well as providing classes to access the stock GDI pens, the WEL library also provides a class to create standard color pens. The class *WEL_STANDARD_PENS* is similar to the class *WEL_STANDARD_COLORS* (see "Using Standard Colors" in this chapter) in that it contains a number of once functions that return a *WEL_PEN* of a particular color. The functions available in this class include

```
Black_pen                   Dark_red_pen
Blue_pen                    Dark_yellow_pen
Cyan_pen                    Green_pen
Dark_blue_pen               Grey_pen
Dark_cyan_pen               Magenta_pen
Dark_green_pen              Red_pen
Dark_grey_pen               White_pen
Dark_magenta_pen            Yellow_pen
```

As described in "Using Standard Colors," you can use this class either by inheritance or through a client-supplier relationship. Each function in the class returns an instance of *WEL_PEN* that you can select into a device context.

Creating a Logical Pen

If your application creates a large number of similar pens, it can be more efficient to create logical pens representing the different pen styles, and then create and select actual pens when needed. This also gives you the advantage of being able to change the settings of a logical pen, which you cannot do with a pen created by *WEL_PEN*.

The class *WEL_LOG_PEN* provides much the same interface as *WEL_PEN*. Additional features, such as *set_style*, *set_width*, and *set_color*, are provided to change the settings. You can create a logical pen either by passing the three settings to the creation procedure *make* or by passing a pen to the *make_by_pen* creation procedure. Feature *make_by_pen* creates a logical pen based on the settings in the pen passed as a parameter.

```
make (a_style, a_width: INTEGER; a_color: WEL_COLOR_REF)
    require
        valid_pen_style_constant: valid_pen_style_constant (a_style);
        positive_width: a_width >= 0;
        color_not_void: a_color /= Void
    ensure
        set_style: style = a_style;
        set_width: width = a_width;
        set_color: color.item = a_color.item

make_by_pen (pen: WEL_PEN)
    require
        pen_not_void: pen /= Void;
        pen_exists: pen.exists
```

Selecting a Pen

Once you have created your pen, you can select it into the device context that you are working with. Four features of *WEL_DC*, *pen*, *pen_selected*, *select_pen*, and *unselect_pen*, are provided to access and set the current pen.

```
pen: WEL_PEN
    -- Current pen selected

pen_selected: BOOLEAN
    -- Is a pen selected?

select_pen (a_pen: WEL_PEN)
        -- Select the 'a_pen' as the current pen.
    require
        exists: exists;
        a_pen_not_void: a_pen /= Void;
        a_pen_exists: a_pen.exists
    ensure
        pen_set: pen = a_pen;
        pen_selected: pen_selected
```

```
unselect_pen
        -- Deselect the pen and restore the old one
    require
        exists: exists;
        pen_selected: pen_selected
    ensure
        pen_not_selected: not pen_selected
```

The function *pen* returns the currently selected pen, if one has been selected (which in turn can be determined by calling *pen_selected*). To select a
pen into the device context, use the feature *select_pen;* and vice versa, to unselect a pen (and reselect the previous pen), use the feature *unselect_pen*. When a
device context is first created, it has a default black pen selected.

Example 10.2 demonstrates the use of both logical and physical pen objects to draw lines of different styles in a window. First, a logical pen is created
with default settings (i.e., a solid black line with a width of one pixel). This
logical pen is used to cycle through the different pen styles and to create a new
pen for each style. A label is drawn at the top of each line to indicate the style.

Example 10.2 Pen Styles (gdi\penstyle)

```
class
    MAIN_WINDOW
inherit
    WEL_FRAME_WINDOW
        redefine
            on_paint
        end
creation
    make
feature
    make is
            -- Initialize the main window
        do
            make_top ("Main Window")
            resize (350, 140)
        end

feature {NONE} -- Implementation

    black: WEL_COLOR_REF is
        once
            create Result.make
        end

    on_paint (paint_dc: WEL_PAINT_DC; invalid_rect: WEL_RECT) is
            -- Draw lines using different pens
        local
```

```
            logical_pen: WEL_LOG_PEN
            pen: WEL_PEN
            rect: WEL_RECT
            count: INTEGER
            x_position: INTEGER
        do
            -- create the logical pen and use it to create a pen
            create logical_pen.make (pen_styles.item (1), 1, black)
            from
                create rect.make (0, 0, client_rect.width //
                    pen_styles.count, 20)
                count := pen_styles.lower
                x_position := (client_rect.width // pen_styles.count) // 2
            variant
                (pen_styles.count) - count
            until
                count > pen_styles.upper
            loop
                -- draw label
                paint_dc.draw_centered_text (pen_style_labels.item
                    (count), rect)
                -- draw line
                logical_pen.set_style (pen_styles.item (count))
                create pen.make_indirect (logical_pen)
                paint_dc.select_pen (pen)
                paint_dc.line (x_position, 20, x_position,
                    client_rect.height)
                -- reposition for the next line and label
                rect.offset (client_rect.width // pen_styles.count, 0)
                x_position := x_position + (client_rect.width //
                    pen_styles.count)
                count := count + 1
            end
        end
    pen_styles: ARRAY [INTEGER] is
            -- Available pen styles
        local
            ps: expanded WEL_PS_CONSTANTS
        once
            Result := << ps.ps_dash, ps.Ps_dashdot, ps.Ps_dashdotdot,
                ps.Ps_dot, ps.Ps_insideframe, ps.Ps_null, ps.Ps_solid >>
        end

    pen_style_labels: ARRAY [STRING] is
            -- Labels for each of the pen styles
        once
            Result := << "Ps_dash", "Ps_dashdot", "Ps_dashdotdot",
                "Ps_dot", "Ps_insideframe", "Ps_null", "Ps_solid" >>
        end

end -- class MAIN_WINDOW
```

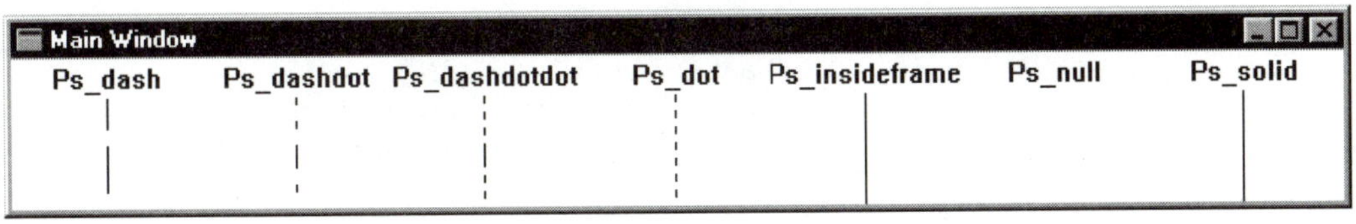

FIGURE 10.3. Pen style examples.

Figure 10.3 shows the output of this example. Notice that there is no apparent difference between the *Ps_insideframe* and *Ps_solid* line styles. The difference lies in how the line is drawn on the screen, not in the style. Similarly, notice that the *Ps_null* line is invisible. Nothing has actually been drawn on the screen for this particular line style.

Regions

Regions define geometric shapes on a device that can be used to perform diverse drawing operations or to perform hit testing (testing whether or not the mouse cursor is inside a region's boundary). The operations that can be executed over a region include painting, filling, inverting, and framing. The basic shapes for a region are rectangle, polygon, or ellipse, and these basic shapes can be combined to produce more elaborate regions.

Creating Regions

A region may initially be empty, a rectangle, a polygon, or an ellipse. The seven *WEL_REGION* creation routines allow you to initialize a region in two different ways for each basic shape. You may specify the required coordinates, or first create a structure that holds the necessary information and pass it to the creation routine. In the case of polygons, the two creation routines present two different ways of defining the surfaces that are part of the region.

```
make_empty
        -- Make an empty rectangle region

make_elliptic (left, top, right, bottom: INTEGER)
        -- Make an elliptical region specified by the
        -- bounding rectangle 'left', 'top', 'right', 'bottom'

make_elliptic_indirect (rect: WEL_RECT)
        -- Make an elliptical region specified by
        -- the bounding rectangle 'rect'
    require
        rect_not_void: rect /= Void
```

```
make_polygon_alternate (points: ARRAY [INTEGER])
            -- Make a polygonal region specified by 'points'
            -- using alternate mode. Fills area between
            -- odd-numbered and even-numbered polygon sides
            -- on each scan line.
    require
        points_not_void: points /= Void
        points_count: points.count \\ 2 = 0

make_polygon_winding (points: ARRAY [INTEGER])
            -- Make a polygonal region specified by 'points'
            -- using winding mode. Fills any region with a nonzero
            -- winding value.
    require
        points_not_void: points /= Void
        points_count: points.count \\ 2 = 0

make_rect (left, top, right, bottom: INTEGER)
            -- Make a rectangle region specified by
            -- 'left', 'top', 'right', 'bottom'.

make_rect_indirect (rect: WEL_RECT)
            -- Make a rectangle region specified by
            -- the rectangle 'rect'.
    require
        rect_not_void: rect /= Void
```

Combining Regions

The true power of regions lies in the ability to create an infinite number of different shapes by combining them. Five different kinds of combination are available: *and, or, xor, diff,* and *copy.* Example 10.3 creates a number of regions using different combination operators to demonstrate their flexibility.

Example 10.3 Region Combination (gdi\region)

```
class
    MAIN_WINDOW
inherit
    WEL_FRAME_WINDOW
        redefine
            on_paint
        end
    WEL_RGN_CONSTANTS
        export
            {NONE} all
        end
    WEL_DT_CONSTANTS
```

```
            export
                {NONE} all
            end
        WEL_HS_CONSTANTS
            export
                {NONE} all
            end
create
    make

feature {NONE} -- Initialization

    make is
            -- Create window.
        do
            make_top (Title)
            resize (650, 450)
        end

feature -- Access

    Source_brush: WEL_BRUSH is
            -- Hatched brush
        once
            create Result.make_hatch (Hs_fdiagonal, Black)
        end

    Destination_brush: WEL_BRUSH is
            -- Hatched brush
        once
            create Result.make_hatch (Hs_bdiagonal, Black)
        end

    Result_brush: WEL_BRUSH is
            -- Hatched brush
        once
            create Result.make_hatch (Hs_diagcross, Black)
        end

    Black: WEL_COLOR_REF is
            -- Black color used for hatches
        once
            create Result.make
        end

    Region_width: INTEGER is 100
            -- Regions width

    Region_height: INTEGER is 100
            -- Regions height
```

```
Space: INTEGER is 50
        -- Empty space (in pixel) between regions

feature {NONE} -- Implementation

    on_paint (paint_dc: WEL_PAINT_DC; invalid_rect: WEL_RECT) is
            -- Draw regions.
        do
            draw_regions (paint_dc, space, space, Rgn_and, And_title)
            draw_regions (paint_dc, 2 * space + 3 * Region_width //
                2, space, Rgn_or, Or_title)
            draw_regions (paint_dc, 3 * space + 3 * Region_width,
                space, Rgn_xor, Xor_title)
            draw_regions (paint_dc, space, 2 * space + 3 *
                Region_height // 2, Rgn_diff, Diff_title)
            draw_regions (paint_dc, 2 * space + 3 * Region_width // 2,
                2 * space + 3 * Region_height // 2, Rgn_copy,
                    Copy_title)
        end

feature {NONE} -- Implementation

    draw_regions (a_dc: WEL_DC; a_x, a_y, mode: INTEGER; a_title:
    STRING) is
            -- Draw regions on dc 'a_dc' at position 'a_x', 'a_y' using
            -- combination mode 'mode'.
            -- Draw text 'a_title' on top of regions.
        require
            non_void_dc: a_dc /= Void
            valid_dc: a_dc.exists
            valid_x: x >= 0
            valid_y: y >= 0
            valid_mode: valid_region_constant (mode)
            non_void_title: a_title /= Void
        local
            source_region, destination_region: WEL_REGION
            title_rect: WEL_RECT
        do
            create source_region.make_rect (a_x, a_y, a_x +
                Region_width, a_y + Region_height)
            create destination_region.make_rect (a_x + (Region_width
                // 2),
                a_y + (Region_height // 2), a_x + 3 * (Region_width //
                    2), a_y + 3 * (Region_width // 2))
            a_dc.fill_region (source_region, Source_brush)
            a_dc.fill_region (destination_region, Destination_brush)
            a_dc.fill_region (source_region.combine (destination_
                region, mode), Result_brush)
            create title_rect.make (a_x, a_y, a_x + 3 * Region_width
                // 2, a_y + 3 * Region_width // 2)
```

```
                a_dc.draw_text (" -" + a_title + "- ", title_rect, Dt_top)
        end

    Title: STRING is "WEL GDI demo"
            -- Window's title

    And_title: STRING is "AND"
            -- And combination title

    Or_title: STRING is "OR"
            -- Or combination title

    Xor_title: STRING is "XOR"
            -- Xor combination title

    Diff_title: STRING is "DIFF"
            -- Diff combination title

    Copy_title: STRING is "COPY"
            -- Copy combination title

end -- class MAIN_WINDOW
```

The interesting feature is *draw_regions,* where the actual combination takes place. The kind of combination is specified in the second argument of the *combine* feature, while the first argument specifies the destination region. Figure 10.4 shows the output of this example, with the result of the region combination represented by the cross-hatch pattern.

The ability to start from a rectangle, an ellipse, or a polygon, along with the possibility of combining these basic shapes, makes it possible to define very complicated shapes for a region.

Selecting a Region

Once the region has the required shape, you can select it into a device context to define the limits of the drawing area. Any drawing performed outside the selected region will not appear on the device. Such a region is called a clipping region.

A clipping region can be defined using either the *select_region* or *select_clip_region* feature from *WEL_DC*. Both features have the same effect. The currently selected region can be retrieved using the *region* query. You may unselect a region by calling the *unselect_region* command, which causes the previously selected region to be restored.

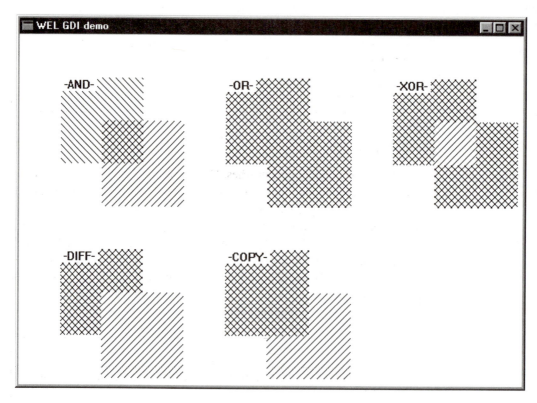

FIGURE 10.4. Region combination example.

```
region: WEL_REGION
        -- Current region selected
region_selected: BOOLEAN
        -- Is a region selected?
select_region (a_region: WEL_REGION)
        -- Select the 'a_region' as the current region.
    require
        exists: exists;
        a_region_not_void: a_region /= Void;
        a_region_exists: a_region.exists
    ensure
        region_set: region = a_region;
        region_selected: region_selected
unselect_region
        -- Deselect the region and restore the old one
    require
        exists: exists;
        region_selected: region_selected
    ensure
        region_not_selected: not region_selected
```

```
select_clip_region (a_region: WEL_REGION)
        -- Select 'a_region' as the current clipping region
    require
        exists: exists;
        a_region_not_void: a_region /= Void;
        a_region_exists: a_region.exists
```

Filling Regions

You can also fill regions with brushes. Once you have created a region and a brush, you can call the feature *fill_region*. Polygon regions can be filled in different ways, depending on the current fill mode of the device context. This mode can be retrieved with the feature *polygon_fill_mode* and changed with *set_polygon_fill_mode*. The valid values are defined in the class *WEL_POLY-GON_FILL_MODE_CONSTANTS* (Table 10.6), which also includes the feature *valid_polygon_fill_mode_constant* that checks whether the integer given as argument is a valid fill mode.

```
polygon_fill_mode: INTEGER
        -- Current polygon fill mode
        -- See class WEL_POLYGON_FILL_MODE_CONSTANTS for values.
    require
        exists: exists
    ensure
        valid_polygon_fill_mode: valid_polygon_fill_mode_constant
            (Result)

valid_polygon_fill_mode_constant (c: INTEGER): BOOLEAN
        -- Is 'c' a valid polygon fill mode constant?
        -- (from WEL_POLYGON_FILL_MODE_CONSTANTS)

set_polygon_fill_mode (mode: INTEGER)
        - Set the polygon fill mode 'polygon_fill_mode' with
        - 'mode'.
        - See class WEL_POLYGON_FILL_MODE_CONSTANTS for
        - 'mode' values.
    require
        exists: exists;
        valid_polygon_fill_mode: valid_polygon_fill_mode_constant
            (mode)
    ensure
        polygon_fill_mode_set: polygon_fill_mode = mode

fill_region (a_region: WEL_REGION; a_brush: WEL_BRUSH)
        - Fill 'a_region' by using 'a_brush' to fill it
    require
```

```
exists: exists
a_region_not_void: a_region /= Void
a_brush_not_void: a_brush /= Void
a_brush_exists: a_brush.exists
```

TABLE 10.6 *Polygon Fill Mode Constants*
(WEL_POLYGON_FILL_MODE_CONSTANTS)

CONSTANT	DESCRIPTION
Alternate	Fills the area between odd-numbered and even-numbered polygon sides on each scan line.
Winding	Fills any region with a nonzero winding value.

DRAWING

The features described in this chapter provide many different ways to draw on a device context—from the basic pixel to the more complex ellipse or polygon.

WEL provides multiple drawing primitives you can use. Each of the primitives uses the currently selected pen to draw. The drawing is also affected by the currently selected region. You can draw on the entire device, but if a region is currently selected into the device, then only the part of the drawing inside the region will be displayed.

Drawing Pixels

The most basic way you can draw is by setting the color of a pixel. The feature *set_pixel* does exactly that—it takes the coordinates of a pixel and a color, and sets the pixel with that color.

```
set_pixel (x, y: INTEGER; color: WEL_COLOR_REF)
        -- Set the pixel at 'x', 'y' position
        -- with the `color' color.
    require
        exists: exists;
        color_not_void: color /= Void
```

Drawing Lines

Drawing pixel by pixel can be very tedious. Fortunately, the Windows API provides ways to draw entire lines in one shot. Even better, the feature *line_to* lets you start from the current position (the last drawing coordinates) and draw a line to a specified coordinate. This way you can draw a series of lines without worrying about matching the coordinates of each line extremity. Independent lines (or the first line of a series) can be drawn using *line*. You can also start a series by specifying the first coordinate, using the feature *move_to*. This moves the pen to the specified coordinate and the next call to *line_to* draws a line between this point and the one passed as an argument.

```
line (x1, y1, x2, y2: INTEGER)
          -- Draw a line from 'x1', 'y1' to 'x2', 'y2'
      require
          exists: exists

move_to (x, y: INTEGER)
          -- Set the current position to 'x', 'y' position
      require
          exists: exists

line_to (x, y: INTEGER)
          -- Draw a line from the current position
          -- to 'x', 'y' position
      require
          exists: exists
```

Drawing Curved Lines

WEL provides three ways of drawing curved lines. You can use *arc* to draw an elliptical arc into a virtual rectangle, or *chord* to draw a chord into a virtual rectangle. Both features take the coordinates of the rectangle and the starting and ending points of the curved line.

```
arc (left, top, right, bottom, x_start_arc, y_start_arc, x_end_arc,
    y_end_arc: INTEGER)
          -- Draw an elliptical arc into a rectangle specified
          -- by 'left', 'top' and 'right', 'bottom', starting
          -- at 'x_start_arc', 'y_start_arc' and ending at
          -- 'x_end_arc', 'y_end_arc'
      require
          exists: exists

chord (left, top, right, bottom, x_start_line, y_start_line,
    x_end_line, y_end_line: INTEGER)
```

```
            -- Draw a chord into a rectangle specified
            -- by 'left', 'top' and 'right', 'bottom', starting
            -- at 'x_start_line', 'y_start_line' and ending at
            -- 'x_end_line', 'y_end_line'
    require
        exists: exists
```

The available curved line primitives also support pie charts consisting of an ellipse and straight lines joining the center of the ellipse to each of its extremities. Again, the ellipse is defined with a virtual rectangle and the two endpoints. Feature *pie* can be used to draw a pie wedge.

```
pie (left, top, right, bottom, x_start_point, y_start_point,
     x_end_point, y_end_point: INTEGER)
            -- Draw a pie-shaped wedge by drawing an elliptical
            -- arc whose center and two endpoints are joined
            -- by lines. The pie is drawn into a rectangle
            -- specified by 'left', 'top' and 'right', 'bottom',
            -- starting at 'x_start_point', 'y_start_point'
            -- and ending at 'x_end_point', 'y_end_point'
    require
        exists: exists
```

Drawing Polygons

The feature *polygon* allows you to draw a polygon. The coordinates are passed as an array of integers. Values at odd indexes represent x coordinates while values at even indexes are the corresponding y coordinates. The precondition of the feature requires that the array contain an even number of values.

```
polygon (points: ARRAY [INTEGER])
            -- Draw a polygon consisting of two or more 'points'
            -- connected by lines.
    require
        exists: exists;
        points_not_void: points /= Void;
        points_count: points.count \\ 2 = 0
```

Drawing Poly Lines

Poly lines are a generalization of polygons, where the endpoint of the last line does not have to be the starting point of the first line. They can be drawn using the feature *polyline*. The extremities of the lines are given in the same way as polygon points—in an array where odd indexes define the x coordinates of the points and even indexes define the y coordinates. Again, the precondition requires that the array contain an even number of values.

Poly lines also include Bézier lines. The feature *poly_bezier* allows you to draw multiple Bézier lines with two control points. The first line is drawn between the first and the fourth points specified in the array; the second and third points define the control points. Subsequent lines require three points—the two control points and the ending point—with the starting point being the ending point of the previous line. The feature *poly_bezier_to* does the same as *poly_bezier,* except it sets the pen position to the last point (useful to continue the drawing with other types of poly lines).

```
polyline (points: ARRAY [INTEGER])
            -- Draws a series of line segments by connecting the
            -- points specified in 'points'.
      require
            exists: exists;
            points_not_void: points /= Void;
            points_count: points.count \\ 2 = 0

poly_bezier (points: ARRAY [INTEGER])
            -- Draw one or more Bezier curves by using the
            -- endpoints and control points specified by `points'.
            -- The first curve is drawn from the first point to the
            -- fourth point by using the second and third points as
            -- control points. Each subsequent curve in the sequence
            -- needs exactly three more points: the ending point of
            -- the previous curve is used as the starting point, the
            -- next two points in the sequence are control points,
            -- and the third is the ending point.
            -- The current position is neither used nor updated by
            -- this procedure.
      require
            points_not_void: points /= Void;
            points_count_ok: points.count \\ 2 = 0

poly_bezier_to (points: ARRAY [INTEGER])
            -- Draw one or more Bezier curves by using the control
            -- points specified by 'points'. The first curve is
            -- drawn from the current position to the third point
            -- by using the first two points as control points.
            -- For each subsequent curve, the procedure needs
            -- exactly three more points, and uses the ending point
            -- of the previous curve as the starting point for the
            -- next.
            -- This procedure moves the current position to the
            -- ending point of the last Bezier curve.
      require
            points_not_void: points /= Void;
            points_count_ok: points.count \\ 2 = 0
```

Drawing Ellipses

The feature *ellipse* allows you to draw an ellipse on a device context. The ellipse is defined with an enclosing rectangle. You can also use this feature to draw circles by using a bounding square.

```
ellipse (left, top, right, bottom: INTEGER)
        -- Draw an ellipse into a rectangle specified by
        -- 'left', 'top' and 'right', 'bottom'
    require
        exists: exists
```

Drawing Rectangles

There are two kinds of rectangles you can draw using GDI. You can draw standard rectangles with *rectangle,* or rounded rectangles with *round_rect.* You can specify how the rounding is done through the last two arguments of the feature *round_rect.* They define the width and height, respectively, of the rounding ellipse.

```
rectangle (left, top, right, bottom: INTEGER)
        -- Draw a rectangle from 'left', 'top'
        -- to 'right', 'bottom'.
    require
        exists: exists

round_rect (left, top, right, bottom, ellipse_width,
    ellipse_height: INTEGER)
        -- Draw a rectangle from 'left', 'top' to
        -- 'right', 'bottom' with rounded corners.
        -- The rounded corners are specified by the
        -- 'ellipse_width' and 'ellipse_height'
    require
        exists: exists
```

Drawing Text

You may also need to draw text directly on a device. This is done in WEL through the features *draw_text* and *draw_centered_text.* The former allows you to specify the position of the text in the rectangle, while the latter automatically draws the text in the center of the specified rectangle.

```
draw_text (string: STRING; rect: WEL_RECT; format: INTEGER)
        -- Draw the text 'string' inside
        -- the 'rect' using 'format'
        -- See class WEL_DT_CONSTANTS for `format' value
    require
        exists: exists;
        string_not_void: string /= Void;
        rect_not_void: rect /= Void

draw_centered_text (string: STRING; rect: WEL_RECT)
        -- Draw the text 'string' centered in `rect'.
    require
        exists: exists;
        string_not_void: string /= Void;
        rect_not_void: rect /= Void
```

You can specify where the text should appear in the rectangle with the last argument of *draw_text*. The possible values for this argument are defined in the class *WEL_DT_CONSTANTS* (see Table 10.7).

TABLE 10.7   *Draw Text Constants (WEL_DT_CONSTANTS)*

CONSTANT	DESCRIPTION
Dt_bottom	When combined with *Dt_singleline*, justifies the text to the bottom of the rectangle.
Dt_calcrect	Determines the width and height of the rectangle. Returns the height of the formatted text but does not draw the text. The result is made available in *message_return_value*.
Dt_center	Centers the text horizontally in the rectangle.
Dt_expandtabs	Expands tab characters. Each tab is expanded to eight characters, by default.
Dt_externalleading	Includes the font external leading in line height. Normally, external leading is not included in the height of a line of text.
Dt_internal	Uses the system font to calculate text metrics.
Dt_left	Aligns text to the left.
Dt_noclip	Draws without clipping.
Dt_noprefix	Turns off processing of prefix characters. Normally, the mnemonic-prefix character & is interpreted as a directive to underscore the character that follows, and && as a directive to print a single &.
Dt_right	Aligns the text to the right.
Dt_singleline	Displays text on a single line only. Carriage returns and linefeeds do not break the line.
Dt_tabstop	Sets tab stops. The default number of characters for each tab is eight.
Dt_top	Top-justifies the text.
Dt_vcenter	Centers text vertically.
Dt_wordbreak	Breaks words. Lines are broken between words if a word would extend past the edge of the rectangle.

Setting the Background Color

You can set the color that Windows uses to fill the background of drawings using *set_background_color*. The feature *set_background_color* takes an instance of *WEL_COLOR_REF* and sets *background_color* accordingly. Windows uses the new background color next time the window receives the message *Wm_erasebkgnd*. If you need the change to occur immediately, you can call the feature *invalidate* from *WEL_WINDOW*. This feature forces the window to repaint itself.

```
background_color: WEL_COLOR_REF
        -- Current color of the background
    require
        exists: exists
    ensure
        result_not_void: Result /= Void

set_background_color (color: WEL_COLOR_REF)
        -- Set the 'background_color' to 'color'
    require
        exists: exists;
        color_not_void: color /= Void
    ensure
        color_set: background_color.item = color.item
```

Drawing Bitmaps, Cursors, and Icons

The feature *draw_bitmap* renders a bitmap directly onto a device context. This features takes the bitmap and the position, width, and height of the rectangle in which it will be rendered. The picture is clipped to fit within the rectangle. If you need the entire picture to be rendered, then you can use the features *width* and *height* from *WEL_BITMAP* to determine the size of the bounding rectangle.

```
draw_bitmap (a_bitmap: WEL_BITMAP; x, y, a_width, a_height: INTEGER)
            -- Draw 'bitmap' at the 'x', 'y' position
            -- using 'a_width' and 'a_height'.
        require
            exists: exists;
            a_bitmap_not_void: a_bitmap /= Void;
            a_bitmap_exists: a_bitmap.exists
```

You can also render cursors directly on a device context using *draw_cursor*. The feature *draw_cursor* takes a cursor and a position, and paints the cursor at the given position.

```
draw_cursor (cursor: WEL_CURSOR; x, y: INTEGER)
    -- Draw 'cursor' at the 'x', 'y' position.
require
    exists: exists;
    cursor_not_void: cursor /= Void;
    cursor_exists: cursor.exists
```

Icons can be rendered in the exact same way, using *draw_icon*.

```
draw_icon (icon: WEL_ICON; x, y: INTEGER)
    -- Draw 'icon' at the 'x', 'y' position.
require
    exists: exists;
    icon_not_void: icon /= Void;
    icon_exists: icon.exists
```

The example located in the *gdi\drawing* folder demonstrates different drawing capabilities of the GDI library.[3] You can draw a series of different figures using the Draw menu items. Figure 10.5 shows the example running after the user has selected to draw a grid of pixels, a filled rectangle and an icon. The example includes a dialog that allows the drawing modes, including the polygon fill mode, the pen style, the ROP2 operation, and brush styles, to be modified.

Performing BIT Block Transfer Operations

The drawing functions described above are generally used to draw static pictures. If you need to render animations, then the following features, although a bit more complicated to use, offer the kind of functionality you require. These features allow you to copy blocks of bits directly from one device context to another. For example, you can draw a figure in a memory device context and then copy the result onto a window device context. This can be very useful for animations, where you want to avoid flickering. If you were using only one device context, you would have to erase the previous image before displaying the next; this would most certainly result in the animation flashing. Using block transfer operations, you can draw the next image in a memory device context and then display the result by copying the corresponding bit block.

There are multiple bit block transfer operations available, ranging from simply copying rectangles to copying a stretched block from one device

---

[3]For brevity, the source code for this example has not been listed. You can find it on the accompanying CD-ROM in the *src* folder.

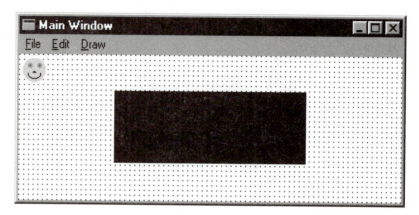

FIGURE 10.5. Drawing example.

context to another. The simplest operation, *pat_blt,* allows you to fill a specified rectangle with the currently selected brush. The operation used to copy the
brush onto the surface depends on the value of the last argument, *raster_op-
eration.* The possible values for this argument are all defined in the class
WEL_RASTER_OPERATIONS_CONSTANTS, listed in Table 10.8.

```
pat_blt (x_destination, y_destination, a_width, a_height: INTEGER;
    raster_operation: INTEGER)
        -- Copy selected brush to rectangle defined by
            'x_destination', 'y_destination'.
        -- 'a_width', 'a_height'.using 'raster_operation'.
        -- See class WEL_RASTER_OPERATIONS_CONSTANTS for
        -- 'raster_operation' values.
    require
        exists: exists;
        positive_width: a_width >= 0;
        positive_height: a_height >= 0
```

If you need to copy a picture rather than a brush into a device, then you
can use the feature *bit_blt.* This feature copies the selected bitmap from the
source device context into the destination device context. Again, the operation
used to copy the rectangle is defined by the last argument, *raster_operation,*
whose values can be found in the class *WEL_RASTER_OPERATIONS_CON-
STANTS* listed in Table 10.8.

TABLE 10.8   *Raster Operation Constants*
(WEL_RASTER_OPERATION_CONSTANTS)

CONSTANT	DESCRIPTION
Pat_copy	Copy the brush onto the surface.
Pat_invert	The color of the destination surface will be the result of a Boolean XOR operation between the colors of the brush and the original colors of the surface.
Pat_paint	The color of the destination surface will be the result of a Boolean OR operation between the colors of the brush and the original colors of the surface.
Merge_copy	The color of the destination surface will be the result of a Boolean AND operation between the colors of the brush and the original colors of the surface.
Srccop	Copy the rectangle onto the surface.
Srcand	The color of the destination surface is the result of a Boolean AND operation between the colors of the rectangle and the original colors of the surface.
Srcerase	The color of the destination surface is the result of a Boolean AND operation between the colors of the rectangle and the original inverted colors of the surface.
Srcinvert	The color of the destination surface is the result of a Boolean XOR operation between the colors of the rectangle and the original colors of the surface.
Srcpaint	The color of the destination surface is the result of a Boolean OR operation between the colors of the rectangle and the original colors of the surface.
Mergepaint	The color of the destination surface is the result of a Boolean OR operation between the colors of the rectangle and the original inverted colors of the surface.
Notsrccopy	Copy inverted rectangle and the original inverted colors of the surface.
Notsrcerase	The color of the destination surface is the inverted result of a Boolean OR operation between the colors of the rectangle and the original colors of the surface.
Dtsinvert	Invert the destination surface colors.
Blackness	Fill the destination surface with the first entry in the color palette (usually black).
Whiteness	Fill the destination surface with the second entry in the color palette (usually white).

```
bit_blt (x_destination, y_destination, a_width, a_height: INTEGER;
    dc_source: WEL_DC;
    x_source, y_source, raster_operation: INTEGER)
            -- Copy block of selected bitmap defined with 'x_source',
            -- 'y_source', 'source_width' and 'source_height' to
            -- 'x_destination',
            -- 'y_destination' using 'raster_operation'.
            -- See class WEL_RASTER_OPERATIONS_CONSTANTS for
            -- 'raster_operation' values.
    require
        exists: exists;
        positive_width: a_width >= 0;
        positive_height: a_height >= 0;
        dc_source_not_void: dc_source /= Void;
        dc_source_exists: dc_source.exists
```

Feature *bit_blt* keeps the size of the copied bitmap untouched. If you need to stretch (or shrink) the bitmap on the destination surface, then you can use the feature *stretch_blt*. The same kinds of operations are available with this feature, the difference being that it takes a size for the destination image.

```
stretch_blt (x_destination, y_destination, width_destination,
    height_destination: INTEGER;
        dc_source: WEL_DC; x_source, y_source, width_source,
            height_source,
            raster_operation: INTEGER)
            -- Copy block of selected bitmap defined with
            -- 'source_width'
            -- and 'source_height' to 'x_destination', 'y_destination'.
            -- using 'raster_operation'. Bitmap is streached to fit in
            -- 'width_destination'x'height_destination'.
            -- See class WEL_RASTER_OPERATIONS_CONSTANTS for
            -- 'raster_operation' values.
    require
        exists: exists;
        positive_width_destination: width_destination >= 0;
        positive_height_destination: height_destination >= 0;
        positive_width_source: width_source >= 0;
        positive_height_source: height_source >= 0;
        dc_source_not_void: dc_source /= Void;
        dc_source_exists: dc_source.exists
```

Setting the Stretch Mode

You have some control of how Windows compresses a bitmap during a *stretch_blt* operation in cases where the resulting size is smaller than the original. By default, any pixels deleted from the original bitmap during the compression are ignored, but you can tell Windows to calculate the value of the existing pixels according to the deleted ones. Windows can use either the *and* or the *or* binary operations on existing and deleted pixels.

The feature *stretch_blt_mode* returns the current stretch mode, which you can set using *set_stretch_blt_mode*. The possible modes of the class *WEL_STRETCH_MODE_CONSTANTS* are listed in Table 10.9. This class also defines the feature *valid_stretch_mode_constant* that checks whether the given constant is a valid stretch mode.

```
stretch_blt_mode: INTEGER
        -- Current stretching mode. The stretching mode
        -- defines how color data is added to or removed from
        -- bitmaps that are stretched or compressed when
        -- 'stretch_blt' is called.
    require
        exists: exists
    ensure
        valid_stretch_mode: valid_stretch_mode_constant (Result)

valid_stretch_mode_constant (c: INTEGER): BOOLEAN
        -- Is 'c' a valid stretch mode constant?
        -- (from WEL_STRETCH_MODE_CONSTANTS)

set_stretch_blt_mode (a_mode: INTEGER)
        -- Set the bitmap stretching mode with 'a_mode'.
        -- See class WEL_STRETCH_MODE_CONSTANTS for 'a_mode'
        -- values.
    require
        exists: exists;
        valid_stretch_mode_constant: valid_stretch_mode_constant
        (a_mode)
    ensure
        stretch_blt_mode_set: stretch_blt_mode = a_mode
```

TABLE 10.9   *Bitmap Stretch Mode Constants (WEL_STRETCH_MODE_CONSTANTS)*

CONSTANT	DESCRIPTION
Stretch_andscans	Performs a Boolean AND operation using the color values for the eliminated and existing pixels. If the bitmap is a monochrome bitmap, this mode preserves black pixels at the expense of white pixels.
Stretch_deletescans	Deletes the pixels. This mode deletes all eliminated lines of pixels without trying to preserve their information. This is the default mode.
Stretch_orscans	Performs a Boolean OR operation using the color values for the eliminated and existing pixels. If the bitmap is a monochrome bitmap, this mode preserves white pixels at the expense of black pixels.

Example 10.4 demonstrates the use of these features to animate a bitmap in a window. It uses a buffer to calculate the new image to avoid flickering when the bitmap is erased and then drawn again. The buffer is an instance of *WEL_MEMORY_DC*, used to draw the new bitmap before it is copied to the window device context. The third device context used for this animation holds the actual bitmap.

Example 10.4 Performing BLIT Operations

```
class
    MAIN_WINDOW
inherit
    WEL_FRAME_WINDOW
    WEL_SYSTEM_METRICS
        export
            {NONE} all
        end
    WEL_DIB_COLORS_CONSTANTS
        export
            {NONE} all
        end
    WEL_RASTER_OPERATIONS_CONSTANTS
        export
            {NONE} all
        end
    DOUBLE_MATH
        export
            {NONE} all
        end
create
    make
feature {NONE} -- Initialization

    make is
            -- Create dcs and load bitmap.
            -- First create window client area device context
            -- Then create two other dc compatible to the former:
            --          - 'mem_dc' is used to calculate the image
            --          - 'bitmap_dc' is used to store the bitmap
        local
            a_file: RAW_FILE
            a_dib: WEL_DIB
            a_bitmap: WEL_BITMAP

        do
            make_top (Title)
            resize (Block_width + 2 * window_border_width,
                Block_height +  2 * window_border_height +
                    title_bar_height)
            create {WEL_CLIENT_DC}win_dc.make (Current)
```

```
        win_dc.get
        create a_file.make_open_read ("wel.bmp")
        create a_dib.make_by_file (a_file)
        create bitmap.make_by_dib (win_dc, a_dib, Dib_rgb_colors)
        create mem_dc.make_by_dc (win_dc)
        create bitmap_dc.make_by_dc (win_dc)
        bitmap_dc.select_bitmap (bitmap)
        create a_bitmap.make_compatible (win_dc, Block_width,
            Block_height)
        mem_dc.select_bitmap (a_bitmap)
        mem_dc.fill_rect (client_rect, Black_brush)
        mem_dc.stretch_blt (bitmap_x, bitmap_y,
            (bitmap.width * (0.5 + dabs (sine (angle)))).
                truncated_to_integer,
            (bitmap.height * (0.5 + dabs (sine (angle)))).
                truncated_to_integer,
            bitmap_dc, 0, 0, bitmap.width, bitmap.height, Srccopy)
        x_direction := 1
        y_direction := 1
    end

feature -- Basic Operations

    go is
            -- Idle action: move bitmap every 'Period' call.
        require
            exists: exists
            win_dc_exists: win_dc.exists
            mem_dc_exists: mem_dc.exists
            bitmap_dc_exists: bitmap_dc.exists
        do
            tick := tick + 1
            if tick = Period then
                mem_dc.stretch_blt (bitmap_x, bitmap_y,
                        (bitmap.width * (0.5 + dabs (sine
                            (angle)))).truncated_to_integer,
                        (bitmap.height * (0.5 + dabs (sine
                            (angle)))).truncated_to_integer, bitmap_dc,
                        0, 0,
                        bitmap.width, bitmap.height, Blackness)
                bitmap_x := bitmap_x + (x_direction * (0.5 + dabs
                    (sine (angle))) * x_speed).truncated_to_integer
                    if (bitmap_x + (1.5 * bitmap.width).truncated_to_
                    integer) > Block_width or bitmap_x < 0 then
                        x_direction := - x_direction
                end
                bitmap_y := bitmap_y + (y_direction * (0.5 + dabs
                    (cosine (angle))) * y_speed).truncated_to_integer
                if (bitmap_y + (1.5 * bitmap.height).trunc-
                    ated_to_
```

```
integer) > Block_height or bitmap_y < 0 then
                y_direction := - y_direction
        end
        angle := angle + increment
        mem_dc.stretch_blt (bitmap_x, bitmap_y,
                (bitmap.width * (0.5 + dabs (sine
                    (angle)))).truncated_to_integer,
                (bitmap.height * (0.5 + dabs (sine
                    (angle)))).truncated_to_integer, bitmap_dc,
                0, 0,
                bitmap.width, bitmap.height, Srccopy)
        win_dc.bit_blt (0, 0, width, height, mem_dc, 0, 0,
            Srccopy)
        tick := 0
    end
end

feature {NONE} -- Implementation

    tick: INTEGER
            -- Number of times 'go' was called since last blit
            -- operation

    Period: INTEGER is 300
            -- Number of times 'go' should be called between two blit
            -- operations

    bitmap: WEL_BITMAP
            -- Rendered bitmap

    bitmap_x, bitmap_y: INTEGER
            -- Position of bitmap

    x_direction, y_direction: INTEGER
            -- X and Y bitmap movement directions
            -- Possible values are 1 or -1.

    angle: DOUBLE
            -- Angle used to calcualte new bitmap position

    increment: DOUBLE is 0.06
            -- Increment added to angle between two blits

    x_speed: DOUBLE is 1.2
            -- Maximum distance (in pixels) from old bitmap x
            -- coordinate to new one
            -- Should be greated than 0

    y_speed: DOUBLE is 1.3
            -- Maximum distance (in pixels) from old bitmap y
            -- coordinate to new one
```

```
                         -- Should be greated than 0

        Block_width: INTEGER is 500
                    -- Blitted block width

        Block_height: INTEGER is 400
                    -- Blitted block height

        Black_brush: WEL_BLACK_BRUSH is
                    -- Black brush used to clear block
            once
                create Result.make
            end

        Title: STRING is "WEL GDI demo"
                    -- Window's title

        win_dc: WEL_CLIENT_DC
                    -- Window client area device context

        mem_dc: WEL_MEMORY_DC
                    -- Memory device context used to calculate image

        bitmap_dc: WEL_MEMORY_DC
                    -- Device context containing the bitmap

invariant
        valid_x_direction: x_direction = 1 or x_direction = -1
        valid_y_direction: y_direction = 1 or y_direction = -1
        valid_x_speed: x_speed > 0
        valid_y_speed: y_speed > 0

end -- class MAIN_WINDOW
```

Filling an Area

There are different ways of filling a surface on a device context using WEL. The easiest is to use *fill_rect*. The two arguments for this feature are the rectangle defining the area you want to fill and the brush you want to use. If you are looking for an equivalent of the so-called bucket in standard drawing software, you can use *flood_fill_surface*. The arguments for that feature are the x and y coordinates of the starting point (where you would have clicked using the bucket) and the color that should be filled. The brush used to fill the color is the currently selected brush.

Feature *flood_fill_border* has the opposite behavior—the color defines the limit of the filling area so that if you draw a black rectangle, and specify a point inside the rectangle and the color black, the rectangle will be filled with the currently selected brush.

```
fill_rect (a_rect: WEL_RECT; a_brush: WEL_BRUSH)
          -- Fill a 'a_rect' by using 'a_brush' to fill it.
   require
       exists: exists;
       a_rect_not_void: a_rect /= Void;
       a_brush_not_void: a_brush /= Void;
       a_brush_exists: a_brush.exists

flood_fill_border (x, y: INTEGER; color: WEL_COLOR_REF)
          -- Fill an area which is bounded by 'color' starting
          -- at 'x', 'y'.
   require
       exists: exists;
       color_not_void: color /= Void
flood_fill_surface (x, y: INTEGER; color: WEL_COLOR_REF)
          -- Fill an area which is defined by 'color' starting
          -- at 'x', 'y'. Filling continues outward in all
          -- directions as long as the color is encountered.
   require
       exists: exists;
       color_not_void: color /= Void
```

Inverting an Area

The features *invert_rect* and *invert_region* invert the colors of each pixel included in a rectangle or region, respectively. Windows uses the Boolean NOT operation on the RGB color value of each pixel.

```
invert_rect (a_rect: WEL_RECT)
          -- Invert 'a_rect' in a window by performing a logical
          -- NOT operation on the color values for each pixel.
   require
       exists: exists;
       a_rect_not_void: a_rect /= Void

invert_region (a_region: WEL_REGION)
          -- Invert the colors in 'a_region'.
   require
       exists: exists;
       a_region_not_void: a_region /= Void;
       a_region_exists: a_region.exists
```

DRAWING MODES

We have seen how you can create and select a pen to draw on a device context. Once a pen has been selected into a device, any call to drawing features uses its color, thickness, and form (dotted, dashed, etc.). There are different ways to draw a figure onto a device context, and you can select how the colors from the figure and the colors of the background should be mixed by choosing between different binary raster operations.

Setting the ROP2 Mode

The default raster operation (ROP2) simply replaces the pixels of the background with those of the figure. You can change the currently selected ROP2 into a device with the feature *set_rop2*. The currently selected ROP2 can be retrieved with *rop2*. The possible operations are integer constants all defined in the class *WEL_ROP2_CONSTANTS*. This class also defines the feature *valid_rop2_constant* that checks whether a given integer is a valid ROP2 constant.

```
rop2: INTEGER
        -- Current drawing mode
   require
        exists: exists
   ensure
        valid_result: valid_rop2_constant (Result)
valid_rop2_constant (c: INTEGER): BOOLEAN
        -- Is 'c' a valid rop2 constant?ki
        -- (from WEL_ROP2_CONSTANTS)
set_rop2 (a_rop2: INTEGER)
        -- Set the current foreground mix mode. GDI uses the
        -- foreground mix mode to combine pens and interiors of
        -- filled objects with the colors already on the screen.
        -- The foreground mix mode defines how colors from the
        -- brush or pen and the colors in the existing image
        -- are to be combined.
        -- For 'a_rop2' values, see class WEL_ROP2_CONSTANTS.
   require
        exists: exists;
        valid_rop2_constant: valid_rop2_constant (a_rop2)
   ensure
        rop2_set: rop2 = a_rop2
```

The available raster operations and their descriptions are all listed in Table 10.10.

TABLE 10.10   *Raster Operation Constants (WEL_ROP2_CONSTANTS)*

CONSTANT	DESCRIPTION
R2_black	Pixel is set with the second entry in the palette (usually black).
R2_copypen	Pixel is the pen color (default).
R2_masknotpen	Pixel is a combination of the colors common to both the screen and the inverse of the pen.
R2_maskpen	Pixel is a combination of the colors common to both the pen and the screen.
R2_maskpennot	Pixel is a combination of the colors common to both the pen and the inverse of the screen.
R2_mergenotpen	Pixel is a combination of the screen color and the inverse of the pen color.
R2_mergepen	Pixel is a combination of the pen color and the screen color.
R2_mergepennot	Pixel is a combination of the pen color and the inverse of the screen color.
R2_nop	Pixel remains unchanged.
R2_not	Pixel is the inverse of the screen color.
R2_notcopypen	Pixel is the inverse of the pen color.
R2_notmaskpen	Pixel is the inverse of the *R2_maskpen* color.
R2_notmergepen	Pixel is the inverse of the *R2_mergepen* color.
R2_notxorpen	Pixel is the inverse of the *R2_xorpen* color.
R2_white	Pixel is set with the first entry in the palette (usually white).
R2_xorpen	Pixel is a combination of the colors in the pen and in the screen, but not in both.

Setting the Background Transparency

You can also specify how the spaces between hatches of a brush, or a line drawn with a nonsolid pen, should be filled. You can either leave the existing background untouched or fill in the spaces with the selected background color. See "Setting the Background Color" earlier in this chapter.

You can retrieve the currently selected mode with the features *is_opaque* (spaces filled with selected background color) and *is_transparent* (background untouched). The features *set_background_opaque* and *set_background_transparent* let you select the current mode.

```
is_opaque: BOOLEAN
        -- Is the background mode opaque?
   require
```

```
            exists: exists

is_transparent: BOOLEAN
            -- Is the background mode transparent?
        require
            exists: exists

set_background_opaque
            -- Set the background mode to opaque
        require
            exists: exists
        ensure
            is_opaque: is_opaque

set_background_transparent
            -- Set the background mode to transparent
        require
            exists: exists
        ensure
            is_transparent: is_transparent
```

LOGICAL VERSUS PHYSICAL COORDINATES

WEL gives you control of the mapping from the size you give when calling a drawing function to the actual size of the resulting figure on the device. Certain applications might require that the size unit be "real life" units, such as inches or centimeters, while other applications might need to map logical size directly into pixels or dots. The GDI API defines two distinct coordinate spaces—the logical coordinate space is where you draw and the physical coordinate space corresponds to the real device coordinates.

Setting the Coordinate Mapping Mode

The mapping mode defines how units are mapped between the logical and the physical coordinate spaces and the direction of the x and y axes. You can retrieve the currently selected mode with the feature *map_mode*. This feature returns an integer with one of the values listed in class *WEL_MM_CONSTANTS*. This class also includes the feature *valid_map_mode_constant* that checks whether the given integer corresponds to a valid mapping mode. You can set the current mode with the feature *set_map_mode*.

```
map_mode: INTEGER
        -- Current mapping mode
        -- See class WEL_MM_CONSTANTS for values.
```

```
require
    exists: exists
ensure
    valid_map_mode: valid_map_mode_constant (Result)

valid_map_mode_constant (c: INTEGER): BOOLEAN
        -- Is 'c' a valid map mode constant?
        -- (from WEL_MM_CONSTANTS)

set_map_mode (mode: INTEGER)
        -- Set the mapping mode 'mode' of the device context.
        -- See class WEL_MM_CONSTANTS for 'mode' values.
    require
        exists: exists;
        valid_map_mode: valid_map_mode_constant (mode)
    ensure
        map_mode_set: map_mode = mode
```

The default mode *Mm_text* is a one-to-one mapping between the logical and physical coordinates—the unit is the pixel. *Mm_loenglish, Mm_hienglish, Mm_himetric,* and *Mm_lometric* allow you to use standard metrics units. For applications that need a fine control on a printer output, the mode *Mm_twips* maps logical units into twips (a twip corresponds to one twentieth of a printer's point). The last mode, *Mm_anisotropic,* lets you set your own extents. See "Setting the Extents and Origins" earlier in this chapter. Table 10.11 provides a detailed description of each mode.

TABLE 10.11   *Mapping Mode Constants (WEL_MM_CONSTANTS)*

CONSTANT	DESCRIPTION
Mm_anisotropic	Logical units are mapped to arbitrary units with arbitrarily scaled axes. The window extent and viewport extent specify the units, orientation, and scaling.
Mm_hienglish	Each logical unit is mapped to 0.001 inch. Positive x is to the right, positive y is up.
Mm_himetric	Each logical unit is mapped to 0.01 millimeter. Positive x is to the right, positive y is up.
Mm_isotropic	Logical units are mapped to arbitrary units with equally scaled axes. The window extent and viewport extent specify the units and the orientation of the axes.
Mm_loenglish	Each logical unit is mapped to 0.01 inch. Positive x is to the right; positive y is up.
Mm_lometric	Each logical unit is mapped to 0.1 millimeter. Positive x is to the right; positive y is up.
Mm_text	Each logical unit is mapped to one device pixel. Positive x is to the right; positive y is down.
Mm_twips	Each logical unit is mapped to one twentieth of a printer's point (1/1440 inch). Positive x is to the right; positive y is up.

Setting the Extents and Origins

We have seen that the GDI API uses two coordinate spaces. The logical coordinate space, also known as window space, defines the coordinates you use when you call the drawing features. The physical coordinate space, also known as viewport space, corresponds to the device coordinate space. Windows automatically maps logical coordinates into physical coordinates using the mapping mode of the device and the origins of both coordinate spaces.

You can manually set the scaling factor between the two spaces by selecting the *Mm_anisotropic* mapping mode. The factor is the result of the division between the viewport and window extents. You can retrieve the current values with the features *window_extent* and *viewport_extent,* and can set their values using the corresponding features *set_window_extent* and *set_viewport_extent.*

The other transformation that occurs when Windows maps the coordinates is a *translation*. The translation is performed according to the origins of both coordinate spaces. The features *window_origin* and *viewport_origin* let you retrieve their current values while the features *set_window_origin* and *set_viewport_origin* let you set them. The resulting formula that gives the physical coordinates from the logical coordinates is the following:

$$P = \left(\frac{(L - WO) \times VE}{WE} \right) + VO$$

where

- *P* is the physical coordinate
- *L* is the logical coordinate
- *WO* is the window space origin
- *VO* is the viewport space origin
- *VE* is the viewport extent
- *WE* is the window extent

```
window_extent: WEL_SIZE
        -- Window extent for the dc
    require
        exists: exists
    ensure
        result_not_void: Result /= Void

window_origin: WEL_POINT
        -- Window origin for the dc
    require
        exists: exists
    ensure
        result_not_void: Result /= Void
```

```
set_window_extent (x_extent, y_extent: INTEGER)
        -- Set the 'x_extent' and 'y_extent' of the window
        -- associated with the device context
    require
        exists: exists;
        valid_current_map_mode: valid_extent_map_mode (map_mode)
    ensure
        x_window_extent_set: window_extent.width = x_extent;
        y_window_extent_set: window_extent.height = y_extent

set_window_origin (x_origin, y_origin: INTEGER)
        -- Set the 'x_origin' and 'y_origin' of the window
        -- associated with the device context
    require
        exists: exists
    ensure
        x_window_origin_set: window_origin.x = x_origin;
        y_window_origin_set: window_origin.y = y_origin

viewport_extent: WEL_SIZE
        -- Retrieve the size of the current viewport for the dc.
    require
        exists: exists
    ensure
        result_not_void: Result /= Void

viewport_origin: WEL_POINT
        -- Viewport origin for the dc
    require
        exists: exists
    ensure
        result_not_void: Result /= Void

set_viewport_extent (x_extent, y_extent: INTEGER)
        -- Set the 'x_extent' and 'y_extent' of the viewport
        -- associated with the device context
    require
        exists: exists;
        valid_current_map_mode: valid_extent_map_mode (map_mode)
    ensure
        x_viewport_extent_set: viewport_extent.width = x_extent;
        y_viewport_extent_set: viewport_extent.height = y_extent

set_viewport_origin (x_origin, y_origin: INTEGER)
        -- Set the 'x_origin' and 'y_origin' of the viewport
        -- associated with the device context
    require
        exists: exists
    ensure
        x_viewport_origin_set: viewport_origin.x = x_origin;
        y_viewport_origin_set: viewport_origin.y = y_origin
```

DEVICE CAPABILITIES

As device-independent as the GDI features can be, certain parts of your system will need to get specific information on the device on which you are drawing. Information such as the supported number of colors, the horizontal and vertical size, the resolution, and so on, can be retrieved through the feature *device_caps*. The unique argument of the feature is an integer that must have one of the values defined in the class *WEL_CAPABILITIES_CONSTANTS* listed in Table 10.12. The result is also an integer whose meaning depends on the capability you are interested in—it can be a size, a count, or a constant with a specific meaning.

The features *height* and *width* call *device_caps* internally and they return the height and width of the device in pixels.

```
device_caps (capability: INTEGER): INTEGER
        -- Give device-specific information about
        -- the current display device.
        -- See class WEL_CAPABILITIES_CONSTANTS for
        -- 'capability' values and results.
    require
        exists: exists

height: INTEGER
        -- Height of screen (in raster lines)
    require
        exists: exists

width: INTEGER
        -- Width of the screen (in pixels)
    require
        exists: exists
```

TABLE 10.12   *Device Capability Constants (WEL_CAPABILITIES_CONSTANTS)*

CONSTANT	DESCRIPTION
Aspect_x	Relative width of a device pixel used for line drawing.
Aspect_x_y	Diagonal width of the device pixel used for line drawing.
Aspect_y	Relative height of a device pixel used for line drawing.
Bits_pixel	Number of adjacent color bits for each pixel.
Clip_caps	Flag that indicates the clipping capabilities of the device. Returns 1 if the device can clip to a rectangle; 0 otherwise.

(continued)

TABLE 1 □.1 2   *Device Capability Constants*
                 (WEL_CAPABILITIES_CONSTANTS) (continued)

CONSTANT	DESCRIPTION
Color_resolution	Actual color resolution of the device in bits per pixel.
Curve_caps	One or more values from Table 10.14 indicating the curve capabilities of the device.
Driver_version	The device driver version.
Horizontal_resolution	Width in pixels of the screen.
Horizontal_size	Width in millimeters of the physical screen.
Line_caps	One or more values from Table 10.15 indicating line capabilities of the device.
Logical_pixels_x	Number of pixels per logical inch along the screen width.
Logical_pixels_y	Number of pixels per logical inch along the screen height.
Num_brushes	Number of driver-specific brushes.
Num_colors	Number of entries in the device's color table, if the device has a color depth of no more than 8 bits per pixel. For devices with greater color depths, −1 is returned.
Num_fonts	Number of device-specific fonts.
Num_markers	Number of device-specific markers.
Num_pens	Number of device-specific pens.
Planes	Number of color planes.
Polygonal_caps	One or more values from Table 10.16 that indicate the polygon capabilities of the device.
Raster_caps	One or more values from Table 10.17 that indicate the raster capabilities of the device.
Size_palette	Number of entries in the system palette.
Technology	One or more values from Table 10.18 indicating the device technology.
Text_caps	One or more values from Table 10.19 indicating the text capabilities of the device.
Vertical_resolution	Height in raster lines of the screen.
Vertical_size	Height in millimeters of the physical screen.

The feature *device_caps* returns a combination of flags for certain capabilities. Tables 10.13 to 10.19 list the flags and describe their meanings.

The first capability to return a combination of flags is *Clip_caps*. It describes the kind of clipping, if any, the device supports. The flags are listed in Table 10.13.

TABLE 10.13 *Clipping Capability Constants (WEL_CLIPPING_CAPABILITIES_CONSTANTS)*

CONSTANTS	DESCRIPTION
Cp_none	Output is not clipped.
Cp_rectangle	Output is clipped to rectangles.
Cp_region	Output is clipped to regions.

Next is *Curve_caps,* which describes the kinds of curves, if any, that can be drawn onto the device. The possible flags for *Curve_caps* are listed in Table 10.14.

The capability *Line_caps* describes the kinds of lines, if any, that can be drawn onto the device. The flags are listed in Table 10.15.

The capability *Polygonal_caps* describes the kinds of polygons, if any, that may be drawn onto the device. These flags are described in Table 10.16.

Raster_caps describes the kinds of raster operations you can apply onto the device. See "Performing BIT Block Transfer Operations" in this chapter. Possible flags are listed in Table 10.17.

The capability *Technology_caps* describes the nature of the device. For once, the value is exactly one flag and not a combination. Table 10.18 lists the possible devices.

TABLE 10.14 *Curves Capability Constants (WEL_CURVES_CAPABILITIES_CONSTANTS)*

CONSTANT	DESCRIPTION
Cc_chord	Supports chords.
Cc_circles	Supports circles.
Cc_ellipses	Supports ellipses.
Cc_interiors	Supports interiors.
Cc_none	Supports no curves.
Cc_pie	Supports pie wedges.
Cc_roundrect	Supports rectangles with rounded corners.
Cc_styled	Supports styled borders.
Cc_wide	Supports wide borders.
Cc_wide_styled	Supports wide-styled borders.

TABLE 10.15 *Line Capability Constants (WEL_LINE_CAPABILITIES_CONSTANTS)*

CONSTANT	DESCRIPTION
Lc_interiors	Supports interiors.
Lc_marker	Supports markers.
Lc_none	Supports no lines.
Lc_polyline	Supports polylines.
Lc_polymarker	Supports polymarkers.
Lc_styled	Supports styled lines.
Lc_wide	Supports wide lines.
Lc_wide_styled	Supports wide-styled lines.

The last capability to return a combination of flags is *Text_caps*. It describes the operations you can apply on fonts and characters on the device. The list appears in Table 10.19.

Copying a Device Context

You should now be able to draw complex figures onto a device. The following feature allows you to reproduce the result onto another device. You have to specify a rectangle that defines the part of the current device that you want to copy. For example, this feature can be useful to output the content of the screen onto a printer.

TABLE 10.16 *Polygonal Capability Constants (WEL_POLYGONAL_CAPABILITIES_CONSTANTS)*

CONSTANT	DESCRIPTION
Pc_interiors	Supports interiors.
Pc_none	Supports no polygons.
Pc_polygon	Supports alternate fill polygons.
Pc_rectangle	Supports rectangles.
Pc_scanline	Supports scan lines.
Pc_styled	Supports styled borders.
Pc_wide	Supports wide borders.
Pc_widestyled	Supports wide-styled borders.
Pc_windpolygon	Supports winding-number-fill polygons.

TABLE 10.17   *Raster Capability Constants*
(WEL_RASTER_CAPABILITIES_CONSTANTS)

CONSTANT	DESCRIPTION
Rc_banding	Requires banding support.
Rc_bigfont	Supports fonts larger than 64K.
Rc_bilblt	Capable of transferring bitmaps.
Rc_bitmap64	Supports bitmaps larger than 64K.
Rc_devbits	Supports device bitmaps.
Rc_di_bitmap	Capable of supporting device-independent bits.
Rc_dibtodev	Capable of supporting device-independent bit to device-dependent bit conversions.
Rc_floodfill	Capable of performing flood fills.
Rc_gdi20_output	Capable of supporting Windows version 2.0 features.
Rc_gdi20_state	Includes a state block in the device context.
Rc_op_dx_output	Supports dev opaque and DX array.
Rc_palette	Specifies a palette-based device.
Rc_savebitmap	Capable of saving bitmaps locally.
Rc_scaling	Capable of scaling.
Rc_stretchblt	Capable of performing stretch BLT operations.
Rc_stretchdib	Capable of performing stretch DIB operations.

TABLE 10.18   *Device Technology Constants*
(WEL_DEVICE_TECHNOLOGY_COSTANTS)

CONSTANT	DESCRIPTION
Dt_charstream	Character stream.
Dt_dispfile	Display file.
Dt_metafile	Metafile.
Dt_plotter	Vector plotter.
Dt_rascamera	Raster camera.
Dt_rasdisplay	Raster display.
Dt_rasprinter	Raster printer.

TABLE 10.19   *Text Capability Constants (WEL_TEXT_CAPABILITY_CONSTANTS)*

CONSTANT	DESCRIPTION
Tc_cp_stroke	Supports stroke-clip precision.
Tc_cr_90	Supports 90-degree, and only 90-degree, character rotation.
Tc_cr_any	Supports character rotation at any degree.
Tc_ea_double	Supports double-weight characters.
Tc_ia_able	Supports italics.
Tc_op_character	Supports character output precision.
Tc_op_stroke	Supports stroke output precision.
Tc_ra_able	Supports raster fonts.
Tc_sa_contin	Supports any multiples for exact scaling.
Tc_sa_double	Supports doubled characters for scaling.
Tc_sa_integer	Supports integer multiples for scaling.
Tc_sf_x_yindep	Supports scaling independent of x and y directions.
Tc_so_able	Supports strikeouts.
Tc_ua_able	Supports underlining.
Tc_va_able	Supports vector fonts.

```
copy_dc (dc_source: WEL_DC; rect: WEL_RECT)
        -- Copy the content of 'rect' in 'dc_source'
        -- to the current dc.
    require
        exists: exists;
        rect_not_void: rect /= Void;
        dc_source_not_void: dc_source /= Void;
        dc_source_exists: dc_source.exists
```

SUMMARY

The GDI chapter is one of the largest because GDI is a large topic. Windows and, consequently, WEL offer many different ways and many degrees of support to draw onto a device. You can draw basic figures with different pens and brushes or fill surfaces with patterns. You can define precise clipping regions to limit the drawing surface. You can also use efficient low-level bit copy functions to create animations. And finally, you can retrieve specific information on a device.

WEL applications do not always need to use the GDI features directly—using controls and specifying their styles is often enough. However, should you need to draw some part of your graphical interface, WEL offers a wide range of tools and functionality that will most certainly cover all your needs.

DIRECTORY TREE ANALYZER

IMPLEMENTING GRAPHICS

Figure 10.6 shows the graphical view of the Directory Tree Analyzer after parsing an ISE Eiffel installation directory. The graphical percentage bars show the size of each directory in relation to the size of the other directories. The largest directory is shown with a full, 100 percent bar; the other directories have smaller bars relative to the size of their content.

The graphical view is drawn whenever a *WM_PAINT* message is received by the control. The view handles this event in the *on_paint* message

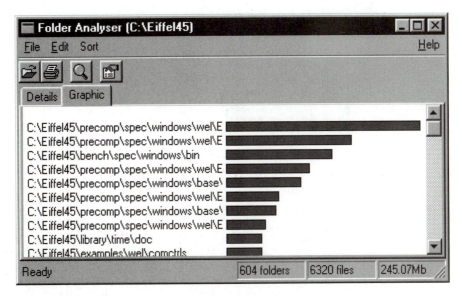

FIGURE 10.6. Directory Tree Analyzer in graphical mode.

hook. In addition to painting the percentage bars and a textual description of each directory, the *on_paint* routine handles scrolling of the view by painting only the area necessary given the current scrolling position.

The Graphical View

The graphical view is implemented as a descendant of *WEL_CONTROL_WIN-DOW*. A *WEL_CONTROL_WINDOW* is a modified frame window that can be used to create custom controls. The features *on_size, on_show, on_vertical_scroll, on_paint,* and *update* are redefined.

In Example 10.5, the creation procedure *make* (lines 29–41) initializes the control window, turns on the vertical scroll bar, and saves the dimensions of the window to be used later.

Example 10.5 GRAPH_VIEW of the Directory Tree Analyzer

```
1    class GRAPH_VIEW
2    inherit
3         WEL_CONTROL_WINDOW
4             rename
5                 make as make_control_window
6             redefine
7                 on_size, on_show, on_vertical_scroll, on_paint, update
8             end;
9         WEL_DT_CONSTANTS
10            export
11                {NONE} all
12            end;
13        WEL_SB_CONSTANTS
14            export
15                {NONE} all
16            end;
17        WEL_DT_CONSTANTS
18            export
19                {NONE} all
20            end;
21        WEL_STANDARD_COLORS
22            export
23                {NONE} all
24            end
25   create
26        make
27   feature -- Initialization
28
29        make (a_parent: WEL_COMPOSITE_WINDOW; a_main_window:
             MAIN_WINDOW) is
30                -- Initialize the graph view
31            require
```

```
32                          a_parent_not_void: a_parent /= void;
33                          a_parent_exists: a_parent.exists;
34                          main_window_not_void: a_main_window /= void
35          do
36              main_window := a_main_window
37              make_control_window (a_parent, "")
38              show_vertical_scroll_bar
39              resize (500, a_parent.height)
40              initialise_text_sizes
41          end;
42
```

The message hooks defined by the *GRAPHIC_VIEW* class include *on_show, on_size, on_vertical_scroll, on_paint,* and *update.* The message hook *on_show* is called when the window is first shown, and its implementation causes the contents of the window to be updated. Message hook *on_size* saves the new dimensions of the window for the *on_paint* routine, *on_vertical_scroll* captures all vertical scroll events and updates the current scrolling position for *on_paint,* and routine *update* forces the client area of the window to be re-painted by sending a *Wm_paint* message (thus causing *on_paint* to be called). The redefinition of *update* in *GRAPHIC_VIEW* calls the precursor version and then stores the new window dimensions for the next paint operation.

In Example 10.6, hook *on_paint* does all of the work to paint the graphical view. During a paint operation, the routine takes into account the current scroll position, the number of *DIRECTORY_INFO* elements collected, and the current dimensions of the client area. Only enough bars required to fill the client area are drawn.

Example 10.6 GRAPHIC_VIEW Events

```
43      feature -- Events
44
45          on_show is
46                  -- Update the initial sizes
47              do
48                  update
49              end;
50
51          on_size (size_y_pospe, a_width, a_height: INTEGER) is
52                  -- Update sizes and metrics for new size
53              do
```

```
54                      if main_window.directory_infos /= void then
55                          initialize_window_sizes (a_width, a_height)
56                      end
57              end;
58
59      on_vertical_scroll (scroll_code, position: INTEGER) is
60                  -- Perform vertical scroll
61          local
62                  ivscrollinc: INTEGER
63          do
64                  if main_window.directory_infos /= void then
65                      if scroll_code = sb_top then
66                          ivscrollinc := - v_scroll_pos
67                      elseif scroll_code = sb_bottom then
68                          ivscrollinc := v_scroll_max - v_scroll_pos
69                      elseif scroll_code = sb_lineup then
70                          ivscrollinc := - 1
71                      elseif scroll_code = sb_linedown then
72                          ivscrollinc := 1
73                      elseif scroll_code = sb_pageup then
74                          ivscrollinc := (- 1).min (- y_client // y_char)
75                      elseif scroll_code = sb_pagedown then
76                          ivscrollinc := (1).max (y_client // y_char)
77                      elseif scroll_code = sb_thumbtrack then
78                          ivscrollinc := position - v_scroll_pos
79                      else
80                          ivscrollinc := 0
81                      end;
82                      ivscrollinc := (- v_scroll_pos).max (ivscrollinc.min
                            (v_scroll_max - v_scroll_pos));
83                      if ivscrollinc /= 0 then
84                          v_scroll_pos := v_scroll_pos + ivscrollinc;
85                          scroll (0, - y_char * ivscrollinc);
86                          set_vertical_position (v_scroll_pos);
87                          update
88                      end
89                  end
90          end;
91
92      on_paint (paint_dc: WEL_PAINT_DC; invalid_rect: WEL_RECT) is
93                  -- Paint the pie chart
94          local
95              font: WEL_ANSI_VARIABLE_FONT;
96              i, y_pos: INTEGER;
97              paint_start, paint_end: INTEGER;
98              info: SORTED_TWO_WAY_LIST [DIRECTORY_INFO];
99              new_rect: WEL_RECT;
100             brush: WEL_BRUSH;
101             border_pen: WEL_PEN;
102             largest_size: INTEGER;
103             percentage_of_largest: REAL;
```

```
104                     bar_size: INTEGER;
105                     current_info: INTEGER
106             do
107                     if main_window.directory_infos /= void then
108                             create font.make;
109                             paint_dc.select_font (font);
110                             create brush.make_solid (red);
111                             create border_pen.make_solid (1, black);
112                             info := main_window.directory_infos;
113                             largest_size := main_window.analyzer.larg-
                                     est_directory_size;
114                             paint_start := (0).max (v_scroll_pos + invalid_rect.top
                                   // y_char - 1);
115                             paint_end := main_window.directory_infos.count.max
                                   (v_scroll_pos
116                                     + invalid_rect.bottom // y_char);
117                     from
118                             i := paint_start
119                     until
120                             i >= paint_end
121                     loop
122                             if (i) < info.count then
123                                 if main_window.sort_reverse then
124                                    current_info := info.count - i
125                                 else
126                                    current_info := i + 1
127                                 end;
128                                 y_pos := y_char * (1 - v_scroll_pos + i);
129                                 create new_rect.make (spacing, y_pos,
                                        component_width, y_pos + y_char);
131                                 paint_dc.draw_text (info.i_th (cur-
                                        rent_info).name, new_rect, dt_left +
                                        dt_vcenter);
133                                 if info.i_th (current_info).total_usage =
                                        0 then
134                                         percentage_of_largest := 0.0
135                                 else
136                                         percentage_of_largest := info.i_th
                                               (current_info).total_usage
137                                                 / largest_size
138                                 end;
139                                 bar_size := (percentage_of_largest *
                                        (component_width - spacing)).rounded;
141                                 paint_dc.select_pen (border_pen);
142                                 paint_dc.select_brush (brush);
143                                 paint_dc.rectangle (component_width + spacing,
                                        y_pos + 2,
144                                         bar_size + component_width + spacing,
                                                y_pos + y_char - 2)
145                             end;
```

```
146                          i := i + 1
147                   end
148              end
149          end;
150
151      update is
152              -- Update the window
153          do
154              Precursor
155              initialize_window_sizes (width, height)
156          end;
157
```

The implementation feature group, shown in Example 10.7, contains attributes to hold the current window dimensions, a reference to the main window object, and two helper routines used to calculate text sizes and window
dimensions.

Example 10.7 GRAPHIC_VIEW Implementation

```
158      feature {NONE} -- Implementation
159
160          main_window: MAIN_WINDOW;
161                  -- The main window of the application
162
163          y_char: INTEGER;
164          y_client: INTEGER;
165          v_scroll_pos: INTEGER;
166          v_scroll_max: INTEGER;
167          component_width: INTEGER;
168          Spacing: INTEGER is 4;
169
170          initialize_text_sizes is
171                      -- Collect initial text metrics and sizes
172              local
173                  font: WEL_ANSI_VARIABLE_FONT
174              do
175                  create font.make;
176                  y_char := font.log_font.height + 2
177              end;
178
179          initialize_window_sizes (a_width, a_height: INTEGER) is
180                      -- Collect current window sizes and
181              local
```

```
182                         info_count: INTEGER
183              do
184                         y_client := a_height;
185                         if main_window.directory_infos /= void
                            then
186                                 info_count := main_window.direc-
                                    tory_infos.count
187                         end;
188                         v_scroll_max := (0).max (info_count + 2 -
                                y_client // y_char);
189                         v_scroll_pos := v_scroll_pos.min
                                (v_scroll_max);
190                         set_vertical_range (0, v_scroll_max);
191                         set_vertical_position (v_scroll_pos);
192                         if has_vertical_scroll_bar then
193                                 component_width := (width - spacing
                                    - 17) // 2
194                         else
195                                 component_width := (width -
                                    spacing) // 2
196                         end
197              end;
198
199      end -- class GRAPH_VIEW
```

CONTROLS

INTRODUCING CONTROLS

A control is a type of window that gives the user a means of interacting with an application. Each type of control provides a different means of input and a different visual representation. Controls are the primary means of interacting with a user interface, and as such, typically represent easily recognizable mechanical or textual controls of everyday life. For example, a button control provides input mechanisms that allow it to be depressed and raised just like the power button on your computer or the eject button on a CD-ROM drive; a check box control can be checked and unchecked just like a box that you need to tick on a paper-based form.

Many different types of controls exist in the Windows operating environment that provide varied and flexible means of interacting with the user. Windows controls vary from very basic push buttons to complex tree view controls and rich text edit controls.

For most of your user interface needs, a control that you can reuse will already exist. If you find you need a control that is not provided with the Windows interface, then you can easily create your own. Additionally, hundreds of controls exist as ActiveX components that you can include in your Eiffel applications. The list of ActiveX controls is enormous and growing every day. You will be hard-pressed not to find the control you need and to have to custom-build one of your own.

TYPES OF CONTROLS

The WEL library classifies controls into a set of related types, including list boxes, buttons, combination boxes, bars, and static controls. The classification also includes the controls for tooltips, tab controls, and tree view controls.

Each of the control types is a descendant of the class *WEL_CONTROL,* and *WEL_CONTROL* itself is a direct descendant of *WEL_WINDOW* (thus providing full window capabilities). The *WEL_CONTROL* class adds the ability to set a text font that will be used for the primary textual component of the control. Typically, each control has a textual part that identifies the purpose of the control. For instance, a button control has a textual part that identifies the purpose of the button. The textual part of each control is generally used in different ways—a button control may display the text in the center of the button, while a check box or radio box may display the text to the right or left of the check image. You are free to change the font, color, and to a lesser degree, the position of the text label.

Figure 11.1 shows the top two levels of the classification of controls supported by the WEL library. As mentioned, each control is a descendant of *WEL_CONTROL* and may also be a descendant of a more specialized control class representing a particular type of control.

The classes *WEL_CONTROL, WEL_BUTTON, WEL_LIST_BOX, WEL_COMBO_BOX,* and *WEL_BAR* are deferred and each has a number of descendants that affect a particular type of specialized control. *WEL_BUTTON,* for example, has descendants that implement push button, group, owner draw, and check box button controls. See "Buttons" in this chapter.

Abstract Control Class

The super class of all controls, *WEL_CONTROL,* introduces a small number of features for retrieving control information and for setting and retrieving the control's font. Each descendant of *WEL_CONTROL* implements specific features for manipulating the respective type of control.

Creating a Control

Each type of control typically has its own creation procedure that is specific to that type of control. In addition, all controls that are situated on a dialog window can be created from a resource, using the creation procedure *make_by_id* as defined in *WEL_CONTROL.*

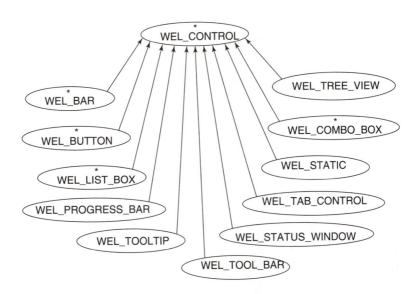

FIGURE 11.1. High-level control classification.

```
make_by_id (a_parent: WEL_DIALOG; an_id: INTEGER)
        -- Make a control identified by 'an_id' with 'a_parent'
        -- as parent.
        -- (export status {NONE})
    require
        a_parent_not_void: a_parent /= void;
        positive_id: an_id > 0
    ensure
        parent_set: parent = a_parent;
        id_set: id = an_id

id: INTEGER
        -- Control id
```

Procedure *make_by_id* takes two arguments, *a_parent* specifying the parent dialog of the control and *an_id* specifying the resource identification number. This procedure loads the control from the application's resources, initializes it, and connects it to the specified parent window. If a control has been created using *make_by_id,* the identification number of the control resource can subsequently be retrieved via the feature *id.*

Changing a Control's Font

Each control has a predefined font that is used to display its textual part. The text is typically used to label the control or to display the control's items. The font of a control can be either the system font (by default) or it can be explicitly set by using the *set_font* feature.

```
font: WEL_FONT
        -- Font with which the control is drawing its text.
    require
        exists: exists
    ensure
        result_not_void: Result /= void

has_system_font: BOOLEAN
        -- Does the control use the system font?
    require
        exists: exists

set_font (a_font: WEL_FONT)
        -- Set `font' with `a_font'.
    require
        exists: exists;
        a_font_not_void: a_font /= void;
        a_font_exists: a_font.exists
    ensure
        font_set: font.item = a_font.item
```

To determine the current font, the function *font* can be called. To determine if the control is using the system font, the *has_system_font* function can be called.

Example 11.1 illustrates the use of a control's font. The example allows you to change the text font of the button, using a standard text selection dialog. The text area below the button displays information about the selected font, including whether it is the system font and what its typeface is.

Example 11.1 Changing a Control's Font (controls\font)

```
class MAIN_WINDOW
inherit
    WEL_FRAME_WINDOW
        redefine
            on_control_command
        end
creation
    make
feature
    make is
            -- Initialize the main window
        do
            make_top ("Main Window")
            resize (350, 120)
            create font_button.make (Current, "Select Font", (width
                // 2) - (90 // 2), 0, 90, 35, -1)
```

```
            create message.make (Current, "", 10, 40, width - 20, 40, -1)
            check_font
       end
   font_button: WEL_PUSH_BUTTON
            -- Push button
   message: WEL_STATIC
            -- Message area
   font_chooser: WEL_CHOOSE_FONT_DIALOG is
            -- Font chooser
       once
            create Result.make
       end
   on_control_command (control: WEL_CONTROL) is
            -- A command has been received from 'control'.
       local
            f: WEL_FONT
       do
            if control = font_button then
                    font_chooser.activate (Current)
                    if font_chooser.selected then
                            create f.make_indirect (font_chooser.log_font)
                            font_button.set_font( f)
                            check_for_system_font
                    end
            end
       end
   check_font is
                    -- Check the font being used by the button?
       local
            s: STRING
       do
            create s.make (20)
            if font_button.has_system_font then
                    s.append ("Using system font!")
            else
                    s.append ("Not using system font.")
            end
            s.append (" Face name: ")
            s.append_string (font_button.font.log_font.face_name)
            message.set_text (s)
       end
   end -- class MAIN_WINDOW
```

The routine *on_control_command* determines if the font button was
pressed, and if so, displays a font selection dialog. If the user selects a font in
the dialog, then the font of the button is changed to the selected font, using a
call to *set_font*. Following a change in the button font, routine *check_font* is
called to update the font information in the text field. First, the button is

checked to determine if the system font is used by calling *has_system_font,* and second, the font's face name is retrieved and displayed by accessing the font's logical font information (via the call chain *font_button.font.log_font. face_name*).

Figure 11.2 shows an execution of this example after selecting the Bauhaus 93 font.

Processing Control Events

The parent window of a control receives notification of events that occur in the control. The control itself does not receive any message directly from Windows. The parent window receives a *Wm_command* message for each control event, and the WEL *process_message* command forwards it to the *on_wm_command* procedure of *WEL_COMPOSITE_WINDOW.* Recall Figure 3.4 from Chapter 3, "Messages." Each message received by a WEL application is - handled by *process_message* and forwarded to the relevant message hook. In the case of the *Wm_command* message, the *on_wm_command* message hook is called. Figure 11.3 illustrates the processing that occurs in this procedure.

First, the origin of the command message is examined to see if it is a control, a menu, or an accelerator. If the command was sent from a control, then the message hook *on_control_id_command* is called followed by *on_control_command,* and if the control object referenced by the message is valid, it is followed by *notify.* Finally, the *process_notification* procedure of the control itself is called to allow the control to process the message.

If the command originated from a menu, then the *on_wm_menu_command* is called (which forwards the message to the appropriate message hook

FIGURE 11.2. Control font example.

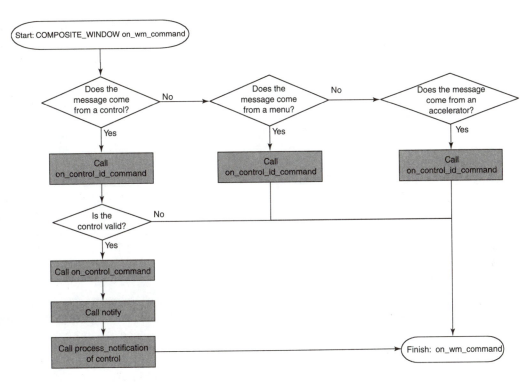

FIGURE 11.3. Control message-processing logic.

for the menu), and similarly, if the command originated from an accelerator, then the *on_accelerator_command* message hook is called.

Color Controls

A number of controls provides the ability to update their background and foreground colors before painting. Each of these controls, including list boxes, edit boxes, static controls, and scroll bars, inherits from the class *WEL_COLOR_CONTROL*.

WEL_COLOR_CONTROL introduces two new features that provide access to the current foreground and background colors. The features are *foreground_color* and *background_color,* each returning a *WEL_COLOR_REF* representing the respective control colors.

See "On a Composite Window Color Control Message" in Chapter 5, "Composite Windows," for information on how to use these color controls and the features provided by *WEL_COLOR_CONTROL*.

```
background_color: WEL_COLOR_REF
        -- Background color used for the background of the
        -- control
    ensure
        color_not_void: background_color /= void

foreground_color: WEL_COLOR_REF
        -- foreground color used for the text of the
        -- control
    ensure
        color_not_void: foreground_color /= void
```

SUMMARY

Controls provide the basic building blocks for user interaction in an application. They include push buttons, lists, edit controls, labels, selection boxes, and many others. The following chapters describe each of the WEL controls in detail.

All controls inherit general window facilities from *WEL_CONTROL* (which itself is a direct descendant of *WEL_WINDOW*), including the ability to set the font of the control's text. Some controls, including list boxes, edit controls, and the like, provide the ability to change the colors that they will be painted with. Each color capable control is a descendant of *WEL_COLOR_CONTROL*.

BUTTONS

INTRODUCING BUTTONS

A button provides a simple way of allowing the user to interact with an application. It gives the user visual feedback that it has been selected and can be used in many situations.

The simplest type of button is the push button. A push button is typically represented graphically as a 3D raised box that appears depressed when the user clicks the mouse within its client area. Other buttons include check boxes and radio buttons, both of which allow the user to select application options. Check boxes provide an on and off status. That is, a check box's status is on when the box is checked, and off otherwise. An extended form of the check box can provide an additional state known as indeterminate.

A radio button is seldom used alone. A group of radio buttons provides a mutually exclusive selection interface whereby only one of the radio buttons in the group can be selected at one time. This is similar to what you would find on a car radio for selecting different radio stations—hence the name radio button.

A third type of button provides a simple interface for creating your own custom buttons by programmatically drawing the graphical representation of the button. An owner-draw button does not define a graphical representation for itself—it only provides the window area in which you can draw your own button representation.

All buttons respond to a user click event when pressed or selected. As you will see below, this event is handled by the *on_bn_clicked* message hook. The click event message hook can be used to perform any action that the button represents, such as committing changes for a Commit button, canceling the current operation for a Cancel button, or updating a database field for a check box or radio box.

One type of button that does not quite fit this mold, but is still recognized as a type of button, is a group box. A group box is typically used to graphically group a selection of controls, such as a group of radio buttons. The grouping of controls may be used to separate different sets of application functionality or to group related controls together. A group box can still behave as a button control and will respond to an *on_bn_clicked* event.

TYPES OF BUTTONS

Figure 12.1 shows the hierarchy of button classes that represent each type of button control. At the first level of the hierarchy, *WEL_CHECK_BOX*, *WEL_OWNER_DRAW_BUTTON*, and *WEL_GROUP_BOX* all inherit directly from the abstract class *WEL_BUTTON*. The remaining classes, *WEL_RA-DIO_BUTTON* and *WEL_CHECK_BOX_3_STATE*, are both specialized check boxes and therefore inherit from *WEL_CHECK_BOX*.

Abstract Button

All button types inherit from the abstract class *WEL_BUTTON*, which provides the general functionality for a button and provides two creation routines for constructing instances of buttons.

Creating a Button

When a button is created it requires a parent, a name, positional coordinates, and dimensions. The parent is the window that the button is attached to and the name is the label that appears on the button. The label is drawn in different positions, depending on the button's type—the label of a push button typically appears in the middle of the button, the label of a radio button or check box appears to the right of the check graphic, and the label of a group box typically appears at the top left of the box.

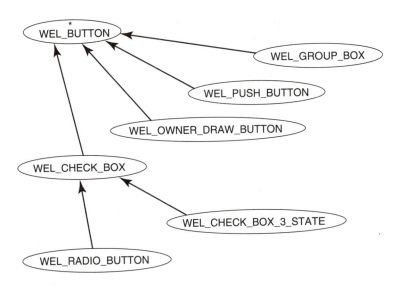

FIGURE 12.1. Button types.

```
make (a_parent: WEL_WINDOW; a_name: STRING; a_x, a_y, a_width,
        a_height, an_id: INTEGER)
        -- (from WEL_BUTTON)
    require -- from WEL_BUTTON
        a_parent_not_void: a_parent /= void;
        a_parent_exists: a_parent.exists;
        a_name_not_void: a_name /= void
    ensure -- from WEL_BUTTON
        parent_set: parent = a_parent;
        exists: exists;
        name_set: text.is_equal (a_name);
        id_set: id = an_id

make_by_id (a_parent: WEL_DIALOG; an_id: INTEGER)
        -- (from WEL_CONTROL)
    require -- from WEL_CONTROL
        a_parent_not_void: a_parent /= void;
        positive_id: an_id > 0
    ensure -- from WEL_CONTROL
        parent_set: parent = a_parent;
        id_set: id = an_id
```

The position of a button is relative to its parent. For example, a coordinate of (10,10) will be positioned 10 pixels from the top and 10 pixels from the left of the top left corner of the parent window. The size dimensions specify the width and height of the button in pixels.

A button can also be defined as a part of a dialog box and linked with an application as a resource. To create an instance of *WEL_BUTTON* (or more specifically, any descendent of *WEL_BUTTON*) from a resource, you need to call *make_by_id*. Procedure *make_by_id* loads the appropriate control resource and initializes the button object to encapsulate it.

On a Button-Clicked Message

Every type of button responds to a click event when the user presses and releases the mouse button while positioned within the button. The clicked event can be handled by the *on_bn_clicked* message hook.

```
on_bn_clicked
        -- Called when the button is clicked
    require
        exists: exists
```

This hook is called whenever the button is clicked. You can redefine the *on_bn_clicked* procedure to perform whatever action is required for the button.

Button Notification Messages

The parent window of a button control can also respond to a selection of notifications raised by the control. Table 12.1 lists the notification codes that can be passed to the *notify* message hook of a button's parent window.

TABLE 12.1   *Button Control Notification Codes (WEL_BN_CONSTANTS)*

NOTIFICATION CODE	DESCRIPTION
Bn_clicked	Sent when a user clicks a button. That is, when the user presses and releases the mouse button within the boundary of the button's client area.
Bn_disable	Sent when the button is disabled. Can be used to perform some action when the button is disabled or to paint the disabled look of the button. However, for an owner-draw button the *on_draw_item* message hook of *WEL_COMPOSITE_WINDOW* should be used.
Bn_doubleclicked	Sent when a radio button or owner-draw button is double-clicked by the user. No other button types send this message.
Bn_hilite	Sent when the user selects the button.
Bn_paint	Sent when the button should be painted.
Bn_unhilite	Sent when the highlight should be removed from the button.

To illustrate the use of push-button notification messages, the following example uses two push buttons—one responds to its clicked event by closing the application, and the other responds by enabling or disabling the first push button. Example 12.1 shows the class text required for the main window of the application.

Example 12.1 Push Button Example, MAIN_WINDOW Class (buttons\push)

```
class MAIN_WINDOW
inherit
    WEL_FRAME_WINDOW
        redefine
            notify
        end
    WEL_BN_CONSTANTS
        export
            {NONE} all
        end
creation
    make
feature
    make is
            -- Initialize the main window
        do
            make_top ("Main Window")
            resize (350, 140)
            create close_button.make (Current, "Close", 10, 30, 90,
                35, -1)
            create enable_button.make (Current, "Disable", 10, 75,
                90, 35, -1)
        end
    enable_button: WEL_PUSH_BUTTON
    close_button: CLOSE_BUTTON
            -- Push buttons
    notify (control: WEL_CONTROL; notify_code: INTEGER) is
            -- Check for a close command
        do
            if control = enable_button
                and notify_code = Bn_clicked then
                if close_button.enabled then
                    close_button.disable
                    enable_button.set_text ("Enable")
                else
                    close_button.enable
                    enable_button.set_text ("Disable")
                end
            end
        end
    end
end -- class MAIN_WINDOW
```

The two push buttons *close_button* and *enable_button* are created and attached to the main window. The main window responds to any events that occur in the buttons by using the *notify* message hook.

The implementation of *notify* determines which control raised the event and what type of event was raised. If a clicked event originated from the *enable_button*, then the enabled status of *close_button* is changed. This illustrates the use of standard window features, including *set_text, enabled, enable,* and *disable,* as defined in *WEL_WINDOW.* Remember that all controls are a descendant of *WEL_WINDOW* and can use all of its functionality. Figure 12.2 shows the main window of the example after *enable_button* has been clicked. The *close_button* object is described in the next section.

Push Buttons

Push buttons are one of the most commonly used controls. Many of the examples you have seen so far have included a push button to allow the user to perform an action such as opening or closing a window, closing an application, or responding to a dialog box.

Creating a Push Button

If a push button is used on a dialog window (and has an associated resource identifier) then it can be created using the creation procedure *make_by_id,* as described in "Creating a Control" earlier in this chapter. You can also create a resource push-button control by using the creation procedure *make,* as defined in *WEL_BUTTON.*

On a Push Button-Clicked Message

When the right mouse button is pressed and released within the boundary of a push button, a clicked event is raised. This event is processed using the *on_clicked* message hook, as defined in *WEL_BUTTON.* Remember that the

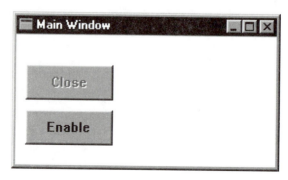

FIGURE 12.2. Push button example.

parent window of the control also receives notification of this event through the *on_control_command, notify,* and *on_notify* message hooks.

Example 12.2 shows the class text of the *CLOSE_BUTTON* class used in Example 12.1. This class implements a push button that responds to its click event by closing the parent window. Together, Example 12.1 and Example 12.2 show two methods of capturing control events. Class *MAIN_WINDOW* uses parent notification via the *notify* message hook, while *CLOSE_BUTTON* uses the *on_bn_clicked* message hook to respond to events itself.

Parent notification-handling is the most common method of capturing control events because it reduces the number of classes that need to be created. The number of controls that may appear on a window can be significant, and creating a separate class for each of the controls can be tedious. Deferring control event-handling to the parent reduces the amount of code that needs to be written and allows you to use the WEL control classes directly rather than defining and using descendant classes.

Using control descendant classes such as *CLOSE_BUTTON* becomes useful when the event-handling logic is complex or when the control (and its associated event-handling) is reusable. A button implemented as a descendant of *WEL_BUTTON* is easier to reuse in another part of the application, or in another application, because it constitutes a self-contained unit without any external code such as parent notification-handling. The close button defined above is a good example. It could be used in any situation where a button that closes

Example 12.2 Push Button Example, CLOSE_BUTTON Class (buttons\push)

```
class
    CLOSE_BUTTON
inherit
    WEL_PUSH_BUTTON
        redefine
            on_bn_clicked
        end
creation
    make
feature
    on_bn_clicked is
            -- Handle button clicked event by closing the
            -- parent window
        do
            parent.destroy
        end
end -- class CLOSE_BUTTON
```

its parent window is required. All that is needed is to instantiate an instance of *CLOSE_BUTTON* and attach it to the parent window.

Check Boxes

Often you may need to ask the users of your applications questions that require a yes or no answer. For example, Do you want to print to a file? Do you want to match letter case for your search? or Do you want to use accrual- or cash-based accounting? Check boxes are perfect for this type of interaction. A check box, implemented in *WEL_CHECK_BOX,* provides a label and a small check mark that contains a tick for an affirmative answer or remains empty for a negative answer.

Creating a Check Box

A check box is created in exactly the same manner as a push button. The creation procedures *make* and *make_by_id* are both available to create a check box usable on any window or a check box usable on a dialog window, respectively.

Setting a Check Box Status

A check box is either checked or unchecked. Querying the status of a check box using the *checked* function returns *True* if the box is checked, and *False* otherwise. You can also change the status of a check box programmatically, using the *set_checked* and *set_unchecked* operations.

```
checked: BOOLEAN
        -- Is the button checked?
    require
        exists: exists

set_checked
        -- Check the button
    require
        exists: exists
    ensure
        checked: checked

set_unchecked
        -- Uncheck the button
    require
        exists: exists
    ensure
        unchecked: not checked
```

Example 12.3 demonstrates the use of check boxes with one check box and two push buttons. The first push button, Change, uses *set_checked* and *set_unchecked* to change the current status of the check box. The second push button, Check, displays a message box that indicates the current status of the check box, using the *checked* query.

Example 12.3 Check Box Example, MAIN_WINDOW Class (buttons\check)

```
class MAIN_WINDOW
inherit
    WEL_FRAME_WINDOW
        redefine
            notify
        end
    WEL_BN_CONSTANTS
        export
            {NONE} all
        end
creation
    make
feature
    make is
            -- Initialize the main window
        do
            make_top ("Main Window")
            create messagebox.make
            resize (350, 140)
            create checkbox.make (Current, "Check Box 1", 120, 50,
                90, 20, -1)
            create change_button.make (Current, "Change", 10, 30, 90,
                35, -1)
            create check_button.make (Current, "Check", 10, 75, 90,
                35, -1)
        end
    checkbox: WEL_CHECK_BOX
            -- Check box
    change_button, check_button: WEL_PUSH_BUTTON
            -- Push buttons
    messagebox: WEL_MSG_BOX
    notify (control: WEL_CONTROL; notify_code: INTEGER) is
            -- Check for button click events
        local
            s: STRING
        do
            if control = change_button
                and notify_code = Bn_clicked then
                if checkbox.checked then
                    checkbox.set_unchecked
                else
```

```
                    checkbox.set_checked
          end
    elseif control = check_button
        and notify_code = Bn_clicked then
        s := "Checked = "
        s.append_boolean (checkbox.checked)
        messagebox.information_message_box (Current,
              s, "Check Box Status")
      end
    end
end -- class MAIN_WINDOW
```

Example 12.3 differs from the previous push button example, as indicated by the shaded code fragments. First, the code creates an instance of a *WEL_CHECK_BOX* and attaches it to the main window. By default, the check box is initially unchecked. The second code change includes modifying the *notify* routine to change the checked status of the check box when the Change button is clicked. This is performed by first determining the current check box status with a call to *checked,* and then checking or unchecking the box, depending on the result, by calling *set_checked* or *set_unchecked,* respectively. Figure 12.3 shows the result of the example after clicking the check box and then clicking the Check button.

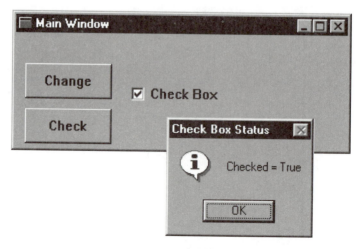

FIGURE 12.3. Check box example.

Three-State Check Boxes

An extended version of check boxes provides an additional state known as indeterminate. This additional state can be used for cases where you need to provide the user with three possible answers to a question. For example, you may associate the indeterminate state of a check box with an undecided or undefined answer from the user.

Setting a Three-State Check Box Status

The three-state check box adds two new features to the standard check box interface. The features are *indeterminate,* used to test whether the check box is set to the indeterminate state, and *set_indeterminate,* used to programmatically set the state of the check box to indeterminate.

```
indeterminate: BOOLEAN
        -- Is the state indeterminate?
    require
        exists: exists

set_indeterminate
        -- Set the indeterminate state.
    require
        exists: exists
    ensure
        indeterminate: indeterminate
```

Changing Example 12.3 to use a three-state check box instead of a standard check box is easy. The type of the *checkbox* attribute is changed from *WEL_CHECK_BOX* to *WEL_CHECK_BOX_3_STATE,* and an additional test for the state *indeterminate* is added to the notify event-processing. Example 12.4 shows the new class text for the *MAIN_WINDOW.*

Example 12.4 Three-State Check Box Example, MAIN_WINDOW Class (buttons\check3)

```
class MAIN_WINDOW
inherit
    WEL_FRAME_WINDOW
        redefine
            notify
        end
    WEL_BN_CONSTANTS
        export
```

```
            {NONE} all
        end
creation
    make
feature
    make is
            -- Initialize the main window
        do
            make_top ("Main Window")
            create messagebox.make
            resize (350, 140)
            create checkbox.make (Current, "Check Box 1", 120, 50,
                90, 20, -1)
            create change_button.make (Current, "Change", 10, 30, 90, 35, -1)
            create check_button.make (Current, "Check", 10, 75, 90, 35, -1)
        end
    checkbox: WEL_CHECK_BOX_3_STATE
            -- Check box
    change_button, check_button: WEL_PUSH_BUTTON
            -- Push buttons
    messagebox: WEL_MSG_BOX
    notify (control: WEL_CONTROL; notify_code: INTEGER) is
            -- Check for button click events
        local
            s: STRING
        do
            if control = change_button
                and notify_code = Bn_clicked then
                if checkbox.checked then
                        checkbox.set_unchecked
                elseif checkbox.indeterminate then
                        checkbox.set_checked
                else
                        checkbox.set_indeterminate
                end
            elseif control = check_button
                and notify_code = Bn_clicked then
                s := "Checked = "
                if checkbox.indeterminate then
                        s.append ("indeterminate")
                else
                        s.append_boolean (checkbox.checked)
                end
                messagebox.information_message_box (Current,
                        s, "Check Box Status")
            end
        end

end -- class MAIN_WINDOW
```

Clicking on the Change button now cycles through the three states of the check box from unchecked to indeterminate to checked. This is performed by adding an additional if statement that checks for the indeterminate state. Figure 12.4 shows the example output with the check box set to indeterminate. To produce this output, click on the check box twice to cycle the check box state from unchecked to indeterminate, and then click Check. You can identify the indeterminate state of a check box by the gray check mark tick.

Radio Buttons

Radio buttons allow the user to choose from a set of mutually exclusive options. Radio buttons always work in groups, and you rarely find a single radio button on a dialog window.

To group radio boxes, all you need to do is attach them to the same parent window. The default event-handling of the parent window manages the selection and deselection of a radio button within the group. A convenient way of grouping radio buttons is to attach them to a group box, as shown in the section "Group Boxes" later in this chapter.

Creating a Radio Button

You create a radio button exactly as you would any other type of button. The creation procedure *make* requires a parent, positioning coordinates, size dimensions, and an identifier (typically −1 for nondialog buttons). Similarly, if the

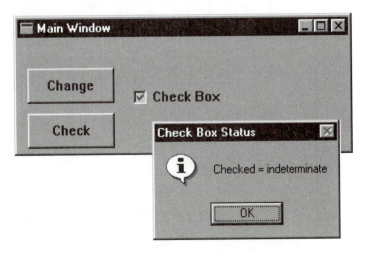

FIGURE 12.4. Three-state check box example.

radio button resides on a dialog window, you can use the *make_by_id* creation
procedure to create an instance of the radio button class that represents the button resource. Example 12.5 uses two radio buttons attached to a window to
demonstrate how they can be used.

**Example 12.5 Radio Button Example, MAIN_WINDOW Class
(buttons\radio)**

```
class MAIN_WINDOW
inherit
    WEL_FRAME_WINDOW
        redefine
            notify
        end
    WEL_BN_CONSTANTS
        export
            {NONE} all
        end
creation
    make
feature
    make is
            -- Initialize the main window
        do
            make_top ("Main Window")
            create messagebox.make
            resize (350, 140)
            create radio_button1.make (Current, "Radio Button 1",
                120, 50, 120, 20, -1)
            create radio_button2.make (Current, "Radio Button 2",
                120, 70, 120, 20, -1)
            radio_button1.set_checked
            create change_button.make (Current, "Change", 10, 30, 90, 35, -1)
            create check_button.make (Current, "Check", 10, 75, 90, 35, -1)
        end
    radio_button1, radio_button2: WEL_RADIO_BUTTON
            -- Radio boxes
    change_button, check_button: WEL_PUSH_BUTTON
            -- Push buttons
    messagebox: WEL_MSG_BOX
    notify (control: WEL_CONTROL; notify_code: INTEGER) is
            -- Check for button click events
        local
            s: STRING
        do
            if control = change_button
                and notify_code = Bn_clicked then
                if radio_button1.checked then
                    radio_button2.set_checked
                    radio_button1.set_unchecked
```

```
            else
                    radio_button1.set_checked
                    radio_button2.set_unchecked
            end
        elseif control = check_button
            and notify_code = Bn_clicked then
            s := "Selected = "
            if radio_button1.checked then
                    s.append (radio_button1.text)
            else
                    s.append (radio_button2.text)
            end
            messagebox.information_message_box (Current,
                    s, "Radio Button Status")
        end
    end
end -- class MAIN_WINDOW
```

Initially, none of the radio buttons in a group are selected. Therefore, you need to choose the initial state of the group by selecting one of the buttons programmatically. For instance, the example selects *radio_button1* in its *make* procedure. As mentioned earlier, the parent window of the radio buttons handles all events necessary for selecting and deselecting buttons in the group. We don't need to add any specific event-handling to our code unless we want to perform additional actions for these events. The Change button now toggles between the two radio buttons depending on which one is selected when the button is clicked. You may have noticed that we need to deselect the radio button that is no longer active. This is because Windows will allow two or more radio buttons in a group to be selected when we change their state programatically. This can cause unexpected results, and you should be careful to include code that maintains a valid state of the radio button group as a whole.

Figure 12.5 shows the example running with *radio_button1* selected.

FIGURE 12.5. Radio button example.

Group Boxes

Group boxes provide the mechanism to group controls visually and functionally. A group box can be used to visually surround one or more controls to separate them from other controls in a window, or a group box can be used to
functionally group one or more controls that must operate together, such as
radio buttons.

The visual representation of a group box includes a rectangular area with
an optional border and label. The label can be used to identify the purpose of
the controls within the group. Any control created with the group box as its
parent will be contained within that group box.

Creating a Group Box

Group boxes are created in the same way as other controls. The creation procedure *make* takes a parent window, a label, positional coordinates, and dimensions.

The creation of controls contained within the group box is more interesting. In this case, each control should be created with the group box as its parent
window. Example 12.6 shows how we can add a group box to the radio button
example shown earlier in the chapter (Example 12.5). First, an attribute *group-
box* of type *WEL_GROUP_BOX* is added to the *MAIN_WINDOW* class and instantiated with its parent window set to the *MAIN_WINDOW*. Second, both of
the radio buttons are created with *their* parents set to the newly instantiated
group box.

Example 12.6 Group Box Example, MAIN_WINDOW Class
(buttons\group)

```
class MAIN_WINDOW
inherit
    WEL_FRAME_WINDOW
        redefine
            notify
        end
    WEL_BN_CONSTANTS
        export
            {NONE} all
        end
creation
    make
feature
    make is
            -- Initialize the main window
```

```
        do
            make_top ("Main Window")
            create messagebox.make
            resize (350, 140)
            create groupbox.make (Current, "Group Box", 110, 30, 140,
                70, -1)
            create radio_button1.make (groupbox, "Radio Button 1",
                10, 20, 120, 20, -1)
            create radio_button2.make (groupbox, "Radio Button 2",
                10, 40, 120, 20, -1)
            radio_button1.set_checked
            create change_button.make (Current, "Change", 10, 30, 90,
                35, -1)
            create check_button.make (Current, "Check", 10, 75, 90,
                35, -1)
        end
    groupbox: WEL_GROUP_BOX
    '        -- Group box
    radio_button1, radio_button2: WEL_RADIO_BUTTON
            -- Radio boxes
    change_button, check_button: WEL_PUSH_BUTTON
            -- Push buttons
    messagebox: WEL_MSG_BOX
    notify (control: WEL_CONTROL; notify_code: INTEGER) is
            -- Check for button click events
        local
            s: STRING
        do
            -- source code as before
        end
end -- class MAIN_WINDOW
```

Figure 12.6 shows the result. The two radio buttons are now surrounded by a thin border representing the group box. The group box is labeled Group Box.

FIGURE 12.6. Group box example.

Owner-Draw Buttons

Occasionally, you may need a control that behaves like a push button but doesn't look like a standard push button. An owner-draw button allows you to specify the appearance (and to some extent, the behavior) of a button.

WEL provides the *WEL_OWNER_DRAW_BUTTON* class as an implementation of an owner-drawn button. The only difference between this class and *WEL_BUTTON* is the redefinition of *default_style* that includes *Bs_owner-draw*, which implies that the control will be drawn by its parent window (the owner). Other control types can specify *Bs_ownerdraw* if you need to override their default appearance and draw them programmatically.

Creating an Owner Draw-Button

An owner-draw button is created with exactly the same code as a normal button. Features *make* and *make_by_id* (for dialog controls) provide the necessary creation procedures. However, each owner-draw button requires a control identification number so that the parent window can identify the control when it needs to be drawn.

If you create owner-draw buttons using *make_by_id*, then they will already have an identification number as defined in the resource. When *make* is used, you need to specify the identification number as the last parameter. Typically, we have passed *–1* as the value of this parameter to indicate that no identifier is required. We now need to pass a meaningful number that can be identified by the parent window.

For instance, we can define a constant *INTEGER* for each type of owner-draw button that we require:

```
Owner_draw_button_1: INTEGER is 1
Owner_draw_button_2: INTEGER is 2
```

These constants can then be used in the creation calls for each button.

```
button_1.make (parent, x, y, width, height, Owner_draw_button_1)
button_2.make(parent, x, y, width, height, Owner_draw_button_2)
```

Painting an Owner-Draw Button

Windows notifies the parent window when an owner-draw button needs to be painted. The parent window can then draw the button or, as we do in the following example, notify the button to draw itself.

The parent window receives the draw notification via the message hook *on_draw_item*. Feature *on_draw_item* receives an *INTEGER* representing the identification number of the control that needs to be drawn and an instance of the class *WEL_DRAW_ITEM_STRUCT* holding information about the draw item event.

```
class interface
      WEL_DRAW_ITEM_STRUCT
creation
      make_by_pointer
feature — Access

      ctl_id: INTEGER
                  -- Control identifier
      ctl_type: INTEGER
                  -- Control type.
                  -- See class WEL_ODT_CONSTANTS.

      dc: WEL_CLIENT_DC
                  -- Device context used when performing drawing
                  -- operations on the control.
      item_action: INTEGER
                  -- Drawing action required.
                  -- See class WEL_ODA_CONSTANTS.
      item_data: INTEGER
                  -- 32-bit value associated with the menu item.

      item_id: INTEGER
                  -- Menu item identifier for a menu item or
                  -- the index of the item in a list box or
                  -- combo box
      item_state: INTEGER
                  -- Visual state of the item after the current
                  -- drawing action takes place.
                  -- See class WEL_ODS_CONSTANTS.

      rect_item: WEL_RECT
                  -- Rectangle that defines the boundaries
                  -- of the control to be drawn.
                  ensure
                  result_not_void: Result /= void
      window_item: WEL_CONTROL
                  -- Identifies the control.
feature -- Measurement

      structure_size: INTEGER
                  -- Size to allocate (in bytes)
invariant
      dc_exists: dc /= void and then dc.exists;
end -- class WEL_DRAW_ITEM_STRUCT
```

The *WEL_DRAW_ITEM_STRUCT* includes information about the type of draw-item event that has occurred, the device context on which to draw the button, the type of owner-draw control, and the state of that control.

As mentioned earlier, different types of controls can be owner-drawn if they include *Bs_ownerdraw* in their default style. The *ctl_type* attribute holds the type of the control that needs to be painted, with possible values of *ctl_type* defined in class *WEL_ODT_CONSTANTS,* listed in Table 12.2.

An owner-draw control can be selected by the user or can gain the input focus. Both of these events are indicated by the *item_action* attribute. A control will also need to be drawn when it is first displayed or when it has been exposed as a result of another window moving or the parent window being restored. The *item_action* values are listed in Table 12.3.

The action of a draw item event is further qualified by the current state of the control. Table 12.4 lists the state values that can be passed in the *item_state* attribute of *WEL_DRAW_ITEM_STRUCT.*

Example 12.7 implements an owner-draw button with behavior and appearance similar to a light switch. The button toggles between two states, on and off, with different graphical bitmaps representing each state. When the switch is on, the bitmap shows the button in the down position, and when off, the bitmap shows the button in the up position.[1]

The owner-draw switch is implemented in the class *SWITCH_BUTTON,* shown in Example 12.8. *SWITCH_BUTTON* is a direct descendant of *WEL_OWNER_DRAW_BUTTON* and implements the routine *on_paint* that provides painting logic needed to draw the button in each of its states. The

TABLE 12.2   *Owner-Draw Type Constants (WEL_ODT_CONSTANTS)*

CONSTANT	DESCRIPTION
Odt_button	Owner-drawn button
Odt_combobox	Owner-drawn combo box
Odt_listbox	Owner-drawn list box
Odt_listview	List view control
Odt_menu	Owner-drawn menu item
Odt_static	Owner-drawn static control
Odt_tab	Tab control

[1]For any European or American readers, this is the Australian way that a light switch operates!

TABLE 12.3 *Owner-Draw Action Constants (WEL_ODA_CONSTANTS)*

CONSTANT	DESCRIPTION
Oda_drawentire	The entire control needs to be drawn.
Oda_focus	The control has lost or gained the keyboard focus. The *item_state* should be checked to determine whether the control has the focus.
Ods_select	The selection status has changed. The *item_state* should be checked to determine the new selection state.

main window of the example, shown in Example 12.7, attaches an instance of *SWITCH_BUTTON,* along with a text label, to its client area. When the window receives an item-draw message, it checks the origin of the message and, if it is from the switch button, delegates the drawing of the button back to the button itself by calling *on_draw*.

TABLE 12.4 *Owner-Draw State Constants (WEL_ODS_CONSTANTS)*

CONSTANT	DESCRIPTION
Ods_checked	Indicates that the menu item is to be checked. Only used for menu items.
Ods_comboboxedit	The drawing takes place in the selection field of an owner-drawn combo box.
Ods_default	The item is the default item.
Ods_disabled	The item is disabled.
Ods_focus	The item has the keyboard focus.
Ods_grayed	The item is to be grayed. Only used in menu items.
Ods_selected	The item's status is selected.

Example 12.7 Owner-Draw Button Example, MAIN_WINDOW Class (buttons\ownerdraw)

```
class
    MAIN_WINDOW
inherit
    WEL_FRAME_WINDOW
        redefine
            on_draw_item,
```

```
                    on_control_command
            end
        WEL_BN_CONSTANTS
            export
                    {NONE} all
            end
creation
    make
feature -- Initialization
    make is
            -- Make the main window
        do
            make_top ("")
            resize (150, 130)
            create button.make (Current, "", 63, 60, 25, 25,
                Switch_button_1)
            create label.make (Current, "", 10, 10, 120, 25, -1)
        end
feature -- Access
    button: SWITCH_BUTTON
            -- Owner draw button
    label: WEL_STATIC
            -- Message label
feature {NONE} -- Implementation
    Switch_button_1: INTEGER is 1
        on_draw_item (control_id: INTEGER;
        struct: WEL_DRAW_ITEM_STRUCT)
is
            -- All owner-draw control identified by 'control_id' has
            -- been changed and must be drawn. 'draw_item' contains
            -- information about the item to be drawn and the type
            -- of drawing required.
        do
            inspect control_id
            when Switch_button_1 then
                button.on_draw (struct)
            else
                - ignore
            end
        end
    on_control_command (control: WEL_CONTROL) is
            -- Control notification
        local
            switch: SWITCH_BUTTON
        do
            if control = button then
                switch ?= control
                check
                        valid_switch_control: switch /= Void
                end
```

```
                        if switch.is_on then
                                label.set_text ("Yippee!")
                        else
                                label.set_text ("")
                        end
                end
        end
end -- class MAIN_WINDOW
```

The *MAIN_WINDOW* class also implements code required to change the label, depending on the current state of the button. Each time the button is activated, the main window checks its state and updates the label.

The switch button itself inherits from *WEL_OWNER_DRAW_BUTTON* and redefines the *on_bn_clicked* message hook to toggle its state from on to off, and vice versa. The button also implements an *on_draw* operation that paints the button when called by its parent. The *on_draw* operation checks the draw-item message information in the *struct* parameter and paints the correct bitmap on the button, depending on its current state. The operation also handles drawing of a focus box (surrounding dotted line) and the drawing of the button's 3D edge.

Example 12.8 Owner-Draw Button Example, SWITCH_BUTTON Class (buttons\ownerdraw)

```
class
    SWITCH_BUTTON
inherit
    WEL_OWNER_DRAW_BUTTON
        redefine
            on_bn_clicked
        end
    WEL_DRAWING_ROUTINES
        rename
            draw_edge as routine_draw_edge
        end
    WEL_DRAWING_ROUTINES_CONSTANTS
        export
            {NONE} all
        end
    WEL_ODA_CONSTANTS
        export
            {NONE} all
        end
    WEL_ODS_CONSTANTS
        export
```

```eiffel
                {NONE} all
        end
    APPLICATION_IDS
        export
                {NONE} all
        end
creation
    make
feature -- Status report
    is_on: BOOLEAN
            -- Is the switch on?
feature -- Access
    on_draw (struct: WEL_DRAW_ITEM_STRUCT) is
            -- Redraw the button
        local
            action: INTEGER
            dc: WEL_DC
            inrect: WEL_RECT
            brush: WEL_WHITE_BRUSH
        do
            action := struct.item_action
            dc := struct.dc
            if action = Oda_focus then
                draw_focus (dc)
            elseif action = Oda_select then
                select_action
                create brush.make
                dc.fill_rect (client_rect, brush)
                dc.draw_bitmap (state_bitmap, 5, 6, width - 5, height - 5)
                draw_edge (dc)
            elseif action = Oda_drawentire then
                create brush.make
                dc.fill_rect (client_rect, brush
                dc.draw_bitmap (state_bitmap, 5, 6, width - 5, height - 5)
                if struct.item_state = Ods_focus then
                    draw_focus (dc)
                end
                draw_edge (dc)
            end
        end
    state_bitmap: WEL_BITMAP is
            -- Select the required bitmap to draw depending on the
            -- current switch state.
        do
            if is_on then
                Result := on_bitmap
            else
                Result := off_bitmap
            end
        end
```

```
        on_bn_clicked is
                -- Toggle the switch state
            do
                is_on := not is_on
            end
        current_state: INTEGER
                -- Current state of the button
        on_bitmap: WEL_BITMAP is
                -- On bitmap for the button
            once
                create Result.make_by_id (Idb_on_constant)
            end
        off_bitmap: WEL_BITMAP is
                -- Off bitmap for the button
            once
                create Result.make_by_id (Idb_off_constant)
            end
    feature {NONE} -- Painting
        is_down: BOOLEAN is
                -- Is the button pressed or not?
            do
                Result := not (current_state = 0)
            end
        select_action is
                -- Toggle the action state
            do
                current_state := (current_state + 1) \\ 2
            end
        draw_edge (dc: WEL_DC) is
                -- Draw the edge of the button.
            do
                if is_on then
                    routine_draw_edge (dc, client_rect, Edge_sunken,
                        Bf_rect)
                else
                    routine_draw_edge (dc, client_rect, Edge_raised,
                        Bf_rect + Bf_soft)
                end
            end
        draw_focus (dc: WEL_DC) is
                -- Draw the focus line around the button.
            local
                rect: WEL_RECT
            do
                create rect.make (3, 3, width - 3, height - 3)
                draw_focus_rect (dc, rect)
            end
    end -- class SWITCH_BUTTON
```

SUMMARY

Buttons are one of the most common controls used in Windows applications. They provide an easy way for the user to answer simple questions (check boxes), answer multiple choice questions (radio boxes), confirm or cancel actions (push buttons), or perform more complicated interactions (such as the *SWITCH_BUTTON* owner-draw button).

Buttons typically send control command-notification messages to their parents when clicked or activated. In most applications, the parent window will perform the necessary action when this notification is received. A button can also respond to its own command messages, if needed.

The next chapter looks at how to receive textual input from a user, using text edit controls.

EDIT CONTROLS

INTRODUCING EDIT CONTROLS

An edit control can be used on a window to permit users to enter and edit textual information using the keyboard. Edit controls can be used in any situation where an application requires text to be entered, edited, or viewed by a user. WEL provides encapsulations of edit controls providing single-line, multiple-line, and formatted text entry, respectively.

TYPES OF EDIT CONTROLS

WEL edit controls inherit from the abstract class *WEL_EDIT,* which provides common edit control features. *WEL_EDIT* is itself a descendant of class *WEL_STATIC,* which encapsulates static controls for displaying information to a user. The direct descendants of *WEL_EDIT,* namely, *WEL_SINGLE_LINE_EDIT* and *WEL_MULTIPLE_LINE_EDIT,* allow you to create two types of edit controls. The final class in this hierarchy, *WEL_RICH_EDIT,* provides capabilities for creating and manipulating rich edit controls, which allow formatted text to be edited and viewed. Figure 13.1 illustrates the hierarchy of edit control types.

419

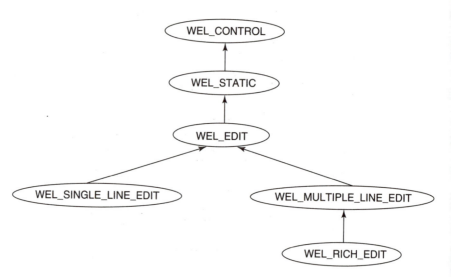

FIGURE 13.1. Edit control types.

Static Text Control

Static textual information can be presented using a static text control. WEL provides an encapsulation of the Windows static text control. This control can be used to present textual information, such as labels, headings and instructions, to the user.

Creating a Static Text Control

A static text control can be created by calling the creation procedures *make* or *make_by_id*. *make_by_id* is used to create a static text control from a resource. The procedure *make* requires arguments that specify the parent window of the control, the text for the control, and its position and size.

We have used static text controls throughout the examples in this book. In particular, see the use of static text controls for labels, shown in Example 13.1 and Example 13.3.

Clearing the Text of a Static Text Control

The static text control provides a feature for clearing the text of the control. Feature *clear* empties the text control, effectively clearing its text. You can reset the text of the control or set the text to something new by calling *set_text* and passing the new text string.

```
clear
        -- Clear the text
    require
        exists: exists
    ensure
        text_empty: text.empty
```

Abstract Edit Control

All edit controls in WEL inherit from the abstract class *WEL_EDIT,* which provides general features including clipboard control, selection, modification, and notification messages. The direct descendants of *WEL_EDIT* are *WEL_SINGLE_LINE_EDIT* and *WEL_MULTIPLE_LINE_EDIT,* which provide single- and multiple-line editing facilities, respectively. *WEL_MULTIPLE_LINE_EDIT* also has one direct descendant, *WEL_RICH_EDIT,* that provides formatted multiple-line editing facilities.

Manipulating the Text Caret in an Edit Control

By clicking at a position in the control's text, the user can position the caret (a vertical bar-shaped cursor that indicates the position at which characters will be added to the text). The current caret position can be determined by calling *caret_position* and, if needed, you can reposition the caret programatically using *set_caret_position.*

```
caret_position: INTEGER
        -- Caret position
    require
        exists: exists

set_caret_position (position: INTEGER)
        -- Set the caret position with 'position'.
    require
        exists: exists;
        position_large_enough: position >= 0;
        position_small_enough: position <= text_length
    ensure
        has_no_selection: not has_selection;
        caret_position_set: caret_position = position
```

The preconditions of *set_caret_position* protect you from trying to position the caret incorrectly. A side effect of setting the caret position is that any selection within the control is removed, as enforced by the postcondition labeled *has_no_selection.*

Text Selection in an Edit Control

Text selections can range from individual characters, words, collections of words, or the entire text of an edit control. The user can select text by pressing the left mouse button and dragging over the desired text. The keyboard can also be used to select text by using the shift and cursor-direction keys. The selection in an edit control is a contiguous sequence of characters with a start and end index. The indexes are inclusive. For example, a selection with start index 2 and end index 4 includes the characters at the positions 2, 3, and 4—not just the character at index position 3.

Class *WEL_EDIT* provides a number of features for manipulating the text selection, including features to determine the start and end indexes of the selection, whether a selection is active, as well as features to activate and deactivate, and change a selection.

```
has_selection: BOOLEAN
        -- Has a current selection?
    require
        exists: exists

selection_end: INTEGER
        -- Index of the last character selected
    require
        exists: exists;
        has_selection: has_selection
    ensure
        result_large_enough: Result >= 0;
        result_small_enough: Result <= text_length + 2

selection_start: INTEGER
        -- Index of the first character selected
    require
        exists: exists;
        has_selection: has_selection
    ensure
        result_large_enough: Result >= 0;
        result_small_enough: Result <= text_length

set_selection (start_position, end_position: INTEGER)
        -- Set the selection between 'start_position'
        -- and 'end_position'.
    require
        exists: exists;
        start_large_enough: start_position >= 0;
        consistent_selection: start_position < end_position;
        end_small_enough: end_position <= text_length
    ensure
        has_selection: has_selection;
```

```
        selection_start_set: selection_start = start_position;
        selection_end_set: selection_end = end_position

delete_selection
        -- Delete the current selection.
    require
        exists: exists;
        has_selection: has_selection
    ensure
        has_no_selection: not has_selection

replace_selection (new_text: STRING)
        -- Replace the current selection with 'new_text'.
        -- If there is no selection, 'new_text' is inserted
        -- at the current 'caret_position'.
    require
        exists: exists;
        new_text_not_void: new_text /= void

select_all
        -- Select all the text.
    require
        exists: exists;
        positive_length: text_length > 0
    ensure
        has_selection: has_selection;
        selection_start_set: selection_start = 0;
        selection_end_set: selection_end <= text_length + 2

unselect
        -- Unselect the current selection.
    require
        exists: exists;
        has_selection: has_selection
    ensure
        has_no_selection: not has_selection
```

A selection can be deleted using *delete_selection,* or it can be replaced by another string using *replace_selection.* The next section describes how to use the selection with the Windows clipboard to provide cut, copy, and paste facilities.

Using the Clipboard with an Edit Control

The Windows clipboard can be used to copy text from an edit control (either in the same application or another application) and paste the text into another edit control. Text can be copied from an edit control into the clipboard using *clip_copy,* or cut from the control using *clip_cut* (effectively removing the original text). To place the text from the clipboard into another text control, use *clip_paste.*

```
clip_copy
        -- Copy the current selection to the clipboard.
    require
        exists: exists;
        has_selection: has_selection

clip_cut
        -- Cut the current selection to the clipboard.
    require
        exists: exists;
        has_selection: has_selection
    ensure
        has_no_selection: not has_selection

clip_paste
        -- Paste at the current caret position the
        -- content of the clipboard.
    require
        exists: exists
```

Both *clip_copy* and *clip_cut* require that the user select some text in the edit control. The selected text, known as a selection, can then be copied or cut to the clipboard. The selection is then removed from the text control.

Undoing an Operation in an Edit Control

The edit controls provide basic undo facilities with which the last operation can be reversed. For instance, if the user accidentally deletes a selection or replaces a selection, then the operation can be undone to restore the original text.

Before calling *undo,* you must determine if the last operation can be undone. Function *can_undo* returns *True* if the last operation can be undone. *False* is returned when there has been no operation performed on the edit control, or when the last operation has already been undone. Function *can_undo* is typically used to set a menu bar or tool bar for an edit control where the Undo menu item is enabled.

```
can_undo: BOOLEAN
        -- Can the last operation be undone?
    require
        exists: exists

undo
        -- Undo the last operation.
        -- The previously deleted text is restored or the
        -- previously added text is deleted.
    require
        exists: exists;
        can_undo: can_undo
```

Setting Modification Status in an Edit Control

Each edit control also maintains a flag indicating whether the text in the control has been modified. The modification flag can be useful when you need to selectively update information in your application from a collection of edit controls in a dialog window. You can update only those fields that have changed by checking the *modified* flag.

The modification flag can be set and unset in your applications by calling the *set_modify* routine and passing the new flag value.

```
modified: BOOLEAN
        -- Has the text been modified?
    require
        exists: exists

set_modify (modify: BOOLEAN)
        -- Set 'modified' with 'modify'
    require
        exists: exists
    ensure
        modified_set: modified = modify
```

Setting Read and Write Permission in an Edit Control

An edit control can allow the user to edit its text (read-write mode) or disallow the user to edit its text (read-only mode). You may wish to use read-only edit controls to display information to the user or to selectively allow users to edit certain fields on a dialog, depending on user authentication levels or application state. You can use static labels for this job, but you would then miss out on the 3D look of the edit control.

The routines *set_read_only* and *set_read_write* change the read-write status of an edit control.

```
set_read_only
        -- Set the read-only state.
    require
        exists: exists

set_read_write
        -- Set the read-write state.
    require
        exists: exists
```

Setting the Text Limit in an Edit Control

The number of characters an edit control will allow a user to enter can be set by calling *set_text_limit*. If the user attempts to enter more than the maximum, then the control will receive an *on_en_maxtext* message indicating that the maximum number of characters has been reached. See "On an Edit Control Maximum Text Message" in this chapter.

For most applications, setting a text limit is unnecessary because Windows will automatically allocate enough memory (up to approximately 32 kilobytes) for the text entered into the control. You may need to set text limits if you need to reduce the amount of memory your application uses or if you need to limit the number of characters for certain data fields.

```
set_text_limit (limit: INTEGER)
        -- Set to 'limit' the length of the text the user
        -- can enter into the edit control.
    require
        exists: exists;
        positive_limit: limit >= 0
```

Setting the Formatting Rectangle of an Edit Control

The formatting rectangle is the area in which the text of a control can be edited. Initially, this area is the same size as the control itself. However, you can change the formatting rectangle to reduce the editing area—for instance, when you want more white space surrounding the text, or to increase the area to allow more text than is visible to be edited.

The formatting rectangle is returned in the form of a *WEL_RECT*.

```
formatting_rect: WEL_RECT
        -- Limiting rectangle the text. It is independent of
        -- the size of the edit-control window.
    require
        exists: exists
    ensure
        result_not_void: Result /= void
```

Message Hooks in an Edit Control

Table 13.1 lists the message hooks that may be called when using an edit control. The message hooks are called for events such as modifying an edit control's text *(on_en_change)*, clicking the scroll bars *(on_en_hscroll* and

Table 13.1   *Text Box Message Operations*

Message Operation	Description
on_en_change	The user has performed an action that may have changed the text within the text control.
on_en_errspace	Windows cannot allocate enough memory to perform the request.
on_en_hscroll	The horizontal scroll bar has been clicked.
on_en_killfocus	The text control is about to lose focus.
on_en_maxtext	The maximum text limit (as set by *set_text_limit*) has been reached.
on_en_setfocus	The text control has gained focus.
on_en_update	The text control is about to display altered text.
on_en_vscroll	The vertical scroll bar has been clicked.

on_en_vscroll), gaining and losing focus *(on_en_setfocus* and *on_en_killfocus)*, and reaching size constraints *(on_en_maxtext* and *on_en_errspace)*.

The following sections describe each message hook in more detail.

On an Edit Control Changed Message

The *on_en_change* message hook is called when the parent window receives an *En_change* message from the control. This message indicates that the user may have changed the text in the control. When this message hook is called, Windows will have already updated the display to reflect the updated text.

```
on_en_change
        -- The user has taken an action
        -- that may have altered the text.
    require
        exists: exists
```

On an Edit Control Error Space Message

The *on_en_errspace* message hook is called if the edit control cannot allocate enough memory for an operation it is trying to perform. You will need to take corrective action if this message is received because your application may have run out of resources.

```
on_en_errspace
          -- Cannot allocate enough memory to
          -- meet a specific request.
     require
          exists: exists
```

On an Edit Control Set Focus Message

If the user selects or tabs to an edit control, the *on_en_setfocus* message hook is called, indicating that the control has gained the input focus.

```
on_en_setfocus
          -- Receive the keyboard focus.
     require
          exists: exists
```

On an Edit Control Kill Focus Message

When the edit control loses focus—for instance, when the user selects or tabs to another control—the *En_killfocus* message is sent to the parent window, and subsequently the *on_en_killfocus* message hook is called. Many applications use this message to perform field validation on the text entered by the user.

```
on_en_killfocus
          -- Lose the keyboard focus.
     require
          exists: exists
```

On an Edit Control Maximum Text Message

If the user attempts to enter more characters than the maximum text limit, then the *on_en_maxtext* message hook is called. Windows automatically truncates the additional characters before this message hook is called.

```
on_en_maxtext
          -- The current text insertion has exceeded
          -- the specified number of characters.
     require
          exists: exists
```

On an Edit Control Update Message

The *on_en_update* message hook can be one of the most useful for performing user input validation. This hook is called whenever the control is about to display updated text in the control. It is called before the *on_en_changed* hook and can be used to validate or format the text entered by the user, before it is actually displayed in the control.

```
on_en_update
        -- The control is about to display altered text.
    require
        exists: exists
```

On an Edit Control Vertical Scroll Message

This message hook is called after the user clicks the vertical scroll bar but before Windows updates the control.

```
on_en_vscroll
        - The user click on the vertical scroll bar.
    require
        exists: exists
```

On an Edit Control Horizontal Scroll Message

The *on_en_hscroll* message hook is called in the same manner as the *on_en_vscroll*. That is, after the user clicks the horizontal scroll bar, but before Windows updates the control.

```
on_en_hscroll
        -- The user click on the horizontal scroll bar.
    require
        exists: exists
```

Single-Line Edit Control

A single-line edit control provides the facilities for a user to enter one line of text of any length or of a fixed length. The single-line edit control is typically sized to fit just one horizontal line of text, and it automatically scrolls horizontally if the user enters a line longer than the controls width.

Creating a Single-Line Edit Control

A single-line edit control can be created by calling the creation procedures
make or *make_by_id*. *make* is used to create a new edit control with a specified
parent, dimensions, initial text, and position. Procedure *make_by_id* is used to
create a *WEL_SINGLE_LINE_EDIT_CONTROL* instance from a resource.

The following example demonstrates the use of single-line edit controls.
The example includes a menu bar that provides typical edit control commands,
including clipboard cut, copy, and paste; selection activation and deactivation,
moving the caret; and undo. The menu bar commands are supported by an accelerator table that provides keyboard shortcuts for some of the commands.

Example 13.1 lists the *MAIN_WINDOW* class. The features *on_menu_com-
mand* and *on_accelerator_command* are redefined to handle menu and
accelerator events. The creation procedure *make* initializes the window, and
creates and positions the edit control instances using the *make* creation
procedure of *WEL_SINGLE_LINE_EDIT*.

**Example 13.1 Single-Line Text Box Example, MAIN_WINDOW Class
(textbox\singleline)**

```
class MAIN_WINDOW
inherit
    WEL_FRAME_WINDOW
        redefine
            on_menu_command, on_accelerator_command
        end
    APPLICATION_IDS
        export
            {NONE} all
        end
creation
    make
feature
    make is
            -- Initialize the main window
        local
            menu_init_command: INITIALISE_MENU_COMMAND
        do
            make_top ("Main Window")
            -- Add CEC command to initialize the popup menu when it appears
            enable_commands
            create menu_init_command.make (main_menu, Current)
            put_command (menu_init_command, Wm_initmenupopup, Current)
            -- add the menu and controls to the window
            set_menu (main_menu)
            resize (360, 220)
            create static1.make (Current, "Edit box 1", 10, 5, 70, 15, -1)
            create edit_text1.make (Current, "", 10, 20, 300, 50, -1)
```

```
            create static2.make (Current, "Edit box 2", 10, 75, 70,
                15, -1)
            create edit_text2.make (Current, "", 10, 90, 300, 50, -1)
        end
    static1, static2: WEL_STATIC
            -- Static text labels
    edit_text1, edit_text2: WEL_SINGLE_LINE_EDIT
            -- Single line edit control
    on_menu_command (menu_id: INTEGER) is
            -- Check for a menu command
        do
            inspect menu_id
            when Id_fileexit_constant then
                destroy
            when Id_editcut_constant then
                edit_text1.clip_cut
            when Id_editcopy_constant then
                edit_text1.clip_copy
            when Id_editpaste_constant then
                edit_text2.clip_paste
            when Id_editselectall_constant then
                edit_text1.select_all
            when Id_editunselect_constant then
                edit_text1.unselect
            when Id_editdelete_constant then
                edit_text1.delete_selection
            when Id_editgotoend_constant then
                edit_text1.set_caret_position (edit_text1.text.count)
            when Id_editgotostart_constant then
                edit_text1.set_caret_position (0)
            when Id_editundo_constant then
                edit_text1.undo
            end
        end
    on_accelerator_command (accelerator_id: INTEGER) is
            -- Perform accelerator command
        do
            if edit_text1.has_selection then
                inspect accelerator_id
                when Ida_editcut_constant then
                        edit_text1.clip_cut
                when Ida_editcopy_constant then
                        edit_text1.clip_copy
                when Ida_editdelete_constant then
                        edit_text1.delete_selection
                else
                        -- ignore
                end
            else
```

```
                    inspect accelerator_id
                    when Ida_editpaste_constant then
                            edit_text2.clip_paste
                    when Ida_editselectall_constant then
                            edit_text1.select_all
                    when Ida_editundo_constant then
                            edit_text1.undo
                    else
                            -- ignore.
                    end
                end
            end
    feature {NONE} -- Implementation
        main_menu: WEL_MENU is
                -- Main menu created from a menu resource
            once
                create Result.make_by_id (Id_mainmenu_constant)
            end
    end -- class MAIN_WINDOW
```

Each of the menu and accelerator commands calls the appropriate edit
control operations. When *Id_editcut_constant* is received, the *clip_cut* operation of the edit control is called to cut the current selection from the control and
insert it into the Windows clipboard.

Recall that *clip_cut* has, as one of its preconditions,

```
    has_selection: has_selection
```

To guarantee that the *clip_cut* operation is called only when a selection has
been made, we initialize and update the menu bar so that the enabled menu
items reflect what the user can validly do. To do this, we need to use a CEC
command class associated with the *Wm_initmenupopup* message to update the
item status of each popup menu just before it is displayed. Class *INITIAL-
IZE_MENU_COMMAND,* listed in Example 13.2, performs this task.

**Example 13.2 Single-Line Text Box Example, INITIALIZE_MENU_
COMMAND Class (textbox\singleline)**

```
class
    INITIALIZE_MENU_COMMAND
inherit
    WEL_COMMAND
```

```
        APPLICATION_IDS
            export
                {NONE} all
            end
creation
    make
feature {NONE} -- Initialization
    make (a_menu: WEL_MENU; a_window: MAIN_WINDOW) is
            -- Hold a reference to the menu that this command
            -- will effect.
        require
            valid_menu: a_menu /= Void
            valid_window: a_window /= Void
        do
            menu := a_menu
            main_window := a_window
        end
feature {ANY} -- Execution
    execute (arg: ANY) is
            -- Initialize the menu
        do
            if main_window.edit_text1.has_selection then
                menu.enable_item (Id_editcut_constant)
                menu.enable_item (Id_editcopy_constant)
                menu.enable_item (Id_editdelete_constant)
                menu.enable_item (Id_editunselect_constant)
            else
                menu.disable_item (Id_editcut_constant)
                menu.disable_item (Id_editcopy_constant)
                menu.disable_item (Id_editdelete_constant)
                menu.disable_item (Id_editunselect_constant)
            end
            if main_window.edit_text1.text.empty then
                menu.disable_item (Id_editselectall_constant)
            else
                menu.enable_item (Id_editselectall_constant)
            end
            if main_window.edit_text1.can_undo then
                menu.enable_item (Id_editundo_constant)
            else
                menu.disable_item (Id_editundo_constant)
            end
        end
feature {NONE} -- Implementation
    menu: WEL_MENU
    main_window: MAIN_WINDOW
end -- class INITIALIZE_MENU_COMMAND
```

The *MAIN_WINDOW* class associates an instance of *INITIAL-IZE_MENU_COMMAND* with the *Wm_initpopupmenu* message and enables CEC command processing by calling

```
enable_commands
create menu_init_command.make (main_menu, Current)
put_command (menu_init_command, Wm_initmenupopup, Current)
```

When the command is executed, it queries the first edit box to determine if it has a selection active, is empty, or has an operation that can be undone. It then initializes the menu items accordingly.

Figure 13.2 shows the window with both edit controls visible. The user has entered a line of text that is longer than the width of the first edit control. The control scrolls when needed so that the user can edit and view the complete line. The user has also selected the first two words of the line, copied the selection to the clipboard, and then pasted it from the clipboard to the second edit control. You will notice when running this example that you can enter only one line of text in the edit control even though the control has sufficient height to show two or more lines.

Multiple-Line Edit Control

The multiple-line edit control is very similar to the single-line edit control, only more than one line of text can be entered. If the user presses enter while typing text in a multiple-line edit control, then a new line will be created in the control's text.

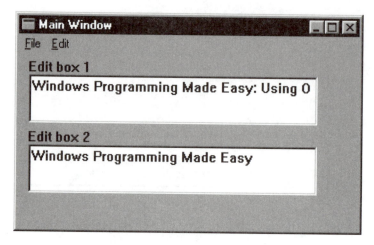

FIGURE 13.2. Single-Line text box example.

Creating a Multiple-Line Edit Control

A multiple-line edit control can be created in exactly the same fashion as a single-line edit control by using the creation procedures *make* and *make_by_id*.

Updating our example to use multiple-line edit controls is very simple. The attribute types for *edit_box1* and *edit_box2* can be changed from *WEL_SINGLE_LINE_EDIT* to *WEL_MULTIPLE_LINE_EDIT*, as shown in Example 13.3.

Example 13.3 Multiple-Line Text Box Example, MAIN_WINDOW Class (textbox\multipleline)

```
class MAIN_WINDOW
inherit
     WEL_FRAME_WINDOW
        redefine
            on_menu_command, on_accelerator_command
        end
     APPLICATION_IDS
        export
            {NONE} all
        end
creation
     make
feature
     make is
            -- Initialize the main window
        local
            menu_init_command: INITIALIZE_MENU_COMMAND
        do
            -- code as before
        end
     static1, static2: WEL_STATIC
            -- Static text labels
     edit_text1, edit_text2: WEL_MULTIPLE_LINE_EDIT
            -- Multiple line edit control
     on_menu_command (menu_id: INTEGER) is
            -- Check for a menu command
        do
            -- code as before
        end
     on_accelerator_command (accelerator_id: INTEGER) is
            -- Perform accelerator command
        do
            -- code as before
        end
  feature {NONE} -- Implementation
     main_menu: WEL_MENU is
            -- Main menu created from a menu resource
        once
```

```
                      -- code as before
            end
   end -- class MAIN_WINDOW
```

The output of this example, shown in Figure 13.3, now allows multiple lines of text to be entered in each edit box. In addition, the edit boxes display horizontal and vertical scroll bars.

Class *WEL_MULTIPLE_LINE_EDIT* introduces additional features particular to a multiple-line control. For instance, a multiple-line edit control supports tab stops, automatic caret positioning, and line manipulation. The following sections describe each of these features and provide examples of their uses.

Setting Tab Stops in a Multiple-Line Edit Control

The tab stops in a multiple-line edit control can be set to regular intervals or to specific positions. The *set_default_tab_stops* sets the tab stop interval to every 32 dialog units, while the *set_tab_stops* operation sets the interval to a specified number. Finally, you can set tab stops at particular positions using the operation *set_tab_stops_array* by passing an array of integers representing each tab stop.

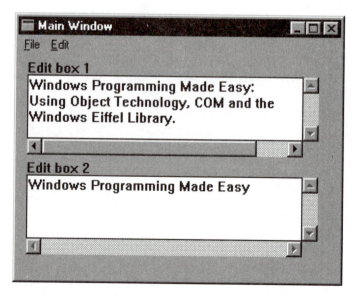

FIGURE 13.3. Multiple-Line text box example

```
set_default_tab_stops
        -- Set tab stops at every 32 dialog box units.
    require
        exists: exists

set_tab_stops (tab: INTEGER)
        -- Set tab stops at every 'tab' dialog box units.
    require
        exists: exists;
        positive_tab: tab > 0

set_tab_stops_array (tab: ARRAY [INTEGER])
        -- Set tab stops using the values of `tab'.
    require
        exists: exists;
        tab_not_void: tab /= void;
        tab_large_enough: tab.count > 1
```

For example, you can set tab stops at positions 30, 45, and 60 using

```
set_tab_stops (<<30, 45, 60>>)
```

In this case we use a manifest array containing the tab stop integers. You could, if needed, build an array using an *ARRAY* class rather than a manifest array.

Manipulating the Text Caret in a Multiple-Line Edit Control

In addition to caret positioning operations, *WEL_MULTIPLE_LINE_EDIT* includes three features that change the way the caret behaves when a selection is made. Feature *enable_scroll_caret_at_selection* causes the edit control to scroll the text so that the selection is visible. You can disable this facility by calling *disable_scroll_caret_at_selection* and determine the current setting using *scroll_caret_at_selection*.

```
scroll_caret_at_selection: BOOLEAN
        -- Will the caret be scrolled at the selection after
        -- a call to 'set_selection'?

disable_scroll_caret_at_selection
        -- Set 'scroll_caret_at_selection' to False.
        -- The caret will not be scrolled at the selection
        -- after a call to 'set_selection'.
    require
        exists: exists
```

```
    ensure
            scroll_caret_at_selection_disabled: not scroll_caret_
            at_selection

enable_scroll_caret_at_selection
            -- Set 'scroll_caret_at_selection' to True.
            -- The caret will be scrolled at the selection after
            -- a call to 'set_selection'.
    require
            exists: exists
    ensure
            scroll_caret_at_selection_enabled: scroll_caret_at_selection
```

Finding the Text Caret in a Multiple-Line Edit Control

Function *current_line_index* gives the number of characters from the start of
the edit control text to the beginning of the line that contains the caret. Feature
current_line_number returns the line number that the caret is located in.

```
current_line_index: INTEGER
        -- Index of the line that contains the caret.
    require
            exists: exists
    ensure
            positive_result: Result >= 0

current_line_number: INTEGER
        -- Line number of the line that contains the caret.
    require
            exists: exists
    ensure
            positive_result: Result >= 0;
            result_small_enough: Result < line_count
```

Manipulating Lines of Text in a Multiple-Line Edit Control

As well as finding line information depending on the caret position, you
can manipulate lines depending on character locations and indexes. Function
line_count gives the current number of lines in an edit control, while *first_vis-
ible_line* returns the index of the line visible at the top of the control.

To retrieve a particular line, the length of a line, or the index of a line
from a character index, use *line, line_length,* and *line_from_char,* respectively.
Finally, you can find the number of characters from the beginning of the control to a particular line using *line_index.*

```
first_visible_line: INTEGER
            -- Upper most visible line
    require
            exists: exists
    ensure
            positive_result: Result >= 0;
            result_small_enough: Result < line_count

line (i: INTEGER): STRING
            -- 'i'th line
    require
            exists: exists;
            i_large_enough: i >= 0;
            i_small_enough: i < line_count
    ensure
            result_exists: Result /= void;
            count_ok: Result.count = line_length (i)

line_count: INTEGER
            -- Number of lines
    require
            exists: exists
    ensure
            positive_result: Result >= 0

line_from_char (i: INTEGER): INTEGER
            -- Index of the line that contains the character
            -- index 'i'. A character index is the number of
            -- characters from the beginning of the edit control.
    require
            exists: exists
    ensure
            positive_result: Result >= 0

line_index (i: INTEGER): INTEGER
            -- Number of characters from the beginning of the edit
            -- control to the zero-based line 'i'.
            -- Retrieve a character index for a given line number.
    require
            exists: exists;
            i_large_enough: i >= 0;
            i_small_enough: i < line_count
    ensure
            positive_result: Result >= 0

line_length (i: INTEGER): INTEGER
            -- Length of the 'i'th line
    require
            exists: exists;
            i_large_enough: i >= 0;
            i_small_enough: i < line_count
    ensure
            positive_result: Result >= 0;
            result_ok: Result = line (i).count
```

To demonstrate the use of these features in Example 13.4, we extend our multiple-line edit control example to display a dialog containing status information about the control.

The dialog is activated by clicking on the Info button, which calls the redefined *on_control_command* message hook. The control information is gathered in *get_text_info* and passed to the *Idd_info_dialog* to display.

Example 13.4 Multiple-Line Text Box Information Example, MAIN_WINDOW Class (textbox\extra)

```
class MAIN_WINDOW
inherit
    WEL_FRAME_WINDOW
        redefine
            on_menu_command, on_accelerator_command, on_control_com-
                mand
        end
    APPLICATION_IDS
        export
            {NONE} all
        end
creation
    make
feature
    make is
            -- Initialize the main window
    local
            menu_init_command: INITIALISE_MENU_COMMAND
    do
            make_top ("Main Window")
            -- Add CEC command to initialize the popupmenu when it
                appears
            enable_commands
            create menu_init_command.make (main_menu, Current)
            put_command (menu_init_command, Wm_initmenupopup, Current)
            -- add the menu and controls to the window
            set_menu (main_menu)
            resize (340, 270)
            create static1.make (Current, "Edit box 1", 10, 5, 70, 15, -1)
            create edit_text1.make (Current, "", 10, 20, 300, 150, -1)
            create info_button.make (Current, "Info", 10, 180, 70, 30, -1)
            -- initialize the dialog
            create info_dialog.make (Current)
        end
    static1: WEL_STATIC
            -- Static text label
    edit_text1: WEL_MULTIPLE_LINE_EDIT
            -- Multiple line edit control
    info_button: WEL_PUSH_BUTTON
```

```
            -- Push button for text box information
    info_dialog: IDD_INFO_DIALOG
            -- Text box information dialog
    on_menu_command (menu_id: INTEGER) is
            -- Check for a menu command
        do
            -- code as before, only Id_editpaste_constant causes a
            -- clipboard paste in
            -- the edit_text1 control.
        end
    on_accelerator_command (accelerator_id: INTEGER) is
            -- Perform accelerator command
        do
            -- code as before, only Id_editpaste_constant causes a
            -- clipboard paste in
            -- the edit_text1 control.
        end
    on_control_command (control: WEL_CONTROL) is
            -- Handle control commands
        do
            if control = info_button then
                info_dialog.set_info_text (get_text_info)
                info_dialog.activate
            end
        end
feature {NONE} -- Implementation
    main_menu: WEL_MENU is
            -- Main menu created from a menu resource
        once
            -- code as before
        end
    get_text_info: STRING is
            -- Return a string representation of the text box
            -- information.
        do
            create Result.make (100)
            Result.append_string ("caret_position: ")
            Result.append_integer (edit_text1.caret_position)
            Result.append_string ("%R%Nhas_selection: ")
            Result.append_boolean (edit_text1.has_selection)
            if edit_text1.has_selection then
                Result.append_string ("%R%Nselection_start: ")
                Result.append_integer (edit_text1.selection_start)
                Result.append_string ("%R%Nselection_end: ")
                Result.append_integer (edit_text1.selection_end)
            end
            Result.append_string ("%R%Ncan_undo: ")
            Result.append_boolean (edit_text1.can_undo)
            Result.append_string ("%R%Nmodified: ")
```

```
            Result.append_boolean (edit_text1.modified)
            Result.append_string ("%R%Ncurrent_line_index: ")
            Result.append_integer (edit_text1.current_line_index)
            Result.append_string ("%R%Ncurrent_line_number: ")
            Result.append_integer (edit_text1.current_line_number)
            Result.append_string ("%R%Nfirst_visible_line: ")
            Result.append_integer (edit_text1.first_visible_line)
            Result.append_string ("%R%Nline_count: ")
            Result.append_integer (edit_text1.line_count)
            Result.append_string ("%R%Nline (line_count / 2): ")
            Result.append_string (edit_text1.line
                (edit_text1.line_count // 2))
            Result.append_string ("%R%Nline_length (line_count / 2): ")
            Result.append_integer (edit_text1.line_length
                (edit_text1.line_count // 2))
            Result.append_string ("%R%Nline_from_char (size // 2): ")
            Result.append_integer (edit_text1.line_from_char
                (edit_text1.text_length // 2))
        end
end -- class MAIN_WINDOW
```

Function *get_text_info* returns a *STRING* representing the available status information of the edit control. Included is the caret position, selection existence and indexes, undo status, and line count and index information.

Figure 13.4 shows the running example with the information dialog showing the caret position at index 56, the *has_selection* status of *False,* and the *can_undo* and *modified* flag status.

Scrolling in a Multiple-Line Edit Control

The last feature available in *WEL_MULTIPLE_LINE_EDIT* is *scroll.* This feature lets you scroll a multiple-line edit control programmatically. When calling scroll, you provide the number of characters that you need to scroll both horizontally and vertically. Windows will reposition the text in the control according to the scroll deltas.

```
scroll (horizontal, vertical: INTEGER)
        -- Scroll the text vertically and horizontally.
        -- 'horizontal' is the number of characters to
        -- scroll horizontally, 'vertical' is the number
        -- of lines to scroll vertically.
```

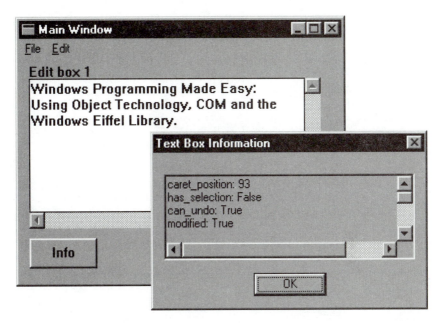

FIGURE 13.4. Multiple-Line text box information example.

Rich Edit Control

Standard edit controls provide only rudimentary formatting capabilities—you can manually include tabs and new lines to align and position the text, but you cannot change any characteristics of the text, such as the font or its alignment and position. The rich text control provides these capabilities. The font style, family, weight, and angle can all be set for particular paragraphs, words, or characters, and lines of text can be aligned or automatically formatted for justification, bulleted lists, or numbered lists.

The rich edit control is implemented in the class *WEL_RICH_EDIT* and relies on a number of helper classes that define paragraph and character ranges, including *WEL_CHARACTER_RANGE, WEL_CHARACTER_FORMAT,* and *WEL_PARAGRAPH_FORMAT.*

Creating a Rich Edit Control

You can create a rich edit control the same way that you create a standard edit control. The creation procedures *make* and *make_by_id* are both available and require the same parameters.

We explore the creation and use of a rich edit control in a detailed example. The example presented is a modified version of the source code found in the *$EIFFEL4\examples\wel\richedit* folder of your ISE Eiffel installation.

The example includes a menu bar and a tool bar created from resources. Both provide complimentary ways of executing rich edit commands. For example, you can activate a file save operation from both the menu bar and the tool bar. You should find the code for manipulating the tool bar relatively straightforward; however, we do not explore this control in detail until later in the book.

When using a rich edit control, you must ensure that your application loads the common control and rich edit control DLLs. This is typically done by redefining *init_application* in the *APPLICATION* class and creating instances of the classes *WEL_COMMON_CONTROLS_DLL* and *WEL_RICH_EDIT_DLL* as shown in Example 13.5.

Example 13.5 Rich Edit Control Example, APPLICATION Class (editbox\richedit)

```
class
    APPLICATION
inherit
    WEL_APPLICATION
        redefine
            init_application
        end
creation
    make
feature
    main_window: MAIN_WINDOW is
            -- Create the application's main window
        once
            create Result.make
        end
    init_application is
            -- Load the common controls dll and the rich edit dll.
        do
            create common_controls_dll.make
            create rich_edit_dll.make
        end
    common_controls_dll: WEL_COMMON_CONTROLS_DLL
    rich_edit_dll: WEL_RICH_EDIT_DLL
end -- class APPLICATION
```

Once you have loaded the required DLLs, you can create and manipulate a rich edit control. Example 13.6 creates a single rich edit control and attaches it to the main window. The main window also creates a menu bar and a tool bar. You will notice that the amount of code associated with using a rich edit control can be significant. This is not because using a rich edit control is overly complicated, but because the control is feature-rich and provides you with facilities for formatting, saving, and loading text. Example 13.6 uses each of these features and provides a fully functional rich text editor.

Most of the logic for using the rich edit control is contained in the *on_menu_command* message hook, which handles events arriving from the menu bar or tool bar. We defer the explanation of the rich text operations used in this message hook until we explore each rich edit control feature in Example 13.6.

Example 13.6 Rich Edit Control Example, MAIN_WINDOW Class (editbox\richedit)

```
class
    MAIN_WINDOW
inherit
    WEL_FRAME_WINDOW
        redefine
            on_menu_command,
            on_control_id_command,
            on_size,
        end
    APPLICATION_IDS
        export
            {NONE} all
        end
    WEL_TTN_CONSTANTS
        export
            {NONE} all
        end
    WEL_CF_CONSTANTS
        export
            {NONE} all
        end
    WEL_IDB_CONSTANTS
        export
            {NONE} all
        end
    WEL_STANDARD_TOOL_BAR_BITMAP_CONSTANTS
        export
            {NONE} all
        end
creation
    make
feature {NONE} -- Initialization
    make is
        local
```

```
    bitmap_index1, bitmap_index2: INTEGER
do
    make_top (Title)
    set_menu (main_menu)
    resize (400, 350)
    -- Create a rich edit control
    create rich_edit.make (Current, "", 0, 35, 200, 200, -1)
    -- Create a toolbar and buttons
    create tool_bar.make (Current, -1)
    create tool_bar_bitmap.make (Bmp_toolbar)
    create standard_tool_bar_bitmap.make_by_predefined_id
        (Idb_std_small_color)
    tool_bar.add_bitmaps (standard_tool_bar_bitmap, 1)
    bitmap_index1 := tool_bar.last_bitmap_index
    tool_bar.add_bitmaps (tool_bar_bitmap, 1)
    bitmap_index2 := tool_bar.last_bitmap_index
    create tool_bar_button1.make_button (bitmap_index1 + Std_filenew,
        Cmd_new)
    create tool_bar_button2.make_button (bitmap_index1 + Std_fileopen,
        Cmd_open)
    create tool_bar_button3.make_button (bitmap_index1 + Std_filesave,
        Cmd_save)
    create tool_bar_button4.make_separator
    create tool_bar_button5.make_button (bitmap_index1 + Std_print,
        Cmd_print)
    create tool_bar_button6.make_separator
    create tool_bar_button7.make_check (bitmap_index2 + 0, Cmd_bold)
    create tool_bar_button8.make_check (bitmap_index2 + 1, Cmd_italic)
    create tool_bar_button9.make_check (bitmap_index2 + 2, Cmd_underline)
    create tool_bar_button10.make_separator
    create tool_bar_button11.make_button (bitmap_index2 + 3, Cmd_font)
    create tool_bar_button12.make_button (bitmap_index2 + 4, Cmd_color)
    create tool_bar_button13.make_separator
    create tool_bar_button14.make_check_group (bitmap_index2 + 5, Cmd_left)
    create tool_bar_button15.make_check_group (bitmap_index2 + 6, Cmd_center)
    create tool_bar_button16.make_check_group (bitmap_index2 + 7, Cmd_right)
    create tool_bar_button17.make_separator
    create tool_bar_button18.make_check (bitmap_index2 + 8, Cmd_bullet)
    tool_bar.add_buttons (<<
        tool_bar_button1,
        tool_bar_button2,
        tool_bar_button3,
        tool_bar_button4,
        tool_bar_button5,
        tool_bar_button6,
        tool_bar_button7,
        tool_bar_button8,
        tool_bar_button9,
        tool_bar_button10,
        tool_bar_button11,
```

```
                    tool_bar_button12,
                    tool_bar_button13,
                    tool_bar_button14,
                    tool_bar_button15,
                    tool_bar_button16,
                    tool_bar_button17,
                    tool_bar_button18>>)
            on_menu_command (Cmd_new)
        end
feature -- Access
    file_name: STRING
            -- File name of the active document
    tool_bar: WEL_TOOL_BAR
            -- Window's tool bar
    tool_bar_bitmap,
    standard_tool_bar_bitmap: WEL_TOOL_BAR_BITMAP
            -- Tool bar Bitmaps
    tool_bar_button1,
    tool_bar_button2,
    tool_bar_button3,
    tool_bar_button4,
    tool_bar_button5,
    tool_bar_button6,
    tool_bar_button7,
    tool_bar_button8,
    tool_bar_button9,
    tool_bar_button10,
    tool_bar_button11,
    tool_bar_button12,
    tool_bar_button13,
    tool_bar_button14,
    tool_bar_button15,
    tool_bar_button16,
    tool_bar_button17,
    tool_bar_button18: WEL_TOOL_BAR_BUTTON
            -- Tool bar buttons
    rich_edit: WEL_RICH_EDIT
            -- Rich edit control
    char_format: WEL_CHARACTER_FORMAT
            -- Structure to format characters
feature {NONE} -- Implementation
    para_format: WEL_PARAGRAPH_FORMAT
            -- Structure to format paragraphs
    on_menu_command (menu_id: INTEGER) is
            -- Execute the command identified by 'menu_id'.
        local
            file: RAW_FILE
        do
            inspect
                menu_id
```

```
when Cmd_exit then
    destroy
when Cmd_new then
    rich_edit.clear
    file_name := Void
    set_window_title
    create char_format.make
    char_format.set_face_name ("Arial")
    char_format.set_height (10)
    char_format.unset_bold
    rich_edit.set_character_format_selection (char_format)
when Cmd_open then
    open_file_dialog.activate (Current)
    if open_file_dialog.selected then
            file_name := clone (open_file_dialog.file_name)
            create file.make_open_read (file_name)
            if file_name.substring_index ("txt", 1) > 0 then
                    rich_edit.load_text_file (file)
            else
                    rich_edit.load_rtf_file (file)
            end
            set_window_title
            rich_edit.set_text_limit ((rich_edit.text_length * 2).max (32000))
    end
when Cmd_save then
    if file_name /= Void then
            create file.make_create_read_write (file_name)
            if file_name.substring_index ("txt", 1) > 0 then
                    rich_edit.save_text_file (file)
            else
                    rich_edit.save_rtf_file (file)
            end
    else
            on_menu_command (Cmd_save_as)
    end
when Cmd_save_as then
    save_file_dialog.activate (Current)
    if save_file_dialog.selected then
            file_name := save_file_dialog.file_name
            set_window_title
            create file.make_create_read_write (file_name)
            if file_name.substring_index ("txt", 1) > 0 then
                    rich_edit.save_text_file (file)
            else
                    rich_edit.save_rtf_file (file)
            end
    end
when Cmd_print then
    print_dialog.activate (Current)
    if print_dialog.selected then
```

```
                    rich_edit.print_all (print_dialog.dc, file_name)
        end
when Cmd_bold then
    create char_format.make
    if tool_bar.button_checked (Cmd_bold) then
            char_format.set_bold
    else
            char_format.unset_bold
    end
    rich_edit.set_character_format_selection (char_format)
when Cmd_italic then
    create char_format.make
    if tool_bar.button_checked (Cmd_italic) then
            char_format.set_italic
    else
            char_format.unset_italic
    end
    rich_edit.set_character_format_selection (char_format)
when Cmd_underline then
    create char_format.make
    if tool_bar.button_checked (Cmd_underline) then
            char_format.set_underline
    else
            char_format.unset_underline
    end
    rich_edit.set_character_format_selection (char_format)
when Cmd_font then
    choose_font.activate (Current)
    choose_font.add_flag (Cf_ttonly)
    if choose_font.selected then
            create char_format.make
            char_format.set_face_name (choose_font.log_font.face_name)
            char_format.set_height (choose_font.log_font.height_
            in_points)
            char_format.set_char_set (choose_font.log_font.char_set)
            char_format.set_pitch_and_family (choose_font.log_font.pitch_
            and_family)
            rich_edit.set_character_format_selection (char_format)
    end
when Cmd_color then
    choose_color.activate (Current)
    if choose_color.selected then
            create char_format.make
            char_format.set_text_color (choose_color.rgb_result)
            rich_edit.set_character_format_selection (char_format)
    end
when Cmd_left then
    create para_format.make
    para_format.set_left_alignment
    rich_edit.set_paragraph_format (para_format)
```

```
        when Cmd_center then
            create para_format.make
            para_format.set_center_alignment
            rich_edit.set_paragraph_format (para_format)
        when Cmd_right then
            create para_format.make
            para_format.set_right_alignment
            rich_edit.set_paragraph_format (para_format)
        when Cmd_bullet then
            create para_format.make
            if tool_bar.button_checked (Cmd_bullet) then
                    para_format.bullet_numbering
            else
                    para_format.no_numbering
            end
            rich_edit.set_paragraph_format (para_format)
        else
            -- ignore
        end
    end
on_control_id_command (control_id: INTEGER) is
    do
        on_menu_command (control_id)
    end
on_size (size_type: INTEGER; a_width: INTEGER; a_height: INTEGER) is
        -- Reposition the status window and the tool bar when
        -- the window has been resized.
    do
        if tool_bar /= Void then
            tool_bar.reposition
        end
        if rich_edit /= Void then
            rich_edit.resize (a_width, a_height - 40)
        end
    end
choose_color: WEL_CHOOSE_COLOR_DIALOG is
        -- Dialog box to choose a text color.
    once
        create Result.make
    ensure
        result_not_void: Result /= Void
    end
choose_font: WEL_CHOOSE_FONT_DIALOG is
        -- Dialog box to choose a text font.
    once
        create Result.make
    ensure
        result_not_void: Result /= Void
    end
open_file_dialog: WEL_OPEN_FILE_DIALOG is
```

```
        -- Dialog box to open a file.
    local
        ofn: WEL_OFN_CONSTANTS
    once
        create ofn
        create Result.make
        Result.set_default_extension ("txt")
        Result.set_filter (<<"Rich Text file (*.rtf)",
            "Text file (*.txt)">>,
            <<"*.rtf", "*.txt">>)
        Result.add_flag (ofn.Ofn_filemustexist)
    ensure
        result_not_void: Result /= Void
    end
save_file_dialog: WEL_SAVE_FILE_DIALOG is
        -- Dialog box to save a file.
    once
        create Result.make
        Result.set_default_extension ("txt")
        Result.set_filter (<<"Rich Text file (*.rtf)",
            "Text file (*.txt)">>,
            <<"*.rtf", "*.txt">>)
    ensure
        result_not_void: Result /= Void
    end
print_dialog: WEL_PRINT_DIALOG is
        -- Dialog box to select the printer.
    once
        create Result.make
    ensure
        result_not_void: Result /= Void
    end
set_window_title is
        -- Set the window's title with 'file_name'.
    local
        s: STRING
    do
        s := clone (Title)
        s.append (" - ")
        if file_name /= Void then
            s.append (file_name)
        else
            s.append ("Untitled")
        end
        set_text (s)
    end
main_menu: WEL_MENU is
        -- Window's menu
    once
```

```
        create Result.make_by_id (Id_main_menu)
      ensure
        result_not_void: Result /= Void
      end
    Title: STRING is "Rich Edit Example"
        -- Window's title
end -- class MAIN_WINDOW
```

Figure 13.5 shows the rich text example running with the title of this book in rich text format. Different fonts, alignments, and font effects have been used to format the text.

Setting Rich Edit Control Events and Options

You can be selective about the events that a rich edit control will raise. For example, you may only be interested in being notified when the text in a rich edit control is changed or updated, or when the control is scrolled. To select the events that the control raises, you need to call *set_event_mask*, passing an integer containing a flag for each event that should be raised. For instance, to enable the changed and updated messages while disabling all other rich text messages use

FIGURE 13.5. Rich text control example.

```
set_event_mask (Enm_change + Enm_update)
```

where *Enm_change* and *Enm_update* are constants from the class *WEL_ENM_CONSTANTS*, as listed in Table 13.2. To determine the current event mask you can call feature *event_mask*.

```
event_mask: INTEGER
        -- Event mask which specifies notification message the
        -- control sends to its parent window.
        -- See class WEL_ENM_CONSTANTS for values.
    require
        exists: exists


set_event_mask (an_event_mask: INTEGER)
        -- Set 'event_mask' with 'an_event_mask'.
        -- See class WEL_ENM_CONSTANTS for values.
    require
        exists: exists
    ensure
        event_mask_set: event_mask = an_event_mask
```

TABLE 13.2   *Edit Notification Mask Constants (WEL_ENM_CONSTANTS)*

CONSTANT	DESCRIPTION
Enm_change	Send notification when the user has taken an action that may have altered the text. Sent after Windows updates the screen.
Enm_correcttext	Send notification from a rich edit control when a SYV_ CORRECT gesture occurs. This notification is only sent when pen capability is enabled.
Enm_dropfiles	Notify the parent of the rich edit control that the user is attempting to drop files into the control.
Enm_keyevents	Notify the parent window of key events.
Enm_mouseevents	Notify the parent window of mouse events.
Enm_none	Do not notify the parent window of any events.
Enm_protected	Notify the parent window when protected text may be changed as a result of a user action.
Enm_requestresize	Notify the parent window that the control's contents are either smaller or larger than the control's window size.
Enm_scroll	Notify the parent window of scroll events.
Enm_selchange	Notify the parent window of selection modification events.
Enm_update	Notify the parent window that altered text is about to be displayed.

A rich edit control can be further customized using options. The options include facilities for automatic scroll bars, automatic word selection, nonhideable selections, read-only settings, and others. The features *options* and *set_options* retrieve the current control options and set new options, respectively. The *set_options* procedure takes, in addition to the *an_options* parameter, another parameter, *operation,* that specifies how the options should be applied to the current settings.

```
options: INTEGER
        -- Give the current set of options.

set_options (operation, an_options: INTEGER)
        -- Set the opetions for the control.
        -- See class WEL_ECO_CONSTANTS for values.
    require
        exists: exists
```

The *operation* parameter can take the value *Ecoop_and, Ecoop_or, Ecoop_set,* or *Ecoop_xor* to set the appropriate combination operator. For instance, *Ecoop_and* retains only those options that are already set and that are also specified in the *an_options* parameter. Other options and operations are listed in Table 13.3.

TABLE 13.3   *Edit Control Options (WEL_ECO_CONSTANTS)*

CONSTANT	DESCRIPTION
Eco_autohscroll	Automatically scroll text horizontally.
Eco_autovscroll	Automatically scroll text vertically.
Eco_autowordselection	Automatic selection of words on double click.
Eco_nohidesel	Specifies that the selection is not hidden when the control loses focus.
Eco_readonly	Makes the control read-only.
Eco_savesel	Preserves the selection when the control loses focus. Normally the entire text of the control is selected when the control regains the focus.
Eco_vertical	Draws text and objects in a vertical direction. Available for Asian languages only.
Eco_wantreturn	Allows carriage-return to be entered as part of the control's text. By default, pressing ENTER will complete the editing action. In a single-line edit control, this option has no effect.
Ecoop_and	Retain only the current options that are also specified in the *set_options* call.
Ecoop_or	Combine the specified options with the current options.
Ecoop_set	Set the options to those specified. Override any options already set.
Ecoop_xor	Retain only those current options that are not specified in the *set_options* call.

In addition, you can completely enable or disable standard rich edit control notifications by calling *enable_standard_notifications* or *disable_notifications*. The standard notifications include *Enm_change, Enm_update,* and *Enm_scroll.*

```
disable_notifications
        -- Disable all notifications.
    require
        exists: exists

enable_standard_notifications
        -- Enable the standard notifications.
        -- (Enm_change, Enm_update and Enm_scroll).
    require
        exists: exists
```

In the rich text example (Example 13.6), we did not specify any particular options, and we left the standard notifications enabled. However, we could have disabled the standard notifications without adverse effects because we do not actually capture and process any of the events.

Setting Background Colors of a Rich Text Control

The background color of a rich edit control can be changed by calling *set_background_color* or *set_background_system_color.* The first procedure sets the color to one you specify, and the second sets the color to the system background color.

```
set_background_color (color: WEL_COLOR_REF)
        -- Set the background color with 'color'.
    require
        exists: exists;
        color_not_void: color /= void

set_background_system_color
        -- Set the background color with the window
        -- background system color.
    require
        exists: exists
```

Manipulating Text Selections in a Rich Edit Control

A rich edit control has the same selection information as a standard edit control. In addition, the currently selected text can be accessed via the *selected_text* function. The selection is also represented by a

WEL_CHARACTER_RANGE via the *selection* function. A rich edit control uses character ranges to apply formatting options to the specified range of characters.

```
selected_text: STRING
        -- Currently selected text
    require
      exists: exists;
      has_selection: has_selection
    ensure
      valid_length: Result.count = selection_end - selection_start

selection: WEL_CHARACTER_RANGE
        -- Structure which contains the starting and ending
        -- character positions of the selection.
    require
      exists: exists
```

A *WEL_CHARACTER_RANGE* holds minimum and maximum character positions that represent the start and end positions of the range. You can create a *WEL_CHARACTER_RANGE* by calling its creation procedure *make,* specifying the minimum and maximum extents of the range, or you can create an empty character range by calling *make_empty.* The minimum and maximum values can also be adjusted by calling *set_range.*

```
class interface
    WEL_CHARACTER_RANGE
creation

    make (a_minimum, a_maximum: INTEGER)
      require
        positive_minimum: a_minimum >= 0;
        valid_maximum: a_minimum = 0 implies a_maximum >= -1;
        positive_maximum: a_minimum > 0 implies a_maximum >= 0
      ensure
        minimum_set: minimum = a_minimum;
        maximum_set: maximum = a_maximum

    make_by_pointer (a_pointer: POINTER)
        -- (from WEL_ANY)
      ensure -- from WEL_ANY
        item_set: item = a_pointer;
        shared: shared
    make_empty
      ensure
        minimum_set: minimum = 0;
        maximum_set: maximum = 0
```

```
feature -- Access

    maximum: INTEGER
            -- Index of last intercharacter position
    minimum: INTEGER
            -- Index of first intercharacter position
feature -- Element change

    set_range (a_minimum, a_maximum: INTEGER)
            -- Set 'minimum' with 'a_minimum' and
            -- 'maximum' with 'a_maximum'
        require
            positive_minimum: a_minimum >= 0;
            valid_maximum: a_minimum = 0 implies a_maximum >= -1;
            positive_maximum: a_minimum > 0 implies a_maximum >= 0
        ensure
            minimum_set: minimum = a_minimum;
            maximum_set: maximum = a_maximum
invariant
    positive_minimum: minimum >= 0;
    valid_minumum_maximum: maximum >= minimum;
end -- class WEL_CHARACTER_RANGE
```

When a selection has been made, either by the user or by your code, you can choose to show or hide it by calling *show_selection* or *hide_selection*, respectively. If a selection is made that is not visible in the client area of the edit control, then you can have the control scroll the text to make the selection visible by calling *move_to_selection*. Calling *move_to_selection* when the selection is already visible has no effect.

```
move_to_selection
        -- Move the selected text to be visible

show_selection
    -- Show selection.
    require
        exists: exists

hide_selection
        -- Hide the selection.
    require
        exists: exists
```

Finding a Character by Position in a Rich Edit Control

Two useful features of a rich edit control are *character_index_from_position* and *position_from_character_index*. The *character_index_from_position* function returns the character position closest to a position in the client area of the control. The inverse of this relation can be determined by calling *position_from_character_index,* which returns a *POINT* representing the coordinate in the client area of the control for a particular character position. As the header comment of *position_from_character_index* mentions, the coordinate may contain negative values if the character position has been scrolled outside of the client area.

```
character_index_from_position (a_x, a_y: INTEGER): INTEGER
          -- Zero-based character index of the character which is
          -- the nearest to 'a_x' and 'a_y' position in the client
          -- area.
          -- A returned coordinate can be negative if the
          -- character has been scrolled outside the edit
          -- control's client area. The coordinates are truncated
          -- to integer values and are in screen units relative
          -- to the upper-left corner of the client area of the
          -- control.
    require
          exists: exists;
          a_x_large_enough: a_x >= 0;
          a_y_large_enough: a_y >= 0

position_from_character_index (character_index: INTEGER): WEL_POINT
          -- Coordinates of a character at 'character_index' in
          -- the client area.
          -- A returned coordinate can be negative if the
          -- character has been scrolled outside the edit
          -- control's client area.
          -- The coordinates are truncated to integer values and
          -- are in screen units relative to the upper-left
          -- corner of the client area of the control.
    require
          exists: exists;
          index_large_enough: character_index >= 0;
          index_small_enough: character_index <= text_length + 2
    ensure
          result_not_void: Result /= void
```

Changing Character Formats in a Rich Edit Control

The flexibility of a rich edit control comes from the ability to apply formatting and layout options to text ranges, paragraphs, and individual characters. Formatting options are applied to text using either a *WEL_CHARACTER_FORMAT* or a *WEL_PARAGRAPH_FORMAT.* A character format specifies the font, font effects (such as bold or italic), offset position (for superscript or subscript characters), height, and color. Paragraph formatting is discussed in "Changing Paragraph Formats in a Rich Edit Control" in this chapter.

The character format for the current selection can be retrieved using *current_selection_character_format*. This function returns an instance of *WEL_CHARACTER_FORMAT* with the current character format settings. The default character format, used for all characters that do not have individual character ranges applied, can be retrieved by calling *default_character_format*.

```
current_selection_character_format: WEL_CHARACTER_FORMAT
        -- Current selection character format information
    require
        exists: exists
    ensure
        result_not_void: Result /= void

default_character_format: WEL_CHARACTER_FORMAT
        -- Default character format information
    require
        exists: exists
    ensure
        result_not_void: Result /= void
```

An instance of the *WEL_CHARACTER_FORMAT* class can be created by calling *make* and then populated with the required format options by calling relevant *set_* operations. Character effects can be applied as a group by calling *add_effects*, using values from Table 13.4, or they can be applied individually by calling *set_* operations for each required effect. For example, a character format for bold italic characters can be created using the *add_effects* operation with the code fragment

```
format: WEL_CHARACTER_FORMAT
...
create format.make
format.set_mask (Cfm_bold + Cfm_italic)
format.add_effects (Cfe_bold + Cfe_italic)
```

or using the individual effect *set_* operations with

```
format: WEL_CHARACTER_FORMAT
...
create format.make
format.set_bold
format.set_italic
```

Using the *set_* operations automatically sets the relevant effect mask values as found in *WEL_CFM_CONSTANTS*, listed in Table 13.5. The *add_effects* operation requires that appropriate effect mask values are also set to ensure that the effect is applied.

```
class interface
    WEL_CHARACTER_FORMAT

creation
    make
    make_by_pointer (a_pointer: POINTER)
            -- (from WEL_ANY)
        ensure -- from WEL_ANY
            item_set: item = a_pointer;
            shared: shared

feature -- Access

    char_set: INTEGER
            -- Character set value. Can be one of the values
            -- specified for the 'char_set' function of the
            -- WEL_LOG_FONT structure.

    effects: INTEGER
            -- Character effects.
            -- See class WEL_CFE_CONSTANTS for values.

    face_name: STRING
            -- Font face name
        ensure
            result_not_void: Result /= void

    height: INTEGER
            -- Character height

    mask: INTEGER
            -- Valid information or attributes to set.
            -- See class WEL_CFM_CONSTANTS for values.
            -- This attribute is automatically set by the
            -- features set_*.

    max_face_name_length: INTEGER
            -- Maximum face name length

    offset: INTEGER
            -- Character offset from the baseline. If the value
            -- is positive, the character is a superscript; if it
            -- is negative, the character is a subscript.

    pitch_and_family: INTEGER
            -- Font pitch and family. This value is the same as
            -- 'pitch and family' of the WEL_LOG_FONT structure

text_color: WEL_COLOR_REF
            -- Text color
        ensure
            result_not_void: Result/=void
```

```
feature -- Status report
    has_effects (an_effects: INTEGER): BOOLEAN
            -- Is 'an effects' set in 'effects'?
            -- See class WEL_CFE_CONSTANTS for 'an_effects' values.
    has_mask (a_mask: INTEGER): BOOLEAN
            -- Is 'a mask' set in 'mask'?
            -- See class WEL_CFM_CONSTANTS for 'a_mask' values.

feature -- Element change
    add_effects (an_effects: INTEGER)
            -- Add 'an_effects' to 'effects'.
            -- See class WEL_CFE_CONSTANTS for 'a_mask' values.
        ensure
            has_effects: has_effects (an_effects)

    add_mask (a_mask: INTEGER)
            -- Add 'a_mask' to 'mask'.
            -- See class WEL_CFM_CONSTANTS for 'a_mask' values.
        ensure
            has_mask: has_mask (a_mask)

    remove_effects (an_effects: INTEGER)
            -- Remove 'an_effects' from 'effects'.
            -- See class WEL_CFE_CONSTANTS for 'a_mask' values.
        ensure
            has_not_effects: not has_effects (an_effects)

    remove_mask (a_mask: INTEGER)
            -- Remove 'a_mask' from 'mask'.
            -- See class WEL_CFM_CONSTANTS for 'a_mask' values.
        ensure
            has_not_mask: not has_mask (a_mask)

    set_all_masks
            -- Set 'mask' with all possible values.

    set_bold
            -- Set bold characters.

    set_char_set (a_char_set: INTEGER)
            -- Set 'char_set' with 'a_char_set'.
        ensure
            char_set_set: char_set = a_char_set

    set_effects (an_effects: INTEGER)
            -- Set 'effects' with 'an_effects'.
            -- See class WEL_CFE_CONSTANTS for 'a_mask' values.
        ensure
            effects_set: effects = an_effects

    set_face_name (a_face_name: STRING)
```

```
                    -- Set 'face_name' with 'a_face_name'.
          require
              a_face_name_not_void: a_face_name /= void;
              valid_count: a_face_name.count <= max_face_name_length
          ensure
              face_name_set: face_name.is_equal (a_face_name)

      set_height (a_height: INTEGER)
              -- Set 'height' with 'a_height'.
          ensure
              height_set: height = a_height

      set_italic
              -- Set italic characters.

      set_mask (a_mask: INTEGER)
              -- Set 'mask' with 'a_mask'.
              -- See class WEL_CFM_CONSTANTS for 'a_mask' values.
          ensure
              mask_set: mask = a_mask

      set_offset (an_offset: INTEGER)
              -- Set 'offset' with 'an_offset'.
          ensure
              offset_set: offset = an_offset

      set_pitch_and_family (a_pitch_and_family: INTEGER)
              -- Set 'pitch_and_family' with 'a_pitch_and_family'.
          ensure
              pitch_and_family_set: pitch_and_family = a_pitch_and_family

      set_protected
              -- Set protected characters.

      set_strike_out
              -- Set strikeout characters.

      set_text_color (a_color: WEL_COLOR_REF)
              -- Set 'text_color' with 'a_text_color'.
          ensure
              text_color_set: text_color.is_equal (a_color)

      set_underline
              -- Set underline characters.

      unset_bold
              -- Unset bold characters.

      unset_italic
              -- Unset italic characters.

      unset_protected
```

```
                -- Unset protected characters.

    unset_strike_out
            -- Unset strikeout characters.

    unset_underline
            -- Unset underline characters.

end -- class WEL_CHARACTER_FORMAT
```

A character format can be applied to a selection, an empty selection, the current word, or to the entire text of a rich edit control. Feature *set_character_format_all* is used to apply a format to the entire text, *set_character_format_word* applies formatting to the current word, and finally, *set_character_format_selection* applies a format to the current selection (empty or not).

```
set_character_format_all (a_char_format: WEL_CHARACTER_FORMAT)
        -- Set the current selection with 'a_char_format'.
    require
        exists: exists;
        a_char_format_not_void: a_char_format /= void

set_character_format_selection (a_char_format: WEL_CHARACTER_FORMAT)
        -- Set the current selection with 'a_char_format'.
    require
        exists: exists;
        a_char_format_not_void: a_char_format /= void

set_character_format_word (a_char_format: WEL_CHARACTER_FORMAT)
        -- Set the current word with 'a_char_format'.
    require
        exists: exists;
        a_char_format_not_void: a_char_format /= void
```

TABLE 13.4 *Character Format Effect Constants (WEL_CFE_CONSTANTS)*

CONSTANT	DESCRIPTION
Cfe_autocolor	The text color is set to the color returned by *Color_windowtext*.
Cfe_bold	Characters are bold.
Cfe_italic	Characters are italic.
Cfe_protected	Characters are protected; an attempt to modify them will cause an *En_protected* notification message.
Cfe_strikeout	Characters are struck out.
Cfe_underline	Characters are underlined.

Table 13.5   *Character Format Mask Constants (WEL_CFM_CONSTANTS)*

Constant	Description
Cfm_bold	Change the bold format effect.
Cfm_charset	Change the character set format effect.
Cfm_color	Change the color.
Cfm_face	Change the font face.
Cfm_italic	Change the italic format effect.
Cfm_offset	Change the character offset.
Cfm_protected	Change the protected format effect.
Cfm_size	Change the size.
Cfm_strikeout	Change the strikeout format effect.
Cfm_underline	Change the underline format effect.

The rich text example uses *set_character_format_selection* to apply formatting that the user has selected either from the menu bar or the tool bar. For example, to toggle the bold effect within the current selection, the following code is used:

```
create char_format.make
if tool_bar.button_checked (Cmd_bold) then
        char_format.set_bold
else
        char_format.unset_bold
end
rich_edit.set_character_format_selection (char_format)
```

Similar code fragments exist for applying italic and underlined character effects.

Changing Paragraph Formats in a Rich Edit Control

A paragraph format provides larger grained formatting of text than a character format. A rich edit control treats a continuous collection of characters terminated by a carriage-return/line-feed pair as a single paragraph. A paragraph can be formatted with automatic word wrapping, alignment, numbering, indentation, and tabulation. The class WEL_PARAGRAPH_FORMAT provides an interface for manipulating paragraph text formatting.

```
class interface
     WEL_PARAGRAPH_FORMAT
creation
     make
     make_by_pointer (a_pointer: POINTER)
            -- (from WEL_ANY)
        ensure -- from WEL_ANY
            item_set: item = a_pointer;
            shared: shared

feature -- Access

    alignment: INTEGER
            -- Alignment type.
            -- See class WEL_PFA_CONSTANTS for values.

    mask: INTEGER
            -- Valid information or attributes to set.
            -- See class WEL_PFM_CONSTANTS for values.
            -- This attribute is automatically set by the
            -- features set_*.

    numbering: INTEGER
            -- Numbering type

    offset: INTEGER
            -- Indentation of the second line and subsequent
            -- lines, relative to the starting indentation. The
            -- first line is indented if this member is negative,
            -- or outdented is this member is positive.

    right_indent: INTEGER
            -- Size of the right indentation, relative to the right
            -- margin

    start_indent: INTEGER
            -- Indentation of the first line in the paragraph

    tabulations: ARRAY [INTEGER]
            -- Contains tab stops
        ensure
            result_not_void: Result /= void

feature -- Measurement

    max_tab_stops: INTEGER

feature -- Status report

    has_mask (a_mask: INTEGER): BOOLEAN
            -- Is 'a_mask' set in 'mask'?
            -- See class WEL_PFM_CONSTANTS for 'a_mask' values.
```

```
feature -- Element change

    add_mask (a_mask: INTEGER)
            -- Add 'a_mask' to 'mask'.
            -- See class WEL_PFM_CONSTANTS for 'a_mask' values.
        ensure
            has_mask: has_mask (a_mask)

    bullet_numbering
            -- Add bullets.

    no_numbering
            -- Remove any numbering.
        ensure
            no_numbering: numbering = 0

    remove_mask (a_mask: INTEGER)
            -- Remove 'a_mask' from 'mask'.
            -- See class WEL_PFM_CONSTANTS for 'a_mask' values.
        ensure
            has_not_mask: not has_mask (a_mask)

    set_alignment (an_alignment: INTEGER)
            -- Set 'alignment' with 'an_alignment'.
            -- See class WEL_PFA_CONSTANTS for values.
        ensure
            alignment_set: alignment = an_alignment

    set_center_alignment
            -- Paragraphs are centered.

    set_default_tabulation
            -- Set the default tabulation.
    set_left_alignment
            -- Paragraphs are aligned with the left margin.

    set_mask (a_mask: INTEGER)
            -- Set 'mask' with 'a_mask'.
            -- See class WEL_PFM_CONSTANTS for 'a_mask' values.
        ensure
            mask_set: mask = a_mask

    set_offset (an_offset: INTEGER)
            -- Set 'offset' with 'an_offset'.
        ensure
            offset_set: offset = an_offset

    set_right_alignment
            -- Paragraphs are aligned with the right margin.

    set_right_indent (a_right_indent: INTEGER)
            -- Set 'right_indent' with 'a_right_indent'.
```

```
    ensure
        right_indent_set: right_indent = a_right_indent

set_start_indent (a_start_indent: INTEGER)
        -- Set 'start_indent' with 'a_start_indent'.
    ensure
        start_indent_set: start_indent = a_start_indent

set_tabulation (tab: INTEGER)
        -- Set a tab stop at every 'tab'.

set_tabulations (tabs: ARRAY [INTEGER])
        -- Set tabulation stops using the values of 'tabs'.
    require
        tabs_not_void: tabs /= void;
        tabs_count: tabs.count <= max_tab_stops
    ensure
        tabulations_set: tabulations.is_equal (tabs)

end -- class WEL_PARAGRAPH_FORMAT
```

WEL_PARAGRAPH_FORMAT operates in the same way that *WEL_CHARACTER_FORMAT* does—individual settings can be applied (with the associated effect mask) by calling *set_* operations. However, combined effects can *not* be applied as a whole using *set_effects*. The only effect that requires an integer value and mask is *set_alignment*. Paragraph alignment can be set to center, left, or right using values *Pfa_center, Pfa_left,* or *Pta_right* as listed in Table 13.6. The *set_* operations of *WEL_PARAGRAPH_FORMAT* ensure that the relevant effect masks, listed in Table 13.7, are set and unset when required. Therefore, you typically do not have to set specific mask values when using this class.

A paragraph format is applied to the current paragraph by calling *set_paragraph_format* and passing an instance of *WEL_PARAGRAPH_FOR-MAT* as the *a_para_format* parameter.

TABLE 13.6 *Paragraph Format Alignment Constants (WEL_PFA_CONSTANTS)*

CONSTANT	DESCRIPTION
Pfa_center	Paragraphs are centered.
Pfa_left	Paragraphs are aligned with the left margin.
Pfa_right	Paragraphs are aligned with the right margin.

TABLE 13.7   *Paragraph Format Mask Constants (WEL_PFM_CONSTANTS)*

CONSTANT	DESCRIPTION
Pfm_alignment	Update the alignment format.
Pfm_numbering	Update the numbering format.
Pfm_offset	Update the offset.
Pfm_offsetindent	Update the offset indent.
Pfm_rightindent	Update the right indent.
Pfm_startindent	Update the start indent.
Pfm_tabstops	Update the tab stops.

```
set_paragraph_format (a_para_format: WEL_PARAGRAPH_FORMAT)
        -- Set the current paragraph with 'a_para_format'.
   require
      exists: exists;
      a_para_format_not_void: a_para_format /= void
```

The rich text example uses *set_paragraph_format* to apply paragraph formatting, including left, center, and right alignment and bullet numbering. For example, to set left alignment for the current paragraph the following code fragment is used:

```
create para_format.make
para_format.set_left_alignment
rich_edit.set_paragraph_format (para_format)
```

Finding Text in a Rich Edit Control

If your applications need to provide text search capabilities, then the feature *find* of *WEL_RICH_EDIT* will be useful. Function *find* provides a convenient way of searching for a particular *STRING* in the text of a rich edit control. You can specify whether the search is to be case-sensitive and from which position the search will begin.

```
find (text_to_find: STRING; match_case: BOOLEAN; start_from:
   INTEGER): INTEGER
      -- Find 'text_to_find' in WEL_RICH_EDIT
```

Printing Text from a Rich Edit Control

The text in a rich edit control, whether it is formatted or not, can be printed on a *WEL_PRINTER_DC* by calling *print_all.* Procedure *print_all* prints the text of the control on as many pages as necessary, with the specified title on each page.

```
print_all (dc: WEL_PRINTER_DC; title: STRING)
        -- Print the contents of the rich edit control on
        -- the printer 'dc'. 'title' is the printer job name.
    require
        exists: exists;
        dc_not_void: dc /= void;
        dc_exists: dc.exists;
        title_not_void: title /= void
```

Recall creating a printer device context in Chapter 10, "Graphics Device Interface." In the example, we created a printer device context using the standard print dialog. All that is needed is to pass the selected device context from the dialog to the *print_all* operation.

```
    print_dialog.activate (Current)
    if print_dialog.selected then
            rich_edit.print_all (print_dialog.dc, file_name)
    end
```

In this case, we also passed the name of the file as the title of the report.

Loading Text into a Rich Edit Control

Our example provides a menu item and a tool bar icon for loading a text file into the rich edit control. When we load text, we need to know what format the text is in. The rich edit control supports both plain text and rich text files with the features *load_rtf_file* and *load_text_file.*

```
load_rtf_file (file: RAW_FILE)
        -- Load a RTF 'file' in the rich edit control.
    require
        exists: exists;
        file_not_void: file /= void;
        file_exists: file.exists;
        file_is_open_read: file.is_open_read
    ensure
        file_closed: file.is_closed

load_text_file (file: RAW_FILE)
        -- Load a text 'file' in the rich edit control.
```

```
require
      exists: exists;
      file_not_void: file /= void;
      file_exists: file.exists;
      file_is_open_read: file.is_open_read
ensure
            file_closed: file.is_closed
```

The example uses a "best guess" approach to determine the format of the file, depending on the extension of the selected file. If the file ends with *.txt* then the file is loaded as plain text; otherwise, the file is loaded as rich text. The following code fragment is used to load a file:

```
open_file_dialog.activate (Current)
if open_file_dialog.selected then
        file_name := clone (open_file_dialog.file_name)
        create file.make_open_read (file_name)
        if file_name.substring_index ("txt", 1) > 0 then
           rich_edit.load_text_file (file)
        else
           rich_edit.load_rtf_file (file)
        end
        set_window_title
        rich_edit.set_text_limit ((rich_edit.text_length *
           2).max (32000))
end
```

The parameter for both *load_text_file* and *load_rtf_file* needs to be an instance of *RAW_FILE* (found in the EiffelBase library). The example creates a *RAW_FILE* from the file selected in the *open_file_dialog*. The control's text limit is also set to the larger of twice the loaded file's length or 32,000 characters.

Saving Text from a Rich Edit Control

Saving the text is similar to loading text. There are two operations available, *save_rtf_file* and *save_text_file,* and both take a *RAW_FILE* as the only parameter. Again, you need to decide whether you are saving the text in plain text format or rich text format.

```
save_rtf_file (file: RAW_FILE)
        -- Save the contents of the rich edit control in RTF
        -- format in 'file'.
    require
        exists: exists;
        file_not_void: file /= void;
```

```
        file_exists: file.exists;
        file_is_open_read: file.is_open_write
    ensure
        file_closed: file.is_closed

save_text_file (file: RAW_FILE)
        -- Save the contents of the rich edit control in text
        -- format in 'file'.
    require
        exists: exists;
        file_not_void: file /= void;
        file_exists: file.exists;
        file_is_open_read: file.is_open_write
    ensure
        file_closed: file.is_closed
```

The Save As option in the example is implemented as

```
save_file_dialog.activate (Current)
if save_file_dialog.selected then
        file_name := save_file_dialog.file_name
        set_window_title
        create file.make_create_read_write (file_name)
        if file_name.substring_index ("txt", 1) > 0 then
            rich_edit.save_text_file (file)
        else
            rich_edit.save_rtf_file (file)
        end
end
```

First, a save file dialog is shown, and if the user selects or enters a save file name, then a new *RAW_FILE* is created to represent the file. Depending on the extension of the file, the control's text is saved in plain text or rich text format.

Internally, WEL uses the classes *WEL_RICH_EDIT_STREAM* and its descendants to load and save text to and from a rich edit control. If you need more control over how text is loaded or saved, you may need to use these classes. For the most part, the features presented above should suffice.

SUMMARY

In this chapter, we have seen the types of edit controls that WEL supports, ranging from single-line edit controls to multiple-line edit controls to rich edit controls. Each of the controls provides the ability to receive textual input from a user.

The current editing position for edit controls is depicted by the caret—a vertical cursor that indicates where the next character will be inserted or appended in the control's current text. In addition, each of the controls supports a text selection that can be used for cut, copy, and paste operations and for formatting.

The following chapter looks at controls that support lists of information, including single-line list boxes, multiple-line list boxes, and list view controls.edit controls

LIST BOXES

INTRODUCING LIST BOXES

When you need to display information in list or tabular form, the list box controls are invaluable. List box controls allow multiple textual (and sometimes graphical) items to be managed. The items are typically shown as a vertical scrolling list that allows the user to select one or more.

TYPES OF LIST BOXES

The WEL library provides an encapsulation of both list boxes and list views. List boxes provide a simple vertical list control that supports the selection of one or more list items. In contrast, a list view provides a more complex control that allows list information to be formatted in a tabular, or spreadsheet, fashion.

WEL_LIST_BOX is a direct descendant of *WEL_CONTROL* and is the common ancestor of *WEL_SINGLE_SELECTION_LIST_BOX* and *WEL_MULTIPLE_SELECTION_LIST_BOX*. The class *WEL_LIST_VIEW* is a direct descendant of *WEL_CONTROL*. Figure 14.1 shows the inheritance relationships between the list box classes.

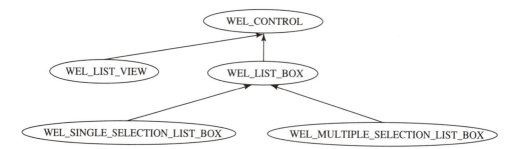

FIGURE 14.1. List box control types.

Abstract List Box Class

The deferred class *WEL_LIST_BOX* defines a set of common list box features that provide general list box functionality. Included are features for adding and removing list items, selecting and finding list items, and processing message hooks. The following sections look at each group of features in more detail.

Adding Text Strings to a List Box

A list box generally contains a set of strings that represent the elements in the list. Three features are available for adding strings to a list box: *add_string,* *add_files,* and *insert_string_at.* Feature *add_string* allows you to add a single string to a list box. If the list is sorted (i.e., the list box has the style *Lbs_sort*), then the string is added to the correct position in the list; otherwise, it is appended to the end.

```
add_string (a_string: STRING)
        -- Add 'a_string' in the list box.
        -- If the list box does not have the
        -- 'Lbs_sort' style, 'a_string' is added
        -- to the end of the list otherwise it is
        -- inserted into the list and the list is
        -- sorted.
    require
        exists: exists;
        a_string_not_void: a_string /= void
    ensure
        count_increased: count = old count + 1

add_files (attribute: INTEGER; files: STRING)
        -- Add 'files' to the list box. 'files' may contain
        -- wildcards (?*). See class WEL_DDL_CONSTANTS for
```

```
          -- 'attribute' values.
    require
        exists: exists;
        files_not_void: files /= void

insert_string_at (a_string: STRING; index: INTEGER)
        -- Add 'a_string' at the zero-based 'index'
    require
        exists: exists;
        a_string_not_void: a_string /= void;
        index_large_enough: index >= 0;
        index_small_enough: index <= count
    ensure
        count_increased: count = old count + 1
```

A simple way of displaying a list of files in a directory is to use the *add_files* feature of a list box. *add_files* includes all files matching a *files* parameter. The *attribute* parameter can be used to narrow the file-matching to particular types of files. For example, to add all read-only files in the root directory of *C:* drive, you could use

```
    list_box.add_files(Ddl_readonly, "c:\");
```

where *Ddl_readonly* is one of the constants defined in *WEL_DDL_CONSTANTS,* listed in Table 14.1.

TABLE 14.1   *Dialog Dir List Constants (WEL_DDL_CONSTANTS)*

CONSTANT	DESCRIPTION
Ddl_archive	File has been archived.
Ddl_directory	File must be a directory name.
Ddl_drives	File must be a drive name.
Ddl_exclusive	If the exclusive flag is set, only files of the specified type are listed. Otherwise files of the specified type are listed in addition to files that do not match the specified type.
Ddl_hidden	File must be hidden.
Ddl_postmsgs	Send this control's messages to the application message queue rather than the control's own queue.
Ddl_readonly	File must be read-only.
Ddl_readwrite	File must be read-write.
Ddl_system	File must be a system file.

A string can be inserted at a particular position in a list box by using the *insert_string_at* routine. This routine takes the string to insert and a zero-based position. The string is inserted at the specified position.

Removing Text Strings from a List Box

Removing strings from a list box can be performed by simply calling *delete_string* and specifying the zero-based index of the string to remove. If all strings are to be removed, then *reset_content* can be called.

```
delete_string (index: INTEGER)
       -- Delete the item at the zero-based 'index'
    require
        exists: exists;
        index_large_enough: index >= 0;
        index_small_enough: index < count
    ensure
        count_decreased: count = old count - 1

reset_content
       -- Reset the content of the list.
    require
        exists: exists
    ensure
        empty: count = 0
```

Accessing Text Strings in a List Box

The strings a list box contains can be accessed in different ways. You can access a particular item, find the length of an item, determine the total number of items that the list box holds, and retrieve an *ARRAY* containing references to all of the items. The features *i_th_text, i_th_text_length, count,* and *strings* provide this functionality, respectively.

```
i_th_text (i: INTEGER): STRING
       -- Text at the zero-based index 'i'
    require
        exists: exists;
        i_large_enough: i >= 0;
        i_small_enough: i < count
    ensure
        result_exists: Result /= void;
        same_result_as_strings: Result.is_equal (strings.item (i))

i_th_text_length (i: INTEGER): INTEGER
```

```
                -- Length text at the zero-based index 'i'
        require
            exists: exists;
            i_large_enough: i >= 0;
            i_small_enough: i < count
        ensure
            positive_result: Result >= 0;
            same_result_as_strings: Result = strings.item (i).count

strings: ARRAY [STRING]
                -- Strings contained in the list box
        require
            exists: exists
        ensure
            result_not_void: Result /= void;
            count_ok: Result.count = count
count: INTEGER
                -- Number of lines
        require
            exists: exists
        ensure
            positive_result: Result >= 0
```

Selecting Text Strings in a List Box

The user typically selects items in a list box by clicking (or control-clicking) on the item's position. You can determine whether an item is currently selected by calling *is_selected* or *selected*. In addition, you can programmatically select items by calling *select_item*, specifying the index position of the item to select.

```
is_selected (index: INTEGER): BOOLEAN
            -- Is item at position `index' selected?
        require
            exists: exists;
            index_large_enough: index >= 0;
            index_small_enough: index < count

selected: BOOLEAN
            -- Is an item selected?
        require
            exists: exists

select_item (index: INTEGER)
            -- Select item at the zero-based `index'.
        require
            exists: exists;
            index_small_enough: index < count;
```

```
        index_large_enough: index >= 0
    ensure
        is_selected: is_selected (index)

top_index: INTEGER
        -- Index of the first visible item
    require
        exists: exists
    ensure
        result_large_enough: Result >= 0;
        result_small_enough: Result <= count

set_top_index (index: INTEGER)
        -- Ensure that the zero-based 'index'
        -- in the list box is visible.
    require
        exists: exists;
        index_large_enough: index >= 0;
        index_small_enough: index < count
    ensure
        top_index_set: top_index = index
```

If a list box has more items than can be displayed in its client area, then a scroll bar is added to the control to allow the user to scroll through items that are not displayed. The user has control over which items are currently visible, but you can also change the view by specifying which item should appear at the top of the client area. *set_top_index* ensures that the specified item is visible in the client area. You can also determine which item is currently at the top of the viewable area by calling the function *top_index*.

Searching for Strings in a List Box

Two functions, *find_string* and *find_string_exact,* can be used to implement search functionality for the users of your applications. *find_string* locates the first list box item that begins with the specified string. Function *find_string_exact* locates an exact string in the list box. Both functions start searching from the item *following* the specified index, and return the index position of the first match or, if the string is not found, −1.

```
find_string (index: INTEGER; a_string: STRING): INTEGER
        -- Find the first string that contains the
        -- prefix 'a_string'. 'index' specifies the
        -- zero-based index of the item before the first
        -- item to be searched.
        -- Returns -1 if the search was unsuccessful.
```

```
    require
        exists: exists;
        index_large_enough: index >= 0;
        index_small_enough: index < count;
        a_string_not_void: a_string /= void
find_string_exact (index: INTEGER; a_string: STRING): INTEGER
            -- Find the first string that matches 'a_string'.
            -- 'index' specifies the zero-based index of the
            -- item before the first item to be searched.
            -- Returns -1 if the search was unsuccessful.
    require
        exists: exists;
        index_large_enough: index >= 0;
        index_small_enough: index < count;
        a_string_not_void: a_string /= void
```

Setting Scrolling Properties in a List Box

A horizontal scroll bar is automatically added to a list box when the length of a list box item is wider than the list box's client area. The user then has the ability to scroll left and right over the wide list items. The extent that a list box can be scrolled horizontally can be controlled by setting the *horizontal_extent* with a call to *set_horizontal_extent*. This procedure sets the width, in pixels, by which the list box can be scrolled horizontally.

```
horizontal_extent: INTEGER
        -- Width, in pixels, by which the list box can be
        -- scrolled horizontally
    require
        exists: exists;
        has_horizontal_scroll_bar: has_horizontal_scroll_bar
    ensure
        positive_result: Result >= 0

set_horizontal_extent (a_width: INTEGER)
        -- Set the width, in pixels, by which a list box can
        -- be scrolled horizontally.
    require
        exists: exists;
        positive_width: width >= 0
    ensure
        horizontal_extent_set: horizontal_extent = a_width
```

Message Hooks in a List Box

Table 14.2 lists the message hooks provided by the *WEL_LIST_BOX* class. Each of these hooks can be used to capture and process list box messages such as double-click events, selection of items, and focus events.

TABLE 14.2   *List Box Message Hooks*

MESSAGE HOOKS	DESCRIPTION
on_lbn_dblclk	A string in the list box has been double-clicked.
on_lbn_errspace	Error allocating memory for the operation.
on_lbn_killfocus	The list box is about to lose focus.
on_lbn_selcancel	The selection has been canceled.
on_lbn_selchange	The selection has been changed.
on_lbn_setfocus	The list box is about to receive focus.

On a List Box Double-Click Message

If a user double-clicks an item in a list box, the *on_lbn_dblclk* message hook is called. Once this message hook has been called, you can determine the item that was selected and perform any appropriate action. See the sections "Accessing Selected Items in a Single Selection List Box" and "Accessing Selected Items in a Multiple Selection List Box" in this chapter for details on determining which item(s) are selected in a list box.

```
on_lbn_dblclk
        -- Double click on a string
    require
        exists: exists
```

On a List Box Error Space Message

The memory needed to store list box items is allocated dynamically at runtime. If the Win32 library finds that it cannot allocate enough memory, then it will send an *Lbn_errspace* message, causing the *on_lbn_errspace* message hook to be executed.

```
on_lbn_errspace
        -- Cannot allocate enough memory
        -- to meet a specific request
    require
        exists: exists
```

On a List Box Set Focus Message

When a list box receives the input focus, Windows sends the *Lbn_setfocus* message to the control. The message hook *on_lbn_setfocus* can be used to process this event.

```
on_lbn_setfocus
        -- Receive the keyboard focus
    require
        exists: exists
```

On a List Box Kill Focus Message

Similarly, if the control loses the input focus, the message *Lbn_killfocus* is sent and the message hook *on_lbn_killfocus* is called.

```
on_lbn_killfocus
        -- Lose the keyboard focus
    require
        exists: exists
```

On a List Box Selection Canceled Message

When a user cancels a selection, the message hook *on_lbn_selcancel* is called. This message hook (in addition to *on_lbn_selchange,* shown next) can be used to detect changes in the user's selection of list items.

This is useful when you want to change that status of other controls, depending on whether a list item is selected or not.

```
on_lbn_selcancel
        -- Cancel the selection
    require
        exists: exists
```

On a List Box Selection Changed Message

Whenever the selected items in a list box change, due to programmatic or user control, the message *Lbn_selchange* is sent, causing the *on_lbn_selchange* message hook to be invoked.

```
on_lbn_selchange
        -- The selection is about to change
    require
        exists: exists
```

Single-Selection List Box

The single-selection list box presents the user with a list of items of which only one may be selected at one time. The class *WEL_SINGLE_SELEC-TION_LIST_BOX* provides the interface for creating such a control.

Creating a Single-Selection List Box

A single-selection list box can be created like any other control, using the creation procedures *make* or *make_by_id*. Example 14.1 demonstrates the use of a single-selection list box. The example displays a window with a list box, a menu bar, and a single push button. The menu bar provides options for adding an item to the list and removing an item from the list. The push button displays a dialog box containing statistical information, such as how many items the list contains, the length of the first item, whether an item is selected, and if so, what the value of the selected item is. The shaded lines in Example 14.1 show the Eiffel code used to manipulate the list box.

Figure 14.2 shows the example running after adding a number of names to the list, selecting an item, and pressing the Info button.

Example 14.1 Single-Selection List Box Example, MAIN_WINDOW Class (listbox\single)

```
class MAIN_WINDOW
inherit
    WEL_FRAME_WINDOW
        redefine
            on_menu_command, on_control_command
        end
    APPLICATION_IDS
        export
            {NONE} all
        end
creation
    make
feature
    make is
            -- Initialize the main window
    local
        menu_init_command: INITIALIZE_MENU_COMMAND
    do
        make_top ("Main Window")
        -- Add CEC command to initialize the popupmenu when it appears
        enable_commands
        create menu_init_command.make (main_menu, Current)
```

```
        put_command (menu_init_command, Wm_initmenupopup, Current)
        -- add the menu and controls to the window
        set_menu (main_menu)
        resize (340, 270)
        create static1.make (Current, "Single Selection List box", 10, 5, 300, 15, -1)
        create list_box.make (Current, 10, 20, 300, 150, -1)
        create info_button.make (Current, "Info", 10, 180, 70, 30, -1)
        -- initialize the dialog
        create info_dialog.make (Current)
        create add_dialog.make (Current)
    end

static1: WEL_STATIC
        -- Static text label
list_box: WEL_SINGLE_SELECTION_LIST_BOX
        -- Single selection list box control
info_button: WEL_PUSH_BUTTON
        -- Push button for text box information
info_dialog: IDD_INFO_DIALOG
        -- List box information dialog
add_dialog: IDD_ADD_DIALOG
        -- Add line dialog
on_menu_command (menu_id: INTEGER) is
        -- Check for a menu command
    do
        inspect menu_id
        when Id_fileexit_constant then
            destroy
        when Id_editadd_constant then
            add_list_line
        when Id_editdelete_constant then
            delete_list_line
        when Id_listgototop_constant then
            if list_box.count > 0 then
                list_box.set_top_index (0)
            end
        when Id_listgotoend_constant then
            if list_box.count > 0 then
                list_box.set_top_index (list_box.count)
            end
        else
            -- ignore
        end
    end

on_control_command (control: WEL_CONTROL) is
        -- Handle control commands
    do
        if control = info_button then
            info_dialog.set_info_text (get_text_info)
```

```
                    info_dialog.activate
            end
        end
feature {NONE} -- Implementation
    add_list_line is
            -- Prompt the user for a text line to add to the listbox
        do
            add_dialog.set_list (list_box)
            add_dialog.activate
        end
    delete_list_line is
            -- Delete the selected list line
        require
            list_box.selected
        do
            list_box.delete_string (list_box.selected_item)
        end
    main_menu: WEL_MENU is
            -- Main menu created from a menu resource
        once
            create Result.make_by_id (Id_mainmenu_constant)
        end
    get_text_info: STRING is
            -- Return a string representation of the text box
            -- information.
        do
            create Result.make (100)
            Result.append_string ("count: ")
            Result.append_integer (list_box.count)
            Result.append_string ("%N%Ri_th_text (list_box.count): ")
            Result.append_string (list_box.i_th_text (list_box.count))
            Result.append_string ("%R%Ni_th_text_length (list_box.count: ")
            Result.append_integer (list_box.i_th_text_length (list_box.count))
            Result.append_string ("%N%Rselected: ")
            Result.append_boolean (list_box.selected)
            if list_box.selected then

                Result.append_string ("%R%Nselected_string: ")
                Result.append_string (list_box.selected_string)
            end
        end
end -- class MAIN_WINDOW
```

Selecting Items in a Single-Selection List Box

As its name suggests, a single-selection list box allows only one item to be selected at a time. The routine *select_item* allows you to select a particular item by specifying its zero-based index. The message hook *on_lbn_selchange* is called as a side effect of this routine.

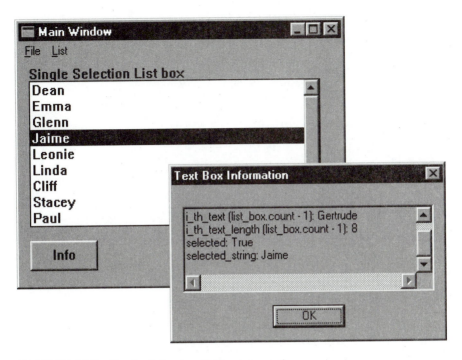

FIGURE 14.2. Single-Selection list box example.

You can also unselect any item that is currently selected by calling *unselect*. If no item is selected at the time of the call, then this routine has no effect. *on_lbn_selchange* is also invoked as a result of this routine.

```
select_item (index: INTEGER)
        -- Select item at the zero-based 'index'.
    ensure
        selected: selected;
        selected_item: selected_item = index;
        selected_string: strings.item (index).is_equal
        (selected_string)

unselect
        -- Unselect the selected item.
    require
        exists: exists
    ensure
        unselected: not selected
```

Accessing Selected Items in a Single-Selection List Box

The example above determined if an item was selected by calling the *selected* function. A result of *True* indicates that an item is currently selected. Once this has been determined, you can retrieve the index of the selected item by calling the function *selected_index,* or you can retrieve the value of the item by calling *selected_string.*

```
selected: BOOLEAN
        -- Is an item selected?

selected_item: INTEGER
        -- Zero-based index of the selected item
    require
        exists: exists;
        selected: selected
    ensure
        result_large_enough: Result >= 0;
        result_small_enough: Result < count

selected_string: STRING
        -- Selected string
    require
        exists: exists;
        selected: selected
    ensure
        result_not_void: Result /= void
```

Multiple-Selection List Box

A multiple-selection list box allows more than one item to be selected at a time. A user can select multiple items by either shift-clicking a range or control-clicking on specific items. The features of *WEL_MULTIPLE_SELEC-TION_LIST* differ from the single-selection form by providing the ability to select multiple items and retrieve the collection of selected items.

Creating a Multiple-Selection List Box

Creating a multiple-selection list box is identical to creating a single-selection type list box. Example 14.2 is very similar to the previous example, only a multiple-selection list box is used rather than a single selection list box. The menu items have been modified to represent multiple-selection operations, such as select all items and delete all selected items. The shaded lines of code highlight the changes from the previous example.

Example 14.2 Multiple-Selection List Box Example, MAIN_WINDOW Class (listbox\multiple)

```
class MAIN_WINDOW
inherit
```

```
        WEL_FRAME_WINDOW
            redefine
                on_menu_command, on_control_command
            end
        APPLICATION_IDS
            export
                {NONE} all
            end
creation
        make
feature
        make is
                -- Initialize the main window
            local
                menu_init_command: INITIALIZE_MENU_COMMAND
            do
                make_top ("Main Window")
                -- Add CEC command to initialize the popupmenu when it
                -- appears
                enable_commands
                create menu_init_command.make (main_menu, Current)
                put_command (menu_init_command, Wm_initmenupopup,
                    Current)
                -- add the menu and controls to the window
                set_menu (main_menu)
                resize (340, 270)
                create static1.make (Current,
                    "Multiple Selection List box", 10, 5, 300, 15, -1)
                create list_box.make (Current, 10, 20, 300, 150, -1)
                create info_button.make (Current, "Info", 10, 180, 70,
                    30, -1)
                -- initialize the dialog
                create info_dialog.make (Current)
                create add_dialog.make (Current)
            end
        static1: WEL_STATIC
                -- Static text label
        list_box: WEL_MULTIPLE_SELECTION_LIST_BOX
                -- Multiple selection list box control
        info_button: WEL_PUSH_BUTTON
                -- Push button for text box information
        info_dialog: IDD_INFO_DIALOG
                -- List box information dialog
        add_dialog: IDD_ADD_DIALOG
                -- Add line dialog
        on_menu_command (menu_id: INTEGER) is
                -- Check for a menu command
            do
                inspect menu_id
                when Id_fileexit_constant then
                    destroy
                when Id_editadd_constant then
```

```
                add_list_line
            when Id_editdelete_constant then
                delete_list_line
            when Id_listselectall_constant then
                list_box.select_all
            when Id_listunselect_constant then
                list_box.unselect_all
            else
                -- ignore
            end
        end
    on_control_command (control: WEL_CONTROL) is
            -- Handle control commands
        do
            if control = info_button then
                info_dialog.set_info_text (get_text_info)
                info_dialog.activate
            end
        end
feature {NONE} -- Implementation
    add_list_line is
            -- Prompt the user for a text line to add to the listbox
        do
            add_dialog.set_list (list_box)
            add_dialog.activate
        end
    delete_list_line is
            -- Delete the selected list line
        require
            list_box.selected
        local
            index: INTEGER
            items: ARRAY [INTEGER]
        do
            from
                items := list_box.selected_items
                index := items.lower
            until
                index > items.upper
            loop
                list_box.delete_string (items.item (index))
                index := index + 1
            end
        end
    main_menu: WEL_MENU is
            -- Main menu created from a menu resource
        once
            create Result.make_by_id (Id_mainmenu_constant)
        end
    get_text_info: STRING is
            -- Return a string representation of the text box
```

```
              -- information.
      local
              index: INTEGER
              strings: ARRAY [STRING]
      do
              create Result.make (100)
              Result.append_string ("count: ")
              Result.append_integer (list_box.count)
              if list_box.count > 0 then
                  Result.append_string ("%R%Ni_th_text (list_box.count -
                      1): ")
                  Result.append_string (list_box.i_th_text
                      (list_box.count - 1))
                  Result.append_string ("%R%Ni_th_text_length
                      (list_box.count - 1): ")
                  Result.append_integer (list_box.i_th_text_length
                      (list_box.count - 1))
              end
              Result.append_string ("%R%Nselected: ")
              Result.append_boolean (list_box.selected)
              if list_box.selected then
                  Result.append_string ("%R%Nselected_strings: ")
                  from
                          strings := list_box.selected_strings
                          index := strings.lower
                  until
                          index > strings.upper
                  loop
                          Result.append_string ("%R%N%T")
                          Result.append_string (strings.item (index))
                          index := index + 1
                  end
              end
      end
end -- class MAIN_WINDOW
```

Figure 14.3 shows the example running with multiple items selected and their values displayed in the information dialog.

Selecting Items in a Multiple-Selection List Box

In contrast to the single-selection list box, the selection features of a multiple-selection list box allow you to manipulate more than one item. Feature *select_all* selects all of the items in a list box, and *select_items* selects a range of

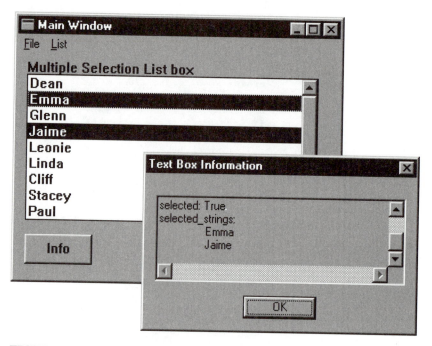

FIGURE 14.3. Multiple-Selection list box example.

items between two zero-based indexes. The routine *select_item* is identical to
the single-selection version.

```
select_all
        -- Select all items.
    require
        exists: exists
    ensure
        all_selected: count_selected_items = count

select_item (index: INTEGER)
        -- Select item at the zero-based 'index'.

select_items (start_index, end_index: INTEGER)
        -- Select items between 'start_index'
        -- and 'end_index' (zero-based index).
        -- For every 'i' in 'start_index'..'end_index',
        -- 'is_selected' ('i') = True
    require
        exists: exists;
        valid_range: end_index >= start_index;
        start_index_small_enough: start_index < count;
```

```
      start_index_large_enough: start_index >= 0;
      end_index_small_enough: end_index < count;
      end_index_large_enough: end_index >= 0;
      valid_range: end_index >= start_index
   ensure
      selected: selected
```

A matching group of features allows you to unselect all items *(unselect_all)*, a specific item *(unselect_item)*, or a range of items *(unselect_items)*.

```
unselect_all
      -- Unselect all the selected items.
   require
      exists: exists
   ensure
      all_unselected: count_selected_items = 0

unselect_item (index: INTEGER)
      -- Unselect item at the zero-based 'index'.
   require
      exists: exists;
      index_small_enough: index < count;
      index_large_enough: index >= 0
   ensure
      is_not_selected: not is_selected (index)

unselect_items (start_index, end_index: INTEGER)
      -- Unselect items between 'start_index'
      -- and 'end_index' (zero-based index).
      -- For every 'i' in 'start_index'..'end_index',
      -- 'is_selected' ('i') = False
   require
      exists: exists;
      valid_range: end_index >= start_index;
      start_index_small_enough: start_index < count;
      start_index_large_enough: start_index >= 0;
      end_index_small_enough: end_index < count;
      end_index_large_enough: end_index >= 0;
      valid_range: end_index >= start_index
```

Accessing Selected Items in a Multiple-Selection List Box

The *selected* function returns *True* if at least one item is selected in the list box. Once it has been determined that at least one item is selected, the item values can be accessed via an *ARRAY* with a call to *selected_strings*. The number of selected items can be determined by querying the count of *selected_strings* or by calling *count_selected_items*.

```
selected: BOOLEAN
        -- Is at least one item selected? selected_items: ARRAY
        -- [INTEGER]
        -- Contains all the selected index
    require
        exits: exists
    ensure
        result_not_void: Result /= void;
        count_ok: Result.count = count_selected_items

selected_strings: ARRAY [STRING]
        -- Contains all the selected strings
    require
        exits: exists
    ensure
        result_not_void: Result /= void;
        count_ok: Result.count = count_selected_items

count_selected_items: INTEGER
        -- Number of items selected
    require
        exits: exists
    ensure
        result_large_enough: Result >= 0;
        result_small_enough: Result <= count
```

Manipulating the Text Caret in a Multiple-Selection List Box

A list item will have input focus if the user has clicked the item to either select or deselect it. The item that currently has input focus can be determined by calling *caret_index,* which returns the index of the item. You can programmatically change the input focus by calling *set_caret_index.* This also has the side effect of making the newly focused item visible.

```
caret_index: INTEGER
        -- Index of the item that has the focus
    require
        exists: exists

set_caret_index (index: INTEGER; scrolling: BOOLEAN)
        -- Set the focus rectangle to the item at the
        -- specified zero-based 'index'. If 'scrolling' is
        -- True the item is scrolled until it is at least
        -- partially visible, otherwise the item is scrolled
        -- until it is fully visible.
    require
        exists: exists;
        index_small_enough: index < count;
        index_large_enough: index >= 0
    ensure
        caret_index_set: caret_index = index
```

List View Control

The *WEL_LIST_VIEW* class provides an encapsulation of the Windows list view control. The default layout of the class uses the report window style, which displays each item in a single row, with columns for row details. The *WEL_LIST_VIEW* class can be used to display tabular information, such as lists of user accounts or stock prices. Our example application uses a list view to display directory size information. See "Implementing List Controls" in this chapter.

Creating a List View Control

A list view control is created in the standard manner, either by creating one directly with a call to *make* or indirectly from a resource with a call to *make_by_id*.

```
make (a_parent: WEL_WINDOW; a_x, a_y, a_width, a_height, an_id:
    INTEGER)
  require
      a_parent_not_void: a_parent /= void
  ensure
      exists: exists;
      parent_set: parent = a_parent;
      id_set: id = an_id

make_by_id (a_parent: WEL_DIALOG; an_id: INTEGER)
      -- (from WEL_CONTROL)
  require -- from WEL_CONTROL
      a_parent_not_void: a_parent /= void;
      positive_id: an_id > 0
  ensure -- from WEL_CONTROL
      parent_set: parent = a_parent;
      id_set: id = an_id
```

Adding Columns to a List View Control

The report list view style allows you to add any number of columns to represent detailed information about your list items. To add a column to a list view, you first need to create an instance of *WEL_LIST_VIEW_COLUMN*, which defines how each column will be formatted, its title, and its initial width. The class interface for *WEL_LIST_VIEW_COLUMN* is shown next.

```
class interface
    WEL_LIST_VIEW_COLUMN

creation
    make,
```

```
        make_by_pointer,
        make_with_attributes

feature -- Initialization

    make
                -- Make a list view column structure

    make_with_attributes (a_mask, a_cx, a_fmt: INTEGER; a_text:
        STRING)
                -- Make a list view column structure with the given
                -- attributes.

feature -- Access

    cx: INTEGER
                -- Specifies the width, in pixel, of the column
        ensure
                positive_result: Result >= 0

    fmt: INTEGER
                -- Specifies the alignment of the column
                -- See class WEL_LVCF_CONSTANTS.
        ensure
                valid_result: valid_lvcfmt_constant (Result)

    mask: INTEGER
                -- Array of flags that indicate which of the other
                -- structure members contain valid data or which are
                -- to be filled in. This member can be a combination
                -- of the Lvcf_* values.
                -- See class WEL_LVCF_CONSTANTS.

    text: STRING
                -- Title of the column
        ensure
                result_not_void: Result /= void
feature -- Element change

    set_cx (a_cx: INTEGER)
                -- Set 'cx' with 'a_cx'.
        require
                positive_cx: a_cx >= 0
        ensure
                cx_set: cx = a_cx
    set_fmt (a_fmt: INTEGER)
                -- Set 'fmt' with 'a_fmt'.
        require
                valid_fmt: valid_lvcfmt_constant (a_fmt)
        ensure
                fmt_set: fmt = a_fmt
    set_mask (a_mask: INTEGER)
```

```
                    -- Set 'mask' with 'a_mask'.
        ensure
                mask_set: mask = a_mask
    set_text (a_text: STRING)
                -- Set 'text' with 'a_text'.
        require
                a_text_not_void: a_text /= void
        ensure
                text_set: text.is_equal (a_text)

end -- class WEL_LIST_VIEW_COLUMN
```

The easiest way to create a list view column is to call *make_with_attributes,* specifying the attribute mask, width, format, and title. The attribute mask should be a combination of one or more *Lvcf_* constants, as listed in Table 14.3. The format can be one of *Lcvfmt_center, Lcvfmt_left,* or *Lcvf_right,* representing a centered, left-justified, or right-justified title, and the title can be any *STRING* value.

Each *WEL_LIST_VIEW_COLUMN* instance then needs to be added to the list view. If you need to append a column to the right side of a list view, use *append_column.* To prepend to the left side of the list view, use *prepend_column.* And to insert a column at a particular position, use *insert_column,* specifying the zero-based position that the column will occupy.

TABLE 14.3 *List View Column Flag and Format Constants (WEL_LVCF_CONSTANTS)*

CONSTANT	DESCRIPTION
Lvcf_fmt	The *fmt* attribute is valid.
Lvcf_image	The *image* attribute is valid.
Lvcf_subitem	The *sub* item attribute is valid.
Lvcf_text	The *text* attribute is valid.
Lvcf_width	The *width* attribute is valid.
Lvcfmt_center	Center-align the column. This flag should not be used for the first column of the list view, which should always be left-aligned.
Lvcfmt_justifymask	Justify the column. Do not use for the first column of the list view.
Lvcfmt_left	Left-align the column.
Lvcfmt_right	Right-align the column. Do not use for the first column of the list view.

```
append_column (column: WEL_LIST_VIEW_COLUMN)
      -- Append 'column' to the list view.
   require
      exists: exists
   ensure
      new_column_count: column_count = old column_count + 1

insert_column (column: WEL_LIST_VIEW_COLUMN; index: INTEGER)
      -- Insert 'column' at the zero-based `index'.
   require
      exists: exists;
      index_large_enough: index >= 0;
      index_small_enough: index <= column_count
   ensure
      new_column_count: column_count = old column_count + 1

prepend_column (column: WEL_LIST_VIEW_COLUMN)
      -- Prepend 'column' to the list view.
   require
      exists: exists
   ensure
      new_column_count: column_count = old column_count + 1
```

Removing Columns from a List View Control

A column can be removed from a list view by specifying its zero-based position in a call to *delete_column*.

```
delete_column (index: INTEGER)
      -- Remove the zero-based 'index'-th column of the list view.
   require
      exists: exists;
      index_large_enough: index >= 0;
      index_small_enough: index < column_count
   ensure
      new_column_count: column_count = old column_count - 1
```

Formatting Columns in a List View Control

If you need to change the format of a column after it has been added to a list view, you can use the routine *set_column_format.* For example, to change the second column's format to left-justified, you could use the call

```
list_view.set_column_format(1, Lvcfmt_left)
```

```
set_column_format (index: INTEGER; fmt: INTEGER)
        -- Set the alignment of the column, cannot be used for
        -- the first column that must be left aligned.
    require
        exists: exists;
        index_large_enough: index > 0;
        index_small_enough: index < column_count;
        good_format: valid_lvcfmt_constant (fmt)
```

Similarly, the title and width of columns can be modified using the calls *set_column_title* and *set_column_width*. Both take the zero-based position of the column and the new attribute value.

```
set_column_title (txt: STRING; index: INTEGER)
        -- Make 'txt' the new title of the 'index'-th column.
    require
        exists: exists;
        index_large_enough: index >= 0;
        index_small_enough: index < column_count

set_column_width (value, index: INTEGER)
        -- Make 'value' the new width of the zero-base 'index'-th
        -- column.
    require
        exists: exists;
        index_large_enough: index >= 0;
        index_small_enough: index < column_count
```

Retrieving Column Information from a List View Control

The number of columns in a list view is accessible via the function *column_count*. In addition, you can get the current width of a particular column with the function *get_column_width*.

```
column_count: INTEGER
            - Number of columns

get_column_width (index: INTEGER): INTEGER
            - Width of the zero-based 'index'-th item.
        require
            exists: exists;
            index_large_enough: index >= 0;
            index_small_enough: index < column_count
```

Adding Items to a List View Control

Each item you add to a list box must be represented by an instance of *WEL_LIST_VIEW_ITEM*. This class holds information about each item, including the text, index position, image, subitem index, and current state. The *iitem* attribute represents the zero-based index of the item, and the *isubitem* attribute, if set to something other than zero, is the one-based index of the subitem. Each subitem represents information that will appear in a column next to the item in the report view. The class interface of *WEL_LIST_VIEW_ITEM* is shown next.

The *lparam* attribute can be used to hold any application-specific *INTEGER* value related to the item.

```
class interface
    WEL_LIST_VIEW_ITEM
creation
    make,
    make_by_pointer,
    make_with_attributes
feature -- Access

    iimage: INTEGER
            -- Index of the icon.

    iitem: INTEGER
            -- Index of the row of the item.

    isubitem: INTEGER
            -- Index of the item in his row. 0 if it is an item and not a
            -- subitem.

    lparam: INTEGER
            -- User parameter.

    mask: INTEGER
            -- Array of flags that indicate which of the other
            -- structure members contain valid data or which are
            -- to be filled in. This member can be a combination
            -- of the Lvif_* values.
            -- See class WEL_LVIF_CONSTANTS.

    state: INTEGER
            - Current state of the item.

    text: STRING
            -- Text of the item
        ensure
```

```
                    result_not_void: Result /= void
feature -- Element change

    set_iimage (value: INTEGER)
                -- Set 'iimage' with 'value'.
        ensure
            iimage_set: iimage = value

    set_iitem (value: INTEGER)
                -- Set 'iitem' with 'value'.
        ensure
            iitem_set: iitem = value

    set_isubitem (value: INTEGER)
                -- Set 'isubitem' with 'value'.
        ensure
            isubitem_set: isubitem = value

    set_mask (value: INTEGER)
                -- Set 'mask' with 'value'.
        ensure
            mask_set: mask = value

    set_state (value: INTEGER)
                -- Set 'state' with 'value'.
        ensure
            state_set: state = value

    set_text (a_text: STRING)
                -- Set 'text' with 'a_text'.
        require
            a_text_not_void: a_text /= void
        ensure
            text_set: text.is_equal (a_text)

end -- class WEL_LIST_VIEW_ITEM
```

The *mask* attribute can take a combination of the constant values found in *WEL_LVIF_CONSTANTS*, listed in Table 14.4. Each constant notifies Windows of which attributes in the *WEL_LIST_VIEW_ITEM* structure are to be used.

TABLE 14.4   *List View Item Flag Constants (WEL_LVIF_CONSTANTS)*

CONSTANT	DESCRIPTION
Lvif_image	The image attribute is valid.
Lvid_param	The param attribute is valid.
Lvif_state	The state attribute is valid.
Lvif_text	The text attribute is valid.

The *istate* variable can be one of the constant values listed in Table 14.5. Each represents one of the states that a list view item can be in, such as having the input focus, performing a cut and paste operation, or performing a drag-and drop-operation.

Each *WEL_LIST_VIEW_ITEM* must be passed to the list view via a call to *insert_item*. Windows uses the information in the item structure and updates the appropriate list view item or subitem.

```
insert_item (an_item: WEL_LIST_VIEW_ITEM)
        -- Insert 'item' in the list view. The zero-based position
        -- of the item is
        -- given by the 'iitem' attribute of the item.
    require
        exists: exists;
        index_large_enough: an_item.iitem >= 0;
        index_small_enough: an_item.iitem <= count
    ensure
        new_count: count = old count + 1
```

You can optimize the addition of many list view items by calling *set_item_count*. This allows the list view control to reallocate its internal list item data structures once, rather than multiple times.

```
set_item_count (value: INTEGER)
        -- Prepares a list view control for adding a large number
        -- of items and make it then faster.
    require
        exists: exists;
        value_big_enough: value >= 0
```

TABLE 14.5   *List View Item State Constants (WEL_LVIS_CONSTANTS)*

CONSTANT	DESCRIPTION
Lvis_cut	The item is marked for a cut and paste operation.
Lvis_drophilited	The item is highlighted as a drag-and-drop target.
Lvis_focuses	The item has the focus.
Lvis_selected	The item is selected.

Removing Items from a List View Control

An item, including all of its subitems, can be removed from a list view control by calling *delete_item* and passing its zero-based index.

```
delete_item (index: INTEGER)
        — Remove the zero-based 'index'-th item of the list view.
    require
        exists: exists;
        index_large_enough: index >= 0;
        index_small_enough: index < count
    ensure
        new_count: count = old count - 1
```

To remove all items in a list view, call *reset_content*.

```
reset_content
        -- Reset the content of the list.
    require
        exists: exists
    ensure
        new_count: count = 0
```

Associating an Image List with a List View Control

Each list view can have an image list registered for small and large icons. Two operations are available to register image lists with a list view: *set_image_list* and *set_small_image_list*. Both features take either a *WEL_IMAGE_LIST* object or *Void* as a parameter. If *Void* is passed, then the image list currently registered for that type of image list will be removed.

```
set_image_list (an_imagelist: WEL_IMAGE_LIST)
        -- Set the current "large" image list to 'an_imagelist'.
        -- If 'an_imagelist' is set to Void, it removes
        -- the current associated image list (if any).

set_small_image_list (an_imagelist: WEL_IMAGE_LIST)
        -- Set the current "small" image list to 'an_imagelist'.
        -- If 'an_imagelist' is set to Void, it removes
        -- the current associated image list (if any).
```

An image list is a collection of icons or bitmaps of the same size. The list is used to efficiently manage large collections of icons or images. All of the icons within an image list must be the same size and color depth. An image list stores all of its images in one contiguous area of memory and accesses images via an index.

The class interface for *WEL_IMAGE_LIST* is shown next.

```
class interface
    WEL_IMAGE_LIST

create
    make,
    make_by_pointer

feature -- Initialization

    make (given_width: INTEGER; given_height: INTEGER;
        image_type: INTEGER)
            -- Initialization with an empty image_list. Images located
            -- in this image_list must have the a width equal to
            -- 'given_width'
            -- and a height equal to 'given_height'.
            -- The flag 'image_type' determines the color depth of
            -- the bitmaps.
            -- (bitmaps with a different color depth than indicated in
            -- 'image_type' will automatically be converted)

feature -- Access

    last_position: INTEGER
            -- Position of last image inserted/deleted.
            -- updated by 'add_image'.

feature -- Status report

    bitmaps_height: INTEGER
            -- height of all bitmaps located in this image_list

    bitmaps_width: INTEGER
            -- width of all bitmaps located in this imageList

    get_background_color: WEL_COLOR_REF
            -- Retrieves the current background color for this
            -- image list.
        ensure
            result_not_void: Result /= void

feature -- Basic operations

    add_bitmap (bitmap_to_add: WEL_BITMAP)
```

```
                         -- Add the bitmap 'bitmap_to_add' into the image list.
        require
             bitmap_not_void: bitmap_to_add /= void;
             compatible_width_for_bitmap: bitmap_to_add.width =
                 bitmaps_width;
             compatible_height_for_bitmap: bitmap_to_add.height =
                 bitmaps_height

    add_color_masked_bitmap (bitmap_to_add: WEL_BITMAP;
        mask_color: WEL_COLOR_REF)
                         -- Add the bitmap 'bitmap_to_add' into the image list.
                         -- 'mask_color' represents the color used to generate the mask.
                         -- Each pixel of this color in the specified bitmap is
                         -- changed to black and the corresponding bit in the
                         -- mask is set to 1.
                         -- Note: Bitmaps with color depth greater than 8bpp
                         -- are not supported
        require
             bitmap_not_void: bitmap_to_add /= void;
             mask_color_not_void: mask_color /= void;
             compatible_width_for_bitmap: bitmap_to_add.width =
                 bitmaps_width;
             compatible_height_for_bitmap: bitmap_to_add.height =
                 bitmaps_height

    add_icon (icon_to_add: WEL_ICON)
                         -- Adds the icon or cursor 'icon_to_add' to this image list
        require
             icon_not_void: icon_to_add /= void

    add_masked_bitmap (bitmap_to_add: WEL_BITMAP;
        bitmap_mask: WEL_BITMAP)
                         -- Add the bitmap 'bitmap_to_add' into the image list.
                         -- 'bitmap_mask' represents the mask for the bitmap.
        require
             bitmap_not_void: bitmap_to_add /= void;
             mask_not_void: bitmap_mask /= void;
             compatible_width_for_bitmap: bitmap_to_add.width =
                 bitmaps_width;
             compatible_height_for_bitmap: bitmap_to_add.height =
                 bitmaps_height;
             compatible_width_for_mask: bitmap_mask.width =
                 bitmaps_width;
             compatible_height_for_mask: bitmap_mask.height =
                 bitmaps_height

    set_background_color (new_color: WEL_COLOR_REF)
                         -- Sets the background color for this image list.
        require
             new_color_not_void: new_color /= void

end -- class WEL_IMAGE_LIST
```

When creating an image list, you must specify the width, height, and color depth of the images that it will contain. The type of image should be defined by one of the constant values found in *WEL_ILC_CONSTANTS,* listed in Table 14.6. You can then add either icons or bitmaps with the correct dimensions and color depth to the list, using *add_bitmap* or *add_icon.* A masked bitmap can also be added to the list, using the features *add_masked_bitmap* or *add_color_masked_bitmap.* The *add_color_masked_bitmap* feature can be used to generate a mask for a bitmap from a specified color.

Once an image list has been registered with the control, the *iimage* attribute of *WEL_LIST_VIEW_ITEM* can reference an image using its zero-based index. If you register both a large and small image list, you should ensure that the small and large images for each item are placed at the same index position.

Updating Items in a List View Control

Once an item has been added to a list view, you can modify its text and state with the features *set_cell_text* and *set_item_state.* Both features take a zero-based index representing the position of the item and the new attribute value.

TABLE 14.6   *Image List Color Constants (WEL_ILC_CONSTANTS)*

CONSTANT	DESCRIPTION
Ilc_color	Default color behaviour. For most display drivers use *Ilc_color4,* but for older drivers use *Ilc_colordb.*
Ilc_color16	Use a 16-bit (32/64K-color) device-independent bitmap (DIB) section as the bitmap for the image list.
Ilc_color24	Use a 24-bit DIB section.
Ilc_color32	Use a 32-bit DIB section.
Ilc_color4	Use a 4-bit (16-color) DIB section.
Ilc_color8	Use an 8-bit DIB section. The colors used for the color table are the same colors as the halftone palette.
Ilc_colorddb	Use a device-dependent bitmap.
Ilc_mask	Use a mask. The image list contains two bitmaps, one of which is a monochrome bitmap used as a mask. If this value is not included, the image list contains only one bitmap.

```
set_cell_text (i, j: INTEGER; txt: STRING)
        -- Set the label of the cell with coordinates 'i', 'j' with
        -- 'txt'.
    require
        exists: exists;
        i_large_enough: i >= 0;
        j_large_enough: j >= 0;
        i_small_enough: i < column_count;
        j_small_enough: j < count

set_item_state (index, value: INTEGER)
        -- Make 'vaue' the new state of the zero-based 'index'-th
        -- item.
        -- See WEL_LVIS_CONSTANTS for the state constants.
    require
        exists: exists;
        index_large_enough: index >= 0;
        index_small_enough: index < column_count
```

If you change an item's attributes or state, you can force Windows to re-draw the item by calling *update_item.*

```
update_item (index: INTEGER)
        -- Update the list view.
    require
        exists: exists;
        index_large_enough: index >= 0;
        index_small_enough: index < count
```

Retrieving Item Information from a List View Control

The list view holds information about the items it contains. You can determine the current number of items, which item has the input focus, the first visible item, and how many items can be visible at one time. Each of these functions returns an *INTEGER* representing either the index position of the item (*focus_item* and *top_index*) or a count (*count* and *visible_count*).

You can also retrieve the details of a specific item or subitem by calling *get_item* and passing the index, and subitem index, if needed, or passing zero, if not. The function returns a *WEL_LIST_VIEW_ITEM* structure holding the item's information, including the *istate, iimage,* and *lparam* value. If you only need to retrieve the state of an item, use *get_item_state.*

```
count: INTEGER
      -- Number of items in the list view.

focus_item: INTEGER
        -- Zero-based index of the item that has the focus
        -- Return -1 if there is none.
    require
      exists: exists
    ensure
      result_large_enough: Result >= 0;
      result_small_enough: Result < count

get_item (index, subitem: INTEGER): WEL_LIST_VIEW_ITEM
        -- Return a representation of the item at the
        -- 'index' position.
    require
      exists: exists;
      index_large_enough: index >= 0;
      index_small_enough: index < column_count

get_item_state (index: INTEGER): INTEGER
        -- State of the zero-based 'index'-th item. See WEL_LVIS_CON-
        -- STANTS for the state constants.
    require
      exists: exists;
      index_large_enough: index >= 0;
      index_small_enough: index < column_count

top_index: INTEGER
        -- Index of the first visible item
    require
      exists
    ensure
      result_large_enough: Result >= 0;
      result_small_enough: Result < count

visible_count: INTEGER
        -- Number of items that will fit in the list view window
    require
      exists: exists
```

Retrieving Selected Items from a List View Control

The user can select one or more items in a list view and the current number of items selected can be determined with the *selected_count* function. You can also retrieve an array of item indexes representing the currently selected items with the function *selected_items*.

```
selected_count: INTEGER
        -- Number of selected items in the list view window
    require
        exists: exists

selected_items: ARRAY [INTEGER]
        -- Contains all the selected index. Only one in
        -- case of a single selection list view.
    require
        exists: exists
    ensure
        result_not_void: Result /= void
```

Searching a List View Control

The list view control provides a flexible function for locating items. It is flexible because it allows you to search for items by attribute, labels, or relative position in the list view. Function *search* takes a *WEL_LIST_VIEW_SEARCH_INFO* structure and a starting index, and returns the index of the first matching item, or −1 if no matching item could be found.

```
search (a_search_info: WEL_LIST_VIEW_SEARCH_INFO;
    a_starting_index: INTEGER): INTEGER
        -- Search list view item according to 'a_search_info'.
        -- Search starts after zero based index `a_starting_index'.
        -- If 'a_starting_index' is -1 then search all items.
        -- Result is zero based index of found item or -1 if item
        -- was not found.
    require
        non_void_search_info: a_search_info /= void;
        valid_search_info: a_search_info.exists;
        valid_starting_index: a_starting_index >= - 1 and a_start-
            ing_index < count
```

The search criteria are specified in the *WEL_LIST_VIEW_SEARCH_INFO* structure. The class interface is shown below. The *flags* attribute specifies what type of search will be performed and can be one of the constant values listed in Table 14.7. A *Lvfi_nearestxy* search uses the *starting_position* attribute and the specified search directions to find the next nearest item. This type of search is most useful when using the icon and list styles of a list view. The *Lvfi_param* search type uses the *lparam* attribute to find the first item with the same *lparam* value. The *Lvif_partial* and *Lvif_string* search types search for an item with either a partially or exactly matching text attribute. The partial match will succeed if the text of the item begins with the specified string. Finally, the *Lvif_wrap* search type can be combined with any of the other search types to allow the search to continue from the top of the list view if the bottom is reached without finding a match.

```
class interface
    WEL_LIST_VIEW_SEARCH_INFO
create
    make

feature -- Access

    downwards: BOOLEAN
            -- Will search be downwards?

    flags: INTEGER
            -- Flags specifying type of search
            -- See class WEL_LVFI_CONSTANTS for possible value

    left: BOOLEAN
            -- Will search direction be left?

    lparam: INTEGER
            -- Search target
            -- Either 'target' or 'lparam' will be used during search
            -- according to 'flags'.
        require
            valid_flags: flag_set (flags, lvfi_param)

    right: BOOLEAN
            -- Will search direction be right?

    starting_position: WEL_POINT
            -- Starting position of search
        require
            valid_flags: flag_set (flags, lvfi_nearestxy)

    target: STRING
            -- Search target
            -- Either 'target' or 'lparam' will be used during search
            -- according to 'flags'.
        require
            valid_flags: flag_set (flags, lvfi_string)

    upwards: BOOLEAN
            -- Will search be upwards?

feature -- Element Change
```

```
    add_flag (a_flag: like flags)
        -- Add 'a_flag' to 'flags'.
      require
        valid_flags: is_valid_list_view_flag (a_flag)
      ensure
        added: flag_set (flags, a_flag)

    set_downwards
        -- Set search direction downwards

    set_flags (a_flags: like flags)
        -- Set 'flags' with 'a_flags'.
      require
        valid_flags: is_valid_list_view_flag (a_flags)
      ensure
        flags_set: flags = a_flags

    set_left
        -- Set search direction left

    set_lparam (a_lparam: like lparam)
        -- Set 'lparam' with 'a_lparam'.
      ensure
        lparam_set: lparam = a_lparam

    set_right
        -- Set search direction right

    set_starting_position (a_starting_position: like
      starting_position)
        -- Set 'starting_position' with 'a_starting_position'.
      require
        non_void_starting_position: a_starting_position /= void;
        valid_starting_position: a_starting_position.exists

    set_target (a_target: like target)
        -- Set 'target' with 'a_target'.
      require
        non_void_target: a_target /= void;
        valid_target: not a_target.empty
      ensure
        target_set: target.is_equal (a_target)

    set_upwards
        -- Set search direction upwards

invariant

    valid_direction: (upwards implies (not downwards and not right
      and not left))
        and (downwards implies (not upwards and not right and not
          left))
```

```
        and (right implies (not upwards and not downwards and not
           left))
        and (left implies (not upwards and not downwards and not
           right));

end -- class WEL_LIST_VIEW_SEARCH_INFO
```

Changing the Style of a List View

The list view control supports four different views: a large icon view, a small icon view, a list view, and a report view. You can change the style of a list view after it has been created by passing a new window style to the *set_style* routine. The list view style can be one of the values listed in Table 14.8.

The following code fragment can be used to change a list view to use the icon view:

```
list_view.set_style (Ws_visible + Ws_child + Ws_group +
    Ws_tabstop + Ws_border + Ws_clipchildren + Lvs_icon)
```

Note that the original window style settings are retained and the only change is to change *Lvs_report* (the default style) to *Lvs_icon.*

Message Hooks in a List View Control

A list view provides sophisticated user interaction capabilities. Depending on the list view mode, a user can drag and drop items, edit item labels, and select items. Table 14.9 lists the message hooks that can be called as a result of user

TABLE 14.7 *List View Search Type Constants (WEL_LVFI_CONSTANTS)*

CONSTANT	DESCRIPTION
Lvfi_nearestxy	Search for item at nearest point in specified direction.
Lvfi_param	Search for item with corresponding lparam attribute.
Lvfi_partial	Search for item with text that begins with specified string.
Lvfi_string	Search for item with text that matches specified string exactly.
Lvfi_wrap	Start search from start when end of list view is reached.

TABLE 14.8   *List View Style Constants (WEL_LVS_CONSTANTS)*

CONSTANT	DESCRIPTION
Lvs_alignleft	Left-align text.
Lvs_aligntop	Top-align text.
Lvs_autoarrange	Auto arrange icons in icon views.
Lvs_editlabels	Allow editing of item labels.
Lvs_icon	Large icon view.
Lvs_list	List view.
Lvs_nocolumnheader	Do not show the column header.
Lvs_nolabelwrap	Do not wrap labels.
Lvs_noscroll	Do not enable scroll bars.
Lvs_ownerdrawfixed	Enable the owner to paint items in report view.
Lvs_report	Report view.
Lvs_shareimagelists	Allow the image lists to be used by multiple controls. Will not destroy image lists when finished with them.
Lvs_showselalways	Always show the selection, if any, even if the control does not have the input focus.
Lvs_singlesel	Only allow one item to be selected at a time.
Lvs_smallicon	Small icon view.
Lvs_shortascending	Sort items in ascending order.
Lvs_sortdescending	Sort items in descending order.

interaction or other list view operation. Each is described in detail in the following sections.

On Drag-and-Drop Messages in a List View Control

When the user begins to drag a list item, the message hook *on_lvn_begindrag* is called. *on_lvn_begindrag* is passed a *WEL_NM_LIST_VIEW* object holding information about the event, including the item or subitem's index, the position at which the event occurred, flags indicating which attributes of the item have changed, and the item's state.

Similarly, when the user drags an item using the right mouse button (rather than the left), the message hook *on_lvn_beginrdrag* is called and passed the same information.

```
on_lvn_begindrag (info: WEL_NM_LIST_VIEW)
        -- A drag-and-drop operation involving the left mouse
        -- button is being initiated.
    require
        exists: exists
on_lvn_beginrdrag (info: WEL_NM_LIST_VIEW)
        -- A drag-and-drop operation involving the right mouse
        -- button is being initiated.
    require
        exists: exists
```

The class interface of *WEL_NM_LIST_VIEW* is shown next. This class is used by many of the list view message hooks to hold information about message events.

TABLE 14.9   *List View Message Operations*

MESSAGE OPERATION	DESCRIPTION
on_lvn_begindrag	A drag-and-drop operation with the left mouse button is being initiated.
on_lvn_beginlabeledit	A label edit operation is being initiated.
on_lvn_beginrdrag	A drag-and-drop operation with the right mouse button is being initiated.
on_lvn_columnclick	A column was clicked with the left mouse button.
on_lvn_deleteallitems	All the items of the list view were deleted.
on_lvn_deleteitem	An item was deleted from the list view.
on_lvn_endlabeledit	A label edit operation has finished.
on_lvn_insertitem	A new item was inserted.
on_lvn_itemchanged	An item was changed.
on_lvn_itemchanging	An item is changing.
on_lvn_keydown	A key has been pressed in the list view control.

```
class interface
    WEL_NM_LIST_VIEW
creation
    make,
    make_by_nmhdr,
    make_by_pointer
feature -- Access
```

```
        hdr: WEL_NMHDR
                -- Information about the Wm_notify message.
        ensure
                result_not_void: Result /= void

        iitem: INTEGER
                -- Information about the list view item or -1 if
                -- not used.

        isubitem: INTEGER
                -- Information about the subitem or 0 if none.

        position: WEL_POINT
                -- Location at which the event occured.
                -- valid argument only for the Lvn_begindrag and
                -- Lvn_beginrdrag notification messages.

        uchanged: INTEGER
                -- Information about the item attributes that
                -- has changed.

        unewstate: INTEGER
                -- Information about the new item state or 0 if
                -- not used.
                -- See class WEL_LVIS_CONSTANTS.

        uoldstate: INTEGER
                -- Information about the old item state or 0 if
                -- not used.
end -- class WEL_NM_LIST_VIEW
```

On Keyboard Messages in a List View Control

If the user clicks a keyboard key while a list view has the input focus, then the message hook *on_lvn_keydown* is called, with the virtual key code passed as the value of the *virtual_key* parameter.

```
on_lvn_keydown (virtual_key: INTEGER)
        -- A key has been pressed.
    require
        exists: exists
```

On Mouse Messages in a List View Control

Clicking the header of a list view column results in the *on_lvn_columnclick* message hook being called. This can be used to implement custom item sorting.

```
on_lvn_columnclick (info: WEL_NM_LIST_VIEW)
        -- A column was tapped.
    require
        exists: exists
```

On Item Edit Messages in a List View Control

A list view control can provide the ability to edit item labels. If this capability is enabled, then the two message hooks *on_lvn_beginlabeledit* and *on_lvn_end-labeledit* are called whenever a user begins and ends a label edit operation. Both of these operations receive an instance of *WEL_LIST_VIEW_ITEM* representing the item being edited.

```
on_lvn_beginlabeledit (info: WEL_LIST_VIEW_ITEM)
        -- A label editing for an item has started.
    require
        exists: exists

on_lvn_endlabeledit (info: WEL_LIST_VIEW_ITEM)
        -- A label editing for an item has ended.
    require
        exists: exists
```

On Item Change Messages in a List View Control

Whenever an item is deleted from a list view, the message hook *on_lvn_de-leteitem* is called. If all items are deleted, perhaps as a result of a call to *reset_content,* then the message hook *on_lvn_deleteallitems* is invoked.

```
on_lvn_deleteallitems (info: WEL_NM_LIST_VIEW)
        -- All the items were deleted.
    require
        exists: exists

on_lvn_deleteitem (info: WEL_NM_LIST_VIEW)
        -- An item was deleted.
    require
        exists: exists
```

In addition, if an item is inserted into a list view, you are notified by a call to the *on_lvn_insertitem* message hook.

```
on_lvn_insertitem (info: WEL_NM_LIST_VIEW)          •
      -- A new item was inserted.
   require
      exists: exists
```

If an item is in the process of being changed, you receive notification via a call to *on_lvn_itemchanging*. Once the item has been changed, you receive a second notification via a call to *on_lvn_itemchanged*.

```
on_lvn_itemchanged (info: WEL_NM_LIST_VIEW)
      -- An item has changed.
   require
      exists: exists

on_lvn_itemchanging (info: WEL_NM_LIST_VIEW)
      -- An item is changing
   require
      exists: exists
```

SUMMARY

List controls provide the functionality to display lists of information to the user. They allow the user to select one or more list items, depending upon the style of the list box. The level of functionality ranges from simple single-selection list boxes to multiple-selection list boxes to relatively complex multiple-mode list views.

DIRECTORY TREE ANALYZER

IMPLEMENTING LIST CONTROLS

Our example application uses a list view control to display directory information in a tabular form. The tabular information includes the name of the directory, its total size, and the number of files and directories it contains.

The List View

The class that implements the list view is called, simply enough, *LIST_VIEW*. *LIST_VIEW* is a direct descendant of *WEL_LIST_VIEW* and implements a creation procedure that initializes required columns and a routine that adds directory information items.

In Example 14.3, the creation procedure *make* (lines 19–46) first calls the creation procedure from *WEL_LIST_VIEW* and then creates a *WEL_LIST_VIEW_COLUMN* for each type of data that will be displayed. The width, format (left, center, or right justification), and heading are set for each column.

The routine *add_info* (lines 70–96) takes a collection of *DIRECTORY_INFO* objects and adds an item representing each one. First, a *WEL_LIST_VIEW_ITEM* is created for each row, with its text set to the name of the directory. Next, the item object is inserted into the list view using *insert_item*. And finally, the subitem information for the directory is set using calls to *set_cell_text*, specifying a different positional index for each piece of information.

Example 14.3 LIST_VIEW of the Directory Tree Analyzer

```
1    class LIST_VIEW
2    inherit
3         WEL_LIST_VIEW
4              rename
5                  make as list_view_make
6              end;
7         SHARED_DATA
8              export
9                  {NONE} all
10             end;
11        WEL_LVCF_CONSTANTS
12             export
13                 {NONE} all
14             end
15   create
16        make
17   feature {NONE} -- Initialization
18
19        make (a_parent: WEL_WINDOW; main: MAIN_WINDOW; a_x, a_y,
             a_width,
20            a_height, an_id: INTEGER) is
21                -- Create the tree and some items in it.
22            local
23                column: WEL_LIST_VIEW_COLUMN
24            do
25                list_view_make (a_parent, a_x, a_y, a_width,
                      a_height, an_id);
```

```
26                      create column.make;
27                      column.set_cx (name_column_width);
28                      column.set_text (name_column_title);
29                      append_column (column);
30                      create column.make;
31                      column.set_cx (size_column_width);
32                      column.set_fmt (lvcfmt_right);
33                      column.set_text (size_column_title);
34                      append_column (column);
35                      create column.make;
36                      column.set_cx (file_count_column_width);
37                      column.set_fmt (lvcfmt_right);
38                      column.set_text (file_count_column_title);
39                      append_column (column);
40                      create column.make;
41                      column.set_cx (directory_count_column_width);
42                      column.set_fmt (lvcfmt_right);
43                      column.set_text (directory_count_column_title);
44                      append_column (column);
45                      main_window := main
46              end;
47
48      feature -- Access
49
50          main_window: MAIN_WINDOW;
51                  -- Main window of application
52          Name_column_title: STRING is "Name";
53                  -- List view name column title
54          Size_column_title: STRING is "Size";
55                  -- List view size column title
56          File_count_column_title: STRING is "Files";
57                  -- List view file count column title
58          Directory_count_column_title: STRING is "Folders";
59                  -- List view directory count column title
60          Name_column_width: INTEGER is 250;
61                  -- List view name column width
62          Size_column_width: INTEGER is 80;
63                  -- List view size column width
64          File_count_column_width: INTEGER is 40;
65                  -- List view file count column width
66          Directory_count_column_width: INTEGER is 50;
67                  -- List view directory count column width
68      feature -- Basic Operations
69
70          add_info (a_directory_info: DIRECTORY_INFO) is
71                  -- Add 'a_directory_info' information to list
view
72              require
73                  non_void_directory_info: a_directory_info /=
                        void
74              local
75                  index: INTEGER;
76                  a_list_view_item: WEL_LIST_VIEW_ITEM;
```

```
77                           size_text: STRING
78              do
79                  index := count;
80                  create a_list_view_item.make;
81                  a_list_view_item.set_text (a_directory_
                        info.name);
82                  a_list_view_item.set_iitem (index);
83                      insert_item (a_list_view_item);
84                  if shared_preferences.size = shared_preferences.
                        size_bytes then
85                    size_text := a_directory_info.total_byte_usage
86                  elseif shared_preferences.size = shared_prefer-
                        ences.size_kilobytes then
87                    size_text := a_directory_info.total_kb_usage
88                  elseif shared_preferences.size = shared_prefer-
                        ences.size_megabytes then
89                    size_text := a_directory_info.total_mb_usage
90                  else
91                    size_text := a_directory_info.total_
                        optimized_usage
92                  end;
93                  set_cell_text (1, index, size_text);
94                  set_cell_text (2, index, a_directory_
                        info.file_count.out);
95                  set_cell_text (3, index, a_directory_info.
                        directory_count.out)
96              end;
97
98      end -- class LIST_VIEW
```

Combo Boxes

Introducing Combo Boxes

Join a single-line edit box and a single-selection list box and you get a combination box, or combo box, with combined functionality—the user can edit text
and select text from a list within the control. Combo boxes can have three different styles—simple, drop-down, and drop-down list. A simple combo box
always displays its list box below the edit control, while a drop-down combo
box only displays the list when the user opens it. A drop-down list box uses a
static text control rather than an edit control.

Combo Box Types

WEL also supports extended combo boxes, available in the common controls
DLL. Descendants of *WEL_COMBO_BOX_EX* provide extended capabilities,
including image handling. Figure 15.1 illustrates the relationships between
each of the combo box classes. *WEL_COMBO_BOX* is a common ancestor of
all combo boxes and is itself a descendant of *WEL_CONTROL*.

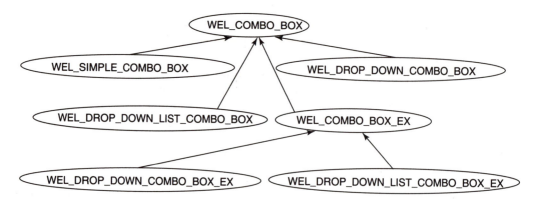

FIGURE 15.1. Combo box control types.

Abstract Combo Box Class

WEL_COMBO_BOX is the common ancestor of all combo box classes and implements the majority of features that a combo box needs. The class defines features for adding and removing list items, selecting items, and searching for items, as well as a set of message hooks for responding to combo box events. The following sections describe each of these features in detail.

Adding Strings to a Combo Box

The combo box list component behaves the same as a list control. Items can be added to the list using the routines *add_string, insert_string,* and *add_files.* Feature *add_string* appends an item to the end of the list, *insert_string* adds an item at a particular position in the list and *add_files* adds file names that match a wildcard pattern and file attributes. See Table 14.1 in Chapter 14, "List Boxes," for possible *attribute* values.

```
add_files (attribute: INTEGER; files: STRING)
        -- Add 'files' to the combo box. 'files' may contain
        -- wildcards (?*). See class WEL_DDL_CONSTANTS for
        -- 'attribut' values.
    require
        exists: exists;
        files_not_void: files /= void

add_string (a_string: STRING)
        -- Add 'a_string' in the combo box.
    require
        exists: exists;
```

```
          a_string_not_void: a_string /= void
      ensure
          new_count: count = old count + 1

  insert_string_at (a_string: STRING; index: INTEGER)
          -- Add 'a_string' at the zero-based 'index'.
      require
          exists: exists;
          a_string_not_void: a_string /= void;
          index_small_enough: index <= count;
          index_large_enough: index >= 0
      ensure
          new_count: count = old count + 1
```

Removing Strings from a Combo Box

Removing a combo box item is a simple case of calling *delete_string* and specifying the zero-based index of the item. Calling *reset_content* removes all items from the combo box.

```
  delete_string (index: INTEGER)
          -- Delete the item at the zero-based 'index'.
      require
          exists: exists;
          index_large_enough: index >= 0;
          index_small_enough: index < count
      ensure
          new_count: count = old count - 1

  reset_content
          -- Reset the content of the list.
      require
              exists: exists
      ensure
          new_count: count = 0
```

Accessing List Text in a Combo Box

Information about each list item and the total count of items is available via the features *i_th_text, i_th_text_length,* and *count.* Function *i_th_text* returns the *STRING* value of the item at the specified index. *i_th_text_length* returns the length of a specified item, and the total number of items in the combo box is given by the function *count.*

```
i_th_text (i: INTEGER): STRING
        -- Text at the zero-based index 'i'
    require
        exists: exists;
        i_large_enough: i >= 0;
        i_small_enough: i < count
    ensure
        result_exists: Result /= void

i_th_text_length (i: INTEGER): INTEGER
        -- Length text at the zero-based index 'i'
    require
        exists: exists;
        i_large_enough: i >= 0;
        i_small_enough: i < count
    ensure
        positive_result: Result >= 0

count: INTEGER
        -- Number of lines
    require
        exists: exists
    ensure
        positive_result: Result >= 0
```

Searching for Strings in a Combo Box

You can search for combo box items using an exact or prefix *STRING* match function. *find_string* attempts to find the first item that begins with the specified *STRING*. In contrast, *find_string_exact* finds the first item that *exactly* matches the specified *STRING*. Both functions need a starting index from which to begin the search and return the index of the matched item, or *−1* if no match was found.

```
find_string (index: INTEGER; a_string: STRING): INTEGER
        -- Find the first string that contains the
        -- prefix 'a_string'. 'index' specifies the
        -- zero-based index of the item before the first
        -- item to be searched.
        -- Returns -1 if the search was unsuccessful.
    require
        exists: exists;
        index_large_enough: index >= 0;
        index_small_enough: index < count;
        a_string_not_void: a_string /= void
```

```
find_string_exact (index: INTEGER; a_string: STRING): INTEGER
        -- Find the first string that matches 'a_string'.
        -- 'index' specifies the zero-based index of the
        -- item before the first item to be searched.
        -- Returns -1 if the search was unsuccessful.
    require
        exists: exists;
        index_large_enough: index >= 0;
        index_small_enough: index < count;
        a_string_not_void: a_string /= void
```

Selecting an Item in a Combo Box

Typically, an item in a combo box is selected by the user. However, you may need to programmatically select an item to give the user a default option or to reflect the state of an application. Routine *select_item* selects the item at the specified index position.

```
select_item (index: INTEGER)
        -- Select item at the zero-based 'index'.
    require
        exists: exists;
        index_large_enough: index >= 0;
        index_small_enough: index < count
    ensure
        selected_item: selected_item = index
```

Accessing the Currently Selected Item in a Combo Box

The item selected by the user (or by your application) can be accessed via the functions *selected_item* and *selected_string,* which return the index or *STRING* value of the currently selected item, respectively. The *STRING* length of the selected item can be determined with a call to *text_length.*

```
selected_item: INTEGER
        -- Zero-based index of the selected item
    require
        exists: exists;
        selected: selected
    ensure
        result_large_enough: Result >= 0;
        result_small_enough: Result < count

selected_string: STRING
        -- String currently selected
```

```
require
    exists: exists;
    selected: selected
ensure
    result_not_void: Result /= void

text_length: INTEGER
        -- Text length
```

Determining the Size of the Drop-Down Rectangle in a Combo Box

You can retrieve the dimensions and position of a combo box's list component by calling *dropped_rect*. This function returns a *WEL_RECT* with the dimensions of the list.

```
dropped_rect: WEL_RECT
        -- Rectangle of the drop down list box
    require
        exists: exists
    ensure
        result_not_void: Result /= void
```

Message Hooks in a Combo Box

Table 15.1 lists the message hooks implemented by *WEL_COMBO_BOX*. The following sections describe each message hook in more detail.

TABLE 15.1   *Combo Box Message Operations*

MESSAGE HOOK	DESCRIPTION
on_cbn_closeup	The list box of a combo box has been closed.
on_cbn_dblclk	A string in the drop-down combo box has been double-clicked.
on_cbn_dropdown	The drop-down list box is about to be shown.
on_cbn_editchange	The user may have changed the contents of the combo box.
on_cbn_editupdate	The edit control of the combo box is about to display changed text.
on_cbn_errspace	The combo box could not allocate enough memory for the operation.
on_cbn_killfocus	The combo box is about to lose focus.
on_cbn_selchange	The selection is about to change.
on_cbn_selendcancel	The user canceled selection of an item by closing the drop-down box or by selecting another control.
on_cbn_selendok	The user selected a list item.
on_cbn_setfocus	The combo box is about to receive focus.

On a Combo Box Close-Up Message

The *on_cbn_closeup* message hook is called when the list box of a drop-down combo box is closed.

```
on_cbn_closeup
        -- The combo box has been closed.
   require
      exists: exists
```

On a Combo Box Double-Click Message

Message hook *on_cbn_cblclk* is called whenever the user double-clicks on an item in the list box.

```
on_cbn_dblclk
        -- The user double-clicks a string in the list box.
   require
      exists: exists
```

On a Combo Box Drop-Down Message

The *on_cbn_dropdown* message hook is called when the drop-down list is about to be shown.

```
on_cbn_dropdown
        -- The list box is about to be made visible.
   require
      exists: exists
```

On a Combo Box Edit Change Message

If the combo box allows the user to edit the value in its edit control, then the message hook *on_cbn_editchange* is called whenever the user takes an action that may have altered the value.

```
on_cbn_editchange
        -- The user has taken an action that may have altered
        -- the text in the edit control portion.
   require
      exists: exists
```

On a Combo Box Edit Update Message

The combo box control calls the *on_cbn_editupdate* message hook when it is about to display altered text. The message hook is called after the control has formatted the text but before it is displayed.

```
on_cbn_editupdate
        -- The edit control portion is about to
        -- display altered text.
    require
        exists: exists
```

On a Combo Box Error Space Message

A combo box needs to dynamically allocate memory to store list items. If at any time the combo box cannot allocate enough memory to meet a request, then the *on_cbn_errspace* message hook will be called to notify you of the problem.

```
on_cbn_errspace
        -- The combo box can not allocate enough memory to
        -- meet a specific request.
    require
        exists: exists
```

On a Combo Box Kill Focus Message

When a combo box loses the input focus, the message hook *on_cbn_killfocus* is called.

```
on_cbn_killfocus
        -- The combo box loses the keyboard focus.
    require
        exists: exists
```

On a Combo Box Selection Change Message

The *on_cbn_selchange* message hook is used to notify the combo box when the user changes the selected item in the list component.

```
on_cbn_selchange
        -- The selection is about to be changed.
    require
        exists: exists
```

On a Combo Box Selection Cancel Message

If the user selects an item and then chooses another control or closes the dialog box, then the selection should be ignored. The message hook *on_cbn_selend-cancel* is called whenever this user interaction sequence occurs so that your application is notified of a canceled selection.

```
on_cbn_selendcancel
        -- The user selects an item, but then selects another
        -- control or closes the dialog box.
    require
        exists: exists
```

On a Combo Box Selection OK Message

In a similar fashion, the *on_cbn_selendok* message hook is called whenever the user selects an item and then closes the list or dialog box—only, in this case, the selection should be processed.

```
on_cbn_selendok
        -- The user selects a list item, or selects
        -- an item an then closes the list.
    require
        exists: exists
```

On a Combo Box Set Focus Message

Message hook *on_cbn_setfocus* is called whenever the combo box receives the input focus.

```
on_cbn_setfocus
        -- The combo box receives the keyboard focus.
    require
        exists: exists
```

Simple Combo Boxes

A simple combo box has an edit control and a list control that are both visible at all times. The user can select an item from the list or can enter a new item using the edit control.

Creating a Simple Combo Box

Example 15.1 demonstrates the use of *WEL_SIMPLE_COMBO_BOX*. This example allows the user to dynamically add and remove items to and from the combo list box via menu items. The user can then select an item or enter a new item using the edit control. When clicked, the Info button displays a dialog box containing information about the contents of the combo box.

Example 15.1 Simple Combo Box Example, MAIN_WINDOW Class (combo\simple)

```
class MAIN_WINDOW
inherit
    WEL_FRAME_WINDOW
        redefine
            on_menu_command, on_control_command
        end
    APPLICATION_IDS
        export
            {NONE} all
        end
creation
    make
feature
    make is
            -- Initialize the main window
        local
            menu_init_command: INITIALIZE_MENU_COMMAND
        do
            make_top ("Main Window")
            -- Add CEC command to initialize the popupmenu when it appears
            enable_commands
            create menu_init_command.make (main_menu, Current)
            put_command (menu_init_command, Wm_initmenupopup, Current)
            -- add the menu and controls to the window
            set_menu (main_menu)
            resize (340, 270)
            create static1.make (Current, "Simple Combo Box", 10, 5,
                300, 15, -1)
            create combo_box.make (Current, 10, 20, 300, 150, -1)
            create info_button.make (Current, "Info", 10, 180, 70, 30, -1)
            -- initialize the dialog
            create info_dialog.make (Current)
            create add_dialog.make (Current)
        end
    static1: WEL_STATIC
```

```
                    -- Static text labe
combo_box: WEL_SIMPLE_COMBO_BOX
        -- Simple Combo box control

info_button: WEL_PUSH_BUTTON
        -- Push button for text box information
info_dialog: IDD_INFO_DIALOG
        -- List box information dialog
add_dialog: IDD_ADD_DIALOG
        -- Add line dialog
on_menu_command (menu_id: INTEGER) is
        -- Check for a menu command
    do
        inspect menu_id
        when Id_fileexit_constant then
            destroy
        when Id_editadd_constant then
            add_list_line
        when Id_editdelete_constant then
            delete_list_line
        when Id_listgototop_constant then
            if combo_box.count > 0 then
                    combo_box.select_item (0)
            end
        when Id_listgotoend_constant then
            if combo_box.count > 0 then
                    combo_box.select_item (combo_box.count - 1)
            end
        else
            -- ignore
        end
    end
on_control_command (control: WEL_CONTROL) is
        -- Handle control commands
    do
        if control = info_button then
            info_dialog.set_info_text (get_text_info)
            info_dialog.activate
        end
    end
feature {NONE} -- Implementation
    add_list_line is
        -- Prompt the user for a text line to add to the listbox
    do
        add_dialog.set_combo (combo_box)
        add_dialog.activate
    end
    delete_list_line is
        -- Delete the selected list line
    require
        combo_box.selected
```

```
        do
            combo_box.delete_string (combo_box.selected_item)
        end
    main_menu: WEL_MENU is
            -- Main menu created from a menu resource
        once
            create Result.make_by_id (Id_mainmenu_constant)
        end

    get_text_info: STRING is
            -- Return a string representation of the text box
            -- information.
        do
            create Result.make (100)
            Result.append_string ("count: ")
            Result.append_integer (combo_box.count)
            if combo_box.count > 0 then
                Result.append_string ("%R%Ni_th_text
                    (combo_box.count - 1): ")
                Result.append_string (combo_box.i_th_text
                    (combo_box.count - 1))
                Result.append_string ("%R%Ni_th_text_length
                    (combo_box.count - 1): ")
                Result.append_integer (combo_box.i_th_text_length
                    (combo_box.count - 1))
            end
            Result.append_string ("%R%Nselected: ")
            Result.append_boolean (combo_box.selected)
            if combo_box.selected then
                Result.append_string ("%R%Nselected_string: ")
                Result.append_string (combo_box.selected_string)
            end
        end
    end
end -- class MAIN_WINDOW
```

Figure 15.2 shows the example running with three list items, Apple, Banana, and Cantaloupe. The Banana item has been selected by the user and the Info button clicked.

Limiting the Text Size of a Simple Combo Box

The only additional public feature that *WEL_SIMPLE_COMBO_BOX* adds is *set_limit_text*. This feature can be used to limit the length of new items that the user enters in the edit control component.

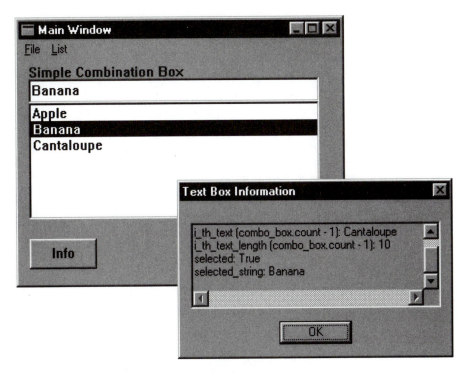

FIGURE 15.2. Simple combo box example.

```
set_limit_text (limit: INTEGER)
        -- Set the length of the text the user may type.
    require
        exists: exists;
        positive_limit: limit >= 0
```

Drop-Down Combo Boxes

A drop-down combo box provides identical functionality to a simple combo box, except that the list component is displayed only when the user opens it. A button is positioned at the end of the edit control to provide for the list to be opened.

Creating a Drop-Down Combo Box

Creating a drop-down combo box is identical to creating a simple combo box. In fact, the only change needed in Example 15.1 is to change the type of the attribute *combo_box* from

```
combo_box: WEL_SIMPLE_COMBO_BOX
```

to

```
combo_box: WEL_DROP_DOWN_COMBO_BOX
```

All other code in the example is identical (see *combo\dropdown* for the example source code). Figure 15.3 shows the difference in appearance between a drop-down combo box and a simple combo box. The list component is not shown unless the button at the right of the edit control is clicked. The user can also enter a new list item without opening the list component.

Limiting the Text Size of a Drop-Down Combo Box

A drop-down combo box also allows the length of the edit control text to be restricted to a certain size via the routine *set_limit_text*.

```
set_limit_text (limit: INTEGER)
        -- Set the length of the text the user may type.
    require
        exists: exists;
        positive_limit: limit >= 0
```

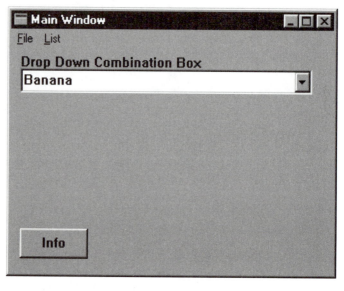

FIGURE 15.3. Drop-down combo box example.

Manipulating the List of a Drop-Down Combo Box

In addition, class *WEL_DROP_DOWN_COMBO_BOX* provides a number of features to manipulate the drop-down list component. You can show and hide the list using *show_list* and *hide_list,* respectively, and you can determine whether the list is currently shown by calling the function *list_shown.*

```
list_shown: BOOLEAN
        -- Is the drop down list shown?
    require
       exists: exists

hide_list
        -- Hide the drop down list.
    require
       exists: exists
    ensure
       list_not_shown: not list_shown

show_list
        -- Show the drop down list.
    require
       exists: exists
    ensure
       list_shown: list_shown
```

Drop-Down List Combo Boxes

A drop-down list combo box does not allow the user to enter a new item in the edit control component. In fact, this type of combo box uses a static text control rather than an edit control.

Creating a Drop-Down List Combo Box

The creation and use of a drop-down list combo box is identical to the other types of combo boxes. Example 15.1 can be modified again, this time to use a drop-down list combo box rather than a simple combo box. In this case, the type declaration for *combo_box* would be

```
combo_box: WEL_DROP_DOWN_LIST_COMBO_BOX
```

Extended Combo Box

The WEL library has recently added support for extended combo boxes. An extended combo box adds the ability to associate images with list items, using image lists. Two classes, namely *WEL_DROP_DOWN_COMBO_BOX_EX* and *WEL_DROP_DOWN_LIST_COMBO_EX*, implement two types of extended combo boxes. Both inherit from the class *WEL_COMBO_BOX_EX*.

Adding an Item to an Extended Combo Box

Adding an item to an extended combo box requires a *WEL_COMBO_BOX_EX_ITEM* structure to be created that represents the item and its formatting details. The *insert_item* routine takes an instance of *WEL_COMBO_BOX_EX_ITEM* and uses the details in the object to position and format the item it represents.

```
insert_item (an_item: WEL_COMBO_BOX_EX_ITEM)
        -- Insert 'an_item' in the combo-box.
    require
        exists: exists;
        an_item_not_void: an_item /= void;
        an_item_exists: an_item.exists;
        index_large_enough: an_item.index >= 0;
        index_small_enough: an_item.index <= count
    ensure
        new_count: count = old count + 1
```

The *WEL_COMBO_BOX_EX_ITEM* holds the details about an extended combo box item, including the item text, index, indent, image index, and overlay image index. Make sure that you set the mask according to which of the attributes should be used when adding the item. Possible attribute mask values are listed in Table 15.2.

```
class interface
    WEL_COMBO_BOX_EX_ITEM
create
    make,
    make_with_index,
    make_by_pointer

feature -- Access

    image: INTEGER
            -- Zero-based index of an image within the image list.
            -- The specified image will be displayed for the item
            -- when it is not selected.
        require
            exists: exists
```

indent: INTEGER
      -- Number of indent space to display for the item.
      -- Each indentation equals 10 pixels.
  require
      exists: exists

index: INTEGER
      -- Zero-based index of the item.
  require
      exists: exists

mask: INTEGER
      -- Array of flags that indicate which of the other
      -- structure members contain valid data or which are
      -- to be filled in. This member can be a combo
      -- of the Cbeif_* values.
      -- See class WEL_CBEIF_CONSTANTS.
  require
      exists: exists

overlay: INTEGER
      -- One-based index of an overlay image within the image
      -- list.
  require
      exists: exists

selected_image: INTEGER
      -- Zero-based index of an image within the image list.
      -- The specified image will be displayed for the item
      -- when it is selected.
  require
      exists: exists

text: STRING
      -- Text of the current item
  require
      exists: exists
  ensure
      result_not_void: Result /= void

feature -- Element change

set_image (value: INTEGER)
      -- Make 'value' the new image index.
  require
      exists: exists
  ensure
      value_set: image = value

set_indent (value: INTEGER)
      -- Make 'value' the new indent.
  require

```
                    exists: exists
             ensure
                    value_set: indent = value

         set_index (value: INTEGER)
                    -- Make 'value' the new index.
             require
                    exists: exists
             ensure
                    value_set: index = value

         set_overlay (value: INTEGER)
                    - Make 'value' the new overlay.
             require
                    exists: exists
             ensure
                    value_set: overlay = value

         set_selected_image (value: INTEGER)
                    -- Make `value' the new selected image index.
             require
                    exists: exists
             ensure
                    value_set: selected_image = value

         set_text (txt: STRING)
                    -- Make 'txt' the new text.
             require
                    exists: exists;
                    valid_text: txt /= void
             ensure
                    text_set: text.is_equal (txt)

  feature -- Basic operation

         clear_mask
                    -- Clear the current 'mask'.
                    -- Call it before to call a set_? feature when you
                    -- want to change only one parameter.
             require
                    exists: exists

  end -- class WEL_COMBO_BOX_EX_ITEM
```

Associating an Image List with an Extended Combo Box

If the items in an extended combo box require images, then you need to register an image list with the control. Routine *set_image_list* registers an image list with the combo box. All item *image* attribute values should then be indices into the registered image list. See "Associating an Image List with a List View Control" in Chapter 14 for more information on image lists.

TABLE 15.2 *Extended Combo Box Item Flag Constants (WEL_CBEIF_CONSTANTS)*

CONSTANT	DESCRIPTION
Cbeif_di_setitem	The control should store the item data and not ask for it again. This flag is used only with the *Cben_getdispinfo* notification message.
Cbeif_image	The *image* attribute is valid or must be filled.
Cbeif_indent	The *indent* attribute is valid or must be filled.
Cbeif_lparam	The *lparam* attribute is valid or must be filled.
Cbeif_overlay	The *overlay* attribute is valid or must be filled.
Cbeif_selectedimage	The *selected_image* attribute is valid or must be filled.
Cbeif_text	The *text* attribute is valid or must be filled.

```
set_image_list (an_imagelist: WEL_IMAGE_LIST)
          -- Set the current image list to 'an_imagelist'.
          -- If 'an_imagelist' is set to Void, it removes
          -- the current associated image list (if any).
```

Setting Extended Combo Box Item Information

Item information can be retrieved or set using the *get_item_info* and *set_item_info* features. *get_item_info* returns a *WEL_COMBO_BOX_EX_ITEM* structure for the requested item. Routine *set_item_info* replaces the attributes of the specified item with all masked values in the *WEL_COMBO_BOX_EX_ITEM* structure.

```
get_item_info (index: INTEGER): WEL_COMBO_BOX_EX_ITEM
          -- Retrieves the information about the zero-based
          -- 'index' item.
    require
          exists: exists;
          index_large_enough: index >= 0;
          index_small_enough: index < count
set_item_info (index: INTEGER; an_item: WEL_COMBO_BOX_EX_ITEM)
          -- Sets the information about the zero-based
          -- 'index' item.
    require
          exists: exists;
          index_large_enough: index >= 0;
          index_small_enough: index < count
```

Message Hooks in an Extended Combo Box

Table 15.3 lists the message hooks defined in *WEL_COMBO_BOX_EX*.

On an Edit Item Message in an Extended Combo Box

You are notified when the user begins or completes an edit operation with the message hooks *on_cben_beginedit_item* and *on_cben_endedit_item*. The *on_cben_endedit_item* message hook is passed a *WEL_NM_COMBO_BOX_EX_ENDEDIT* structure detailing what has changed and why.

```
on_cben_beginedit_item
        -- The user activated the drop-down list or clicked in the
        -- control's edit box.

on_cben_endedit_item (info: WEL_NM_COMBO_BOX_EX_ENDEDIT)
        -- The user has concluded an operation within the edit box
        -- or has selected an item from the control's drop-down list.
```

The *why* attribute in the *WEL_NM_COMBO_BOX_EX_ENDEDIT* structure indicates what type of edit operation was performed. Table 15.4 lists the constants used to define the reason.

On an Insert Item Message in an Extended Combo Box

When an item is inserted into the control list, the *on_cben_insert_item* message hook is called. The *WEL_COMBO_EX_ITEM* structure used to insert the item is passed to the message hook.

TABLE 15.3   *Extended Combo Box Message Hooks*

MESSAGE OPERATION	DESCRIPTION
on_cben_beginedit_item	Called when the user activates the list or clicks in the edit control.
on_cben_delete_item	Called when an item is removed from the list.
on_cben_endedit_item	Called when the user concludes an edit operation or selects an item from the list.
on_cben_insert_item	Called when an item is added to the list.

TABLE 15.4 *Extended Combo Box Notification Constants (WEL_CBEN_CONSTANTS)*

CONSTANT	DESCRIPTION
Cbenf_dropdown	The user activated the drop-down list.
Cbenf_escape	The user pressed the ESCAPE key.
Cbenf_killfocus	The edit box lost the keyboard focus.
Cbenf_return	The user completed the edit operation by pressing the ENTER key.

```
on_cben_insert_item (an_item: WEL_COMBO_BOX_EX_ITEM)
        -- An item has been inserted in the control.
```

On a Delete Item Message in an Extended Combo Box

You are notified when an item is deleted by the message hook *on_cben_delete_item.* The parameter *an_item* contains the details about the deleted item.

```
on_cben_delete_item (an_item: WEL_COMBO_BOX_EX_ITEM)
        -- An item has been deleted from the control.
```

SUMMARY

Combo boxes provide an interface for a user to select or create an item. They are useful when you need to provide a compact user interface that enables the user to select one option from a list. The extended combo boxes provide the ability to include images with each list item, with the potential for a higher-impact user interface.

Bar Controls

Introducing Bar Controls

This chapter looks at a group of controls that provides a wide variety of user interface functionality but still exhibit similar behavior. The general bar controls supported by WEL include scroll bars, up-down controls, progress bars, and track bars. Each has a very distinct user interface. However, they all provide the same basic abstraction—the ability to adjust a numeric scale from a minimum to a maximum.

We also look at another control that is related only by name. The ReBar control provides a repositionable control bar on which other controls can be attached. The ReBar control is commonly used in recent style applications, such as Microsoft's Internet Explorer and Developer Studio, to provide a highly customizable user interface.

Types of Bar Controls

The four general bar controls all inherit from *WEL_BAR,* which implements the generic features that each of the controls must support. *WEL_BAR* itself inherits from *WEL_CONTROL* and, therefore, implements all of *WEL-CONTROL's*

541

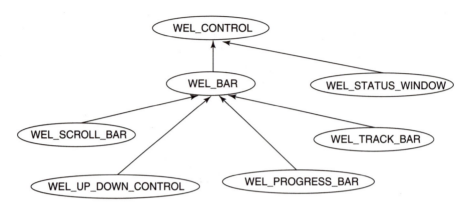

FIGURE 16.1. Types of bar controls.

functionality. The implementation of ReBar controls, class *WEL_REBAR,* also inherits from *WEL_CONTROL.* Figure 16.1 illustrates the inheritance hierarchy of the bar control classes.

Abstract Bar Class

As mentioned above, the class *WEL_BAR* defines and implements the features shared by all of the bar controls.[1] All bar controls have an integer range, specified by a maximum and minimum, and a current position within the range. Both the range and position can be adjusted at any time. However, they must meet certain constraints defined by the class—the maximum must be greater than or equal to the minimum, and the position must fall between the maximum and minimum, inclusively.

Setting the Range of a Bar

The range of a bar control is defined by the current *maximum* and *minimum* values. It can be adjusted by calling *set_range* and specifying new maximum and minimum values. The two values can be identical, thus specifying a range of only one value.

---

[1]We exclude *WEL_REBAR* from these discussions for the moment. Remember, the ReBar control is only included in this chapter because of a similarity in name, not in function.

```
maximum: INTEGER
      -- Maximum position
   require
      exists: exists
   ensure
      maximum_ok: maximum >= minimum
minimum: INTEGER
      -- Minimum position
   require
      exists: exists
   ensure
      minimum_ok: minimum <= maximum

set_range (a_minimum, a_maximum: INTEGER)
      -- Set 'minimum' and 'maximum' with
      -- 'a_minimum' and 'a_maximum'
   require
      exists: exists;
      valid_range: a_minimum <= a_maximum
   ensure
      minimum_set: minimum = a_minimum;
      maximum_set: maximum = a_maximum
```

Setting the Position of a Bar

The *position* specifies the control's current position within the range. It can be changed by calling *set_position,* specifying a new position value that must reside within the range.

```
position: INTEGER
         -- Current position
    require
         exists: exists
    ensure
         valid_minimum: Result >= minimum;
         valid_maximum: Result <= maximum

set_position (new_position: INTEGER)
         -- Set 'position' with 'new_position'
    require
         exists: exists;
         valid_minimum: new_position >= minimum;
         valid_maximum: new_position <= maximum
    ensure
         position_set: position = new_position
```

Scroll Bar

A scroll bar provides a user interface suitable for selecting a relative position within a document. A document, in this context, is typically represented by a graphical view in another control, such as a scrolling window, and can be any arbitrary concept supported by your application. For example, a document may be a book or even a graphical view of a house floor plan.

Scroll bars give the user a familiar way of navigating through a document, whether it be by pages in the case of a book or by rooms in the case of a floor plan. The range of a scroll bar is typically related to the logical length of the document, and the position determines what portion of the document the user wishes to view.

Scroll bars are implemented by the class *WEL_SCROLL_BAR*.

Creating a Scroll Bar

A scroll bar can be positioned either vertically or horizontally. The creation procedures *make_vertical* and *make_horizontal* create a vertical or horizontal scroll bar of the specified dimensions, attached to *a_parent*.

```
make_vertical (a_parent: WEL_WINDOW; a_x, a_y, a_width, a_height,
an_id: INTEGER) is
        -- Make a vertical scroll bar.
        -- (export status {NONE})
    require
        a_parent_not_void: a_parent /= void
    ensure
        parent_set: parent = a_parent;
        exists: exists;
        id_set: id = an_id;
        position_equal_zero: position = 0;
        minimum_equal_zero: minimum = 0;
        maximum_equal_zero: maximum = 0

make_horizontal (a_parent: WEL_WINDOW; a_x, a_y, a_width,
    a_height, an_id: INTEGER) is
        -- Make a horizontal scroll bar.
        -- (export status {NONE})
    require
        a_parent_not_void: a_parent /= void
    ensure
        parent_set: parent = a_parent;
        exists: exists;
        id_set: id' = an_id;
        position_equal_zero: position = 0;
        minimum_equal_zero: minimum = 0;
        maximum_equal_zero: maximum = 0
```

Determining Line Settings of a Scroll Bar

The scroll bar interface allows the user to scroll by lines or by pages. Clicking the end buttons scrolls by one line, while clicking in the area between buttons scrolls by a page, as illustrated in Figure 16.2. The line and page magnitudes are logically related to the range of the scroll bar.

The *line magnitude* can be set by calling *set_line* and should be the number of units the scroll bar will move when scrolling by lines. For example, in a word processing application, you might set the range of a scroll bar to be the total number of lines in a document, and if you want the user to scroll three lines at a time to give the user a sense of context when scrolling, the line magnitude would be set to *3*.

```
line: INTEGER
        -- Number of scroll units per line

set_line (line_magnitude: INTEGER)
        -- Set 'line' with 'line_magnitude'.
    require
        positive_line: line >= 0
    ensure
        line_set: line = line_magnitude
```

Determining Page Settings of a Scroll Bar

When scrolling by pages, the page magnitude is used. A scroll bar scrolls the correct number of units, up or down, whenever the user clicks the page scroll areas. The page magnitude can be set using the routine *set_page*.

```
page: INTEGER
        -- Number of scroll units per page

set_page (page_magnitude: INTEGER)
        -- Set 'page' with 'page_magnitude'.
    require
        positive_page: page >= 0
    ensure
        page_set: page = page_magnitude
```

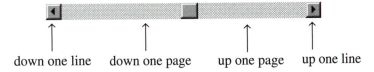

down one line   down one page   up one page   up one line

FIGURE 16.2. Scrolling magnitude.

On a Scroll Bar Scroll Message

The *on_scroll* message hook implements standard scrolling functionality for changing a scroll bar's position. You normally need to call *on_scroll* when you have created your own scroll bars and receive notification of a scroll event via the message hooks *on_vertical_scroll_control* or *on_horizontal_scroll_control* (see "On a Composite Window Control Scroll Message" in Chapter 5, "Composite Windows"). The implementation of *on_scroll* provided by WEL performs all necessary processing to update the position of the scroll bar, depending on the type of scroll event and position. Therefore, you rarely have to redefine this routine.

```
on_scroll (scroll_code, pos: INTEGER)
        -- Process the scroll messages.
        -- Typically, this routine will be called from
        -- 'on_vertical_scroll_control' or
        -- 'on_horizontal_scroll_control' of the parent window.
    require
        exists: exists
```

Example 16.1 shows how this is done. First, we create an instance of *WEL_SCROLL_BAR* and attach it to our main window. When the *on_horizontal_scroll_command* message hook receives a scroll event from our scroll bar, we forward the event parameters to its *on_scroll* routine. The *on_scroll* routine only updates the scroll bar to its new position. In a complete application, we should scroll the target document appropriately. For example, we may need to repaint a graphical view of a document so that it appears to have scrolled in the direction chosen by the user.

The example sets the range of the scroll bar from *0* to *100* (a total of 101 units). The line magnitude is set to *1,* indicating that a line scroll event should move the position by one unit, and the page magnitude is set to *10.* Clicking the Info button displays a dialog box containing information about the scroll bar, including its range and current position.

Example 16.1 Scroll Bar Example, MAIN_WINDOW Class (bar\scrollbar)

```
class MAIN_WINDOW
inherit
    WEL_FRAME_WINDOW
        redefine
            on_menu_command, on_control_command,
            on_horizontal_scroll_control
        end
```

```
        APPLICATION_IDS
            export
                {NONE} all
            end
creation
        make
feature
        make is
                -- Initialize the main window
            do
                make_top ("Main Window")
                -- add the menu and controls to the window
                set_menu (main_menu)
                resize (340, 270)
                create static1.make (Current, "Scroll Bar", 10, 5, 300, 15, -1)
                create scroll_bar.make_horizontal (Current, 10, 25, 300, 20, -1)
                create info_button.make (Current, "Info", 10, 180, 70, 30, -1)
                -- initialize the scrollbar
                scroll_bar.set_range (0, 100)
                scroll_bar.set_line (1)
                scroll_bar.set_page (10)
                -- initialize the dialog
                create info_dialog.make (Current)
            end
        static1: WEL_STATIC
                -- Static text label
        scroll_bar: WEL_SCROLL_BAR
                -- Scroll bar control
        info_button: WEL_PUSH_BUTTON
                -- Push button for text box information
        info_dialog: IDD_INFO_DIALOG
                -- List box information dialog
        on_menu_command (menu_id: INTEGER) is
                -- Check for a menu command
            do
                inspect menu_id
                when Id_fileexit_constant then
                    destroy
                else
                    -- ignore
                end
            end
        on_control_command (control: WEL_CONTROL) is
                -- Handle control commands
            do
                if control = info_button then
                    info_dialog.set_info_text (get_text_info)
                    info_dialog.activate
                end
```

```
        end
    on_horizontal_scroll_control (scroll_code: INTEGER; position: INTEGER;
        bar: WEL_BAR) is
            -- handle scroll events
        do
            if bar = scroll_bar then
                scroll_bar.on_scroll (scroll_code, position)
            end
        end
feature {NONE} -- Implementation

    main_menu: WEL_MENU is
            -- Main menu created from a menu resource
        once
            create Result.make_by_id (Id_mainmenu_constant)
        end
    get_text_info: STRING is
            -- Return a string representation of the text box
            -- information.
        do
            create Result.make (100)
            Result.append_string ("minimum: ")
            Result.append_integer (scroll_bar.minimum)
            Result.append_string ("%R%N")
            Result.append_string ("maximum: ")
            Result.append_integer (scroll_bar.maximum)
            Result.append_string ("%R%N")
            Result.append_string ("line magnitude: ")
            Result.append_integer (scroll_bar.line)
            Result.append_string ("%R%N")
            Result.append_string ("page magnitude: ")
            Result.append_integer (scroll_bar.page)
            Result.append_string ("%R%N")
            Result.append_string ("position: ")
            Result.append_integer (scroll_bar.position)
            Result.append_string ("%R%N")
        end
end -- class MAIN_WINDOW
```

Figure 16.3 shows the scroll bar attached to the main window and the information dialog displaying scroll bar information, including the current position of 50.

Track Bar

A track bar is similar to a scroll bar in that it can be used both vertically and horizontally. However, rather than providing an interface for scrolling a document, a track bar provides a user interface for choosing a value between a certain range. For example, a track bar is commonly used as a way for the user

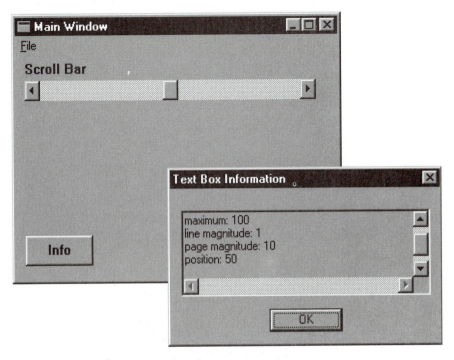

FIGURE 16.3. Scroll bar example.

to select volume levels for playing sound effects or music. Figure 16.4 shows an example track bar and an information dialog showing its current settings. Just like a scroll bar, a track bar supports both line and page magnitudes. The differences lie in its appearance and the ability to modify its appearance using *tick marks.*

Creating a Track Bar

To create a track bar, you need to call either *make_vertical* or *make_horizontal.* Both creation procedures require a reference to the parent window and dimensions.

```
make_vertical (a_parent: WEL_WINDOW; a_x, a_y, a_width, a_height,
    an_id: INTEGER) is
        -- Make a vertical track bar.
        -- (export status {NONE})
    require
        a_parent_not_void: a_parent /= void
```

```
      ensure
         exists: exists;
         parent_set: parent = a_parent;
         id_set: id = an_id;
         position_equal_zero: position = 0

make_horizontal (a_parent: WEL_WINDOW; a_x, a_y, a_width,
   a_height, an_id: INTEGER) is
         -- Make a horizontal track bar.
         -- (export status {NONE})
      require
         a_parent_not_void: a_parent /= void
      ensure
         parent_set: parent = a_parent;
         exists: exists;
         id_set: id = an_id;
         position_equal_zero: position = 0
```

Determining Tick Mark Settings of a Track Bar

A tick mark can be added to any arbitrary position within the range of the track
bar. A tick mark provides a visual about a significant track bar position. For

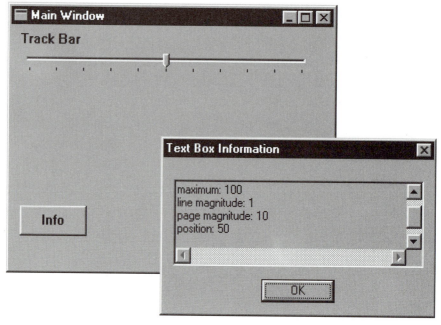

FIGURE 16.4. Track bar example.

example, you may want to add regular tick marks equivalent to the page magnitude to indicate page positions.

A single tick mark can be added using the routine *set_tick_mark* and specifying its position. Therefore, to add regular tick marks you will need to call *set_tick_mark* a number of times (most likely within a loop). All tick marks can be cleared by calling *clear_tick_marks,* and the position of individual tick marks can be determined by calling *tick_mark_position* and specifying a zero-based index of the tick mark in question.

```
tick_mark_position (index: INTEGER): INTEGER
        -- Tick mark position at the zero-based `index'
    require
        exists: exists;
        valid_index: valid_index (index)
    ensure
        positive_result: Result >= 0

valid_index (index: INTEGER): BOOLEAN
        -- Is 'index' valid?
    require
        exists: exists

clear_tick_marks
        -- Clear the current tick marks from the track bar.
    require
        exists: exists

set_tick_mark (pos: INTEGER)
        -- Set a tick mark at 'pos'.
    require
        exists: exists;
        pos_large_enough: pos > minimum;
        pos_small_enough: pos < maximum
```

Example 16.2 modifies the previous example to use a track bar. The creation of the track bar is identical to a scroll bar, including setting the range and magnitudes. A loop has been added to place tick marks at regular positions equal to the page magnitude. The result is the track bar shown in Figure 16.4.

Example 16.2 Track Bar, MAIN_WINDOW Class (bar\trackbar)

```
class MAIN_WINDOW
inherit
    WEL_FRAME_WINDOW
        redefine
```

```
            on_menu_command, on_control_command
        end
    APPLICATION_IDS
        export
            {NONE} all
        end
creation
    make
feature
    make is
            -- Initialize the main window
        local
            tick_count: INTEGER
        do
            make_top ("Main Window")
            -- add the menu and controls to the window
            set_menu (main_menu)
            resize (340, 270)
            create static1.make (Current, "Track Bar", 10, 5, 300, 15, -1)
            create track_bar.make_horizontal (Current, 10, 25, 300, 20, -1)
            create info_button.make (Current, "Info", 10, 180, 70, 30, -1)
            -- initialize the track bar
            track_bar.set_range (0, 100)
            track_bar.set_line (1)
            track_bar.set_page (10)
            -- add tick marks
            from
                tick_count := 10
            until
                tick_count > 90
            loop
                track_bar.set_tick_mark (tick_count)
                tick_count := tick_count + 10
            end
            -- initialize the dialog
            create info_dialog.make (Current)
        end
    static1: WEL_STATIC
            -- Static text label
    track_bar: WEL_TRACK_BAR
            -- Track bar control
    info_button: WEL_PUSH_BUTTON
            -- Push button for text box information
    info_dialog: IDD_INFO_DIALOG
            -- List box information dialog
    on_menu_command (menu_id: INTEGER) is
            -- Check for a menu command
        do
            inspect menu_id
            when Id_fileexit_constant then
                destroy
```

```
        else
            -- ignore
        end
    end
on_control_command (control: WEL_CONTROL) is
        -- Handle control commands
    do
        if control = info_button then
            info_dialog.set_info_text (get_text_info)
            info_dialog.activate
        end
    end
feature {NONE} -- Implementation

    main_menu: WEL_MENU is
            -- Main menu created from a menu resource
        once
            create Result.make_by_id (Id_mainmenu_constant)
        end
    get_text_info: STRING is
            -- Return a string representation of the text box
            -- information.
        do
            create Result.make (100)
            Result.append_string ("minimum: ")
            Result.append_integer (track_bar.minimum)
            Result.append_string ("%R%N")
            Result.append_string ("maximum: ")
            Result.append_integer (track_bar.maximum)
            Result.append_string ("%R%N")
            Result.append_string ("line magnitude: ")
            Result.append_integer (track_bar.line)
            Result.append_string ("%R%N")
            Result.append_string ("page magnitude: ")
            Result.append_integer (track_bar.page)
            Result.append_string ("%R%N")
            Result.append_string ("position: ")
            Result.append_integer (track_bar.position)
            Result.append_string ("%R%N")
        end
end -- class MAIN_WINDOW
```

Up-Down Control

An up-down control provides a simple two-button interface for incrementing
and decrementing an integer value. A window, known as a buddy-window, can
be linked with an up-down control to display the current value using its text attribute.

Creating an Up-Down Control

An up-down control can be created normally with the creation procedure *make* or from a resource with the creation procedure *make_by_id*. Both procedures require a parent window, positional coordinates and dimensions.

Setting the Buddy Window of an Up-Down Control

The buddy window can be set by calling *set_buddy_window* by passing a window object. The buddy window can be any type of window that has a text attribute. Typically, a text control is set as the buddy window of an up-down control. Once a buddy window has been set, it can be accessed via the function *buddy_window*.

```
buddy_window: WEL_WINDOW
        -- Current buddy window
    require
        exists: exists


set_buddy_window (a_window: WEL_WINDOW)
        -- Set the buddy window with 'a_window'.
    require
        exists: exists;
        a_window_not_void: a_window /= void;
        a_window_exists: a_window.exists
    ensure
        window_set: buddy_window = a_window
```

Setting the Number Base of an Up-Down Control

The text in a buddy window can be displayed in either decimal or hexadecimal notation. The default number base is decimal and this can be changed to hexadecimal by calling *set_hexadecimal_base*. You can return to a decimal base by calling *set_decimal_base*. The functions *decimal_base* and *hexadecimal_base* can be used to determine which number base the up-down control is currently using.

```
decimal_base: BOOLEAN
        -- Is the base decimal?
    require
        exists: exists


hexadecimal_base: BOOLEAN
        -- Is the base hexadecimal?
    require
        exists: exists
```

```
set_decimal_base
        -- Set the radix base to decimal.
    require
        exists: exists
    ensure
        decimal_base: decimal_base

set_hexadecimal_base
        -- Set the radix base to hexadecimal.
    require
        exists: exists
    ensure
        hexadecimal_base: hexadecimal_base
```

Example 16.3 creates an up-down control with a text control as its buddy window. The range of the up-down control is set like any other bar control with a call to *set_range*. Clicking the up arrow button on the up-down control increments the position of the control and displays the new value in the buddy window. Similarly, clicking on the down arrow button decrements and displays the control's position. The edit control buddy window also allows a value to be entered using the keyboard. If the value entered is outside the range of the control, then it is set to the maximum or minimum value, whichever is closer.

Example 16.3 Up-Down Control, MAIN_WINDOW Class (bar\updown)

```
class MAIN_WINDOW
inherit
    WEL_FRAME_WINDOW
        redefine
            on_menu_command, on_control_command
        end
    APPLICATION_IDS
        export
            {NONE} all
        end
creation
    make
feature
    make is
            -- Initialize the main window
        local
            tick_count: INTEGER
        do
            make_top ("Main Window")
            -- add the menu and controls to the window
            set_menu (main_menu)
```

```
            resize (340, 270)
            create static1.make (Current, "Up/Down Bar", 10, 5, 300,
                15, -1)
            create text_control.make (Current, "", 10, 25, 100, 25, -1)
            create updown_bar.make (Current, 110, 25, 0, 25, -1)
            create info_button.make (Current, "Info", 10, 180, 70,
                30, -1)
            -- initialize the updown control
            updown_bar.set_buddy_window (text_control)
            updown_bar.set_range (0, 100)
            -- initialize the dialog
            create info_dialog.make (Current)
        end
    static1: WEL_STATIC
            -- Static text label
    text_control: WEL_SINGLE_LINE_EDIT
            -- Text control to buddy with updown control
    updown_bar: WEL_UP_DOWN_CONTROL
            -- Track bar control
    info_button: WEL_PUSH_BUTTON
            -- Push button for text box information
    info_dialog: IDD_INFO_DIALOG
            -- List box information dialog
    on_menu_command (menu_id: INTEGER) is
            -- Check for a menu command
        do
            inspect menu_id
            when Id_fileexit_constant then
                destroy
            else
                -- ignore
            end
        end
    on_control_command (control: WEL_CONTROL) is
            -- Handle control commands
        do
            if control = info_button then
                info_dialog.set_info_text (get_text_info)
                info_dialog.activate
            end
        end
feature {NONE} -- Implementation
    main_menu: WEL_MENU is
            -- Main menu created from a menu resource
        once
            create Result.make_by_id (Id_mainmenu_constant)
        end
    get_text_info: STRING is
            -- Return a string representation of the text box
            -- information.
        do
```

```
        create Result.make (100)
        Result.append_string ("minimum: ")
        Result.append_integer (updown_bar.minimum)
        Result.append_string ("%R%N")
        Result.append_string ("maximum: ")
        Result.append_integer (updown_bar.maximum)
        Result.append_string ("%R%N")
        Result.append_string ("position: ")
        Result.append_integer (updown_bar.position)
        Result.append_string ("%R%N")
    end
end -- class MAIN_WINDOW
```

Figure 16.5 shows the example running after incrementing the position to 50 and clicking on the Info button. The information dialog shows the range of the up-down control and the current position value of 50.

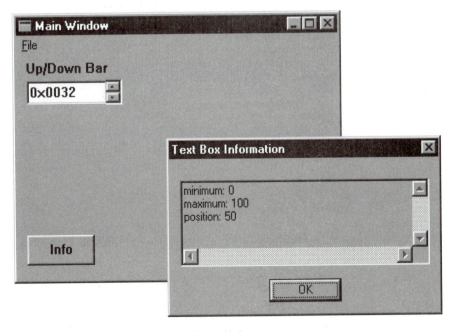

FIGURE 16.5. Up-down control example.

Progress Bar

A progress bar can be used to indicate the progress of an operation. In addition to indicating that an application is working by changing the cursor to an hourglass shape, you can indicate *actual* progress by incrementing a progress bar at appropriate points. For example, during a lengthy file save operation, you may want to increment a progress bar to show the percentage of the file that has actually been written to disk. The user receives visual feedback about the progress of the operation and will not get the impression that an application has "locked-up" or is "hung."

Updating Progress Bar Settings

The position of a progress bar can be adjusted by a delta value using the routine *set_delta_pos*. For example, if you need to change the position by 4, you can call *set_delta_pos* with the value 4, causing the current position to be incremented by 4.

```
set_delta_pos (increment: INTEGER)
        -- Advance the current position by a specified
        -- 'increment'.
    require
        exists: exists

set_step (step: INTEGER)
        -- Set the step increment with 'step'.

step_it
        -- Advance the current position by the step increment.
```

A progress bar also supports a *step* increment that can be used to increment the position. For example, a progress bar with a range of 1 to 100 might have a step increment of 10 to indicate progress at a steady rate. That is, the progress of an operation can be indicated at 10 percent increments. The routine *set_step* is used to set the step increment value, and *step_it* increments the progress bar by the step increment.

Example 16.4 demonstrates the use of a progress bar. In this example we link the position of a progress bar with the position of a track bar. Whenever the track bar is moved, the progress bar is adjusted accordingly.

Example 16.4 Progress Bar, MAIN_WINDOW Class (bar\progress)

```
class MAIN_WINDOW
inherit
    WEL_FRAME_WINDOW
        redefine
            on_menu_command, on_control_command,
            on_horizontal_scroll_control
        end
    APPLICATION_IDS
        export
            {NONE} all
        end
creation
    make
feature
    make is
            -- Initialize the main window
        local
            tick_count: INTEGER
        do
            make_top ("Main Window")
            -- add the menu and controls to the window
            set_menu (main_menu)
            resize (340, 270)
            create static1.make (Current, "Track Bar", 10, 5, 300,
                15, -1)
            create track_bar.make_horizontal (Current, 10, 25, 300,
                20, -1)
            create progress_bar.make(Current, 10, 50, 300, 20, -1)
            create info_button.make (Current, "Info", 10, 180, 70,
                30, -1)
            -- initialize the track bar
            track_bar.set_range (0, 100)
            track_bar.set_line (1)
            track_bar.set_page (10)
            -- add tick marks
        from
            tick_count := 10
        until
            tick_count > 90
        loop
            track_bar.set_tick_mark (tick_count)
            tick_count := tick_count + 10
        end
            -- initialize the progress bar
            progress_bar.set_range (0, 100)
            -- initialize the dialog
            create info_dialog.make (Current)
        end
    static1: WEL_STATIC
```

```
                        -- Static text label
        track_bar: WEL_TRACK_BAR
                        -- Track bar control
        progress_bar: WEL_PROGRESS_BAR
                        -- Progress bar control
        info_button: WEL_PUSH_BUTTON
                        -- Push button for text box information
        info_dialog: IDD_INFO_DIALOG
                        -- List box information dialog
        on_menu_command (menu_id: INTEGER) is
                        -- Check for a menu command
            do
                inspect menu_id
                when Id_fileexit_constant then
                    destroy
                else
                    -- ignore
                end
            end
        on_control_command (control: WEL_CONTROL) is
                        -- Handle control commands
            do
                if control = info_button then
                    info_dialog.set_info_text (get_text_info)
                    info_dialog.activate
                end
            end
        on_horizontal_scroll_control (scroll_code: INTEGER;
            position: INTEGER; bar: WEL_BAR) is
                        -- Handle child scroll events
            do
                if bar = track_bar then
                    progress_bar.set_position (track_bar.position)
                end
            end
    feature {NONE} -- Implementation
        main_menu: WEL_MENU is
                        -- Main menu created from a menu resource
            once
                create Result.make_by_id (Id_mainmenu_constant)
            end -- main_menu
        get_text_info: STRING is
                        -- Return a string representation of the text box
                        -- information.
            do
                create Result.make (100)
                Result.append_string ("minimum: ")
                Result.append_integer (progress_bar.minimum)
                Result.append_string ("%R%N")
                Result.append_string ("maximum: ")
                Result.append_integer (progress_bar.maximum)
                Result.append_string ("%R%N")
```

```
                Result.append_string ("position: ")
                Result.append_integer (progress_bar.position)
                Result.append_string ("%R%N")
        end

end -- class MAIN_WINDOW
```

As you can see in Figure 16.6, the progress bar is half-filled when the track bar is positioned at the middle. The information dialog shows the range of the progress bar and the current position of 50.

Status Window

A status window attaches itself to the bottom of a window and is typically used to display application information to the user. The status window extends across the full width of its parent window's client area and resizes and repositions itself automatically when the parent is resized. You might use a status window to display the current state of your application. For example, a word

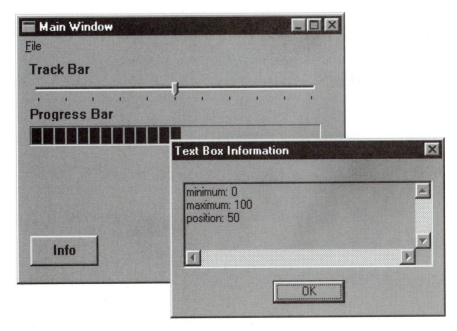

FIGURE 16.6. Progress bar example.

processing application might use a status window to display the position of the editing caret, the current page, and the current editing mode.

Setting the Mode of a Status Window

A status window can be used in two modes—simple mode, in which the window has only one part that can contain text, or multiple mode, in which the window has multiple text parts. Changing the mode of a status window is accomplished by calling either *set_multiple_mode* or *set_simple_mode*.

```
set_multiple_mode
        -- Switch to multiple parts mode.
    require
        exists: exists

set_simple_mode
        -- Switch to simple mode.
    require
        exists: exists
```

Different status window operations are permitted, depending on the selected mode of operation. For instance, in multiple mode you can specify the number and position of parts and text content of parts, while in simple mode, you can only operate with one predefined part.

Setting Simple Mode Text for a Status Window

In simple mode the entire status window consists of one part. The text for the part can be set by calling *set_simple_text*. This routine displays the specified text in the default style, which consists of the text displayed within a sunken three-dimensional border.

```
set_simple_text (a_text: STRING)
        -- Set 'a_text' for the simple mode
    require
        exists: exists;
        a_text_not_void: a_text /= void

set_simple_text_with_style (a_text: STRING; a_style: INTEGER)
        -- Set the text 'a_text' with style 'a_style' for a part
        -- identified by 'Simple_part'.
        -- See class WEL_SBT_CONSTANTS for 'a_style' values.
    require
        exists: exists;
        a_text_not_void: a_text /= void
```

TABLE 16.1   *Status Window Text Style Constants (WEL_SBT_CONSTANTS)*

CONSTANT	DESCRIPTION
Sbt_borders	The text is drawn with a border to appear lower than the plane of the window.
Sbt_noborders	The text is drawn without borders.
Sbt_ownerdraw	The text is drawn by the parent window.
Sbt_popout	The text is drawn with a border to appear higher than the plane of the window.

The status window supports a number of text styles, and the *set_simple_text_with_style* routine can be used to display text in a style other than the default. Class *WEL_SBT_CONSTANTS*, listed in Table 16.1, defines the styles supported by status windows.

Setting Parts to a Multiple Mode Status Window

If you select multiple mode, you need to specify the position of each part, using the *set_parts* routine. *set_parts* requires an array of integers as its sole parameter. Each value in the array is used to position the right edge of a part. If the last value is -1, then the right edge of the last value will be positioned at the far right of the window. For example, if you need to add two evenly spaced parts to a status window (perhaps for the current column and current line for a word processing application), you need to specify an array with the values *parent.width // 2* and -1,[2] thus positioning the first edge at half the width of the status window's parent, and the second at the far right edge.

A simple way to pass the array of edge positions is to use a manifest array. For example, the following code fragment would set the part edges as required:

```
set_parts (<<parent.width // 2, -1>>)
```

```
set_parts (a_edges: ARRAY [INTEGER])
        -- Set the parts for a multiple parts status window
        -- according to the edged defined in 'a_edges'.
        -- If an element is -1, the position of the right edge
        -- for that part extends to the right edge of the
        -- window.
    require
        exists: exists;
        a_edges_not_void: a_edges /= void;
        count_large_enough: a_edges.count > 0;
        count_small_enough: a_edges.count < 255
```

---

[2]Recall that // is the Eiffel integer division operator.

```
     ensure
          edges_set: edges.is_equal (a_edges)

set_part_owner_drawn (index, value, a_style: INTEGER)
          -- Set a part identified by the zero-based 'index' to
          -- be owner drawn using 'a_style' as extended style.
          -- 'value' will be present in the 'on_draw_item'
          -- routine of the 'parent' as 'item_data' in class
          -- WEL_DRAW_ITEM_STRUCT.
          -- See class WEL_SBT_CONSTANTS for 'a_style' values.
     require
          exists: exists;
          index_small_enough: index < number_of_parts;
          index_large_enough: index >= 0
```

A part can be drawn by the parent window. For example, if you need to add an icon to the text of the part, you can have the parent, rather than the status window, draw the contents. To designate a part as owner-drawn, you need to call *set_part_owner_drawn,* specifying the zero-based index of the part to draw, an arbitrary data value (passed to the paint routine), and a style. The parent receives notification whenever the part needs to be drawn and also receives a *WEL_DRAW_ITEM_STRUCT* structure containing the details about the part and the graphics context on which to draw.

Setting Multiple Mode Text for a Status Window

To set the text of a part in multiple mode, you must specify the zero-based index of the part to change. Routine *set_text_part* changes the text of the part at the specified index position. Each part can also display its text in different styles. Use *set_text_part_with_style* to specify a display style other than the default.

```
set_text_part (index: INTEGER; a_text: STRING)
          -- Set the text for a part identified by the
          -- zero-based 'index'.
     require
          exists: exists;
          index_small_enough: index < number_of_parts;
          index_large_enough: index >= 0;
          a_text_not_void: a_text /= void
     ensure
          text_set: a_text.is_equal (text_for_part (index))

set_text_part_with_style (index: INTEGER; a_text: STRING; a_style:
   INTEGER)
          -- Set the text for a part identified by the
```

```
            -- zero-based 'index'.
            -- See class WEL_SBT_CONSTANTS for 'a_style' values.
    require
        exists: exists;
        index_small_enough: index < number_of_parts;
        index_large_enough: index >= 0;
        a_text_not_void: a_text /= void
    ensure
        text_set: a_text.is_equal (text_for_part (index));
        style_is_set: a_style = text_style_for_part (index)
```

Accessing Part Attributes of a Multiple Mode Status Window

The current number of parts in a status window can be determined by calling the function *number_of_parts*. In addition, you can determine the display rectangle, text, length of text, and text style for particular parts, using the routines *rect_for_part*, *text_for_part*, *text_length_for_part*, and *text_style_for_part*, respectively.

```
number_of_parts: INTEGER
        -- Current number of parts
    require
        exists: exists
    ensure
        positive_result: Result > 0

rect_for_part (index: INTEGER): WEL_RECT
        -- Rectangle for a part identified by the
        -- zero-based 'index'.
    require
        exists: exists;
        index_small_enough: index < number_of_parts;
        index_large_enough: index >= 0
    ensure
        result_not_void: Result /= void

text_for_part (index: INTEGER): STRING
        -- Text for the part identified by the zero-based
        -- 'index'.
    require
        exists: exists;
        index_small_enough: index < number_of_parts;
        index_large_enough: index >= 0
    ensure
        result_not_void: Result /= void;
        consistent_count: Result.count = text_length_for_part
            (index)
```

```
text_length_for_part (index: INTEGER): INTEGER
        -- Length of the text in the part identified by the
        -- zero-based 'index'.
    require
        exists: exists;
        index_small_enough: index < number_of_parts;
        index_large_enough: index >= 0
    ensure
        positive_result: Result >= 0

text_style_for_part (index: INTEGER): INTEGER
        -- Style of the text in the part identified by the
        -- zero-based 'index'
    require
        exists: exists;
        index_small_enough: index < number_of_parts;
        index_large_enough: index >= 0
    ensure
        positive_result: Result >= 0
```

Accessing Status Window Attributes

The collection of edges set by the *set_edges* routine are accessible via the function *edges*. You can also determine the width of horizontal and vertical borders—perhaps to help draw an owner-drawn part. In addition, function *width_between_rectangles* specifies the spacing between rectangles.

```
edges: ARRAY [INTEGER]
        -- Zero-based integer array which contains
        -- all the edges currently present.
    require
        exists: exists
    ensure
        result_not_void: Result /= void;
        consistent_count: Result.count = number_of_parts

horizontal_border_width: INTEGER
        -- Width of the horizontal border
    require
        exists: exists
    ensure
        positive_result: Result > 0

vertical_border_width: INTEGER
        -- Width of the vertical border
    require
        exists: exists
    ensure
        positive_result: Result > 0
```

```
width_between_rectangles: INTEGER
        -- Width between the rectangles
    require
        exists: exists
    ensure
        positive_result: Result > 0
```

Setting the Minimum Height of a Status Window

The minimum height of a status window is normally set by Windows when you create the control. However, you can change the minimum height by calling *set_minimum_height* and specifying the new height of the drawing area. The drawing area is the area containing the text but not including the borders. Adjusting the minimum drawing area is useful if you have owner-drawn parts that require more vertical space than normal.

```
set_minimum_height (a_height: INTEGER)
        -- Set the minimun height with 'a_height' in pixels.
        -- To let the change take effect, call
        -- the 'reposition' procedure.
    require
        exists: exists;
        minimum_height: a_height >= 2 * vertical_border_width
```

Repositioning a Status Window

Whenever the parent window changes size, you should reposition (and effectively resize) the status window by calling *reposition*. The *reposition* routine adjusts the *y* coordinate of the status bar so that it is correctly positioned at the bottom of the parent window. If the width of the parent window changes, you may also need to reposition the parts by calling *set_parts* again.

```
reposition
        -- Reposition the window according to the parent.
        -- This function needs to be called in the
        -- 'on_size' routine of the parent.
    require
        exists: exists
```

To demonstrate the use of a status bar, Example 16.5 adds a status window and two track bars to a main window. The position attribute of each track bar is displayed in the two status bar parts. The message hook *on_size* is redefined to ensure that the status window's parts and the status window itself are repositioned whenever the parent window changes size.

Example 16.5 Status Window, MAIN_WINDOW Class (bar\status)

```
class MAIN_WINDOW
inherit

    WEL_FRAME_WINDOW
        redefine
            on_menu_command, on_control_command,
            on_horizontal_scroll_control,
            on_size
        end
    APPLICATION_IDS
        export
            {NONE} all
        end
creation
    make
feature

    make is
            -- Initialize the main window
        do
            make_top ("Main Window")
            -- initialize the status bar
            create status_bar.make(Current, -1)
            initialize_status_bar (width)
            -- add the other controls
            set_menu (main_menu)
            create track_bar.make_horizontal (Current, 10, 25, 300,
                20, -1)
            create track_bar1.make_horizontal (Current, 10, 50, 300,
                20, -1)
            create info_button.make (Current, "Info", 10, 130, 70,
                30, -1)
            initialize_track_bars
            create info_dialog.make (Current)
            resize (340, 270)
        end

    track_bar, track_bar1: WEL_TRACK_BAR
            -- Track bar controls
    status_bar: WEL_STATUS_WINDOW
            -- Status bar control
    info_button: WEL_PUSH_BUTTON
            -- Push button for text box information
    info_dialog: IDD_INFO_DIALOG
            -- List box information dialog

    on_menu_command (menu_id: INTEGER) is
            -- Check for a menu command
        do
```

```
            inspect menu_id
            when Id_fileexit_constant then
                destroy
            else
                -- ignore
            end
        end

    on_control_command (control: WEL_CONTROL) is
            -- Handle control commands
        do
            if control = info_button then
                info_dialog.set_info_text (get_text_info)
                info_dialog.activate
            end
        end

    on_horizontal_scroll_control (scroll_code: INTEGER;
        position: INTEGER; bar: WEL_BAR) is
            -- Handle child scroll events
        do
            if bar = track_bar then
                status_bar.set_text_part (Part_one,
                    track_bar.position.out)
            elseif bar = track_bar1 then
                status_bar.set_text_part (Part_two,
                    track_bar1.position.out)
            end
        end
    on_size (size_type, new_width, new_height: INTEGER) is
            -- Reposition controls
        do
            initialize_status_bar (new_width)
            status_bar.reposition
        end
feature {NONE} -- Implementation

    Part_one: INTEGER is 0;
    Part_two: INTEGER is 1;

    initialize_status_bar (new_width: INTEGER) is
            -- Build the status bar
        do
            status_bar.set_multiple_mode
            status_bar.set_parts (<<new_width // 2, -1>>)
        end

    initialize_track_bars is
            -- Build the track bar
        local
```

```eiffel
          tick_count: INTEGER
    do
          track_bar.set_range (0, 100)
          track_bar.set_line (1)
          track_bar.set_page (10)
          track_bar1.set_range (0, 100)
          track_bar1.set_line (1)
          track_bar1.set_page (10)
          -- add tick marks
          from
              tick_count := 10
          until
              tick_count > 90
          loop
              track_bar.set_tick_mark (tick_count)
              track_bar1.set_tick_mark (tick_count)
              tick_count := tick_count + 10
          end
      end

  main_menu: WEL_MENU is
          -- Main menu created from a menu resource
      once
          create Result.make_by_id (Id_mainmenu_constant)
      end

  get_text_info: STRING is
          -- Return a string representation of the text box
          -- information.
      local
          count: INTEGER
      do
          create Result.make (100)
          Result.append ("number_of_parts: ")
          Result.append_integer (status_bar.number_of_parts)
          from
              count := 0
          until
              count >= status_bar.number_of_parts
          loop
              Result.append ("%R%N")
              Result.append ("text_for_part(")
              Result.append_integer (count)
              Result.append ("): ")
              Result.append(status_bar.text_for_part (count))
              count := count + 1
          end
      end

end -- class MAIN_WINDOW
```

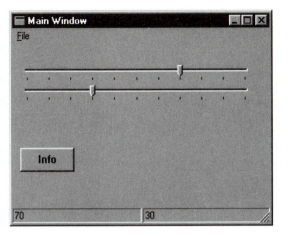
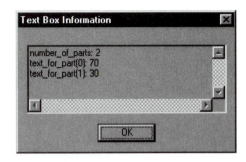

FIGURE 16.7. Status window example.

Figure 16.7 shows the example running with the first track bar at position 30 and the second at position 70. The positions are displayed in the status window at the bottom of the main window. The information dialog displays the number of parts in the status window and their values.

Tool Bar

A tool bar is commonly used to provide the user with easy access to application functionality. The most common operations are often represented by buttons on a tool bar. This is normally in addition to menu items and/or accelerator keys representing the operations. For example, you often find a tool bar containing buttons that allow you to open, save, and print a document.

A tool bar can contain standard push buttons (with or without an icon and text), check buttons, and grouped check buttons that behave like a radio button group.

Setting Button Properties on a Tool Bar

Each tool bar button is associated with a control command identifier. The identifier is passed to the *on_control_id_command* message hook of the parent when the button is clicked. The identifier is normally set when a button is created; however, you can change a button's command identifier after the fact by calling *set_identifier*—you need to specify the zero-based index of the button to be modified and the new command identifier value.

```
set_identifier (index, an_id: INTEGER)
        -- Set the identifier for the button at zero-based
        -- `index' to 'an_id'.
    require
        exists: exists;
        index_large_enough: index >= 0;
        index_small_enough: index < button_count
```

The size of buttons added to a tool bar can be specified by calling *set_button_size*. You must call this routine before adding any buttons for it to take effect. If you do not call *set_button_size* explicitly, then Windows will assume a button size of 24 by 22 pixels.

```
set_button_size (a_width, a_height: INTEGER)
        -- Set the size of the buttons to be added to the
        -- toolbar.
        -- The size can be set only before adding any buttons
        -- to the tool bar. If an application does not
        -- explicitly set the button size, the size defaults
        -- to 24 by 22 pixels.
    require
        exists: exists;
        positive_width: a_width >= 0;
        positive_height: a_height >= 0;
        no_existing_buttons: button_count = 0
```

Adding Buttons to a Tool Bar

An array of tool bar buttons can be added with a single call to *add_buttons,* or a single button can be added at a particular position with a call to *insert_button.* Each button is represented by an instance of *WEL_TOOL_BAR_BUTTON.* Routine *insert_button* also requires a zero-based index, which is used to position the new button.

Once you have initialized a *WEL_TOOL_BAR_BUTTON* instance for each button, you can easily add all of the buttons with a call to *add_buttons,* using a manifest array to quickly create the array parameter. For instance, the following line of code will add the buttons *button1, button2,* and *button3* to the tool bar referenced by *tool_bar:*

```
tool_bar.add_button(<<button1, button2, button3>>)
```

The *WEL_TOOL_BAR_BUTTON* objects referenced by *button1, button2,* and *button3* must be initialized and valid (see below). In addition, *tool_bar* must be initialized and must *exist*. Each of the buttons is added in the order specified—*button1* at index position 0, *button2* at position 1, and *button3* at position 2.

A button can be removed at any time by calling *remove_button* and specifying its zero-based index. All remaining buttons to the right of the removed button are moved one position to the left.

```
add_buttons (buttons: ARRAY [WEL_TOOL_BAR_BUTTON])
        -- Add buttons.
    require
        exists: exists;
        buttons_not_void: buttons /= void;
        buttons_not_empty: not buttons.empty;
        no_void_button: not buttons.has (void)
    ensure
        count_increased: button_count = old button_count +
            buttons.count

insert_button (index: INTEGER; button: WEL_TOOL_BAR_BUTTON)
        -- Insert 'button' to the left of the button
        -- at the zero-based 'index'.
    require
        exists: exists;
        button_not_void: button /= void;
        index_large_enough: index >= 0;
        index_small_enough: index <= button_count
    ensure
        buttons_increased: button_count = old button_count + 1

delete_button (index: INTEGER)
        -- Delete the button at the zero-based 'index'.
    require
        exists: exists;
        index_large_enough: index >= 0;
        index_small_enough: index < button_count
    ensure
        buttons_decreased: button_count = old button_count - 1
```

The *WEL_TOOL_BAR_BUTTON* class supports different types of tool bar buttons, including push buttons, check buttons, check button groups (radio buttons), and separator buttons. Each type of button can be created by calling an appropriate creation procedure. For example, to create a tool bar push button, use

```
button: WEL_TOOL_BAR_BUTTON
...
create button.make_button (Bitmap_index, Command_id)
```

where *Bitmap_index* represents the index to an icon stored in the tool bar bitmap (see below for more detail) and the *Command_id* is the command value that will be passed to the parent when the button is activated. A check button can be created with

```
create button.make_check (Bitmap_index, Command_id)
```

Finally, a separator tool bar button can be used to add horizontal space between related button groups and is created with the creation procedure *make_separator.*

All tool bar buttons have a bitmap icon, an optional string label, a command identification number, a style, a state, and a user defined *INTEGER* data value. Each of these attributes can be accessed by the routines in the feature group labeled *Access* and set by the routines in group *Element Change.* The icon and string label are indexes into an internal bitmap image list and string array stored by the tool bar itself. See "Setting Bitmaps on a Tool Bar" and "Setting Strings on a Tool Bar" in this chapter. The command identification number is passed to the *on_control_id_command* and *notify* message hooks when the tool bar button is activated.

The class interface of *WEL_TOOLBAR_BUTTON* is shown next.

```
class interface
    WEL_TOOL_BAR_BUTTON
create

    make_button (a_bitmap_index, a_command_id: INTEGER)
        ensure
            bitmap_index_set: bitmap_index = a_bitmap_index;
            command_id_set: command_id = a_command_id

    make_check (a_bitmap_index, a_command_id: INTEGER)
        ensure
            bitmap_index_set: bitmap_index = a_bitmap_index;
            command_id_set: command_id = a_command_id

    make_check_group (a_bitmap_index, a_command_id: INTEGER)
        ensure
            bitmap_index_set: bitmap_index = a_bitmap_index;
            command_id_set: command_id = a_command_id

    make_group (a_bitmap_index, a_command_id: INTEGER)
        ensure
            bitmap_index_set: bitmap_index = a_bitmap_index;
            command_id_set: command_id = a_command_id

    make_separator
```

```
feature -- Access

    bitmap_index: INTEGER
            -- Zero-based index of button image

    command_id: INTEGER
            -- Command identifier associated with the button. This
            -- identifer is used in a Wm_command message when the
            -- button is chosen.

    data: INTEGER
            -- Application-defined value

    state: INTEGER
            -- Button state flags.
            -- See class WEL_TB_STATE_CONSTANTS for values

    string_index: INTEGER
            -- Zero-based index of button string.
        ensure
            positive_result: Result >= 0

    style: INTEGER
            -- Button style flags.
            -- See class WEL_TB_STYLE_CONSTANTS for values

feature -- Element change

    set_bitmap_index (a_bitmap_index: INTEGER)
            -- Set 'bitmap_index' with 'a_bitmap_index'.
        ensure
            bitmap_index_set: bitmap_index = a_bitmap_index

    set_command_id (a_command_id: INTEGER)
            -- Set 'command_id' with 'a_command_id'.
        ensure
            command_id_set: command_id = a_command_id

    set_data (a_data: INTEGER)
            -- Set 'data' with 'a_data'.
        ensure
            data_set: data = a_data

    set_state (a_state: INTEGER)
            -- Set 'state' with 'a_state'.
        ensure
            state_set: state = a_state

    set_string_index (a_string_index: INTEGER)
            -- Set 'string_index' with 'a_string_index'.
        require
            positive_index: a_string_index >= 0
```

```
        ensure
            string_index_set: string_index = a_string_index

    set_style (a_style: INTEGER)
            -- Set 'style' with 'a_style'.
        ensure
            style_set: style = a_style

end -- class WEL_TOOL_BAR_BUTTON
```

The *state* attribute of a tool bar button can be one of the values listed in Table 16.2. When creating buttons, this value determines what initial state the button will take. For example, creating a button with *Tbstate_hidden* state will initially hide the button on the tool bar.

The *state* attribute is also used to indicate the current state of buttons, when accessed. For example, a call to *i_th_button* (shown below) returns a *WEL_TOOL_BAR_BUTTON* structure with the state attribute set to the current state of the button.

The shape and function of a tool bar button is determined by its *style* attribute. A button can use a combination of the style constants listed in Table 16.3 to determine how the button looks and behaves. The main tool bar button styles include *Tbstyle_button* for standard push buttons, *Tbstyle_check* for check box buttons, *Tbstyle_group* for radio buttons, and *Tbstyle_dropdown* for drop down list buttons. Additional style values can be used to allow user-customization of tool bars *(Tbstyle_altdrag)*, tool tips *(Tbstyle_tooltip)*, and customized drawing and painting *(Tbstyle_customerase, Tbstyle_flat, and Tbstyle_wrapable)*.

TABLE 16.2 *Tool Bar Button State Constants (WEL_TB_STATE_CONSTANTS)*

CONSTANT	DESCRIPTION
Tbstate_checked	The button has the *Tbstyle_checked* style and is being pressed.
Tbstate_enabled	The button accepts user input.
Tbstate_hidden	The button is not visible and cannot receive user input.
Tbstate_indeterminate	The button is grayed.
Tbstate_pressed	The button is being pressed.
Tbstate_wrap	A line break follows the button. The button must also have the *Tbstate_enabled* state.

TABLE 16.3 *Tool Bar Style Constants (WEL_TB_STYLE_CONSTANTS)*

CONSTANT	DESCRIPTION
Tbstyle_altdrag	Allows the user to change the position of a tool bar button by dragging it while holding down the ALT key. If this style is not specified, the user must hold down the SHIFT key while dragging a button. Note that the *Ccs_adjustable* style must be specified to enable tool bar buttons to be dragged.
Tbstyle_button	Creates a standard push button.
Tbstyle_check	Creates a button that toggles between the pressed and not pressed states each time the user clicks it. The button has a different background color when it is in the pressed state.
Tbstyle_checkgroup	Creates a check button that stays pressed until another button in the group is pressed.
Tbstyle_customerase	Generates *Nm_customdraw* notification messages when it processes *Wm_erasebkgnd*.
Tbstyle_dropdown	Creates a drop-down list button. If the tool bar has the *Tbstyle_ex_drawddarrows* extended style, an arrow will be displayed next to the button.
Tbstyle_flat	Creates a transparent toolbar with flat buttons. The appearance of the button changes when the user moves the mouse over the button.
Tbstyle_group	Creates a button that stays pressed until another button in the group is pressed.
Tbstyle_list	Places button text to the right of the button bitmaps. To avoid repainting problems, this style should be set before the tool bar becomes visible.
Tbstyle_sep	Creates a separator, providing a small gap between button groups. A button that has this style does not receive user input.
Tbstyle_tooltips	Creates a tool tip control that an application can use to display descriptive text for the buttons in the tool bar.
Tbstyle_wrapable	Creates a tool bar that can have multiple lines of buttons. Tool bar buttons can "wrap" to the next line when the tool bar becomes too narrow to include all buttons on the same line. Wrapping occurs on separation and nongroup boundaries.

Accessing Buttons on a Tool Bar

You can determine the number of buttons, the rectangular area each button occupies, and the state and style of buttons using the features *button_count, button_rect,* and *i_th_button* respectively. The function *i_th_button* can be used to retrieve a *WEL_TOOL_BAR_BUTTON* structure for a specific button identified by its zero-based index.

```
button_count: INTEGER
        -- Number of buttons in tool bar
    require
        exists: exists
    ensure
        positive_result: Result >= 0

button_rect (index: INTEGER): WEL_RECT
        -- Rectangle of button at the zero-based 'index'.
    require
        exists: exists;
        index_large_enough: index >= 0;
        index_small_enough: index < button_count
    ensure
        result_not_void: Result /= void

i_th_button (index: INTEGER): WEL_TOOL_BAR_BUTTON
        -- Button at the zero-based 'index'.
    require
        exists: exists;
        index_large_enough: index >= 0;
        index_small_enough: index < button_count
    ensure
        result_not_void: Result /= void
```

Accessing the Status of Buttons on a Tool Bar

A number of features provide a shorthand way to check a button's state. Each of the routines takes the command identifier for the button and returns *True* or *False,* depending on whether the button is in the specified state. For example, you can determine if a button with the command identifier *Command_id* is enabled on a tool bar referenced by the variable *tool_bar* with the call

```
tool_bar.button_enabled (Command_id)
```

The states you can check for include checked, enabled, hidden, indeterminate, and pressed.

```
button_checked (command_id: INTEGER): BOOLEAN
        -- Is the button identified by 'command_id' checked?
    require
        exists: exists

button_enabled (command_id: INTEGER): BOOLEAN
        -- Is the button identified by 'command_id' enabled?
    require
        exists: exists
```

```
button_hidden (command_id: INTEGER): BOOLEAN
        -- Is the button identified by 'command_id' hidden?
    require
        exists: exists

button_indeterminate (command_id: INTEGER): BOOLEAN
        -- Is the button identified by 'command_id'
        -- indeterminate?
    require
        exists: exists

button_pressed (command_id: INTEGER): BOOLEAN
        -- Is the button identified by 'command_id' pressed?
    require
        exists: exists
```

Changing the Status of Buttons on a Tool Bar

In a similar fashion, given a specific command identifier, you can change the state of individual buttons. For example, to check or uncheck a button, you can call *check_button* or *uncheck_button;* to hide or show a button, call *hide_button* or *show_button.*

```
check_button (command_id: INTEGER)
        -- Checks a button identified by 'command_id'.
    require
        exists: exists
    ensure
        button_is_checked: button_checked (command_id)

uncheck_button (command_id: INTEGER)
        -- Unchecks a button identified by 'command_id'
    require
        exists: exists
    ensure
        button_unchecked: not button_checked (command_id)

hide_button (command_id: INTEGER)
        -- Hide the button identified by 'command_id'.
    require
        exists: exists
    ensure
        button_hidden: button_hidden (command_id)

show_button (command_id: INTEGER)
        -- Show the button identified by 'command_id'.
    require
        exists: exists
```

```
      ensure
          button_shown: not button_hidden (command_id)

disable_button (command_id: INTEGER)
          -- Disable the button identified by 'command_id'.
      require
          exists: exists
      ensure
          button_disabled: not button_enabled (command_id)

enable_button (command_id: INTEGER)
          -- Enable the button identified by 'command_id'.
      require
          exists: exists
      ensure
          button_enabled: button_enabled (command_id)

press_button (command_id: INTEGER)
          -- Press the button identified by 'command_id'.
      require
          exists: exists
      ensure
          button_pressed: button_pressed (command_id)

release_button (command_id: INTEGER)
          -- Release the button identified by 'command_id'.
      require
          exists: exists
      ensure
          button_not_pressed: not button_pressed (command_id)

clear_indeterminate_state (command_id: INTEGER)
          -- Clear the indeterminate state of the button
          -- identified by 'command_id'.
      require
          exists: exists
      ensure
          button_not_indeterminate: not button_indeterminate (com-
              mand_id)

set_indeterminate_state (command_id: INTEGER)
          -- Set the indeterminate state of the button
          -- identified by 'command_id'.
      require
          exists: exists
      ensure
          button_indeterminate: button_indeterminate (command_id)
```

Setting Bitmaps on a Tool Bar

Each tool bar button can display a bitmap image. The tool bar stores the information for each button image in an internal list. The list contains bitmap images of the same size, with indexes starting at zero. You can add bitmaps to a tool bar by calling *add_bitmaps* and passing a *WEL_TOOL_BAR_BITMAP* structure. If you need to add more than one bitmap at a time, you can create a large bitmap image with each smaller bitmap arranged horizontally. The *bitmap_count* parameter lets Windows know how many smaller bitmaps the bitmap contains.

The *add_bitmaps* routine sets the *last_bitmap_index* to the index of the first bitmap image added in each call to *add_bitmaps*. For instance, if we create a *WEL_TOOL_BAR_BITMAP* structure with a large bitmap containing four smaller bitmap images, and then call

```
tool_bar.add_bitmaps (bitmaps, 4)
```

then the zero-based value of *last_bitmap_index* will be 0. A subsequent call to *add_bitmaps* would set *last_bitmap_index* to 4.

```
add_bitmaps (bitmap: WEL_TOOL_BAR_BITMAP; bitmap_count: INTEGER)
        -- Add bitmaps.
    require
        exists: exists;
        bitmap_not_void: bitmap /= void;
        positive_bitmap_count: bitmap_count > 0

last_bitmap_index: INTEGER
        -- Last bitmap index added by 'add_bitmaps'.
```

Normally, tool bar bitmap images have the dimensions 16 by 15 pixels. You can call *set_bitmap_size* to change the default dimensions, but you must do so before the first call to *add_bitmaps*.

```
set_bitmap_size (a_width, a_height: INTEGER)
        -- Sets the size of the bitmapped images to be added to
        -- the toolbar.
        -- The size can be set only before adding any
        -- bitmaps to the toolbar. If an application does
        -- not explicitly set the bitmap size, the size
        -- defaults to 16 by 15 pixels.
    require
        exists: exists;
        positive_width: a_width >= 0;
        positive_height: a_height >= 0
```

The *WEL_TOOL_BAR_BITMAP* structure can be created from a bitmap defined as a resource, a predefined bitmap image, or from a bitmap represented by the WEL class *WEL_BITMAP,* using the creation procedures *make_by_id, make_by_predefined_id,* and *make_by_bitmap.* The structure basically holds a reference to the underlying bitmap image via its *bitmap_id* and *instance* attributes.

```
class interface
     WEL_TOOL_BAR_BITMAP
create

     make (a_bitmap_id: INTEGER)
         require
             positive_bitmap_id: a_bitmap_id > 0
         ensure
             bitmap_id_set: bitmap_id = a_bitmap_id

     make_from_bitmap (a_bitmap: WEL_BITMAP)
         require
             bitmap_not_void: a_bitmap /= void;
             bitmap_exists: a_bitmap.exists
         ensure
             bitmap_set: bitmap_id = a_bitmap.to_integer

     make_by_predefined_id (a_bitmap_id: INTEGER)
         require
             valid_tool_bar_bitmap_constant:
             valid_tool_bar_bitmap_constant (a_bitmap_id)
         ensure
             bitmap_id_set: bitmap_id = a_bitmap_id

feature -- Access

     bitmap_id: INTEGER
             -- Resource identifier of the bitmap resource that
             -- contains the button images.

     instance: WEL_INSTANCE
             -- Instance that contains the bitmap resource
             -- 'bitmap_id'
         ensure
             result_not_void: Result /= void

feature {ANY} -- Status report

     valid_tool_bar_bitmap_constant (c: INTEGER): BOOLEAN
             -- Is 'c' a valid tool bar bitmap constant?
             -- (from WEL_IDB_CONSTANTS)

feature -- Element change
```

```
set_bitmap_id (a_bitmap_id: INTEGER)
        -- Set 'bitmap_id' with 'a_bitmap_id'.
    require
        positive_bitmap_id: a_bitmap_id > 0
    ensure
        bitmap_id_set: bitmap_id = a_bitmap_id

set_predefined_bitmap_id (a_bitmap_id: INTEGER)
        -- Set 'bitmap_id' with the system predefined resource
        -- bitmap identifier 'a_bitmap_id'.
        -- See class WEL_IDB_CONSTANTS for 'a_bitmap_id' values.
    require
        valid_tool_bar_bitmap_constant: valid_tool_bar_bitmap_
        constant (a_bitmap_id)
    ensure
        bitmap_id_set: bitmap_id = a_bitmap_id

end -- class WEL_TOOL_BAR_BITMAP
```

Commonly, a *WEL_TOOL_BAR_BITMAP* structure is created from a predefined Windows bitmap. The predefined bitmaps provide standard tool bar icon collections that can be used in your applications, and include standard file manipulation and view bitmaps. The *WEL_IDB_CONSTANT* values are listed in Table 16.4.

Setting Strings on a Tool Bar

Each tool bar button can have a textual label in addition to its bitmap image. Tool bar button labels are defined in the same way as bitmaps—each button defines a zero-based index into a collection of strings. The tool bar holds the collection of strings internally.

To set strings for tool bar button labels, you need to call *add_strings,* passing an array of *STRING* objects. The zero-based index of the first string is stored in the *last_string_index* attribute.

TABLE 16.4 *System-Defined Tool Bar Bitmap Constants (WEL_IDB_CONSTANTS)*

CONSTANT	DESCRIPTION
Idb_std_large_color	Large color standard bitmaps.
Idb_std_small_color	Small color standard bitmaps.
Idb_view_large_color	Large color view bitmaps.
Idb_view_small_color	Small color view bitmaps.

```
add_strings (strings: ARRAY [STRING])
          -- Add strings to the tool bar.
    require
          exists: exists;
          string_not_void: strings /= void;
          strings_not_empty: not strings.empty

last_string_index: INTEGER
          -- Last string index added by 'add_strings'.
```

Sizing a Tool Bar

The parent window of a tool bar automatically sets the size and position of the tool bar. The width of the tool bar is set to the width of the parent window's client area, and the height is based on the height of the tool bar buttons.

If the parent window changes size or the tool bar bitmap size has changed, then the *auto_size* routine should be called so that the tool bar can resize itself accordingly (see the next section for an example).

```
auto_size
          -- Resize tool bar after changes.
          -- An application sends the Tb_autosize message after
          -- causing the size of a tool bar to change either by
          -- setting the button or bitmap size or by adding strings
          -- for the first time.
    require
          exists: exists
```

Repositioning a Tool Bar

A tool bar must also be repositioned if its parent window changes size, particularly if the tool bar is positioned at the bottom of the window (using the *Ccs_bottom* common control style). The routine *reposition* moves a tool bar to the correct position within its parent window when called.

```
reposition
          -- Reposition the bar according to the parent.
          -- This function needs to be called in the
          -- `on_size' function of the parent.
    require
          exists: exists
```

For example, to manage the resizing and repositioning of a tool bar, a common implementation of *on_size* in the parent window is

```
on_size (size_type, new_width, new_height: INTEGER) is
        -- Resize tool bar
  do
        tool_bar.auto_size
        tool_bar.reposition
  end
```

Message Hooks in a Tool Bar

A tool bar supports customization internally. That is, your applications can provide complete tool bar customization facilities by responding to a selection of notification messages. Customization can involve moving buttons to new positions, adding buttons, and removing buttons. Table 16.5 lists the notification message hooks defined by *WEL_TOOL_BAR* that are used to support customization. The following sections describe how and when to use them.

On a Tool Bar Query Delete Message

A tool bar can be customized in two different ways—the user can drag tool bar buttons using the mouse and the shift key to reposition or delete a button, or the user can double-click the mouse to open a tool bar customize dialog box. The level of customization supported by a tool bar is configurable by your applications. You can specify which buttons can be deleted as well as what buttons can be inserted and at what position.

TABLE 16.5   *Tool Bar Messages*

MESSAGE	DESCRIPTION
on_tbn_beginadjust	The user has begun customizing the tool bar.
on_tbn_begindrag	The user has begun dragging a button in the tool bar.
on_tbn_custhelp	The user has chosen the Help button in the customize tool bar dialog box.
on_tbn_endadjust	The user has stopped customizing the tool bar.
on_tbn_enddrag	The user has stopped dragging a button in the tool bar.
on_tbn_getbuttoninfo	Retrieves tool bar customization.
on_tbn_querydelete	A button may be deleted from the tool bar while the user is customizing.
on_tbn_queryinsert	A button may be inserted to the left of the specified button while the user is customizing the tool bar.
on_tbn_reset	The user has reset the content of the customize tool bar dialog box.
on_tbn_toolbarchange	The user has customized the tool bar.

When the user begins dragging a tool bar button (with the shift key pressed), the *on_tbn_querydelete* message hook is called to determine if the button can be deleted. If this message hook returns *True,* then Windows continues the drag operation; otherwise, the drag operation is aborted.

```
on_tbn_querydelete (info: WEL_NM_TOOL_BAR)
        -- A button may be deleted from the tool bar while
        -- the user is customizing the tool bar.
    require
        exists: exists
```

The message hook *on_tbn_querydelete* is also used during the initialization of the tool bar customization dialog box. See "On a Tool Bar Adjustment Message" in this chapter.

The *on_tbn_querydelete* message hook is passed a reference to a *WEL_NM_TOOL_BAR* object. As shown in the class interface below, *WEL_NM_TOOL_BAR* holds information about the notification message that occurred and the button referred to by the message.

```
class interface
    WEL_NM_TOOL_BAR

feature -- Access
    button: WEL_TOOL_BAR_BUTTON
            -- Button associated with the notification. This
            -- member contains valid information only with the
            -- Tbn_queryinsert and Tbn_querydelete notification
            -- messages.
        require
            exists: exists
        ensure
            result_not_void: Result /= void

    button_id: INTEGER
            -- Information about the command identifier of the
            -- button associated with the notification.
        require
            exists: exists

    hdr: WEL_NMHDR
            -- Information about the Wm_notify message.
        require
            exists: exists
        ensure
            result_not_void: Result /= void
```

```
        text: STRING
                -- Text of the button associated with the notifica-
tion.
            require
                exists: exists
        text_count: INTEGER
                -- Count of characters in the button text.
            require
                exists: exists
            ensure
                positive_result: Result >= 0
feature -- Element change
        set_button (new_button: WEL_TOOL_BAR_BUTTON)
                -- Set the button to 'button'. When on_tbn_get-
                -- buttoninfo is called
                -- it is passed an empty WEL_NM_TOOL_BAR structure.
                -- Use this routine to set the tbButton element.
            require
                exists: exists;
                button_not_void: new_button /= void;
                button_exists: new_button.exists
            ensure
                button_set: button.is_equal (new_button)
        set_text (new_text: STRING)
                -- Set the text to 'text'. When on_tbn_getbuttoninfo
                -- is called it is passed an empty WEL_NM_TOOL_BAR
                -- structure. Use this routine to set the pszText
                -- and cchText elements.
            require
                exists: exists;
                text_not_void: new_text /= void
            ensure
                text_set: text.is_equal (new_text);
                text_count_set: text_count = new_text.count
end -- class WEL_NM_TOOL_BAR
```

On a Tool Bar Query Insert Message

When the user releases the button during a tool bar button drag operation, Windows first determines the position of the mouse cursor. If the mouse cursor resides outside the tool bar, then the button is deleted. If the mouse cursor resides within the tool bar, then the message hook *on_tbn_queryinsert* is called to determine if the dragged button can be inserted to the left of the button at or near the mouse cursor. If *on_tbn_queryinsert* returns *True,* then the button is inserted; otherwise, it is left at its original position.

```
on_tbn_queryinsert (info: WEL_NM_TOOL_BAR)
         -- A button may be inserted to the left of the
         -- specified button while the user is customizing
         -- the tool bar.
   require
      exists: exists
```

The message hook *on_tbn_querydelete* is also used during the initialization of the tool bar customization dialog box (see "On a Tool Bar Adjustment Message").

On a Tool Bar Change Message

Once a tool bar button drag operation is completed, the *on_tbn_toolbarchange* message hook is called. This hook is called whenever a button is repositioned or deleted.

```
on_tbn_toolbarchange
         -- The user has customized the tool bar.
   require
      exists: exists
```

On a Tool Bar Adjustment Message

Windows provides a Customize dialog that is displayed whenever the user double-clicks the tool bar. Note, the tool bar must have the *Ccs_adjustable* style to allow it to be customized. The *on_tbn_beginadjust* message hook is called after the user double-clicks, but before the dialog box is created.

During the execution of this message hook, you can save the current state of the tool bar to allow the user to restore the tool bar to its original configuration before customization began. The message *Tb_saverestore* can be used to save and restore the state of a tool bar.

```
on_tbn_beginadjust
         -- The user has begun customizing the tool bar.
   require
      exists: exists
```

Windows determines which tool bar buttons appear in the customize dialog by sending a series of query messages. The message hook *on_tbn_queryinsert* is called to determine if the tool bar allows buttons to be inserted. As soon as *on_tbn_queryinsert* returns *True,* Windows stops calling the message hook. If *False* is returned for all buttons, then the customize dialog is destroyed. Next, Windows calls *on_tbn_querydelete* for each button in the tool bar to determine if it can be deleted. Tool bar buttons that cause *False* to be returned by *on_tbn_querydelete* are grayed in the customize dialog box. Finally, whenever Windows requires information about a button, such as its icon, command identifier, and text, the *on_tbn_getbuttoninfo* message hook is called (see "On a Tool Bar Get Button Info Message").

The *on_tbn_endadjust* message hook is called once the user has completed the customization and dismissed the dialog box.

```
on_tbn_endadjust
        -- The user has stopped customizing the tool bar.
    require
        exists: exists
```

On a Tool Bar Get Button Info Message

Windows assigns a zero-based index to each button it requests information about. Your applications can associate this zero-based index with a collection of tool bar buttons that you allow the user to use. The *info* parameter holds the Windows-assigned index in the *button_id* parameter.

When your application receives this message, you can determine which button Windows needs information about using the *button_id,* set the requested information in the *info* structure using *set_button* and *set_text,* and set the message return value to *True.* Windows does not know how many buttons your application supports, so it will continue to call *on_tbn_getbuttoninfo* messages until the message hook returns *False.*

```
on_tbn_getbuttoninfo (info: WEL_NM_TOOL_BAR)
        -- Retrieves tool bar customization.
    require
        exists: exists
```

On a Tool Bar Help Message

The tool bar customize dialog box contains a Help button. Whenever the user clicks this button, the *on_tbn_custhelp* message hook is called. You can then display your own application help information for customizing the tool bar.

```
on_tbn_custhelp
        -- The user has chosen the Help button in the
        -- customize tool bar dialog box.
    require
        exists: exists
```

On a Tool Bar Reset Message

A Reset button also exists on the customize dialog box that can be used to allow the user to reset the tool bar configuration to what it was before the customization dialog box was displayed. The message hook *on_tbn_reset* is called whenever the Reset button is clicked. Your application must implement any necessary code to save and restore the state of a tool bar.

```
on_tbn_reset
          -- The user has reset the content of the customise
          -- tool bar dialog box.
      require
          exists: exists
```

On a Tool Bar Drag Message

A tool bar also supports customized drag-and-drop operations. If the user attempts to drag a tool bar button without holding the shift key, then the message hooks *on_tbn_begindrag* and *on_tbn_end_drag* are called at the beginning and end of the drag operation. You can implement customized drag-and-drop operations using these message hooks.

```
on_tbn_begindrag (info: WEL_NM_TOOL_BAR)
          -- The user has begun dragging a button in the tool bar.
      require
          exists: exists

on_tbn_enddrag (info: WEL_NM_TOOL_BAR)
          -- The user has stopped dragging a button in the tool bar.
      require
          exists: exists
```

The following example creates a fully customizable tool bar that provides access to all of the standard Windows tool bar buttons as defined in *WEL_STANDARD_TOOL_BAR_BITMAP_CONSTANTS*. The class *TOOL_BAR* listed in Example 16.6 provides a reusable tool bar abstraction for creating standard tool bars and provides a simple interface for creating tool bars for file operations, edit operations, and other standard tool bar operations. We reuse this class in the ReBar example at the end of this chapter.

The creation procedure *make* initializes an empty tool bar with a collection of buttons stored in the attribute *buttons*. Individual buttons can be added to the tool bar by retrieving them from the *buttons* collection and calling *add_buttons*. Two additional creation procedures initialize a tool bar with a predefined selection of buttons. For instance, *make_edit* adds common edit buttons to the new tool bar and *make_file* adds file buttons. Additional creation procedures could be added in the future to create tool bars for other common button combinations.

The initialize routine does most of the initialization work—it creates each of the buttons using a *WEL_TOOL_BAR_BUTTON* structure and adds them to the buttons collection for later use. Each button uses one of the standard bitmap icons and a unique command identifier.

Example 16.6 Tool Bar Control, TOOL_BAR Class (bar\toolbar)

```
class TOOL_BAR
inherit
    WEL_TOOL_BAR
        redefine
            make, default_style,
            on_tbn_querydelete,
            on_tbn_queryinsert,
            on_tbn_getbuttoninfo
        end
    WEL_WINDOWS_ROUTINES
        export
            {NONE} all
        end
    APPLICATION_IDS
        export
            {NONE} all
        end
    WEL_STANDARD_TOOL_BAR_BITMAP_CONSTANTS
        export
            {NONE} all
        end
    WEL_IDB_CONSTANTS
        export
            {NONE} all
        end
    WEL_CCS_CONSTANTS
        export
            {NONE} all
        end
create
    make, make_edit, make_file
```

```
feature {NONE} -- Initialization

    make (a_parent: WEL_WINDOW; an_id: INTEGER) is
            -- Initialize the tool bar with no buttons. Buttons can
            -- be added from the 'button' array.
        do
            Precursor (a_parent, an_id)
            initialize
        end

    make_edit (a_parent: WEL_WINDOW; an_id: INTEGER) is
            -- Initialize the tool bar with edit buttons including
            -- copy, paste, cut and delete.
        do
            make (a_parent, an_id)
            add_edit_buttons
        end

    make_file (a_parent: WEL_WINDOW; an_id: INTEGER) is
            -- Initialize the tool bar with file buttons including
            -- new, open, save, print and print preview.
        do
            make (a_parent, an_id)
            add_file_buttons
        end

feature -- Access

    buttons: ARRAY [WEL_TOOL_BAR_BUTTON]
            -- Available buttons.

feature -- Status setting

    add_edit_buttons is
            -- Add edit buttons to tool bar including copy, paste,
            -- cut, and delete.
        do
            add_buttons (<<
                buttons.item (8),
                buttons.item (9),
                buttons.item (10),
                buttons.item (11)
                >>)
        end

    add_file_buttons is
            -- Add file buttons to tool bar including new, open,
            -- save, print, print preview.
        do
                add_buttons (<<
                buttons.item (0),
```

```
                        buttons.item (1),
                        buttons.item (2),
                        buttons.item (3),
            buttons.item (4)
                        >>)
           end


    feature -- Events

        on_tbn_querydelete (info: WEL_NM_TOOL_BAR) is
                -- Can the button be deleted?
           do
                -- All buttons can be deleted
                set_return_value (1)
           end

        on_tbn_queryinsert (info: WEL_NM_TOOL_BAR) is
                -- Can the button be inserted?
           do
                -- All buttons can be inserted
                set_return_value (1)
           end

        on_tbn_getbuttoninfo (info: WEL_NM_TOOL_BAR) is
                -- Return information for the requested button
           do
                if info.button_id <= buttons.upper then
                     info.set_button (buttons.item (info.button_id))
                     -- get the resource string for the button id and use
                     -- it as the description string
                     info.set_text (resource_string_id (buttons.item
                     (info.button_id).command_id))
                     set_return_value (1)
                end
           end

    feature {NONE} -- Implementation

        std_bitmaps, view_bitmaps: WEL_TOOL_BAR_BITMAP

        std_bitmap_index, view_bitmap_index: INTEGER

        Number_std_bitmaps: INTEGER is 14

        Number_view_bitmaps: INTEGER is 8

        initialize is
                -- Initialize the tool bar
           local
                file_new_button, file_open_button, file_save_button,
```

```
            print_button, print_preview_button: WEL_TOOL_BAR_BUTTON
        find_button, undo_button, redo_button, copy_button,
            paste_button, cut_button: WEL_TOOL_BAR_BUTTON
        edit_delete_button, replace_button, properties_button,
            view_large_icons_button: WEL_TOOL_BAR_BUTTON
        view_small_icons_button, view_list_button,
            view_details_button, view_sort_name_button:
            WEL_TOOL_BAR_BUTTON
        view_sort_size_button, view_sort_date_button,
            view_sort_type_button: WEL_TOOL_BAR_BUTTON
    do
        -- add the standard bitmaps
        create std_bitmaps.make_by_predefined_id
            (Idb_std_small_color)
        add_bitmaps (std_bitmaps, Number_std_bitmaps)
        std_bitmap_index := last_bitmap_index
        -- add the view bitmaps
        create view_bitmaps.make_by_predefined_id
            (Idb_view_small_color)
        add_bitmaps (view_bitmaps, Number_view_bitmaps)
        view_bitmap_index := last_bitmap_index
        -- create the std buttons
        create file_new_button.make_button (std_bitmap_index +
            Std_filenew, Id_filenew_constant)
        create file_open_button.make_button (std_bitmap_index +
            Std_fileopen, Id_fileopen_constant)
        create file_save_button.make_button (std_bitmap_index +
            Std_filesave, Id_filesave_constant)
        create print_button.make_button (std_bitmap_index +
            Std_print, Id_print_constant)
        create print_preview_button.make_button (std_bitmap_index
            + Std_printpre, Id_printpre_constant)
        create find_button.make_button (std_bitmap_index +
            Std_find, Id_find_constant)
        create undo_button.make_button (std_bitmap_index +
            Std_undo, Id_undo_constant)
        create redo_button.make_button (std_bitmap_index +
            Std_redow, Id_redow_constant)
        create copy_button.make_button (std_bitmap_index +
            Std_copy, Id_copy_constant)
        create paste_button.make_button (std_bitmap_index +
            Std_paste, Id_paste_constant)
        create cut_button.make_button (std_bitmap_index +
            Std_cut, Id_cut_constant)
        create edit_delete_button.make_button (std_bitmap_index +
            Std_delete, Id_delete_constant)
        create replace_button.make_button (std_bitmap_index +
            Std_replace, Id_replace_constant)
        create properties_button.make_button (std_bitmap_index +
            Std_properties, Id_properties_constant)
        -- create the view buttons
```

```
        create view_large_icons_button.make_button
            (view_bitmap_index +
        View_largeicons, Id_viewlargeicons_constant)
        create view_small_icons_button.make_button
            (view_bitmap_index + View_smallicons,
        Id_viewsmallicons_constant)
        create view_list_button.make_button (view_bitmap_index +
            View_list, Id_viewlist_constant)
        create view_details_button.make_button (view_bitmap_index
            + View_details, Id_viewdetails_constant)
        create view_sort_name_button.make_button
        (view_bitmap_index + View_sortname,
            Id_viewsortname_constant)
        create view_sort_size_button.make_button
        (view_bitmap_index + View_sortsize,
            Id_viewsortsize_constant)
        create view_sort_date_button.make_button
        (view_bitmap_index + View_sortdate,
            Id_viewsortdate_constant)
        create view_sort_type_button.make_button
        (view_bitmap_index + View_sorttype,
            Id_viewsorttype_constant)
        -- store buttons in array
        create buttons.make (0, Number_std_bitmaps +
            Number_view_bitmaps - 1)
        buttons.put (file_new_button, 0)
        buttons.put (file_open_button, 1)
        buttons.put (file_save_button, 2)
        buttons.put (print_button, 3)
        buttons.put (print_preview_button, 4)
        buttons.put (find_button, 5)
        buttons.put (undo_button, 6)
        buttons.put (redo_button, 7)
        buttons.put (copy_button, 8)
        buttons.put (paste_button, 9)
        buttons.put (cut_button, 10)
        buttons.put (edit_delete_button, 11)
        buttons.put (replace_button, 12)
        buttons.put (properties_button, 13)
        buttons.put (view_large_icons_button, 14)
        buttons.put (view_small_icons_button, 15)
        buttons.put (view_list_button, 16)
        buttons.put (view_details_button, 17)
        buttons.put (view_sort_name_button, 18)
        buttons.put (view_sort_size_button, 19)
        buttons.put (view_sort_date_button, 20)
        buttons.put (view_sort_type_button, 21)
    end
default_style: INTEGER is
        -- Default style used to create the control
    once
```

```
        Result := Precursor + Ccs_adjustable
    end

set_return_value (value: INTEGER) is
        -- Set the return value of the parent. If the parent is a
        -- WEL_UNPOSITIONABLE_CONTROL_CONTAINER then set the re-
        -- turn value of its parent. This is required because of
        -- problems in the processing of control return values.
    local
        unpositionable: WEL_UNPOSITIONABLE_CONTROL_CONTAINER
    do
        unpositionable ?= parent
        if unpositionable = Void then
            parent.set_message_return_value (value)
        else
            parent.parent.set_message_return_value (value)
        end
    end

end -- class TOOL_BAR
```

The default style of the tool bar is redefined to include *Ccs_adjustable.*
This indicates to Windows that the tool bar will allow customization via drag-
and-drop operations and the Customize dialog box. The message hooks
on_tbn_querydelete, on_tbn_queryinsert, and *on_tbn_getbuttoninfo* are implemented to support full customization of the tool bar, given the complete collection of standard tool bar buttons. The customization facilities allow all buttons
to be deleted and all buttons to be inserted at any position. The complete collection of buttons can be added to any tool bar created using this class.

The main window, Example 16.7 utilizes the customizable tool bar by
creating an instance in its creation procedure *make.* The message hook *on_size*
is used to reposition and resize the tool bar when the main window changes
size, and the *on_notify* hook is used to provide tool tip information for tool bar
buttons.

Example 16.7 Tool Bar Control, MAIN_WINDOW Class (bar\toolbar)

```
class MAIN_WINDOW
inherit
    WEL_FRAME_WINDOW
        redefine
            on_menu_command,
            on_size, on_notify
        end
    APPLICATION_IDS
```

```
            export
                {NONE} all
            end
        WEL_TTN_CONSTANTS
            export
                {NONE} all
            end
        WEL_TBN_CONSTANTS
            export
                {NONE} all
            end
creation
    make
feature

    make is
            -- Initialize the main window
        do
            make_top ("Main Window")
            -- initialize the toolbar
            create tool_bar.make_file (Current, -1)
            -- initialize other controls
            set_menu (main_menu)
            resize (340, 270)
        end

    tool_bar: TOOL_BAR
            -- Tool bar

    on_menu_command (menu_id: INTEGER) is
            -- Check for a menu command
        do
            inspect menu_id
            when Id_fileexit_constant then
                destroy
            else
                -- ignore
            end
        end

    on_size (size_type, new_width, new_height: INTEGER) is
            -- Reposition tool bar
        do
        tool_bar.auto_size
            tool_bar.reposition
        end

    on_notify (control_id: INTEGER; info: WEL_NMHDR) is
            -- Display tooltips
        local
```

```
            tt_text: WEL_TOOLTIP_TEXT
      do
          if info.code = Ttn_needtext then
              create tt_text.make_by_nmhdr (info)
              tt_text.set_text_id (tt_text.hdr.id_from)
          end
      end

feature {NONE} -- Implementation
    main_menu: WEL_MENU is
          -- Main menu created from a menu resource
      once
          create Result.make_by_id (Id_mainmenu_constant)
      end
end -- class MAIN_WINDOW
```

Figure 16.8 shows the tool bar created by this example with the Customize Tool bar dialog box open. The buttons listed in the right pane can be removed from the tool bar, while the buttons on the left can be added. In addition to the standard buttons, a separator button can be added to any position in the tool bar to separate related groups of buttons or just to add spacing between buttons.

ReBar Controls

A ReBar is a container for child controls and windows that provides the ability to reposition and resize each child. Each child of a ReBar control is assigned to a ReBar band, which defines the style and behavior traits of the band itself. A ReBar is often used to hold a number of tool bars (each in its own band) that can be repositioned by the user. This provides an extensive range of user customization for applications—tool bars can be moved to separate rows of the ReBar moved beside another tool bar on the same row, and removed from the ReBar altogether. Used with the standard tool bar customization facilities, the ReBar provides an almost unlimited range of user customization.

Creating a ReBar

A ReBar is created as a child of another window, typically an instance of WEL_FRAME_WINDOW. The creation procedure make takes two parameters—a reference to the parent window and an identification number.

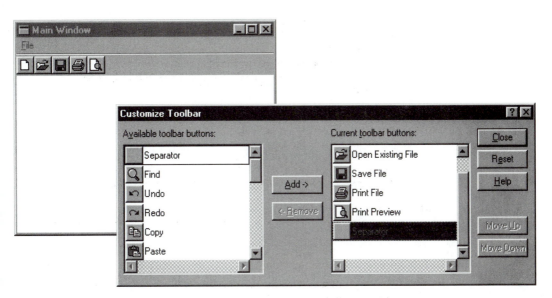

FIGURE 16.8. Tool bar example.

Before using the *WEL_REBAR* class, you must ensure that the appropriate Windows DLL has been loaded correctly. The class *WEL_INIT_COMM-CTRL_EX* can be used to initialize the common control DLL with the required parameters *Icc_bar_classes* and *Icc_cool_classes* (see Example 16.8).

Determining Bar Information in a ReBar

The ReBar style is stored in an instance of *WEL_REBARINFO*. This information can be accessed via the function *get_bar_info,* which returns an appropriately initialized ReBar information structure. The information contained in this structure includes a handle to the ReBar's image list.

```
get_bar_info: WEL_REBARINFO
        -- Retrieve all the information about the current rebar
        -- control
    require
        exists: exists
```

TABLE 16.6   *ReBar Mask Message Constants (WEL_RBIM_CONSTANTS)*

CONSTANT	DESCRIPTION
Rbim_imagelist	The image list member is valid and should be used.

The interface of *WEL_REBARINFO* is shown next. You will notice that the only public feature is *mask*. All other features are used internally by the *WEL_REBAR* control. Table 16.6 lists the values that the attribute *mask* can include.

```
class interface
      WEL_REBARINFO

create
      make,
      make_by_pointer

feature -- Access

      mask: INTEGER
              -- Array of flags that indicate which of the other
              -- structure members contain valid data or which are
              -- to be filled in. This member can be a combination
              -- of the Rbim_* values (only one for now).
              -- See class WEL_RBIM_CONSTANTS.
          require
              exists: exists

feature {WEL_REBAR} -- Implementation

      set_cbsize (value: INTEGER)
              -- Set `cbSize' (size of the structure) as `value'.

      set_mask (value: INTEGER)
              -- Set `mask' with `value.
          ensure
              mask_set: mask = value

end -- class WEL_REBARINFO
```

Setting Bar Information in a ReBar

The rebar information can be changed by calling *set_bar_info* and passing an initialized instance of *WEL_REBARINFO*.

```
set_bar_info (info: WEL_REBARINFO)
        -- Make 'info' the new information about the rebar.
    require
        exists: exists;
        info_not_void: info /= void;
        info_exists: info.exists
```

Determining Row Information in a ReBar

The current number of rows in a ReBar control can be determined by the function *row_count*. Each row may contain one or more bands and can have an arbitrary height. The height of each individual row can be determined by calling *row_height* and passing the zero-based index of the row.

```
row_count: INTEGER
        -- Number of rows of bands in the rebar control.
    require
        exists: exists
    ensure
        positive_result: Result >= 0
row_height (index: INTEGER): INTEGER
        -- Retrieve the height of the zero-based 'index' band.
    require
        exists: exists
    ensure
        positive_result: Result >= 0
```

Adding Bands to a ReBar

Each child widow is contained in a ReBar band. The band holds the window, the style in which the window will be displayed, an optional background image, band dimensions, and optional text. The class interface of *WEL_REBARBAND-INFO* follows.

```
class interface
        WEL_REBARBANDINFO

create
        make,
        make_with_id,
        make_by_pointer

feature -- Access

        background_color: WEL_COLOR_REF
                -- Background color used for the background of the
                -- control
```

```
    require
        exists: exists
    ensure
        color_not_void: Result /= void
```

child: WEL_WINDOW
```
        -- Child currently in the rebar.
    require
        exists: exists
```

child_minimum_height: INTEGER
```
        -- Minimum width required by the child.
    require
        exists: exists
    ensure
        positive_result: Result >= 0
```

child_minimum_width: INTEGER
```
        -- Minimum width required by the child.
    require
        exists: exists
    ensure
        positive_result: Result >= 0
```

foreground_color: WEL_COLOR_REF
```
        -- Foreground color used for the text of the
        -- control
    require
        exists: exists
    ensure
        color_not_void: Result /= void
```

id: INTEGER
```
        -- 'id' of the band.
    require
        exists: exists
```

length: INTEGER
```
        -- Current 'length' of the band.
    require
        exists: exists
    ensure
        positive_result: Result >= 0
```

mask: INTEGER
```
        -- Array of flags that indicate which of the other
        -- structure members contain valid data or which are
        -- to be filled in. This member can be a combination
        -- of the Rbbim_* values.
        -- See class WEL_RBBIM_CONSTANTS.
    require
        exists: exists
```

```
        style: INTEGER
                -- Array of flags that specify the band style.
                -- This value can be a combination of RBBS_*
                -- constants. See class WEL_RBBS_CONSTANTS.
            require
                exists: exists


        text: STRING
                -- Item text
            require
                exists: exists

feature -- Element change

        set_background_bitmap (bmp: WEL_BITMAP)
                -- Set 'background_bitmap' with 'bmp'.
            require
                exists: exists;
                bitmap_not_void: bmp /= void

        set_background_color (color: WEL_COLOR_REF)
                -- Set 'background_color' as 'color'.
            require
                exists: exists;
                color_not_void: color /= void
            ensure
                color_set: background_color.is_equal (color)

        set_child (window: WEL_WINDOW)
                -- Set 'child' as 'window'.
                -- Do not use this feature for controls as tool bars
                -- that reposition themselves automatically at a
                -- specific place. Use 'set_reposition_child'.
            require
                exists: exists;
                window_not_void: window /= void;
                window_is_inside: window.is_inside
            ensure
                window_set: child.is_equal (window)

        set_child_minimum_height (value: INTEGER)
                -- Set 'child_minimum_height' as 'value'.
            require
                exists: exists;
                valid_value: value >= 0
            ensure
                value_set: child_minimum_height = value

        set_child_minimum_width (value: INTEGER)
                -- Set 'child_minimum_width' as 'value'.
            require
                exists: exists;
```

```
                valid_value: value >= 0
        ensure
            value_set: child_minimum_width = value

set_foreground_color (color: WEL_COLOR_REF)
            -- Set 'foreground_color' as 'color'.
        require
            exists: exists;
            color_not_void: color /= void
        ensure
            color_set: foreground_color.is_equal (color)

set_id (value: INTEGER)
            -- Set 'id' as 'value'.
        require
            exists: exists
        ensure
            id_set: id = value

set_length (value: INTEGER)
            -- Set 'length' as 'value'.
        require
            exists: exists;
            valid_value: value >= 0
        ensure
            length_set: length = value

set_style (value: INTEGER)
            -- Set 'cbSize' (size of the structure) as 'value'.
        require
            exists: exists
        ensure
            style_set: style = value

set_text (txt: STRING)
            -- Set 'text' as 'txt'.
        require
            exists: exists;
            a_text_not_void: txt /= void
        ensure
            text_set: text.is_equal (txt)

set_unpositionable_child (window: WEL_WINDOW)
            -- Set 'child' as 'window'.
            -- Use this feature for controls as toolbars
            -- that reposition themselves automatically at a
            -- specific place. Use 'set_reposition_child'.
            -- Do not use for usual controls.
        require
            exists: exists;
            window_not_void: window /= void;
            window_is_inside: window.is_inside
```

```
            ensure
                window_set: child.is_equal (window.parent)

    feature -- Basic operation

        clear_mask
                -- Clear the current 'mask'.
                -- Call it before to call a set_? feature when you
                -- want to change only one parameter.
            require
                exists: exists

    end -- class WEL_REBARBANDINFO
```

To add a child window, you first need to create a *WEL_REBARBAND-INFO* instance and set any required attributes. The minimum you need to do is set the child window using the call *set-child*. You can also set the colors, background bitmap, dimensions, and style. The style value can be a combination of the constants defined in *WEL_RBBS_CONSTANTS,* listed in Table 16.7.

Once you have created and initialized a *WEL_REBARBANDINFO* structure, you can add it to a rebar control by calling *append_band, insert_band,* or *prepend_band.* Routine *append_band* adds the new band to the end of the rebar, while *insert_band* positions the new band at the specified index. *prepend_band* adds the new band before all other bands in the rebar.

TABLE 16.7   *(WEL_RBBS_CONSTANTS)*

CONSTANT	DESCRIPTION
Rbbs_break	The band should be drawn on a new line.
Rbbs_childedge	The band has an edge at the top and bottom of the child window.
Rbbs_fixedbmp	The background bitmap does not move when the band is resized.
Rbbs_fixedsize	The band cannot be resized. No resize gripper appears on the band.
Rbbs_hidden	The band is hidden.
Rbbs_novert	The band does not display its text attribute.

```
append_band (band: WEL_REBARBANDINFO)
        -- Insert 'band' in the rebar.
    require
        exists: exists;
        valid_band: band /= void and then band.exists
```

```
insert_band (band: WEL_REBARBANDINFO; index: INTEGER)
        -- Insert 'band' in the rebar.
    require
        exists: exists;
        band_not_void: band /= void;
        band_exists: band.exists;
        index_large_enough: index >= 0;
        index_small_enough: index < band_count

prepend_band (band: WEL_REBARBANDINFO)
        -- Insert 'band' in the rebar.
    require
        exists: exists;
        valid_band: band /= void and then band.exists
```

Removing Bands from a ReBar Control

Once a band has been added to a ReBar, it can subsequently be removed by calling *delete_band* and specifying its zero-based index.

```
delete_band (index: INTEGER)
        -- Delete the zero-based 'index' band from the rebar.
    require
        exists: exists;
        index_large_enough: index >= 0;
        index_small_enough: index < band_count
```

Determining Band Information in a ReBar

The number of bands contained by a ReBar can be determined by calling the function *band_count*. Information about each individual bar can be accessed via the function *get_band_info* and specifying the zero-based index of the band.

```
band_count: INTEGER
        -- Number of bands in the rebar control.
    require
        exists: exists
    ensure
        positive_result: Result >= 0
get_band_info (index: INTEGER): WEL_REBARBANDINFO
        -- Retrieve all the informations about the zero-based
        -- 'index' band of the rebar.
    require
        exists: exists;
        index_large_enough: index >= 0;
        index_small_enough: index < band_count
```

Setting Band Information in a ReBar

The information for a band can be changed after it has been added to the ReBar control by calling *set_band_info,* passing a new *WEL_REBARBANDINFO* structure, and specifying the zero-based index of the band.

```
set_band_info (info: WEL_REBARBANDINFO; index: INTEGER)
        -- Make 'info' the new information about the zero-based
        -- 'index' band of the rebar.
    require
        exists: exists;
        index_large_enough: index >= 0;
        index_small_enough: index < band_count;
        info_not_void: info /= void;
        info_exists: info.exists
```

Repositioning a ReBar

A ReBar control will automatically position itself according to the parent window's dimensions. If the parent window changes size, then the ReBar should be informed by calling *reposition* so that it can adjust its own dimensions and position accordingly.

```
reposition
        -- Reposition the window according to the parent.
        -- This function needs to be called in the
        -- 'on_size' routine of the parent.
    require
        exists: exists
```

On a Height Changed Message in a ReBar

The WEL_REBAR control implements only one message hook. The message hook *on_rbn_heightchanged* is called whenever the ReBar height changes either as a result of a reposition call, when new bands are added, or when the user causes a row to be added or removed while reconfiguring the ReBar.

```
on_rbn_heightchanged
        -- The height of the rebar has changed.
    require
        exists: exists
```

The following example extends our tool bar example to use a ReBar to hold more than one repositionable tool bar. Each tool bar is contained in its own ReBar band using the default ReBar band styles.

Before using the ReBar control, we must initialize the common control DLL with two flags to ensure that the correct control definitions are loaded. The *init_application* routine of the *APPLICATION* class (Example 16.8) uses the *WEL_INIT_COMMCTRL_DLL* class to initialize the common controls DLL.

Example 16.8 ReBar Example, APPLICATION Class (bar\rebar)

```
class APPLICATION
inherit
    WEL_APPLICATION
        redefine
            init_application
        end
    APPLICATION_IDS
        export
            {NONE} all
        end
    WEL_ICC_CONSTANTS
        export
            {NONE} all
        end
creation
    make
feature

    main_window: MAIN_WINDOW is
            -- Main window
        once
            create Result.make
        end

    common_ctl_dll_ex: WEL_INIT_COMMCTRL_EX
            -- Common controls dll

feature {NONE} -- Implementation

    init_application is
            -- Load common controls dlls
        do
            create common_ctl_dll_ex.make_with_flags (Icc_bar_classes
            + Icc_cool_classes)
        end

end -- class APPLICATION
```

The implementation of the *MAIN_WINDOW* creates two tool bars—one with file manipulation buttons and the other with edit buttons. Both tool bars are created using the *TOOL_BAR* class from Example 16.6. The style of both tool bars is modified to include *Ccs_nodivider* and *Tbstyle_flat* by calling *set_style* after the creation instruction. *Ccs_nodivider* suppresses the drawing of a two-pixel divider that normally appears above tool bar buttons and *Tbstyle_flat* draws the tool bar using a flat button style.

As shown in Example 16.9, the tool bars are then added to the ReBar in the routine *initialize_rebar*. A ReBar band is created for each with minimum dimensions suitable for holding all of the tool bar's buttons. The tool bar window itself is added to the band using the call *set_unpositionable_child*, because the tool bar manages its own sizing and positioning. If the child window was a normal window or control, then a call to *set_child* would suffice.

Example 16.9 ReBar Example, MAIN_WINDOW Class (bar\rebar)

```
class MAIN_WINDOW
inherit
    WEL_FRAME_WINDOW
        redefine
            on_size, background_brush
        end
    WEL_COLOR_CONSTANTS
        export
            {NONE} all
        end
    APPLICATION_IDS
        export
            {NONE} all
        end
    WEL_CCS_CONSTANTS
        export
            {NONE} all
        end
    WEL_TB_STYLE_CONSTANTS
        export
            {NONE} all
        end
creation
    make
feature

    make is
            -- Initialize the main window
        do
            make_top ("Main Window")
            -- initialize the toolbars
            create tool_bar.make_file (Current, -1)
            tool_bar.set_style (tool_bar.style + Ccs_nodivider + Tb-
                style_flat)
            create tool_bar2.make_edit (Current, -1)
```

```
            tool_bar2.set_style (tool_bar2.style + Ccs_nodivider +
                Tbstyle_flat)
            -- create rebar
            create rebar.make (Current, -1)
            initialize_rebar
            set_menu (main_menu)
            resize (340, 270)
        end

    tool_bar, tool_bar2: TOOL_BAR
            -- Tool bars

    rebar: WEL_REBAR
            -- ReBar

feature -- Events

    on_size (size_type, new_width, new_height: INTEGER) is
            -- Reposition tool bar
        do
            rebar.reposition
        end

feature {NONE} -- Implementation

    main_menu: WEL_MENU is
            -- Main menu
        once
            create Result.make_by_id (Id_mainmenu_constant)
        end

    background_brush: WEL_BRUSH is
            -- Use a gray background brush to fill background
        once
            create Result.make_by_sys_color (Color_appworkspace)
        end

    initialize_rebar is
            -- Initialize the rebar
        local
            rebar_info: WEL_REBARBANDINFO
        do
            -- add tool bar
            create rebar_info.make
            rebar_info.set_unpositionable_child (tool_bar)
            rebar_info.set_child_minimum_width
                ((tool_bar.button_count * 22) + 12)
            rebar_info.set_child_minimum_height (26)
            rebar.append_band (rebar_info)
            -- add second tool bar
            create rebar_info.make
            rebar_info.set_unpositionable_child (tool_bar2)
```

```
            rebar_info.set_child_minimum_width
                ((tool_bar2.button_count * 22) + 12)
            rebar_info.set_child_minimum_height (26)
            rebar.append_band (rebar_info)
            -- reposition the rebar
            rebar.reposition
        end

    end -- class MAIN_WINDOW
```

Each band is appended to the ReBar, and finally, the ReBar is repositioned by calling *reposition*. The *background_brush* of the main window has been redefined to draw the background in gray (actually the current application workspace color) to improve the appearance of the window.

Figure 16.9 shows the two tool bars after the edit bar has been repositioned below the file bar. You will notice the resizing gripper at the left edge of each tool bar.

SUMMARY

Bar controls provide a wide variety of user interaction capabilities, ranging from simple up-down controls to tool bars and rebars. The controls can be put to many uses in your applications.

The first set of bar controls includes up-down controls, scroll bars, track bars, and progress bars. All are related in taxonomy and provide the ability to

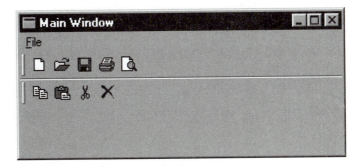

FIGURE 16.9. ReBar example.

represent a value within a specified range. You can use these controls to display a value within a range or to allow the user to select a value within a range.

The second set of bar controls, although not related in taxonomy, provide user interface components that are displayed in a horizontal (and sometimes vertical) bar-like fashion. This set of controls includes status windows, tool bars, and ReBar controls.

DIRECTORY TREE ANALYZER

IMPLEMENTING BAR CONTROLS

The DTA application uses two bar controls—a tool bar and a status bar. The tool bar is used to provide access to the most commonly required operations, such as parsing a new directory, setting application properties, and printing results. Each of the operations can be invoked by clicking on one of the buttons on the tool bar.

The status bar is used to display operational information, including the current progress of a directory parse and the total results for a parse, such as the number of directories, total number of files, and total size.

The Tool Bar

The *TOOL_BAR* class is a direct descendant of *WEL_TOOL_BAR* and makes use of the standard tool bar bitmaps available via *WEL_STANDARD_TOOL_BAR_BITMAP_CONSTANTS*. In Example 16.10, the *initialize* routine (lines 46–69) creates the tool bar buttons and assigns each an appropriate bitmap icon and command identifier. The standard tool bar bitmaps are first registered with the control with the call *add_bitmaps* (line 55) and the index to the bitmap array is stored in the variable *standard_bitmap_index*. Once registered, an offset to each of the bitmaps can be used during the creation of each button.

Example 16.10 TOOL_BAR for the Directory Tree Analyzer

```
1    class TOOL_BAR
2    inherit
3         WEL_TOOL_BAR
4              rename
5                   make as tool_bar_make
```

```
 6                    end;
 7            APPLICATION_IDS
 8                    export
 9                        {NONE} all
10                    end;
11            WEL_STANDARD_TOOL_BAR_BITMAP_CONSTANTS
12                    export
13                        {NONE} all
14                    end;
15            WEL_IDB_CONSTANTS
16                    export
17                        {NONE} all
18                    end
19   create
20          make
21   feature
22
23          make (a_parent: WEL_WINDOW) is
24                    -- Initialization
25            do
26                    tool_bar_make (a_parent, - 1)
27                    initialize
28            end;
29
30   feature
31
32          update_icons (directory_infos: CONTAINER [ANY]) is
33                    -- Element change
34            do
35                    if directory_infos = void then
36                      disable_button (idm_file_print_constant)
37                      disable_button (idm_edit_find_constant)
38                    else
39                      enable_button (idm_file_print_constant)
40                      enable_button (idm_edit_find_constant)
41                    end
42            end;
43
44   feature {NONE} -- update_icons
45
46          initialize is
47                    -- Implementation
48            local
49                    standard_bitmaps: WEL_TOOL_BAR_BITMAP;
50                    standard_bitmap_index: INTEGER;
51                    open_button, print_button, find_button,
                            properties_button,
52                            separator1_button, separator2_button:
                            WEL_TOOL_BAR_BUTTON
53            do
54                    create standard_bitmaps.make_by_predefined_id
                        (idb_std_small_color);
```

```
55                              add_bitmaps (standard_bitmaps, 1);
56                              standard_bitmap_index := last_bitmap_index;
57                              create open_button.make_button
58                                  (standard_bitmap_index + std_fileopen,
                                       idm_file_open_constant);
59                              create print_button.make_button
60                                  (standard_bitmap_index + std_print,
                                       idm_file_print_constant);
61                              create separator1_button.make_separator;
62                              create find_button.make_button
63                                  (standard_bitmap_index + std_find,
                                       idm_edit_find_constant);
64                              create separator2_button.make_separator;
65                              create properties_button.make_button (stan-
                                  dard_bitmap_index + std_properties,
66                                       idm_edit_preferences_constant);
67                              add_buttons (<<open_button, print_button,
                                  separator1_button, find_button,
68                                       separator2_button, properties_button>>)
69              end;
70
71  end -- class TOOL_BAR
```

The *update_icons* routine is used by the *MAIN_WINDOW* to update the status of tool bar buttons, given the current state of the application. In this case, if no directory parsing operation has occurred, the print and find buttons are disabled.

The Status Bar

The DTA status bar, shown in Example 16.11, contains four parts—the first part displays the application status, including the progress of a parsing operation. The second, third, and fourth parts display totals of folders, files, and file sizes for the last parsing operation.

We allocated one-half of the window width for the first part and one-sixth of the width for the remaining parts. The call to *set_parts* (lines 80–85) initializes the edges at one-half, two-thirds, and five-sixths. The final edge *(−1)* indicates that the last part should extend to the right side of the window.

The *STATUS_BAR* class also includes a set of helper routines for updating the text in each of the parts. For example, routine *set_status_part* updates the text in the first part. In this case, the text is also truncated using *truncate_path_for_width,* if necessary. This routine also sets the part text using a nondefault style *Sbt_noborders,* effectively displaying the text without borders.

Example 16.11 STATUS_BAR for the Directory Tree Analyzer

```
1     class STATUS_BAR
2     inherit
3            WEL_STATUS_WINDOW
4                 rename
5                      make as status_window_make
6                 end;
7            APPLICATION_IDS
8                 export
9                      {NONE} all
10                end;
11           WEL_SBT_CONSTANTS
12                export
13                     {NONE} all
14                end;
15           WEL_WINDOWS_ROUTINES
16    create
17           make
18    feature -- Initialization
19           make (a_parent: WEL_WINDOW) is
20                     -- make
21               do
22                    status_window_make (a_parent, - 1)
23                    initialize (a_parent.width)
24               end;
25
26    feature -- Element change
27
28           set_status_part (t: STRING) is
29                     -- Set status part
30               require
31                    str_exists: t /= void
32               local
33                    str: STRING;
34                    part_char_width: INTEGER
35               do
36                    part_char_width := rect_for_part (status_part).width //
                          average_status_bar_char_width;
37                    if t.count > part_char_width then
38                        str := truncate_path_for_width (t, part_char_width)
39                    else
40                        str := t
41                    end;
42                    set_text_part_with_style (status_part, str, sbt_noborders)
43               end;
44
45           set_folders_part (t: STRING) is
46                     -- Set folders part
47               require
48                    text_exists: t /= void
49               do
50                    set_text_part (folders_part, t)
```

```
51              end;
52
53          set_size_part (t: STRING) is
54                  -- Set size part
55              require
56                  text_exists: t /= void
57              do
58                  set_text_part (size_part, t)
59              end;
60
61          set_files_part (t: STRING) is
62                  -- Set files part
63              require
64                  text_exists: t /= void
65              do
66                  set_text_part (files_part, t)
67              end;
68
69  feature -- Initialization
70
71          initialize (new_width: INTEGER) is
72                  -- Initialize
73              require
74                  status_bar_exists: exists;
75                  valid_width: new_width >= 0
76              local
77                  part_size: INTEGER
78              do
79                  set_multiple_mode
80                  part_size := new_width // 6
81                  set_parts (<<
82                      new_width - (part_size * 3),
83                      new_width - (part_size * 2),
84                      new_width - part_size,
85                      -1>>)
86              end;
87
88  feature {NONE} -- Implementation
89
90          Status_part: INTEGER is 0;
91          Folders_part: INTEGER is 1;
92          Files_part: INTEGER is 2;
93          Size_part: INTEGER is 3;
94          Average_status_bar_char_width: INTEGER is 6;
95
96          truncate_path_for_width (path: STRING; new_width: INTEGER): STRING is
97                  -- Truncate `path' to fit in `width' characters.
98                  -- Precede `path' with ellipses to indicate preceding path
99              require
100                 path_not_void: path /= void;
101                 valid_width: new_width > 0
102             do
103                 Result := clone (path)
```

```
104                    if path.count > new_width then
105                            if new_width <= min_path_length then
106                                    Result.tail (ellipses.count)
107                                    Result.prepend (ellipses)
108                            else
109                                    Result.tail (new_width - ellipses.count)
110                                    Result.prepend (ellipses)
111                            end
112                    end
113            ensure
114                    specified_width: Result.count <= new_width
115            end;
116
117        ellipses: STRING is
118            once
119                    Result := resource_string_id (ids_ellipses_constant)
120            end;
121
122        Min_path_length: INTEGER is 6;
123
124 end -- class STATUS_BAR
```

ADVANCED CONTROLS

INTRODUCING ADVANCED CONTROLS

This chapter explores the use of advanced controls. The controls presented here include the tab control, tree view control, and header control. They each provide very flexible and different functionality for you and the user.

TYPES OF ADVANCED CONTROLS

All of the controls presented in this chapter inherit directly from *WEL_CONTROL*. Figure 17.1 shows the inheritance hierarchy for all of the classes.

Tab Control

The Windows tab control is commonly used to partition a large number of child controls into related groups. Each group appears in a separate tab window, known as a tab item. Only one tab item is visible at a time because each is positioned at the same x and y coordinates and all have the same dimensions. The user can choose another tab item by clicking on its button positioned at the top of the tab control. Each tab has its own button.

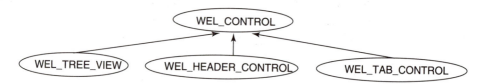

FIGURE 17.1. Advanced control types.

One of the most common uses of a tab control is to present property sheets to the user. Each related set of controls for an application's properties and settings can be located on a single tab item. The user can be presented with a tab item for each group of properties.

The tab control is implemented by the class *WEL_TAB_CONTROL.*

Creating a Tab Control

The creation procedures *make* and *make_by_id* are both available to create tab controls. The parent of the tab controls must be specified and, in the case of *make,* the position and dimensions of the tab control should also be specified.

The tab control requires the common controls DLL to be loaded for it to function correctly. Therefore, your *APPLICATION* class should initialize the DLL using either *WEL_COMMON_CONTROLS_DLL* or *WEL_INIT_COMM-CTRL_EX* classes.

Adding a Tab Item to a Tab Control

Each tab item is represented by an instance of *WEL_TAB_CONTROL_ITEM.* The *WEL_TAB_CONTROL_ITEM* structure identifies the child window that will appear on the tab and either the text of the tab button or an index for an image that will appear on the button. You can also specify both a text string and an image for tab buttons.

To insert a tab item into the tab control, call *insert_item,* passing an instance of *WEL_TAB_CONTROL_ITEM* and a zero-based index representing the position that the tab will occupy within the control.

```
insert_item (index: INTEGER; an_item: WEL_TAB_CONTROL_ITEM)
            -- Insert 'an_item' at the zero-based 'index'.
      require
            exists: exists;
            an_item_not_void: an_item /= void;
            index_large_enough: index >= 0;
            index_small_enough: index <= count
      ensure
            count_increased: count = old count + 1
```

To instantiate *WEL_TAB_CONTROL_ITEM* objects, you need to call either *make* or *make_with_window*. Feature *make* instantiates an empty structure that you must fill by calling appropriate *set_* features, such as *set_text, set_image,* and *set_window*. The *mask* attribute will be set appropriately when each of these features is called.

The value passed to *make_with_window* or *set_window* should be a reference to the tab control in which the item will reside. As mentioned earlier, the *text* and *image* attributes determine the text of the tab button for the item and also whether an image appears on the button.

```
class interface
     WEL_TAB_CONTROL_ITEM

create
     make,
     make_with_window,
     make_by_pointer

feature -- Access

     mask: INTEGER
             -- Array of flags that indicate which of the other
             -- structure members contain valid data or which are
             -- to be filled in. This member can be a combination
             -- of the Tcif_* values.
             -- See class WEL_TCIF_CONSTANTS.

     text: STRING
             -- Item text
         ensure
             result_not_void: Result /= void

     image: INTEGER
             - Index of the icon

     window: WEL_WINDOW
             - The current window associated to the item.
feature - Measurement

     structure_size: INTEGER
             - Size to allocate (in bytes)

feature - Element change

     set_mask (a_mask: INTEGER)
             - Set 'mask' with 'a_mask'.
         ensure
             mask_set: mask = a_mask
```

```
set_text (a_text: STRING)
        -- Set 'text' with 'a_text'.
    require
        a_text_not_void: a_text /= void
    ensure
        text_set: text.is_equal (a_text)

set_image (image_index: INTEGER)
        -- Set the image to the image at position 'index'
    ensure
        image_set: image= image_index

set_window (a_window: WEL_WINDOW)
        -- Associate 'a_window' to the current item.
    require
        a_window_not_void: a_window /= void;
        inside_window: a_window.is_inside
    ensure
        window_set: window = a_window

end -- class WEL_TAB_CONTROL_ITEM
```

Deleting a Tab Item from a Tab Control

Tab items can be removed from a tab control in two ways—all items can be removed by calling *delete_all_items,* or individual items can be removed by calling *delete_item.* Feature *delete_item* requires the zero-based index of the item to delete.

Tab controls often have a fixed set of tab items—they are created when the control is first instantiated and are not changed. However, by using the *insert_item* and *delete_item* features, you can add and remove items dynamically at runtime. You could use this facility to dynamically add property sheets to a property editing dialog, depending on the state of an application.

```
delete_all_items
        -- Delete all items.
    require
        exists: exists
    ensure
        empty: count = 0

delete_item (index: INTEGER)
        -- Delete the item at the zero-based 'index'.
    require
        exists: exists;
```

```
        index_large_enough: index >= 0;
        index_small_enough: index < count
ensure
        count_decreased: count = old count - 1
```

Selecting Tab Items in a Tab Control

A tab control can have one tab selected at a time. The tab that is selected is visible and all other tabs are hidden. The appearance of each tab button is adjusted to visually indicate which tab item is active.

You can determine which tab item is active by calling *current_selection*. This function returns the zero-based index of the active item. You can also change the active item, perhaps to bring a certain property sheet into focus, by calling *set_current_selection*.

```
current_selection: INTEGER
        -- Selected zero-based tab
    require
        exists: exists
    ensure
        consistent_result: Result >= 0 and Result < count

set_current_selection (index: INTEGER)
        - Set the zero-based tab `index'.
    require
        exists: exists;
        index_large_enough: index >= 0;
        index_small_enough: index < count
    ensure
        current_selection_set: current_selection = index
```

Retrieving Tab Control Status Information

The number of items in a tab control and the number of rows the item buttons take can be determined by calling *count* and *row_count* respectively. The number of rows used by tab buttons can be greater than one if the tab control allows multiple button rows and if there are more buttons than fit in the width of the control.

You can also retrieve the dimensions of different parts of the tab control itself. First, you can retrieve the dimensions of the area where labels are drawn by calling *label_index_rect*. Second, you can find the dimensions of the tab item sheet (on which child controls are drawn) by calling *sheet_rect*. Both results are returned as an instance of *WEL_RECT*.

```
count: INTEGER
        -- Number of tabs in the tab control
    require
        exists: exists
    ensure
        positive_result: Result >= 0

row_count: INTEGER
        - Number of tab rows in the tab control
    require
        exists: exists
    ensure
        positive_result: Result >= 0

label_index_rect: WEL_RECT
        -- Labeled index area of selected tab
        -- (excluding the tab sheet)

sheet_rect: WEL_RECT
        -- Client area of each tab sheet
        -- (excluding the labeled index)
        -- Windows requires in multiline mode, that at least
        -- two elements in the notebook  have access to this
        -- data or  be currently showing in the tab control.
        -- If these conditions are not satisfied, Windows will
        -- raise a segmentation violation.
    require
        exists: exists
```

Adjusting Tabs in a Tab Control

A tab control item can be updated by retrieving its *WEL_TAB_CON-TROL_ITEM* structure via the *get_item* call, changing the attributes within the structure, and calling *set_item*. Note that the *get_item* call restricts the size of tab button labels to 30 characters. A button label of more than 30 characters will be truncated.

If the tab control positions its buttons on the left or right side (because the *Tbs_vertical* style has been specified), then the font used for the buttons can be set by calling *set_vertical_font*. The normal routine *set_font* is used to set the font of horizontal buttons that appear at the top or bottom of the control.

A tab control automatically sizes the tab buttons to fit both the icon and the label. You can force Windows to use a particular size by calling *set_label_index_size* and specifying the new width and height. Windows then positions the icon and label so that it fits within the specified area.

```
get_item (index: INTEGER): WEL_TAB_CONTROL_ITEM
        -- Give the item at the zero-based index of tab.
        -- As we must give a maximum size for the retrieving
        -- of the label, we allow only 30 letters. If the
        -- label is longer, it will be cut.
    require
        exists: exists

set_vertical_font (fnt: WEL_FONT)
        -- Assign 'font' to the vertical tabs of this tab control.
        -- (Cannot use 'set_font' since its postcondition is not
        -- always fulfilled)
        -- To use for a notebook with the tabs on the left or
        -- the right.

set_label_index_size (new_width, new_height: INTEGER)
        -- Set size of labeled index area of each tab
        -- Width is only reset if tabs are fixed-width; height is
           always reset
```

Setting the Image List of a Tab Control

To use icons in tab buttons, you must first register an image list that contains the bitmap images. The list can be registered by calling *set_image_list* and passing an instance of *WEL_IMAGE_LIST*. The *image* attribute of each *WEL_TAB_CONTROL_ITEM* must then be a valid index into the image list.

```
set_image_list (an_imagelist:WEL_IMAGE_LIST)
        -- Set the current image list to 'an_imagelist'.
        -- If'an_imagelist' is set to Void, it removes
        -- the current associated image list (if any).
```

Message Hooks in a Tab Control

A tab control responds to three messages, *Tcn_keydown*, *Tcn_selchange*, and *Tcn_selchanging*. Each has a corresponding message hook that can be redefined to perform appropriate actions. Table 17.1 lists the message hooks and describes when each is called. The following sections describe the use of each hook in more detail.

Tab control events are usually confined to the tab button area—the area of the tab items themselves typically handle their own events.

TABLE 17.1 *Tab Control Message Hooks*

MESSAGE HOOK	DESCRIPTION
on_tcn_keydown	A key has been pressed by the user.
on_tcn_selchange	The selected tab has changed.
on_tcn_selchanging	The selected tab is about to change.

On a Key Down Message in a Tab Control

If the user presses a key while the tab control has focus, then the *on_tcn_keydown* message hook is called. The virtual key code and key event data are passed as a parameter to the hook. The key data contains flags representing control keys and other modifiers.

```
on_tcn_keydown (virtual_key, key_data: INTEGER)
        -- A key has been pressed
    require
        exists: exists
```

On a Selection Message in a Tab Control

When the selected tab changes, two message hooks are invoked. After the user clicks on a nonactive tab, the *on_tcn_selchanging* message hook is called. You can use this notification to implement tab control access policies or to initialize the new tab item, depending on changes made by the user.

Once the selected tab item has changed, the *on_tcn_selchange* message hook is called.

```
on_tcn_selchange
        -- Selection has changed.
        -- Shows the current selected page by default.
    require
        exists: exists

on_tcn_selchanging
        -- Selection is about to change.
        -- Hides the current selected page by default.
    require
        exists: exists
```

As mentioned earlier, you must initialize the common controls DLL before you can use *WEL_TAB_CONTROL*. Example 17.1 lists an *APPLICATION* class that initializes the DLL during its *init_application* routine. All that is required is for an instance of *WEL_COMMON_CONTROLS_DLL* to be initialized and held in a reference of the class.

Example 17.1 Tab Control Example, APPLICATION Class (advanced\tab)

```
class APPLICATION
inherit
    WEL_APPLICATION
        redefine
            init_application
        end
creation
    make
feature

    main_window: MAIN_WINDOW is
            -- Main window
        once
            create Result.make
        end

    init_application is
            -- Load the common controls dll
        do
            create common_controls_dll.make
        end

    common_controls_dll: WEL_COMMON_CONTROLS_DLL

end -- class APPLICATION
```

A tab control can now be created and used in any window of your application. Example 17.2 attaches a *WEL_TAB_CONTROL* to the main window of an application. The control is initialized in the *initialize_tab_control* routine to contain three tabs. Each tab is assigned a label and an icon from the registered image list. A multiple-line edit control is added to the client area of each tab item.

Example 17.2 Tab Control Example, MAIN_WINDOW Class (advanced\tab)

```
class MAIN_WINDOW
inherit
    WEL_FRAME_WINDOW
        redefine
            on_size
        end
    WEL_SIZE_CONSTANTS
        export
            {NONE} all
        end
    WEL_ILC_CONSTANTS
        export
            {NONE} all
        end
    APPLICATION_IDS
        export
            {NONE} all
        end
creation
    make
feature

    make is
            -- Initialize the main window
        do
            make_top ("Main Window")
            initialize_tab_control
        end

feature -- Events

    on_size (size_type, new_width, new_height: INTEGER) is
            -- Resize controls
        do
            -- ignore minimized resize events
            if size_type = Size_maximized or
                    size_type = Size_restored or
                    size_type = Size_maxshow then
                tab_control.move_and_resize (0, 0, new_width,
                    new_height, True)
            end
        end

feature {NONE} -- Implementation

    tab_control: WEL_TAB_CONTROL
            -- Tab control
    initialize_tab_control is
            -- Initialize the tab control
```

```
local
        image_list: WEL_IMAGE_LIST
        tab: WEL_TAB_CONTROL_ITEM
        edit: WEL_MULTIPLE_LINE_EDIT
        background_color: WEL_COLOR_REF
        icon: WEL_ICON
        icon1, icon2, icon3: INTEGER
do
        -- create the image list
        create image_list.make(16, 16, Ilc_color32, False)
        -- First match the background color of the imagelist with
        -- the background color of the tab control.
        create background_color.make_system(Color_btnface)
        image_list.set_background_color(background_color)
        -- Add bitmaps to the image list.
        create icon.make_by_id(Idi_icon1_constant)
        image_list.add_icon(icon)
        icon1 := image_list.last_position
        create icon.make_by_id(Idi_icon2_constant)
        image_list.add_icon(icon)
        icon2 := image_list.last_position
        create icon.make_by_id(Idi_icon3_constant)
        image_list.add_icon(icon)
        icon3 := image_list.last_position

        create tab_control.make (Current, 0, 0, width, height, -1)
        tab_control.set_image_list (image_list)

        -- create tab 1
        create tab.make_with_window (tab_control)
        tab.set_text ("Tab 1")
        tab.set_image (icon1)
        create edit.make (tab_control, "Edit control 1", 0, 0,
            0, 0, -1)
        tab.set_window (edit)
        tab_control.insert_item (0, tab)

        -- create tab 2
        create tab.make_with_window (tab_control)
        tab.set_text ("Tab 2")
        tab.set_image (icon2)
        create edit.make (tab_control, "Edit control 2", 0, 0,
            0, 0, -1)
        tab.set_window (edit)
        tab_control.insert_item (1, tab)

        -- create tab 3
        create tab.make_with_window (tab_control)
        tab.set_text ("Tab 3")
        tab.set_image (icon3)
        create edit.make (tab_control, "Edit control 3", 0, 0,
            0, 0, -1)
```

```
        tab.set_window (edit)
        tab_control.insert_item (2, tab)
    end

end -- class MAIN_WINDOW
```

Figure 17.2 shows the example executing with the second tab selected. The control uses the default style—horizontal tab buttons appearing at the top of the window and the icon and label for each button displayed right-to-left.

Tree View

As its name suggests, a tree view can be used to present information to the user that is structured hierarchically or in a tree structure. For example, a tree view is commonly used to display hierarchical file system information such as folders and files. You can use a tree view to display any type of information that is hierarchically structured.

The tree view control requires the common controls DLL to be initialized; therefore, you must ensure that you have loaded the DLL in your *APPLICATION* class.

The class *WEL_TREE_VIEW* implements tree view controls. It is supported by the classes *WEL_TREE_VIEW_INSERT_STRUCT* and *WEL_TREE_VIEW_ITEM*.

Creating a Tree View

The creation procedures *make* and *make_by_id* are both available to create a tree view object. Once the tree view object has been created, you need to

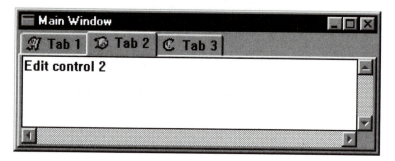

FIGURE 17.2. Tab control example.

populate the control with tree view items that represent a single item within the hierarchy. The tree view itself serves as a container for these items and manages how each item and its children are displayed.

Adding an Item to a Tree View

The *insert_item* routine is used to add a tree view item. The routine requires an instance of *WEL_TREE_VIEW_INSERT_STRUCT* that holds the new item and describes how it is to be added to the tree.

```
insert_item (an_item: WEL_TREE_VIEW_INSERT_STRUCT)
        -- Insert 'an_item' in the tree.
    require
        exists: exists;
        an_item_not_void: an_item /= void;
        an_item_exists: an_item.exists
    ensure
        new_count: count = old count + 1
```

An item can be added as a root item of the tree or as a child of another item in a particular position or order. For example, to add an item as a root item, you need to instantiate a *WEL_TREE_VIEW_INSERT_STRUCT* (interface shown below), set the item by calling *set_item,* and set the position by calling *set_root.* To add an item as a child of another item, you need to call *set_parent,* passing a pointer to the parent item (accessed by the object's *item* function) and then calling *set_first, set_last, set_insert_after,* or *set_sort* to determine the position.

```
class interface
    WEL_TREE_VIEW_INSERT_STRUCT
create
    make
feature -- Access

    insert_after: POINTER
            -- Handle to the item after which the new item is to
            -- be inserted or one of the Tvi_* values.
            -- See class WEL_TVI_CONSTANTS.

    parent: POINTER
            -- Handle to the parent item. If this member is
            -- the Tvi_root value or NULL, the item is inserted
            -- at the root of the tree-view control.
```

```
        tree_view_item: WEL_TREE_VIEW_ITEM
                -- Item to insert
        ensure
                result_not_void: Result /= void

feature -- Element change

    set_first
                -- Insert the item at the beginning of the list.

    set_insert_after (a_insert_after: POINTER)
                -- Set 'insert_after' with 'a_insert_after'.
        ensure
                insert_after_set: insert_after = a_insert_after

    set_last
                -- Insert the item at the end of the list.

    set_parent (a_parent: POINTER)
                -- Set 'parent' with 'a_parent'.
        ensure
                parent_set: parent = a_parent

    set_root
                -- Insert the item as the root of the list.

    set_sort
                -- Insert the item into the list in alphabetical order.

    set_tree_view_item (a_tree_view_item: WEL_TREE_VIEW_ITEM)
                -- Set 'tree_view_item' with 'a_tree_view_item'.
                -- In this case, Windows copies the structure we
                -- send into another structure. Therefore, we need
                -- to keep a reference on the first structure in case
                -- the user is using it.
                -- At insertion time, the h_item paremeter of both
                -- structures will be set at the good value.

end -- class WEL_TREE_VIEW_INSERT_STRUCT
```

Each tree view item is represented by an instance of *WEL_TREE_VIEW_ITEM*. Instances of this class are used to insert new items and to retrieve information about existing items.

Each item contains a text string, an application-defined state value, and an icon index. The text string is displayed in the tree view as the label of the item. If an icon index is specified, the icon referenced by the index is displayed at the left side of the label.

When adding a new item, you need to instantiate a *WEL_TREE_VIEW_ITEM* (shown below) and call *set_text* to set the item's label. Optionally, you can call *set_image* and *set_state* to set the icon index and the application-defined state. The item can then be added to the tree view using a *WEL_TREE_VIEW_INSERT_STRUCT*, as previously described.

```
class interface
     WEL_TREE_VIEW_ITEM

create
     make,
     make_by_pointer

feature -- Access

     children: INTEGER
               -- Information about the children of the item
          require
             valid_member: children_is_valid

     h_item: POINTER
               -- Item to which this structure refers.

     mask: INTEGER
               -- Array of flags that indicate which of the other
               -- structure members contain valid data or which are
               -- to be filled in. This member can be a combination
               -- of the Tvif_* values.
               -- See class WEL_TVIF_CONSTANTS.

     state: INTEGER
               -- Current state of the item.
          require
             valid_member: state_is_valid

     text: STRING
               -- Item text
          require
             valid_member: text_is_valid
          ensure
             result_not_void: Result /= void

feature -- Status report

     children_is_valid: BOOLEAN
               -- Is the structure member 'children' valid?

     state_is_valid: BOOLEAN
               -- Is the structure member 'state' valid?
```

```
        text_is_valid: BOOLEAN
              -- Is the structure member 'text' valid?

 feature -- Element change

     add_mask (a_mask_value: INTEGER)
           -- add 'a_mask_value' to the current mask.

     set_h_item (a_h_item: POINTER)
           -- Set 'h_item' with 'a_h_item'.
        ensure
           h_item_set: h_item = a_h_item

     set_image (image_normal: INTEGER; image_selected: INTEGER)
           -- Set the image for the tree item to 'image_normal'.
           -- and 'image_selected' for the image displayed when this
           -- item is selected.
           -- 'image_normal' and 'image_selected' are the index of
           -- an image in the image list associated with the treeview.

     set_mask (a_mask_value: INTEGER)

           -- Set 'mask' with 'a_mask_value'.

     set_state (a_state: INTEGER)
           -- Set 'a_state' as current 'state'.
        ensure
           state_set: state = a_state

     set_text (a_text: STRING)
           -- Set 'text' with 'a_text'.
        require
           a_text_not_void: a_text /= void
        ensure
           text_set: text.is_equal (a_text)

 end -- class WEL_TREE_VIEW_ITEM
```

Removing an Item from a Tree View

To remove an item, you need to call *delete_item,* passing an instance of
WEL_TREE_VIEW_ITEM that represents the item to remove. You can retrieve
the instance of *WEL_TREE_VIEW_ITEM* from the *selected_item* or *last_item*
calls by holding the item structures as they are created or by creating a new
WEL_TREE_VIEW_ITEM and initializing its *h_item* attribute by calling
set_h_item.

```
delete_item (an_item: WEL_TREE_VIEW_ITEM)
        -- Remove 'an_item' from the tree.
    require
        exists: exists;
        item_not_void: an_item /= void;
        valid_item: has_item (an_item);
        has_items: count > 0
```

Accessing an Item in a Tree View

When an item is added using the *insert_item* routine, its handle is stored in the *last_item* attribute of the tree view control. This attribute can be used to set the *h_item* attribute of *WEL_TREE_VIEW_ITEM* structures used in retrieval or deletion operations.

You can determine via its handle whether a tree view contains a particular item by calling *has_item* and passing an appropriately initialized *WEL_TREE_VIEW_ITEM* structure. You can also retrieve the parent of an item by calling *get_parent_item*.

```
get_parent_item (an_item: WEL_TREE_VIEW_ITEM): WEL_TREE_VIEW_ITEM
        -- Return the parent item of the given item.

last_item: POINTER
        -- Handle of the last item inserted

has_item (an_item: WEL_TREE_VIEW_ITEM): BOOLEAN
        -- Does 'an_item' exist in the tree?
    require
        exists: exists;
        item_not_void: an_item /= void;
        item_valid: an_item.exists
    ensure
        mask_unchanged: an_item.mask = old an_item.mask
```

Selecting Items in a Tree View

The user normally selects tree view items by clicking on their labels or icons in the tree view window. In addition, you can programmatically select items and determine which item is currently selected using the features listed below.

```
is_selected (an_item: WEL_TREE_VIEW_ITEM): BOOLEAN
        -- Is 'an_item' selected?
    require
        exists: exists;
        valid_item: has_item (an_item)

selected: BOOLEAN
        -- Is an item selected?
    require
        exists: exists

selected_item: WEL_TREE_VIEW_ITEM
        -- Return the currently selected item.
    require
        exists: exists;
        selected: selected
    ensure
        item_valid: Result.exists

deselect_item (an_item: WEL_TREE_VIEW_ITEM)
        -- Deselect the given item
    require
        exists: exists;
        valid_item: has_item (an_item)
    ensure
        item_deselected: not is_selected (an_item)

select_first_visible (an_item: WEL_TREE_VIEW_ITEM)
        -- Scrolls the tree view vertically so that
        -- the given 'an_item' is the first visible item.
    require
        exists: exists;
        valid_item: has_item (an_item)

select_item (an_item: WEL_TREE_VIEW_ITEM)
        -- Set the selection to the given 'an_item'.
    require
        exists: exists;
        valid_item: has_item (an_item)
    ensure
        item_selected: is_selected (an_item)
```

The *selected, is_selected,* and *selected_item* functions can be used to determine if any item is selected, if a particular item is selected, and the details about a selected item respectively. To select an item programmatically call *select_item* passing a *WEL_TREE_VIEW_ITEM* instance with its *h_item* attribute initialized to the handle of the item.

Similarly, to deselect an item, call *deselect_item.* You can also select an item and ensure it is visible in the tree view control by calling *select_first_visible.* This routine will select the item and then scroll the tree view so that the item is the first visible item.

Accessing Status Information for a Tree View

The tree view control retains information about each item and about the collection of items as a whole. For instance, you can determine how many items a tree view contains by calling *count* or the number of items currently visible in the control by calling *visible_count.*

An item is displayed below its parent and indented a certain number of pixels to the right. The level of indentation can be determined by calling the function *indent.*

Each individual item can be queried to determine its current state, including whether it is bold, participating in a cut and paste operation, participating in a drag-and-drop operation, is expanded, or is a parent of other items. The functions *is_bold, is_cut, is_drophilited, is_expanded,* and *is_parent* implement the queries.

```
count: INTEGER
        -- Number of items in the tree view window
    require
        exists: exists
    ensure
        positive_result: Result >= 0

visible_count: INTEGER
        -- Number of items that will fit into the tree
        -- view window
    require
        exists: exists
    ensure
        positive_result: Result >= 0

indent: INTEGER
        -- Amout, in pixels, that child items are indented
        -- relative to their parent items.
    require
        exists: exists

is_bold (an_item: WEL_TREE_VIEW_ITEM): BOOLEAN
        -- Is 'an_item' bold?
    require
        exists: exists;
        valid_item: has_item (an_item)

is_cut (an_item: WEL_TREE_VIEW_ITEM): BOOLEAN
```

```
        -- Is 'an_item' selected as part of a cut and paste
        -- operation?
    require
        exists: exists;
        valid_item: has_item (an_item)

is_drophilited (an_item: WEL_TREE_VIEW_ITEM): BOOLEAN
        -- Is 'an_item' selected as a drag-and-drop target?
    require
        exists: exists;
        valid_item: has_item (an_item)

is_expanded (an_item: WEL_TREE_VIEW_ITEM): BOOLEAN
        -- Is 'an_item' expanded?
    require
        exists: exists;
        is_parent: is_parent (an_item);
        valid_item: has_item (an_item)

is_parent (an_item: WEL_TREE_VIEW_ITEM): BOOLEAN
        -- Is 'an_item' a parent of other items?
    require
        exists: exists;
        valid_item: has_item (an_item)
```

Setting Status Information in a Tree View

When first displayed, a tree view lists only the root items. If the control style includes *Tvs_hasbuttons,* then each parent item includes an additional icon to the left that indicates that the item can be expanded or collapsed.

To expand the child list of a parent item, the user can double-click the item's icon or label, or click on the expansion icon to the left. You can also expand or collapse an item using the features *collapse_item* and *expand_item* respectively.

The level of indentation of child items can be changed by calling *set_indent,* passing the number of pixels to indent for the *an_indent* parameter.

```
collapse_item (an_item: WEL_TREE_VIEW_ITEM)
        -- Collapse the given item.
    require
        exists: exists;
        is_parent (an_item);
        valid_item: has_item (an_item)
```

```
     ensure
          item_collapse: not is_expanded (an_item)
expand_item (an_item: WEL_TREE_VIEW_ITEM)
          -- Expand the given item.
     require
          exists: exists;
          is_parent: is_parent (an_item);
          valid_item: has_item (an_item)
     ensure
          item_expanded: is_expanded (an_item)

set_indent (an_indent: INTEGER)
          -- Set 'indent' with 'an_indent'.
     require
          exists: exists
```

Associating an Image List with a Tree View

When your tree view items use images, you need to register an image list with the control using *set_image_list*. You can retrieve the current image list by calling *get_image_list*.

Each item that specifies a value for its image attribute in the *WEL_TREE_VIEW_ITEM* structure will use that value to index into the registered image list.

```
set_image_list (an_imagelist: WEL_IMAGE_LIST)
          -- Set the current image list to 'an_imagelist'.
          -- If 'an_imagelist' is set to Void, it removes
          -- the current associated image list (if any).

get_image_list: WEL_IMAGE_LIST
          -- Get the image list associated with this treeview.
          -- Returns Void if none.
```

Message Hooks in a Tree View

The tree view control implements a number of message hooks for responding to events such as drag-and-drop operations, label editing, item insertion, updates and deletions, changes in the display of items, and key press events. Table 17.2 lists the message hooks and describes when they are called.

TABLE 17.2   *Tree View Message Hooks*

MESSAGE HOOK	DESCRIPTION
on_tvn_begindrag	A drag operation involving the left mouse button is being initiated.
on_tvn_beginrdrag	A drag operation involving the right mouse button is being initiated.
on_tvn_beginlabeledit	Label editing for an item has started.
on_tvn_deleteitem	An item has been deleted.
on_tvn_endlabeledit	Label editing for an item has ended.
on_tvn_getdispinfo	The parent window must provide information needed to display or sort an item.
on_tvn_itemexpanded	A parent item's list of child items has expanded or collapsed.
on_tvn_itemexpanding	A parent item's list of child items is about to expand or collapse.
on_tvn_keydown	The user pressed a key and the tree view control has the input focus.
on_tvn_selchanged	Selection has changed from one item to another.
on_tvn_selchanging	Selection is about to change from one item to another.
on_tvn_setdispinfo	The parent window must update the information it maintains about an item.

On a Drag Event in a Tree View

A tree view can support drag-and-drop operations. The control is notified whenever the user begins a drag operation using either the left or right mouse buttons. For example, your application may allow the user to change the order or position of items, using the mouse. To do this, you need to implement appropriate logic in the *on_tvn_begindrag* and/or *on_tvn_beginrdrag* operations.

The message hook *on_tvn_beginrdrag* is called when the drag operation is performed using the right mouse button; otherwise *on_tvn_begindrag* is called.

```
on_tvn_begindrag (info: WEL_NM_TREE_VIEW)
      -- A drag-and-drop operation involving the left mouse
      -- button is being initiated.
   require
      exists: exists

on_tvn_beginrdrag (info: WEL_NM_TREE_VIEW)
      -- A drag-and-drop operation involving the right mouse
      -- button is being initiated.
   require
      exists: exists
```

Many of the tree view message hooks receive an instance of *WEL_ NM_TREE_VIEW* as a parameter. This structure contains information about the notification message, including the notification message itself, any items in-volved, the position of the mouse, and how the action was performed. The possible actions are listed in Table 17.3.

The public interface of *WEL_NM_TREE_VIEW* is shown next.

```
class interface
    WEL_NM_TREE_VIEW

create
    make,
    make_by_nmhdr,
    make_by_pointer

feature -- Access

    action: INTEGER
            -- Information about the notification-specific action
            -- flag.
            -- See class WEL_TVAF_CONSTANTS for the meaning of this
            -- parameter.

    hdr: WEL_NMHDR
            -- Information about the Wm_notify message.
        ensure
            result_not_void: Result /= void

    new_item: WEL_TREE_VIEW_ITEM
            -- Information about the new item state
        ensure
            result_not_void: Result /= void

    old_item: WEL_TREE_VIEW_ITEM
            -- Information about the old item state
        ensure
            result_not_void: Result /= void

    position: WEL_POINT
            -- Mouse coordinates when notification occurred.
        ensure
            result_not_void: Result /= void

end -- class WEL_NM_TREE_VIEW
```

On a Label Edit Event in a Tree View

If the *Tvs_editlabels* style is used, then the user can edit labels directly within the control itself. The user begins a label edit operation by selecting a label and then clicking on the label for a second time. Your application is notified of this event via the message hook *on_tvn_beginlabeledit*.

TABLE 17.3   *Tree View Action Flags (WEL_TVAF_CONSTANTS)*

CONSTANT	DESCRIPTION
Tvc_bykeyboard	Used for the *Tvn_selchanged* and *Tvn_selchanging* notification messages. Action performed by a key stroke.
Tvc_bymouse	Used for the *Tvn_selchanged* and *Tvn_selchanging* notification messages. Action performed by a mouse click.
Tvc_unknown	Used for the *Tvn_selchanged* and *Tvn_selchanging* notification messages. Action performed by a mouse click.
Tvc_collapse	Used for the *Tvn_expand* and *Tvn_expanding* messages. Action performed by collapsing the list.
Tvc_collapsereset	Used for the *Tvn_expand* and *Tvn_expanding* messages. Action performed by collapsing the list and removing the child items.
Tvc_expand	Used for the *Tvn_expand* and *Tvn_expanding* messages. Action performed by expanding the list.
Tvc_toggle	Used for the *Tvn_expand* and *Tvn_expanding* messages. Action performed by changing the list between collapse and expand.

The user can then edit the value of the label at its position within the tree view. Once **Enter** is pressed, the operation is completed and you are notified with a call to *on_tvn_endlabeledit*. You can then collect the new value from the *WEL_TREE_VIEW_ITEM* structure that has been passed to the message hook, and store it appropriately.

```
on_tvn_beginlabeledit (info: WEL_TREE_VIEW_ITEM)
        -- A label editing for an item has started.
    require
      exists: exists

on_tvn_endlabeledit (info: WEL_TREE_VIEW_ITEM)
        -- A label editing for an item has ended.
    require
      exists: exists
```

On an Item Expansion Event in a Tree View

When the user expands an item, the message hook *on_tvn_itemexpanding* is called before the operation, and *on_tvn_itemexpanded* is called after. If you need to build a tree view as needed, then the *on_tvn_itemexpanding* message hook can be very useful. For instance, if you need to add child items to a tree view only when the parent item is expanded, you can add them when you receive notification of the parent expanding.

```
on_tvn_itemexpanded (info: WEL_NM_TREE_VIEW)
        -- a parent item's list of child items has expanded
        -- or collapsed.
    require
        exists: exists


on_tvn_itemexpanding (info: WEL_NM_TREE_VIEW)
        -- a parent item's list of child items is about to
        -- expand or collapse.
    require
        exists: exists
```

On a Delete Item Event in a Tree View

When an item is deleted, you receive notification via the message hook *on_tvn_deleteitem*. The *info* parameter references a *WEL_NM_TREE_VIEW* structure containing information about the item that was deleted, including its handle.

```
on_tvn_deleteitem (info: WEL_NM_TREE_VIEW)
        -- An item has been deleted.
    require
        exists: exists
```

On a Key Event in a Tree View

A tree view key press event is indicated by a call to the *on_tvn_keydown* message hook. The virtual key code for the pressed key is passed to the hook.

```
on_tvn_keydown (virtual_key: INTEGER)
        -- The user pressed a key and the tree-view control
        -- has the input focus.
    require
        exists: exists
```

On a Selection Event in a Tree View

The last two message hooks defined by *WEL_TREE_VIEW* provide notification of a change to the selected item, both before the change occurs and afterwards. The message hooks *on_tvn_selchanged* and *on_tvn_selchanging* indicate that the selection has changed and that the selection is changing, respectively.

```
on_tvn_selchanged (info: WEL_NM_TREE_VIEW)
        -- Selection has changed from one item to another.
    require
        exists: exists

on_tvn_selchanging (info: WEL_NM_TREE_VIEW)
        -- Selection is about to change from one item to
        -- another.
    require
        exists: exists
```

Example 17.3 illustrates the use of a tree view control. An instance of *WEL_TREE_VIEW* is attached to the main window and initialized via the *initialize_tree_vew* routine. One root item and three parent items, each with five children, are added to the control.

The child items are each created in a nested loop that iterates five times for the children and three times for the parents. Each item is given an appropriate label that identifies its position in the tree and an icon from a registered image list.

Example 17.3 Tree View Example, MAIN_WINDOW Class (advanced\tree)

```
class MAIN_WINDOW
inherit
    WEL_FRAME_WINDOW
    WEL_ILC_CONSTANTS
        export
            {NONE} all
        end
    APPLICATION_IDS
        export
            {NONE} all
        end
creation
    make
feature

    make is
            -- Initialize the main window
```

```
        do
          make_top ("Main Window")
          create tree_view.make (Current, 0, 0, width, height, -1)
          initialize_tree_view
        end

    feature {NONE} -- Implementation
      tree_view: WEL_TREE_VIEW
            -- Tree view control
      Number_children: INTEGER is 5
            -- Number of children for each parent
      Number_parents: INTEGER is 3
            -- Number of parents

      initialize_tree_view is
            -- Initialize the tree view
        local
          tree_item: WEL_TREE_VIEW_ITEM
          tree_insert: WEL_TREE_VIEW_INSERT_STRUCT
          image_list: WEL_IMAGE_LIST
          icon: WEL_ICON
          icon1, icon2: INTEGER
          root_item_handle, parent_item_handle: POINTER
          background_color: WEL_COLOR_REF
          parent_count, count: INTEGER
        do
          -- create image list
          create image_list.make (16, 16, Ilc_color32, False)
          -- set the background color
          create background_color.make_system(Color_window)
          image_list.set_background_color(background_color)
          -- add icon 1
          create icon.make_by_id(Idi_icon1_constant)
          image_list.add_icon(icon)
          icon1 := image_list.last_position
          -- add icon 2
          create icon.make_by_id(Idi_icon2_constant)
          image_list.add_icon(icon)
          icon2 := image_list.last_position
          -- set the image list
          tree_view.set_image_list(image_list)
          -- Add root item
          create tree_insert.make
          tree_insert.set_root
          create tree_item.make
          tree_item.set_text ("Root 1")
          tree_item.set_image (icon1, icon2)
          tree_insert.set_tree_view_item (tree_item)
          tree_view.insert_item (tree_insert)
          root_item_handle := tree_view.last_item
          -- Add parents
```

```
from
      parent_count := 1
until
      parent_count > Number_parents
loop
      create tree_insert.make
      tree_insert.set_parent (root_item_handle)
      tree_insert.set_last
      create tree_item.make
      tree_item.set_text ("Parent " + parent_count.out)
      tree_item.set_image (icon1, icon2)
      tree_insert.set_tree_view_item (tree_item)
      tree_view.insert_item (tree_insert)
      parent_item_handle := tree_view.last_item
      -- Add children
      from
            count := 1
      until
            count > Number_children
      loop
            create tree_insert.make
            tree_insert.set_parent (parent_item_handle)
            tree_insert.set_last
            create tree_item.make
            tree_item.set_text ("Child " + count.out)
            tree_item.set_image (icon1, icon2)
            tree_insert.set_tree_view_item (tree_item)
            tree_view.insert_item (tree_insert)
            count := count + 1
      end
      parent_count := parent_count + 1
end
end

end -- class MAIN_WINDOW
```

Figure 17.3 shows the example executing with the root item and the first parent item expanded to show its children.

Header Control

A header control is usually positioned above columns of text and can be split into parts that can be individually labeled and sized. Each part contains a label and optionally an icon, and can be sized by dragging the dividers between parts.

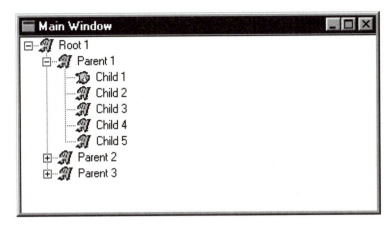

FIGURE 17.3. Tree view example.

If a header control is used above text, then the events produced by it can be used to size and position the columns. The behavior is similar to the list view control (see "List View Control" in Chapter 14, "List Boxes").

The header control is implemented by the class *WEL_HEADER_CON-TROL.*

Creating a Header Control

To use header controls in your applications, you must ensure that the common controls DLL is loaded by your *APPLICATION* class.

Header controls themselves can be instantiated using the creation procedures *make* and *make_by_id.*

Adding Header Items to a Header Control

Each part of a header control is represented by a header item that contains a text label, an icon, or both. The header item also has a width, a formatting style, and a position.

To create a header item with just a text label, you can call *insert_text_header_item.* You need to specify the label, the initial width of the part, the format (see Table 17.4), and the item number to insert after.

To create a header item with a text label and an icon, you need to use the routine *insert_header_item* and create an instance of *WEL_HD_ITEM* that represents the item. This routine is actually used by *insert_text_header_item* internally.

```
insert_text_header_item (a_label: STRING; a_width, a_format:
   INTEGER; insert_after_item_no: INTEGER)
         -- Insert a text item to the header control after the
         -- 'insert_item_item_no' item. If there is no item in the
            list
         -- yet, or you want to insert the new item as the first
         -- one, use 0 for 'insert_item'
         -- The item will be 'a_width' broad and use 'a_format' as
         -- format.
         -- For possible formats please look into WEL_HDF_CONSTANTS.
         -- (Hdf_string will be set automatically)
   require
      exists: exists;
      label_not_void: a_label /= void;
      insert_after_item_no_positive: insert_after_item_no >= 0
   ensure
      item_count_increased: item_count = old item_count + 1

insert_header_item (hd_item: WEL_HD_ITEM; insert_after_item_no:
INTEGER)
         -- Insert an item to the header control after the
         -- 'insert_item_item_no' item. If there is no item in the
         -- list
         -- yet, or you want to insert the new item as the first
         -- one, use 0 for 'insert_item'
   require
      exists: exists;
      hd_item_not_void: hd_item /= void;
      insert_after_item_no_positive: insert_after_item_no >= 0
   ensure
      item_count_increased: item_count = old item_count + 1
```

TABLE 17.4   *Header Item Format Constants (WEL_HDF_CONSTANTS)*

CONSTANT	DESCRIPTION
Hdf_bitmap	The item displays a bitmap.
Hdf_center	Centers the contents of the item.
Hdf_ownerdraw	The owner window of the header control draws the item.
Hdf_right	Right-aligns the contents of the line.
Hdf_rtl_reading	Displays text using right-to-left reading order for Hebrew or Arabic systems.
Hdf_string	The item displays a string.

The class *WEL_HD_ITEM* is used to represent a new header item, including its label, format, bitmap, and width. The attributes *text, format, image,* and *width* are used. In addition, the item can hold an *INTEGER* in the *custom_data* attribute for application-specific state information.

```
class interface
    WEL_HD_ITEM

create
    make,
    make_by_pointer

feature -- Access

    bitmap_handle: POINTER
            -- Handle to item bitmap.
        require
            exists: exists;
            good_mask: flag_set (mask, hdi_bitmap)

    custom_data: INTEGER
            -- Application-defined item data.
        require
            exists: exists;
            good_mask: flag_set (mask, hdi_lparam)

    format: INTEGER
            -- A set of bit flags that specify the item's format.
            -- Constants are defined in class WEL_HDF_CONSTANTS.
            -- Constants may be combined.
        require
            exists: exists;
            good_mask: flag_set (mask, hdi_format)

    height: INTEGER
            -- Height of item (Only available when mask contains
            -- 'Hdi_height')
        require
            exists: exists;
            good_mask: flag_set (mask, hdi_height)
        ensure
            positive_result: Result >= 0

    mask: INTEGER
            -- Mask flags that indicate which of the other structure
            -- members contain valid data.
            -- Constants may be combined.
            -- The valid constants can be found in class
            -- WEL_HDI_CONSTANTS
        require
            exists: exists
```

```
       text: STRING
             -- Text of the button associated with the notification.
         require
             exists: exists

       text_count: INTEGER
             -- Count of characters in the button text.
         require
             exists: exists
         ensure
             positive_result: Result >= 0

     width: INTEGER
             -- Width of item (Only available when mask contains
             -- 'Hdi_width')
         require
             exists: exists;
             good_mask: flag_set (mask, hdi_width)
         ensure
             positive_result: Result >= 0

     image: INTEGER
             -- Index to image list icon

feature -- Element change

   set_bitmap (a_bitmap: WEL_BITMAP)
             -- Sets item bitmap.
             -- Also updates 'mask'
         require
             exists: exists;
             bitmap_exsits: a_bitmap.exists

   set_custom_data (value: INTEGER)
             -- Sets application-defined item data.
             -- Also updates 'mask'
         require
             exists: exists

   set_format (value: INTEGER)
             -- Sets a set of bit flags that specify the item's format.
             -- Constants are defined in class WEL_HDF_CONSTANTS.
             -- Constants may be combined.
             -- Also updates 'mask'
         require
             exists: exists

   set_height (value: INTEGER)
             -- Sets height of item with 'value'
             -- Also updates 'mask'
             -- Note: You can only specify either the width or the height
         require
             exists: exists;
```

```
          positive_value: value >= 0

     set_mask (value: INTEGER)
             -- Sets mask flags that indicate which of the other
             -- structure
             -- members contain valid data.
             -- Constants may be combined.
             -- The valid constants can be found in class
             -- WEL_HDI_CONSTANTS
         require
             exists: exists

     set_text (a_text: STRING)
             -- Set 'text' with 'a_text'.
             -- Also Updates 'text_count' and 'mask'
         require
             text_not_void: a_text /= void
         ensure
             text_set: text.is_equal (a_text);
             text_count_set: a_text.count = text_count;

     set_width (value: INTEGER)
             -- Sets width of item with 'value'
             -- Also updates 'mask'
             -- Note: You can only specify either the width or the height
         require
             exists: exists;
             positive_value: value >= 0

     set_image (image_index: INTEGER)
             -- Sets image index.
             -- Also updates 'mask'.
         require
             exists: exists
end -- class WEL_HD_ITEM
```

Removing Header Items from a Header Control

A header item can be deleted by specifying its zero-based index in a call to
delete_header_item. The number of header items is reduced by one and the
items to the right are moved one position to the left.

```
delete_header_item (index: INTEGER)
        -- delete item from header control at index 'index'
    require
        exists: exists;
        valid_index: valid_index (index)
    ensure
        item_count_decreased: item_count = old item_count - 1
```

Accessing Header Control Items

The number of header items is accessible via the function *item_count.*

You can also retrieve information about an item at a particular position on the screen. Feature *item_info_from_point* requires a *WEL_POINT* parameter and returns an instance of *WEL_HD_HIT_TEST_INFO* representing the header item at the position, if any.

```
item_count: INTEGER
        -- Retrieves the number of items that are in the header
        -- control
    require
        exists: exists
    ensure
        positive_result: Result >= 0

item_info_from_point (a_point: WEL_POINT): WEL_HD_HIT_TEST_INFO
        -- Tests a point to determine which header item, if any, is
        -- at the specified point.
    require
        exists: exists;
        a_point_exists: a_point /= void and then a_point.exists
```

The *WEL_HD_HIT_TEST_INFO* structure contains the point at which the hit test was performed and the index of the header at that position. The *point* attribute identifies what part of the header item the point is on. It can be one of the values listed in Table 17.5.

```
class interface
    WEL_HD_HIT_TEST_INFO

create
    make,
    make_by_pointer

feature -- Access

    flags: INTEGER
            -- Variable that receives information about the results of
            -- a hit test.
            -- This member can be one or more of the values defined in
            -- WEL_HHT_CONSTANTS
        require
            exists: exists

    index: INTEGER
            -- Retrieves the index of the item at 'point' if any
```

```
      require
          exists: exists
      ensure
          positive_result: Result >= 0

  point: WEL_POINT
          -- Points to test, in client coordinates
      require
          exists: exists

feature -- Element change

  set_flags (value: INTEGER)
          -- Sets variable that receives information about the
          -- results of a hit test.
          -- This member can be one or more of the values defined
          -- in WEL_HHT_CONSTANTS
          -- (Usually set by the OS)
      require
          exists: exist

  set_index (value: INTEGER)
          --- Sets the index of the item at 'point' if any
          -- (Usually set by the OS)
      require
          exists: exists;
          positive_value: value >= 0

  set_point (a_point: WEL_POINT)
          -- Sets the point to test, in client coordinates
      require
          exists: exists;
          point_exists: a_point /= void and then a_point.exists

end -- class WEL_HD_HIT_TEST_INFO
```

TABLE 17.5 *Header Control Hit Test Constants (WEL_HHT_CONSTANTS)*

CONSTANT	DESCRIPTION
Hht_nowhere	The point is inside the bounding rectangle of the header control but is not over a header item.
Hht_on_div_open	The point is on the divider of an item that has a width of zero. Dragging the divider reveals the item instead of resizing the item to the left of the divider.
Hht_on_divider	The point is on the divider between two header items.
Hht_on_header	The point is inside the bounding rectangle of the header control.
Hht_to_left	The point is to the left of the bounding rectangle of the header control.
Hht_to_right	The point is to the right of the bounding rectangle of the header control.

Updating a Header Item

An existing header item can be modified by calling *set_header_item*, passing the index of the item to change and a new *WEL_HD_ITEM* structure with the values to change initialized.

```
set_header_item (index: INTEGER; hd_item: WEL_HD_ITEM)
      -- This windows message sets the attributes of the specified
      -- item in a header control.
   require
      exists: exists;
      hd_item_exists: hd_item /= void and then hd_item.exists;
      valid_index: valid_index (index)
```

Message Hooks in a Header Control

Once a header control has been initialized and the header items added, it performs very little in terms of functionality—the control displays the header items and responds to user events for resizing and selection.

In an application, the notification events generated by a header control are significant and need to be processed accordingly. For example, if you have a header control associated with columns of text, then you need to process changes in the size of header items and possibly in the selection of items. A single column of text may be associated with a header item and when that header item changes size, the column of text may need to change size equally.

The message hooks defined in *WEL_HEADER_CONTROL*, listed in Table 17.6, respond to changes in item sizes, selection, and mouse click events.

TABLE 17.6   *Header Control Message Hooks*

MESSAGE	DESCRIPTION
on_hdm_begin_track	The user has begun dragging a divider in the control.
on_hdm_divider_dbl_click	The user double-clicked the divider area of the control.
on_hdm_end_track	The user has finished dragging a divider.
on_hdm_item_changed	The attributes of a header item have changed.
on_hdm_item_changing	The attributes of a header item are about to change.
on_hdm_item_click	The user clicked a header item.
on_hdm_item_dbl_click	The user double-clicked a header item.
on_hdm_track	The user is dragging a divider in the header control.

On a Track Event in a Header Control

The user can change the width of individual header items by dragging the separator line displayed between items. When the user begins a divider drag operation, the *on_hdn_begin_track* message hook is called, identifying the mouse button pressed, the item selected, and the notification event. During the drag operation, the hook *on_hdn_track* is called. Once the user drops the divider, the *on_hdn_end_track* operation is called.

```
on_hdn_begin_track (info: WEL_HD_NOTIFY)
        -- The user has begun dragging a divider in the control
        -- (that is, the user has pressed the left mouse button while
        -- the mouse cursor is on a divider in the header control).
    require
        exists: exists;
        info_exists: info /= void and then info.exists

on_hdn_end_track (info: WEL_HD_NOTIFY)
        -- The user has finished dragging a divider.
    require
        exists: exists;
        info_exists: info /= void and then info.exists
on_hdn_track (info: WEL_HD_NOTIFY)
        -- The user is dragging a divider in the header control.
    require
        exists: exists;
        info_exists: info /= void and then info.exists
```

The divider drag message hooks receive information in the form of a *WEL_HD_NOTIFY* structure. This structure holds a code identifying the mouse button pressed, the index of the item selected, and the actual notification event being processed. Its public interface is shown below.

An instance of this class is passed to all of the header control message hooks.

```
class interface
    WEL_HD_NOTIFY

create
    make,
    make_by_pointer,
    make_by_nmhdr

feature -- Access

    button_index: INTEGER
            -- Specifies the index of the mouse button involved in
```

```
                -- generating the notification message.
                -- This member can be one of these values:
                --
                -- Value          Meaning
                -- 0                 Left button
                -- 1                 Right button
                -- 2                 Middle button
        require
            exists: exists

    header_item: WEL_HD_ITEM
                -- a WEL_HD_ITEM object that contains information about
                -- the header item associated with the notification
                -- message.
        require
            exists: exists

    item_index: INTEGER
                -- Specifies the index of item associated with notification.
        require
            exists: exists

    nmhdr: WEL_NMHDR
                -- Specifies a NMHDR structure.
                -- The code member of this object identifies the notification
                -- message being sent.
        require
            exists: exists

feature -- Element change

    set_button_index (value: INTEGER)
                -- Sets the index of the mouse button involved in
                -- generating the notification message.
                -- This member can be one of these values:
                --
                -- Value          Meaning
                -- 0                 Left button
                -- 1                 Right button
                -- 2                 Middle button
                -- (Usually set by the OS)
        require
            exists: exists;
            good_value: value >= 0 and value <= 2

    set_header_item (hd_item: WEL_HD_ITEM)
                -- Sets the WEL_HD_ITEM object that contains
                -- information about
                -- the header item associated with the notification
                -- message.
                -- (Usually set by the OS)
```

```
    require
          exists: exists;
          hd_item_exists: hd_item /= void and then hd_item.exists
  set_item_index (value: INTEGER)
          -- Sets the index of item associated with notification.
          -- (Usually set by the OS)
    require
          exists: exists

end -- class WEL_HD_NOTIFY
```

On a Mouse Click Event in a Header Control

If the user double-clicks a divider between header items, the *on_hdn_divider_dbl_click* message hook is called. The standard behavior of a header control when this event occurs is to resize the header item so that the longest line of text in the associated column can be viewed.

A single or double-click on a header item is indicated by either the *on_hdn_item_click* or *on_hdn_item_dbl_click* message hooks.

```
on_hdn_divider_dbl_click (info: WEL_HD_NOTIFY)
      -- The user double-clicked the divider area of the control.
   require
      exists: exists;
      info_exists: info /= void and then info.exists

on_hdn_item_click (info: WEL_HD_NOTIFY)
      -- The user clicked the control.
   require
      exists: exists;
      info_exists: info /= void and then info.exists

on_hdn_item_dbl_click (info: WEL_HD_NOTIFY)
      -- The user double-clicked the control.
   require
      exists: exists;
      info_exists: info /= void and then info.exists
```

On an Item Change Event in a Header Control

You are notified before and after a header item changes. The message hook *on_hdn_item_changing* is called when an item is about to be updated and *on_hdn_item_changed* is called after the updates have been applied.

```
on_hdn_item_changed (info: WEL_HD_NOTIFY)
        -- The attributes of a header item have changed.
    require
        exists: exists;
        info_exists: info /= void and then info.exists

on_hdn_item_changing (info: WEL_HD_NOTIFY)
        -- The attributes of a header item are about to change.
    require
        exists: exists;
        info_exists: info /= void and then info.exists
```

The next example creates a header control with three items and attaches it to a frame window. Example 17.4 creates each header item using the call *insert_header_item*, with a new *WEL_HD_ITEM* structure for each. The items contain a text label and an index to an icon in the registered image list. The call to *retrieve_and_set_windows_pos* repositions the header control at the top of the window automatically.

Example 17.4 Header Control Example, MAIN_WINDOW Class (advanced\header)

```
class MAIN_WINDOW
inherit
    WEL_FRAME_WINDOW
        redefine
            on_size
        end
    WEL_ILC_CONSTANTS
        export
            {NONE} all
        end
    WEL_COLOR_CONSTANTS
        export
            {NONE} all
        end
    APPLICATION_IDS
        export
            {NONE} all
        end
creation
    make
feature

    make is
            -- Initialize the main window
        do
```

Example 17.4 Header Control Example, MAIN_WINDOW Class (advanced\header) *(Continued)*

```
            make_top ("Main Window")
            create header_control.make (Current, 0, 0, width, 0, -1)
            initialize_header_control
    end

feature -- Events
    on_size (type, new_width, new_height: INTEGER) is
            -- Resize child controls
        do
            header_control.retrieve_and_set_windows_pos (client_rect)
        end
feature {NONE} -- Implementation

    header_control: WEL_HEADER_CONTROL
            -- Header control

    initialize_header_control is
            -- Initialize the header control
        local
            header_item: WEL_HD_ITEM
            count: INTEGER
            image_list: WEL_IMAGE_LIST
            icon: WEL_ICON
            icon1, icon2, icon3: INTEGER
            background_color: WEL_COLOR_REF
        do
            -- create image list
            create image_list.make (16, 16, Ilc_color32, False)
            -- set the background color
            create background_color.make_system(Color_btnface)
            image_list.set_background_color(background_color)
            -- add icon 1
            create icon.make_by_id(Idi_icon1_constant)
            image_list.add_icon(icon)
            icon1 := image_list.last_position
            -- add icon 2
            create icon.make_by_id(Idi_icon2_constant)
            image_list.add_icon(icon)
            icon2 := image_list.last_position
            -- add icon 3
            create icon.make_by_id(Idi_icon3_constant)
            image_list.add_icon(icon)
            icon3 := image_list.last_position
            -- set the image list
            header_control.set_image_list(image_list)
            -- add header item 1
            create header_item.make
            header_item.set_text ("Header 1")
            header_item.set_width (width // 3)
```

Example 17.4 Header Control Example, MAIN_WINDOW Class (advanced\header) *(Continued)*

```
                    header_item.set_image (icon1)
                    header_control.insert_header_item (header_item, 0)
                    -- add header item 2
            create header_item.make
                    header_item.set_text ("Header 2")
                    header_item.set_width (width // 3)
                    header_item.set_image (icon2)
                    header_control.insert_header_item (header_item, 1)
                    -- add header item 3
            create header_item.make
                    header_item.set_text ("Header 3")
                    header_item.set_width (width // 3)
                    header_item.set_image (icon3)
                    header_control.insert_header_item (header_item, 2)
                    -- size according to parent window
                    header_control.retrieve_and_set_windows_pos (client_rect)
        end

    end -- class MAIN_WINDOW
```

Figure 17.4 shows the resulting header control with each of the header items. Each header item is sized to one-third of the parent window's width.

SUMMARY

This chapter explored three of the more advanced controls available in the WEL library. Tab controls provide a way of presenting multiple windows in the same area, for use in property sheets or notebook-type applications. Tree controls provide functionality to display hierarchical information to the user in the form of an expandable tree, and header controls provide a flexible control that can be use to represent headings for columnar information.

FIGURE 17.4. Header control example.

THE COMPONENT OBJECT MODEL

INTRODUCING COM

The goal of this chapter is to cover enough information on COM so that you can use development tools such as the EiffelCOM Wizard to build COM applications. We do not cover all aspects of COM since this would require an entire book by itself. Instead we focus on the core of the technology.

Simply put, the Component Object Model is a Microsoft binary standard that establishes how two binary units can call each other at runtime. Such binary units can run in the same process, in different processes on the same machine, or even on different machines, and are more commonly referred to as components. Components can be implemented in any language as long as the compiler produces COM standard compliant binaries. The advantages of such an approach include increased reusability (binary reuse), better version management (the COM standard implies that new component versions will still be compatible with older versions), and a built in runtime environment that takes care of synchronization issues, transactional behavior, and other contextual settings.

But before you become comfortable with all these topics, we need to focus on the core of COM—what the binary standard is and how it affects the design of COM components.

THE MODEL

One of the main difficulties involved with learning COM consists of understanding the relationships between the concepts and the actual implementation. We first examine the COM object model and how it relates to the object model of Eiffel. After we have described this model, it should be easier to understand the actual implementation of components.

Interfaces

Interfaces are at the heart of any COM component. Interfaces consist of a group of semantically related functions that the component exposes to its clients. They are the only way a client can access a component—any implementation function used internally by the component is not accessible to a client. This is how COM enforces information-hiding.

Interfaces also define the type of a component. Each interface corresponds to a specific view of the component. It is the equivalent of polymorphism in the object-oriented world. Whenever an interface from a component is requested, only the functions defined on that interface are accessible to the client, as if the component were polymorphically cast into an object of that type. Interfaces do not include any implementation; they only expose a set of functions without actually implementing them. The implementation lies in the class (note, unless otherwise specified, classes refer to COM classes in this chapter). As such, an interface really corresponds to a deferred class in the Eiffel model. Different classes can implement the interface functions in their own way.

The COM specification forces the use of single inheritance between interfaces. This is mainly for efficiency reasons and does not limit the expressive power since classes can inherit multiple interfaces. The COM specification also ensures that once you get hold of an interface, you can access any other interface on the same class. All the COM interfaces are identified uniquely by their interface identifier (IID)—this identifier is a globally unique identifier (GUID) statistically guaranteed to be unique in time and space.

Classes

Classes define the behavior of the interfaces they implement and are identified by a globally unique identifier called a class identifier (CLSID). Conceptually, classes inherit from all the interfaces they implement and polymorphism is achieved by accessing different interfaces on the class. A component can include more than one class.

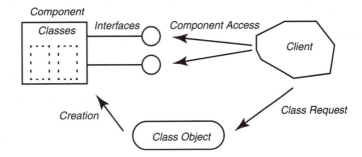

FIGURE 18.1. The COM conceptual model.

Class Objects

COM follows the class factory pattern for the creation of classes. The class factory is called a class object. Clients of a component can retrieve the class object associated with a given COM class and they can then ask the class object to spawn instances of the class and pass back interfaces. Depending on the component settings, the same class object can be used to spawn multiple instances of a class; otherwise a single instance is created each time the client requests one. Class objects are not identified by themselves; instead they are associated with one or more classes. The client uses a class identifier to get the corresponding class object.

Summary

Figure 18.1 shows how the different conceptual parts of the COM model interact with each other. Keeping this figure in mind should help in understanding the rest of this chapter. Essentially, a component consists of interface implementations in the form of classes. The component's interfaces expose the functions callable by clients. A client can request the creation of a component via its class object and can receive an interface in return. The client can then call the functions defined in the interface.

THE MICROSOFT INTERFACE DEFINITION LANGUAGE

Since COM components can be written in many different languages, there needs to be a language-neutral representation of a component. Tools for each language can then use this representation to get information about the components. COM uses the Microsoft Interface Definition Language (MIDL) to describe components. The MIDL syntax is very similar to C and fairly easy to learn. Each MIDL file contains the declarations for data types, interfaces, and libraries.

Data Types

MIDL supports a group of preset data types that roughly corresponds to the set of C data types listed in Table 18.1. It also supports the declaration of custom data types through the *struct, enum, union,* and *array* constructs.

The main difference between MIDL constructs and their C equivalents is the ability to use attributes to qualify the fields of the structure. The attributes usually define the behavior, at runtime, of the construct they are associated with. They are placed between square brackets in front of the construct they qualify. Attributes can qualify data types as well as interfaces, classes, and libraries.

The *enum* construct is the equivalent to a C enumeration. It defines a set of named integers and has the same syntax as C. By default, enumeration elements are passed between interfaces as 16-bit integers. If you need to handle the enumeration elements as 32-bit integers, you can specify the attribute **v1_enum** in front of the **enum** keyword.

Example 18.1 declares two enumerations. The first enumeration includes 16-bit integers and the second uses the attribute **v1_enum,** consequently including 32-bit integers.

TABLE 18.1   *Main MIDL Basic Data Types*

DATA TYPE	DESCRIPTION
boolean	8 bits representing a Boolean value
byte	8 bits
char	8 bits representing a character
double	64-bit floating point number
float	32-bit floating point number
hyper	64-bit integer
int	32-bit integer
long	32-bit integer
short	16-bit integer
small	8-bit integer
wchar_t	16 bits representing a wide character

Example 18.1 MIDL Enum Declaration

```
// Enum of 16-bit integers
typedef enum
{
    MinValue = 0, MaxValue = 32767
} Enum;

// Enum of 32-bit integers
typedef [v1_enum] enum
{
    MinValue = 0, MaxValue = 2147483647
} Enum;
```

The *union* construct is a bit different from the standard C union because it can be of two types: encapsulated or nonencapsulated. Encapsulated unions are contained in a structure with their discriminant, while nonencapsulated unions are not contained within a structure.

Example 18.2 shows how unions can be declared in MIDL. The first union is encapsulated within *UnionContainer*. The switch keyword precedes the declaration of the union discriminant (*UnionDiscriminant* in the example). The second union is nonencapsulated and very similar to a standard C union. You can specify the type of the discriminant of nonencapsulated unions with the attribute **switch_type.** The discriminant may be an integer, character, or enumeration (respectively *int, char,* or *enum*).

Example 18.2 MIDL Unions

```
// Encapsulated union
typedef union _UnionContainer switch (long UnionDiscriminant) Union-
    Name
{
    case 0:
        boolean b;
    case 1:
        double d;
} UnionContainer;

// Non-encapsulated union
typedef [switch_type( int )] union _UnionName
{
    case 0:
        boolean b;
    case 1:
        double d;
} UnionName;
```

The next construct, *struct,* is also very similar to its C equivalent. The only difference lies in the ability to add attributes before the declaration of any field. Apart from the attributes you can use in conjunction with enumerations, unions, and arrays with the string and ignore attributes, as shown in Example 18.3, you can also qualify structure fields with the **string** and **ignore** attributes. The attribute string specifies that the array of characters (*char[ ], wchar_t[ ],* or *byte[ ]*) it precedes should be treated as a string when transmitted and the attribute **ignore** specifies that the pointer it precedes should be ignored when the structure is transmitted. Neither the pointer nor the data it points to will be transmitted. The other attributes you can use in MIDL structures qualify the types of the pointers they precede. There are three different types of pointers in MIDL.

- ▶ *Reference pointers* cannot be null. They can always be dereferenced, they are constant throughout a call, and they cannot be reallocated. This means that the implementation of a function that receives such a pointer cannot allocate new memory and has to use the storage defined by the pointer. Finally, such pointers cannot cause aliasing; there should not be other pointers pointing to the same data. The keyword preceding a reference pointer is **ref.**
- ▶ *Unique pointers* can be null. They can be assigned to a null value and they can be reallocated (but do not have to be). If the original value was null, then the pointer is reallocated by the function it was given to. If the original value was non-null then the same memory storage is used for the data given to the function and the new data the function writes. Unique pointers cannot cause aliasing, thus the name *unique.* The keyword preceding unique pointers is **unique.**
- ▶ *Full pointers* are equivalent to unique pointers except that they can cause aliasing. Full pointers are more costly to use since the code that extracts the data to be transmitted has to handle possible cycles. The keyword preceding full pointers is **ptr.**

Example 18.3 MIDL Structures

```
typedef stuct _StructureName
{
    [unique] char * UniquePointer;
    [ignore] int * NonTransmittedData;
    [string, ptr] wchar_t * UnicodeString;
}
```

MIDL arrays are also quite different from standard C arrays. The Microsoft remote procedure call (RPC) protocol that COM uses to transmit data between interfaces requires that their lower bound be set to 0. They can be of four natures.

- *Conformant arrays* have their upper bound of any dimension determined at runtime.
- *Varying arrays* have the range of transmitted elements determined at runtime. Their bounds are determined at compile time.
- *Open arrays* have both their upper bound and range of transmitted elements determined at runtime.
- *Static arrays* have both their bounds and range of transmitted elements determined at compile time.

Conformant and open arrays can be embedded in at most one *struct* construct and have to be the last element of the structure. The attributes **max_is** or **size_is** specify the upper bound of such arrays. The range of elements transmitted for varying and open arrays is set using the attributes **length_is, first_is,** or **last_is.** All of these attributes, from **max_is** to **last_is,** take an integer argument. If the array is part of the parameters of a function, then the integer argument of any associated attribute needs to be a parameter as well. If the array is encapsulated into a structure, then any attribute argument needs to be a field of the same structure. The attribute **max_is** specifies the index of the last item in the array, while the attribute **size_is** specifies the size of the array. Since the lower bound of MIDL arrays needs to be equal to 0, giving the value n to the argument of **size_is** is equivalent to giving the value $n-1$ to the argument of **max_is.** These two attributes cannot be used together on the same array. The attribute **first_is** specifies the index of the first element in the array to be transmitted. The attribute **last_is** specifies the index of the last element in the array to be transmitted, while the attribute **length_is** specifies the number of elements to be transmitted. These two attributes cannot be used together on the same array. The arguments of the attributes **first_is, last_is,** and **length_is** are bound with the relationship.

```
length = last-first
```

Example 18.4 shows how to declare different types of arrays in MIDL.

Example 18.4 MIDL Arrays

```
// Conformant array
typedef struct
```

Example 18.4 MIDL Arrays (*Continued*)

```
{
     unsigned short size;
     [size_is( size )] int Array[];
} ConformantArray;

// Varying array
typedef struct
{
     unsigned short first;
     unsigned short last;
     [first_is( first ), last_is( last )] int Array[];
} VaryingArray;

// Open array
typedef struct
{
     unsigned short size;
     unsigned short first;
     unsigned short last;
     [size_is( size ), first_is( first ), last_is( last )] int
Array[];
} OpenArray;

// Static array
typedef struct
{
     int Array[10];
} StaticArray;
```

Interfaces

Now that we know how to define the data types that our component can transmit, we can describe the interfaces that hold the functions using them. The description includes the signature of the functions and the attributes associated with the interface. These attributes can include information such as the interface identifier, its version number, and a short description. Attributes appear before the declaration of the interface (between square brackets) and apply to any item declared in the interface body. There are two kinds of interfaces you can declare in IDL: standard interfaces and dispatch interfaces, also known as dispinterfaces. Dispatch interfaces are used for Automation and are nothing more than standard interfaces inheriting from *IDispatch*. See "Automation" later in this chapter.

Example 18.5 MIDL Interface Header Declaration

```
[
        object,
        uuid (9A483B80-AA39-11d2-B961-00403392AC95),
        helpstring ("String manipulation interface"),
        version (1.0)
]
interface IString : IUnknown
```

Example 18.5 is an extract from the IDL file associated with the Eiffel-COM *StringManipulator* example. It shows the declaration of the interface header for *IString*. The first attribute *object* is compulsory for all COM interfaces. It tells the IDL compiler that this interface is a COM interface since IDL is also used to declare Distributed Computing Environment (DCE) RPC interfaces. The second attribute is the interface identifier. **uuid** stands for universally unique identifier. The attribute **helpstring** includes a short description associated with the interface. This attribute can be associated with any MIDL construct (functions, interfaces, classes, and libraries). The last attribute is the version number of the interface. This interface inherits from the interface *IUnknown*. See "From Pointers to Interfaces" later in this chapter. Another useful interface attribute that does not appear in this example is **default_pointer.** This attribute takes one argument that specifies the type of pointers used in the interface functions. The possible values for this argument are **ref, unique,** and **ptr** that correspond to reference, unique, and full pointers respectively. Function parameter attributes can override this default and specify their own pointer types.

The body of the interface declaration lists the functions exposed by the interface. All the functions on an interface should return a status value called HRESULT. This value is a 32-bit integer that describes the return status of the function.

Figure 18.2 describes the layout of an HRESULT. The severity bit (*S* in the figure) specifies whether the function call was successful (bit set to 0) or a failure (bit set to 1). Bits 29 and 30 are reserved. The facility code indicates the group of status codes that the HRESULT belongs to, as listed in Table 18.2.

Your component can define its own HRESULT, in which case the facility code should be set to *FACILITY_ITF*. The last 16 bits of the HRESULT define the actual status code. The meaning of the code depends on the facility.

Each function on the interface can be qualified with the idempotent attribute, which specifies that the result of the function is independent from the

31	30-29	28-16	15-0
S	R	Facility	Code

FIGURE 18.2. HResult layout.

state of the component. Two calls with identical parameter values will yield the same result. This allows COM to optimize the calls by caching the return value on the client side.

Every parameter should be qualified with a directional attribute. This attribute specifies the direction in which the data is being transmitted. The possible values for the directional attribute are **in, out,** or a combination of the two. The COM documentation advises to avoid the use of both the **in** and **out** attributes at the same time because it adds an overhead to remote calls. The other attribute you can apply to function parameters is **retval.** This attribute must appear only once per function and should be associated only with an outgoing parameter. Since functions must return an HRESULT, any result the function needs to return should be passed as an out parameter. The attribute **retval** allows you to specify which out parameter is semantically the return value of the function. Certain languages such as Eiffel will use this parameter as the actual return value, with the language runtime taking care of transmitting the HRESULT and mapping the return value into an out parameter.

Example 18.6 shows the full declaration of the interface *IString* from the *StringManipulator* example.

TABLE 18.2   *Facility Codes*

FACILITY CODE (VALUE)	DESCRIPTION
FACILITY_NULL (0)	Common status codes. Includes S_OK and S_FALSE.
FACILITY_ITF (4)	Status codes specific to the interface. Should be used for user-defined HRESULTS.
FACILITY_RPC (1)	RPC error codes.
FACILITY_DISPATCH (2)	IDispatch status codes.
FACILITY_STORAGE (3)	Persistent storage error codes.
FACILITY_WIN32 (7)	Win32 error codes.
FACILITY_WINDOWS (8)	Microsoft interfaces error codes.
FACILITY_CONTROL (10)	OLE controls error codes.

Example 18.6 Full MIDL Interface Declaration

```
[
    object,
    uuid (9A483B80-AA39-11d2-B961-00403392AC95),
    helpstring ("String manipulation interface"),
    version (1.0)
]
interface IString : IUnknown
{
    [helpstring ("Manipulated string")]
    HRESULT String ([out, retval] LPSTR *a_string);

    [helpstring ("Set manipulated string with 'a_string'.")]
    HRESULT SetString ([in] LPSTR a_string);

    [helpstring ("Copy the characters of 's' to positions
        'start_pos' .. 'end_pos'.")]
    HRESULT ReplaceSubstring ([in] LPSTR s, [in] int start_pos,
        [in] int end_pos);

    [helpstring ("Remove all occurrences of 'c'.");
    HRESULT PruneAll ([in] CHAR c);
};
```

Libraries

The information included in the IDL file is useful for tools that can produce language-dependent representations of the component. Microsoft provides the Microsoft IDL compiler that can be used to compile an IDL file into a binary type library. Windows then provides a set of API function calls to access the information held in the type library. The use of a compiler has two main advantages. First, it checks the validity of the IDL source. Therefore, if you have written inconsistent MIDL, the compiler will catch it and report the errors. Second, the information in a type library is exposed in a convenient way so that tools can use it efficiently.

The content of a type library is controlled via the *library* construct in IDL. Any entity declared inside the library definition will be generated into the type library. A library can include the definitions of another library thanks to the **importlib** statement. The argument of this statement is the filename of the other type library, including any required definitions. The library is associated with a unique identifier and thus is qualified with a **uuid** attribute. You can also specify the version of the library with the version attribute and associate a short description with the **helpstring** attribute.

The library construct is how you define the classes that implement the interfaces of a component. Apart from the standard **uuid, version,** and **helpstring** attributes, you can also use the **hidden, control,** and **appobject** attributes. You should use **hidden** when you do not want the class to appear in the component browser. The **control** attribute declares the class as an ActiveX control implementation. Finally, you should associate the **appobject** attribute with classes that implement an OLE application object.

Interfaces are listed one by one inside the class declaration. Each is declared with the keywords **interface** or **dispinterface,** depending on whether it is a direct or a dispatch interface. See "Interfaces" earlier in this chapter. The interface must have been described previously for the IDL file to compile correctly. Possible attributes that apply to interfaces include **default** and **source.** The former indicates that the interface is the default interface of the component. Only one interface should be qualified with the **default** attribute. The latter indicates that the qualified interface is a source interface. A source interface is meant to be given to the component as opposed to exposed from the component. This allows for callbacks between the component and the client.

Example 18.7 shows the library declaration of the *StringManipulator* example. The library imports the definitions included in *stdole32.tlb*. Any library should do the same since all the standard COM types are defined within this standard type library.

Example 18.7 MIDL Library Declaration

```
[
    uuid(6C39F541-F349-11d2-B965-00403392AC95),
    helpstring ("String Manipulator Library"),
    version (1.0)
]
library StringManipulatorLib
{
    importlib ("stdole32.tlb");

    [
      uuid(2DB86EC0-9672-11D2-B961-00403392AC95),
      helpstring ("String Manipulator")
    ]
    coclass StringManipulator
    {
      [default] interface IString;
    };
};
```

IMPLEMENTING COM COMPONENTS

We have seen the object model of COM and how you can describe components in a language-neutral way, using MIDL. We will now look at the actual implementation of components and how they interact with the COM runtime.

The Secret: Virtual Tables

The trick that makes everything work lies in the binary layout of the component. The functions of interfaces are all referenced from a table of pointers known as a virtual table. One virtual table per interface exists. When a client requests a pointer to an interface, it is given a pointer to such a table. Since the layout of these tables is directly deduced from the description of the interfaces in the MIDL file, COM knows the offset of each function pointer in the table.

Figure 18.3 describes the virtual table layout of the interface *IString* from the EiffelCOM *StringManipulator* example. The first three entries in the table are functions belonging to the interface *IUnknown* (see "From Pointers to Interfaces"). They appear first because they are functions inherited from a parent interface. You can see now why single inheritance between interfaces makes things a lot easier. The layout of the virtual table consists of the inherited interface functions pointers appended with the derived interface functions pointers. This layout is the same that C++ follows for derived classes; this is why COM interfaces and classes can be directly written as C++ classes.

From Pointers to Interfaces

Virtual tables are the bridge between the implementation and the model. Once you have obtained a pointer to one of the virtual tables of the component, the COM specification ensures that you can get hold of any other virtual table

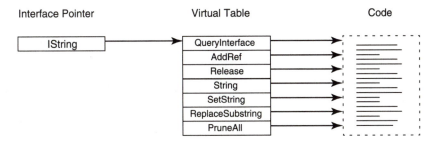

FIGURE 18.3. Virtual table.

THE COMPONENT OBJECT MODEL

pointer that the component exposes. Thus, there needs to be a function that lets you query any interface from the component. This function is called *Query-Interface* and is one of the functions of the interface *IUnknown*. This special interface contains functions that any valid COM interface should expose. For this reason, any COM interface inherits *IUnknown*. In other words, *QueryInterface* is the function whose pointer always appears first in any virtual table. The C prototype of this function is the following:

```
HRESULT QueryInterface(
                REFIID iid,          // Interface identifier
                void ** ppvObject    // Out parameter, resulting interface
                                     pointer
);
```

QueryInterface returns an HRESULT, which indicates if the function was successful or failed. The first parameter is the identifier of the interface you need to get a pointer to, while the second parameter is a pointer to the interface pointer that acts as an out parameter—the function sets the interface pointer with a valid value. Notice that this parameter is declared as *void ***, which means that this function, one of the key functions of COM, is not type-safe. Fortunately, higher level languages such as Eiffel alleviate this problem and expose a type-safe equivalent to *QueryInterface*.

The *IUnknown* interface holds two more functions that any valid COM interface must expose. The function *AddRef* increments the reference count on the interface—any client that copies an interface pointer should call *AddRef* before calling anything else, and when the client does not need the interface anymore, it should call *Release,* which decrements the reference count. The following rules dictate when these functions should be called:

▶ A client should call *AddRef* when it duplicates a valid interface pointer.
▶ A client should call *Release* when it overrides a valid interface pointer with other data.

Note that *QueryInterface* calls *AddRef* and that it is the client's responsibility to call the corresponding *Release.* Manual reference counting is prone to errors and higher level languages tend to hide it from the developer. The C prototypes for *AddRef* and *Release* are the following:

```
ULONG AddRef();
ULONG Release();
```

These two functions, although exposed through interfaces, do not return HRESULTs. Instead, they return the number of references currently held on the interface, although this is not guaranteed for all interfaces and should not be relied upon (you may use this number for debug purposes only).

Objects

We have seen that getting an interface on a component is logically equivalent to casting the component to the type of the interface. This conceptual representation often maps to the implementation of COM components. A standard implementation technique consists of making the class inherit from the interfaces and implement their abstract functions. Interfaces are pure abstract classes that define the functions exposed by the component. The classes then implement these functions. This is the schema used in Eiffel, where each interface corresponds to a deferred class. The Eiffel class that implements the COM class then inherits from these deferred classes and implements the deferred features.

A single component can hold multiple classes. When a client requests an interface for the first time, it provides both the identifier of the interface and the identifier of the class. Once instantiated, components are identified with their pointers on the *IUnknown* interface. The COM specification requires that any client calling the function *QueryInterface* with the identifier of *IUnknown* on a given instance always receives the same pointer. This ensures that you can compare instances of a component by comparing the pointers to *IUnknown*.

Activation

Now that we know how interfaces and classes are implemented, we can focus on the creation of classes. Any client that needs to get an interface pointer to a given component will first access the *class object*. The name of this module should really be class factory, since its goal is to spawn instances of a class on request. A class object is just another class that implements interfaces needed for the lifetime management of the component. The same class object can create instances of multiple classes. The association between the class and its class object is done in the registry, when the component is registered. The *Service Control Manager* (SCM) is able to read the information in the registry and locate the class object whenever a client requests a new instance of the component.

The way a class object is loaded in memory (known as *activation*) depends on the location of the component. See "Location" in this chapter for a description of the possible locations of a component. If the component is an in-process server (i.e., a DLL) then the pointer to the class object can be directly retrieved through the DLL exported function *DllGetClassObject*. If the component is an out-of-process server (i.e., a standard executable), then it registers its class object when loaded in memory. The SCM can then hand the pointer back to the client that requested it. Figure 18.4 illustrates this process.

A client can request to access the class object of a component with the function *CoGetClassObject*.

```
HRESULT CoGetClassObject (
            REFCLSID rclsid,               // Class identifier
            DWORD dwClsContext,            // Expected component location
            COSERVERINFO * pServerInfo,    // Remote server information
            REFIID riid,                   // Interface identifier
            LPVOID * ppv );                // Out parameter, resulting
                                               interface pointer
```

The parameters of this function include the identifiers for the class and the expected pointer. Note that the requested interface pointer is an interface pointer on the class object, not on the class itself. This function returns an HRESULT that indicates the success or failure of the call. The second parameter is a flag that indicates the expected location of the server. The same class can be implemented in different modules with different locations. That is, you can compile the same class in a DLL and then in an EXE and let the client decide which version is more appropriate for its use. If the client requests an out-of-process version of the component, then it can provide information on where the component is expected to run. This is the role of the third parameter, which describes the machine on which the class object should be loaded. The last parameter is an out parameter that holds the resulting pointer to the interface of the class object.

Each component is free to implement its own class object with custom interfaces. However, environments such as COM+ require that the class object

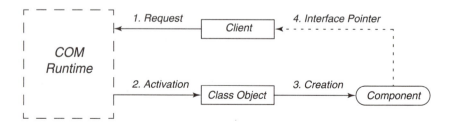

FIGURE 18.4. Component creation.

exposes the *IClassFactory* interface. This interface is used by the majority of components since it exposes only two functions. The first function, *CreateInstance,* is the function that spawns new instances of a given class. The other function, *LockServer,* allows you to keep the class object in memory even if clients hold references to any of its interface.

```
HRESULT CreateInstance(
                IUnknown *pUnkOuter,  // Pointer to aggregated component,
                                      //    if any
                REFIID riid,          // Interface identifier
                void **ppv            // Out parameter, resulting interface
                                      //    pointer
);
```

The function *CreateInstance* returns an HRESULT. The first argument is used for aggregation. Aggregation is a special technique where you can embed (aggregate) a component into another. The second argument is the interface identifier, which is handed back to the client once the instance has been loaded. The last argument is a placeholder for the resulting interface pointer.

Clients can retrieve an interface pointer in two steps. They should first call *CoGetClassObject* to get a pointer on *IClassFactory* and then use this pointer to call *CreateInstance.* The COM API exposes a shortcut function that combines the two calls into one. The function *CoCreateInstance* requests the *IClassFactory* interface on the component and then calls *CreateInstance* and returns the resulting pointer.

```
HRESULT CoCreateInstance(
                REFCLSID clsid,       // Class identifier
                IUnknown * pUnkOuter, // Pointer to aggregated component,
                                      //    if any
                DWORD grfContext,     // Expected location of component
                REFIID iid,           // Interface identifier
                void * ppvObj         // Out parameter, resulting interface
                                      //    pointer
);
```

This function takes the identifiers for both the class and its interface. Note that in this case it is the interface identifier of the component itself, not its class object. The second argument is used for aggregation. The third argument is a flag that indicates the expected location of the component. The last argument is a placeholder for the resulting pointer.

TYPES OF COMPONENTS

A large collection of technologies, including ActiveX, DirectX, OCX, COM+, ADO, and ASP, use the COM standard. This section focuses on categorizing COM components according to their properties as well as the context in which they are used.

Location

The first criteria that defines the type of component is the location—will the component be loaded in the client process or will the component be a remote server for a distributed application? In the former case, the component is compiled as a dynamic-link library (DLL), while in the latter case it is a standard executable.

In-Process Components

Typical instances of DLL components are found in technologies such as OCX, ActiveX, or ASP. These are small, downloadable binaries that are loaded and executed in a container. The container acts as a client of the component. One main difference between an out-of-process component and an in-process component (other than the nature of the module—DLL versus executable) is the activation process. In the case of out-of-process components, the component must notify COM when it is ready to receive calls from clients. In the case of an in-process server, the call comes directly from COM. COM first loads the DLL into the client process and then calls the exported function *DllGetClassObject* to access the component class object.

There are four exported functions that an in-process component must expose. The function *DllRegister* is called at install time and should register the component in the Windows registry. The utility *Regsvr32.exe* allows you to register COM DLLs by loading them in memory and calling the function *DllRegister*. *DllUnregister* does exactly the opposite—it uninstalls the component from the registry. If you add the command line argument *-u* after *Regsvr32,* then the utility loads the DLL and calls *DllUnregisterServer*. Finally, *DllCanUnloadNow* gets called by COM whenever it tries to unload the component from memory. If the result of the function is *S_OK,* then Windows unloads the DLL from memory. These four functions must be accessible from outside the DLL for the in-process component to work correctly.

```
HRESULT DllGetClassObject(
                REFCLSID rclsid,      //CLSID for the class object
                REFIID riid,          //Interface identifier
                LPVOID * ppv,         //Out parameter, Interface pointer holder
);

HRESULT DllRegisterServer();

HRESULT DllUnregisterServer();

HRESULT DllCanUnloadNow();
```

Out-of-Process Components

This type of component is a standard executable that can act as a remote server. Out-of-process components can be COM-compliant applications, such as the Microsoft Office programs, or remote servers in a three-tier client-server architecture. Out-of-process components must notify COM when they are loaded in memory and give the SCM a pointer to their class objects. The function *CoRegisterClassObject* is the function used by such components to register their class object. The COM runtime keeps track of all running instances of out-of-process components in its Running Object Table (ROT). There are multiple API functions used to access the ROT on a machine and query for components.

```
HRESULT CoRegisterClassObject(
                REFCLSID rclsid,        //Class identifier to be
                                              registered
                IUnknown * pUnk,        //Pointer to the class object
                DWORD dwClsContext,     //Location of component
                DWORD flags,            //How to connect to the class
                                              object
                LPDWORD lpdwRegister    //Pointer to the value
                                              returned
);
```

The function *CoRegisterClassObject* returns a token in its last argument. This token should be given to the function *CoRevokeClassObject* when the component is shutting down. This function removes the class object from the entries of the ROT.

```
HRESULT CoRevokeClassObject( DWORD dwRegister );
```

COM applications should handle the arguments */RegServer* and */Un-regServer* on the command line. They indicate that the component should be registered or unregistered from the registry, respectively. They are the equivalent of the functions *DllRegisterServer* and *DllUnregisterServer* of in-process components.

Access Type

Regardless of its location, you can access a COM component either directly through its interfaces or with Automation. We have already seen how you can get hold of one of the component interfaces using the component class object. Automation allows you to expose the component functionality to scripting environments where the COM machinery is hidden from the developer.

Automation

Automation consists of using a well-known interface to provide access to a group of methods and properties. This interface, called *IDispatch,* includes the function *invoke* that allows you to call a method, set a property, or get a property. One advantage of this approach is that the interface is a standard interface whose functions and methods are well known. As a result, Windows can include a built-in marshaller for that interface (see "Marshalling" in this chapter). *IDispatch* exposes four functions to its clients.

- ► *GetTypeInfoCount* specifies whether the component implements the interface *ITypeInfo*. This interface allows the client to retrieve information about the component. If the component is associated with a type library, this interface gives access to the information held in it.
- ► *GetTypeInfo* allows you to retrieve a pointer to an *ITypeInfo* interface. You can specify the locale in which you would like the information to be represented and the index of the type information. The index of the information on the dispatch interface is always 0.
- ► *GetIDsOfNames* allows you to retrieve the identifiers of functions and the arguments from their names. You should use this function for late binding.
- ► Last but not least, *invoke* allows you to call functions and retrieve or set the value of properties on an Automation component. The function or property is identified with the dispatch identifier (DISPID). You can retrieve the available DISPIDS with *GetIDsOfNames*. The arguments of functions called through *invoke* must be packed into a *DISPPARAMS* (dispatch parameters) structure. This structure consists of two arrays, one for the values of the arguments and one for their dispatch identifiers. The

result of the function is handed back as an out parameter. The memory holding the value of the result must be allocated by the caller of *invoke* and the client must also allocate the memory for the exception information and the index of the first argument with an error. The exception information is packed in an *EXCEPINFO* structure. This structure holds information such as the nature and description of the exception. It also points to an associated help file.

```
HRESULT GetTypeInfoCount (
            unsigned int FAR*  pctinf // Out parameter, number of type
            information provided.

);


HRESULT GetTypeInfo (
        unsigned int  iTInfo,       // Type information index (0 for IDispatch)
        LCID  lcid,                 // Expected locale
        ITypeInfo FAR* FAR*  ppTInfo // Out parameter, resulting interface pointer.

);


HRESULT GetIDsOfNames (
        REFIID  riid,               // Must be IID_NULL
        OLECHAR FAR* FAR*  rgszNames, // Array of names to be mapped
        unsigned int  cNames,       // Count of elements in array
        LCID    lcid,               // Locale of given names
        DISPID FAR*  rgDispId       // Out parameter, resulting array of ids.

);


HRESULT Invoke (
        DISPID  dispIdMember,       // Dispatch identifier of member
        REFIID  riid,               // Must be IID_NULL
        LCID    lcid,               // Locale of arguments
        WORD    wFlags,             // Type of operation, function call or
                                    property set/put
        DISPPARAMS FAR*  pDispParams, // Arguments
        VARIANT FAR*  pVarResult,   // Out parameter, result of function call
        EXCEPINFO FAR*  pExcepInfo, // Out parameter, Exception information, if
                                    any
        unsigned int FAR*  puArgErr // Out parameter, Index of first argument with
                                    error, if any
);
```

Automation allows for dynamic discovery of the methods and properties of a component at runtime. This process, called late binding, consists of calling *GetIDsOfNames* to retrieve the dispatch identifier of the member the client needs to access, as well as any argument identifier. The client can then call *invoke* with the retrieved identifiers. This approach also has some drawbacks. First, late binding is not an efficient way of calling a function on an interface since it requires two round trips, which can be expensive in a distributed environment. Second, since the marshaller is built in, it has to know in advance all the possible types that a function can accept to be able to marshal the corresponding data. There is consequently a limitation on the number of types that you can use in signatures of functions on an Automation-compatible interface. The set of available types is called Variant and covers most of the standard types. However, the marshaller does not allow the passing of complex user-defined data types. For these reasons, Automation is mostly used in scripting environments where speed is not a critical factor and data types are simple. The supported types (known as *Automation types*) and their Eiffel equivalents are listed in Table 18.3.

TABLE 18.3 *Type Mappings*

COM TYPE	EIFFEL EQUIVALENT	DESCRIPTION
boolean	BOOLEAN	Standard Boolean
unsigned char	CHARACTER	Standard character
double	DOUBLE	Standard double
float	REAL	2 bytes real
int	INTEGER	Standard integer
long	INTEGER	4 bytes integer
short	INTEGER	2 bytes integer
BSTR	STRING	Standard string
CURRENCY	ECOM_CURRENCY	Currency value
DATE	DATE	Standard date
SCODE	INTEGER	Return status
Interface IDispatch *	ECOM_QUERIABLE	Automation interface
Interface IUnknown *	ECOM_QUERIABLE	Generic interface
dispinterface	ECOM_QUERIABLE	Automation interface
Coclass TypeName	TYPE_NAME	Component coclass
SAFEARRAY	ARRAY	Automation array
TypeName*	CELL [TypeName]	Pointer to type
Decimal	ECOM_DECIMAL	Decimal value

Direct Access

Direct interface access is the preferred way to access remote servers if speed is a concern and data types are specific to the application. The first interface pointer to the component is obtained through the class object, and other interfaces of the component are obtained by calling the *QueryInterface* function.

As information on any interface is not accessible dynamically, the description of the interfaces must be provided to tools that need to handle the components, such as the EiffelCOM wizard. The official way to describe components and interfaces is through the IDL (see "The Microsoft Interface Definition Language" earlier in this chapter). Once an IDL file has been written to describe a component, it can be compiled with the MIDL compiler to generate both a type library and the code for the marshaller specific to that interface.

EiffelCOM

The idea behind EiffelCOM is to hide the implementation details of COM components. Of course, the developer should be able to choose what kind of access to use, but this choice should have no impact on the design of the Eiffel system itself. For that reason, the Eiffel code generated by the EiffelCOM wizard follows the same architecture, independently of the choice made for interface access and marshalling. The difference lies in the runtime and generated C code, where the actual calls to the components are implemented.

DEEPER INTO COM

This section gives a bit more detail on the internals of COM. The understanding of these details is not required to use the EiffelCOM wizard, but can help when making decisions about the design of components.

Apartments

The first interesting subject that requires more in-depth coverage is the execution context of a component. Components can run in the same process as the client, or they can run in a separate process, possibly on a different machine.

This superficial description only takes in-processes into account. What happens if a component uses multithreading to achieve its tasks? In the case of a remote server, this scenario does not seem too esoteric. The problem is that a server does not (and should not) know what type of client is trying to access it. It cannot assume that the client will be able to take advantage of its multi-threading capabilities. Conversely, a multithreaded client should not rely on the server's ability to handle concurrent access.

The solution chosen in the COM specification consists of defining an additional execution context called an apartment. When COM loads a component, it creates the apartment in which the component will run. Multiple instances of a multithreaded component live together in the same apartment, since asynchronous calls should be handled correctly and there is no need to add any synchronization layer. On the other hand, single-threaded components live alone in their apartments and any concurrent calls coming from clients are first synchronized before executing. These two behaviors define two different kinds of apartments: multithreaded apartments (MTA) and single-threaded apartments (STA) (see Figure 18.5).

Apartments solve the concurrency problem by removing the necessity of knowing the multithreaded capability of a component and its clients. Multi-threaded clients can always make asynchronous calls, and depending on whether the component handles concurrent access or not, they will be forwarded directly or first synchronized and then forwarded. There can be multiple instances of STAs running in one process while there will be at most one MTA.

A component specifies the type of apartment in which it runs when it initializes the COM runtime. This initialization is done through the API function *CoInitializeEx*. The first argument of this function is reserved and should be *null,* while the second argument is a flag that specifies the threading nature of the component.

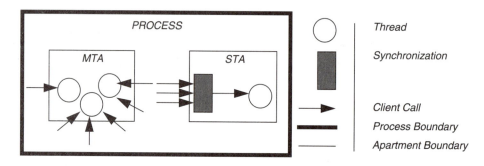

FIGURE 18.5. Apartments.

```
HRESULT CoInitializeEx(
                 void *pvReserved,     // Reserved, must be null
                 DWORD dwFlags         // Threading nature of component (see
                                       //    Table 18.4)
);
```

The possible values that the *dwFlags* argument can take are listed in Table 18.4.

Marshalling

At this point you might wonder how calls can "cross" apartment boundaries. Components from an STA can make calls to components running in an MTA, and vice versa. These apartments might be running in different processes, or even on different machines. COM uses the proxy and stub techniques to call across apartments.

The idea is to trick the client of an interface by providing an interface proxy in its apartment. The proxy includes exactly the same functions as the interface itself, but their implementation just forwards the call to the actual interface. The client has no idea whether the entity it is dealing with is the actual interface or just a proxy. One of the most interesting implications of this approach is that the client implementation is independent from the location of the component.

This last explanation is not totally accurate—the call will not be forwarded to the actual interface but to its stub. The stub is the counterpart of the proxy. It represents the client for the interface. The interface doesn't know whether it is communicating with the actual client or with a stub. Although it is

TABLE 18.4   *COM Runtime Initialization Flags*

FLAG (HEXADECIMAL VALUE)	DESCRIPTION
COINIT_APARTMENTTHREADED	Runs the component in a single-threaded apartment.
COINIT_MULTITHREADED	Runs the component in a multithreaded apartment
COINIT_DISABLE_OLE1DDE	No support for DDE (OLE1). Can be combined with any of the first two flags.
COINIT_SPEED_OVER_MEMORY	Implies faster calls across apartment boundaries but more memory usage. Can be combined with any of the first two flags.

not completely true that the component implementation is independent from the location of the client, the stub pattern still helps to keep code identical for the implementation of the interfaces themselves. The implementation of a component is still different, depending on whether it is an in-process or out-of-process component, since the activation code differs in both cases. The design of the interfaces might also be different since out-of-process servers tend to avoid many round trips.

Figure 18.6 illustrates the cross-apartment call process.

There is one proxy/stub pair per interface. The proxy or the stub is loaded dynamically only when needed. This proxy/stub pair constitutes the marshaller. The reason for having a single name for two different things comes from how the MIDL compiler generates its code. MIDL produces the source files for one DLL in which both the proxy and the stub are included. This DLL is the marshaller.

Summary

Although COM might seem a bit awkward at first, it is a very powerful technology. The ability to reuse entire binaries, written in different languages, can really increase the productivity of a software development. COM is the base for diverse technologies found in the Windows environment. Such technologies include ActiveX, ADO, ASP, COM+, and an increasing number of others. One of the drawbacks of COM is the amount of so-called plumbing code required to produce a working solution. COM requires the writing of code not directly related to the problem domain, but rather to the support of the technology. Fortunately, higher level languages such as Visual Basic and Eiffel provide tools that automate the generation of such code. Using these languages, you can focus on solving the given problem rather than spend time chasing reference leaks or misaligned virtual tables.

The following chapter describes the use of the EiffelCOM library and wizard to produce and use COM components in Eiffel.

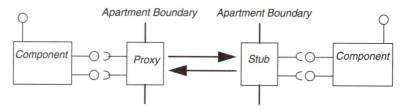

FIGURE 18.6. Cross-apartment calls.

EiffelCOM

Introducing EiffelCOM

This chapter focuses on the use of COM with Eiffel. If you are not familiar with COM, it is strongly advised that you read Chapter 18, "The Component Object Model." This chapter is the only chapter of the book that contains examples that are not included on the accompanying CD-ROM. If you plan to use EiffelCOM, please contact Interactive Software Engineering (www.eiffel.com).

The EiffelCOM environment allows for both the creation of new components and the reuse of existing components. If you decide to create a new component in Eiffel, you can either start from an existing Eiffel system and wrap it into a COM component or start from a component definition in the form of a MIDL file or a type library.

The heart of EiffelCOM lies in the EiffelCOM wizard tool. The wizard allows Eiffel developers, with little COM knowledge, to develop and reuse COM components. The wizard takes a type library describing a component as input and generates code consisting of Eiffel classes, C++ files, and library files. The design of the Eiffel-generated code follows the Eiffel standards so that it looks familiar to experienced Eiffel users. Moreover, the wizard automatically produces library files from the generated C++ code so that you do not need to modify the generated C++ code to build your EiffelCOM system. Figure 19.1 shows the general process that the EiffelCOM wizard uses to build a COM component.

For the remainder of the chapter, COM Definition File refers to the input file given to the wizard (either a MIDL file or a type library). If you start from an Eiffel system to generate a COM component, the wizard automatically generates an MIDL file from a given Eiffel class.

THE WIZARD

This chapter describes the wizard and the code it generates. The wizard consists of seven different dialogs. Each dialog asks for different information about the component and the kind of generation you need. Once the dialogs have been completed, the wizard compiles the MIDL file, if any, then analyzes the type library and generates the code.

The Introduction Dialog

The EiffelCOM wizard can be launched from the Windows start menu using

```
Start -> Programs -> EiffelXX -> EiffelCOM Wizard
```

where EiffelXX corresponds to your Eiffel installation (e.g., Eiffel46). The window in Figure 19.2 appears after you have launched the wizard.

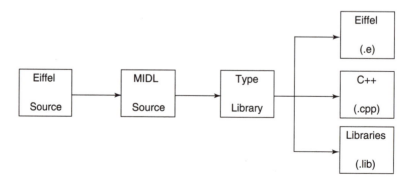

FIGURE 19.1. Generation process.

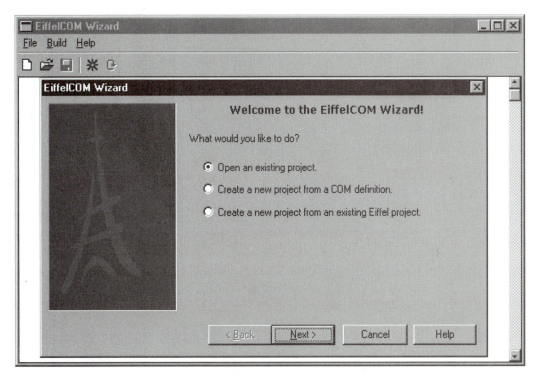

FIGURE 19.2. First dialog.

The introduction dialog lets you choose between opening an existing project or creating a new one, either from a COM definition or from an Eiffel project. Creating a new project opens the Generated Code Type Dialog. Opening an existing project displays an Open File Dialog from which you can select a previously saved EiffelCOM project.

The four buttons at the bottom of the dialog, **Back, Next, Cancel,** and **Help,** are common to all dialogs displayed throughout the execution of the wizard. **Next** validates all the values entered in the current dialog and activates the next dialog, **Back** discards all the values entered in current dialog and displays the previous dialog, **Cancel** exits the dialog and discards all the values entered, and finally, **Help** displays the EiffelCOM wizard manual.

The Main Window

The main window, shown in Figure 19.3 includes a tool bar and a menu. The first three buttons on the tool bar correspond to the first three entries in the File menu: New, Open, and Save. New resets all the information previously entered

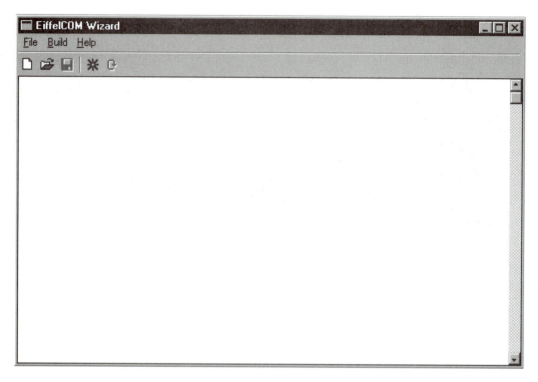

FIGURE 19.3. Main window.

in the wizard, Open brings up an Open File Dialog that can be used to retrieve a previously saved EiffelCOM project, and Save is used to save the current project. A saved project includes all of the values entered into the wizard. A project can be saved only after the wizard has been run successfully. The file extension for an EiffelCOM project is *.ewz*.

The second menu, Build, includes the entries Launch Wizard and Generate (no wizard) corresponding, respectively, to the last two tool bar buttons. The former activates the Generated Code Type Dialog while the latter launches the generation with the current settings and bypasses the dialogs. This last button can be used only when a project has been loaded or when the wizard has been run successfully at least once.

The third menu, Help, includes Help and About EiffelCOM. Help shows the manual. About EiffelCOM shows the About EiffelCOM Dialog (Figure 19.4).

The Generated Code Type Dialog

The first dialog asks whether you want to reuse or build a component. If you want to reuse an existing component, then the generated code will be for a client. If you choose to build a new one, the generated code will be for a COM

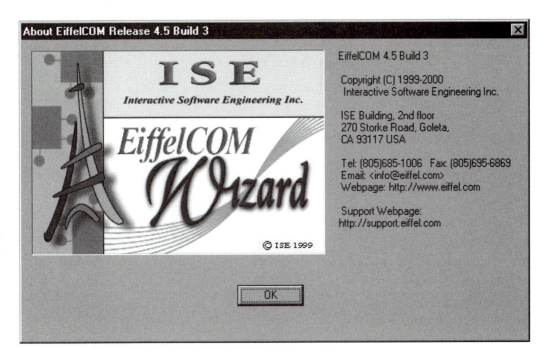

FIGURE 19.4. About box.

server. Choose the server or client radio button to specify which kind of project you want to work on. The Generated Code Type dialog is shown in Figure 19.5.

EiffelCOM supports the following component executable types:

- ▶ *In-process.* These components are implemented as DLLs that are loaded into the client process. The server runs in the same process as the client.
- ▶ *Out-of-process.* These components are executable files that can be accessed through the network. Clients and servers run in different processes and may even run on different machines.

If you do not want to compile the generated code automatically, you should check the check boxes at the bottom of the dialog. If you decide not to compile the C code automatically, then you will not be able to compile the Eiffel code since the latter relies on the former.

The Definition File Dialog

The Definition File dialog, shown in Figure 19.6 asks for the location of a COM definition file for the project. An IDL file is usually provided when building a new component. However, when you need to access an existing

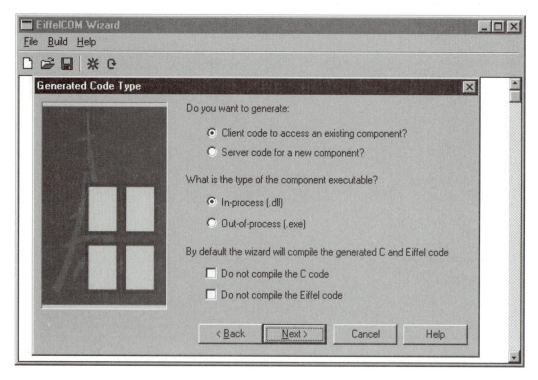

FIGURE 19.5. Generated Code Type dialog.

component, the original source code might not be available. In this case a type library is often embedded within the component and includes enough information for the wizard to generate the code.

The wizard accepts the following type extensions: *idl, tlb, ocx, olb, dll,* and *exe,* as shown in Figure 19.7.

The destination folder is the directory where the wizard saves the generated files, which should be empty. If the wizard were to overwrite an existing file, it first makes a copy and then emits a warning message. If any of the entered values are not correct when the Next button is pressed, then the wizard displays a warning message.

The Eiffel Project File Dialog

The Eiffel Project File dialog (Figure 19.8) asks for the location of an Eiffel project file *(*.epr),* the Ace file of the project, the name of the Eiffel class that will be converted into an IDL file, and the cluster name to which the Eiffel class belongs.

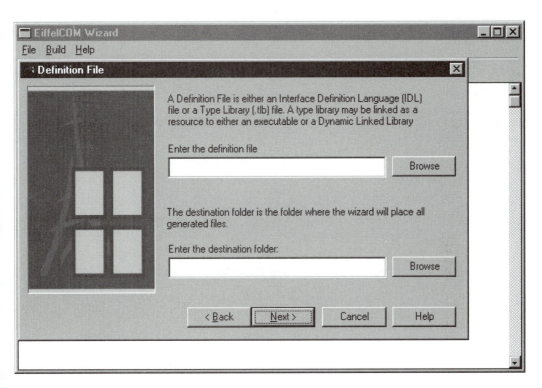

FIGURE 19.6. Definition File dialog.

The Destination Folder Dialog

The Destination Folder dialog (Figure 19.9) asks for the destination folder path where the wizard saves the generated files.

The IDL Marshalling Definition Dialog

The IDL Marshalling Definition dialog, shown in Figure 19.10 is displayed only for a server project and if the chosen definition file is an IDL file. It is used to determine how marshalling will be implemented for the component. The first choice that has to be made is whether the component will be called through Automation (using *IDispatch*) or through the interface's virtual table.

If you choose Automation, then the Universal Marshaller will be used. If you specify Virtual Table access, then you have the choice between using the Windows Universal Marshaller and the marshaller generated from the definition file. Since this dialog is displayed only when the definition file is an IDL file, choosing Standard Marshalling forces the wizard to compile the

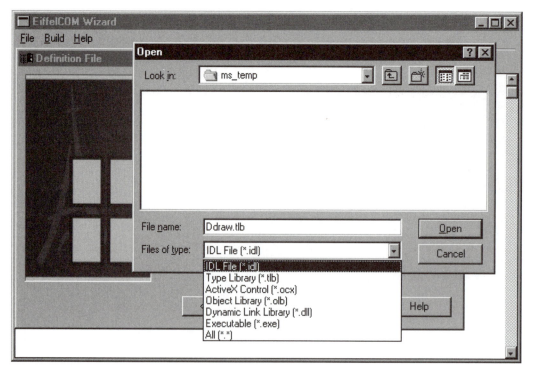

FIGURE 19.7. Definition File dialog, file extensions.

marshaller from the code generated with the MIDL compiler. Standard marshalling should be used whenever interface functions make use of non-Automation types.

The Type Library Marshalling Definition Dialog

The Type Library Definition dialog (Figure 19.11) is displayed only for a server project when the definition file is a type library. You have to choose between Automation and Virtual Table access and between Universal and Standard marshalling.

Because the definition file is a type library, the wizard cannot compile the Standard marshaller without additional information. This is the reason for having an extra text field for the path to the marshaller (also known as Proxy/Stub pair or just Proxy/Stub). The Proxy/Stub is a DLL that is used to marshall the data on the wire for a given component.

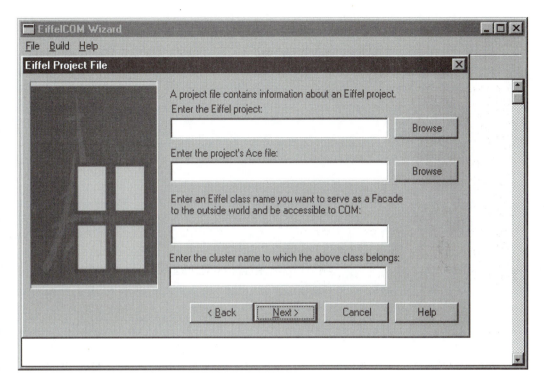

FIGURE 19.8. Eiffel Project File dialog.

The Final Dialog

The last dialog, shown in Figure 19.12 offers a choice of different output levels. By default, the wizard will display errors, warnings, and generic information. You can choose not to see warnings and/or extra information.

This dialog also asks whether you wish to continue after an error occurs during compilation. The Finish button closes the dialog and starts the processing. You can save the project after the wizard finishes.

COM Definition File Processing

Six phases are involved in the COM definition file processing.

1. *IDL Compilation.* If the definition file is an IDL file, the wizard compiles the IDL file into a type library, and if Standard Marshalling has been chosen, produces the marshaller from the generated C files.

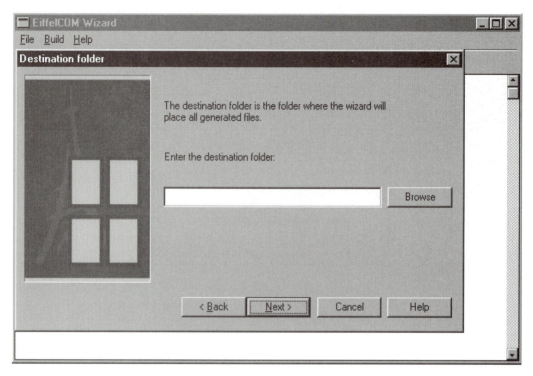

FIGURE 19.9. Destination Folder dialog.

2. *Type Library Parsing.* The wizard analyzes the type library and transforms the information it needs to generate the code into an internal representation.
3. *Code Generation.* The wizard generates both the Eiffel and C++ code from the information gathered during the previous steps.
4. *C++ Compilation.* The wizard compiles the generated C++ code into object files and libraries that will be linked with the Eiffel system.
5. *Eiffel Compilation.* For a client project, the wizard compiles the generated Eiffel code into a precompiled library that can be reused from other projects. For a server project, the wizard compiles the generated Eiffel code into a standard project with the registration class as its root class. If the location is in-process, then the project corresponds to a DLL, whereas if the location of the server is out-of-process, then the project corresponds to a standard executable.
6. *Eiffel Bench Launch.* Finally, the wizard launches EiffelBench and automatically opens the generated Eiffel system.

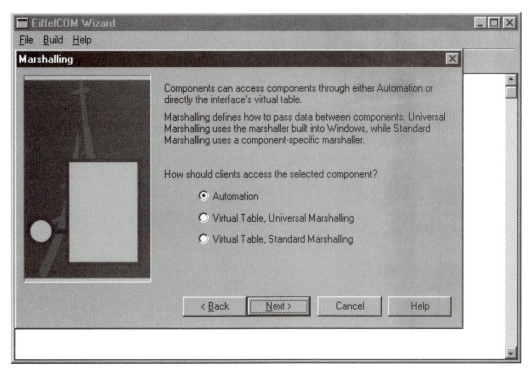

FIGURE 19.10. IDL Marshalling Definition dialog.

While processing, the wizard displays information in real time in the main window. The information includes output of calls to external compilers (C, Eiffel, and MIDL) and a description of the currently analyzed or generated type library item.

Generated Files

The wizard generates code into the specified destination folder. The file hierarchy is displayed in Figure 19.13.

- ▶ The root folder has two files and four subclusters.
- ▶ The file *generated.txt* includes a list of all the files generated by the wizard.
- ▶ The file *component.log* contains a summary of the processing done by the wizard. The name of the file is the name of the definition file, appended with *log* (so Figure 19.13 presumes that the definition file was *component.idl*).
- ▶ The folder idl contains the generated IDL file.

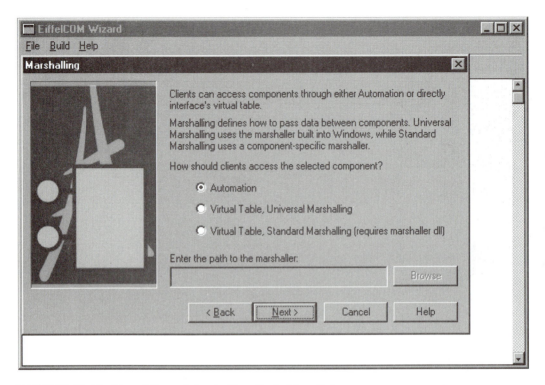

FIGURE 19.11. Type Library Marshalling Definition dialog.

▶ The folders Client and Server include the files generated for reusing a component or creating a new component. Each consists of three sub-directories—Include comprises header files needed to compile the Eiffel code, CLib contains the generated C++ code as well as the library files, and Component holds Eiffel code that wraps or defines the component. The Component subfolder of Server also includes the registration class. This Eiffel class contains the code needed to activate the component. The Client and Server folders also include an Ace file used to compile the generated Eiffel code.

▶ The Common folder comprises code that is used for both the server and the client parts. The Include and CLib directories contain the header files and the C++ code. The Interfaces subdirectory includes Eiffel classes that correspond to the component interfaces, and the Structures sub-directory includes Eiffel classes that wrap data structures specified in the definition file.

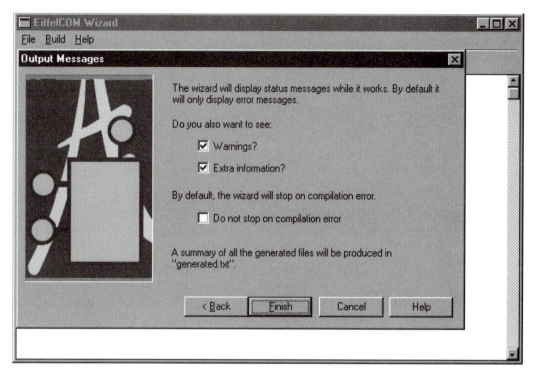

FIGURE 19.12. Final dialog.

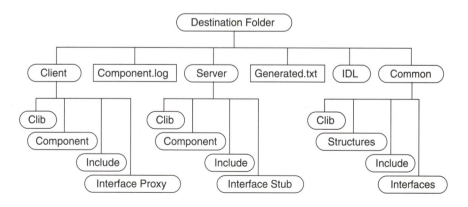

FIGURE 19.13. Generated files hierarchy.

Class Hierarchy

The generated Eiffel code reflects the architecture of the component described in the definition file. As shown in Figure 19.14, each interface corresponds to a deferred Eiffel class that includes one deferred feature per interface function. The deferred features are implemented in the heir inheriting from all interfaces. This central class is referred to as the Eiffel coclass in the rest of this chapter.

In a client application, the Eiffel coclass inherits from the class *ECOM_QUERIABLE,* which is part of the EiffelCOM library. This class includes the feature *make_from_other,* used to initialize the component from another instance of *ECOM_INTERFACE.*

In a server application, the Eiffel coclass inherits from the class *ECOM_STUB* as shown in Figure 19.15. This class includes the feature *create_item,* which initializes the component.

The Interface_proxy folder includes Eiffel classes that wrap interfaces sent to or received by the component. Such interfaces are referred to as client-implemented interfaces in the rest of the chapter. These classes inherit from both the deferred interface class and *ECOM_QUERIABLE* as shown in Figure 19.16.

The Interface_stub folder includes Eiffel classes implementing interfaces that are sent by the component. Such interfaces are referred to as server-implemented interfaces in the rest of the chapter. Figure 19.17 illustrates how these classes inherit from both the deferred interface class and *ECOM_STUB.*

For both the Eiffel coclass and the implemented interfaces, the *ECOM_INTERFACE* class contains no implementation—it only defines the signatures of the functions that are part of the interface. The actual implementation lies in the heirs of that class.

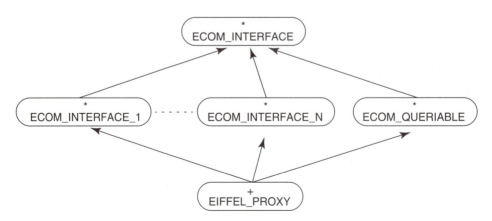

FIGURE 19.14. EiffelCOM system basic architecture, client side.

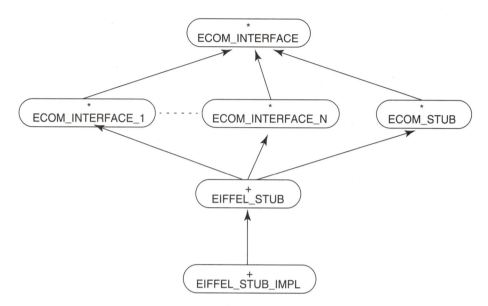

FIGURE 19.15. EiffelCOM system basic architecture, server side.

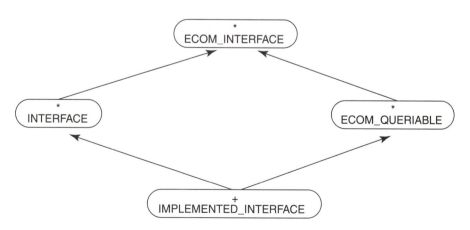

FIGURE 19.16. Client-implemented interfaces.

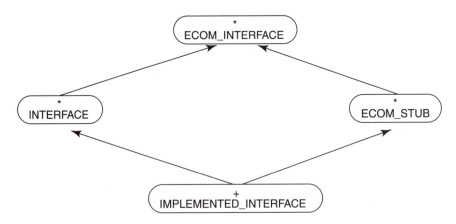

FIGURE 19.17. Server-implemented interfaces.

ACCESSING A COMPONENT

The wizard generates all the necessary code to access the existing component. The plumbing is already done, so instantiating an Eiffel coclass actually initializes the COM runtime and does all the necessary registrations.

Using the Generated Code

To access the component, you need to call the features of the coclass. The data types of the function arguments are either Eiffel types defined in the Eiffel data structure libraries (EiffelBase), standard COM data types defined in the Eiffel-COM library, or component COM data types specified in the definition file. For example, from the following IDL line,

```
HRESULT InterfaceFunction( [in] int a, [out, retval] MyStruct *b );
```

the wizard generates the following feature in the Eiffel coclass,

```
interface_function (a: INTEGER): MY_STRUCT_RECORD
```

where *MY_STRUCT_RECORD* is a generated Eiffel class wrapping *MyStruct*. Here is another, more complex example.

```
HRESULT a_function( [in]ISomeInterface * p_interface );
```

In this case, the wizard generates the following Eiffel feature,

```
a_function (p_interface: ISOME_INTERFACE_INTERFACE )
```

where *ISOME_INTERFACE_INTERFACE* is a generated deferred class. You can obtain an instance of this class from the result of another function on the component or by creating an implemented server interface *ISOME_INTER-FACE_IMPL_STUB*. In the latter case, you need to provide your own implementation.

Contracts

The wizard cannot generate fully specified contracts. Indeed, the tool has no domain-specific knowledge and can only generate contracts that are domain-independent. Such contracts, although useful, are not enough to describe entirely the behavior of a component.

Generated contracts include void Eiffel object checking as well as C++ pointer validity checking. There might be other conditions that allow calls to an Eiffel coclass feature. Invariants and postconditions can be enforced in an heir of the generated Eiffel coclass. Preconditions, however, cannot be strengthened. A workaround provided by the wizard consists of generating a precondition function (*interface_function_use_precondition* in the next example) for each feature in the interface. The default implementation of these functions always returns *True*. They should be redefined in a descendant to implement the correct behavior.

```
interface_function (a: INTEGER): MY_STRUCT is
      -- Example of a generated Eiffel coclass feature
   require
      interface_function_user_precondition:
         interface_function_user_precondition
   do
      ...
   ensure
      non_void_my_struct: Result /= Void
   end
```

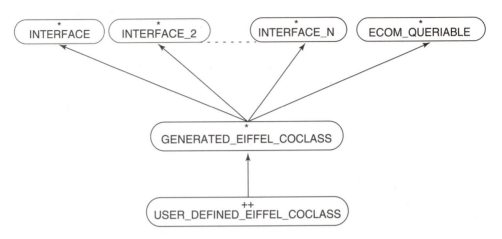

FIGURE 19.18. Full EiffelCOM client system hierarchy.

The complete class hierarchy for an Eiffel client coclass is shown in Figure 19.18.

Another advantage of the hierarchy is that it makes the EiffelCOM system more incremental. Indeed, should the definition file be modified and the wizard run once more against it, your code will not need to be changed. Only the generated Eiffel coclass is modified and it suffices to adapt your heir accordingly.

Exceptions

The COM standard requires that any interface function returns a status value, known as an HRESULT. This leads to side effect features which the Eiffel methodology tends to avoid. The workaround used in EiffelCOM systems consists of mapping these return values into Eiffel exceptions. If the server returns an error code, the EiffelCOM runtime raises an Eiffel exception that your code needs to catch. Figure 19.19 shows the flaw of events between the generated classes. As a result, any feature in the coclass client making calls to a user-defined Eiffel coclass should include a **rescue** clause. The processing performed in this clause will depend on the nature of the exception.

All the standard COM exceptions can be found in the library class *ECOM_EXCEPTION_CODES*, which is inherited from by *ECOM_EXCEPTION*. The latter also inherits from the kernel class *EXCEPTIONS*, and can consequently be used by the coclass client to catch exceptions. The feature

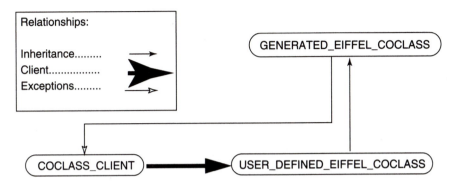

FIGURE 19.19. Raising exceptions in an EiffelCOM client system.

hresult from *ECOM_EXCEPTION* extracts the HRESULT from the exception
tag. You can then compare its value with the values found in *EXCEPTION_
CODES*. The following code fragment illustrates how a client can process exceptions raised in the Eiffel coclass.

```
indexing
    description: "Eiffel coclass client example"
class
    COCLASS_CLIENT
inherit
    ECOM_EXCEPTION
        export
            {NONE} all
        end

create
    make

feature {NONE} -- Initialization
    make is
            -- Initialize Eiffel coclass.
        do
            create coclass.make
        end

feature -- Basic Operations

    coclass_feature_client is
            -- Example of a coclass feature caller
        local
            retried: BOOLEAN
            coclass: EIFFEL_COCLASS_PROXY
        do
```

```
            create coclass.make
            if not retried then
               coclass.coclass_feature -- Actual call
            end
            rescue
              if hresult = E_notimpl then
                      -- Process nonimplemented function error.
                      retried := True
                      retry
              elseif hresult = E_invalidarg then
                      -- Process invalid argument error.
                      retried := True
                      retry
              else
                      -- Forward exception to caller.
              end
            end

end -- class COCLASS_CLIENT
```

BUILDING A COMPONENT

You can build COM components from scratch thanks to the EiffelCOM wizard, either starting from a definition file or from an Eiffel project. In the latter case, the wizard generates an MIDL file.

Choosing an Eiffel Class

If you start building a COM component from an Eiffel system, you need to give an Eiffel class to the wizard. The wizard translates the flat-short form of that class into an MIDL file, which is a formal specification of the COM component. Clients of the component are able to access only the features specified in the MIDL file. You need to supply the wizard with a facade class that provides clients with a higher-level, single-class interface to the facilities of the component. The facade class should satisfy the following requirements:

► It should have a creation routine *make* without arguments. The wizard does not enforce the rule, but breaking it causes a runtime error.
► Features of the class may only have arguments and return values of the following types: *CHARACTER, INTEGER, REAL, DOUBLE, BOOLEAN, INTEGER_REF, BOOLEAN_REF, REAL_REF, CHARACTER_REF, DOUBLE_REF, STRING, DATE_TIME, ECOM_CURRENCY, ECOM_DECIMAL, ECOM_UNKNOWN_INTERFACE, ECOM_AUTOMATION_INTERFACE, CELL or ECOM_ARRAY* (with a

generic parameter of one of the above types). Features with arguments or return values of other types are excluded from the generated IDL file and are not accessible to the COM runtime.

► Feature names should not be C++ keywords or names of standard library functions such as *min, max,* and so on. The wizard is able to handle this correctly when creating a COM component. However, other languages may not be able to access it.

► The class must belong to a compiled Eiffel project.

In most Eiffel systems, functionality is spread throughout many classes. A system may not natively contain a class that can serve as a facade to the outside world. You might have to write this class before running the wizard.

Using the Generated Code

If you start from an Eiffel project, the wizard produces a ready-to-use component, and you do not need to modify or implement any generated code.

If you start from a COM definition file, you are able to design a more flexible component that has more than one interface and/or coclass and user defined types. In that case, the generated features are empty and you need to provide the implementation. You should redefine them in the heir to implement the intended behavior. Unlike client-generated code, the server-generated code differs depending on whether you have chosen to implement an in-process or an out-of-process component. The difference lies in the component activation code in the class *ECOM_<Name of system>_REGISTRATION*. If the component is in-process, then this class includes the four functions that need to be exported from an in-process COM component (*DllRegisterServer, DllUnregisterServer, DllGetClassObject,* and *DllCanUnloadNow*). If the component is out-of-process, then the registration class includes a feature that initializes the component and its graphical user interface.

The architecture of the generated code for the server is similar to the one for the client—the generated Eiffel coclass should be inherited and the contract features redefined. The default feature implementations for the generated Eiffel coclass are empty. Features should be redefined to implement the intended behavior. These features are called by the EiffelCOM runtime whenever a client accesses the interface.

Component's GUI

In the case of an out-of-process server, you can add a graphical user interface to your component. There are two different scenarios in which the component can be activated: either an end user launched it explicitly (e.g., by double-clicking the executable icon) or it was launched by the COM runtime to satisfy a client request. The GUI should appear only in the former case, when the user has explicitly launched the application. The generated registration class for an out-of-process server includes the feature

```
main_window: WEL_FRAME_WINDOW
```

This feature is a once function that can be redefined in a child class to return the class corresponding to the component window. This window is displayed only if COM does not start the component. When COM loads an out-of-process component, it appends the option -embedding to the executable. The generated registration class looks for this option and if it is part of the process argument list, then it sets the default window appearance to hidden.

As a summary, when building a server from a COM definition, you need to implement classes that inherit from coclasses and implement interface functions. The names of the child classes should be the names of the parent classes appended with _IMP. You also have to inherit from the registration class in the case of an out-of-process component to provide the class that implements the component GUI.

Exceptions

When creating a component, it will be your code that raises exceptions and the EiffelCOM runtime that catches them. Here is what the Eiffel code for a server should look like.

```
indexing
    description: "Eiffel coclass server example"
class
    ECOM_SERVER_COCLASS_IMP
inherit
    ECOM_SERVER_COCLASS -- Generated by the EiffelCOM wizard

    ECOM_EXCEPTION
      export
          {NONE} all
      end

feature -- Basic Operations

    coclass_feature (an_argument: ARGUMENT_TYPE) is
            -- Example of a coclass feature
```

```
      do
      if not is_valid (an_argument) then
              trigger (E_invalidargument)
      else
              -- Normal processing
      end
      end
feature   {NONE} -- Implementation

    is_valid (an_argument: ARGUMENT_TYPE): BOOLEAN is
            -- Is 'an_argument' a valid argument?
      do
                    -- Test of validity of 'an_argument'
      end

end -- class ECOM_SERVER_COCLASS_IMP
```

This class inherits from the generated Eiffel coclass and from *ECOM_EXCEPTION*. It redefines the feature *coclass_feature* from the generated coclass. This feature is part of the interface functions that can be called by clients of the component. Its implementation uses the feature *trigger* from *ECOM_EXCEPTION* to raise exceptions in case the feature cannot be executed normally (e.g., an invalid argument). The EiffelCOM runtime catches the exception and maps it into an HRESULT that is sent back to the client.

SUMMARY

The EiffelCOM wizard is a powerful tool that takes care of all the "plumbing code" needed to build COM applications. There are only a few things you have to worry about when using it. If you build a wrapper for a COM component, then you have to make sure your code is ready to handle any exception that the EiffelCOM runtime may raise. If you build a server, you have to choose between creating the component from an Eiffel project or from a COM definition file. The former might seem more attractive, particularly if the Eiffel system you want to "componentize" already exists, but the latter offers more control over the layout of the component. The choice really depends on your needs; if you do not mind the actual COM implementation of your component, then you might as well just start from an Eiffel system, write a facade class, and feed it into the wizard. But if you want your component to expose specific interfaces and/or need to transmit custom data types, you have to write your own MIDL file.

DIRECTORY TREE ANALYZER

ENHANCEMENTS AND IMPROVEMENTS

No application should be considered complete without a generalization activity—an analysis of the final application design and structure in order to improve it and to discover potentially reusable abstractions. This chapter describes the results of just such an activity. The DTA application was reviewed with particular attention paid to how it could be improved and what abstractions (if any) could be reused in other applications.

To begin, the DTA application was developed as an ongoing process during the construction of the book. At the end of each relevant chapter, additional work was done to build the example. This resulted in a working, but not perfect, piece of software. Surprisingly, the application is actually fairly useful—an attribute we think is rarely found in textbook examples! You could say that we worked in a similar fashion to how we would build a software application in an industrial environment—the application was constructed in a limited time period, with unclear requirements, and with a focus on building a working, rather than perfect, solution.

We can now look back and see what can be improved. In addition, with our newly found knowledge of the WEL library, we can use more advanced controls and design techniques.

Improving the User Interface

The first and most obvious improvements can be made to the user interface. The DTA tool bar looks and feels dated. We can improve its appearance and provide user customization capabilities by using the *TOOL_BAR* class created in Chapter 16, "Bar Controls" (see Example 16.6) and a ReBar control in which to hold it. This would also give us the opportunity to easily use other standard tool bar icons, such as sort and view icons.

The code changes required to make these changes would be isolated to the *MAIN_WINDOW* class. In particular, the initialization routines would need to include the creation of the *TOOL_BAR* instances and creation and initialization of a *WEL_REBAR*.

A second user interface change could include the creation of a *WEL_TREE_VIEW* that represented the parsed directory structure rather than a flat list. This would improve the information presented to the user by including directory hierarchy information. The tree view could be constructed during the parsing processes (possibly using a callback mechanism) or afterwards, by iterating through the generated information (possibly stored in a *TREE*-like data structure).

Multithreaded Directory Parsing

The directory parsing operation is currently not interruptible. That is, during a parsing operation, the user cannot stop or interrupt the process. Two possible solutions exist. First, given that the main window responds effectively to events (as indicated by the fact that the progress messages are actually drawn in the main window), we could add a Cancel button to the interface to flag that a parsing process should finish.

Second, we could implement our parsing class (*DIRECTORY_PARSER*) so that it makes use of a second thread in which to perform the parsing. This would allow the user interface to continue operating without interruption, with the ability to respond quickly to a Cancel request. This could be done using the EiffelThread library or the forthcoming SCOOP (Simple Concurrent Object-Oriented Programming) implementation.

COM Parsing Component

Using EiffelCOM, we could convert our *DIRECTORY_PARSER* into a COM component that would be reusable in other (possibly non-Eiffel) applications. In addition, the component could be deployed and used in a distributed environment using technology such as Microsoft Transaction Server.

The merits of converting our parser into a COM component should be investigated further. Whether the abstraction would be more useful as a COM component than an Eiffel class is difficult to determine without additional requirements for its use in either scenario.

Platform Independence

The DTA application is currently limited to use in the Windows environment. As a demonstration of the WEL library and as a supporting example for this book, the current implementation is appropriate. However, we could port the application to the EiffelVision library to provide platform independence. Chapter 1, "The Windows Eiffel Library," briefly described EiffelVision as a library that sits on top of WEL and GEL (the GTK Eiffel Library).

Porting our application to EiffelVision would be a relatively simple exercise. Each of the WEL user interface components we have used has a corresponding class in EiffelVision. However, we have also used a number of

Windows-specific behaviors and capabilities, such as resources, that would need conversion when using EiffelVision.

Summary

You have done well to reach this point. If you skipped a few sections along the way, that is understandable. Refer to them when you need the components they describe. By now you should have a thorough understanding of what the WEL library supports, how it works, and what it can do for you in your applications. You should now be able to build sizable and complex Windows applications with relatively little trouble using the Eiffel language as the vehicle and WEL as one of the building blocks.

INDEX

LICENSE AGREEMENT AND LIMITED WARRANTY

READ THE FOLLOWING TERMS AND CONDITIONS CAREFULLY BEFORE OPENING THIS SOFTWARE PACKAGE. THIS LEGAL DOCUMENT IS AN AGREEMENT BETWEEN YOU AND PRENTICE-HALL, INC. (THE "COMPANY"). BY OPENING THIS SEALED SOFTWARE PACKAGE, YOU ARE AGREEING TO BE BOUND BY THESE TERMS AND CONDITIONS. IF YOU DO NOT AGREE WITH THESE TERMS AND CONDITIONS, DO NOT OPEN THE SOFTWARE PACKAGE. PROMPTLY RETURN THE UNOPENED SOFTWARE PACKAGE AND ALL ACCOMPANYING ITEMS TO THE PLACE YOU OBTAINED THEM FOR A FULL REFUND OF ANY SUMS YOU HAVE PAID.

1.   **GRANT OF LICENSE:** In consideration of your payment of the license fee, which is part of the price you paid for this product, and your agreement to abide by the terms and conditions of this Agreement, the Company grants to you a nonexclusive right to use and display the copy of the enclosed software program (hereinafter the "software") on a single computer (i.e., with a single CPU) at a single location so long as you comply with the terms of this Agreement. The Company reserves all rights not expressly granted to you under this Agreement.

2.   **OWNERSHIP OF SOFTWARE:** You own only the magnetic or physical media (the enclosed software) on which the software is recorded or fixed, but the Company retains all the rights, title, and ownership to the software recorded on the original software copy(ies) and all subsequent copies of the software, regardless of the form or media on which the original or other copies may exist. This license is not a sale of the original software or any copy to you.

3.   **COPY RESTRICTIONS:** This software and the accompanying printed materials and user manual (the "Documentation") are the subject of copyright. You may <u>not</u> copy the Documentation or the software, except that you may make a single copy of the software for backup or archival purposes only. You may be held legally responsible for any copying or copyright infringement which is caused or encouraged by your failure to abide by the terms of this restriction.

4.   **USE RESTRICTIONS:** You may <u>not</u> network the software or otherwise use it on more than one computer or computer terminal at the same time. You may physically transfer the software from one computer to another provided that the software is used on only one computer at a time. You may <u>not</u> distribute copies of the software or Documentation to others. You may <u>not</u> reverse engineer, disassemble, decompile, modify, adapt, translate, or create derivative works based on the software or the Documentation without the prior written consent of the Company.

5.   **TRANSFER RESTRICTIONS:** The enclosed software is licensed only to you and may <u>not</u> be transferred to any one else without the prior written consent of the Company. Any unauthorized transfer of the software shall result in the immediate termination of this Agreement.

6.   **TERMINATION:** This license is effective until terminated. This license will terminate automatically without notice from the Company and become null and void if you fail to comply with any provisions or limitations of this license. Upon termination, you shall destroy the Documentation and all copies of the software. All provisions of this Agreement as to warranties, limitation of liability, remedies or damages, and our ownership rights shall survive termination.

7.   **MISCELLANEOUS:** This Agreement shall be construed in accordance with the laws of the United States of America and the State of New York and shall benefit the Company, its affiliates, and assignees.

8.   **LIMITED WARRANTY AND DISCLAIMER OF WARRANTY:** The Company warrants that the software, when properly used in accordance with the Documentation, will operate in substantial conformity with the description of the software set forth in the Documentation. The Company does not warrant that the software will meet your requirements or that the operation of the software will be uninterrupted or error-free. The Company warrants that the media on which the software is delivered shall be free from defects in materials and workmanship under normal use

for a period of thirty (30) days from the date of your purchase. Your only remedy and the Company's only obligation under these limited warranties is, at the Company's option, return of the warranted item for a refund of any amounts paid by you or replacement of the item. Any replacement of software or media under the warranties shall not extend the original warranty period. The limited warranty set forth above shall not apply to any software which the Company determines in good faith has been subject to misuse, neglect, improper installation, repair, alteration, or damage by you. EXCEPT FOR THE EXPRESSED WARRANTIES SET FORTH ABOVE, THE COMPANY DISCLAIMS ALL WARRANTIES, EXPRESS OR IMPLIED, INCLUDING WITHOUT LIMITATION, THE IMPLIED WARRANTIES OF MERCHANTABILITY AND FITNESS FOR A PARTICULAR PURPOSE. EXCEPT FOR THE EXPRESS WARRANTY SET FORTH ABOVE, THE COMPANY DOES NOT WARRANT, GUARANTEE, OR MAKE ANY REPRESENTATION REGARDING THE USE OR THE RESULTS OF THE USE OF THE SOFTWARE IN TERMS OF ITS CORRECTNESS, ACCURACY, RELIABILITY, CURRENTNESS, OR OTHERWISE.

IN NO EVENT, SHALL THE COMPANY OR ITS EMPLOYEES, AGENTS, SUPPLIERS, OR CONTRACTORS BE LIABLE FOR ANY INCIDENTAL, INDIRECT, SPECIAL, OR CONSEQUENTIAL DAMAGES ARISING OUT OF OR IN CONNECTION WITH THE LICENSE GRANTED UNDER THIS AGREEMENT, OR FOR LOSS OF USE, LOSS OF DATA, LOSS OF INCOME OR PROFIT, OR OTHER LOSSES, SUSTAINED AS A RESULT OF INJURY TO ANY PERSON, OR LOSS OF OR DAMAGE TO PROPERTY, OR CLAIMS OF THIRD PARTIES, EVEN IF THE COMPANY OR AN AUTHORIZED REPRESENTATIVE OF THE COMPANY HAS BEEN ADVISED OF THE POSSIBILITY OF SUCH DAMAGES. IN NO EVENT SHALL LIABILITY OF THE COMPANY FOR DAMAGES WITH RESPECT TO THE SOFTWARE EXCEED THE AMOUNTS ACTUALLY PAID BY YOU, IF ANY, FOR THE SOFTWARE.

SOME JURISDICTIONS DO NOT ALLOW THE LIMITATION OF IMPLIED WARRANTIES OR LIABILITY FOR INCIDENTAL, INDIRECT, SPECIAL, OR CONSEQUENTIAL DAMAGES, SO THE ABOVE LIMITATIONS MAY NOT ALWAYS APPLY. THE WARRANTIES IN THIS AGREEMENT GIVE YOU SPECIFIC LEGAL RIGHTS AND YOU MAY ALSO HAVE OTHER RIGHTS WHICH VARY IN ACCORDANCE WITH LOCAL LAW.

ACKNOWLEDGMENT

YOU ACKNOWLEDGE THAT YOU HAVE READ THIS AGREEMENT, UNDERSTAND IT, AND AGREE TO BE BOUND BY ITS TERMS AND CONDITIONS. YOU ALSO AGREE THAT THIS AGREEMENT IS THE COMPLETE AND EXCLUSIVE STATEMENT OF THE AGREEMENT BETWEEN YOU AND THE COMPANY AND SUPERSEDES ALL PROPOSALS OR PRIOR AGREEMENTS, ORAL, OR WRITTEN, AND ANY OTHER COMMUNICATIONS BETWEEN YOU AND THE COMPANY OR ANY REPRESENTATIVE OF THE COMPANY RELATING TO THE SUBJECT MATTER OF THIS AGREEMENT.

Should you have any questions concerning this Agreement or if you wish to contact the Company for any reason, please contact in writing at the address below.

Robin Short
Prentice Hall PTR
One Lake Street
Upper Saddle River, New Jersey 07458

About the CD-ROM

The accompanying CD-ROM contains complete example source and the full ISE Eiffel compiler and IDE. The top-level directory of the CD-ROM contains a readme.txt file that you should read to get started. It describes how to install the example source and ISE Eiffel environment onto your computer.

Each set of examples for each chapter is located in its own folder. For instance, example source for the Windows chapter is located in the windows folder. Each example listing in the book includes a description of where the example source is located on the CD-ROM.

Installing the Example Source Code

To install the example source code to a folder on your hard drive, double-click the set_up.exe file located in the example folder. You will need to select a folder to install the files into.

The installation includes build scripts that you can use to quickly compile all the examples from a given chapter.

Important Note: For the scripts to work correctly, you need to make sure that the Eiffel compiler es4.exe can be run from the command line. The compiler is located in $EIFFEL4\bench\spec\windows\bin where $EIFFEL4 is the path to your Eiffel4 directory (e.g. c:\Eiffel4). To call es4 from the command line, add the previous path to the PATH environment variable. If you have installed the Eiffel compiler in C:\, type the following line:

```
set %PATH%=%PATH%;c:\eiffel4\bench\spec\windows\bin
```

in the dos console where you will run the scripts.

INSTALLING THE ISE EIFFEL ENVIRONMENT

To install the ISE Eiffel environment, double-click the setup.exe file located in the Eiffel folder. This will begin the setup program. Follow the on screen prompts to install the product. Some examples need C compilation to be correctly compiled. To run these examples, you need to install first a C compiler on your machine (Microsoft Visual C++ or Borland C++ Builder). If you do not possess a C compiler, you can download the free Borland C++ compiler at http://www.inprise.com/bcppbuilder/freecompiler/cppc55steps.html.

TECHNICAL SUPPORT

Prentice Hall does not offer technical support for any of the programs on the CD-ROM. However, if the CD is damaged, you may obtain a replacement copy by sending an email describing the problem to: disc_exchange@phptr.com.